WORD AND ACTION

By the same author

THE HEROIC TEMPER
OEDIPUS THE KING (translation)
OEDIPUS AT THEBES

WORD AND ACTION
Essays on the Ancient Theater

Bernard Knox

The Johns Hopkins University Press
Baltimore and London

The Johns Hopkins University Press, Baltimore, Maryland 21218
The Johns Hopkins Press Ltd., London

Originally published, 1979
Second printing, 1980

Library of Congress Catalog Number 79-11277
ISBN 0-8018-2198-3

Library of Congress Cataloging in Publication data will be found on the last printed page of
this book.

FOR BIANCA

σύν τε δύ' ἐρχομένω

CONTENTS

PREFACE

This collection of essays and reviews dealing with ancient (mainly Greek) drama contains only one new item—the first; the others have all appeared in periodical or book form during the last twenty-five years. They are here arranged roughly by subject, rather than in the order of their composition; since they appear unaltered (except for minor corrections), the critical reader is respectfully asked to bear in mind the date of publication in each case. Some items were omitted as too trivial or overly polemical; I hope that those here presented make enough of a contribution to learning or appreciation to justify their revival.

Part I: Prologue

ONE

Myth and Attic Tragedy

Any title which includes the word "myth" is almost certain, these days, to raise expectations, entertained by some with enthusiasm and by others with dismay, that the writer will deal in wide, if not universal, terms of reference—the complexes, displacements, and sublimations of Sigmund Freud; the somewhat arbitrary archetypes of Jung; the Indo-European tripartite functions of Dumézil; or the codes, contradictions, and mediations of Claude Lévi-Strauss—and also that the article will come equipped with at least one complicated diagram. This essay is less ambitious. It tries to deal in specific, pragmatic terms with a limited area—the myths preferred by the Attic tragic poets of the fifth century B.C.

The thirty or so Greek tragedies we still possess (as well as many others we know only in fragmentary form) were performed in Athens some 2,500 years ago at a citywide festival which was a religious ceremony and also a political occasion, a celebration of the imperial power and social cohesion of the Athenian people. It is hard to think of any period since then in which the theater has expressed so clearly and directly the mood and mind of a whole community; this is in fact the ideal relationship between stage and audience to which all theaters look back in envy. And yet, as is well known, the subject matter of the plays, far from reflecting the immediate concerns, the everyday life of the audience, dealt almost exclusively with the action and suffering of mythical figures who were believed to have lived and died in a far-off past. With a few exceptions at the beginning of the century (excursions into recent history), the tragedies of the great age of Athenian drama dealt exclusively with the figures and events of myth.

Drama, since it can function only as a contact between poet and audience through the medium of actors, can never be a hermetic art, one that demands time and interpretation for its understanding; it may be outrageous, it may be unexceptional or even dull, but whatever else it is, it *must* be immediately intelligible to a mass audience on some level, must appeal at once to that audience's deepest sympathies, its secret fears, its ambitions, its hopes. The fifth-century Athenian dramatist, at the very birth of the theater, succeeded in doing so by using, in the main, story material handed down from the immemorial past. How was this possible? In other words, what resources, what strengths, did the tragic poets find in myth? An attempt to answer that question may perhaps explain what myth—at least the kind of myth tragedy made peculiarly its own—meant to the fifth-century Athenians, why it had such a hold on their imaginations, and how it functioned in their social, religious, and political life.

It is often assumed (even in contexts where it is not explicitly stated) that the use of such mythical themes was imposed on the dramatists by the force of tradition and the religious nature of the occasion; myth is seen as the natural, indeed inevitable, content for a dramatic medium which, to use the terms of Aristotle's influential metaphor, was an organic growth from Dionysiac ritual to perfection of form. Most modern theorists of tragedy's origin, as if relieved to find one aspect of Aristotle's account they could all agree on, have laid great stress on the ritual, religious origin of the performance in the theater of Dionysus. And a process of gradual evolution from some kind of Dionysiac ritual performance—dithyrambic, satyric, phallic—to fully dramatic presentation rides easily in harness with a parallel theory of the development of content, from "sacred tales" of Dionysus to myths that may indeed have "nothing to do with Dionysus" but still deal with gods and men imagined in the far-off past and represented in the same social religious mode.

One influential theory of the origin of tragedy emphasized the ritual element by reconstructing out of airy nothing a full-fledged Dionysiac passion play and saw its continued pervasive influence in the structure and tone of fully developed drama, even in that of Euripides (in fact, one of the weaknesses of the theory was that the "ritual structure" was most clearly discerned in Euripides, left little traces of its presence in Sophocles, and was almost invisible in the plays of Aeschylus). Frazer and Jane Harrison laid the foundations for the theory; Cornford in an exciting book, *The Origin of Attic Comedy*,[1] and Murray in his excursus on the ritual origins of Greek tragedy (an appendix to Jane Harrison's *Themis*[2]) built an elaborate structure on this foundation. It was, however, a shaky structure at best, not the least wobbly of its pillars the addition to an already overcrowded Greek pantheon of a new divinity, the *eniautos daimon*, the Year Spirit.

A meticulous and destructive analysis of this theory in Pickard-Cambridge's indispensable book *Dithyramb, Tragedy and Comedy*[3] (now, alas, unobtainable) left the "ritual structure" of developed tragedy in ruins more desolate than those of Pentheus' palace in *The Bacchae* and laid forever the ghost of the *eniautos daimon*. Or so one happily thought.

But in T. B. L. Webster's revised edition of Pickard-Cambridge's great book, the work is undone. Webster's edition has its merits—the addition of new evidence, the discussion of the vase paintings, a field in which he was an acknowledged authority—but his attempt to cancel out Pickard-Cambridge's exorcism of the *daimon* is regrettable. "With our extended knowledge of the history of the Dionysus cult," he says, "the theory can be restated in a form both tenable and valuable." This form is as follows: "ritual of the *eniautos daimon* type in the Mycenaean age very early (and certainly before Homer) gave rise to myths which were dramatized very early and so established a rhythm which was so satisfying that stories from other mythological cycles were approximated to it." This sounds more like a simple repetition than a restatement; in any case, that second "very early," though less precise than one could wish, seems to claim the existence of dramatized Dionysiac ritual, complete with pathos, threnos, and epiphany, long before tragedy as we know it began some time in the second half of the sixth century. If so, the problem of the origin of tragedy is solved and its later preoccupation with myth perfectly comprehensible and almost inevitable. But the evidence for this restatement "in a form both tenable and valuable" is not impressive. It consists of "the likeness of the ecstatic dances of Dionysus' Maenads to the ecstatic dances which appear on Minoan and Mycenaean works of art," a likeness which, we are told, "is obvious." Apart from the fact that ecstatic dancing Maenads do not appear in Aristotle's account of Dionysiac origins, the likeness is not obvious to everyone. The Mycenaean works of art on which these scenes are found are rings, and these rings, Webster tells us, "can be arranged by the variation of the foliage on the trees in the background as a cycle proceeding from winter through spring to summer and harvest time. The cycle starts with mourning for the dead and a hope that the young god (who may perhaps be called Dionysus) will appear and possibly ends with the departure of goddess or god and goddess in a boat. The cycle is certainly a Year God cycle ... the ritual is designed to overcome the forces of nature which resist the new growth of vegetation and in story this resistance is translated into the resistance of human Kings to the worship of Dionysus and his Maenads ... Pentheus ..." and so on.[4]

This is "evidence" which will impress some more than others; it would have appalled Pickard-Cambridge, who limited himself to "what can really be said to be proved or probable." The interpretation of the tiny figures on Mycenaean seal rings is a guessing game at best, but it requires the eye of blind faith to detect seasonal changes of vegetation on those crude schematic designs. And the method of this argument leaves much to be desired. "The rings can be arranged ... as a cycle"; of course they can. They can also be arranged in any way you wish, depending on what you want to prove. The "arrangement" becomes a "cycle" which emerges as a "rite"; "the resistance" of the forces of nature (how is *that* represented on the rings?) is translated into "the resistance of human beings"—a transformation, to use the terms of a more recent anthropology, of the vegetable code to the social.

Webster's attempt to push the origin of tragedy back in time into what he assumes was a more "ecstatic," barbaric context is of course in the spirit of our age; interestingly enough, performances of Greek tragedy in recent years have followed suit. Tyrone Guthrie's company, when still located in Stratford, Ontario, produced a famous version of the *Oedipus Tyrannos* (widely known through the film adaptation) in which actors and chorus wore hideous rubber masks, like the Halloween goblin masks American children put on at that season, and the grim proceedings on stage gave the audience the impression they were watching some kind of Druidical human sacrifice. Some years ago, in a garage in New York City, a theatrical group staged *The Bacchae* of Euripides under the title *Dionysus in 69*.[5] It did take place in 1969, but some of the stage action suggested that the title was chosen with an eye to the sexual connotations of that number. In the Dionysus-Pentheus scene, for example, Dionysus exerted his power over the king by persuading him to commit fellatio on him (needless to say, the text of Euripides had long since been left behind in favor of creative improvisation). The killing of Pentheus took place onstage (except that there was no stage—the spectators, who had had to remove their shoes before they were let in, sat on the floor in a circle), and the Maenads (rather hefty girls most of them) stripped naked, splashed themselves with tomato ketchup, and proceeded to pass the equally naked Pentheus through their legs in what was billed as an African rebirth rite.

It seems clear enough, of course, that the origin of tragedy did have something to do with Dionysus, perhaps even with Dionysiac ritual, though no one seems to be sure what that ritual was. But the problem is: how did something like *The Oresteia* develop from it? It does not seem likely, given that the essential fact about ritual is that it does not change, that the process was an orderly, evolutionary progression, an organic growth; some new elements must have been added, some violent disruptions of continuity effected.

It was once possible (and indeed almost general) to argue for the smooth evolution from ritual to drama by arguing backward from the formal evolution observable in extant tragedy—from a choral, lyrical tragedy to a vehicle dominated by actors. This argument depended of course on the early date of the Aeschylean *Supplices*. It was obviously early because it was clearly, from the standpoint of fully evolved drama, apprentice work; the second actor was so clumsily used that he must have been recently introduced, the actor's *epeisodia* were short, the choral odes long, involved, and magnificent. But a papyrus fragment has removed the play to the sixties of the fifth century from the nineties in which it had so confidently been placed. Exhibit A for the idea that early tragedy was, as Kitto named it, "lyrical tragedy" vanished into thin air and left us with the maverick *Persae* as the earliest extant play—maverick in its nonmythical content, the inordinate length of the first *epeisodion*, the switch from iambic trimeter to trochaic tetrameter and back again in the Darius scene, and some other peculiarities as well.

In recent years the whole theory of orderly evolution has been subjected to searching criticism. Gerald Else, in his radical and brilliant book, *The Origin and Early Form of Greek Tragedy*,[6] has made the iconoclastic suggestion (and it is not the only one in the book) that "the origin of tragedy was not so much a gradual 'organic' development as a sequence of two creative leaps, by Thespis and Aeschylus." He goes on to stress the importance for the formative period of tragedy of Homeric recitations at the Panathenaea, and the impact of the personal (i.e., self-dramatizing) poetry of Solon—in iambic verse. He sees Thespis' achievement as "a new creation" which "brought together three different things which had never been joined before: the epic hero, impersonation, and iambic verse." Dionysus and ritual form no part of his picture of the origin of tragedy.

Whatever may be thought of the theory as a whole (and it does depend to some extent on the exclusion of a crucial sentence in Aristotle's *Poetics* as an interpolation), there is much to be said for the idea that the early stages of Attic tragedy were not an "organic" growth but a series of daring experiments. One successful experiment, for example, was the addition to the Dionysiac festival of the satyr play by Pratinus of Phlius, which, it is now generally agreed, came toward the end of the sixth century. There may have been experiments which had no imitators: the Aeschylean *Aitnaiai*, it now appears, had frequent changes of scene. In any case, the experimental openness of early Attic tragedy is clear from the fact that, among the few tragedies produced prior to 470 B.C. of which we know anything at all, three deal not with mythical but with contemporary themes. Phrynichus' *Capture of Miletus*, probably produced in 492, moved the audience to tears and resulted in a fine for the author; his *Phoenissae*—its subject the arrival at the Persian court of the news of Salamis—was produced in 477–76; and in 472 Aeschylus produced *The Persians*, a fresh treatment of the same subject. The recently discovered fragment of a Gyges drama may also come under this head; it has even been suggested that its author was Phrynichus.[7] Be that as it may, the evidence suggests firmly that in the first decades of the fifth century, Attic tragedy was far from being locked on a fixed course of dramatic adaptation of myth. But, as it turned out, the drama based on recent history seems to have been an experiment that was not repeated; we hear no more of such subjects for tragedy until the late fourth century. The fifth-century tragic poets, with the exception of the three plays already mentioned, drew their themes, as far as we know, from the great body of traditional mythology.

What kind of myth did they prefer? Since the plays which have survived intact are only a pitiful remnant of the hundreds of tragedies staged in the course of the century, this may seem like an idle question. But in fact we are not so badly off as at first appears. We have 31 complete tragedies which were produced before the end of the fifth century. But we know by fragments, by title, or both, 61 more plays of Aeschylus, 81 of Sophocles and 52 of Euripides. To this we can add titles and fragments from ten other dramatists who we know were at work in the fifth century—a total of 54 plays.[8] And there are 14 plays of which we have indicative fragments or titles but no author's name and which have a fifth-century look about them. This gives us a total of 293 plays. If we end our period with B.C. 402 (the date of the posthumous production of Sophocles' *Oedipus at Colonus*) and assume, with much probability, that no performances took place in 479, 478 and 404, years of destruction and revolution, we come up with a total of just over a thousand tragic plays[9] (9 at each Dionysia, 4 at the Lenaea from 440 B.C. on). So we have some knowledge of the subjects of close to one-third of the century's tragic production. Since our sample was produced by processes as varied as selection for school use in the Byzantine empire, citation by rhetoricians and lexicographers, inclusion in encyclopedic lists, and the fortuitous preservation of inscribed stone fragments or torn pieces of papyrus, our one-third is a random sample. Its nature as well as its size justify some generalizations about tragic subject matter in the great age of Athenian drama.

The first striking fact about the plays of this sample is that not one of them deals exclusively (and only two of them—the *Prometheus* plays—extensively) with gods. The whole cycle of myths which told of the birth, marriages, and wars of the Olympian divinities, the material of Hesiod's *Theogony*, was left almost untouched by the tragic poets; even the *Prometheus* has one prominent human character (though it is true that, as Housman put it, she is provided with four hooves, two horns, one tail), and in the *Prometheus Unbound* the hero Heracles plays a key role. The normal material of Attic tragedy is the complex of myths which told the stories of the men and women of the Greek past. The gods may, indeed often do, appear on stage, but though their role may be, theologically speaking, causal, it is, dramatically speaking, secondary.

This exclusive preoccupation of tragedy with human as opposed to divine myth is emphasized by a contrasting phenomenon, the fairly frequent appearance of divine, even cosmogonical, myths in comedy and satyr plays. Hermippus wrote a comedy called *The Birth of Athena* [*Athenas gonai*]; the fragments contain a speech by Athena herself and part of an account of how Zeus gave her her name. In the *Nemesis* of Cratinus, Zeus is told to change into a big bird in order to seduce Nemesis; Nemesis subsequently lays an egg and Leda is told to get to work, Λήδα, σὸν ἔργον, "act exactly like a rooster and hatch it out." She does, and it produces Castor, Polydeuces, Clytemnestra, and Helen of Troy. In satyr plays, too, the gods have prominent roles. There are no human characters in Sophocles' *Ichneutae*, and his *Judgement* [*Krisis*] seems to have brought the three goddesses on stage for the beauty contest on Mount Ida. Achaeus wrote a satyric *Hephaestus*, in which Dionysus persuades Hephaestus to come back to Olympus; the many representations of Hephaestus' return on the vases suggest that this was a hilarious and drunken scene. Achaeus also wrote an *Iris,* Astydamas a *Hermes*, Timesitheus (who may have produced in the fifth century) a *Birth of Zeus*—all satyr plays.

Tragedy, however, avoids such themes and concentrates on human, heroic myth. But even within this category, it is highly selective; the bulk of the tragedies we can identify draw their themes from a surprisingly small segment of the vast mythological repertoire. The Trojan War and its ramifications account for no less than 68 of the known plays; the voyage of the Argo, its antecedents and consequences, for 21. The house of Cadmus and the story of Thebes down to its capture by the Epigonoi give us 33 titles, the house of Tantalus, from Pelops through Atreus to Iphigeneia, 31. Heracles and his children are the subject of 14 dramas; Athenian myth (including Theseus) contributes 19, Crete and the line of Europa 10, Calydon and the famous hunt 8. The Perseus cycle was used in 10 tragedies, the adventures of Odysseus in 10 more; Bellerophon and family appear in 7 plays, Ixion and his descendents in 6. The remaining 54 titles of our sample include the two Prometheus plays and 2 each for Melanippe, Phaethon, and Tyro.

This body of traditional material is a closely woven pattern of human lives, the action and suffering of men and women in their relationships with one another and with the gods, organized in a complex of interlocking family histories and grouped round a number of great central events: the Trojan War, the founding and the siege of Thebes, the voyage of the Argo, the Calydonian boar hunt—events with repercussions that spread, like circles from a stone thrown into a pond, outwards through the whole to the extreme borders of the pattern.

It will be obvious from this description of "tragic myth" that one of the things the poets found in it, one of the sources of its powerful hold on them and their audience, was the authority of what we would call "history." Tragic myth, for the fifth-century Greeks, was the story of their past, their history—for early times the only history they knew. It was not of course history in our sense of the word. The Greek alphabet, adapted from a North Phoenician syllabary,[10] makes its appearance in the archeological record some time in the late eighth century B.C., and writing does not seem to have been used for literary rather than commercial purposes until the start of the century after that. All the events of tragic myth are thought of as many centuries back in time. There was no written record of these events, no conceivable way to find out what actually happened. There were only the myths—"what they say," ὅσα μυθέονται.

M. I. Finley has stressed the fact that myths have no real chronology and that "dates and a coherent dating scheme are as essential to history as exact measurement is to physics." It is also true that, as he goes on to point out, the time of the mythical events is not fixed chronologically with regard to known historical events. Herodotus, he says, "was able ... to establish some kind of time-sequence for perhaps two centuries of the past, roughly from the middle of the seventh century B.C. on. All that came before remained as it had been when he began his work, epic tales and myths believed to be true, at least in essence, but incorrigibly timeless." And yet, in spite of Herman Fränkel's statement (which Finley quotes) that in the epic "there is no interest in chronology, whether relative or absolute,"[11] his conclusion that the myths are "incorrigibly timeless"[12] seems to go too far. They were timeless in the sense that fifth-century Greeks could not relate them chronologically to known events of the immediate past, but they did have a rough internal chronology of their own, a fixed sequence of main events. The labors and death of Heracles and the siege of Thebes preceded the Trojan War; the trial of Orestes and the return of the Heraclidae followed it. And often the internal chronology of individual myths is quite precise: the Trojan War lasted ten years, as did the wanderings of Odysseus; Orestes returned to Argos to kill his mother in the eighth year after the murder of Agamemnon. Heracles' last and fatal absence from home was one year and three months.

These, it may be objected, are conventional mythical numbers, not chronological statements; this is of course true, but the statements are not timeless. To see what a timeless myth is like, one has only to look at Hindu mythology—for example, the *Mahabharata* story of the death goddess and her attempt to avoid her odious duties. She "slipped away without having promised to destroy creatures, and returned to Dhenuka. There the goddess practised the supreme asceticism that is hard to practise: for fifteen thousand million years she stood on one foot ... Brahma ... again spoke to her, saying, 'Death, obey my command!' But she disregarded him and immediately began to practise asceticism on one foot for another twenty thousand million years, and then yet another ten million million years she dwelt with the wild animals."[13] She ends up standing on one big toe for a thousand million years before she gives in and gets to work.

It was the elementary chronological structure of Greek mythology which tempted later scholars in Alexandria—Eratosthenes and Callimachus in particular—to pursue cross-references in order to establish an internally coherent chronology of the whole body of heroic myth, anchored to the capture of Troy. The attempt was of course a failure, for there are too many contradictions. Laios of Thebes, for example, carried off Chrysippus, the young son of Pelops, from Argos (or Mycenae), an event which will put his son Oedipus in the same generation as Atreus, and so Polynices and Eteocles in the same generation as Agamemnon—which is manifestly impossible since, according to other cross-references, they had been dead a long time when Agamemnon gathered the fleet at Aulis. Yet the fact that scholars as well-read as Eratosthenes and Callimachus thought it worthwhile to try to systematize the heroic myths in a valid chronological relationship shows that, even for the sophisticated intellects of the Hellenistic age, heroic myth appeared to be the raw material of history. But for the fifth-century Greeks, before Herodotus began his inquiries into the past and Thucydides established strict standards for writing the history of contemporary events, it was their only vision of their own past.

How far it was a true vision is another matter. Opinions are divided today on whether there was in fact a Trojan War or not, but the Greeks believed that there was. Herodotus tells us that when, in the face of Xerxes' preparations for invasion, Spartan and Athenian envoys were sent to Gelon of Syracuse to ask for help, they were promised it on condition that Gelon should be appointed commander in chief of the Greek forces.[14] The Spartan envoys' reply was an indignant negative, expressed in Homeric phrase: "Surely Pelops' son Agamemnon would wail with anguish if he could hear that command was taken away from Sparta by Gelon and the men of Syracuse." When Gelon, evidently a reasonable man, offered to settle for the command of the fleet, the Athenians replied, equally indignant; they invoked their claim to be the oldest people in Greece, the only ones who had never migrated, and reminded Gelon that they were mentioned by Homer as sending to Troy the best man to dispose and marshal an army. (He would have needed a reminder, since the man in question, Menestheus, is one of the least conspicuous figures of *The Iliad*.) As a result, the Greeks had to do without help from Syracuse. Agamemnon and the obscure Athenian king (whose qualifications may be an interpolation)[15] were for the Greeks historical facts, with, as this instance suggests, the power that historical facts which have acquired symbolic significance can exert on present action.

An even more striking example of this attitude toward myth can be found in Herodotus' account of the arguments between the Tegeans and the Athenians before the battle of Plataea.[16] Both contingents demanded the honor of fighting on the left wing of the Greek forces; their speeches are addressed to the Spartans, whose king commanded the whole force and who fought on the most exposed flank, the right. The Tegeans' claim to the post rests on an exploit of their king Echemus, who, chosen to represent the Peloponnesians in single combat, killed Hyllus, king of the invading Heraclidae. The Athenian answer counters with not one but four mythical feats of arms: their protection of the Heraclidae against Eurystheus; their defeat of the Thebans, who refused burial to Polynices and the rest of the seven champions; their defeat of the Amazons, who had invaded Attica; and their part in the Trojan War. They concede that these events are long past and admit the objection that a people who had been brave once might be cowardly now. But they can add a recent feat of arms to meet this objection: the battle of Marathon, fought only eleven years before. And the only distinction they make between this event and the battles of the far-off past is one between ancient and recent (*palaia te kai kaina*). For them, as for their hearers (and for Herodotus and his), all these exploits are equally historical: the hard-riding one-breasted Amazon invaders are as real as the Persians who had been routed in 490 B.C. by the fathers of many in Herodotus' audience.

That unrecorded events, believed to have been preserved by collective memory over centuries, should be accepted as fact, myth as history, is something hard for the modern age to understand. It is especially hard for Americans, for America is the youngest of the western nations and has no myth of this type at all. America was born in the seventeenth century and came of age in the eighteenth century, the Age of Reason. There is no dim, unrecorded past in the American memory: no Achilles and Hector, no David and Goliath, no Beowulf, no King Arthur, Guinevere, and Lancelot, no *poema del mio Cid*, no Roland or Roncesvaux, no Siegfried and Brünnhilde. There is no American time for which myth is the only authority.

When the poet Henry Wadsworth Longfellow tried to create an American mythical memory, he had to go back beyond the birth of the nation and draw on the traditions of the displaced and subjected Indians.

But the attempt was a failure, not only because of the pedestrian quality of Longfellow's muse and his monotonous adaptation of the trochaic line of the Finnish *Kalevala* (the target of dozens of hilarious parodies), not only because, in a final canto few have read, he lost his nerve and made Hiawatha welcome the arrival of the Christian missionaries ("told them of the Virgin Mary, and her infant son, the Savior"). It failed also because Manitaw the Mighty, the shores of Gitchee Goomee and Minnehaha, Laughing Water, cannot possibly stir in American (or for that matter Indian) hearts that mysterious sense of continuity, even identity, which Arthur can produce in the Englishman, Roland in the Frenchman, or, more potent and terrifying (as my generation learned to its cost), Siegfried, die Walküre, and Götterdämmerung in the German.

Of course there are American myths—George Washington and the cherry tree for example—but they do not command the power inherent in stories which go back to remote antiquity. They are all of them subject to correction, if not destruction, by the evidence; in the face of the evidence, no one can persist in the belief that George Washington said "I did it with my little hatchet"—the evidence is all too clear that the story was fabricated by one Parson Weems. The modern historical myth is choked at birth by the modern historical sensibility and the wealth of evidence which can be marshaled against it.

In the Capitol in Washington, visitors can see in the Rotunda a huge painting of a much-loved story from the early days of the Virginia Colony: the rescue of Captain John Smith from execution through the intervention of Pocohontas, the daughter of an Indian chief. The story is told at length and in vivid detail by John Smith himself in a book published in 1624 entitled *The General History of Virginia, New England and the Summer Isles*. Captain Smith is brought before Powhatan, the Indian chief. "Then," he tells us, "as many as could, laid hands on him, dragged him to two great stones and thereon laid his head and being ready with their clubs to beat out his brains, Pocohontas, the king's dearest daughter, when no intreaty could prevail, got his head in her arms and laid her own on his to save him from death, whereat the Emperor was content he should live." Now Captain John Smith and Pocohontas are historical characters with a real existence; in fact, Pocohontas was taken to England in 1616 to be presented at court, died there, and was buried at Gravesend. And Captain John Smith, on the occasion of the visit, wrote a letter (or says he did) to the Queen telling the same romantic story of his escape from execution. Unfortunately, he had published an account of his adventures among what he calls the "salvages" eight years before the letter to the Queen and sixteen years before the published account of the incident. It is called *A True Relation ... of Virginia 1608*, and it does not mention Pocohontas at all. Here is his first account of his meeting with the Emperor Powhatan: "The next night I lodged at a hunting town of Powhatan's and the next day arrived at Aranamoco upon the river of Pamaunke, where the great king is resident. Arriving at Weramocomoco their Emperor ... kindly welcomed me with sundry victuals, assuring me his friendship and my liberty within four days."[17]

Take a more recent instance. In 1917, a United States Marine division went into the attack at Belleau Wood in northern France. A sergeant climbed out of the trench into heavy fire, then realized that his men were hanging back. He turned and shouted to them: "Come on, you sons of bitches, do you want to live forever?" This is a story which was reported by correspondents at the time and is believed by every United States Marine. Unfortunately, this memorable phrase had been used before. At one of the many bloody engagements he directed on the Spanish peninsula, the Duke of Wellington, observing that the Forty-fifth Light Infantry was not advancing as ordered, yelled at them: "What's the matter, Forty-fifth, do you want to live forever?" And in the century before that, in one of the many battles fought by the Prussian soldiers of Frederick the Great, the king, standing on the Feldherrenhügel, the hill from which Prussian kings surveyed the battlefield—well in the rear—saw his guards retreating. He screamed at them: "Ihr Hunde, Wollt Ihr ewig leben?" ("You curs, do you want to live forever?"). That story, a version with the punchline verbally identical with that of the Marine sergeant except for the difference of one canine generation, is to be found in Carlyle's life of Frederick the Great, a book most newspaper correspondents of the 1917 generation would have read, and one is entitled to doubt, especially if one has known any rank-and-file U.S. Marines, that the sergeant said any more than the first six of the words attributed to him.

The modern myth is hindered if not completely checked at the very beginning of its metamorphosis into history. But in fifth-century Athens there was no such damning evidence, no records, no archives, no one to question the reality of the Trojan War, no one even ready to cut it down to size and treat it as a poverty-stricken piratical raid until Thucydides, for reasons that had little to do with history, did just that right at the end of the century—in a book which, to judge by the references to history made by the orators of the next century, seems to have had no influence whatever on popular opinion. All through the fourth century for example, orators praising Athenian dead who had fallen in battle continued to invoke, in their appeal to tradition, the mythical precedents: the Athenian victory over the Amazons, the rescue of the Heraclidae, the defeat of the Thebans and burial of the Argives. This is clear from the literary imitations in Lysias, Plato's *Menexenus* and pseudo-Demosthenes; Aristotle, in fact, in the *Rhetoric*, says that a reference to the rescue of the Heraclidae is essential in such a speech. All this in spite of the example given by Thucydides, who makes his Pericles say, as the later orators do, "I shall begin with our ancestors," but goes no farther back than the Persian Wars.[18]

For the fourth-century Athenians, as for those of the fifth, myth, and therefore tragedy, which gave it dramatic form, had the unquestioned authority which we grant to history; the masked actors on stage were the great figures of the audience's past. But it is history in which the original core of genuine memory, if indeed that ever existed, had been transformed by the selective emphasis of the oral tradition. Over many generations of oral transmission, stories change on the lips of tellers to reflect new preoccupations, new attitudes. And in such a process only what remains meaningful and relevant will survive. The oral tradition, myth, "what they say," emphasizes and preserves only what is memorable. A witty book by two English history teachers, *1066 and All That*,[19] stated in joking fashion a profound truth: "History is what you can remember." And it is remembered only because it has meaning (or is given new meaning by adaptation and addition); it embodies a view of life, an attitude, an ideal, a warning; it has contemporary significance. In the absence of records only what continues to have significance will survive in the communal memory.

What myth, the popular memory, preserves is not historical fact, not the particular details, the multiplicity, complexity, and ambiguity of any *real* happening. It preserves, creates, and recreates symbolic figures and situations, persons and events which typify recurring dilemmas and challenges, heroes whose relations to gods and to their fellow men embody permanent religious and social problems, whose actions present an ideal by which men can live and die or a monitory example of conduct to be avoided. Myth, in other words, is indeed history for the fifth-century Athenians, but it is history transformed by the selective emphasis of a long tradition, shaped and concentrated, and so endowed with universal significance. In other words, it is a kind of poetry.

Even today, in the age of records, of computer banks which remember the date of birth, credit status, and Social Security number of every one of us, even today, undaunted by the easily ascertainable historical facts, a poetic, a mythical history of this kind is not dead. For most of us, history is indeed "what we can remember." And what we can remember is not very much and not even that little will always stand up to critical examination. I take an American example again. What does the popular memory say of one Patrick Henry, a prosperous lawyer who lived in Virginia in the eighteenth century? That he forced the royal officials in Virginia to pay three hundred pounds for the gunpowder they had removed form the colony's stores? That he bitterly opposed the ratification of the Federal Constitution in 1788? It says none of these things; in order to find them, one has to consult the historical record. But if that record disappeared forever, the popular memory would still credit Patrick Henry with two unforgettable phrases. Speaking at Williamsburg against the Stamp Act, he said: "Caesar had his Brutus, Charles I his Cromwell, and George III ... ". Interrupted by cries of "Treason!" he continued, "and George III might profit by their example—and if this be treason, make the most of it." And he also said: "Give me liberty or give me death." And after all, these two phrases are the most important thing about him. If he had not said these things his name would hardly be remembered, and there would certainly not be an aircraft carrier named after him.

We can go farther. Though it now seems fairly certain that he did *not* in fact pronounce the first of these two memorable phrases in exactly the canonical form,[20] the oral tradition will not abandon him; the myth will live on—they will go on saying it—as the myth of Belleau Wood lives on among the Marines. That Marine sergeant's words sum up a grim ideal by which thousands of brave men have lived and died, on Pacific islands, Korean mountains, and in Vietnam jungles, and Patrick Henry's defiant words are an unforgettable expression of the fierce American devotion to independence. They are both symbolic figures, belonging, to use the terms of Aristotle's distinction between poetry and history, to the area of the universal and so are superior to the particular—even to the awkward particular that one of them may have expressed himself in much more diplomatic terms and the other may never have existed.

Today, of course, few will agree with Aristotle's statement that poetry is more philosophical and valuable than history since poetry deals with the universal and history the particular. Yet, in terms of his own distinctions, he is not so far wrong. For history itself becomes more philosophical and valuable as it moves from the establishment and collection of particular facts to the generalizations which can be extracted from them. What distinguishes the great historian from the mere compiler is precisely the ability to discern patterns of order in the chaos of detail—to emphasize, select, and synthesize. What the great historian does, paradoxically, is to create a myth. So Gibbon created from the fantastic agglomeration of the facts and fancies of 1,200 years of European history the eighteenth century myth of the Decline and Fall of the Roman Empire: a vision of an empire "governed ... by absolute power under the guidance of virtue and wisdom" which, however, carried within it the seeds of its own death, its vast extent ("immoderate greatness"), and the corruption of overcivilization. Threatened by barbarian invasion from without and undermined by Christian fanaticism within, "the stupendous fabric yielded to the pressure of its own weight." So Macaulay created out of the particulars of the English civil war and revolution of the seventeenth century the powerful nineteenth-century myth which has since been called "the Whig interpretation of history": the story of the rise to power of the English landed gentry, seen as the triumph of universal freedom over an oppressive and regressive autocracy. This was a powerful myth all through the nineteenth century and even beyond; it was the charter myth of modern English parliamentary democracy. And Gibbon's great myth, demolished piecemeal and as a whole by historians ever since his death, comes back to haunt us now, as western civilization fears the future and begins to doubt its own ability to survive.

Every people has to have a vision of its past to live by, and even today, in the age of the record, that vision is as much mythical as scientific, in spite of the evidence and prestige of historians devoted to the search for "the untutored incident, that actually occurred." But for the fifth-century Athenians, there was no check of any kind on the mythopoeic creation and adaptation of tradition; their vision of the past, of their own history, was fully poetic from the start, its personages and events symbolic representations of every aspect of man's life on earth, his strength and weakness in the struggle against his fellow men, the forces of nature, and the bleak fact of his own mortality. Myth and its tragic adaptation have, besides the authority of history, the power of poetry. The masked actors in the theater of Dionysus present to the audience not only the historical figures of the past but also poetic symbols of its own life and death, its ambitions and its fate.

But the myth has still another source of power: its religious content. It re-creates the past as a time when men and gods were in closer relationship than they have ever been since. For the fifth-century audience, communication with its gods was possible only through sacrifice, prayer, consultation at oracular shrines, "through a glass darkly," but then, in the vision of the past, men and gods met "face to face." The myths are, besides history and poetry, the sacred tales of Greek religion, the equivalent for them of the Hebrew Bible.

"Bible," of course, is the Greek word for "book." The Hebrews have been justly called "the people of the Book"; it was the repository of their deepest beliefs as well as their laws, it played its part in their communications with their unseen, mysterious God. Consequently, as their laws and religious ideas changed in response to new situations, the Book was revised. Priests and religious and social reformers constantly brought it up to date, suppressing and expanding; the various components which went into the making of what became the final version have been isolated by the work of generations of Biblical scholars, with the suppressions, additions, adaptations, and occasional oversights of the revisors meticulously exposed. One such oversight gives us a glimpse of earlier beliefs which seem incompatible with the religious feeling of the Book in its final version: the opening verses of the sixth chapter of Genesis, popularly known as "The Angel Marriages":

> And it came to pass, when men began to multiply on the face of the earth, and daughters were born unto them, that the sons of God saw the daughters of men that they were fair, and that they took wives of all which they chose. ... There were giants in the land in those days: and also after that, when the sons of God came in unto the daughters of men and they bare children to them, the same became mighty men, which were of old, men of renown.

This sounds for all the world like a prologue to a Hesiodic catalogue of the loves of gods and mortal women, the births of heroes. But such lapses are rare; the revisors did their work well enough so that when the final version was completed after the return from the Babylonian exile, the Book became canonical; from that point on it might be, indeed *had* to be, interpreted, but it could not be changed.

But the Greeks are the people not of the Book but of the myth. How can you revise, correct, or suppress "what they say"? You may try, but they are perfectly free to go on saying it, even if by changing moral standards it is wrong, even if to new ways of thought it is ridiculous. You cannot correct or suppress, you can only enlarge, add one more version—a more powerful one, you hope—to the limitless complexity and variety of traditional story. A constant process of such enlargement and attempts at correction was inevitable: the myths, all concerned to a greater or lesser extent with the relation between men and gods, imply each one a view of the divine nature and its governance of the world; new moral and religious views had to come to terms with them. So the fifth-century poet Pindar tries to correct the famous and scandalous story of the banquet of Tantalus. Tantalus, king of Lydia, was a friend of the gods, who condescended to eat at his table. He began to think that they were no better than he was, and, to test his idea, served them up a dish which consisted of the flesh of his own son Pelops. The gods realized what the meat was and drew back, except for Demeter, the goddess of the wheat crops and cereal harvests; she was hungry and ate Pelops' shoulder. Tantalus was punished, Pelops was put back together again (except for the shoulder—he was given a prosthetic one of ivory) and went on to found the Olympic games and give his name to the Peloponnese. Pindar is appalled at this story (as well he might be); he rejects the idea that the blessed gods were gluttonous cannibals and substitutes what seems to him a more decorous tale: he will tell the story of Pelops "in opposition to those who went before" (*antia proteron*). What really happened was this: Poseidon fell in love with young Pelops and carried him off to Olympus, to serve the same purpose as Ganymede later did for Zeus. And when Pelops could not be found, some neighbor, in envious spite, invented the story of the cannibalizing feast.

Pindar rejects the myth, accounts in remarkably rationalizing terms for its existence, and tries to supplant it with what seems to him a more moral and dignified version. But he clearly is not confident that he will succeed: he knows what he is up against. "Myths, ornate with the embroidery of lies, are deceivers [*exapatonti muthoi*]. And the charm of poetry, which creates all delights for men, adds its prestige and time and again makes the incredible believed." Quite apart from the charm of poetry, Pindar was flying in the face of the difficulty that his story was much less memorable; who could forget Demeter gobbling that shoulder?

It is, of course, true, as Elroy Bundy demonstrated, that many things in Pindar which were once blithely assumed to be personal or general statements are really (though one should perhaps more cautiously say "are also") sophisticated techniques for praising the *laudandus*. And Köhnken has pointed out that Pindar's implied comparison of Hieron to young Pelops made some correction of the Tantalus myth politic if not necessary.[21] But even with all these factors taken into consideration, Pindar's procedure is, in terms of any other known socioreligious context, extraordinary, to say the least.

What is striking about the passage is not so much the nature of his attempt to revise the myth as the fact that the task is undertaken by a poet, and a poet, at that, who was writing, on commission for pay, an ode celebrating a victory in an athletic contest. With not the slightest hint that he thinks he is doing anything exceptional, he attacks a problem which in Israel lay in the province of the high priest and rabbi, which in Christian Europe was the restricted domain of bishops and theologians. Of course there were priests in Greece too, but their expertise and authority were confined to matters of ritual: the formulas of prayer, the ceremonies of sacrifice and purification, the celebration of the mysteries. In this area there was no deviation from immemorial custom, no laxity, no variation. But these observances were not, as in Israel and the Christian church, indissolubly wedded to an organized and canonical vision of the nature of divinity, its operation in human affairs and its concern with human morality, nor, as in Egypt and Mesopotamia, to charter myths of ritual and royal ceremonial which guaranteed the stability of central governments administering the complicated technology of river valley civilizations. These larger questions of man's relationship to gods, the nature of those gods, and the human morality appropriate or possible given the nature of those gods—all this in Greece was the province of myth, and so of the epic and tragic poets, until the philosophers claimed it for their own, and either replaced the myths with more seemly fictions, like Plato, or abandoned them entirely, like Aristotle and his successors. Any presentation of a myth which involved gods as well as men (and all of them did) implied an attitude to these great questions; any important modification of the story was a fresh contribution to the continual search for an understanding of the nature of divine government and the proper place and conduct of man in the world. "Homer and Hesiod," says Herodotus, "were the first ... to give the gods their epithets, to allot them their several offices and occupations and describe their forms"; they also raised difficult questions of the attitude of the gods to man and man's society, and man's proper attitude toward them. The moral and philosophical problems inherent in the religious tradition were already posed by the myths, and the tragic poets accepted the challenge: Attic tragedy from the first extant play, *The Persians*, to the last, the *Oedipus at Colonus*, wrestles with these same problems. The masked actors on stage presented to the audience not only figures molded by the oral tradition into shapes symbolic of all human hopes and fears, all human victory and defeat, but also, invoked at every turn if not actually present on stage, those gods who dispensed both good and evil in ways that seemed to pass all understanding.

There was still one more source of power in tragic myth, one which worked strongly on the deepest individual emotions. The myths are set from first to last in the framework of the family, that close unit—closer in ancient Greece than it is today—which sets an indelible mark on our formative years and stays with us, backward and forward, a burden and support, until we die. The family, its hates and loves, its unity and its discord, has of course been the main source of energy for western fiction ever since. "All happy families are similar: every unhappy family is unhappy in its own way." So runs the opening sentence of one of the great Russian novels, which records the tragic disintegration of one family and the foundation of another.

I once saw, in a small theater in Piraeus, a magnificent performance, in modern Greek, of Sophocles' *Electra*. The audience was audibly and visibly in tears during Electra's great speech over the urn which she thinks contains her brother's ashes and was profoundly moved by the joy of the recognition scene. When, during the offstage murder of Clytemnestra by her son, Electra, left on stage, screamed to Orestes: "Strike her twice, if you have the strength" (*paison ei stheneis diplen*, though what the actress actually said was more like *htip' an boreis thipla*), a well-dressed, middle-aged man sitting next to me (he looked rather like a bank manager) jumped to his feet and, applauding vigorously, shouted "Bravo! Bravo!" As people looked around in astonishment, he sat down, embarrassed. But clearly Sophocles had touched some unhealed wound in the man, a wound inflicted in the everlasting hates and loves of family life.

A French literary critic who had just returned from Communist China once began a lecture with the sentence: "Les Chinois sont en train d'abolir la famille. Ce sera la fin de la littérature." In its epigrammatical exaggeration and its implication that *la fin de la littérature* will be *la fin du monde*, it was a typically French statement, but there is more than a grain of truth in it. It is hard to think of a masterpiece of western literature that has not drawn at least part of its power to move us from the deep well of those conflicting emotions which are engendered in us by our existence in a family.

Greek tragic myth is a web of interlocking family histories. Within the families, as well as in their relations with each other, the whole spectrum of the passions family life can breed is displayed. And these passions, as is to be expected of material shaped by oral tradition, are exemplary in their extreme intensity. "When it is in the family relationships [*en tais philiais*]" says Aristotle, "that violence occurs, as for example when murder or some similar action is committed or planned by brother against brother, son against father, mother against son or son against mother—this should be the objective."[22] This advice is addressed to the tragic poet; it was easy advice to follow, for the myths provided a rich array of such incidents. Even a short list will make the point: Orestes and Alcmaeon, the matricides; Clytemnestra, Eriphyle, Deianira, husband-killers; Oedipus the patricide; Medea, Ino, Althaea, Procne, and Agave, who brought about the deaths of their own sons; Agamemnon, a father who kills his daughter; Scylla, a daughter who kills her father; Heracles, who butchers his sons, and Oedipus and Theseus, whose curses have the same effect on theirs; the fratricidal brothers Polynices and Eteocles and the only slightly less murderous Atreus and Thyestes; twin sons who kill their stepmothers, Pelias and Neleus, Amphion and Zethus; mothers who expose their children, Creusa, Hecuba, Jocasta. In addition to acts of violence perpetrated by one family member against another, the myths offer a variety of sexual trespasses within the family bounds: incest, mother and son (Oedipus and Jocasta), brother and sister (Canace and Macareus), father and daughter (Atreus and Pelopeia—their son was Aegisthus); adultery, Helen, Clytemnestra; seduction, Stheneboea, Phaedra; desertion, Jason, Theseus. And the myths also presented family ties that are not broken but closely knit in love: brother and sister, Orestes and Electra, Antigone and Polynices; father and son, Odysseus and Telemachus; husband and wife, Admetus and Alcestis, Laodamia and Protesilaus, Hector and Andromache; father and daughter, Oedipus and Antigone and Ismene.

In their loves, as in their hates, the mythic figures of tragedy are extreme cases; the daily life of the audience was not so sensational. Yet they must have known the same impulses and passions in muted form in their own family relationships; the tragic figures are larger than life but true to it. Exposure of children was not an unknown practice in Athens; Creusa's heartbroken lyric lament in the *Ion* when she thinks she will never again see the child she left in the cave on the Acropolis would find an echo in the hearts of those who had been forced by circumstances to abandon their own children. The bitter hatred of Polynices and Eteocles for each other was an emotion many would recognize from their own lives; in the legal cases we know from the fourth-century orations, brothers (or half-brothers) pursue each other to the limits allowed by the law in their fierce quarrels over their inheritance, and Isaeus tells us of two brothers, Euthycrates and Thoudippos, whose quarrel over the division of their father's estate ended in the death of one brother at the hands of the other.[23]

We do not have to believe the story that Sophocles in his old age was prosecuted by his son for incompetence in the management of family property. Nevertheless, the enraged curse which Oedipus pronounces on his son in Sophocles' last play may well have stirred up violent emotions in some members of the audience, for such a prosecution was possible, in the old man's life or after his death, to upset his will. "This law," says an authority on the Greek family, "may have provided an incentive to men to divest themselves of their property to their adult sons," and he adds later, with notable understatement, that "the balance of such a father/son relationship was obviously delicate."[24] In the speech Antiphon wrote for the son whose dying father had charged him with the duty to avenge him, the wife, who, according to the prosecution, contrived his death through a poison disguised as a love philter, is compared to Clytemnestra. And a passage from Andocides' speech in his own defense delivered in 399 B.C., an attack on the character of his legal opponent, suggests that sometimes Athenian family relationships could in fact be as lurid as those of the mythical prototypes:

> Let us just see, gentlemen of the jury, whether anything of this kind has ever happened in Greece before. A man marries a wife, and then marries the mother as well as the daughter. The mother turns the daughter out. Then while living with the mother, he

wants to marry the daughter of Epilycus, so that the granddaughter can turn the grandmother out. Why, what ought his child to be called? Personally I do not believe that there is anyone ingenious enough to find the right name for him. There are three women with whom his father would have lived: and he is alleged son of one of them, the brother of another, and the uncle of the third. What ought a son like that to be called? Oedipus, Aegisthus, or what?[25]

These echoes of the tragic stage in speeches delivered before the juries of law courts give some idea of how deeply rooted and influential tragic myth was in the mind of the ordinary Athenian. It is hardly to be wondered at. Tragic myth, to recapitulate, was a people's vision of its own past, with all that such a vision implies for social and moral problems and attitudes in its present. It was a vision of the past shaped by the selective adaptation of the oral tradition to forms symbolic of the permanencies in human nature and the human condition. It was rich in religious significance, for its interweaving of human action and divine purpose explored the relation of man to his gods. And the political, moral, and religious questions it raised were given a passionate intensity and a powerful grip on the emotions by their grounding in the loves and hates of family life.

Notes

1. F. M. Cornford, *The Origin of Attic Comedy* (London, 1914).

2. Jane E. Harrison, *Themis* (Cambridge, 1912), pp. 341ff.

3. Arthur Pickard-Cambridge, *Dithyramb, Tragedy and Comedy* (Oxford, 1927).

4. Ibid., ed. T. B. L. Webster (2d ed., Oxford, 1962), p. 128.

5. Photographs and descriptions (with sample texts) in *Dionysus in 69* (New York, 1970).

6. G. F. Else, *The Origin and Early Form of Greek Tragedy* (Cambridge, Mass., 1965).

7. E. Lobel, *Proceedings of the British Academy*, XXXV (1950), 1-12; cf. also D. L. Page, *A New Chapter in the History of Greek Tragedy* (Cambridge, 1951).

8. Choerilus, Phrynichus, Pratinas, Polyphrasmon, Aristias, Aristarchus of Tegea, Ion of Chios, Achaeus, Iophon, Philocles.

9. Horst-Dieter Blume, in *Einführung in das antike Theaterwesen* (Darmstadt, 1978), p. 7, concludes that "die Summe der aufgeführten Stücke [in the fifth century] die Grenze der Tausend weit überschritt . . . ," but he is including comedies and satyr plays in the total.

10. On this point, see E. Havelock, "Prologue to Greek Literacy," in *University of Cincinnati Classical Studies* II, pp. 335ff.

11. M. I. Finley, *The Use and Abuse of History* (London, 1975), p.15; Herman Fränkel, *Wege und Formen frühgriechischen Denkens*[2] (Munich, 1960), p. 2.

12. Finley, *The Use and Abuse of History*, p. 18.

13. W. D. O'Flaherty, *Hindu Myths: A Sourcebook Translated from the Sanskrit* (Harmondsworth, 1975), pp. 41–42.

14. Hdt. 7.159.

15. The lines quoted by the Athenians (*Iliad* 2.553–54) were athetized by Zenodotus. Menestheus is mentioned in passing in book 4, calls on the two Aiantes for help and helps carry a wounded man out of the line in book 12, and later in the same book is mentioned in a list of the defenders of the ships against Hector. In book 15, Hector kills an unnamed companion of his, and he is not mentioned again.

16. Hdt. 9.26–27.

17. I am indebted for this example of myth in the process of creation to L. A. Fiedler and A. Zeiger, *O Brave New World: American Literature from 1600 to 1840* (New York, 1968), pp. 17–26.

18. Th. 2.22.6.

19. W. C. Sellar and R. J. Yeatman, *1066 and All That* (London, 1930).

20. For two different accounts of this famous incident, cf. Page Smith, *A New Age Now Begins* (New York, 1976), pp. 195–96.

21. A. Köhnken, "Pindar as Innovator," *CQ* 24 (1974), 199ff.

22. Arist. *Po.* 1453b, 19ff.

23. Is. 9.17.

24. W. K. Lacey, *The Family in Classical Greece* (Ithaca, 1968), p. 118.

25. And. 1.128–29.

Part II: Aeschylus

TWO

The Lion in the House
(Agamemnon 717–36 [Murray])

This parable[1] of the lion in the house, in the third stasimon of the *Agamemnon*, comes unannounced from the mouth of the chorus with all the abruptness and dark ambiguity of an oracular response. The opening phrase abandons the theme of the preceding lines, Helen and Troy (the connecting word οὕτως comes seventh in the sentence); the closing words provide no verbal link[2] with the following strophe, which resumes the abandoned theme. The parable's apparent thematic independence of its context is emphasized by a formal device, the reappearance in its end of its opening words, ἔθρεψεν ... δόμοις, δόμοις προσεθρέφθη; this is a well-known technique for marking off a self-contained digression, which is already fully developed in Homer—it appears, for instance, in the long digression which explains the origin of Odysseus' scar in *Odyssey* 19.[3] The lioncub parable is a separate unity formally marked off from its context, and this, together with its emphatic position, central in the central stasimon of the tragedy, suggests that its meaning is of more than local importance.

It has, of course, its local application. The context suggests that the lioncub is Helen, and the man who takes it into his house Paris,[4] or more generally, Troy. This interpretation, demanded by the context in which the parable appears, is discussed and developed at length by the modern critics.[5]

The parallel is exact and significant. Troy adopts and maintains, ἔθρεψεν, Helen, and at the outset of her life at Troy, ἐν βιότου προτελείοις, she is gentle, ἄμερον. The phrase ἐν βιότου προτελείοις has a striking appropriateness, for προτέλεια, "preliminaries," are strictly "ceremonies previous to the consummation of marriage";[6] this is a sarcastic reflection on the γάμος, the "marriage" of Helen and Paris. The connotations of the word προτέλεια also suggest the incongruous idea of virginity, an ironical reference to the promiscuity of Helen, which the chorus has already referred to specifically earlier in the play; πολυάνορος ... γυναικός they call her in the parodos (62).[7] She was

This chapter originally appeared in *Classical Philology*, 47 (January 1952). © 1952 by The University of Chicago.

delightful to those who are held in honor, to the elders (each of the disputed readings γεραροῖς and γεραιοῖς suggests the other); the phrase refers, as Headlam points out,[8] to the famous passage in *Iliad* 6, where even the old men of Troy are for a moment swayed by Helen's beauty. The epic forms and usages found in these lines, the locative δόμοις, the forms πολέα, ποτί, and (adopting Casaubon's reading) ἔσκ᾽ emphasize the reference to the Homeric scene.

The antistrophe describes the destruction brought to Troy by Helen, the lioncub. When the time came, χρονισθείς, she repaid those who had sheltered her, χάριν ... τροφεῦσιν ἀμείβων, with blood, αἵματι δ᾽ οἶκος ἐφύρθη. She was μέγα σίνος πολύκτονον for the Trojans; μία τὰς πολλάς, τὰς πάνυ πολλὰς ψυχὰς ὀλέσασ᾽ ὑπὸ Τροίᾳ are the words the chorus uses of her later in the play (1456–57).

This is the immediate dramatic relevance of the parable of the lioncub, and with this interpretation of it the modern commentators have, so far as I have been able to ascertain, rested content.[9] But even within the limits of the stasimon in which the parable appears another significance, an abstract one, is suggested by parallel and echo. The lioncub is a type of the ὕβρις νεάζουσα of the fourth strophe of the stasimon (763–70). Just as the lioncub, when the time comes, χρονισ-θείς, reveals the temper of its parents, ἀπέδειξεν ἦθος τὸ πρὸς τοκέων, so the new hubris, νεάζουσαν ... ὕβριν, appears, when the time comes, ὅτε τὸ κύριον μόλῃ φάος τόκου, a spirit invincible, ἄμαχον (769), like the lioncub, ἄμαχον ἄλγος, black ruin for the house, μελαίνας μελάθροισιν Ἄτας, like the lioncub which is a priest of ruin, ἱερεύς τις ἄτας, and this black ruin, like the lioncub, resembles its parents, εἰδομένας τοκεῦσιν (771). The lioncub image is thus associated with the process of the reappearance of evil from generation to generation which is the central problem of the trilogy; and thus indirectly associated with the house of Atreus and the individual characters in whom the whole process is worked out to an end and the problem to a solution.

That this apparently simple and direct story of the lioncub should contain complicated and indirect significance ought to surprise no one; the characteristic ambiguity of the choral odes of the *Agamemnon* is well known. It is particularly striking in passages where the dramatically obvious meaning is, as in this case, a justification of the Trojan war and its hero, Agamemnon. The lines in the parodos, for example, which compare Agamemnon and Menelaus, robbed of Helen, to eagles robbed of their young (49–59), cannot fail to suggest to the audience Clytemnestra robbed of her daughter Iphigenia, for the image is more appropriate to her situation than it is to theirs. The lines of the second stasimon which in general terms condemn Paris and Troy (369–80) are equally applicable to Agamemnon, so much so that the chorus, as if realizing where its words are leading, pulls up short and emphatically repeats the name of Paris οἶος καὶ Πάρις (399). In both cases a confident statement of support for the war and the war aims of its leaders has, as it develops, suggested to the audience, if not to the chorus itself, the dark and complicated reality behind the bright façade of the "official" view. The lioncub parable is equally "official" on the surface—Troy which took in Helen has got what it deserved—but below the surface there is conscious foreboding and unconscious prophecy of disaster to come. And this is made clear as the pattern of the whole trilogy unfolds; this parable is the center of one of the main designs, an elaborate pattern of imagery which extends throughout the *Agamemnon* and into the central and final play of the trilogy. It is a complex knot of suggestions which evoke simultaneously all the principal human figures of the *Oresteia*.

Headlam, who saw so much, seems to have glimpsed this too. At any rate, in his pioneering article "Metaphor" (1902),[10] he remarked, with reference to this passage, "There are more parallels than have commonly been observed in *Agamemnon* 718 seq." He did not discuss them in this article, and in his later comment on the passage he seems to have abandoned his earlier view, for he states there, with exclusive emphasis, "the lion-cub is Helen and the herdsman Paris." He adopts Wecklein's conjecture βούτας for the ουτ$_{ος}^{ως}$ of the MSS, and this conjecture, brilliant though it is, has the effect of limiting the significance of the parable, for it puts an overwhelming emphasis on the surface meaning—Helen the lioncub and Paris the shepherd, who took her into his house.[11] This is the best reason for suspecting it, for it may safely be said of the text of the choral odes of the *Agamemnon* that any conjecture which lessens or removes dramatic ambiguity is for that reason alone suspect. Headlam's adoption of βούτας is a rare example of the pitfall into which his brilliant critical method led him when carried to extremes; his insistence on the traditional and proverbial element in Greek poetry[12] (an admittedly correct emphasis) led him in this case to create a "commonplace,"[13] to use his characteristic word, where it did not exist, and to impoverish the text.

The received text, οὕτως ἀνήρ,[14] suggests initially Paris or Troy, just as the lioncub, in the context of the stasimon, suggests Helen. But ἀνήρ is indefinite in the proper manner of the parable, and may be any man; for example, Menelaus, who took the lioncub into his house when he married Helen. The reference to marriage ceremonies in the words ἐν βιότου προτελείοις is even more appropriate for Menelaus and Helen than for Paris and Helen. The parable as a whole is rich in meaning when so understood; in return for her bed and board, χάριν γὰρ τροφεῦσιν ἀμείβων, she brought her husband's house blood and ruin, αἵματι δ' οἶκος ἐφύρθη, she is μέγα σίνος πολύκτονον for the Greeks no less than for the Trojans, she is indeed a priest of ruin, ἱερεύς τις ἄτας, for the Pelopidae. This implication of the story of the lioncub reveals the mental disturbance that lies behind the confident tone of the chorus' comparison. Menelaus is to blame for marrying Helen; the chorus hints at the general discontent with the war, its unworthy cause and its disproportionate losses—a subdued echo of the strong disapproval which the chorus expressed openly in the second stasimon.

Of this meaning of the lioncub parable the chorus, as a character in the play, is perhaps half, perhaps fully conscious. But the parable means much more than this, much more than the old men, in dramatic time and place, can possibly realize. As so often in the *Agamemnon*, they say more than they know, ἔτι γὰρ θεόθεν καταπνεύει πειθώ, μολπᾶν ἀλκάν, ξύμφυτος αἰών, the force of their singing comes from on high. And in this ode perhaps more than any other in the play, they are the unwitting medium of a superior knowledge.

The full import of the parable is made clear enough to the audience as the play progresses. Lions have already been mentioned in a significant context, the sacrifice of Iphigenia (μαλερῶν λεόντων, 141), and in the scene which immediately follows the stasimon containing the parable Agamemnon boasts of his achievements at Troy in a figure which recalls the conclusion of the story of the lioncub. He speaks of the Greek army at Troy as a raw-fed lion leaping over the wall to lap its fill of the blood of kings (827–28):

ὑπερθορὼν δὲ πύργον ὠμηστὴς λέων
ᾅδην ἔλειξεν αἵματος τυραννικοῦ.

These two suggestions that the lioncub is connected with Agamemnon, (these references to the lion connect the two contexts most significant for Agamemnon's past, the sacrifice of Iphigenia and the slaughter at Troy) are confirmed by the one human character who sees clearly in the murky atmosphere of the play. Cassandra calls Agamemnon the "noble lion," λέοντος εὐγενοῦς (1259), and not content with this she calls Aegisthus (1224) and Clytemnestra (1258) lions too. She explains the full implications of the parable at a moment in which her prophetic frenzy brings before our eyes the past, present, and future of the house of Atreus, a moment too in which the unconscious prophecies contained in the parable of the lioncub are about to be fulfilled.

"The lion," says Headlam, "which is common on Lydian coins and still extant on the ancient gates of Mycenae, was probably the badge of the Lydian dynasty of Pelops. That seems to be the reason why the

term is appied to the various members of the family."[15] Headlam's
guess that the lion was the badge of the dynasty of Pelops is supported
by a more specific piece of evidence. In Pausanias' description of the
chest of Cypselus (5.19), Agamemnon's shield, which appeared on one
of the panels, is described in the following words: Φόβος δὲ ἐπὶ τοῦ
Ἀγαμέμνονος τῇ ἀσπίδι ἔπεστιν ἔχων τὴν κεφαλὴν λέοντος.[16] But this
connection of the lion with the house of Pelops can hardly be "the
reason why the term is applied to the various members of the family";
Headlam's statement explains how it was possible to call Agamemnon,
Clytemnestra, and Aegisthus lions; it does not explain what effect is so
produced. The fact that the lion was the heraldic device of the house of
Pelops may have been the germ of the Aeschylean conception, but the
significance of these repeated lion images is surely their reference to the
central parable of the lioncub, and the identification of the lioncub of
the parable with Agamemnon, Clytemnestra, and Aegisthus.

Aegisthus the lion is of course a sarcasm. He is no true lion, as
Cassandra's phrase makes clear; λέοντ' ἄναλκιν she calls him, a
strengthless lion; he is rather a wolf, as she says later (1259) or a
woman, as the chorus calls him in vs. 1625. Yet, like the lioncub, he
was taken into the house, by Clytemnestra, and kept there, ἔθρεψε; that
this connotation of the English word "kept" is also possible for τρέφειν
is clear from such phrases as τρέφειν γυναῖκα, τρέφειν πορνάς.[17]

Χρονισθεὶς δ' ἀπέδειξεν ἦθος τὸ πρὸς τοκέων, in time he showed
himself a true son of Thyestes, and he is ἄμαχον ἄλγος οἰκέταις,
invincible bane to the household, in the final scene of the play where,
in the moment of victory, he browbeats and threatens the chorus.

This is an ironic suggestion, and one which is not immediately suggested by the words of the chorus; it does not emerge clearly until Cassandra supplies the connection. But the two chief figures of the tragedy
are linked to the lioncub in so many ways that the parallel is unmistakable. And in the case of Agamemnon it presents itself immediately. It is
suggested in the opening words of the parable by a striking echo.

The opening words ἔθρεψε δὲ λέοντος ἶνιν recall the only previous
mention of lions in the play; the verbal echo is precise. The echo in
λέοντος ἶνιν ... φιλόμαστον of δρόσοις μαλερῶν λεόντων, πάντων τ'
ἀγρονόμων φιλομάστοις θηρῶν ὀβρικάλοισι τερπνά is clear. The
opening words of the parable contain a reminiscence of Calchas' prayer
to Artemis (141–43), a fruitless attempt to avert the evil that follows,
the death of Iphigenia. This echo of the first stasimon brings into the
context of the lioncub parable Agamemnon's great crime, which is also
Clytemnestra's justification for the murder she is planning.

The same ominous suggestion is made again in the next line ἐν
βιότου προτελείοις. This repeats the unusual metaphor of lines 224–27,

ἔτλα δ' οὖν θυτὴρ γενέσθαι θυγατρός ... πολέμων ἀρωγὰν καὶ προτέλεια ναῶν, "he had the daring to become the sacrificer of his daughter, to further his warlike ambitions, a preliminary ceremony for the sailing of his ships." This brings into connection with the lioncub the same crime, but by an even more direct allusion than before; at the same time it recalls an earlier appearance of this same metaphor, vss. 65–66, διακναιομένης τ' ἐν προτελείοις κάμακος, "the spear shattered in the preliminaries of the fighting," which adds to the suggestions with which the parable is loaded the memory of the ten years of battle at Troy. In this one word προτέλεια Aeschylus reminds us of the two counts on which Agamemnon is guilty, the two acts for which he is shortly to die, the murder of Iphigenia and his responsibility for the general slaughter of the war.

This is only the beginning; as the parable unfolds the full wealth of its allusive narrative, the identification of Agamemnon with the lioncub becomes startlingly clear. For the lion is the emblem of the dynasty of Pelops. Hence, the young Agamemnon in his father's house is appropriately described as λέοντος ἶνιν, "the lion's whelp," the pride and hope of the royal line. In his childhood he was gentle, a delight to his elders, fondled in their arms. This idyllic description of the childhood of the young prince is disturbed by yet a third intrusion of the same terrible theme which haunts the opening lines, the murder of Iphigenia; the lioncub is called εὐφιλόπαιδα, fond of children. As a description of a lioncub it is an awkward word, a lioncub is not usually fond of children, though children may be fond of a lioncub, and most of the translators render the word by some such phrase as "by the children loved."[18] Yet the force of the verb in compounds of this type is generally active, and applied to Agamemnon the adjective bears its proper meaning and produces a savagely ironical effect. Agamemnon may have loved his child, but he killed her to further his warlike ambitions.

Χρονισθεὶς δ' ἀπέδειξεν ἦθος τὸ πρὸς τοκέων. When the time came, when he grew up, he reverted to the temper of his forebears, Atreus and Pelops. Unbidden he contrived a feast, δαῖτ' ἀκέλευστος ἔτευξεν; Iphigenia's sacrifice again, for these words contain a reminiscence of that same prayer of Calchas which has been recalled before. "May Artemis contrive no windless calm" prays Calchas, "hastening a second sacrifice ... which shall be no feast," μή τινας ... ἀπλοίας τεύξῃ, σπευδομένα θυσίαν ἑτέραν τιν' ... ἄδαιτον (150–51). The lioncub brought to the house blood and confusion, αἵματι δ' οἶκος ἐφύρθη, Iphigenia's blood, the blood of all those who fell at Troy, and the blood still to be shed. Like the lioncub, Agamemnon is a great evil that kills many, μέγα σίνος πολυκτόνον; this word πολύκτονος has been used by the chorus before, in a context which clearly refers to

Agamemnon (461); he is blamed for the losses at Troy: τῶν πολυ-κτόνων γὰρ οὐκ ἄσκοποι θεοί.

The four distinct references to the death of Iphigenia (φιλόμαστον, προτελείοις, εὐφιλόπαιδα, δαῖτ᾽ ἔτευξεν) bring Clytemnestra, as well as Agamemnon to mind, for Iphigenia's death is the most important link between these two. And Clytemnestra, like her husband, is symbolized in the parable of the lioncub; its allusive phrases present her past, her present, and her future. Agamemnon took her in, like the man who took in the lioncub; προτελείοις refers to Clytemnestra's marriage as well as Iphigenia's death and Agamemnon's crime. Clytemnestra at first was gentle, ἅμερον; it was Agamemnon's misfortune that he failed to realize that the lioncub had grown up, failed so badly that he told Clytemnestra to take his concubine into the house and treat her kindly. Εὐφιλόπαιδα is magnificently appropriate, for Clytemnestra's driving passion is her love for her daughter and hatred for that daughter's murderer. When the time came she showed her lion heart—the chorus is unconsciously prophecying things to come—in return for her bed and board, χάριν ... τροφεῦσιν ἀμείβων, unbidden she contrived a feast, δαῖτ᾽ ἀκέλευστος ἔτευξεν, with slaughter of sheep, μηλοφόνοισι σὺν ἄταις. What the sheep stand for is made clear many lines later (1057) when Clytemnestra, failing in her attempt to make Cassandra follow Agamemnon into the palace, tells the chorus that she herself must go inside, she has no leisure to remain, the sheep are standing ready for the sacrifice, ἕστηκεν ἤδη μῆλα πρὸς σφαγάς. She is speaking of Agamemnon.

Αἵματι δ᾽ οἶκος ἐφύρθη, the house was a bloody confusion; later Clytemnestra speaks in exultant metaphor of the rain of blood[19] that soaked her as she struck Agamemnon for the first, second, and third times. The lioncub is ἱερεύς τις ἄτας, a sort of priest of ruin; Clytemnestra later uses the priestly language of sacrificial technique when she tells how she killed her husband (1384–87), and then claims that the deed was done by "the ancient spirit of revenge," παλαιὸς ἀλάστωρ (1501), who, in her shape, made the final sacrifice, ἐπιθύσας.

Before she goes into the palace to her death Cassandra in her final prophetic frenzy sees that she will herself fall a victim to Clytemnestra, and couches this prophecy in terms of the parable of the lioncub. "This two-footed lioness, who sleeps with the wolf while the noble lion is away, will kill me ... ":

αὕτη δίπους λέαινα συγκοιμωμένη
λύκῳ λέοντος εὐγενοῦς ἀπουσίᾳ
κτενεῖ με τὴν τάλαιναν ...

The two-footed lioness is the lioncub grown up and about to become ἱερεύς τις ἄτας, a priest of ruin.

The parable of the lioncub is a central reference point for the recurrent lion image of the play. The context in which it appears suggests the official interpretation, a specific identification, Helen the lioncub who brings disaster on those who give her shelter. But the following strophe and antistrophe, which echo the words and ideas of the parable, suggest an abstract significance: the lioncub is a symbol of reversal to type, of hubris that resembles its parent, and this connects the parable with the house of Pelops, where in each generation the evil strain in the race comes out. The specific references to the individual members of that house emphasize a new series of identifications, and for each of them the parable has a wealth of meaning. They are initially suggested by the significant echoes with which the words of the parable are packed and finally confirmed by Cassandra, who speaks out clearly, no longer from under veils, as she says, καὶ μὴν ὁ χρησμὸς οὐκέτ' ἐκ καλυμμάτων. . . . The lioncub is not only Helen, but Aegisthus, Agamemnon, and Clytemnestra.

It is characteristic of the *Oresteia* that not even this rich complexity exhausts the significance of the parable. Another identification of the lioncub, which, more sinister and of longer prophetic range than those already discussed, is far beyond the comprehension of the chorus, is suggested by the terms of the parable, developed as the trilogy moves on towards the second act of violence, and confirmed by a specific reference of the chorus of the *Choephoroe* at the moment when Clytemnestra has just been led off to her death at the hands of her son. The lioncub is also Orestes.

This parallel is the most strikingly exact of all five. In the dramatic time of the *Agamemnon* it is Orestes who is the lion's whelp, the young heir of the house that took the lion as its heraldic device. It is to him that the description of the lioncub's childhood is most immediately appropriate, for he is still a child. Τρέφειν, the word which appears in the parable, in one form or another, four times (ἔθρεψε, νεοτρόφου, τροφεῦσιν, προσεθρέφθη), implies childhood, and it is this word which Clytemnestra, speaking of Orestes, uses in the following scene when she explains to Agamemnon that Orestes has been sent abroad (880–81):

τρέφει γὰρ αὐτὸν εὐμενὴς δορύξενος
Στρόφιος ὁ Φωκεύς . . .

'Εν βιότου προτελείοις, in the preliminaries of his life he was gentle, a delight to his elders, often held in the arms, like a nursling child; Orestes was fondled in the arms like a nursling child, but he was no ordinary child, he was the lion's whelp.

Many of these particulars of the lioncub's childhood are recalled much later, in the *Choephoroe*, when the nurse Kilissa, grieving over

Orestes' reported death, remembers how she took care of him in his infancy. Ὀρέστην ... ὅν ἐξέθρεψα, "Orestes ... whom I reared." At the moment when the lioncub, now full grown, is about to kill his mother, the nurse recalls the helplessness of his childhood, the crying in the night, the work he caused her; "for a child that has no intelligence must be looked after like a dumb beast," τὸ μὴ φρονοῦν γὰρ ὡσπερεὶ βοτὸν τρέφειν ἀνάγκη. This is a reference to the parable, the dumb beast that was looked after like a child. And in her famous complaint about the indiscipline of the child's belly, νέα δὲ νηδὺς αὐτάρκης τέκνων, "the child's young belly is its own law," she recalls, though in a different sense, the words of the lioncub parable, γαστρὸς ἀνάγκαις.

Χρονισθεὶς δ᾽ ἀπέδειξεν ἦθος τὸ πρὸς τοκέων. In the fullness of time he showed the temper of his parents, Agamemnon and Clytemnestra. Χρονισθείς is one of the most significant words in the passage; "in time" is the characteristic cry of all the characters of the trilogy: "in time" says Calchas, "this expedition captures Priam's city," χρόνῳ μὲν ἀγρεῖ Πριάμου πόλιν ἅδε κέλευθος; "though it took time, it came," says Clytemnestra of her revenge, ἦλθε, σὺν χρόνῳ γε μήν; "in time has justice come for Priam's sons," ἔμολε μὲν δίκα Πριαμίδαις χρόνῳ, sings the chorus of the *Choephoroe*, as Clytemnestra is led off to her death.

Χάριν γὰρ τροφεῦσιν ἀμείβων, returning thanks to those that reared him, the opening of the *Choephoroe* shows us Orestes dedicating a lock of hair on Agamemnon's tomb; this is the θρεπτήρια, a symbolic thanks-offering which children made to their parents on coming of age.[20] Orestes gives his mother thanks for his upbringing later in the play.

The physical intimacy of the bond between mother and child is suggested in the parable by the words ἀγάλακτον, "torn from its mother's milk," and φιλόμαστον, "loving the breast." Whatever the precise meaning of ἀγάλακτον, it suggests the mother's milk, γάλα, just as φιλόμαστον suggests her breast, μαστός. And these two words, closely associated, as here, recur in three of the most terrible passages of the *Choephoroe*.

When the chorus describes Clytemnestra's dream (526–29), it tells Orestes how, in the dream, she gave suck to a serpent to which she had given birth. "She herself, in her dream gave it the breast ... and with the milk it drew a clot of blood":

Χο. αὐτὴ πρόσεσχε μαστὸν ἐν τὠνείρατι.
Ορ. καὶ πῶς ἄτρωτον οὖθαρ ἦν ὑπὸ στύγους;
Χο. ὥστ᾽ ἐν γάλακτι θρόμβον αἵματος σπάσαι.

A few lines later (544–46), Orestes identifies himself with the serpent of the dream and resolves on his mother's death. He repeats the significant words, "the breast that nourished me ... the kind milk":

οὖφις . . .

. . . μαστὸν ἀμφέχασκ᾽ ἐμὸν θρεπτήριον
θρόμβῳ τ᾽ ἔμειξεν αἵματος φίλον γάλα.

Much later, at the climactic moment of the play, when Clytemnestra, facing death at her son's hands, points to her breast and reminds him of the bond between them, the same words appear. "This breast . . . from which you drew the nourishing milk" (896–98):

Ἐπίσχες, ὦ παῖ, τόνδε δ᾽ αἴδεσαι τέκνον
μαστόν, πρὸς ᾧ σὺ πολλὰ δὴ βρίζων ἅμα
οὔλοισιν ἐξήμελξας εὐτραφὲς γάλα.

Two of these passages refer directly to the dream of the serpent, but all three use the words of the parable of the lioncub. And when Clytemnestra is led off to her death, the chorus, in its song of triumph, emphasizes the connection by referring directly to the lioncub parable of the *Agamemnon*. "It has come to the house of Agamemnon, the double lion . . . " (937–38):

ἔμολε δ᾽ ἐς δόμον τὸν Ἀγαμέμνονος
διπλοῦς λέων . . .

The words recall not only the δίπους λέαινα[21] of Cassandra, but the opening words of the parable itself, λέοντος ἶνιν δόμοις.

In the final play of the trilogy, when the chorus of Furies pursues Orestes to Delphi to exact blood for blood, Apollo expels them from his shrine. "For such beings as you" he says, "this oracle is no fit dwelling-place, you should inhabit the cave of a blood-supping lion" (193–94):

λέοντος ἄντρον αἱματορρόφου
οἰκεῖν τοιαύτας εἰκός.

They might have replied that the house of Pelops, which they have inhabited for generations, answers his description precisely. In each generation, the children of the house have gone through the cycle of the parable, from auspicious beginning to bloody end; each generation has carried one step farther the sequence of blood for blood, made unbidden a feast, and taken its turn as a priest of ruin.

This speech of Apollo, which occurs in the opening scene of the *Eumenides*, is the last reference to the lion. As the action of the final play develops towards the solution of all the conflicts of the trilogy, human and divine, the familiar cycle is interrupted. The parable is no longer appropriate. Orestes, tried and acquitted by a court of law, a new institution which stands for a new concept of justice, leaves the stage a free man, free of the curse, of that repetitive pattern imposed on the lives of Pelops' descendants by the system of private vengeance, a pattern which is metaphorically represented, both as a general phenomenon and as a complex of individual destinies, in the parable of the lioncub.

Notes

1. Walter Headlam refers to it as a "fable," the accepted equivalent of λόγος, the word employed by Aristotle in his discussion of rhetorical "examples," παραδείγματα, *Rhet.* 2.20. Of invented examples (as distinct from historical ones) Aristotle proposes two classifications, παραβολή and λόγος. The two examples he gives of λόγοι both concern animals which think and talk in the Aesopian manner; as examples of παραβολή he instances τὰ Σωκρατικά, the everyday comparisons which are typical of Socratic teaching. The lioncub story falls somewhere in between the two types; it is not an everyday occurrence, but it is not, like the talking hedgehogs and horses of the λόγοι, an impossibility. (Martial [2.75] relates a story similar to that told by Aeschylus; Maximus Tyrius [31.3 (Hobein, Teubner text)] describes a young Carthaginian who brought up a lion as a pet; Plutarch [*De cohibenda ira* 14.462e] mentions lioncub pets as something common and makes a similar statement in *De fraterno amore* 8.482c, πολλοὶ δὲ ... , λέοντας τρέφοντες καὶ ἀγαπῶντες; Aelian [περὶ ζῴων 5.39] speaks of the docility of lioncubs, ἡμερωθεὶς γε μὴν ... πραότατός ἐστι ... καὶ φιλοπαίστης, and gives a list of famous people who brought them up as pets: Hanno, Berenice, Onomarchus the tyrant of Catana, and the sons of Cleomenes.) The connotations of the English word "parable" make it preferable to "fable" in this particular case, for the story, like the parables of the Old and New Testaments, means much more than appears at first sight. It is only when the parable is applied to specific persons that the full meaning emerges. In this respect, it is like Christ's parable of the wicked husbandmen (Matt. 21:33–41), which the high priests and elders accept because they do not realize that it applies to them. (For an enlightening discussion of biblical parables see T. W. Manson, *The Teaching of Jesus* [2d. ed., Cambridge, 1945], pp. 57ff.).

2. The old interpretation of πάραντα (738) as "so" is now generally discredited. (See Liddell and Scott *ad verb.*) Hesychius glosses πάραντα with παραχρῆμα εὐθέως παραυτίκα.

3. *Od.* 19.392–94.

> αὐτίκα δ᾽ ἔγνω
> οὐλὴν τήν ποτέ μιν σῦς ἤλασε λευκῷ ὀδόντι
> Παρνησόνδ᾽ ἐλθόντα μετ᾽ Αὐτόλυκόν τε καὶ υἷας

and *Od.* 19.464–66:

> ὁ δ᾽ ἄρα σφίσιν εὖ κατέλεξεν
> ὥς μιν θηρεύοντ᾽ ἔλασεν σῦς λευκῷ ὀδόντι
> Παρνησόνδ᾽ ἐλθόντα σὺν υἱάσιν Αὐτολύκοιο

This type of "Ringkomposition" is discussed at length by W. A. A. van Otterlo in *Untersuchungen über Begriff, Anwendung und Entstehung der griechischen Ringkomposition* (Med. Kon. Neder. Aka. van Wet., Afd. Let. Deel 7, no. 3 [Amsterdam, 1944], reviewed in *CR*, LX [1946], 96). The Homeric passage is discussed on pp. 16–18.

4. For N. Wecklein's conjecture βούτας for οὕτως (718), which makes the parable point almost exclusively to Paris, see below.

5. Walter Headlam and George Thomson, *The Oresteia of Aeschylus*, II (Cambridge, 1938), pp. 81–83; A. W. Verrall, *Agamemnon* (2d. ed., Macmillan, 1904), p. 92; Gilbert

Murray, *Aeschylus* (Oxford, 1940), p. 215; Franz Stoessl, *Die Trilogie des Aischylos* (Baden bei Wien, 1937), p. 17.

6. Headlam and Thomson, *Oresteia*, p. 11 (on vs. 65).

7. The same tradition appears in E., *Cy.* 181:

ἐπεί γε πολλοῖς ἥδεται γαμουμένη.

8. Headlam and Thomson, *Oresteia*, p. 82.

9. Not so the ancient. In the scholia which Triclinius calls σχόλια παλαιά (published by Wilhelm Dindorf in *Philologus*, XX [1863], 17–29, and printed as scholia to this portion of the play by Wecklein) there occurs a note on 718 ἔθρεψεν δὲ λέοντος which runs as follows: ἤγουν ἀνέθρεψεν αὐτὸν ἀνήρ τις ἐκτεθέντα· τὸν Ἀλεξάνδρον λέγει.

10. *CR*, XVI (1902), 434ff.

11. Headlam and Thomson (*Oresteia*, p. 82) quote with approval Wecklein's defense of his conjecture—"without this word (βούτας) we should not know what 731 μηλοφόνοισιν meant." But sheep are the traditional victims of the lion (cf. *Il.* 5.554–56; 10.485; 12.299–301, 303; 24.41–43, and *Od.* 6.130–34), and μηλοφόνοισιν supplies an expected detail.

12. See for example Headlam and Thomson, *Oresteia*, nn. on 228–31, 339–40, 389–91 (p. 47), 1269–71, 1360; *CR*, XIV (1900), 12, col. 2.

13. See for example Headlam and Thomson, *Oresteia*, nn. on 349, 707–10 (p. 81).

14. For οὕτως used to introduce a parable, see Ar., *V.* 1182, Plato, *Phdr.* 237b (both cited by Headlam), and Ar., *Lys.* 785.

15. Headlam and Thomson, *Oresteia*, p. 29. Cf. also A. Y. Campbell, *Agamemnon* (London, 1940), p. 77. "There is reason to suppose that every mention of a lion in this play glances at some member of the family." This would have been a familiar figure to the Athenian audience of the fifth century; Herodotus has several passages in which a man is spoken of (or to) as a lion, cf. Hdt. 6.13 ἐδόκεε δὲ λέοντα τεκεῖν (Pericles), 5.56 τλῆθι λέων (addressed to Hipparchus), 5.92 αἰετός ... τέξει ... λέοντα καρτερὸν ὠμηστήν (Cypselus).

16. Phobos appears on Agamemnon's shield in *Iliad* 11.37.

17. Τρέφειν γυναῖκα, E., *I.A.* 749; ταύτας (i.e., πορνάς) τρέφειν, Diphilus 87 (Kock); ἔστιν δ᾽ ἑταίρα τῷ τρέφοντι συμφορά, Antiphanes 2 (Kock). Aegisthus is later addressed as γύναι (1625), and Clytemnestra is ἀνδρόβουλον κέαρ (11).

18. "The happy children loved him well," (Murray); "By the children loved" (Plumptre); "a fondling for the childrens' play" (Morshead); "the childrens' pet" (A. Y. Campbell); "the innocent sport of children" (Thomson). Headlam writes "the friend of childhood" and Verrall "made friends with youth."

19. Αἵματι δ᾽ οἶκος ἐφύρθη is reminiscent of Agamemnon's account of his own murder in *Od.* 11.420 δάπεδον δ᾽ ἅπαν αἵματι θῦεν.

20. Headlam and Thomson, *Oresteia*, on vss. 729–30.

21. So effectively that the MSS at Agamemnon 1258 read δίπλους λέαινα, usually corrected to δίπους. (Porzig, *Die attische Tragödie des Aischylos* [Leipzig, 1926], argues unconvincingly for reading διπλοῦς.)

THREE

Aeschylus and the Third Actor

"Three and scene-painting Sophocles." So runs a typically crabbed sentence of Aristotle's *Poetics* (1449ª). Exactly what he meant by "scene painting" is still a subject for debate, but the "three" refers to actors. Sophocles introduced into the tragic performance a third speaking actor; before him there had been only two.

We know almost nothing about this important aspect of the tragic theater of the fifth century B.C.: we have no ancient explanation of the fact that Aeschylus increased the number of actors to two, no reason given for the Sophoclean addition of a third, no comment on what seems, on the evidence, to be the fact that nobody added a fourth.[1]

Aristotle's evolutionary account of the growth of tragedy makes it seem inevitable that tragedy should develop until, as he says, "it found its nature"—one aspect of its "nature" being, presumably, three actors. But this does not really explain why Aeschylus did not invent a third actor as he had earlier in his career added a second.[2] Why was it Sophocles who introduced a third?[3] Why did Euripides not introduce a fourth? And for that matter, being Euripides, a fifth? Tragedy was, of course, always a religious ceremony; it might be argued that like everything associated with cult and ritual, it was tradition bound and stubbornly resistant to change. But democratic Athens was a place in which experiment and innovation set a breathless pace in the development of politics, literature, philosophy, education, the plastic arts, and the theater: the creation of what we know as tragedy at Athens, and at Athens alone, out of a Dionysiac cult which was celebrated in a variety of forms all over the Greek world, is in fact one of the most revolutionary advances in the history of human endeavor.

The reason why the step from two actors to three came comparatively late, and why no further addition was made, may possibly have been economic. The actors, unlike the members of the chorus, were professionals, paid, as far as we can tell, by the state,[4] and they must have been expensive. The theater of Dionysus made almost impossible demands; the performance took place in the open air before an audience

This chapter originally appeared in the *American Journal of Philology*, 93, no. 1 (1972). ©1972 by The Johns Hopkins University Press. Reprinted by permission of the *Journal*.

which might reach the figure of fourteen thousand. As any visitor to Epidaurus knows, the acoustics of the Greek theaters are astonishing, but the actor still needs great skill and long training before he can speak and—without shouting—make every word tell[5] in a theater one half the size of an American football stadium. There cannot have been too many well-trained actors available, for tragedy in the early part of the fifth century was a purely Athenian affair, and even in Athens there seems to have been, in the first half of the fifth century, only one yearly festival at which they could find employment.[6] At that time they were indispensable and could demand high wages. Though the burden of expense for the costumes and training of the chorus was assigned to prominent and wealthy citizens—an enlightened method of taxation— the city magistrates were responsible for payments to actors (as well as for the prizes awarded to the dramatists whose plays were selected for production).[7] Since these magistrates were elected officials who had to present their accounts to the scrutiny of the citizen assembly at the end of their year of office, they were not likely to look with favor on the additional expense of three more actors for the tragic festival (for obviously, if one dramatist was granted a third actor, his competitors had to be given the same privilege).

Two actors had been enough for Aeschylus to produce master- pieces: he had in fact, as great artists always do, made what seems like a limitation into a source of strength. Two actors did not, of course, mean that his *dramatis personae* were restricted to two characters; the mask meant that one man could play several parts. *The Persians*, with its cast of Atossa, the messenger, the ghost of Darius, and Xerxes, used only two actors. The *Seven Against Thebes*, with its long central scene in which the six champions are sent to their respective gates, is all done with two actors; the champions (if indeed they appear on stage at all)[8] do not speak and can be played by extras. The magistrates must have been hard to convince that another actor was needed; only a dramatist who knew he *had* to have a third actor, who thought and talked of nothing else, and brought pressure to bear, would in the end get one.

It was Sophocles who did, and his plays show us why. He wanted that third actor to produce a completely new effect: a scene with three speaking actors on stage, a dramatic triangle, like the prologue of the *Ajax*, with its hero exposed in his madness by Athena to Odysseus, whom Ajax cannot see—like the great scene of the *Oedipus* in which the king, the Corinthian messenger, and the herdsman lock in an intricate three-cornered pattern to produce the dreadful revelation, or that even more terrifying scene just before, in which Jocasta, listening to Oedipus and the Corinthian messenger, suddenly realizes the truth.

We do not know when Sophocles got his third actor. His first production, with which he won the first prize against Aeschylus, was in

468 B.C.; it does not seem possible that his plays for that year employed three actors—he must have won his spurs as a dramatist before he could start changing the rules of the game. The *Suppliants* of Aeschylus, it now seems proved, was produced in the late sixties; it calls for two actors only—if Aeschylus had three actors, he was not making much use of them.[9] But we do know that Sophocles must have obtained his third actor in the next few years, in fact before 458, for in that year Aeschylus produced his trilogy, the *Oresteia*, which employs a third actor in all three of the plays. Once the magistrates authorized a third actor, he had to be used: the theater of Dionysus, like all Athenian institutions, was fiercely competitive, and once the breakthrough had been made, it was no use to carry on with the old formula. Aeschylus, almost at the end of a great career, was presented, willy-nilly, with a new instrument—an old dog obliged to learn new tricks.

In the final play of the trilogy, the *Eumenides*, he brings three speaking actors together for one scene only, the trial scene. Athena is on stage, presiding over the trial; so is Orestes, the defendant; the chorus of Furies acts as prosecutor. As the trial begins, Apollo enters; he comes, he says, as a witness for Orestes. And when Orestes breaks down under the stern, logical questions of the Furies, he turns to Apollo, who takes his place and carries on the defense. How would Aeschylus have managed this scene without the third actor? He would have had to get Orestes off stage and bring back the same actor with the mask of Apollo. It would have been awkward, perhaps, but the scene is a little awkward as it is: one actor relieves another who remains silent and waits his turn—they do not lock in the revealing three-way dialogue of the Sophoclean stage.

In the *Eumenides*, Aeschylus uses the third actor, if not with Sophoclean brilliance, at least along Sophoclean lines. But in the other two plays of the trilogy he does something quite different with him—something Aeschylean, something huge, strange, and magnificent.

In *The Libation Bearers*, the second play, Orestes is accompanied throughout by Pylades, who is carefully identified for the audience in the opening scene (vs. 20) but remains silent as the play develops toward its climax. He stands silent, unaddressed, unmentioned, all through the recognition scene and the long lament in which brother and sister draw strength from their hideous invocations of the corpse of Agamemnon in the grave; he is mentioned again (561) when Orestes describes his plan for vengeance but says nothing either here or during Orestes' scene with Clytemnestra; still silent he goes with Orestes into the palace. If the audience ever expected him to speak, it must have renounced that hope by now and indeed may well have forgotten him as the nurse comes out of the house to play her scene with the chorus, and as Aegisthus, boastful and exultant, walks into the trap.

A slave rushes on stage with news for Clytemnestra: Aegisthus is dead. This small part must be played by the third actor, for in a few moments Orestes, blood-stained sword in hand, will appear at the door to confront his mother. She is still the magnificent, if deadly, creature of the first play, and as the slave makes his exit, she calls for "a man-killing axe." But too late; Orestes appears at once. There is no hope of rescue, and after an agonized cry of farewell to Aegisthus, Clytemnestra turns to face her son. Always a gambler, she risks everything on one throw; she bares her breast and dares him to kill his mother. And Orestes breaks. The command of the god Apollo, the unavenged blood of Agamemnon murdered in his bath, Orestes' own exile and poverty, all the forces behind him—gods, family, and his own ambition—fail him at this supreme moment. He turns to the silent figure who has followed him step for step throughout the play. Πυλάδη, τί δράσω; "Pylades, what shall I do? Show mercy—spare my mother?" And Pylades is there behind him. It is the third actor who went off as a slave, resumed the mask and costume of Pylades,[10] and followed Orestes on stage. And now, at last, Pylades speaks. Three lines, no more, but they are enough. "Then what becomes in the future of Apollo's oracles, what meaning in the sworn pledge of faith? Better offend the whole human race than the gods."

It is the voice of Apollo himself; these three lines seal Clytemnestra's death warrant. Orestes proceeds with his task, his duty, his destiny. Aeschylus has saved up his third actor for this dramatic explosion; further speech from Pylades would be anticlimax, and he says no more. The third actor in *The Libation Bearers* is used to dominate the stage for one tremendous moment in which mother and son hang on his words for life or death.

But in the *Agamemnon*, the first play of the trilogy, Aeschylus' use of this new theatrical resource is stranger still. The third actor is employed to portray a character who remains silent throughout a long tense scene, like Pylades, who is begged to speak, like Pylades, but unlike him, does not answer, and who then, when the other actors have quit the stage, leaving the chorus alone with this obstinately mute figure, bursts out in a torrent of speech and song which races on its frenzied course, checked only by the questions of the chorus, for 250 lines, one of the longest scenes in the play. This strange part, which Aeschylus wrote for his third actor, is the part of the Trojan princess Cassandra.[11]

She comes on stage with Agamemnon in the chariot when Clytemnestra and the chorus welcome the victorious king. Her name is not pronounced, her presence not explained, not even mentioned, as she sits there silent through the long dramatic confrontation, through

Agamemnon's haughty and insensitive speech of greeting, through Clytemnestra's baleful speech of welcome, overloaded with flattering superlatives and laced with threatening ambiguities, through the tussle of wills between husband and wife which ends in the wife's victory and Agamemnon's consent to enter the palace treading on the blood-red carpet she has spread for him. Cassandra sits silent as she hears Agamemnon explain at last to his wife that she is his concubine: "Gift of the army, chosen flower of all my many possessions, she comes home with me." She gives no sign, makes no sound as she hears Clytemnestra's final prayer before going into the palace to murder her husband: "Zeus, Zeus accomplisher, accomplish my prayers. . . . " And then, still sitting motionless in the chariot from which Agamemnon descended to walk the blood-red carpet to his death, she is all but forgotten as the chorus sings, and the audience watches the palace door waiting for a messenger to announce the death of Agamemnon, or for Clytemnestra herself, fresh from that sacrifice she spoke of, or perhaps simply for a scream of agony as Agamemnon is cut down. The choral ode ends with words that seem expressly designed to announce the catastrophe—"My heart . . . frets in the dark, anguished and without hope . . . " and out of the stage door comes Clytemnestra.

But she surprises us. "Cassandra," she says, identifying the silent figure in the chariot for the first time in the play,[12] "get inside the house, you too." Agamemnon is still alive then, and this girl *is* important. The whole play has been moving with the slow sureness of some natural force towards the moment of Agamemnon's death, and now, when that moment seems at hand, the rhythm of the action is brusquely interrupted. This silent Cassandra must have something to say. She does indeed, but not yet. Clytemnestra orders her into the palace, threatens, storms, blusters, the chorus urges and pleads, but Cassandra makes no reply, no movement, no sign of understanding. Perhaps she is deaf and dumb, perhaps, as Clytemnestra suggests, she does not know Greek—perhaps she is not a speaking actor. Whatever the reason, the queen cannot afford to waste more time. "The sheep are standing, ready for the sacrifice. . . . " Agamemnon too is waiting, and if she leaves him alone too long he may hear something; one word, "Aegisthus," would be enough. She goes back in, leaving the chorus the task of sending Cassandra into the palace to share her master's fate.

It does not seem likely that they will succeed. If Clytemnestra cannot make her speak or obey, who can? The chorus repeats its plea, with words of sympathy: "Step down, poor girl, leave the chariot empty. . . . " And suddenly, just as we begin to think that she will never speak, she does. Or rather, she screams. "*Otototoi popoi da*." It is a formulaic cry of grief and terror, one of those cries ancient Greek is so rich in, not words at all but merely syllables,[13] which express emotion no words could adequately convey. But her next utterance is clearer. She addresses the god whose statue stands before the stage door, the god Apollo, who will impose on Orestes the dreadful duty of killing his mother and who will appear in person in the last play to defend his action.

To the chorus, the invocation of the name of Apollo accompanied by a cry of agony makes no sense; for them, in their innocence, Apollo is a god "whose presence is not appropriate at scenes of mourning." They pity Cassandra's ignorance: this foreign captive "needs some interpreter who speaks clear." And when she asks the god, "Where have you brought me? To what house?" they answer for him: "To the house of Atreus' sons. If you don't know that...." As if she did not know that, and all it means. She needs no interpreter, she *is* the interpreter, and now she tells them what the house of Atreus is—"a house that hates gods, with many guilty secrets, murder of next of kin. ..." She knows the hideous story of its past ... "the small children wailing over their slaughter, the roasted flesh eaten by the father..." and its future, too, for in a vivid, cryptic phrase, she foreshadows Agamemnon struck down in his bath ... "slaughterhouse of a husband, the sprinkled floor...."[14] The chorus which looked on her with pity now feels only fear and revulsion; she has brought out into the open everything they have been trying to forget. They reject the prophet. "We seek no prophets in this place at all." But a prophet they have, one who sees the immediate future happening before her inward eye, who in the frantic rhythm of her song shows them fragments from the pictures that race before her possessed mind, her vision of Agamemnon's death as it will take place when this scene is over. "The sprinkled floor ... the hands groping forward ... take him in a black-horned trap of robes and strike. And he falls in the water of the bath."

Her inward eye can see the immediate future, the details of Agamemnon's murder which is now only a matter of minutes; but her knowledge ranges far into the past, too, into the causes of the event. Agamemnon's death is no accident. It takes its due place in a long chain of causes and effects, and Cassandra can follow that chain far back, all the way back to the seduction of Atreus' wife by his brother, which led to the murder of the children, to "the original sin ... that man who trampled his brother's marriage bed. Did I miss," she asks the chorus, "or hit the mark, like a real archer?" She hit the mark. The causes of Agamemnon's death reach back over generations. But this does not mean that he himself bears no responsibility. There are other causes too, and one, she suggests by her presence (though she never actually states it), is all the Trojan blood on Agamemnon's hands. "The gods," the chorus sang earlier in the play, "do not ignore those who have done much killing ... Not for me the sack of cities, nor capture and slavery, eating the bread of a master." In the chariot which came on stage we saw them both, the man who had done much killing and sacked the city, and the captive, whose life is in the power of another.

Agamemnon's death is some measure of payment for what he has done to Troy; Cassandra's silent figure in the chariot all through his exultant victory speech reminded us of what he had done. She takes comfort from the knowledge of his imminent death to face her own. "Since I have seen the fate of the city of Ilion, and the outcome for those who took it, the judgment of the gods ... I will go and face my own fate." But her vision sees not only far back into causes and forward to immediate effect. It ranges far into the future, seven years ahead. She foresees the day when Orestes will come back to avenge his father. Agamemnon's death, and her own, will be paid for. "We shall lie dead, but not unavenged; the gods will see to that. There will come one to avenge us in our turn, a man born to kill his mother and to punish his father's murderer."

There was a reason for this strange and entirely unexpected scene. It delays, unaccountably at first, the catastrophe for which every line of the play has been preparing us—the death of Agamemnon. But that death is precisely the burden of Cassandra's song; before we hear his death cry offstage she weaves into the texture of her mysterious vision cause, effect, and result—the children murdered long ago, the husband who will be struck down by his wife as soon as Cassandra leaves the stage, and far off in time and still to come, the murder of a mother by her son. We do not see Agamemnon's death; we see much more. This strange scene which interrupts the dramatic action blurs and almost suspends dramatic time; in Cassandra's possessed song the past, present, and future of Clytemnestra's action and Agamemnon's suffering are fused in a timeless unity which is shattered only when Agamemnon in the real world of time and space (which is also the false world of mask and stage) screams aloud in mortal agony.

Aeschylus has taken the third actor Sophocles introduced to make the dialogue more flexible, complicated, and realistic, and has used him to make the drama transcend the limits of space and time. This tremendous scene depends of course on the fact that Cassandra is a prophet. She knows the future, the present, the past, sees them clearly as actual and present; she is close to reality, has a concrete vision of what happens and what will happen. It is a terrible burden she bears. "Human beings," says Eliot, "cannot bear very much reality," and Cassandra is no exception. The weight of her knowledge is too much for her. She is either totally absorbed in her vision, inaccessible to other

human beings—"in the passion of her own wild thoughts," as Clytemnestra truly says—or else so overcome by the terror of her vision that
she pours it out in a stream of disconnected images which pass the
comprehension of her hearers, or, if they do strike home, inspire only
fear and revulsion. When she is silent, she is an object for pity—"come
down poor girl . . . "—but when she speaks, only two reactions are
possible: bewilderment—"I can make nothing of these prophecies"—or
rejection—"We seek no prophets in this place at all."

She tells the chorus later how she came to be a prophet. The god
Apollo gave her the gift of true prophecy but she refused him the love
which he desired. He did not take back his gift but he added it to the
proviso that although she would always see the truth, she would never
be believed. It is a simple story,[15] but like all simple Greek stories it
presents in symbolic form a great truth. Those people who from time to
time in the world's history do have this vision, this knowledge, are
always rejected. The prophets of the Old Testament, who told Israel
what was coming, were not believed either. "I was a derision to all my
people," says Jeremiah, "and their song all the day—I am in derision
daily, every one mocketh me."[16] So Cassandra speaks of her lot among
the Trojans: "mocked by my dearest ones,—they hated me with all their
hearts." And the prophets of Israel poured out their horrifying visions
of destruction in the same incoherent, vivid language that Cassandra
uses; Nahum's vision of the fall of Niniveh, like Cassandra's vision of
the death of Agamemnon, is a swift flow of detailed images which
convey the shock of things present and seen: "The noise of a whip and
the rattling wheels and of the prancing horses and of the jumping
chariots. The horseman lifteth up both the bright sword and the
glittering spear . . . a multitude of slain and a great number of carcasses,
no end of the corpses, they stumble on their corpses. . . . "[17]

The language and figure of the prophet are the same from age to
age and nation to nation. The clarity of his vision and the burden of his
knowledge are too great a load for human senses, and the disbelief and
mockery of his hearers tip the balance so that what might have been
merely a strange urgency comes close to madness; the apocalyptic vision
is expressed in magnificent but unconnected images which to the
workaday mind of the hearer seem only to confirm the suspicion that
the prophet is deranged. "I am like a drunken man, and like a man
whom wine has overcome" says Jeremiah "because of the Lord and
because of the words of his holiness."[18] So with Cassandra. "Your wits
are crazed, you are god possessed," the chorus sings to her, "some evil-
intentioned spirit falls heavily on you." But when they can understand
the burden of her song their mood hardens. "What good has ever come
to men from prophecy?" "We seek no prophets in this place at all." So

Israel too turned from its prophets—"Prophesy not in the name of the Lord, that thou die not by our hand"[19]—and so do all peoples in their time and place.

But there is one striking difference between the Old Testament prophets and Cassandra. She has the same concrete vision of reality past, present, and future, the same charged and clotted imagery, the same desperate urgency. Like them, she is the tortured mouthpiece of a higher knowledge, but unlike them, she has no purpose: she has no advice to give, no call to action or repentance, no moral judgment, nothing except the vision of reality, of what has been, is, and will be. She has no wish to speak at all; she remains silent as Clytemnestra taunts and scolds her and when she does at last open her mouth it is to utter a scream of agony and address a series of questions to the god whose spirit rides her and whose image stands on stage. Only when the chorus answers the question she addresses to the god—"What house is this?"—does she turn to speak to them, and a few lines later she is again oblivious of their presence as she shrieks at the phantom figures in her vision of Agamemnon's death. "So hard hearted—can you do this thing? Keep him away—the bull from his mate!"

Cassandra is not intent on forcing her knowledge on others. She has had enough of that at Troy among her own people: "like a vagrant witch, I had to endure the names they called me—beggar-woman, starveling. . . . " She has no moral compulsion to prophesy to the Greeks, her conquerors. She has her spells of prophetic fury, when "the dread pain of true prophecy scatters my wits in chaotic preludes . . . ," but also her sober moments of indifference—"What does it matter if I am believed or not? What will be, will be." Her knowledge is not a message she forces on unwilling ears, a ministry, a gospel to be preached. The speech that unlocks the secret of the future is not offered to Agamemnon; it is refused to Clytemnestra; it is reserved for the chorus alone, for the feeble old men who, as they say themselves, have no strength, no power for action, nothing but "the power of song." The great scene which has been made possible by the Sophoclean third actor is so far from being a complex three-cornered confrontation of the type Sophocles invented that it is in fact the oldest and simplest dramatic form of all, a dialogue between one actor and the chorus.

But this is not a missed opportunity, not the failure of an older technique to take full advantage of a new dramatic resource. This meeting of the third actor and the chorus is a crucial point in the *Agamemnon*. For the chorus, right from the beginning, when it invokes Zeus as the only being who can "cast the dead weight of ignorance off at last from my thought," has needed precisely the knowledge of reality which Cassandra alone can give them. This chorus, which consists of men who were too old to fight even ten years ago, men incapable of action, is yet one of the most important characters of the play. For in the splendor and scope of the long odes the chorus sings there is a dramatic development, a development of ideas, which parallels the development of the action on stage.

On the stage we see acted out the fulfillment of a purpose, Clytemnestra's purpose. Concealed from the chorus, the herald, and her victim by the resolution of that "male-thinking" brain, dangerously close to the ironic surface of her speech of welcome, triumphantly fulfilled when she stands with blood-stained sword over Agamemnon's corpse—this inflexible purpose, openly confessed only when it is finally achieved, is the straight line along which the whole action moves. But on the dancing floor, when the actors have retired and in the chorus there surges that "power of song" which is all that age has left them, a different purpose is revealed. The object of the chorus is not to act, but to understand, to understand what is happening, and what will happen and why, to pierce through uncertainty to the moral law. They struggle to find some light in the darkness which throughout the play shrouds the will not only of Clytemnestra but also of Zeus.

The blaze of the sacrificial fire kindled at Clytemnestra's order to hail the fall of Troy and Agamemnon's imminent return fills them with puzzled misgivings. In their first effort to understand the present they probe back into the past: ten years back, to the army's departure, the portent of the eagles interpreted by Calchas, which brings them to the sacrifice of Iphigenia. And here their agony of soul begins. They know that something menacing is afoot; they fear Clytemnestra and hope that Agamemnon's return will restore order to the house. But they cannot completely blind themselves to the fact that Agamemnon, their hope of rescue and order, has much to answer for, not least the sacrifice of his own daughter Iphigenia to speed the ships to Troy. This is the "merciless pondering of sorrow" that eats their heart. And that is why at this point in their re-creation of the past they break off abruptly and call on the name of Zeus, who is their only resource if they are to cast the dead weight of ignorance off at last from their thought. Their trust is that all the bloodshed and confusion they have seen and fear they yet may see is Zeus' will and therefore somehow good. "Zeus has established this law, that wisdom comes only through suffering." The suffering has a meaning, then, the violence and disorder are the expression of a divine purpose; they can, they must, be understood. That purpose is the will of Zeus, "who set men on the road to understanding." It is characteristic of Greek fifth-century religious feeling that in one of its most profound formulations the god to whom men turn for comfort demands that they use their minds.[20]

And this is what the chorus does for the rest of the play: it ranges over the past, surveys the present, broods on the future, trying to understand. It returns after its invocation of Zeus to the subject it dared not face before, Iphigenia's death. Every dreadful detail is rehearsed, until the actual moment when the knife was drawn across her throat; there the chorus's nerve fails. "What happened after that I did not see: I will not speak of it." For the moment, they give up the attempt to understand the past, for it seems to demand that they resign their hope for the present, Agamemnon. They end their song with an almost incoherent patter of generalities as they turn to hear Clytemnestra announce the fall of Troy.

The sudden shock of such good news—Agamemnon's return will not be long delayed—lulls their anxieties, and they launch into a hymn of thanksgiving to Zeus. In the exaltation of victory and the prospect of Agamemnon's immediate return all doubts vanish. The war was just, the Trojans deserve what they got. It was the fault of Paris who robbed Menelaus of his bride. . . . But Menelaus' loss reminds them that for that one woman, stolen or seduced, all Hellas is full now of wives robbed of husbands and mothers robbed of sons. Their joyful note turns to one of apprehension—Argos is "a people cursing its rulers . . . "; they are back again with their doubts and fears. "The gods do not ignore those who have done much killing . . . "; Agamemnon is such a man. "Great reputation is a dangerous thing . . . the thunderbolt of Zeus is hurled . . . "; Agamemnon, sacker of the greatest city of the East, is now at the pinnacle of human fame and greatness. The ode which began as a thanksgiving for victory ends with a repudiation of the war ("not for me the sack of cities . . . ") and a prophetic vision of Cassandra, the conquered victim ("nor capture and slavery, eating the bread of another").

Two attempts to face the reality of the past and yet clear Agamemnon of guilt have failed; the old men cannot absolve him of responsibility for the death of Iphigenia and for the Greek blood shed at Troy. After the herald's announcement that Agamemnon has landed and is on his way, they try again. This time they place the blame for the war and all the suffering it has caused on the shoulders of Helen, and they pursue this theme obstinately through some of the most beautiful and complex poetry of the play. But they can hardly believe that this is the real explanation.[21]

As the ode proceeds, the language becomes ambiguous; the parable of the lioncub, though it is applicable to Helen, is also a symbol of the recurrent violence in the line of Atreus—each generation in its turn tears at the vitals of the house like the full-grown lion.[22] Soon their language grows more ominous still. They talk in generalities, but the relevance to Agamemnon is all too plain. "When a man's wealth is built up to greatness, it bears children . . . from good fortune there blossoms for his race sorrow insatiable." It is a fresh expression of the idea which occurred to them in the previous ode: "Great reputation is a dangerous thing . . . the thunderbolt of Zeus is hurled. . . . " Even if Agamemnon *is* free of moral responsibility for all the blood shed at home and at Troy, perhaps he is doomed merely because he is now a man so wealthy, so exalted, so high, that he must fall.

They state this archaic doctrine only to reject it: "I stand apart from others, hold my own mind. For it is the *act* of impiety which breeds others to follow. . . . " Not the state of great prosperity, but the act of evil is what brings disaster. They are expecting Agamemnon's return in triumph and magnificence from moment to moment—that is why they reject the old idea; they forget that by the other standard too, the *act* of evil, Agamemnon still stands condemned. The plain fact is that Agamemnon is doomed by both standards; he is responsible for the death of his daughter and all the dead at Troy, and also, in his chariot and later as he walks on the precious tapestry, he is the classic figure of the man whose lofty eminence and overwhelming success invite destruction.

The chorus cannot pursue its search for understanding to the end because it cannot face the possibility of Agamemnon's death. Its lofty vision of Zeus and the working of his will, its formulation of the moral law—"wisdom comes alone through suffering"—: all this remains abstract. Zeus has set them on the road to understanding but they still have far to go. The chorus cannot apply the law to its own situation because it does not dare contemplate the possibilities of the future. The will of Zeus may include Agamemnon's death, and more besides—and all of it deserved; unless the old men of the chorus can face that dreadful prospect, they will never cast the dead weight of ignorance off at last from their thought.

And this is what Cassandra does for them. She brings them brutally face to face with the future, set in its pattern of the past which gives it meaning; she offers them the concrete vision of things to come which could join with their intuition of the moral law to bring light into the darkness in which they grope for understanding. The meeting of the chorus and the third actor brings together the two elements, the moral understanding and the knowledge of reality, which must combine to produce true wisdom.

But they cannot combine. The prophet is rejected, as always. When she talks of the past, they understand. But her vision of the future leaves them bewildered: "These prophecies . . . I understand nothing . . . I am at a loss. . . . " When she mourns for Troy and prophesies her own death, they have no difficulty: "a word too clear . . . a child could hear and understand." It is only the one thing they *must* understand which eludes them. And in the end she speaks clearly to them—no longer in song and visionary language, "no more from behind veils ... or from riddles." First, the past.[23] They are amazed at her exact knowledge of things she could not be expected to know: "raised from childhood beyond the sea you speak unerringly of a foreign city, as though you had been there." And when she tells them no one believes her prophecies, they protest: "But to us, you seem to utter oracles worthy of trust." She goes on, from past to future: "The woman will cut down the man." And they are lost again. "I heard it but I am a runner off the track." She tells them now in words that cannot be misunderstood. "I tell you you shall see Agamemnon's death." And their answer this time is to reject her utterly, with pity and reproof: "Silence, wretched woman! Put those ill-omened lips to sleep." As she launches now on her last, long, prophetic outpouring, she throws off the ornaments that mark her as Apollo's priestess; she is preparing herself for death. Her vision of the future leaps to its outmost limit; she sees seven years ahead to the homecoming of Orestes and the murder of Clytemnestra. And then, as the chorus—which understands only that she is prophesying her own death—speaks to her with respectful pity, she goes in through the door of the palace to join the sheep who are ready, waiting for the sacrifice.

The old men of the chorus have been offered the knowledge that would convert their moral formula into true, if bitter, understanding. "Wisdom comes alone through suffering ... "—more suffering than they were prepared to face. They did not recognize what they were offered, and when finally it was made unmistakably clear, they rejected it. But now, at the very last moment, after Cassandra has gone into the house, they bring themselves to face the prospect which, before this, they have not dared to think of. Is Agamemnon, who has returned in victory and honor, doomed to die? "Now if he shall pay for the blood of those who went before, die, and bring the dead retribution for their deaths, what man alive could boast that his birth was free of misfortune?" It has taken them the whole length of the play to phrase that question and the answer comes at once. The answer is "Yes." It is Agamemnon's death cry from inside the house. "Ah, I am struck, a deep and mortal blow." We know too that Cassandra has died with him. Time has caught up with her vision. Her task is done.

Her body is laid on the steps next to Agamemnon's and Clytemnestra pronounces her epitaph. "This captive woman, who saw strange visions, and shared his bed ... sang like a swan her last dying song and now lies here, his lover; she has added a keen relish to the wanton luxury of my bed." This fierce, exultant dismissal is the last mention of

Cassandra in the play. And we are left to wonder: is that all? Was there no meaning to her suffering? Is she only, as she said herself, "a slave-girl dead, killed lightly and with ease"? Was her vision, her prophecy, pointless and was she right when she said: "one wipe of a sponge blots the whole picture out"? Not quite. Her prophecy does have its effect, too late, as is her destiny, but we in the audience see it. It has its effect on the chorus.

"That man by suffering shall learn. . . . " It has often been pointed out that this idea, the only hint of comfort in the murk and terror of the action, has no relevance for the principal characters. Agamemnon is given no time to learn, Clytemnestra learns nothing, and Aegisthus is incapable of learning. The phrase has been taken to apply only in a larger sense—to the whole human race, which learns from the example of these great dramatic prototypes of human action and suffering. But it is true also of the chorus. They do learn, in the end, and from Cassandra, to face reality, bitter though it may be, to see things as they actually are and must and will be.

In the altercation with Clytemnestra which follows her triumphant speech over the corpses of Agamemnon and Cassandra, the old men of the chorus, broken in spirit and incoherent at first, struggle painfully to see things clearly, and in the end they do. Though they mourn for Agamemnon, they can at last admit his responsibility. "The case is hard to judge," they say after Clytemnestra's arraignment of her husband, "force suffers force; the killer pays." But they know also that payment does not end with Agamemnon. "The law stands fast . . . the doer shall suffer." They are telling Clytemnestra that her turn will come. They have learned from Cassandra to look reality in the face. And before the play is over, stung to furious disgust by the cowardly boasting of Aegisthus, they look forward to the farthest edge of Cassandra's vision of the future. "Oh, does Orestes somewhere see the light of day, to return here . . . and kill them both . . . ?"

It is their only hope now, for Clytemnestra and Aegisthus rule Argos as tyrants. They have the power. "You and I," says Clytemnestra to her lover, "will bring order to the house at last." But more disorder is to come, the worst yet, the avenging son, commissioned by a god to cut his own mother down. "From the gods who sit in majesty on the helmsman's deck" the chorus sang early in the play, "there comes a grace which is somehow violent." We have seen some of the violence and will see more; the grace, which is to be the replacement of individual vengeance by community justice, lies far in the future, beyond the range of Cassandra's vision, beyond the vision even of the god Apollo, who, like his priestess, is an instrument of the mysterious will of Zeus, "universal cause and mover."

Notes

1. The "Rule of Three Actors" has been questioned by some scholars (the distribution of the parts in Sophocles' *Oedipus at Colonus*, for example, can be made for three speaking actors, but only if the part of Theseus is taken first by one and then by another). But the weight of the ancient evidence is heavily in favor of three speaking actors for tragedy (comedy is a different matter). Aristotle clearly had never heard of a fourth actor. For the most recent and thorough discussion, see Arthur Pickard-Cambridge, *The Dramatic Festivals of Athens* (2d ed., rev. by J. Gould and D. M. Lewis, Oxford, 1968), pp. 135ff.

2. On the function of Aeschylus' second actor, see the perceptive remarks of G. F. Else, *The Origin and Form of Early Greek Tragedy* (Cambridge, Mass., 1965), pp. 86ff.

3. Else (*TAPA*, LXXVI [1945], 1–10; *Wiener Studien*, LXXII [1959], 75ff.) has made out a case for Aeschylus as the first to use a third actor; undeterred by much adverse criticism, he still maintains this position in his latest book: "it was his development as a dramatist that made the third actor necessary" (Else, *Origin and Form*, p. 96). For a detailed discussion of this theory, see Pickard-Cambridge, *Dramatic Festivals²*, pp. 130–32.

4. There is practically no ancient evidence on this point; payment by the state seems the most likely procedure and is generally accepted.

5. For a discussion of this point, see B. Hunningher, "Acoustics and Acting in the Theatre of *Dionysus Eleuthereus*," *Med. Kon. Nederl. Akad. van Wet.*, Afd. Lett., N. R., XIX, 9.

6. "The evidence of inscriptions makes it practically certain that the organization of contests at the Lenaia in tragedy and comedy (parallel to those at the city Dionysia) goes back no farther than the middle of the fifth century B.C. . . . probably about 440 B.C. . . . " (Pickard-Cambridge, *Dramatic Festivals²*, p. 40). The earliest evidence for tragic performances at the rural Dionysia is for the end of the fifth century at Piraeus and Eleusis and an earlier (but unspecified) date in the same century for Ikarion.

7. Once again the evidence is almost nonexistent. Ar., *Ra.* 367 speaks of an orator "eating up the payments made to the poets" (cf. Sch. Ar., *Ec.* 102) and if the comic poets were given a money prize, it is to be presumed that the tragic poets were also rewarded for their pains.

8. Strong arguments against their appearance are in Eduard Fraenkel, *Die sieben Redepaare im Thebanerdrama des Aeschylus* (*Bayerische Akad. der Wissenschaften*, Phil.-hist. Kl., 1957, 3), pp. 6–7; cf. also p. 13, n. 33 and p. 32.

9. He did not make brilliant use even of the two he had. Before the publication of the papyrus fragment which redates the play, "the insignificance of the second actor" (A. E. Haigh, *Tragic Drama of the Greeks* [Oxford, 1896], p. 101, n. 2) was one of the reasons regularly cited for dating the play in the first decade of the century. With the new date, the ineffectiveness of the figure of Danaus is puzzling: "it remains an awkward fact that the actors were used in a way which suggested that the dramatist had not long had the use of two actors" (D. W. Lucas, *The Greek Tragic Poets²* [London, 1959], p. 83). Lucas suggests that "features of the play which could plausibly be interpreted as primitive might in fact be due to the use of one of the few myths in which it was possible to give the chorus this unusual predominance" (Ibid., p. 83). For a different explanation see Else, *Origin and Form*, p. 94.

10. So the scholium, vs. 899, μετεσκεύασται ὁ ἐξάγγελος εἰς Πυλάδην, ἵνα μὴ δ' λέγωσιν. This has been questioned, but see Pickard-Cambridge, *Dramatic Festivals²*, p. 140. There is ample time for a change of costume: the slave can go into the house at 887 (889ff. are addressed to one of Clytemnestra's attendants, but there is no time to execute the order) and Pylades need not appear until 899.

11. There is no scene in *Agamemnon* which has three actors speaking (as in the Pylades and trial scenes). But without a third speaking actor Cassandra could not come on stage with Agamemnon (and there was no other time to bring her on), and it is only for this entrance that a third actor is required.

12. Eduard Fraenkel, *Aeschylus, Agamemnon* (Oxford, 1950) suggests (on vs. 950 τὴν ξένην δὲ κτλ.) that Aeschylus did not wish "to make her identity clear to the audience before the beginning of the Cassandra scene" [i.e., 1035]—if he had "he would presumably have written 950 in a different form." "And even now" he says earlier, "the words τὴν ξένην serve up to a point to conceal her identity." Up to what point? There was no need to mention her at all if the audience was not meant to wonder who she was; knowing their *Odyssey* (λ 422) they would not have wondered long.

13. Fraenkel's thorough discussion in *Aeschylus, Agamemnon* (at vs. 1072) should lay to rest forever the persistent ghost of the scholiast's suggestion that δᾶ is a Doric form of γᾶ.

14. Whether one reads ἀνδρὸς σφαγεῖον or ἀνδροσφαγεῖον, Cassandra's words cannot fail to suggest the death of Agamemnon (cf. Fraenkel, *Aeschylus, Agamemnon*). D. L. Page, in *Aeschylus, Agamemnon* (ed. by J. D. Denniston and D. L. Page, Oxford, 1957) takes πέδον ῥαντήριον to mean "ground sprinkled (with blood)" and the whole line to refer exclusively to the mutilation of Thyestes' children. This is in accordance with his view that "Cassandra's visions . . . form a continuous series of events. Cause and effect, the crime of Atreus and the murder of Agamemnon are revealed to her stage by stage in a stream of visions, past and future in orderly sequence" (p. 164). Consequently, any reference to Agamemnon's death in Cassandra's first vision "would be wholly premature, for we are at this time farther back in the past, about to witness a vision of the mutilation of Thyestes' children."

15. It sounds like a folk tale motif, but Stith Thomson, in *Motif-Index of Folk Literature* (Bloomington, Ind., 1955), lists only one parallel, from India (M301.0.1). Similar in form (the transformation of a gift or curse rather than its cancellation) is the story that Poseidon, angered at his defeat in the contest for Athens, laid on the city the curse that it would always make the wrong decision; Athena added the proviso (προσθεῖναι) that, even so, the result would always be success. This story seems to be attested only by the scholium to Ar., *Ec.* 473, but it does not sound like a Byzantine invention (though it may well be an Athenian invention of the fifth century B.C.).

For an argument that Cassandra's refusal to yield to Apollo is a crucial decision which makes her a "transgressor" and one whom we are to regard "as being in the wrong," see D. M. Leahy, "The Role of Cassandra in the *Oresteia* of Aeschylus," *Bulletin of the John Rylands Library*, LII (1969), 145–77. "She chose wrongly and thereby ensured her murder . . . " (p. 175). Leahy's article is valuable (especially for its examination of Aeschylus' treatment of the loves of gods for mortal women, pp. 161ff.), but Cassandra's "responsibility" does not seem to me as important a theme in the play as he makes out.

16. Jeremiah 20:7.

17. Nahum 3:2–3.

18. Jeremiah 23:9.

19. Jeremiah 11:21.

20. φρονεῖν, in Attic, as Fraenkel (at vs. 176) says, "comes very close to the meaning of σωφρονεῖν and of ὑγίεια φρενῶν." But in this passage it refers also to mental activity, as Fraenkel himself implies in his eloquent explanation of χάρις (at 182ff.): "There might have been a world—so far the poet's thinking seems to have progressed—in which man had only to suffer, struck down by obscure powers *without ever understanding why, without ever recognizing any connexion between* doing and suffering [italics mine]. As things are, this is not so . . . the god . . . has opened a way to φρονεῖν. . . . "

21. Later (1455ff.), when they revert to this false comfort, Clytemnestra calmly dismisses it as irrelevant, and they do not protest.

22. cf. chapter 2 of this book.

23. As Fraenkel points out in *Aeschylus, Agamemnon* (p. 625), Cassandra "discloses her knowledge of the past to prove the trustworthiness of her prophecies ... Thus the customary ideas about the nature of true seership provided the dramatic poet with an excellent means of widening his story beyond the time of the actual plot and strengthening the links between the past and the future."

Review

AESCHYLUS: SUPPLIANTS. *Translated by Janet Lembke. Oxford University Press, 1975.*

AESCHYLUS: SEVEN AGAINST THEBES. *Translated by Anthony Hecht and Helen Bacon. Oxford University Press, 1975.*

AESCHYLUS: PROMETHEUS BOUND. *Translated by James Scully and C. John Herington. Oxford University Press, 1975.*

Ever since Greek tragedy was rediscovered by the West in the early Renaissance, it has been more widely read in translation than in the original. Greek in the modern world has always been an elite accomplishment and the Renaissance editions of Greek tragedy, like many of their modern counterparts, were bilingual—Latin translation on the facing page. What is surprising is that when the time came for English translation, tragedy was so badly served: unlike Homer, it did not attract the poets—it has no interpreter even remotely comparable with Chapman or Pope. Dryden, the translator-general of his age, Englished all of Vergil, much of Lucretius, Ovid, Juvenal, and Persius, some of Horace, Theocritus, and Homer; he versified Boccaccio, modernized Chaucer, and even converted *Paradise Lost* into an opera "in Heroickal Verse," but he never laid a finger on Aeschylus, Sophocles, Euripides.

Shelley translated a play of Euripides but it was the satyr play *Cyclops* (bowdlerized at that), and Browning produced a sentimental travesty of the *Alcestis* and a typically eccentric version of the *Agamemnon*. But these two poet-translators are the exception: for the whole of the eighteenth and nineteenth centuries, the Greekless reader saw Attic tragedy through the distorting spectacles of verse written by scholars whose acute perception of the nuances of ancient Greek was exactly matched by their crass insensitivity to the sound and sense patterns of English. Aeschylus paraded in the rococo trappings of Potter—"But you, my friends, amid these rites / Raise high your solemn warblings ... "— or played the reluctant clown in the archaic shreds and patches of

This chapter originally appeared in the *New York Review of Books*, November 27, 1975.

Morshead—"I rede ye well, beware!" "Speak now to me his name, this greybeard wise!"

By the early years of this century, those Greekless readers (a condescending Victorian equivalent of "deserving poor") were no longer an embarrassed minority of the educated; they were now an important intellectual constituency to be won over for the classics. For tragedy, this task was undertaken with enthusiasm and success by the Regius Professor at Oxford, Gilbert Murray, a great Hellenist and also a public figure whose impact on the life of his time, like that of Jowett before him, was not confined to Oxford—as Shaw's affectionate caricature of him in *Major Barbara* testifies. Murray's verse translations (of Euripides and Aeschylus) were intended for performance and were in fact extremely successful on stage: they were also accepted by the public at large and some of the critics as English poetry in their own right.

This is a judgment time has rescinded. Murray would occasionally in the choral passages rise to giddy Swinburnian heights (he could also sink to nameless bathetic depths), but for the dramatic dialogue he adopted a form which only Donne could handle successfully—rhymed couplets which are, for the most part, not closed. One can understand his recourse to rhyme as a protest against the lifeless blank verse of his predecessors ("Blanker verse ne'er was blunk," to quote Walt Kelly), and in this he had the enthusiastic support of Granville Barker (who demanded for Greek tragedy "a formal decorative beauty, scarcely attainable in English without the aid of rhyme"). But, quite apart from the faintly spastic effect of rhymes which usually do not point up and sometimes work against the sense, the insistence on rhyme over hundreds of lines of dramatic dialogue exacts a heavy price in warped syntax, violent inversions, and, above all, fulsome padding. This was the target of one of Eliot's lethal shots: he pointed out that Medea's prosaic six (Greek) words—"I am a dead woman, have lost all joy in life"—were transformed by Murray into the rococo jewel, "I dazzle where I stand / The cup of all life shattered in my hand."

Most of Murray's translations predate World War I: as Western civilization plunged deeper into its own tragic age, the poets were drawn to Greek tragedy. Yeats made a stage version of Sophocles' *Oedipus* (in prose—except for the choruses, which, though magnificent, recall the Liffey more than the Ilissus) and formulated the modern program: "The one thing I kept in mind was that a word unfitted for living speech, out of its natural order or unnecessary to our modern technique, would check emotion and tire attention." In the next generation MacNeice (so great a poet that few realize he was also a professor of Greek) produced a spare, virile *Agamemnon*, and Pound published (1954) a typically aggressive version of *Trachiniae*; in America, Fitzgerald turned out a memorable *Oedipus at Colonus* (1941) and Lattimore began, with a fine *Agamemnon*, the translations of Aeschylus and Euripides which became standard versions for their time.

Lattimore is of course a joint editor, with David Grene, of the *Complete Greek Tragedies* published by Chicago; it contains the surviving Greek tragedies in versions made and commissioned by the editors (eight by Lattimore and five by Arrowsmith)—the earliest done in 1941, the most recent in 1958. Oxford has now begun to issue, under the general editorship of Arrowsmith, a series called The Greek Tragedy in New Translations, which is, presumably, going to translate the whole corpus of thirty-three plays over again.

Apart from the fact that poetic fashions change (more rapidly in the twentieth century than the nineteenth), there are good reasons for going back over the ground. The Chicago translations, though infinitely superior to anything else available in the immediate postwar decades, have their bad spots. Lattimore and Arrowsmith can be depended on to produce English verse that, while it does not always scale the heights of Parnassus, never stumbles into a pratfall, and they are both careful, accurate scholars. But their collaborators are in a different league. There are some real blunders in translation, some of them badly misleading in passages crucial to interpretation; there are passages of grotesque translationese which seem to have come from the hand of Potter's ghost—"What will befall me? I swoon / Beholding the citizens agèd"; but worse than the occasional outrage is the steady bleat of dramatic verse doggedly penned by professors whose normal medium of self-expression is the footnote.

The aim of the Oxford series is, to quote its general editor, to produce "a re-*creation* of these plays—as though they had been written, freshly and greatly, by a master fully at home in the English of our own times" (so Fitzgerald in 1941 said of the *Oedipus at Colonus*: "it can be rendered only in what might be called the English of Sophocles"). Since there are few contemporary poets who know Greek well enough to bring over into their versions what Arrowsmith calls "that crucial *otherness* of Greek experience . . . its remoteness from us," some of the plays are tackled by poet-scholar teams. The first three Aeschylus plays to appear in the series present us with one scholar-poet, Janet Lembke (*Suppliants*) and two teams: Helen Bacon-Anthony Hecht (*Seven against Thebes*) and John Herington-James Scully (*Prometheus Bound*).

For a translator, Aeschylus is of course the most formidable of the three tragedians. Even his own countrymen, in the next generation, blended admiration for his archaic grandeur with amused appreciation of what their more rhetorical taste thought crude and gigantic. The modern translator has to find an English equivalent for a dramatic idiom which, though distant enough from the talk of the street to serve as the language of gods and heroes, still preserved the contemporary resonance essential for popular drama. The problem is of course insoluble for many reasons, one of them the lamentable fact that since the early seventeenth century, English has had no poetic drama worth the name, has developed no verse style suitable for the stage and acceptable to a mass audience. The Shakespearian achievement, dramatic poetry which possessed both high solemnity and a contemporary rasp, remains unique—and inimitable. The translator of Aeschylus has no pilot to help him steer a course between the Scylla of archaic silliness and the Charybdis of swiftly obsolescent colloquialism.

These two extremes once assumed for this reviewer a paradigmatic form which suggested a private terminology for judging translations of Greek tragedy. I was collaborating with a gifted actor-director on a prose translation of Sophocles' *Oedipus* which was to be used by actors in an educational film. We were in a hurry: working directly from the Greek, I fed him the lines to test for their speakability. I was concerned to be swift, clear, and direct, no matter what other values might be lost, and when we came to the great scene in which Oedipus forces the truth out of the reluctant herdsman, I gave my collaborator the line: "Grab him! Tie his hands behind his back! Quick!" He looked at me malevolently, pulled an imaginary fedora down over his forehead, stuck a real cigar in the corner of his mouth, and snarled the line back at me in what passes on the English stage for a Chicago accent. "What *is* this," he asked, "a gangster epic?" Challenged to do better, he put down the cigar, waved a hand that transformed the fedora into the likeness of a kingly crown, rose to his full height, and, pointing a menacing finger down at me, bellowed: "Pinion him!"

We eventually compromised on "seize," but I have ever since thought of the horns of the translator's dilemma as Pinion and Grab. With Aeschylus the main danger is obviously Pinion: the characteristic blemishes of Aeschylus-in-translation are archaisms (biblical preferred), complicated inversions, and distressing echoes of the fashionable poetic strains of yesteryear (if not of yestercentury). It is a pleasure to be able to say that the three translations under review are all written, for better or for worse, in twentieth-century English.

Lembke, the only scholar-poet of the three, has the most intractable of the plays. The suppliants of the title are dark-hued Egyptian daughters (fifty of them) who, led by their father Danaos, seek the protection of the Greek city of Argos against the violent courtship of their fifty cousins, sons of Egyptus. Their claim on Argos is that their great-grandmother Io was a princess of that city before—loved by Zeus but persecuted by his wife Hera—she was transformed into a cow and driven, half-mad, round the eastern Mediterranean to Egypt. In the play, the Argive king gives way before their passionate appeals and threats of suicide on the altars; he takes up their cause against their cousins. In the next play of the trilogy (now lost) he was defeated in battle; the Suppliants were forced to marry their cousins, but all of them (except one) cut their husbands' throats on their wedding night. How the third, final play developed, we do not know; we have only a few lines of it, part of a speech by Aphrodite, which give divine justification to that sexual union the Suppliants so fiercely refused. The motivation of this fanatic hatred of marriage is not clear from the text of the play and the text itself is hideously corrupt (some passages are a mosaic of modern and Byzantine corrections and guesswork). The translator's difficulties are compounded by the fact that this is, of all the Aeschylean plays, the most profuse and violent in its imagery.

Lembke has met these multiple challenges magnificently. Image and metaphor are translated with fidelity: "If Aeschylus implies that Zeus' gaze is a bird, then the gaze is not *like* bird but *is* bird." Greek meters are not reproduced, but replaced by "English ... rhythms that seem affective equivalents." And everywhere the verse moves with the energy and harmony, the language with the precision and opulence, of a poet speaking her own tongue. "But Aphrodite is not scanted here / nor do her rites lack eager celebrants. / ... And she is thanked, guile-dazzling / goddess, for her solemn games. / And in her motherlight soft daughters walk. . . . "

There are of course occasional passages which will send scholars back to the Greek with raised eyebrows. For most of them, she supplies a note explaining her interpretation (or reading) and provides a literal translation where she has taken "great liberties in order to make evocative English poetry." Sometimes the liberties degenerate into license, as, for example, when "land of Argos" becomes "earth cupped in the day's hand." It is true that the name of the city is identical (except for accentuation) with an adjective that means (among other things) "bright"—but that cup and hand are pure Pinion. And by a weird coincidence they are the same extraneous objects Eliot shot down from Murray's high-flying *Medea*. But such extravagances are rare. For page after page, Lembke's *Suppliants* creates the illusion that it is written in the English of Aeschylus.

The *Seven* (another play avoided by most translators) is the work of a team. Helen Bacon is a scholar well known as a sensitive critic of

Greek tragic poetry; Anthony Hecht is of course an acknowledged master of his craft. The result of their teamwork is technically dazzling as well as deeply moving. Hecht, unlike Lembke, has used rhyme as the armature of the elaborate choral odes, but rhyme, the despotic master of the versifying professor, is here the vibrant but subtle instrument of a musician. "It is a bitter sight for the housewife / to see, spilled piecemeal from her cherished store, / the foison and wealth of the earth, the harvest riches, / grain, oil, and wine, dashed from their polished jars, / sluicing the filthy ditches. / And by the rule of strife, / the pale, unfamilied girl become the whore / and trophy of her captor. . . . "

The shock effect of "ditches" and "whore" provides an English equivalent for the Greek's re-creation, in relentlessly formal metrical patterns, of the waste and horror of the city's fall. Hecht sustains this high level throughout; this is an English poem in its own right. At times, he seems to have left Aeschylus far behind; I can find, for example, little basis in the Greek for the splendid lines: "You were yourselves misfortune's instruments, / the silenced theme infecting these laments." And yet, on reflection, one sees what he is doing. Aeschylus, in this passage, was relying for his effect on music, dance, and the psychological tension, familiar to the audience, of the hysterical yet formal wailing over the dead; Hecht has only printed words to work with, so they must work three times as hard.

Translators may not be always traitors but they are, whether they like it or not, interpreters: both of these versions, as their authors candidly state, are new interpretations. Lembke sees the solution of the Suppliants' motivation—their wild disgust for marriage—in a "refusal to assume adulthood" which has its roots in the fact that they are "archetypal victims of a father fixation." The villain of the piece is their father; "the play has a madman, and it is Danaos, author of his daughters' lives and their . . . deepening insanity." Those who know the play in the original will search it in vain for traces of this Egyptian Barrett of Wimpole Street; Danaos is a faceless tritagonist, a dramatic nonentity whose function is to report what happens off stage, a puppet ineffective in action and Polonian in speech. Unfortunately Lembke's strange vision of Danaos has colored her translation: the very first reference to him—his daughters' "Danaos, father"—becomes the brilliantly suggestive but quite unjustified "Our father on earth."

Bacon and Hecht take similar liberties. One example will suffice. It is important for their staging of the central scene (and interpretation of the play) that the six Theban champions should appear on stage and that each one, like his Argive opponent, should have a symbolic blazon on his shield. The text mentions only one (Zeus on the shield of Hyperbios), but our translators assume that the others also carry images of the gods, the seven gods prayed to in the opening choral ode, whose statues are represented on stage. Except that Eteocles, who should have carried the image of Aphrodite, surprises us by revealing on his shield the Fury. This is already complicated and conjectural enough to raise the hackles on the critic's back, but there is worse to come. The chorus in the Greek text prays not to seven but to eight gods: this inconvenient fact is dealt with by the lordly expedient of leaving one of them, Hera, out of the translation. The technical reasons given for this omission in a note will not satisfy most scholars, who will await with interest the defense, promised "elsewhere," of "such liberties as we may be thought to have taken."

The third volume, *Prometheus Bound*, offers no such wayward interpretations: the scholar of the team is a recognized authority on the problems posed by this play and its lost successors (or successor). The illuminating introduction, informative notes, and valuable appendix are a distillation for the general reader, as well as the scholar, of original research and critical evaluation maturing over many years. The translation is, of the three, the closest to the Greek. It is also the least exciting. It is of course true that the language of this play shows so little of the metaphorical exuberance and complexity typical of Aeschylus that (for this and other reasons) many scholars have doubted its Aeschylean provenance—doubts finally laid to rest, in most scholars' minds, by Herington's work on the subject.

The style is direct and simple, even in the uncharacteristically short choral odes. Here the demon menacing the translator is not Pinion but Grab, and Scully seems to have had trouble fighting him off. His translation, he says, is "more idiomatic, yet more literal than other versions of the play." More idiomatic it certainly is: "Clamp this troublemaking bastard to the rock. . . . MOVE damn it! . . . OK OK I'm doing my job. . . . I see this bastard getting what he deserves. . . . The boss checks everything out. . . . So *be* a bleeding heart! . . . You cocky bastard. . . . " What is this, a gangster epic?

It is true that this colloquial banter occurs mainly (though not exclusively) in the prologue and is an attempt to re-create in contemporary terms the Aeschylean vision of intelligence crucified by brute power. But though Aeschylus assaults the audience's sensitivity with all the pathos, terror, and savagery of the situation, he does so with language which, for all its force, never loses dignity. If naked Power itself could speak Greek, Aeschylus persuades us, it would sound like this. Can we believe that if it spoke English it would have to fall back on "bastard" three times in one short scene? Scully also has what seems now (so many years since the Cantos) an old-fashioned fondness for capitals and typographic pranks: what is gained by printing

MAJESTY OF MY MOTHER
and of
SKY SKy Sky sky

—the last line looking like a neon sign with circuits going out of phase? Unlike Hecht, he rarely uses rhyme; one passage in which he does leaves one wishing he hadn't. "You're all so young," says his Prometheus to Hermes, "newly in power, you dream / you live in a tower / too high up for sorrow." The similar rhythm and length of the two rhymed phrases leads the ear to connect them—and to recognize with dismay that their form is that of the two short lines of the limerick. Edith Hamilton did not claim to be a poet but her version of these remarkable lines is much better: "Young, young, your thrones just won / you think you live in citadels grief cannot reach." But elsewhere Scully's translation reads very well, especially in the long Io scenes:

> *Having crossed the stream between*
>   *Europe and Asia*
> *— towards that dawnworld where*
>   *the sun*
>   *walks, flare-eyed—*
> *you'll move on*
>   *over swells of an unsurging sea.*
>
>   *These*
> *are dunes, it's desert!*

And, taken as a whole, it is better than any other *Prometheus* now in print.

The Oxford series is off to a good start. Murray in his day built a bridge between the Greek text and the modern reader; in less than two decades, Eliot found it "a barrier more impenetrable than the Greek language." All translations share this fate in the end; in the case of these versions of Aeschylus, it can be confidently predicted that they will have many decades to run before they have to be replaced.

FIVE

Review

THE ORESTEIA, by Aeschylus. Translated by Robert Fagles. Viking, 1975.

THE BACCHAE OF EURIPIDES, A COMMUNION RITE. By Wole Soyinka. Norton, 1974.

Thirty-two Greek tragedies have come down to us intact, a pitiful remnant of the Athenian theater's great century; it is about one-tenth of the known work of the three great tragedians, who were, however, only three among many. The composition of this remnant was determined by factors which are hardly ideal from a purely aesthetic standpoint; suitability as school texts in early Byzantium was a governing consideration, for example. And it was blind chance which decided that over half of our sample should be from the pen of Euripides; one volume of a complete edition of his work somehow survived the sack of Byzantium by the licensed brigands of the Fourth Crusade and their destructive fifty-year occupation of the city. Given this hit-and-miss process of selection, it seems almost miraculous that, although three of the Aeschylean plays we still possess are dramatic fragments, torn from the trilogic frame for which they were composed, three others, *Agamemnon*, *The Libation Bearers*, and *Eumenides*, constitute the trilogy Aeschylus produced in the competition of 458 B.C., the *Oresteia*.

We have very little evidence (apart from its survival) that the ancient world thought very highly of it, and in modern times it had to wait until the nineteenth century for full appreciation. Swinburne's praise—"the greatest achievement of the human mind"—is well known, and Swinburne, witness his admiration for Baudelaire, was a better judge of poetry than some of his own compositions might suggest. Wagner, working on *Lohengrin* in 1847, read the *Oresteia* (in Droysen's translation) and found himself overwhelmed: " ... right up to the end of the *Eumenides* I lingered in a state of ecstasy from which I have never fully returned to reconcile myself to modern literature."

In our own century, its prestige has risen as fast as the number of people able to read it in the original has declined. The modern liberal

This chapter originally appeared in the *New York Review of Books*, February 5, 1976.

conscience recognized themes that echoed its own aspirations: the law of learning by suffering seen as a force driving toward human progress under a divine dispensation mysterious, apparently merciless, yet ultimately benevolent; the transition from vengeance exacted by the family of the victim to the assumption of responsibility by society, the court of law which allowed consideration of motive and extenuating circumstance; the voices of both Athena and the Furies raised in praise of democracy, the mean between anarchy and despotism. The fact that the dark past is associated with the female principle—Clytemnestra, the Furies—and the new democratic justice with male domination—Apollo, Athena—was accepted, not without a certain complacency, as a reflection of fifth-century historical conditions.

We are no longer so sure of ourselves, and our reactions have changed. Progress is no longer a word to conjure with, especially when it is associated with national aggrandizement; modern audiences may feel nothing but apprehension as Athena proclaims the greatness of Athens to come: "As time flows on, the honors flow through all / my citizens. . . . Let our wars / rage on abroad, with all their force, to satisfy / our powerful lust for fame." At a performance of the trilogy by Guthrie's Minnesota Company in New York some years ago, it was very noticeable that the audience in the trial scene of the *Eumenides* was roused to a high pitch of emotion not by the pleas of extenuating circumstance and the acquittal of Orestes for murder but by the Furies' warning, later repeated by Athena: "There is a time when terror helps . . . ," "Never / banish terror from the gates. . . . " Apollo's male biology—"the woman you call the parent of the child / is not the parent, just a nurse to the seed . . . the *man* . . . the source of life . . . "—though it has been accepted as historical necessity by Marxist interpreters (it can be reconciled with Engels's imaginative anthropology) has not found favor in other quarters—Kate Millett made an understandably savage attack on it in her *Sexual Politics.*

And yet the trilogy still imposes itself as one of the great dramatic achievements of all time. For one thing, it is close to the sources of power that lie hidden in myth. In the *Eumenides*, the gods, men, and Furies meet face to face in alliance or enmity, trade attacks and promises, all with a grave simplicity which can only have existed in the first days of the world; there is no trace of the Sophoclean barrier between heroic and divine, of the Euripidean ironic distance from both. The Aeschylean characters converse in a language honed to perfection before the invention and triumph of formal oratory; innocent of the rhetorical patterns which, insistent in Sophocles, dominant in Euripides, and obsessive in Seneca, came to life again on the Renaissance and classical stage, the speeches of Aeschylus' awesome figures are shaped exclusively by the poetry of their emotion and the logic of the dramatic movement—they have a disconcerting originality, a constant unexpectedness.

Above all, the *Oresteia* is the work of a great poet composing at the height of his powers to produce not only, in the choral odes, some of the greatest lyric poetry in Greek but also, throughout the whole trilogy, a dense pattern of magnificent images which, like the repetitive revenges of the action, return again and again, always with renewed significance—"images which yet / fresh images beget. . . . " The language of the trilogy is as convoluted, overloaded with meaning, and rich in cross-reference as that of the great Shakespearean tragedies, *Antony* and *Lear*.

Robert Fagles's translation is the product of many years of experimentation; a preliminary version of the first 300 lines of *Agamemnon* was published in *Arion* as early as 1966. Fagles does not discuss his aims as a translator; he would have the work "speak for itself instead of introducing it with any principles." Speak for itself it does, and eloquently; the praises of Robert Fitzgerald, Kenneth Burke, and others, printed on the dust cover, are fully merited. But the question most readers will want an answer to (and which must have been on Fagles's mind throughout) is this: what is the difference between this *Oresteia* and that of Richmond Lattimore, a version which, greatly (and justly) admired, has been the authorized version for the postwar years?

The first impression that emerges from a comparison of individual passages is that Fagles is more solicitous of the needs of the Greekless reader. Aeschylus can be difficult and obscure, often is so, in fact, in his most magnificent flights of poetry (at times of course the obscurity stems from corruption of the text). In many such passages, Lattimore presents the reader with a *tour de force*, English lines which uncannily reproduce the mantic denseness of the original—this, one feels, is what Aeschylus would have written if he had been one of us. This is of course one of the qualities in Lattimore for which Greek scholars feel professional admiration, but it must be admitted that many an American student has reacted with something less than enthusiasm to passages such as: "The female force, the desperate / love crams its resisted way / on marriage and the dark embrace / of brute beasts, of mortal men." The context, a lyric recital of notorious female crimes, sheds some general light but the details are hazy (as they are indeed in the Greek).

Fagles, with the Greekless reader in mind, is clearer: "Woman's passion, overpowered by lust, / twists the soft, warm harness / of wedded love that strengthens man and beast." And so throughout the trilogy, Fagles has, in the last analysis, asked himself: "Is this passage fully intelligible English, without reference to the Greek?" I suspect that Lattimore was intrigued not only by the problem of bringing over into English the murky magnificence of the original but also, poet that he is, by the poetic dividend, the unprecedented English combinations that may emerge from the process. "Crams its resisted way on marriage" is a phrase hard to forget, and that would have been hard to invent.

The overall result of Fagles's bias toward the Greekless reader is not only greater immediate intelligibility but also, as Fitzgerald rightly claims, English verse which is "actable." It has been the experience of many directors of the play that Lattimore's version is not easy material for actors. And this is mainly due, once again, to Lattimore's desire to preserve as much as he can of the form and texture of the original. For the dialogue he developed a line corresponding in length to the Greek—one based roughly on twelve syllables instead of the usual (for English) ten. Incidentally, it is the same line Droysen used in the German translation Wagner read. This line enabled Lattimore to reproduce the architecture of the Aeschylean dialogue, the building blocks of the speeches corresponding closely; it is especially useful where the actors converse in *stichomythia*, the thrust, parry, and riposte of line-for-line dialogue, where Lattimore is able to reproduce the archaic strictness of the form in all its strangeness.

But the line has one great disadvantage. In spite of Lattimore's skillful efforts to make it a unit, it is always in danger of fragmenting at the point where the ear, especially the actor's ear, raised on Shakespearean cadences, expects it to end. "Almighty herald of the world above, the world / below: Hermes, lord of the dead, help me: announce / my prayers to the charmed spirits underground, who watch. ... " Fagles turns to the normal English length, variable, resolved, relaxed, but still recognizably Shakespeare's: "Herald King / of the world above and the quiet world below / lord of the dead, my Hermes, help me now. / Tell the spirits underground to hear my prayers. ... "

One more difference. Lattimore aimed at a modern English which, while fully idiomatic, would still preserve the decorum of Aeschylean tragic diction, that *onkos* (literally "weight, bulk") which was the poet's distinguishing mark. Sometimes the result seems a little stiff and artificial. "We have been sold, and go as wanderers / because our mother bought herself, for us, a man, / Aegisthus, he who helped her hand to cut you down. / Now I am what a slave is, and Orestes lives / outcast from his great properties, while they go proud / in the high style and luxury of what you worked / to win."

Contrast Fagles: "We're auctioned off, drift like vagrants now. / Mother has pawned us for a husband, Aegisthus, / her partner in her murdering. / I go like a slave, / Orestes driven from his estates while they, / they roll in the fruits of all your labors, / magnificent and sleek." It does seem more like what Dryden aimed at in translation—"the living language of the day"—though perhaps the difference is simply a reflection of the fact that the translations are two decades apart.

There can never be too many good translations—the chairman-poet of Peking called for "a hundred flowers" (in a different context, it is true)—and in any case each generation calls for its own. Fagles has given us an *Oresteia* for the seventies. He has also, "with W. B. Stanford," given us a brilliant (if sometimes erratic) introductory essay over eighty large pages long, and some very useful notes at the end of this beautifully designed and produced book.

The *Oresteia*, produced as Athens moved into an age of radical democracy at home and naval empire abroad, celebrated mankind's emergence from the anarchy of individual violence to the civilized order of the city state. Fifty years later, as Athens, near the end of a long war, faced defeat and possible extinction, Euripides wrote a play, the *Bacchae*, which presents the overthrow of the city state's order by a god-priest of emotional anarchy and ecstasy. It was a subject Aeschylus had handled in a play now lost; perhaps it was a legacy from the Dionysiac origins of the theater itself (but about that we know next to nothing); in any case, the Euripidean play is a terrifying masterpiece. The Dionysiac cult, non-Greek in origin and in its primitive form a threat to social stability, had long since been institutionalized in Athens; the dancing on the mountains, the feasts of raw flesh had been replaced by city festivals, the most splendid of them the theatrical contests in the spring. But Euripides in the play brings back to terrifying life the raw savagery of Dionysus as he once was.

The play's action is a ghastly ritual sequence: the mockery of the god, his escape from prison, his assertion of power over his oppressor, who becomes a substitute for him and, clothed in the god's attributes— long hair and female dress—is torn apart by the wild women, led by his mother, who in Dionysiac ecstasy has no more idea of his identity than of her own. As a counterpart to this frenzied action, the chorus celebrates, in some of the most exquisite of Greek lyrics, the peace, the ecstasy, the joy that come from total surrender to the god.

We do not know what moved Euripides to re-create this Dionysiac frenzy; E. R. Dodds has suggested that the impulse may have come from the growing popularity in Athens, during the desperate last years of the war, of new foreign deities worshiped with orgiastic rites. What one can be fairly sure of is that it had nothing to do with industrial mining, as suggested by Wole Soyinka in the introduction to his adaptation of the *Bacchae.* "Silver and gold mines were opened up," he says, "and with them a group consciousness among urban labour.... And when, in the wake of the wars of Greek colonialism, the mining industry expanded in Attica, a similar Dionysiac movement swept through mainland Greece.... Dionysus ... was eminently suited to the social and spiritual needs of the new urban classes...."

This is of course hopelessly unhistorical, but it does not matter. Soyinka's *Bacchae* is not Euripides' but his own—a third-world revolutionary communion rite, in which Dionysus sometimes speaks with the voice of Frantz Fanon. The stage for the opening shows "a road ... lined by the bodies of crucified slaves mostly in the skeletal stage ...," and the audience sees "dim figures of slaves flailing and treading." Grafted onto the Euripidean text (based on the Arrowsmith and Murray translations—Soyinka disarmingly admits to "a twenty-year rust on my acquaintanceship with classical Greek") are scenes and characters drawn from Soyinka's own imagination to flesh out his vision of "a prodigious barbaric banquet ... the more than hinted-at cannibalism" corresponding "to the periodic needs of humans to swill, gorge and copulate on a scale as huge as Nature's...." Soyinka is a dramatist of great power, and his own contact with Dionysus is a real one, as his fascinating description of the Yoruba deity Ogun in his introduction makes clear. The play was commissioned for the Old Vic and first staged in 1973. It must have been an electrifying performance.

It was not the first time the *Bacchae* was resurrected in exotic circumstances. Three and a half centuries after Euripides' death, the Roman multimillionaire Crassus led a Roman army into Syria, was defeated by the Parthians, and killed. When the messenger arrived at the Parthian capital with his head, the court was watching a Greek company perform the *Bacchae.* They had reached the scene in which Pentheus' mother Agave, still in Dionysiac frenzy, comes on stage carrying her son's severed head. The head of Crassus was thrown on the floor; Jason, the actor playing Agave, substituted it for the prop he had been carrying and resumed the performance, singing the famous aria "I bring from the mountain, this bough fresh-cut...." The audience went wild.

One cannot help thinking that Euripides, who had a penchant for baroque violence and an interest in odd religions, would have been fascinated by both performances and, in particular, would have been very eager to question Soyinka more fully about Ogun, the Yoruba "god of metals, creativity, the road, wine and war."

SIX

Review

AGAMEMNON, by Aeschylus. Directed by Andrei Serban at the Vivian Beaumont Theater, New York City, 1977.

A great deal of enthusiasm goes into the production of Greek tragedies for the modern stage, both academic and professional; unfortunately, the same enthusiasm is rarely in evidence on the house side of the footlights. Playgoers watching a Greek tragedy usually manage to refrain from looking too often at their wrist watches, but the expression on their faces is one of self-congratulation at the steady accumulation of cultural Brownie points. They greet the barely intelligible chanting of the chorus and its inert choreography with simulated rapture and affect a connoisseur's taste for rhetoric as the long descriptive speeches roll on uninterrupted; only their applause for the end of the proceedings is heartfelt. Most productions of Greek tragedy, though I should be the last person to say so, are a crashing bore.

Excuses lie ready to hand. We have only the bare words of the text; we have lost the original music of the choral odes and the mimetic gestures of the dancers, as well as the enigmatic immobility of the masks. We cannot experience the tension generated by the awesome size of the ancient audience (the theater at Athens had a capacity of 14,000); we cannot even imagine the religious fears and ecstasy to which the participants in this Dionysiac festival appealed. We have only the bare bones, a magnificent armature, of course, but not living flesh and blood.

The more courageous among the modern directors have refused to resign themselves to such an admission of defeat and have determined to make these bones live. The usual approach has been to poise against the decorous rhetoric of the dialogue and the allusive obscurity of the lyric a violence in action, staging, and costume which draws eclectically from all the modern stage innovators—Brecht, Artaud, Grotowski, Brook—and from any source, provided the result will compel audience attention. One school favored a jarring contemporaneity: Menelaus

This chapter originally appeared in the *New York Review of Books*, July 14, 1977.

returning from the Trojan war in combat boots with six-inch soles, cigar in mouth; Orestes and Pylades juvenile delinquents in light-colored sunglasses and black motorcycle jackets.

Others, influenced perhaps by Francis Fergusson's chapter on *Oedipus* in his *Idea of a Theater*, followed the opposite tack: to present Greek tragedy as a sort of primeval scapegoat rite. The most distinguished effort along these lines was the Guthrie *Oedipus* produced at Stratford, Ontario; the hideous masks, primeval decor, and weirdly stylized movements invested the most relentlessly secular of Sophoclean dramas with overtones of some Stone Age ceremony of human sacrifice. The most sensational was undoubtedly the New York extravaganza called *Dionysus in 69*, which, claiming the *Bacchae* as its base—"of the 1,300 lines in Arrowsmith's translation we use nearly 600, some of them more than once"—splashed pints of stage blood on many square yards of nude female anatomy, and spiced the mixture with simulated fellatio and a naked New Guinea "birth ritual," to produce a dish which would have given Euripides, that most civilized of dramatists, an acute case of indigestion.

Whatever their success as theater of cruelty, metatheater, or unintentional farce, these solutions to the problem posed by Greek tragedy in performance were all wide of the mark. For the problem has nothing to do with the loss of the original music and choreography, which were the humble servants of the word, not its equals, and for which, with proper care and talent, modern substitutes can be created. The problem lies in the words themselves. They were aimed at an audience which listened to them in a way no modern audience can, an audience which was sensitively attuned to the living word as an art form, or rather—to use their own evaluation of it—as a kind of magic. Fifth-century Athens was a city in which books existed to be read aloud; Homeric epics as well as lyric poetry and the drama were heard, not read; state policy was influenced by the eloquence of orators, not by the cogency of position papers or the brute force of statistics; the philosopher Socrates made his indelible impression on the mind of a whole generation by speech alone—he never wrote a word.

Pindar, a contemporary of Aeschylus, wrote victory odes for athletes which are so difficult for a modern reader to follow that Cowley, who translated some of them, remarked that if a man translated Pindar literally, readers would think that one madman was translating another; Voltaire ironically complimented Pindar on writing "*des vers que personne n'entend / Et qu'il faut toujours qu'on admire.*" Yet these poems, so rich, concentrated, and allusive in their diction and content, so subtle and complicated in their meter, so lightning-swift in their elliptical transitions, were commissioned (and paid for at high prices) by the families of young men victorious at the national games—for performance at a private celebration. Whitman demanded great audiences for poetry; the Greek poets had them.

The lyric portions of Attic tragedy are from the same poetic mold as the Pindaric odes; those of Aeschylus were already famous in antiquity for the magnificence of their vocabulary, the audacity of their imagery, their length, and what seemed to later ages like lapses into occasional magniloquent obscurity. But his audience understood and was swayed by them; no Attic dramatist, in the fierce competition for popular favor imposed by the festival, could afford to leave his audience puzzled.

If the lyric sections of the drama were merely ornamental, the modern producer could skirt the difficulty. But they are not. In most Greek tragedy and especially in Aeschylus, they are essential for the audience's understanding of the drama as a whole. Yet to modern ears, no matter how reductively simple the translations, they are hard to follow even if they are intelligibly delivered (which is often not the case); and even if they are understood they cannot make that direct appeal to the senses which the original audience experienced. And no amount of naked writhing and *sacre-du-printemps* screaming, no display of motorcycles, cigars, or machine guns is going to be any help toward a full appreciation of these lyrics, which present not only the mythic background but also the moral and religious context of the words and actions of the masked players.

In his choice of the *Agamemnon*, Serban has taken the bull by the horns; the lyric sections of the play are not only the most sublime passages of Aeschylean poetry, they are also the longest such sequences extant in Greek drama—they constitute almost exactly one half of the text. The *Agamemnon* comes close to justifying the jeering assessment of Aeschylus' dramaturgy offered by "Euripides" in Aristophanes' *Frogs*: after a prologue "the chorus would then churn out / four consecutive chains of unbroken odes, while the actors kept their mouths shut." It does, in fact, contain four stasima, set pieces performed by the chorus in song and dance (the first of them the longest in Greek tragedy); it also presents in this lyric mode two long dramatic scenes—the prophetic ravings of Cassandra and the choral mourning for Agamemnon, interrupted by Clytemnestra's increasingly insecure attempts at self-justification.

To add to the difficulties faced by the modern director, the dramatic action of the first half of the play is not motion along a line but development of a single theme. In the prologue, a watchman announces the fall of Troy and prays for the return of Agamemnon; the first episode consists of Clytemnestra's announcement of the fall of Troy and the imminent return of Agamemnon; the second presents a herald who gives thanks for the fall of Troy and announces Agamemnon's arrival in Argos; and in the third, Agamemnon returns and describes the fall of Troy. Anything farther removed from the modern conception of dramatic action would be hard to conceive.

Serban's response to the challenge of this recalcitrant text is restrained and intelligent. He avoids both fake modernism and self-indulgent primitivism; the tone is hieratic, not savage. Above all, he avoids nudity; in fact, the actors are padded out with multiple layers of clothing—the one instance of partial nudity is reserved for an appallingly successful dramatic effect. He has his actors deliver the spoken lines with distinct, almost meticulous, elocution and deliberate slowness; his aim is clearly full intelligibility. That aim is furthered by the choice of Edith Hamilton's translation, which, in spite of occasional archaisms, is distinguished by its simplicity and straightforwardness. The choral odes are performed by a chorus which both sings and dances, but it does so in a way which puts to shame most previous efforts in this line; after this production, there should be no excuse for posturings in the style of Isadora Duncan and pale imitations of plainsong or—the usual alternative to these genteelisms—aboriginal howling and primeval jigs.

Serban's chorus not only sings well, it has something to sing; Elizabeth Swados has composed for these voices music which, reminiscent at times of Byzantine church music and at times of Mikis Theodorakis, is authoritative, exquisitely adjusted to the dramatic tempo, and compelling in its own right. And the chorus as dancer is a disciplined instrument; it moves with that reassuring speed and precision which comes only from training; the figures of the dance, ranging from solemn processional to the abandon of funeral lament, impose themselves throughout as appropriate to the situation. A great deal of thought and work has obviously gone into the creation of these effects, but, satisfying though the results are, they are the product of refinement rather than invention. What is truly original is Serban's attempt to deal with the real problem, the poetic and intellectual content of the lyric portions of the play.

Since a modern audience, unused to hearing poetry even of the simplest sort, cannot see in imagination or experience in emotion the events over which the chorus broods in the choral lyrics, Serban puts those events before their eyes, on stage. The sacrifice of Iphigenia, for example, which is re-created in merciless detail and magnificent poetry in the first stasimon, is, in this version, acted out before the spectators' eyes in what the Elizabethans called "dumb show." A similar technique is adopted for many other lyric passages, in particular for Cassandra's

horrendous visions of the past, present, and future of the house of
Atreus.

Now that the work once done by the words alone is given to the
actors, the words themselves become superfluous; indeed, if recited at
full length and so as to be intelligible to the audience they might
constitute a dangerous distraction. So Serban cuts the text considerably
and has his chorus sing the words in what is billed as a mixture of the
Edith Hamilton translation and "fragments of ancient Greek." And, of
course, since the words are no longer all-important, the music is given
free rein. In the first stasimon, which has as its climax the sacrifice of
Iphigenia, the English translation emerged from the music into full
intelligibility only at the passages essential for an understanding of the
mimed action; the rest of it was impenetrable, sometimes because of
the volume of the music, sometimes because whatever the chorus was
singing it was not Edith Hamilton, or, for that matter, English. I wish I
could say that it was Greek, but though I know most of the choral lyric
of the play by heart in the original and though I am familiar with many
of the different modern ways of pronouncing ancient Greek (sloppy
English, harsh Prussian, soft modern Greek, and Chinese-singsong
purist being the main varieties), I managed to identify only three words.
Two of them, *iou* and *popax*, are not words at all, but exclamations (and
the second one does not occur in *Agamemnon*); the other, *kai*, a savage
choral cry of anger with which the chorus punctuated Clytemnestra's
keening over her daughter's body, is Greek all right, but it is the Greek
word for "and."

This is of course an unfair scholarly cavil; 99 percent of the
audience was perfectly content—it was Greek to them. And I would
have been equally content if the program had told me that the chorus
was singing in Zulu. For the fact is that the enactment of Iphigenia's
sacrifice is a theatrical *tour de force*, an irresistible assault on the
emotions of the audience. The frenetic gestures of the priest as he
declares for the sacrifice; the monstrous padded figure of Agamemnon,
wearing a mask suggestive both of cruelty and of agony; the wordless,
shocked grief of Clytemnestra; and the innocence of the child in her
saffron wedding dress—all build the tension toward the moment when
the armed men surround the girl and strip off her robe; the frail
adolescent body, naked except for white loincloth and breastband, the
mouth stopped with a black gag, is lifted high up over Agamemnon's
sword, "as you lift a kid above the altar," to create, for one instant of
unbearable intensity, that pity and fear which Aristotle named as the
emotions proper to tragedy. After this scene, no one in the audience
can fail to understand the force which drives Clytemnestra on to her
revenge. Here at last, a director has found a way to penetrate the

modern spectator's insensitivity to spoken poetry and expose him to the beauty and terror which, for the ancient audience, stemmed from the words alone.

Now for the bad news. The same technique is less successful elsewhere. The second choral ode begins as a hymn of thanks to Zeus for the victory at Troy: "you cast over Troy and her towered walls / a close-meshed net none could win through"; it proceeds through an indictment of Paris and Helen, the cause of the war, to lamentation for the Greek losses, and ends in foreboding for the future. Serban's chorus operates with a real net, one as wide as a tennis court; dancers who appear to represent Paris and Helen are snared, released, and finally caught as the mazes of the dance reach their end. This is heavy-handed literalism and ineffective theater; it is also not very clear—there were many puzzled faces in the audience. My own disenchantment was increased by the fact that this was one net too many (number four, in fact). Every schoolboy knows (well, every undergraduate who has taken a course in classical civilization) that the dominant image of the *Agamemnon* is the net; but there was no need to rub it in by dressing Clytemnestra in a black net shawl, giving her a net to play with as she makes her speech about the fall of Troy, and using for a stage a huge construction made of steel netting.

The technique of what might be called the visual correlative is employed with a lavish hand in one other lyric area of the play, the Cassandra scene. This is certainly a proper place for it. Cassandra's lines in the original—disjointed fragments of a whirling vision of past, present, and future—are allusive in the extreme; in the play they are for the most part unintelligible to the chorus but of course they were understood by the audience, which was familiar with the story of the house of Atreus. The modern audience, however, has to read up on it quickly in the lobby of the Vivian Beaumont theater, where it is displayed on a large chart; inside the theater, the audience needs all the help it can get. It does not get enough. Serban does put most of Cassandra's visions on stage, but without the sureness of touch which made the sacrifice of Iphigenia so electrifying. The Fury dancing with her blazing torch is impressive enough, but the children carrying their own cooked entrails are merely grotesque, especially since the objects they have in their hands look more like dried-out lobster shells than liver and lights. When Cassandra realizes that Apollo is sending her to her death in the house, a contraption that looks like the platform used by window cleaners on the World Trade Center descends from the flies carrying a muscular man dressed only in a black jockstrap; he proceeds to prod Cassandra from above with a spear longer than anything seen in

Greece until Philip of Macedon's troops came south with their fourteen-foot *sarisas*. Who is it? Apollo? I suppose so. But the man sitting behind me whispered to his companion that it was Superman.

Cassandra's most spectacular vision is the murder of Agamemnon in his bath. The bath (a little small for Jamil Zakkai, its occupant) duly appears on stage and Agamemnon is killed in it (after having net number five thrown over him by Clytemnestra). So far so good, but then Clytemnestra kills Cassandra. Not the Cassandra who is seeing this happen in a vision, but the one in the vision; they are both on stage. This is confusing enough but is made worse by the fact that Priscilla Smith, who has so far played Clytemnestra, is now playing Cassandra (the one having the vision), so that the Clytemnestra who kills Cassandra (the one in the vision) is somebody else. These complications are a by-product of the decision to use only two actors for the four principal roles.

It is hard to think of reasons for such a procedure. It was surely not a shortage of competent actors, and though there might be some slight symbolic value in having Agamemnon and Aegisthus played by the same man, to emphasize the repetitive pattern of justice by revenge, there is no similar dividend to be expected from doubling the roles of Clytemnestra and Cassandra. It has been suggested that Serban is striving for authenticity by accepting the limit of two speaking actors which early tragedy imposed on the Attic dramatist. If so, there has been a failure of communication somewhere, for the *Agamemnon* is the first play we know of in which the third speaking actor, introduced to the repertoire by Sophocles, is used by Aeschylus—used, in fact, to bring Cassandra on stage together with Agamemnon and Clytemnestra.

This is not the only case of tampering with the structure of the original. Much more serious is the rearrangement of the final sequence. In the Greek play, Cassandra's exit is followed by Agamemnon's famous death cries offstage; the door opens and Clytemnestra appears to make her triumphant speech over the bodies of the king and the Trojan princess. As the chorus laments their dead king and accuses the queen, she defends herself, but, retreating from her original assumption of full responsibility, finally claims that it was not she who killed Agamemnon but the spirit of vengeance which haunts the house. She prays that this spirit will depart, offers to sacrifice part of her wealth, to bargain with it, in fact, and at this moment, Aegisthus, its living embodiment, comes on stage to exult over his enemy's corpse. The chorus, stung to fury, defies him; he threatens them with his armed bodyguard, but Clytemnestra intervenes to prevent "more bloodshed." The stage is set for the next play, in which more blood will indeed be shed, that of Aegisthus and her own.

What happens in Serban's version is very different. When the door opens it is Aegisthus who walks out to make his victory speech. He quarrels with the chorus and Clytemnestra intervenes. Only then does the queen, over the bodies of her two victims, buried in a shallow grave in the steel netting, make her great speech of triumph while the chorus mourns its king. This radical reshuffling (reminiscent of Marowitz, who played similar havoc with Shakespeare in an attempt to abolish his "relentless *narrativeness*") deprives the play of two of its great lines (Agamemnon's offstage death cries) and one of its great tableaux (the confrontation of the aged chorus and the tyrant's bodyguard); it also destroys the logic of the Aeschylean development.

Nothing in the production so far has suggested that Serban is merely capricious; there must be some reason for this. Perhaps it is connected with the fact that the *Agamemnon* is not a self-contained play but the first part of a trilogy, which goes on to present the insoluble dilemma faced by Orestes and, in the last play, the solution which can come only from divine intervention. The *Agamemnon* cannot stand alone; some hint of the future is indispensable. Too far into the future Serban cannot go; what he does is to bring Orestes on in dumb show, equip him with a sword (handed to him from Agamemnon's grave by Electra), and send him into the house to murder his mother. Serban may have felt that this silent miming of Orestes' return and revenge made most sense if it followed directly on Clytemnestra's speech over the corpse of the king, and so he transposed the final scenes of the play.

This sequence is visually and in every other way an anticlimax, but it is at least fairly intelligible. There is, however, another dumb show, which serves as prologue to the play, for which the same claim cannot be made. In it, Agamemnon pushes what looks like a baton against Iphigenia's stomach; she lies down, whereupon Clytemnestra does the same thing to him, with the same result. A young man, naked to the waist and dressed in baggy white trousers, appears and does the same thing to her. This is, presumably, Orestes (at least he is the same character we see at the end of the play), but there were few in the audience who could be sure of it. In any case, this is an unimpressive piece of business; it seems to come from a different mind than the one that conceived the terrifying scene of Iphigenia's sacrifice.

In retrospect, the weaknesses recede as the production's tremendous images reassert their hold on the imagination. The play has a wealth of stunning visual effects, many of which have an authentic antique Greekness: one such scene has Clytemnestra light the torches of the chorus women as they file slowly past her looking like figures from an Attic vase. And it would be hard to imagine a more convincing Clytemnestra than Priscilla Smith. She is magnificent and deadly throughout: in her incredulous agony as she watches her daughter die, her mouth wide open in a soundless scream; in her slow delivery of the baleful speech of welcome, loaded with flattering superlatives and laced with menacing ambiguities; in the struggle of wills as Agamemnon balks at treading the purple carpet; above all in her exultation over Agamemnon's corpse. "Croaking your song, ravenlike" the chorus says, and, as she rasps out her hymn of triumphant hate, she jumps on the steel netting, her legs wide apart, like some hideous bird of prey.

The production has its victories as well as its defeats; the critic, to adapt an Aeschylean refrain, may at times cry "Alas," but the good prevails. The richness of its music, the care that has been taken with the training of the chorus, the insistence on clear delivery in the spoken dialogue, the restraint of the actors, whose passionate intensity is somehow raised rather than lowered by the solemnity of their gestures, above all the imaginative attack on the problem posed by choral lyric—all this means that Serban has set standards against which future productions of Greek tragedy will be measured.

SEVEN

Review

THE STAGECRAFT OF AESCHYLUS: THE DRAMATIC USE OF EXITS AND ENTRANCES IN GREEK TRAGEDY. By Oliver Taplin. Oxford University Press, 1977.

Aiskhylos edidaske ... "Aeschylus was the teacher ... " So runs the entry for the year we call 472 B.C. on the great inscription which lists the victors in the Athenian tragic contest. It is an urgent reminder that, in addition to writing the four plays (one of which was *The Persians*), Aeschylus taught the actors their lines and the chorus their words and music (which he had composed); he also directed stage movement and grouping as well as acting in the plays himself. Of all this theatrical activity, the only record which has come down to us is the script, in the form of medieval manuscripts and pitiful fragments of papyrus. But the script contains no stage directions, not even for those basic elements of the dramatic structure, exits and entrances. To complicate matters still further, the attributions of lines to speakers are problematical, since the papyri use a notation system so vulnerable to misunderstanding and corruption that we are now sure (what was in many passages already clear) that such attributions in the medieval manuscripts are worth much less than the parchment they are written on.

The Athenian dramatist was a complete man of the theater: playwright, composer, director all in one and, in the case of Aeschylus, actor too, fully aware that the drama appeals as much to the eye as to the ear. The plays cannot be completely experienced without some attempt to visualize the original performance, an attempt which demands the exercise of disciplined imagination. Unfortunately, there is more imagination than discipline at work in the editions, discussions, and translations of Greek plays which have tried to deal with this problem. The questions raised by the determination of actors' movements have often, when not silently ignored, been given answers which show too much respect for late, suspect information about the fifth-century theater of Dionysus and too little for the sobering results of excavation on the site. It is in the reconstitution of Aeschylus'

This chapter originally appeared in the *Times Literary Supplement*, October 6, 1978.

dramaturgy, in particular, that imagination has run riot. Taking their cue from a corrupt and obscure reference to a *Prometheus* in Aristotle's *Poetics* (1459[a]) and—as Oliver Taplin tellingly points out in this new book, *The Stagecraft of Aeschylus*—the first half of a sentence in the ancient *Life* (the second half is clearly rubbish), scholars have filled the Aeschylean stage with signs and wonders.

Gilbert Murray, for example, believed that there were no fewer than 153 people visible in the climactic scene of *The Suppliants*, and in *Prometheus Bound* he entertains the possibility that "the winged car" containing the chorus "and the flying griffin" on which Okeanos rides "balanced one another at opposite ends of a double crane"; not content with this flying circus, he brings Hermes in to end the play on the machine. As for Prometheus, he is a "wooden structure," a "gigantic figure ... crucified against a gigantic crag" which, at the finale, "sinks into the abyss."

Taplin's Aeschylus has much less equipment to work with: no huge extra choruses, not even (before *The Oresteia*) a stage building with a practicable door (and so no *ekkyklema* to roll out for "interior" scenes). As for the *mechane*, Taplin sympathizes with "those who try to eliminate the flying machine altogether" from the theater of Aeschylus. For him, "inessential visual effects—particularly crowds, machines and massive 'happenings'" have "nothing to do with the authentic Aeschylus."

This "authentic Aeschylus" is a playwright-director whose stage resources are minimal but who is nonetheless a master of "scenic presentation," and Taplin is confident that this presentation—"an inextricable element of his communication and hence of his meaning"—can be recovered. It can be "elicited with more or less confidence from close consideration of the text and from comparative study of recurrent or conventional dramatic methods." Taplin's claim is "that all, or at least most, stage actions of significance can be worked out from what we have." In this book he concentrates his attention on one type of action: exits and entrances. These are in any case the basic elements of all drama and "in the huge Greek theatre" they were "large and lengthy stage movements."

They are also, in the innovative analysis proposed in this book, the key to an understanding of the structure of the plays. Some recognized "ground-pattern" of structure is, as Taplin says, a prerequisite for dramaturgy; the audience must have a sense of the units which compose the whole, a set of formal expectations which the dramatist can count on. The modern audience waits for the emphatic line or the striking tableau which brings the curtain down and the house lights up to end an act; Shakespeare's audiences recognized the clearing of the stage and a fresh entry (Flourish; Exeunt; Enter Macbeth's wife, alone, with a letter) as the end of one dramatic unit and the beginning of another. But Greek tragedy in the fifth century was "debarred from this kind of straightforward structural basis by its peculiar formal continuity, which is largely due to the continuous presence of the chorus."

The chorus, however, does provide a basic framework by punctuating the action with strophic choral songs (usually, but by no means always, with the stage clear of actors), and this is in effect the structural formula proposed in chapter 12 of Aristotle's *Poetics*, a chapter which, Taplin argues in a cogent appendix, is "as good as useless for a meaningful analysis of surviving tragedy." For not only is there one strophic choral song which is clearly part of a continuing action (*Supp.* 418ff); there are also many obvious breaks in the action which are marked by astrophic anapaests, astrophic dochmiac lyrics, an actor's monody, or even the exit and reentry of the chorus without benefit of any song whatsoever. The basis for Taplin's theory is what he modestly calls "the rather simple observation" that all these recognizable structural breaks have one thing in common: the songs, strophic or not, are preceded by an exit and followed by an entry, and the scene breaks of a different type also involve entry following close on an exit. "The formal structure ... is founded on a basic pattern: enter actor(s) — actors' dialogue — exeunt actor(s)/choral strophic song/enter new actor(s) — actors' dialogue ... and so on." Exits and entrances are not only, given the visual setup of the Greek theater, impressive dramatic moments in themselves, they are also the signals for the opening and closing of the "acts" of which the play is composed; this is why Taplin can claim that his book is an attempt to show "how the precise handling of the action may throw light on the playwright's larger dramatic purpose."

This is, as Taplin is quick to emphasize, no more than a "basic pattern": "there are a multitude of variations on it." But "in every tragedy the ground pattern also asserts itself and thus supplies a norm for the structural variations to work upon." Since it is "in the departures and variations that we may detect artistic purposes," the 355 pages which follow, an analysis of exits and entrances which constitutes a theatrical commentary on the Aeschylean plays, are as much concerned with significant variations, apparent exceptions, and possible textual corruption as with the norm.

It is a fascinating commentary. Every controversial passage (and there are many) is discussed with incisive intelligence, great learning, and also good-humored respect for opposing views; from the entry of the chorus in *The Persians* to the final processional-exeunt of *The Eumenides*, every important exit and entrance (real or imagined) provides the cue for an essay which, firmly based on the principles enunciated in the first chapter, enlightens and stimulates the reader even where it fails to command full agreement.

Taplin is in effect surveying the Aeschylean text from a new point of view, or rather, from a point of view which has never before been so consciously and consistently developed. The results are both negative and positive. On the one hand, a great many widely accepted Aeschylean scenic effects are subjected to withering criticism, and fresh ammunition is provided against targets already under fire; on the other, new facets of Aeschylus' mastery of stage action are brought to light.

The negative effects derive mainly from the application of Taplin's principle that "the significant stage instructions are implicit in the words." By this standard, strictly applied, Clytemnestra's entrance during the *parodos* of *Agamemnon* is rejected, as is the presence of the six Theban champions during the long central scene of *Seven against Thebes* (hereafter *Seven*); rejected also is Schadewalt's brilliant suggestion that Eteocles puts on his armor on stage, his fatal resolve to fight his brother hardening as each piece of his panoply is fitted on. The singing chorus of handmaids is excised from *The Suppliants* (their lines are given to the Argive bodyguard or to Danaos), and Hermes no longer appears on stage in *The Eumenides*.

In addition, Taplin's new (and persuasive) structural analysis contributes to the indictment of passages already suspect. On this basis, Taplin concludes that in the last scenes of the *Seven* "the sisters, the introductory anapaests (861–74), and the entire scene from 1005 to the end have been added, presumably by actors, to Aeschylus' original play." By the same criterion, the *Prometheus*, even apart from the fact that it presents problems of staging insoluble in terms of the fifth-century theater's resources, emerges as structurally erratic; Taplin isolates dramatic techniques which are "inexplicably unlike Aeschylus as we know him from the other plays." Elsewhere, abnormalities of technique are removed by emendation, excision, transposition, or a combination of all three; in discussing one such passage, Taplin remarks that "questions of dramatic technique may be sufficient to be the chief—or even sole—grounds for textual emendation." In *The Eumenides*, for example, he suspects large-scale disruption in the trial scene: "678–710 have been displaced and altered and lines 712–14 are the corrupted edges of a large lacuna ... perhaps 40 lines" which "will have contained Athena's inaugural speech, much of it preserved in 681–706, and it will have included the arrival of Apollo" and possibly also "the oath of the jurors, the summoning of witnesses, and perhaps a formal announcement by the Herald."

It will appear to many that new criteria for impugning the text of the dramatists are something that we can do without, and even Taplin admits that he finds it "hard to believe wholeheartedly in this hypothesis"; but he claims that the alternative is to conclude that Aeschylus "was, or was sometimes, a crude and undeveloped crafts- man"—a conclusion which he has all through the book persuasively rejected as false. The main stumbling block here is the entry of Apollo, which he finds "disruptive, hurried and informal." This is, it is true, disruptive (it interrupts the speech which Athena was about to address to the court), and it is not treated with the solemnity and due preparation usual for an important entry. But *The Eumenides*, as Taplin himself stresses, is full of technical surprises (the word "unique" recurs frequently in his discussion), and this entry may be defended as dramatically effective. For Apollo's appearance is completely unex- pected; he promised Orestes protection from afar but gave no hint that he would appear as a witness in the trial. His appearance and approach from the side entrance during the last line of Athena's proclamation would be a visual surprise to the audience and, in terms of dramatic situation, a new factor important enough to "disrupt" the trial to the extent of postponing Athena's general instructions to the court.

The "arming scene" in the *Seven* is dismissed on the grounds that "the action would not in any proper sense be accompanied by the words"; but this leaves Taplin with the impossible situation that Eteocles calls for his greaves at line 676 and goes into battle at 711 without the rest of his armor. Taplin's solution is to suppress 675–76 and have Eteocles come on in full armor at the very beginning of the scene. But are his objections to Schadewalt's suggestion well founded? "The putting on of armour or of any costume is a difficult thing to manage on stage," says Taplin, but nevertheless it is by no means rare. Shakespeare does it frequently, and in any case Eteocles has attendants with him (they are sent to get his greaves); they can hand him his spear, helmet, and shield, and clasp the breastplate round him—such a scene is a favorite subject of vase painters. "Even Shakespeare," says Taplin, speaking of his arming scenes, "does not normally pay no verbal attention to the stage action." But in the famous scene in Brecht's *Galileo* where the once-liberal pope is clothed in full regalia by attendants, and with each fresh garment yields more ground before the Inquisitor's demand that Galileo be forced to retract, the dialogue contains no hint whatsoever of the spectacular stage action. Taplin's objection that Eteocles's "powerful words" should not be "accompanied by action independent of them" does not deal adequately with the suggestion that Eteocles puts on his armor not while he speaks but during the choral appeals; he answers them negatively by action before he does so in words.

It is a measure of the authority of this book that these disagree- ments with its author on points of detail are phrased in terms of the critical approach which he has developed with such mastery; Taplin imposes on the reader his own conviction that "the critic of a work which is only fully realized in performance should always keep his mind's eye on the work in action." And in the positive aspects of his criticism, where he undertakes the "extension into interpretative criticism" of the detailed study of exits and entrances, it is not too much to say that he has revealed unsuspected dramatic power and thematic relevance in many an Aeschylean scene which was thought to have yielded all of its secrets long ago. His scheme of movements for Clytemnestra in *Agamemnon*, for example, which has her on stage less than any other discussion I know of (enter 258, exit 350, enter 587, exit 614, enter 855), is the basis for a brilliant discussion of a theme Taplin calls "Clytemnestra's control of the threshold." She "controls the doorway. She is the watchdog . . . and the threshold may only be crossed under her eyes." She forestalls the herald's entry into the palace, as later she forestalls Agamemnon's; she seems to be in complete control and knows everything that needs to be known. When Agamemnon does enter, treading the purple cloth, he does so on her terms: "he enters a conqueror and goes off himself conquered." Taplin's rich discussion of this and many other passages justifies the claim he makes at the beginning of the book that some exits and entrances "may be only a matter of a few paces, but these paces may convey victory or defeat, death or life, a world of suffering or of joy."

It remains only to add that the commentary is followed by five appendixes on special subjects (among the most important are those on the fifth-century theater and the authenticity of the *Prometheus Bound*), and the work concludes with an index of topics which, unlike so many such productions, is intelligently organized and constitutes a serviceable guide to the wealth of material contained in this indispensable book.

Part III: Sophocles

EIGHT

Why Is Oedipus Called Tyrannos?

This is not the same question as that asked by one of the ancient hypotheses—"Why is it entitled *tyrannos?*"—for the title by which the tragedy is known is clearly post-Aristotelian.[1] But the title owes its origin, as Jebb points out,[2] to the frequent occurrence of the word *tyrannos* in the play.

It is of course true that this word *tyrannos* (partly perhaps because of its greater adaptability to iambic meter) is sometimes used in tragedy (especially in Euripides)[3] as a neutral substitute for *basileus*, king. But in the Sophoclean play it is used in at least one passage with the full import of its historical and political meaning—an unconstitutional ruler, who generally abuses the power he has seized. Jebb, who translates the word *tyrannos* and its cognates as "king," "prince," "royalty," "empire," "crown," and "throne" elsewhere in the play, comments on vs. 873 (*hubris phuteuei tyrannon*—Violence and pride engender the *tyrannos*) as follows: "Here not a prince, nor even, in the normal Greek sense, an unconstitutionally absolute ruler (good or bad), but in our sense a 'tyrant.'" Other passages, too, insist on the historical figure of the *tyrannos*, a despot who has won power through "friends . . . masses and money" as Oedipus himself says (541–42). The word cannot then be considered neutral in any of its appearances in the play; it is colored by the reflections of these emphatic references to the traditional Athenian estimate of the *tyrannos*.

In what sense is Oedipus a *tyrannos?* There is one aspect of his power in Thebes which fully justifies the term; he is not (as far as is known at the beginning of the action) the hereditary successor to the throne of Thebes, but an outsider, a *xenos*, as he says himself,[4] who, not belonging to the royal line, for that matter not even a native Theban, has come to supreme power. This is one of the fundamental differences between the historical *tyrannos* and the king, *basileus*. Thucydides, for example, makes this distinction in his reconstruction of

This chapter originally appeared in the *Classical Journal*, 50, no. 3 (1954).

early Greek history. "Tyrannies were established in the cities as the revenue increased ... previously there was kingship with fixed preroga-tives handed down from father to son."[5]

This sense of the word *tyrannos* is exact and appropriate for Oedipus (as far as he understands his own situation at the beginning of the play); he is an intruder, one whose title to power is individual achievement, not heredity. But, though exact, it is a double-edged word, and Creon, whose sophistic defense later marks him as the subtle politician of the play, seems to be aware of its implications; for in the opening scene he refers to Laius, who was king, not *tyrannos*, in terms which avoid pointing the contrast between Oedipus' title to power and the hereditary title of his predecessor. "We once, my lord, had a ... leader (*hegemon*) called Laius" is his formula to avoid what might have been an odious comparison (103).

Oedipus, in reply, carries on this diplomatic misnomer of Laius: he refers to the power of his predecessor by a word which equates it with his own—*tyrannis* (128). Later in the play, he twice calls Laius himself *tyrannos* (799, 1043): and the reason why he calls him *tyrannos* instead of *basileus* in these lines is all too clear—by this time he suspects that Laius may have been the man he killed many years before where the three roads meet, and it is only natural that in these circumstances he should avoid the use of a word which would invest his violent action with a darker guilt. The psychological nuance of his use of the word *tyrannos* here emerges clearly from the comparison of this situation with that in which, for the only time in the play, he gives Laius his proper title. "It was not right" he tells the chorus "that you should leave this matter unpurified, the death of a good man—and a king" (*Basileos t' ololotos*, 256–57). The context explains his choice of terms. For in these lines, which follow the pronouncement of the curse on the unknown murderer, Oedipus is dwelling, with terrible unconscious irony, on the close connection between himself and Laius. "Since now it is I that am in authority, holding the powers which he formerly held,— ... married to his wife ... and if his line had not met with disaster we would have been connected by children born in common to us both ... for all these reasons I shall fight on his behalf or as if he were my father ... seeking the murderer ... on behalf of the son of Labdacus, whose father was Polydorus son of Cadmus before him, whose father in ancient time was Agenor" (258–68).

The involved irony of these lines has aroused much admiring comment: their motivation also deserves attention. The resounding, half-envious recital of Laius' royal lineage emphasizes Oedipus' feeling of inadequacy in this matter of birth: though he claims the royal line of Corinth as his own, he cannot in his inmost heart be sure of his parentage.[6] And he tries in these lines to insert himself into the honored line of Theban kings. "Having his powers"—his successor then, "married to his wife"—Oedipus feels himself almost legitimized by this fact[7] and his children completely so: "we would have been connected by children." The presence of an heir of Laius would have drawn attention to the royal blood in the veins of his own children, born of the same mother. Then, inconsistently (the typical inconsistency of deep unconscious desires forcing themselves violently and disturbingly up into the surface of rational speech): "as if he were my father." In this context, where Oedipus' buried misgivings about his birth express themselves as a fantasy that he is, in one sense or another, of the line of Laius, Labdacus, Polydorus, Cadmus, and Agenor, it is only natural that he should give Laius his proper title, king, *basileus*: it is what he would dearly like to be himself.

The terrible fact is that he *is* king: no man more legitimately. He is the son of Laius, direct descendant of Cadmus and Agenor. But it is only when he and all Thebes know the truth that he is finally addressed by this title. "You rose up like a fortified wall against death for my city," sings the chorus in the tremendous ode which follows the recognition, "since then you are called my king, *basileus emos kalei*" (1202).[8] Once he was called Oedipus, famous among all men, and now "you are called my king." But this transformation from *tyrannos* to king is his reversal; the revelation that he is king is the overthrow of the *tyrannos*. The proof of his legitimacy is at the same time the exposure of his unspeakable pollution.

The title *tyrannos* has then a magnificent ironic function, but if it makes a great contribution to the complexity of the play's texture, it raises some problems as well. For the word meant more to the fifth-century audience than a usurper who replaced the hereditary king: the *tyrannos* was an adventurer who, however brilliant and prosperous his regime, had gained power by violence and maintained it by violence. The connection of the *tyrannos* with violence is forced on the spectator when the chorus sings, "Violence and pride (*hybris*) engender the *tyrannos*." The succeeding sentences of this choral ode are an estimate of the origin, nature, and end of the *tyrannos* in terms of the current moral and political tradition of the late fifth century.

What is the reason for the chorus's attack on Oedipus? And why does it take this particular form? According to Jebb,[9] "the strain of warning rebuke" is suggested by "the tone of Oedipus towards Creon," but this does not seem an adequate explanation. The chorus's last word on the subject of Creon was a declaration of complete loyalty to Oedipus. "I should be clearly insane, incapable of intelligence, if I turned my back on you" (690–91). The change from this to "Violence and pride engender the *tyrannos*" is clearly a decisive change: it must be due to something that has happened since the quarrel with Creon.

Not much has happened, but much has been revealed. Oedipus came to Thebes with blood on his hands, and one of the men he had just killed was a person of some importance, for he rode in a carriage and was accompanied by a herald. True, Oedipus struck in self-defense, but none the less the chorus has come to know an Oedipus they had not suspected, a man of violence, who can say, with almost a touch of pride, "I killed the whole lot of them" (*Kteino de tous xumpantas*, 813). *Hubris phuteuei tyrannon.* The elevation of Oedipus to the throne of Thebes was preceded by the bloody slaughter on the highway.

But this is not all. Oedipus has good reason to suspect that the man in the carriage was Laius, the hereditary king of Thebes, and the chorus is afraid that he is right.[10] If he is, then Oedipus won his power by killing the hereditary king and taking his place both on his throne and in his marriage bed—like Gyges of Lydia, one of the classic types of the *tyrannos*; Gyges is in fact the first man to whom the title is applied in extant Greek literature.[11] *Hubris phuteuei tyrannon*—violence engenders him, for it is the instrument of his accession to power.

These aspects of Oedipus' present title to power and his past actions, together with the choral ode on the *tyrannos*, clearly raise the whole issue of *tyrannis* in terms of the current political tradition. Why? The play cannot be an attack on *tyrannis* as an institution, for not only was *tyrannis* universally detested, it was also, at the beginning of the Peloponnesian war, a dead issue;[12] though he was to be a typical phenomenon of the next century, in the last half of the fifth century the *tyrannos* was a bitter memory of the past rather than a fear of the future. And in any case, Oedipus is not a figure which conforms to the pattern of the *tyrannos*. He does not defy ancestral laws, outrage women, put men to death without trial,[13] plunder his subjects,[14] distrust the good and delight in the bad,[15] nor does he live in fear.[16] He is not equipped with the armed bodyguard, which is the salient characteristic of the *tyrannos* in real life[17] and of Aegisthus, for example, on the tragic stage.[18] Oedipus comes directly to his people—"not through messengers," as he says himself (6); he is loved, not feared. And the political actions which he carries out in the play are decidedly untyrannic. He rejects Creon's strong hint that the oracular response should be discussed in private,[19] calls an assembly of the people of Thebes,[20] and on a matter which he considers vital, the condemnation of Creon, he gives way to Jocasta and to the chorus which represents the people he has summoned in the opening scene. Thebes under Oedipus may be a *tyrannis*, but it works surprisingly like a democracy, led by its most gifted and outstanding citizen. What are we to make of this combination of democracy and *tyrannis*?

It was no puzzle to members of the Athenian audience, who were themselves citizens of exactly such a state. "We are called a democracy," says Pericles,[21] but he also tells the Athenians, "you hold your empire (*arche*, Oedipus' word!) as a *tyrannis*."[22] Cleon calls the Athenian empire a *tyrannis*, too,[23] and it is the word used not only by Athenians, but by the enemies of Athens: the Corinthians at Sparta twice characterize Athens as the city "which has been established as *tyrannos* in Hellas."[24] It is clear that in the late fifth century the idea of Athens as *tyrannos* was a commonplace both at Athens and abroad. Oedipus talks about his power (*arche*) in terms that vividly recall the fifth-century estimates, both hostile and admiring, of Athenian power. "O wealth and *tyrannis*," he exclaims, "and skill surpassing skill in the competition of life, how much envy and hatred (*phthonos*) are stored up in you ..." (380–83). Wealth was the Athenian boast, and the terror of her enemies:[25] skill, especially technical and naval skill, was the guarantee of Athenian commercial and naval supremacy,[26] and the Athenians knew how they were envied and hated. "Do we deserve," say the Athenian ambassadors at Sparta, "the excessive hatred and envy (*phthonos*) the Greeks feel for us?"[27] "The possession of power," says Pericles, "has always brought envy: when the power involved is great, the envy must be accepted."[28]

The Athenian *arche*, like that of Oedipus, is not an inherited power, but something new in the Greek world, gained by self-exertion. Pericles proudly refers to the fathers of the Athenians whom he is addressing, "who by their own efforts and not by inheriting it, gained this power and maintained it."[29] And, like the power of Oedipus, it was originally offered, not sought. "This power," says Oedipus, "which the city put into my hands, as a free gift, not something I asked for" (303–4). "We did not take power by force," the Athenian ambassadors remind the Spartans, "the allies themselves came to us and asked us to be their leaders ... an empire was offered to us, and we accepted it."[30]

These resemblances between the Athenian supremacy in Greece and Oedipus' peculiar power in Thebes are enough to suggest that the word *tyrannos*, applied to Oedipus, is part of a larger pattern of image and emphasis which compares Oedipus with Athens itself. They are strengthened by the fact that the character of Oedipus is the character of the Athenian people. Oedipus in his typical reactions and capacities, his virtues and defects, is a microcosm of the people of Periclean Athens, the audience which watched the play. That such a generalized conception, the Athenian character, was current in the late fifth century is clear from the speeches in Thucydides alone (especially the brilliant contrast of Athenian and Spartan character made by the Corinthians in Book I): and for an example of a national type portrayed on the tragic stage we have only to look at Euripides' *Andromache*, where Menelaus is clearly a hostile portrait, verging on caricature, of the worst aspects of the Spartan character as seen by the Athenians in war time. The character of Oedipus, one of the most complicated and fully developed in Greek tragedy, bears a striking resemblance to the Athenian character as we find it portrayed in the historians, dramatists, and orators of the late fifth century.

Oedipus' magnificent vigor and his faith in action are markedly Athenian characteristics. "Athens," says Pericles, "will be the envy of the man who has a will to action,"[31] and the boast is supported by Thucydides' breath-taking summary of the action of the "fifty years." The enemies of Athens have a different view of Athenian vigor. "Their nature," say the Corinthians, "not only forbids them to remain inactive, but denies the possibility of inaction to the rest of mankind."[32] This is an apt description of Oedipus in the tragedy: his will to action never falters and forces Tiresias, Jocasta, and the shepherd, in spite of their reluctance, to play their part in the dynamic progress towards the discovery of the truth and his own fall.

The priest appeals to Oedipus as "experienced," the state which results from constant action, and this too is a source of Athenian pride and of caution for her enemies.[33] And like Oedipus, Athens is magnificently courageous:[34] Athenian courage, in fact, rises to its greatest heights when circumstances seem most adverse,[35] and this again is a characteristic of Oedipus.

Oedipus' action is swift (he has already sent to Delphi when the priest hints that he should, he has already sent for Tiresias when the chorus advises him to); he prefers to forestall rather than react (as he says when condemning Creon) (618–21). This speed in decision and action is the Athenian characteristic which the Corinthians fear above all others. "They are the only people who simultaneously hope for and have what they plan, because of their quick fulfillment of decision."[36]

But Oedipus' swift action is not rash, it is based in reflection. Even his most impulsive act, his self-blinding, is shown to be based on a careful deliberation.[37] And this too is typically Athenian. "We are unique," says Pericles, "in our combination of the most courageous action and rational discussion of our projects."[38] Oedipus' reflection is the working of a great intelligence, and this is his greatest pride, *gnomei kuresas.* "I found the answer by intelligence" (398), he says of his solution of the Sphinx's riddle. So Pericles claims that the Athenians defeated the Persians "by intelligence rather than chance" (*gnomei te pleoni e tuchei*).[39]

All these qualities and the record of success which they have produced generate in Oedipus an enormous self-confidence (a mood that informs all the Periclean speeches in Thucydides, even the last one)[40] and also unlimited hopes. Athenian hopes are highest in the face of danger and even impending disaster. "In terrible circumstances they are full of good hope" say the Corinthians;[41] this reads like a comment on Oedipus' hopeful outburst which follows Jocasta's last words.

Oedipus, speaking of the riddle of the Sphinx, boasts that he was the amateur (*ho meden eidos Oidipous*, 397) who put the professional (Tiresias) to shame. This is of course the proud boast of the Funeral Speech; the Athenians are amateurs in war but are confident of their ability to beat the Spartan professionals.[42] And Oedipus' adaptability—he was a homeless exile and became the loved and admired ruler of a foreign city—is another Athenian characteristic. "The individual Athenian," says Pericles, "addresses himself to the most varied types of action with the utmost versatility and charm."[43]

Oedipus' devotion to the city, the mainspring of his dedicated action in the first half of the play, is the great Athenian virtue which Pericles preaches[44] and Athens' enemies fear. "In the city's service"—the Corinthians again—"they use their bodies as if they did not belong to them."[45]

Oedipus' quick suspicion and keen nose for a plot is of course one of the outstanding traits of the Athenian *demos*.[46] And so is his terrible anger, which at its height seems uncontrollable by force and reason alike. This rage of Oedipus is the rage of Athens which even Pericles feared,[47] which condemned the people of Mitylene and the generals at Arginusae.[48] But like the Athenian anger, it does not last: Creon gets a reprieve, as Mitylene did.[49]

Oedipus *tyrannos*, then, is more than an individual tragic hero. He represents, by the basis of his power, his character, and his title, the city which aimed to become (and was already on the road to becoming) the *tyrannos* of Greece, the splendid autocrat of the whole Hellenic world. Sophocles' use of the word *tyrannos* and the relationships it points up, add an extra dimension to the heroic figure of Oedipus, and also to the meaning of his fall.

Notes

1. Aristotle calls it simply "The Oedipus," cf. *Po.* 1452^{a}24, 1453^{b}7, etc.
2. p. 4, n. 2.
3. Euripides goes so far as to make a chorus of Athenian citizens refer to Demophon, son of Theseus, an Attic King and pattern of Athenian bravery and piety, as *tyrannos* (*Heracl.* 111).
4. cf. 219–20 and 222.
5. Th. 1.13 *patrikai basileiai*; cf. also *Pol.* 1285^{a}3.
6. He left Corinth to settle his doubts once and for all by consulting the Delphic oracle, but was sent away unanswered—*atimon* (789) is his word, which in the context

simply means "with my request disregarded" (cf. 340 *atimazeis*) but also implies "without honor," i.e., the doubt about his birth still unresolved.

7. cf. the situation on Ithaca in the *Odyssey*, where the hand of Penelope is evidently regarded as a stepping stone to royal power.

8. *ex hou ... basileus kalei emos kai ta megist' etimathes*. *Kalei* is ambiguous, for it refers in such a construction to both past and present (cf. Goodwin, sec. 26), but the present reference is emphasized by the change in tense of the next verb *etimathes*, which permits no ambiguity at all (naturally, for the statement cannot refer to the present, only to the past). Normal construction, however, would demand that this verb, too, be in the present tense. The effect is to stress the present reference of *kalei*, which might not have been emphatic without the sudden change of tense.

9. at vs. 873.

10. cf. 834.

11. Archil., *Fr.* 25 (Bergk⁴) and cf. the second hypothesis of the *O.T.*

12. True, the meetings of the Assembly were preceded by the recital of prayers which included curses on those who aimed to restore the *tyrannos*, but the frequent Aristophanic parodies of this prayer indicate that it was an antiquarian survival (cf. *Av.* 1074, *Th.* 334–40), and a celebrated passage in *V.* 488–502 suggests that, although demagogues and unscrupulous persecutors made free with the accusation of tyranny, it was not to be taken seriously.

13. For these three characteristic actions, see Hdt. 3.80 and E., *Supp.* 447–49.

14. cf. Hdt. 3.39 (Polycrates); 5.92, sec. 2 (Cypselus); Arist., *Pol.* 1311ᵃ; E., *Fr.* 605 (N²); Pl., *Phd.* 82a; E., *Supp.* 450–51.

15. Hdt., 3.80; E., *Ion* 627–8; Pl., *R.* 8.567.

16. E., *Ion.* 621–28. Cf. also *Fr.* 605 (N²). X., *Hier.* 2.8–10.

17. Pl., *R.* 8.567d.; Arist., *Pol.* 1285ᵃ, 1311ᵃ; Th. 1.130.

18. A., *A.* 1650, *Ch.* 768–69; S., *El.* 1369–71; E., *El.* 798, 845.

19. 93 *es pantas auda*.

20. 144 *allos de Kadmou laon hod' athroizeto*.

21. Thuc. 2.37. From here on, all references are to Thucydides if not otherwise indicated.

22. 2.63.

23. 3.37; cf. also 6.85 (Euphemus, Athenian ambassador in Sicily).

24. 1.122, 124.

25. 1.80, 2.13, 64, 6.31.

26. 1.102, 142, 1.71, 2.87, 1.121.

27. 1.75. *Ar' axtoi esmen ... kai prothumias heneka tes tote kai gnomes xuneseos arches ge hes echomen tois Hellesi me houtos agan epiphthonos diakeisthai?* The parallels to the Oedipean phrases are striking: 48. *tes paros prothumias*, 398 *gnomei kuresas*, 381 *hosos phthonos*, 382 *tesde g' arches hounek'*.

28. 2.64; cf. also (Lysias) *Epitaphios* 48.

29. 2.62.

30. 1.75, 76.

31. 2.64.4; cf. also 6.

32. 1.70.9; cf. also 8.

33. 7.61; 2.84, 85, 89; 1.142. Hdt. 9.46.

34. Hdt. 9.27; Th. 1.9, 102, 2.88, 2.41, 7.28.

35. 1.74 (Lysias) *Epitaphios* 58.

36. 1.70. For parallels to Oedipus' "forestalling" cf. 1.57, 3.3.

37. cf. 1371ff.—Oedipus' defense of his self-blinding: note the past tenses (1372, 1375, 1385) and the correspondence of the argument with the words of Oedipus before the action, as reported by the messenger (1271–74).

38. 2.40.
39. 1.144; cf. also 1.75, 2.40 *philosophoumen*, 2.62 *xunesis* and *gnome*.
40. 2.62.
41. 1.70 *en tois deinois euelpides*; cf. Euelpides, the Athenian of Aristophanes' *Aves*. Cf. also Th. 7.77.
42. 2.39 *rathumiai mallon e ponon meletei* and 1.133. (Themistocles) *hon d' apeiros eie, krinai hikanos.*
43. 1.41 *ton auton andra ... epi pleist' an eide ... malist' an eutrapelos ...* and also 1.138 (Themistocles at Sardis).
44. 2.43; cf. 2.60 *philopolis.*
45. 1.70.
46. cf. e.g., 6.28, 53; 2.13; 3.43; Ar., *V.* 343–45 (with which cf. *O.T.* 124–5).
47. 2.60 and Ar., *Pax* 606–7.
48. For Athenian *orge* cf. 6.60, 8.1; Ar. *Eq.* 41–42 *despotes agroikos orgen ... Demos ... duskolon gerontion*, Ibid. 537, *V.* 243, Antiphon *Herodes* 69, 71.
49. 3.36 *metanoia*; cf. 1.65 and X., *HG.* 1.7.35.

NINE

Sophocles' Oedipus

Sophocles' *Oedipus* is not only the greatest creation of a major poet and the classic representative figure of his age: he is also one of the long series of tragic protagonists who stand as symbols of human aspiration and despair before the characteristic dilemma of western civilization— the problem of man's true nature, his proper place in the universe.

In the earlier of the two Sophoclean plays which deal with the figure of Oedipus, this fundamental problem is raised at the very beginning of the prologue by the careful distinctions which the priest makes in defining his attitude toward Oedipus, the former savior of Thebes, its absolute ruler, and its last hope of rescue from the plague. "We beg your help," he says, "regarding you not as one equated to the gods, θεοῖσι . . . οὐκ ἰσούμενον, but as first of men."

"Not equated to the gods, but first of men." The positive part of the statement at any rate is undeniably true. Oedipus is *tyrannos* of Thebes, its despotic ruler. The Greek word corresponds neither to Shelley's "tyrant" nor to Yeats' "king": tyrannos is an absolute ruler, who may be a bad ruler or a good one (as Oedipus clearly is), but in either case he is a ruler who has seized power, not inherited it. He is not a king, for a king succeeds only by birth; the *tyrannos* succeeds by brains, force, influence. "This absolute power, τυραννίς," says Oedipus in the play, "is a prize won with masses and money." This title of Oedipus, *tyrannos*, is one of the most powerful ironies of the play, for, although Oedipus does not know it, he is not only *tyrannos*, the outsider who came to power in Thebes, he is also the legitimate king by birth, for he was born the son of Laius. Only when his identity is revealed can he properly be called king, and the chorus refers to him by this title for the first time in the great ode which it sings after Oedipus knows the truth.

But the word *tyrannos* has a larger significance. Oedipus, to quote that same choral ode, is a παράδειγμα, a paradigm, an example to all men; the fact that he is *tyrannos*, self-made ruler, the proverbial Greek

This chapter originally appeared in *Tragic Themes in Western Literature*, ed. Cleanth Brooks (New Haven and London, 1955). ©1955 by The Yale University Press.

example of worldly success won by individual intelligence and exertion, makes him an appropriate symbol of civilized man, who was beginning to believe, in the fifth century B.C., that he could seize control of his environment and make his own destiny—become, in fact, equated to the gods. "Oedipus shot his arrow far beyond the range of others"—the choral ode again—"and accomplished the conquest of complete prosperity and happiness."

Oedipus became *tyrannos* by answering the riddle of the Sphinx. It was no easy riddle, and he answered it, as he proudly asserts, without help from prophets, from bird signs, from gods; he answered it alone, with his intelligence. The answer won him a city and the hand of a queen. And the answer to the Sphinx's riddle was—Man. In Sophocles' own century the same answer had been proposed to a greater riddle. "Man," said Protagoras the sophist, "is the measure of all things."

Protagoras' famous statement is the epitome of the critical and optimistic spirit of the middle years of the fifth century; its implications are clear—man is the center of the universe, his intelligence can overcome all obstacles, he is master of his own destiny, *tyrannos*, self-made ruler, who has the capacity to attain complete prosperity and happiness.

In an earlier Sophoclean play, *Antigone*, the chorus sings a hymn to this man the conqueror. "Many are the wonders and terrors, and nothing more wonderful and terrible than man." He has conquered the sea, "this creature goes beyond the white sea pressing forward as the swell crashes about him"; and he has conquered the land, "earth, highest of the gods . . . he wears away with the turning plough." He has mastered not only the elements, sea, and land, but the birds, beasts, and fishes; "through knowledge and technique," sings the chorus, he is yoker of the horse, tamer of the bull. "And he has taught himself speech and thought swift as the wind and attitudes which enable him to live in communities and means to shelter himself from the frost and rain. Full of resources he faces the future, nothing will find him at a loss. Death, it is true, he will not avoid, yet he has thought out ways of escape from desperate diseases. His knowledge, ingenuity and technique are beyond anything that could have been foreseen." These lyrics describe the rise to power of *anthropos tyrannos*; self-taught, he seizes control of his environment, he is master of the elements, the animals, the arts and sciences of civilization. "Full of resources he faces the future"—an apt description of Oedipus at the beginning of our play.

And it is not the only phrase of this ode which is relevant; for Oedipus is connected by the terms he uses, and which are used to and about him, with the whole range of human achievement which has raised man to his present level. All the items of this triumphant catalog recur in the *Oedipus Tyrannos*; the images of the play define him as helmsman, conqueror of the sea, and ploughman, conqueror of the land, as hunter, master of speech and thought, inventor, legislator, physician. Oedipus is faced in the play with an intellectual problem, and as he marshals his intellectual resources to solve it, the language of the play suggests a comparison between Oedipus' methods in the play and the whole range of sciences and techniques which have brought man to mastery, made him *tyrannos* of the world.

Oedipus' problem is apparently simple: "Who is the murderer of Laius?" But as he pursues the answer, the question changes shape. It becomes a different problem: "Who am I?" And the answer to this problem involves the gods as well as man. The answer to the question is not what he expected, it is in fact a reversal, that *peripeteia* which Aristotle speaks of in connection with this play. The state of Oedipus is reversed from "first of men" to "most accursed of men"; his attitude from the proud ἀρκτέον, "I must rule," to the humble πειστέον, "I must obey." "Reversal," says Aristotle, "is a change of the action into the opposite," and one meaning of this much disputed phrase is that the action produces the opposite of the actor's intentions. So Oedipus curses the murderer of Laius and it turns out that he has cursed himself. But this reversal is not confined to the action; it is also the process of all the great images of the play which identify Oedipus as the inventive, critical spirit of his century. As the images unfold, the inquirer turns into the object of inquiry, the hunter into the prey, the doctor into the patient, the investigator into the criminal, the revealer into the thing revealed, the finder into the thing found, the savior into the thing saved ("I was saved, for some dreadful destiny"), the liberator into the thing released ("I released your feet from the bonds which pierced your ankles," says the Corinthian messenger). The accuser becomes the defendant, the ruler the subject, the teacher not only the pupil but also the object lesson, the example—a change of the action into its opposite, from active to passive.

And the two opening images of the *Antigone* ode recur with hideous effect. Oedipus the helmsman, who steers the ship of state, is seen, in Tiresias' words, as one who "steers his ship into a nameless anchorage," who, in the chorus's words, "shared the same great harbour with his father." And Oedipus the ploughman—"How," asks the chorus, "how could the furrows which your father ploughed bear you in silence for so long?"

This reversal is the movement of the play, parallel in the imagery and the action: it is the overthrow of the *tyrannos*, of man who seized power and thought himself "equated to the gods." The bold metaphor of the priest introduces another of the images which parallel in their development the reversal of the hero and suggest that Oedipus is a figure symbolic of human intelligence and achievement in general. He is not only helmsman, ploughman, inventor, legislator, liberator, revealer, doctor—he is also equator, mathematician, calculator; "equated" is a mathematical term, and it is only one of a whole complex of such terms which present Oedipus in yet a fresh aspect of man *tyrannos*. One of Oedipus' favorite words is "measure," and this is of course a significant metaphor: measure, mensuration, number, calculation—these are among the most important inventions which have brought man to power. Aeschylus' Prometheus, the mythical civilizer of human life, counts number among the foremost of his gifts to man. "And number, too, I invented, outstanding among clever devices." In the river valleys of the East, generations of mensuration and calculation had brought man to an understanding of the movements of the stars and of time: in the histories of his friend Herodotus, Sophocles had read of the calculation and mensuration which had gone into the building of the pyramids. "Measure"—it is Protagoras' word: "Man is the measure of all things." In this play man's measure is taken, his true equation found. The play is full of equations, some of them incomplete, some false; the final equation shows man equated not to the gods but to himself, as Oedipus is finally equated to himself. For there are in the play not one Oedipus but two.

One is the magnificent figure set before us in the opening scenes, *tyrannos*, the man of wealth and power, first of men, the intellect and energy which drive on the search. The other is the object of the search, a shadowy figure who has violated the most fundamental human taboos, an incestuous parricide, "most accursed of men." And even before the one Oedipus finds the other, they are connected and equated in the name which they both bear, Oedipus. Oedipus—Swollen-foot; it emphasizes the physical blemish which scars the body of the splendid *tyrannos*, a defect which he tries to forget but which reminds us of the outcast child this *tyrannos* once was and the outcast man he is soon to be. The second half of the name πούς, "foot," recurs throughout the play, as a mocking phrase which recalls this other Oedipus. "The Sphinx forced us to look at what was at our feet," says Creon. Tiresias invokes "the dread-footed curse of your father and mother." And the choral odes echo and re-echo with this word. "Let the murderer of Laius set his foot in motion in flight." "The murderer is a man alone with forlorn foot." "The laws of Zeus are high-footed." "The man of pride plunges down into doom where he cannot use his foot."

These mocking repetitions of one-half the name invoke the unknown Oedipus who will be revealed: the equally emphatic repetition of the first half emphasizes the dominant attitude of the man before us.

Oidi—"swell," but it is also *Oida*, "I know," and this word is often, too often, in Oedipus' mouth. His knowledge is what makes him *tyrannos*, confident and decisive; knowledge has made man what he is, master of the world. Οἶδα, "I know"—it runs through the play with the same mocking persistence as πούς, "foot," and sometimes reaches an extreme of macabre punning emphasis.

When the messenger, to take one example of many, comes to tell Oedipus that his father, Polybus, is dead, he inquires for Oedipus, who is in the palace, in the following words:

> "Strangers, from you might I learn where
> is the palace of the *tyrannos* Oedipus,
> best of all, where he is himself if you know where."

Here it is in the Greek:

ἆρ' ἄν παρ' ὑμῶν ὦ ξένοι μάθοιμ' ὅπου (oimopou)
τὰ τοῦ τυράννου δώματ' ἐστὶν Οἰδίπου (oidipou)
μάλιστα δ' αὐτὸν εἴπατ' εἰ κάτισθ' ὅπου (isthopou)

Those punning rhyming line endings, μάθοιμ' ὅπου, Οἰδίπου, κάτισθ' ὅπου, "learn where," "Oedipus," "know where," unparalleled elsewhere in Greek tragedy, are a striking example of the boldness with which Sophocles uses language: from the "sweet singer of Colonus" they are somewhat unexpected, they might almost have been written by the not-so-sweet singer of Trieste-Zurich-Paris.

Οἶδα, the knowledge of the *tyrannos*, πούς, the swollen foot of Laius' son—in the hero's name the basic equation is already symbolically present, the equation which Oedipus will finally solve. But the priest in the prologue is speaking of a different equation, ἰσούμενον, "We beg your help, not as one equated to the gods ... " It is a warning, and the warning is needed. For although Oedipus in the opening scenes is a model of formal and verbal piety, the piety is skin deep. And even before he declares his true religion, he can address the chorus, which has been praying to the gods, with godlike words. "What you pray for you will receive, if you will listen to and accept what I am about to say."

The priest goes on to suggest a better equation: he asks Oedipus to equate himself to the man he was when he saved Thebes from the Sphinx. "You saved us then, be now the equal of the man you were." This is the first statement of the theme, the double Oedipus; here there is a contrast implied between the present Oedipus, who is failing to save his city from the plague and the successful Oedipus of the past who answered the riddle of the Sphinx. He must answer a riddle again, be his old self, but the answer to this riddle will not be as simple as the answer to the first. When it is found, he will be equated, not to the foreigner who saved the city and became *tyrannos*, but to the native-born king, the son of Laius and Jocasta.

Oedipus repeats the significant word, "equal," ὅστις ἐξ ἴσου νοσεῖ. "Sick as you are, not one of you has sickness equal to mine," and he adds a word of his own, his characteristic metaphor. He is impatient at Creon's absence. "Measuring the day against the time, ξυμμετρούμενον χρόνῳ, I am worried. . . . " And then as Creon approaches, "He is now commensurate with the range of our voices"—ξύμμετρος γὰρ ὡς κλύειν.

Here is Oedipus the equator and measurer; this is the method by which he will reach the truth: calculation of time and place, measurement and comparison of age and number and description—these are the techniques which will solve the equation, establish the identity of the murderer of Laius. The tightly organized and relentless process by which Oedipus finds his way to the truth is the operation of the human intellect in many aspects; it is the investigation of the officer of the law who identifies the criminal, the series of diagnoses of the physician who identifies the disease—it has even been compared by Freud to the process of psychoanalysis—and it is also the working out of a mathematical problem which will end with the establishment of a true equation.

The numerical nature of the problem is emphasized at once with Creon's entry. "One man of Laius' party escaped," says Creon, "he had only one thing to say." "What is it?" asks Oedipus. "One thing might find a way to learn many." The one thing is that Laius was killed not by one man but by many. This sounds like a problem in arithmetic, and Oedipus undertakes to solve it. But the chorus which now comes on stage has no such confidence: it sings of the plague with despair, but it makes this statement in terms of the same metaphor; it has its characteristic word which, like the priest and like Oedipus, it pronounces twice. The chorus's word is ἀνάριθμος, "numberless," "uncountable." "My sorrows are beyond the count of number," and later, "uncountable the deaths of which the city is dying." The plague is something beyond the power of "number . . . outstanding among clever devices."

The prologue and the first stasimon, besides presenting the customary exposition of the plot, present also the exposition of the metaphor. And with the entry of Tiresias, the development of the metaphor begins, its terrible potentialities are revealed. "Even though you are *tyrannos*," says the prophet at the height of his anger, "you and I must be made equal in one thing, at least, the chance for an equal reply," ἐξισωτέον τὸ γοῦν ἴσ' ἀντιλέξαι. Tiresias is blind, and Oedipus will be made equal to him in this before the play is over. But there is more still. "There is a mass of evil of which you are unconscious which shall equate you to yourself and your children":

ἅ σ᾽ ἐξισώσει σοί τε καὶ τοῖς σοῖς τέκνοις.

This is not the equation the priest desired to see, Oedipus present equated with Oedipus past, the deliverer from the Sphinx, but a more terrible equation reaching farther back into the past, Oedipus son of Polybus and Merope equated to Oedipus son of Laius and Jocasta; "equate you with your own children," for Oedipus is the brother of his own sons and daughters. In his closing words, Tiresias explains this mysterious line and connects it with the unknown murderer of Laius. "He will be revealed, a native Theban, one who in his relationship with his own children is both brother and father, with his mother both son and husband, with his father, both marriage partner and murderer. Go inside and reckon this up, λογίζου, and if you find me mistaken in my reckoning, ἐψευσμένον, then say I have no head for prophecy."

Tiresias adopts the terms of Oedipus' own science and throws them in his face. But these new equations are beyond Oedipus' understanding; he dismisses them as the ravings of an unsuccessful conspirator with his back to the wall. Even the chorus, though disturbed, rejects the prophet's words and resolves to stand by Oedipus.

After Tiresias, Creon; after the prophet, the politician. In Tiresias, Oedipus faced a blind man who saw with unearthly sight, but Creon's vision, like that of Oedipus, is of this world. They are two of a kind, and Creon talks Oedipus' language. It is a quarrel between two calculators. "Hear an equal reply," says Creon, and "Long time might be measured since Laius' murder." "You and Jocasta rule in equality of power." And finally, "Am I not a third party equated, ἰσοῦμαι, to you two?" Creon and Oedipus are not equal now, for Creon is at the mercy of Oedipus, begging for a hearing; but before the play is over Oedipus will be at the mercy of Creon, begging kindness for his daughters, and he then uses the same word. "Do not equate them with my misfortunes":

μηδ᾽ ἐξισώσῃς τάσδε τοῖς ἐμοῖς κακοῖς

With Jocasta's intervention, the inquiry changes direction. In her attempt to comfort Oedipus, whose only accuser is a prophet, she indicts prophecy in general, using as an example the unfulfilled prophecy about her own child, who was supposed to kill Laius. The child was abandoned on the mountainside and Laius was killed by robbers where three wagon roads meet. "Such were the definitions, διώρισαν, made by prophetic voices," and they were incorrect. But Oedipus is not, for the moment, interested in prophetic voices. "Where three wagon roads meet"—he once killed a man at such a place and now in a series of swift questions he determines the relation of these two events. The place, the time, the description of the victim, the number in his party—five—all correspond exactly. His account of the circumstances includes Apollo's prophecy that he would kill his father and be his mother's mate. But this does not disturb him now. That prophecy has not been fulfilled, for his father and mother are in Corinth, where he will never go again. "I measure the distance to Corinth by the stars," ἄστροις . . . ἐκμετρούμενος. What does disturb him is that he may be the murderer of Laius, the cause of the plague, the object of his own solemn excommunication. But he has some slight ground for hope. There is a discrepancy in the two events. It is the same numerical distinction which was discussed before, whether Laius was killed by one man or many. Jocasta said robbers, and Oedipus was alone. This distinction is now all-important, the key to the solution of the equation. Oedipus sends for the survivor, who can confirm or deny the saving detail. "If he says the same number as you then I am not the murderer. For one cannot equal many":

οὐ γὰρ γένοιτ' ἂν εἷς γε τοῖς πολλοῖς ἴσος

which may fairly be rendered, "In no circumstances can one be equal to more than one." Oedipus' guilt or innocence rests now on a mathematical axiom.

But a more fundamental equation has been brought into question, the relation of the oracles to reality. Here are two oracles, both the same, both unfulfilled; the same terrible destiny was predicted for Jocasta's son, who is dead, and for Oedipus, who has avoided it. One thing is clear to Jocasta. Whoever turns out to be Laius' murderer, the oracles are wrong. "From this day forward I would not, for all prophecy can say, turn my head this way or that." If the equation of the oracles with reality is a false equation, then religion is meaningless. Neither Jocasta nor Oedipus can allow the possibility that the oracles are right, and they accept the consequences, as they proceed to make clear. But the chorus cannot, and it now abandons Oedipus the calculator and turns instead to those "high-footed laws, which are the children of Olympus and not a creation of mortal man." It calls on Zeus to fulfill the oracles. "If these things do not coincide," ἁρμόσει, if the oracles do not equal reality, then "the divine order is overthrown," ἔρρει τὰ θεῖα. The situation and future of two individuals has become a test of divine power: if they are right, sings the chorus, "why reverence Apollo's Delphi, the center of the world? Why join the choral dance?" τί δεῖ με χορεύειν; and with this phrase the issue is brought out of the past into the present moment in the theater of Dionysus. For this song itself is also a dance, the choral stasimon which is the nucleus of tragedy and which reminds us that tragedy itself is an act of religious worship. If the oracles and the truth are not equated, the performance of the play has no meaning, for tragedy is a religious ritual. This phrase is a *tour de force* which makes the validity of the performance itself depend on the denouement of the play.

The oracles are now the central issue; the murder of Laius fades into the background. A messenger from Corinth brings news, news which will be greeted, he announces, "with an equal amount of sorrow and joy." "What is it," asks Jocasta, "which has such double power?" Polybus is dead. The sorrow equal to the joy will come later; for the moment, there is only joy. The oracles are proved wrong again: Oedipus' father is dead. Oedipus can no more kill his father than the son of Laius killed his. "Oracles of the gods, where are you now?" Oedipus is caught up in Jocasta's exaltation, but it does not last. Only half his burden has been lifted from him. His mother still lives. He must still measure the distance to Corinth by the stars, still fear the future.

Both Jocasta and the messenger now try to relieve him of this last remaining fear. Jocasta makes her famous declaration in which she rejects fear, providence, divine and human alike, and indeed any idea of order or plan. Her declaration amounts almost to a rejection of the law of cause and effect, and it certainly attacks the basis of human calculation. For her, the calculation has gone far enough: it has produced an acceptable result; let it stop here. "Why should man fear?" she asks. "His life is governed by the operation of chance. Nothing can be accurately foreseen. The best rule is to live blindly, at random, εἰκῇ, as best one can." It is a statement which recognizes and accepts a meaningless universe. And Oedipus would agree, but for one thing. His mother lives. He must still fear.

Where Jocasta failed, the messenger succeeds. He does it by destroying the equation on which Oedipus' life is based. And he uses familiar terms. "Polybus is no more your father than I, but equally so." Oedipus' question is indignant: "How can my father be equal to a nobody, to zero? τῷ μηδενί" The answer: "Polybus is not your father, neither am I." But that is as far as the Corinthian's knowledge goes; he was given the child Oedipus by another, a shepherd, one of Laius' men. And now the two separate equations begin to merge. "I think," says the chorus, "that that shepherd was the same man that you already sent for," the eyewitness to the death of Laius. He was sent for to say whether Laius was killed by one or many, but he will bring more important news. He will finally lift from Oedipus' shoulders the burden of fear he has carried since he left Delphi. Chance governs all. Oedipus' life history is the operation of chance; found by one shepherd, passed on to another, given to Polybus who was childless, brought up as heir to a kingdom, self-exiled from Corinth, he came to Thebes a homeless wanderer, answered the riddle of the Sphinx, and won a city and the hand of a queen. And that same guiding chance will now reveal to him his real identity. Jocasta was right. Why should he fear?

But Jocasta has already seen the truth. Not chance, but the fulfillment of the oracle; the prophecy and the facts coincide (ἁρμόσει), as the chorus prayed they would. Jocasta is lost, but she tries to save Oedipus, to stop the inquiry. But nothing can stop him now. Her farewell to him expresses her agony and knowledge by its omissions: she recognizes but cannot formulate the dreadful equation which Tiresias stated. "ἰού, ἰού, δύστηνε, Unfortunate. This is the only name I can call you." She cannot call him husband. The three-day-old child she sent out to die on the mountainside has been restored to her, and she cannot call him son.

Oedipus hardly listens. He in his turn has scaled the same heights of confidence from which she has toppled, and he goes higher still. "I will know my origin, burst forth what will." He knows that it will be good. Chance governs the universe and Oedipus is her son. Not the son of Polybus, nor of any mortal man but the son of fortunate chance. In his exaltation he rises in imagination above human stature. "The months, my brothers, have defined, διώρισαν, my greatness and smallness"; he has waned and waxed like the moon, he is one of the forces of the universe, his family is time and space. It is a religous, a mystical conception; here is Oedipus' real religion, he is equal to the gods, the son of chance, the only real goddess. Why should he not establish his identity?

The solution is only a few steps ahead. The shepherd is brought on. "If I, who never met the man, may make an estimate (σταθμᾶσθαι), I think this is the shepherd who has been the object of our investigation (ζητοῦμεν). In age he is commensurate σύμμετρος with the Corinthian here." With this significant prologue, he plunges into the final calculation.

The movement of the next sixty lines is the swift ease of the last stages of the mathematical proof: the end is half foreseen, the process an automatic sequence from one step to the next until Oedipus *tyrannos* and Oedipus the accursed, the knowledge and the swollen foot, are equated. "It all comes out clear," he cries, τὰ πάντ' ἂν ἐξήκοι σαφῆ. The prophecy has been fulfilled. Oedipus knows himself for what he is. He is not the measurer but the thing measured, not the equator but the thing equated. He is the answer to the problem he tried to solve. The chorus sees in Oedipus a παράδειγμα, an example to mankind. In this self-recognition of Oedipus, man recognizes himself. Man measures himself and the result is not that man is the measure of all things. The chorus, which rejected number and all that it stood for, has learned to count and states the result of the great calculation. "Generations of man

that must die, I add up the total of your life and find it equal to zero,"
ἴσα καὶ τὸ μηδὲν ζώσας ἐναριθμῶ.

The overthrow of the *tyrannos* is complete. When Oedipus returns
from the palace he is blind and, by the terms of his own proclamation,
an outcast. It is a terrible reversal, and it raises the question, "Is it
deserved? How far is he responsible for what he has done? Were the
actions for which he is now paying not predestined?" No. They were
committed in ignorance, but they were not predestined, merely predicted. An essential distinction, as essential for Milton's Adam as for
Sophocles' Oedipus. His will was free, his actions his own, but the
pattern of his action is the same as that of the Delphic prophecy. The
relation between the prophecy and Oedipus' actions is not that of cause
and effect. It is the relation suggested by the metaphor, the relation of
two independent entities which are equated.

Yet no man can look on Oedipus without sympathy. In his moment
of exaltation—"I am the son of fortune"—he is man at his blindest, but
he is also man at his most courageous and heroic: "Burst forth what
will, I will know." And he has served, as the chorus says, to point a
moral. He is a paradigm, a demonstration. True, Oedipus, the independent being, was a perfectly appropriate subject for the demonstration.
But we cannot help feeling that the gods owe Oedipus a debt. Sophocles
felt it too, and in his last years wrote the play which shows us the
nature of the payment, *Oedipus at Colonus*.

This play deals with Oedipus' reward, and the reward is a strange
one. How strange can be seen clearly if we compare Oedipus with
another great figure who also served as the subject of a divine
demonstration, Job. After his torment, Job had it all made up to him.
"The Lord gave Job twice as much as he had before. For he had 14,000
sheep, and 6,000 camels and 1,000 yoke of oxen and 1,000 she-asses.
He had also 7 sons and 3 daughters. And after this lived Job an
hundred and forty years, and saw his sons and his sons' sons, even four
generations." This is the kind of reward we can understand—14,000
sheep, 6,000 camels. Job, to use an irreverent comparison, hit the
patriarchal jackpot. Oedipus' reward includes no camels or she-asses, no
long life, in fact no life at all; his reward is death. But a death which Job
could never imagine. For in death Oedipus becomes equated to the
gods. The ironic phrase with which the first play began has here a literal
fulfillment. Oedipus becomes something superhuman, a spirit which
lives on in power in the affairs of men after the death of the body. His
tomb is to be a holy place, for the city in whose territory his body lies
will win a great victory on the field where Oedipus lies buried. By his
choice of a burial place he thus influences history, becomes a presence
to be feared by some and thanked by others. But it is not only in his

grave that he will be powerful. In the last hours of his life, he begins to assume the attributes of the divinity he is to become; the second play, *Oedipus at Colonus*, puts on stage the process of Oedipus' transition from human to divine.

"Equated to the gods." We have not seen the gods, but we know from the first play what they are. That play demonstrated that the gods have knowledge, full complete knowledge, the knowledge which Oedipus thought he had. He was proved ignorant; real knowledge is what distinguishes god from man. Since the gods have knowledge, their action is confident and sure. They act with the swift decision which was characteristic of Oedipus but which was in him misplaced. Only gods can be sure, not a man, and their action is just. It is a justice based on perfect knowledge, is exact and appropriate, and therefore allows no room for forgiveness—but it can be angry. The gods can even mock the wrongdoer as Athena does Ajax, as the echoes of his name mocked Oedipus. This sure, full, angry justice is what Oedipus tried to administer to Tiresias, to Creon, but his justice was based on ignorance and was injustice. These attributes of divinity—knowledge, certainty, justice—are the qualities Oedipus thought he possessed—and that is why he was the perfect example of the inadequacy of human knowledge, certainty, and justice. But in the second play Oedipus is made equal to the gods, he assumes the attributes of divinity, the attributes he once thought his, he becomes what he once thought he was. This old Oedipus seems to be equal to the young, confident in his knowledge, fiercely angry in his administration of justice, utterly sure of himself— but this time he is justified. These are not the proper attitudes for a man, but Oedipus is turning into something more than man; now he knows surely, sees clearly; the gods give Oedipus back his eyes, but they are eyes of superhuman vision. Now, in his transformation, as then, in his reversal, he serves still as an example. The rebirth of the young, confident Oedipus in the tired old man emphasizes the same lesson; it defines once more the limits of man and the power of gods, states again that the possession of knowledge, certainty, and justice is what distinguishes god from man.

The opening statement of Oedipus shows that as a man he has learned the lesson well. "I have learned acquiescence, taught by suffering and long time." As a man Oedipus has nothing more to learn. With this statement, he comes to the end of a long road. The nearby city whose walls he cannot see is Athens, and here is the place of his reward, his grave, his home. The welcome he receives is to be ordered off by the first arrival; he has trespassed on holy ground, the grove of the Eumenides. He knows what this means, this is the resting place he was promised by Apollo, and he refuses to move. His statement recalls the *tyrannos*, a characteristic phrase: "In no circumstances will I leave this place." The terms of his prayer to the goddesses of the grave foreshadow his transition from body to spirit. "Pity this wretched ghost of Oedipus the man, this body that is not what it once was long ago."

As a body, as a man, he is a thing to be pitied; he is blind, feeble, ragged, dirty. But the transformation has already begun. The first comer spoke to him with pity, even condescension, but the chorus of citizens which now enters feels fear: "dreadful to see, dreadful to hear." When they know his identity, their fear changes to anger, but Oedipus defends his past. He sees himself as one who was ignorant, who suffered rather than acted. But now he is actor, not sufferer. He comes with knowledge and power. "I come bringing advantage to this city."

He does not yet know what advantage. His daughter Ismene comes to tell him what it is, that his grave will be the site of a victory for the city that shelters him. And to tell him that his sons and Creon, all of whom despised and rejected him, now need him and will come to beg his help. Oedipus has power over the future and can now reward his friends and punish his enemies. He chooses to reward Athens, to punish Creon and his own sons. He expresses his choice in terms which show a recognition of human limitations; Athens' reward, something which lies within his will, as an intention; his sons' punishment, something over which he has no sure control, as a wish. "May the issue of the battle between them lie in my hands. If that were to be, the one would not remain king, nor the other win the throne."

Theseus, the king of Athens, welcomes him generously, but when he learns that Thebes wants Oedipus back and that he refuses to go, Theseus reproaches the old man. "Anger is not what your misfortune calls for." And the answer is a fiery rebuke from a superior. "Wait till you hear what I say, before you reproach me." Oedipus tells Theseus that he will bring victory over Thebes at some future time, and Theseus, the statesman, is confident that Athens will never be at war with Thebes. Oedipus reproaches him in his turn. Such confidence is misplaced. No man should be so sure of the future: "Only to the gods comes no old age or death. Everything else is dissolved by all-powerful time. The earth's strength decays, the body decays, faith dies, mistrust flowers and the wind of friendship changes between man and man, city and city." No man can be confident of the future. Man's knowledge is ignorance. It is the lesson Oedipus learned in his own person, and he reads it to Theseus now with all the authority of his blind eyes and dreadful name—but he does not apply it to himself. For he goes on to predict the future. He hands down the law of human behavior to Theseus speaking already as a *daemon*, not one subject to the law but one who administers it. And with his confident prediction, his assump-

tion of sure knowledge, goes anger, but not the old human anger of
Oedipus *tyrannos*. As he speaks of Thebes' future defeat on the soil
where he will be buried, the words take on an unearthly quality, a
demonic wrath:

ἵν᾽ οὑμὸς εὕδων καὶ κεκρυμμένος νεκύς
ψυχρὸς ποτ᾽ αὐτῶν θερμὸν αἷμα πίεται
εἰ Ζεὺς ἔτι Ζεὺς χὡ Διὸς Φοῖβος σαφής.

"There my sleeping and hidden corpse, cold though it be, will drink
their warm blood, if Zeus is still Zeus and Apollo a true prophet." What
before was wish and prayer is now prediction. But the prediction is
qualified: "if Apollo be a true prophet." He does not yet speak in the
authority of his own name. That will be the final stage.

And when it comes, he speaks face to face with the objects of his
anger. Creon's condescending and hypocritical speech is met with a blast
of fury that surpasses the anger he had to face long ago in Thebes. The
final interview is a repetition of the first. In both Creon is condemned,
in both with the same swift vindictive wrath, but this time the
condemnation is just. Oedipus sees through to the heart of Creon, he
knows what he is; Creon proceeds to show the justice of Oedipus'
rejection by revealing that he has already kidnapped Ismene, by
kidnapping Antigone, and laying hands on Oedipus himself. Oedipus is
helpless, and only the arrival of Theseus saves him. This is the man
who is being equated to the gods, not the splendid *tyrannos*, the man of
power, vigor, strength, but a blind old man, the extreme of physical
weakness, who cannot even see, much less prevent, the violence that is
done him.

There is physical weakness but a new height of spiritual strength.
This Oedipus judges justly and exactly, knows fully, sees clearly—his
power is power over the future, the defeat of Thebes, the death of his
sons, the terrible reversal of Creon. One thing Creon asks Oedipus
clarifies the nature of the process we are witnessing: "Has not time
taught you wisdom?" Creon expected to find the Oedipus of the
opening scene of the play, whom time had taught acquiescence, but he
finds what seems to be the *tyrannos* he knew and feared. "You harm
yourself now as you did then," he says, "giving way to that anger which
has always been your defeat." He sees the old Oedipus as equal to the
young. In one sense they are, but in a greater sense they are no more
equal than man is equal to the gods.

With the next scene, the whole story comes full circle. A suppliant
begs Oedipus for help. Our last sight of Oedipus is like our first. This
suppliant is Polynices, his son, and the comparison with the opening
scene of the first play is emphasized by the repetitions of the priest's

speech—words, phrases, even whole lines—which appear in Polynices' appeal to his father. It is a hypocritical speech which needs no refutation. It is met with a terrible indictment which sweeps from accusation through prophecy to a climax which, with its tightly packed explosive consonants resembles not so much human speech as a burst of demonic anger:

θανεῖν κτανεῖν θ' ὑφ' οὗπερ ἐξελήλασαι
τοιαῦτ' ἀρῶμαι καὶ καλῶ τὸ Ταρτάρου
στυγνὸν πατρῷον ἔρεβος ὥς σ' ἀποικίσῃ

"Kill and be killed by the brother who drove you out. This is my curse, I call on the hideous darkness of Tartarus where your fathers lie, to prepare a place for you. . . . " This is a superhuman anger welling from the outraged sense of justice not of a man but of the forces of the universe themselves.

Creon could still argue and resist, but to this speech no reply is possible. There can be no doubt of its authority. When Polynices discusses the speech with his sisters, the right word for it is found. Oedipus speaks with the voice of an oracle. "Will you go to Thebes and fulfill his prophecies?" (μαντεύματα) asks Antigone. Oedipus, who fought to disprove an oracle, has become one himself. And his son now starts on the same road his father trod. "Let him prophesy. I do not have to fulfill it." Polynices leaves with a phrase that repeats his mother's denunciation of prophets. "All this is in the power of the divinity ἐν τῷ δαίμονι, it may turn out this way or that." In the power of a god—in the power of chance—whatever he means, he does not realize the sense in which the words are true. The demon, the divinity, in whose power it lies is Oedipus himself.

Oedipus has stayed too long. Power such as this should not walk the earth in the shape of a man. The thunder and lightning summon him, and the gods reproach him for his delay. "You Oedipus, you, why do we hesitate to go? You have delayed too long":

ὦ οὗτος οὗτος Οἰδίπους τί μέλλομεν
χωρεῖν; πάλαι δὴ τἀπὸ σοῦ βραδύνεται.

These strange words are the only thing the gods say in either play. And, as was to be expected of so long delayed and awful a statement, it is complete and final. The hesitation for which they reproach Oedipus is the last shred of his humanity, which he must now cast off. Where he is going vision is clear, knowledge certain, action instantaneous and effective; between the intention and the act there falls no shadow of hesitation or delay. The divine "we"—"Why do *we* hesitate to go"—completes and transcends the equation of Oedipus with the gods; his identity is merged with theirs. And in this last moment of his bodily life they call him by his name, *Oidipous*, the name which contains in itself the lesson of which not only his action and suffering but also his apotheosis serve as the great example—*oida*—that man's knowledge, which makes him master of the world, should never allow him to think that he is equated to the gods, should never allow him to forget the foot, *pous*, the reminder of his true measurement, his real identity.

TEN

The Date of the Oedipus Tyrannus of Sophocles

There is almost no external evidence:[1] until and unless an inscription or a papyrus fragment is unearthed which will confirm one (or none) of the dates which have been proposed, we have nothing to work from but the text of the play itself.

Internal evidence, then, and the arguments from metrical and stylistic chronology are not decisive.[2] Such arguments will, at best, serve as a secondary support or a minor objection to dates arrived at by other means. These means are, in the main, allusions in the text to historical circumstances, and all of the attempts to date the play, beginning with Karl Friedrich Hermann's *Disputatio* (1834), rest on this type of foundation.

Many features of the plot and passages in the text have been interpreted as historical allusions,[3] but the most impressive is the plague which afflicts Thebes at the opening of the play. At the present time, this dramatic plague seems to be recognized as the most important element which may reflect a historical event with enough strength and clarity to be used for dating. It is seriously discussed by all writers on the subject whether they deny a connection between the dramatic and historical plagues,[4] or feel that such a connection exists.[5] This essay attempts to offer new evidence for such a connection, and suggests a date for the play which differs from that proposed by other upholders of the connection between the plague in Athens and the plague in Thebes.

Our evidence (admittedly incomplete) goes to show that the plague is not a traditional feature of the Oedipus story. Homer makes no mention of a plague. "Presently the gods made these things [i.e., the real identity of Oedipus] known to men," he says, but he does not tell us how.[6] Pindar does not mention the plague,[7] and the summary of the Aeschylean *Oedipus* given in the final stasimon of *The Seven against Thebes* does not mention it either. "But when he came to knowledge of his fateful marriage ... " runs the relevant passage (778–80). It does

This chapter originally appeared in the *American Journal of Philology*, 77, no. 2 (1956). ©1956 by The Johns Hopkins Press. Reprinted by permission of the *Journal*.

not explain how. From what little we know and can surmise about the lost epic, the *Oedipodea*, the plague seems to play no part in that version.[8] Moreover, there is no reference to the plague in Euripides' *Phoenissae*, although in several passages, as is the manner of the later Euripidean tragedies, the legend as a whole is recapitulated.[9] There is no trace of the plague in later authorities. The Attic historian Androtion, whose account is quoted at some length in the scholium on *Odyssey* 11.271, does not mention it. "Later," he says, "Jocasta, realizing that she had had intercourse with her own son, hanged herself." And there is no mention of the plague in the much later accounts of Apollodorus[10] and Diodorus.[11]

All these, it must be admitted, are arguments *ex silentio*; yet it should be noticed that Homer, Aeschylus, Euripides, and Androtion all mention the discovery of the truth, the point at which they would be expected to refer to the plague if it had been a traditional feature of the Oedipus story. The plague in Thebes seems to be a Sophoclean invention;[12] to the extent that this is accepted, the connection between the Theban and the Attic plagues becomes more probable.

But is the Sophoclean plague comparable to the plague in Athens? There are of course some verbal resemblances between the Sophoclean and the Thucydidean descriptions,[13] but many of them can be discounted as phrases which are almost inevitable in any description of a plague. And in any case, it has been argued,[14] the Sophoclean plague has the marks of a literary and religious, rather than a historical, phenomenon; it is the traditional threefold blight (often the effect of a curse), not a real epidemic like that which struck the Athenians in 430 B.C. The plague in the *Oedipus Tyrannus* is not only a disease which attacks the population (168), it includes also a blight on the crops (25, 171), the death of the cattle (26), and the abortive birth pangs of the women (26–27, 173–74).

These last three features are common in descriptions of supernatural afflictions and are also a regular formula of curses. "When the Pelasgians had killed their children," says Herodotus 6.139, "the earth refused to bring forth its crops for them, their wives bore fewer children, and their herds increased more slowly than before. . . ." "Do this," says Cambyses to the Persians (Hdt. 3.65), "and then may your land bring forth crops abundantly, and your wives bear children and your herds increase . . . but if you do not . . . then my curse be on you, and may the opposite of all these things happen to you." These same three features are found also in the blessings of the Eumenides in Aeschylus (naturally in negative form),[15] in the text of the "Amphictyonic curse" given by Aeschines,[16] and in Philostratus' account of the blight which attacked the Ethiopians after they killed Ganges their king;[17] two of them are found as part of a curse in a papyrus fragment of Eupolis' *Demoi*.[18]

It is clear enough that Sophocles is drawing on a literary and religious tradition which goes back far beyond the Athenian plague; the plague in Thebes has three features which are closely associated with supernatural forces and appear in religious contexts. This fact has been used to suggest that there is no connection between the plague in Thebes and the plague in Athens. Surely it suggests exactly the opposite. The blight which affects Thebes has indeed the three traditional features, failure of crops, cattle, and human births, but it also has something else which is not part of the traditional blight at all—the plague. In none of the passages which describe the traditional blight is there a reference to a disease (νόσος, λοιμός, are the terms used by Sophocles—and Thucydides) which attacks the whole population: the traditional blight is confined to crops, cattle, and pregnant women. What Sophocles has done is to take the traditional threefold blight and add to it the plague. "We have thus, as it were," runs Mortimer Lampson Earle's brilliant note, "λιμός and λοιμός combined."[19]

This surely requires an explanation. Sophocles had a dramatic problem—to find an imperative factor which would set in motion the process of discovery; he could not say "and suddenly they realized the truth," for the plot of his play consists of that discovery. He needed something that would impel Oedipus to search for the murderer of Laius. But surely the threefold blight would have been enough. It would have served the purpose admirably; the supernatural associations of such a blight were precisely what the dramatic situation demanded. But he added to the blight the plague. There can surely be only one reason why he did so: the plague at Athens.

If the plague which is added to the traditional blight is a reference to a contemporary situation, why, it may be asked, did Sophocles bother with the blight at all? Why not just the plague? Part of the answer to that question is that the three features of the religious blight did actually correspond to conditions in plague-stricken Attica; Sophocles introduced a contemporary detail, the plague, and was able to suggest contemporary applications for the traditional religious details as well.

"The whole host of my city is sick," the chorus sings, "and the products of our famous soil do not increase" (169–71). There was, so far as we know, no failure of the crops in Attica in the early plague years (though, as we shall see, there was later), but these words of the chorus are a good description of what was happening to the Attic farms. Year after year, the Peloponnesian armies cut down olive and fruit trees, burned crops, and trampled down vines; "men dying inside and the land devastated outside" is Thucydides' laconic description of the condition of Athens and Attica during the early years of the war (2.54). The land might well be described as "blighted in the crop-laden blossoms of the soil"—the phrase used by the priest to picture the effects of the plague in Thebes.

What happened to the Athenian cattle during the invasions and the plague? According to Thucydides, they were removed to Euboea and the neighboring islands at the beginning of the war (2.14), but it seems unlikely that such a policy can have been fully enforced over so large an area against the passive resistance which farmers, in all ages and places, have exerted against attempts to part them from their livestock. There is a fragment of Andocides, in fact, which gives a vivid picture of the refugees coming into Athens bringing their cattle with them. "May we never see again the charcoal-burners and their sheep and cattle and wagons coming from the hills. . . . "[20] What cattle there were in Athens must have suffered, whether from plague or neglect,[21] and Thucydides, when he wants to describe the miserable end of the men who were left untended, says that they died "like sheep" (ὥσπερ τὰ πρόβατα, 2.25). Or do these words mean "like the sheep"—the sheep brought into the city by the farmers?

As for the abortive births, it is very possible that in the inferno described by Thucydides they were unusually numerous, if not a product of the plague itself.[22] Certainly any that occurred would be interpreted as another sign that the plague was a manifestation of divine anger or a curse. There must have been many in Athens who so regarded it; even Pericles, in his last speech, refers to it in these terms: "the visitations of heaven (τὰ δαιμόνια) we must bear with resignation" (2.64). And Thucydides tells us that many Athenians connected the plague with the hostile and menacing pronouncement of the Delphic oracle, made just before hostilities began;[23] they saw the plague as something sent by the god, and would so naturally see in it features of the traditional religious blight on the land.

The fact that the plague is an addition to the legendary material and to the threefold blight may be said to establish a strong probability that Sophocles had the Athenian plague in mind. There is a puzzling phrase in the text of the play which makes sense only in terms of such a reference, and which goes far towards turning the probability into a certainty. In the third strophe of the first stasimon the chorus prays for the defeat of "raging Ares" (Ἄρεά τε τὸν μαλερόν, 190). This is an extraordinary prayer. For one thing it completely ignores the fictive dramatic situation; this chorus cannot in these lines be thought of as a chorus of Theban elders. Ares, whom they go on to call "the god without honor among the gods" (τὸν ἀπότιμον ἐν θεοῖς θεόν, 215), is perhaps the most important patron deity of Thebes, associated with the city in myth and cult. In Aeschylus' *Seven against Thebes*, the chorus of Theban women calls on Ares in its hour of danger, begging him not to abandon his own city. "Ares, guard the city of Cadmus ... show your care for it manifestly" (135–36); "Golden-helmeted divinity, look down, look down on this city which you once made your best-beloved" (106–7); "Will you betray, Ares, your own city?" (104–5). But the Theban chorus of the Sophoclean play speaks of Ares not as a protector but as a hostile invader, and they speak of him (not *to* him) with fear and hatred. They actually conclude the strophe with a prayer to Zeus to destroy Ares with his thunderbolt (202). The Theban origin of the chorus has clearly been forgotten; the only possible explanation of so dramatically inappropriate a prayer is that Sophocles was thinking not of Thebes, but of Athens.

And in any case, what is Ares doing here at all? His invocation by the Aeschylean chorus is fully appropriate, for Thebes is under armed attack, but the Thebes of Oedipus is not at war. Ares in this passage is identified with the plague; "he burns me" ($\phi\lambda\epsilon\gamma\epsilon\iota$ $\mu\epsilon$, 192), sings the chorus, and "the flame of pain" ($\phi\lambda\acute{o}\gamma\alpha$ $\pi\acute{\eta}\mu\alpha\tau\circ\varsigma$, 166) is one of the many phrases in the ode which refer to the plague in terms of fire. This identification of Ares with the plague is unprecedented and found no imitators; the labor and ingenuity of generations of commentators has been unable to find even the ghost of a parallel to it.[24]

But the phrase cries aloud for explanation. And a simple explanation lies ready to hand in the conditions in Athens during the early years of the war, the combination of plague and armed invasion which was year after year a feature of the spring season. To the stricken Athenians, the plague seemed to be simply an aspect of the war, Ares. They were assailed by plague within the walls and the Peloponnesian armies without. "The plague attacked them and the war too," as Thucydides puts it (2.59).[25] The imagery which Sophocles employs to evoke the onslaught of the plague is such as to suggest the movement of an invading army, which attacks and burns, with shouts of battle ($\phi\lambda\acute{\epsilon}\gamma\epsilon\iota$ $\mu\epsilon$ $\pi\epsilon\rho\iota\beta\acute{o}\alpha\tau\circ\varsigma$ $\dot{\alpha}\nu\tau\iota\acute{\alpha}\zeta\omega\nu$, 191). The prayer for the defeat of the plague maintains the metaphor: "may he turn his back and run from the land of our fathers" ($\delta\rho\acute{\alpha}\mu\eta\mu\alpha$ $\nu\omega\tau\acute{\iota}\sigma\alpha\iota$, 193). Surely the words of this strophe cannot be considered appropriate to anything in the play, nor even to anything outside it, except after 430 B.C., the first outbreak of the plague in an Athens beleaguered by invading armies. In fact, except in this situation, the words of this strophe are hardly intelligible.

This argument, if accepted, gives us a *terminus post quem* of 430. But this same first stasimon contains a number of phrases which, like the description of Ares, seem to demand explanation in contemporary terms and suggest a more definite, and later, date.

The first stasimon, which in its dramatic place and time is a prayer of the people of Oedipean Thebes for relief from the plague, is full of expressions, emphases, and references which suggest an Athenian rather than a Theban atmosphere. It begins with a dramatically appropriate address to the oracular message which the chorus is waiting for and proceeds by a natural transition to Apollo. But it calls him "Delian Healer" (Δάλιε Παιάν, 154). This title, though it is not inappropriate for a Theban chorus (as Jebb points out), is yet significant for an Athenian audience; the Athenian connotations of the word "Delian" need no emphasis. And since Jebb's time, a papyrus fragment of Pindar has presented us with an almost identical refrain—ἰήιε Δάλι' Ἄπολλον—in what seems to be part of a paean composed for the Athenians.[26]

In the antistrophe, the prayer proper begins: "First I call upon you, daughter of Zeus, immortal Athena" (158–59). This address to the Athenian goddess is repeated later (185): "send rescue, golden daughter of Zeus," an epithet[27] which would surely recall to the audience Phidias' magnificent statue and the gold-plate on it which was not only a symbol of Athenian wealth, but also the war reserve of the Athenian state.

The next deity invoked is Artemis, and the words of the invocation, though their exact meaning is disputed, contain Athenian as well as Theban references. "Artemis who sits in her circular seat in [or, consisting of] the market place, the goddess of Fair Fame" (161–62).[28] There was a temple of Fair Fame (Εὔκλεια) at Athens, built, Pausanias tells us, from the spoils taken at Marathon (1.14.5); Pindar refers to the Athenian market place as "fair-famed" (εὐκλέ' ἀγοράν, frag. 63, Bowra); and a part of the Athenian market place was known as "the circle" (κύκλος).[29] Clearly the effect of these details is to suggest a parallel between the situation in Thebes and that in Athens, a parallel which is, for that matter, maintained throughout the play.[30]

Athena, Artemis, and Apollo are called upon to appear; "if ever against former ruin attacking the city you drove the flame of pain beyond our borders, come now also" (προτέρας ἄτας ὕπερ, 164). The "flame of pain" is the plague, which is described in terms of fire throughout. Why should the Theban chorus talk like this? There had been no "former" visitation of the plague in Thebes. Bruhn (one of the few who notices the problem raised by this phrase) attempts to side-step the difficulty by explaining "former ruin" as the depredations of the Sphinx;[31] but this does not fit the expression "flame of pain," which refers to the plague, and in any case the Sphinx was dealt with not by Athena, Artemis, and Apollo, but by Oedipus, whether with the help of some unnamed god (as the priest suggests) or by his own unaided intelligence (as Oedipus claims). There is no explanation possible in terms of the myth or the dramatic situation. The phrase must refer to Athens, and it suggests a state of affairs in which the plague has appeared for a second time.

Thucydides' account of the plague presents us with exactly such a situation. "In the following winter," he says (i.e., the winter of 427–26), "the plague, which had never entirely disappeared, although abating for a time, again attacked the Athenians. It continued on this second occasion not less than a year, having previously (τὸ δὲ πρότερον) lasted for two years" (3.87). Although the plague never entirely disappeared during the whole period, there was yet enough of a relief from the epidemic for Thucydides to call the outbreak in the winter of 427–26 a "second occasion"—"it attacked again," he says. This second outbreak, or a time near enough to it for the emotions of the occasion to be vividly remembered, is a situation in which the lines under consideration are fully apposite as a description of conditions in Athens. "Appear to me, you triple defenders against death, if ever against former ruin attacking the city you drove beyond our borders the flame of pain, come now too."

This second outbreak of the plague began in the late autumn of 427 and ended in the winter of 426–25. Our new *terminus post quem* is autumn 427, and the first date possible for the production of the play is the spring of 426 (if, that is, it was produced at the Dionysia).

There is some evidence to suggest an even later date. In this same first stasimon there is another phrase which demands explanation. "Ares the raging, who now unbronzed with shields burns me . . . " (ὅς νῦν ἄχαλκος ἀσπίδων . . . , 190–91). This Ares is the plague, which to the Athenians seems to be simply another form of the war; but what is meant by "who *now* unbronzed with shields"? The plague is an Ares who attacks without military panoply, but the word "now" suggests that on a previous occasion he *had* been "bronzed with shields." That is to say, the present occasion seems to be an attack by plague alone as distinguished from a previous attack, or attacks, by plague and war combined. Such an occasion, plague alone, is to be found in the summer of 426, when, with the plague raging anew in Athens, the Peloponnesian armies turned back before crossing the Attic frontier.[32]

There are some additional indications that this stasimon refers to the summer of 426. Thucydides gives us no details about the second outbreak of the plague, but in Diodorus there is a full and fascinating account of it.[33] "The Athenians," he says,

> after a certain period of relief from the pestilential disease, were again subjected to the same misfortunes. . . . In the previous winter there had been very heavy rains, and consequently the soil was

soaked; many hollows received a large quantity of water and turned into swamps—they held stagnant water exactly like permanent marshes. . . . In addition to the disease there was the bad condition of the crops which came up. For the crops this year were completely watery and corrupted in their essence (διεφθαρμένην ἔχοντες τὴν φύσιν). A third cause of the disease was the failure of the Etesian winds, which normally in the hot season reduce the heat to a large extent. As the temperature rose, the air became fiery . . . (τοῦ ἀέρος ἐμπύρου γενομένου . . .).

This description of the condition of Attica in the summer of 426 has many features which illuminate the Sophoclean plague. There was disease in the city, the crops were a failure (and in the conditions Diodorus describes it is hardly likely that the cattle remained healthy), and Diodorus' description of the unprecedented heat suggests an added appropriateness for the Sophoclean reference to the plague as fire and its action as burning.

If the Sophoclean plague is conceived in terms of the second outbreak in Athens, and particularly of the terrible summer of 426, the earliest possible date for the production of the play is the spring of 425. The first stasimon supplies one more piece of evidence, which tends to confirm that date. "Delian Healer," sings the chorus (155–57), "I stand in awe of you—what thing will you accomplish [or, exact], something new, or something repeated in the revolutions of the seasons?" (τί μοι ἢ νέον ἢ περιτελλομέναις ὥραις πάλιν ἐξανύσεις χρέος) "What expiation"—so runs Jebb's paraphrase—"wilt thou prescribe as the price of deliverance from the plague? Will it be an expiation of a new kind? Or will some ancient mode of atonement be called into use once more?"

What is this all about? It does not seem to refer to anything specifically Theban, or any known detail of the myth, and yet it is too precise and emphatic a formula to be dismissed as a mere piece of tragic or religious atmosphere. But if the play was produced in the spring of 425, the passage makes very good sense. For in the winter of 426–25 the Athenians had in fact tried to obtain relief from the plague by expiation made to Delian Apollo.

"The Athenians," says Diodorus' account, "because of the excessive ravages of the disease, referred the origins of the disaster to the divine. For this reason, and in accordance with a certain oracle (κατά τινα χρησμόν), they purified the island of Delos." Thucydides, in his account of the purification of Delos, also mentions "some oracle" (κατὰ χρησμὸν δή τινα, 3.104), though he does not specifically connect the purification of the island with the plague.

An act of expiation, then, had been demanded from the Athenians by oracular authority, and this act was the purification of the island of Delos. But it was not a new form of expiation for the Athenians. Pisistratus the *tyrannos*, as Thucydides tells us, had already purified the island, though incompletely (3.104). And he did it, according to Herodotus, as a result of prophecies (ἐκ τῶν λογίων, 1.64). The expiation corresponds closely to the terms of the Sophoclean chorus; it is connected with Delian Apollo, and it is not "new" but something done "again in the revolution of the seasons."

If the *Oedipus Tyrannus* was produced at the Greater Dionysia in 425, or even in the next year, all these puzzling expressions are explained; not only that, they can be seen as adding to the effect of the play, when it was first produced, a whole dimension of immediate reference which must have heightened the effectiveness of the performance enormously. It is possible, however, to choose between these two dates. There is some evidence to show that the date of the play's performance was 425, not 424.

In the opening months of 424, at the Lenaea, Aristophanes produced his comedy *The Knights*. And in this comedy it is possible to point out (as one would expect if the *Oedipus Tyrannus* was produced the year before) some parodic references to and echoes of the Sophoclean masterpiece.[34]

The central factor of the *Oedipus Tyrannus* is a prophecy—a prophecy made by the Delphian Apollo, apparently false, and finally triumphantly vindicated. And in *The Knights* also the core of the plot is a Delphic prophecy, a prophecy about the fate of Cleon which he fears and conceals but which is in the end fulfilled. Demosthenes steals and reads the prophecy at the beginning of the play. "Damned Paphlagonian" he says "so this is what you have been keeping secret and guarding against for so long.... It's all in here, how he is to be destroyed" (125–27). Demosthenes tells the sausage seller who is to replace Cleon—"you are to become, this oracle says here, the greatest man" (ἀνὴρ μέγιστος, 177–78). Oedipus, explaining his past to Jocasta, describes himself in the same phrase—"I was thought to be the greatest man of the citizens there" (ἀνὴρ ἀστῶν μέγιστος, 775–76). In the figure of the Paphlagonian there seems to be more than a touch of the Oedipus who raged against Tiresias and Creon as conspirators. "By the twelve gods," he shouts, "you will not get away with it—you are conspirators against the people from of old" (οὔ τοι ... χαιρήσετον, 235). "But you will not get away with it" (ἀλλ᾽ οὔ τι χαίρων, 313), says Oedipus to Tiresias. Oedipus' angry dismissal of Creon—"Get out" (οὐκ αὖ μ᾽ ἐάσεις, 676)—is repeated by Cleon in his quarrel with the sausage seller—"Get out" (οὐκοῦν μ᾽ ἐάσεις, 338)—and Cleon flings at his

opponent the word Oedipus uses against both Creon and Tiresias—
"Fool" (μῶρος, *Kn.* 350, *O.T.* 540, 433).

These verbal resemblances are of course easily explicable as
coincidence; the expressions used are also found, and frequently,
elsewhere. But they begin to appear as something more than a
coincidence when Cleon and the sausage seller get to work on each
other's parentage. "I say," says Cleon, "that you belong to the family of
those accursed by the goddess" (445–46), that is, the Alcmaeonidae,
the family of Pericles—a highly ridiculous charge, considering the
insight we have been given into the sausage seller's birth and education.
The sausage seller, unabashed, brings a countercharge. "And I say that
your grandfather was one of the body-guard of ... " "Of whom, say,"
Cleon interrupts (ποίων, φράσον, 448). This sounds very like a
reminiscence of the Sophoclean play. "I seem a fool to you," says
Tiresias, "but I seemed sane to the parents who begot you." "What
parents? Wait," Oedipus replies (ποίοισι, μεῖνον, 437). And there is
another passage in which Oedipus asks an anxious question about his
parents. Told that his name derives from his swollen feet, he asks: "In
the gods' name who did it? My mother or my father? Say" (πρὸς
μητρὸς ἢ πατρὸς, φράσον, 1037). Cleon's agitated ποίων, φράσον
sounds like an echo of both these questions of Oedipus.

Later in the comedy, pleading with Demos, Cleon urges him not to
be influenced by whoever happens to be speaking (μὴ τοῦ λέγοντος
ἴσθι, 860); this is exactly Jocasta's phrase to describe Oedipus in his
confusion (ἀλλ' ἐστι τοῦ λέγοντος, 917). Cleon's collapse comes when
he recognizes, like Oedipus, that the oracle has been fulfilled. And in
this passage, the climax of the play, the language is deliberately parodic
of a tragic *anagnorisis*.[35] When Cleon is told by Demos and his adversary
the sausage seller to put down his crown, he replies: "No. I have a
Pythian oracle which describes the only man by whom I can be
defeated" (1229–30). He questions the sausage seller about his antecedents, and finds that the answers one after another correspond to the
oracle's specifications. The questions he puts are very like those which
Oedipus asks the herdsman at the beginning of the climactic scene of
the *Oedipus Tyrannus.* "What trade did you pursue as you came to
manhood?" asks Cleon (1241). "What work were you employed in,
what way of life?" Oedipus asks the herdsman (1124). The answers are,
of course, different, but the next question is essentially the same in
both cases: "Did you sell your sausages right in the market place, or at
the gates?" (1245–46) and "What places chiefly did you range with your
flocks?" (1126). "Cithaeron and the neighboring country," replies the
shepherd (1127), and the sausage seller answers, "At the gates, where
the salt fish is sold" (1247). The questions and answers in *The Knights*

present an urban parodic version of the pastoral scenes conjured up by the questions and answers in the *Oedipus Tyrannus*.

Cleon's reactions to the sausage seller's replies are in high tragic style. "O Phoebus, Lycian Apollo, what will you do to me?" (ὦ Φοῖβ' Ἄπολλον Λύκιε, τί ποτε μ' ἐργάσει; 1240). A parody of a line in the *Bellerophon* of Euripides, says the scholiast, but it sounds also like an echo of the tragic cry of Oedipus when he hears Jocasta's account of the death of Laius: "O Zeus, what have you planned to do to me?" (ὦ Ζεῦ τί μου δρᾶσαι βεβούλευσαι πέρι; 738).[36] After the discovery of the sausage seller's trade, Cleon is convinced that he is lost (1243). But he recovers. He has one hope, one question more. "There is a slim hope on which we ride at anchor. Tell me just this much" (λεπτή τις ἐλπίς ἐστ' ἐφ' ἧς ὀχούμεθα· καί μοι τοσοῦτον εἰπέ, 1244–45). So Oedipus, after the revelations of Jocasta, has one remaining hope, one question to put to the herdsman, the answer to which will ruin or save him. "I have in fact just this much hope" (καὶ μὴν τοσοῦτον ἐστί μοι τῆς ἐλπίδος, 836). The answer to Cleon's question convinces him that the oracle has been fulfilled. "Alas, the god's prophecy has been carried out" (1248). So Oedipus recognizes the truth: "Oh, it all comes out clear and true" (1182).

Each one of these Aristophanic resemblances to the language and situations of the *Oedipus Tyrannus* is slight enough in itself, but taken all together they seem suggestive. If they can be considered convincing, they fix the date January 424 as the *terminus ante quem*, and the first performance of the *Oedipus Tyrannus* must then have taken place in 425. If not, the date of the performance must still be close enough to the summer of 426 for the allusions to the second outbreak of the plague and the purification of Delos to be timely, and the best date for those requirements is still 425.

Notes

1. All that we have is contained in the second hypothesis: ἡττηθέντα ὑπὸ Φιλοκλέους, ὥς φησι Δικαίαρχος (cf. Aristid. 2.334, Dindorf). Philocles was a nephew of Aeschylus; he wrote a trilogy, the *Pandionis*, and also an *Oedipus* (cf. Nauck, *TGF.*, s.v. "Philocles").

2. cf. H. D. F. Kitto, "Sophocles, Statistics, and the *Trachiniae*," *AJP*, LX (1939), 178–193.

3. Especially, of course the "*tyrannos*" stasimon (vss. 863–910), which Ewald Bruhn (*König Oedipus* [Berlin, 1910], p. 36) connects with the events of 457, R. C. Jebb and others with the events of 415, and Mortimer Lampson Earle (*The Oedipus Tyrannus* [New York, 1901], p. 240, note on vs. 885) with the "scandal about Phidias and the statue of Athena Parthenos." For a negative attitude to the passage as evidence for dating cf. Ulrich von Wilamowitz-Moellendorff, *Hermes*, XXXIV, 59 (cited by Bruhn, p. 37).

4. e.g., Schmid-Stählin, *Gesch. d. gr. Lit.*, I, 2, p. 361, n. 3; Maurice Croiset,

L'Oedipe-Roi de Sophocle (Paris, 1931), pp. 30f.; J. T. (now Sir John) Sheppard, *The Oedipus Tyrannus* (Cambridge, 1920), note on vs. 25, p. 100.

5. e.g., Max Pohlenz, *Die gr. Tragödie*² (Göttingen, 1954), p. 220 (also Erläuterungen, p. 93); Cedric H. Whitman, *Sophocles* (Cambridge, Mass., 1951), pp. 49ff.

6. *Od.* 11.274ff.

7. Pi., *O.* 2.42ff.

8. See Paus. 9.5, 10–11.

9. cf. the very full exposition of the legend in the prologue of the play. The discovery of the truth is described in the same terms as those used by pre-Sophoclean writers: μαθὼν δὲ τἀμὰ λέκτρα, etc. (59); there is no mention of plague. Tiresias' phrase νοσεῖ γὰρ ἥδε γῆ πάλαι, Κρέον (867) is clearly metaphorical; he continues ἐξ οὗ 'τεκνώθη Λάϊος βίᾳ θεῶν.

10. Apollod. *Bibliotheca* 3.9: φανέντων δὲ ὕστερον τῶν λανθανόντων....

11. Diodorus 4.65: τῶν περὶ τὴν οἰκίαν ἀσεβημάτων γνωσθέντων....

12. Bruhn (p. 11) points to the full exposition given to the subject of the plague in the opening scenes as a sign of its novelty to the audience; cf. also Carl Robert, *Oedipus* (Berlin, 1915), p. 69.

13. Most of them will be found in Sheppard's commentary. They do not, of course, imply that Sophocles had read Thucydides; both of them may be expressing independent personal observation. For that matter, it is possible that Thucydides is echoing Sophocles.

14. This argument is most thoroughly presented by Sheppard.

15. A., *Eu.* 939–49.

16. Aeschines, *In Ctes.* 111. For parallels in inscriptions cf. Louis Robert, *Etudes épigraphiques et philologiques* (Paris, 1938), pp. 313ff. It seems strange that Bruhn did not cite the Aeschines passage to strengthen his case for dating the play around the time of the Athenian interference in Delphic affairs.

17. Philostratus, *V.A.* 3.20.

18. *P. Oxy.* 6 (1908), no. 862 (p. 172); cf. also Hdt., 9.39 (Apollonia, cattle and crops only) and Paus. 6.11.7 (Thasos, crops only).

19. p. 144. The preceding sentences run: "The addition of the plague to blight and the subsequent raising to exclusive importance of the plague (vs. 167ff.) suggest the possibility that in an earlier version of the story of Oedipus (that of Aeschylus?) there may have been a blight but no plague and that Sophocles added this feature with reference to the plague at Athens. . . . "

20. cf. Suid., s.v. σκάνδιξ.

21. Th. (2.50) mentions the infection of carnivorous birds and animals.

22. One of the features of a mysterious epidemic at Thasos described Hp., *Epid.* 1.13–26 was "difficult childbirth" (ἐδυστόκεον δὲ πλεῖσται, 16). "All who chanced to fall ill while pregnant, that I know of, aborted" (Ibid.: διέφθειραν πᾶσαι ἃς ἐγὼ οἶδα).

23. Th. 2.54.

24. The Homeric hymn to Ares, which contains sixteen epithets of Ares in the first five lines, has nothing which even vaguely hints at plague. The closest approximation to this striking identification is to be found in the *Suppliants* of Aeschylus. In two passages (659–66 and 678–85) the chorus couples plague and Ares; λοιμός . . . Ἄρης in the first case, and Ἄρη . . . νούσων in the second. But, though associated, they are here clearly separate things.

25. ἡ νόσος ἐπέκειτο καὶ ὁ πόλεμος; cf. also Th. 3.3.

26. C. M. Bowra, frag. 39.

27. This is the only example of the application of this epithet to Athena in Sophocles. It is also rarely found elsewhere (cf. Karl Bruchmann, *Epitheta Deorum* [Leipzig, 1893], p. 16).

28. For the Theban reference of this passage, see Jebb *ad loc.*

29. cf. Sch. Ar., *Eq.* 137; E., *Or.* 919; Th. 3.74.

30. For the general parallel cf. "Why is Oedipus Called *Tyrannos*?" (chapter 8 in this book).

31. Note on vs. 165 (p. 72).

32. Earle (p. 53 and note on vs. 190) was, as far as I can tell, the first to see the implication of the word νῦν; for him it is evidence for the correctness of the "traditional" date, 429.

33. Diodorus 12.58. A. E. Zimmern, *The Greek Commonwealth* (Oxford, 1931), p. 36, refers Diodorus' description to 430 (an error which is still uncorrected in the fifth edition, the latest I have been able to consult).

34. A few of the parallels of phrase and situation between the *anagnorisis* in *The Knights* and that of the Sophoclean play have been noticed by Valerio Milio in his article "Per la cronologia dell' Edipo Re," *Boll. Fil. Class.*, XXXV (1928–29), 203–5. On this basis he too suggests a *terminus ante quem* of 424 for the *Oedipus Tyrannus*. Of the resemblances discussed below, he mentions *Eq.* 1240−*O.T.* 738 and *Eq.* 1244−*O.T.*, 834–35 and points out some minor verbal coincidences (e.g., πῶς εἶπας, *Eq.* 1237−πῶς εἶπας, *O.T.* 942, 1018) which do not carry much weight. His general statement on the resemblances puts the case well: "si tratta non della parodia di una frase ma della imitazione di tutta una situazione tragica" (p. 205).

35. "*Sequitur ἀναγνώρισις vere tragica numeris et verbis insignis,*" says J. Van Leeuwen, *Aristophanis Equites* (Leyden, 1900).

36. The Sophoclean line is clearly parodied in the later *Peace.* cf. 62 ὦ Ζεῦ τί δρασείεις ποθ' ἡμῶν τὸν λεών; and 106 ὅ τι ποιεῖν βουλεύεται [*sc.* Ζεύς] ʽΕλλήνων πέρι. The parody here is surely clear enough to rule out any date for the *Oedipus Tyrannus* later than 422.

ELEVEN

The Ajax *of Sophocles*

The key to an understanding of this harsh and beautiful play is the great speech in which Ajax debates his course of action and explores the nature of man's life on earth (646–92). These lines are so majestic, remote, and mysterious, and at the same time so passionate, dramatic, and complex, that if this were all that had survived of Sophocles he would still have to be reckoned as one of the world's greatest poets. They are the point from which this discussion starts and to which it will return, for in the play all the poetic and thematic threads which make up the stark pattern of the *Ajax* start from and run back to this speech. These magnificent, enigmatic lines, alternately serene and passionate, and placed almost dead center in the action, offer us the only moment of repose and reflection in a play which begins in monstrous violence and hatred and maintains that atmosphere almost unbroken to the end.

It is a puzzling play. Ever since scholars started to work on it, it has been criticized as faulty in structure, and the schoolmasterish remarks of the ancient scholiast on this point[1] have often been echoed, though in more elegant and conciliatory terms, in the writings of modern critics. Apart from the structural problem, it is only too easy for the modern critic and reader to find the characters repellent: to see in Athena a fiendish divinity,[2] in Ajax a brutalized warrior,[3] in the Atridae and Teucer undignified wranglers, and in Odysseus a cold self-seeker.

In recent years, a host of new and more sympathetic critics have tried to rehabilitate the play;[4] most influential among them is H. D. F. Kitto, who, working on the unassailable basis that Sophocles knew more about dramaturgy than both Schlegels and Tycho von Wilamowitz rolled into one, assumes that the play is a dramatic success and then attempts to explain why. In his best-known book[5] (though he has modified the position considerably in his latest work on the subject),[6] he found the solution of the difficulty in the importance of Odysseus, which he called the "keystone" of the play.[7] Kitto's chapter on the *Ajax* is so well written (and so welcome a relief after the self-satisfied strictures of nineteenth-century critics) that it is at first reading overwhelmingly

This chapter originally appeared in *Harvard Studies in Classical Philology*, 65 (1961).

persuasive, but when the reader changes books and gets back to Sophocles, his difficulties return. For Ajax, dead and alive, imposes his gigantic personality on every turn of the action, every speech. When he is not speaking himself, he is being talked about; there is only one subject discussed in this play, whether the speaker is Ajax, Athena, Odysseus, Tecmessa, the messenger, Teucer, Menelaus, or Agamemnon—and that subject is Ajax. Ajax is on stage in every scene, first alive, then dead. The rest of the characters follow him wherever he goes; Odysseus tracks him to his tent, and later Tecmessa and the chorus follow his tracks to the lonely place on the shore where he has killed himself.[8] The hero's death, which normally in Attic tragedy is described by a messenger who accompanies the body onstage, takes place before our eyes in the *Ajax*, and to make this possible Sophocles has recourse to the rare and difficult expedient of changing the scene; when Ajax moves, the whole play follows after him. Further, as Kitto indeed points out, the poetry of the play (and it contains some of Sophocles' most magnificent lines) is all assigned to Ajax. Brutal and limited he may be, but there can be no doubt that Sophocles saw him as heroic. The lamentations of Tecmessa, Teucer, and the chorus express our own sense of a great loss. The tone of the speeches made over his body in the second half of the play emphasizes the fact that the world is a smaller, meaner place because of his death. The last half of the play shows us a world emptied of greatness; all that was great in the world lies there dead, impaled on that gigantic sword, while smaller men, with motives both good and bad, dispute over its burial. The unheroic tone of the end of the play (with its threats and boasts and personal insults)[9] has often been criticized as an artistic failure; surely it is deliberate. Nothing else would make us feel what has happened. A heroic age has passed away, to be succeeded by one in which action is replaced by argument, stubbornness by compromise, defiance by acceptance. The heroic self-assertion of an Achilles, an Ajax, will never be seen again; the best this new world has to offer is the humane and compromising temper of Odysseus, the worst the ruthless and cynical cruelty of the Atridae. But nothing like the greatness of the man who lies there dead.

The poetry of the play is in the speeches of Ajax, and there is one speech of Ajax which is Sophoclean poetry at its greatest: ἅπανθ' ὁ μακρὸς κἀναρίθμητος χρόνος. . . . "All things long uncounted time brings forth from obscurity and buries once they have appeared. . . . " The opening lines of the speech raise the problem which the play as a whole explores: the existence of man in time and the changes which time brings. It is significant that the *Ajax*, contrary to Sophoclean practice as we know it from the extant plays, brings an Olympian god on stage,[10] for the difference between men and gods is most sharply defined in their relationship to time—mortality and immortality are conditions of subjection to and independence of time.

This difference between man and the gods, the transitory and the permanent, is a theme which Sophocles returns to in his last play, where Oedipus, at Colonus, spells out for Theseus what the difference is. "Dearest son of Aegeus, only for the gods is there no old age or death. Everything else is confounded by all-powerful time." He goes on to describe the changes which time brings to all things human in terms strikingly reminiscent of lines written many years before, in the *Ajax*.[11] The theme of man, the gods, and time is from first to last one of the main concerns of Sophoclean tragedy.

In the *Ajax*, this theme is developed through the exploration of one particular aspect of human activity, the working of an ethical code. This code was already a very old one in the fifth century B.C., and although more appropriate to the conditions of a heroic society, it was still recognized in democratic Athens as a valid guide to conduct. Τοὺς μὲν φίλους εὖ ποιεῖν, τοὺς δ᾽ ἐχθροὺς κακῶς—to help your friends and harm your enemies: a simple, practical, natural rule. From the point of view of a Christian society it is a crude and cynical rule, but for all that, it is often followed. But whereas we today pay at least lip service to a higher ideal of conduct, the fifth-century Athenian accepted this simple code as a valid morality.[12] It was a very old rule (a strong point in its favor for a people in whose language the word νέος, "new," had a "collateral notion of *unexpected, strange, untoward, evil*");[13] it seemed like sound common sense; and it had the authority of the poets, who were, for fifth-century Athens, the recognized formulators of ethical principles, the acknowledged legislators.

Plato's Socrates, who begins the great argument of the *Republic* by rejecting this formula as a definition of justice, denies that the poets could have said any such thing. "We shall fight them, you and I together," he says to Polemarchus, "—anyone who says that Simonides or Bias or Pittacus or any other of the wise and blessed men said it. . . . Do you know whose saying I think this is, that justice consists of helping your friends and harming your enemies? I think it is a saying of Periander, or Perdiccas, or Xerxes or Ismenias the Theban or some other such man. . . . "[14]

Plato, of course, when he tries to make this saying the exclusive property of a bloodthirsty Corinthian tyrant, a Macedonian barbarian, a Persian despot, or a Theban intriguer, is writing with his tongue in his cheek. For the maxim "Help your friends, harm your enemies" stares out at us from the pages of the poets. It is to be found in Archilochus,[15] in Solon,[16] in Theognis,[17] in Pindar,[18] and was attributed to Simonides.[19] It continued to be a rule of conduct universally accepted and admired in spite of Plato's rejection of it, and something very like it is rejected by Christ in the first century A.D.: "Ye have heard that it hath been said, Thou shalt love thy neighbor and hate thine enemy. But I say unto you, love your enemies."[20]

This is of course *our* ideal of conduct, the ideal to which, in our better moments most of us try to rise. Even if, regrettably, we continue to live by the old rule, we have the vision of a higher ideal. But this was not the case in the Athens of Sophocles. The simple formula, "Help your friends, harm your enemies," was generally accepted, not just as hard-headed practical advice, but as a moral principle, a definition of justice, a formulation of the *arete*, the specific excellence, of man.

The *Ajax* of Sophocles examines the working of this code. It is a theme which springs naturally from the figure of Ajax as Sophocles found it already formed in saga and drama, the figure of a man of fierce impulse and action, whose hate for his enemies led him to attempt a monstrous act of violence and, when it failed, to kill himself.

Sophocles' treatment of this theme, however, reveals an attitude which differs from that of Christ and of Plato. It is thoroughly Sophoclean and fifth century; that is to say, it is at once intellectual and practical, and at the same time ironic and tragic. Christ's rejection of the way of the world (and the interpretation of the Mosaic law which was used to support it) is justified by a summons to a higher morality: "Love thine enemy. If ye love them which love you, what reward have ye?" Plato's rejection of the ancient maxim is based on its inadequacy as a definition of justice: the enemy you harm may be a just man, and in any case, even if he is unjust, harming him will only make him more so.[21] But the Sophoclean presentation of the old code in action makes the comparatively simple point that it is unworkable. The objective may be good, but in the world in which we live, it is unattainable. The old morality is exposed as a failure in practice.

Τοὺς μὲν φίλους εὖ ποιεῖν, to do good to your friends—no one objects to that (though Christ rejects it as not enough); it is the other half of the commandment, τοὺς ἐχθροὺς κακῶς, that raises problems. "To harm your enemies": this accepts and justifies hatred. The *Ajax* is full of hatred and enmity. The hatred of Ajax for Odysseus was proverbial; it is immortalized in one of the greatest passages of the *Odyssey*, and in Sophocles' play it is given full expression, together with his hatred for the Atridae, their hatred for him, and the hatred between them and Teucer. No other play of Sophocles contains so many bitter speeches; Ajax dies cursing his enemies (and his curses are repeated by Teucer at the end of the play), and after his death the venomous disputes between the Atridae and Teucer make the last half of the play a noisy, scurrilous quarrel to which only the last-minute intervention of

Odysseus restores some measure of dignity. The Greek words for enmity and hate (and there are many of them, with a great range of subtle distinctions)[22] dominate the vocabulary of the play. "I see you," says Athena, addressing Odysseus, in the first lines of the play, "I see you always hunting for some occasion against your enemies." This prologue sets before us, with brilliant dramatic economy, three attitudes toward the traditional code, and, as is to be expected of the superb dramaturgy of Sophocles, they are not described but expressed in action.

The simplest attitude is that of Ajax, who has lived in this faith and is shortly to die in it.[23] He represents the savagery of "harm your enemies" in an extreme form; he glories in the violence he is dispensing to the animals he takes for his enemies. He believes that he has killed the sons of Atreus, and is proud of it;[24] he relishes in advance the pleasure he will feel in whipping Odysseus before killing him. When Athena urges him to spare the torture, he tells her sharply to go about her own business. He goes back to his butcher's work with evident gusto: χωρῶ πρὸς ἔργον—"back to work" (116).[25]

He is mad, of course, and the madness has been inflicted on him by Athena. But it consists only in his mistaking animals for men; the madness affects his vision more than his mind.[26] All the verbs used by Athena make it clear that she is not producing the intention to murder the Achaean kings; she merely diverts, hinders, checks, limits, and encourages a force already in motion.[27] The intent to torture and murder was present in Ajax sane; when he recovers from his delusions, his only regret is that his victims were sheep instead of men, his disgrace is that he failed in his murderous attempt. Ajax did not need to be driven mad to attempt to harm his enemies; once restored to sanity, he never for a moment doubts that his attempt was justified. We learn later from Tecmessa that he laughed loudly in the midst of his cruelties.[28] This enjoyment of the shame and helplessness of his enemies is, of course, according to the old morality, his right and privilege. If it is right to harm your enemies, there is no reason why you should not enjoy it. There is in fact every reason why you should.

There is a goddess on stage throughout this scene, and in her we are shown a divine attitude to the traditional morality. It is exactly the same, point for point, as that of Ajax. Τοὺς ἐχθροὺς κακῶς. Ajax is her enemy. As we learn later in the play, he has angered her by an insulting and contemptuous reply. She harms her enemy. She exposes him in his madness before his adversary Odysseus and lets him convict himself out of his own mouth.[29] Athena mocks Ajax as he mocks *his* enemies, calling herself his "ally"[30] and ironically accepting his insulting commands. She harms and mocks her enemy Ajax and helps her friend Odysseus, who in this scene emphasizes his devotion to her and is assured by the goddess of her continued favor.[31] Athena is the traditional morality personified, in all its fierce simplicity.

The third figure on stage during the prologue, Odysseus, has come hunting his enemy. He is told by the goddess that Ajax intended to kill him, and then he hears Ajax insist on torturing the animal he takes to be Odysseus himself. Odysseus is given the mandate to inform the Achaeans of Ajax's criminal intentions, and so becomes the instrument of his enemy's fall. And he is invited by the goddess to rejoice in his enemy's disaster, to mock, to echo Ajax's laughter at the imagined sufferings of his enemies. Odysseus has every reason in the world to rejoice at the spectacle revealed to him by Athena, but he cannot do it. "I pity him," he says, "although he is my enemy." The authority of the ancient heroic code and the explicit invitation of the goddess both fail, overwhelmed by this sudden feeling of pity. Odysseus abandons the traditional morality at the moment of victory and exultation. He does so because he puts himself, in imagination, in his enemy's place, "considering not so much his case as my own," to use his own words.[32] In the ruin of Ajax he sees, beyond the fall of a man who was and still is,[33] his most dangerous enemy, a proof of the feeble and transitory condition of all men, himself included.[34] "All of us who live are images, or weightless shadows."[35] That the great Ajax has been reduced to this state of deluded impotence is no occasion for triumph for a fellow man, but rather a melancholy reminder of the instability and tragic frailty of all things human.

Of these three attitudes to the traditional morality, the most disturbing for the modern reader is that of the goddess. The audience in the theater of Dionysus had seen gods on stage before, but, as far as we can tell, they had seen nothing as vengeful and fierce as this Athena since Aeschylus put the Eumenides on stage; this Athena seems to derive from the same concept of divinity as that which later inspired the Aphrodite and Dionysus of Euripides.[36] Her rigid adherence to the traditional code and the added refinement of mockery of her victim seem all the more repellent by contrast with the enlightened attitude of Odysseus.

But we must remember that for Sophocles and his contemporaries, gods and men were not judged by the same standards.[37] The Christian ideal, "be ye therefore perfect, even as your father in heaven is perfect,"[38] would have made little or no sense to a fifth-century Athenian, whose deepest religious conviction would have been most clearly expressed in opposite terms: "Do not act like a god." Sophocles clearly admires the attitude of Odysseus, but we must not therefore assume that he criticizes the attitude of Athena. She is a goddess, and her conduct must be examined in a different light.

Her attitude is consistent. Odysseus, whom she helps and rewards, has always been her friend, and Ajax, whom she thwarts and mocks, is an enemy of fairly long standing. His insulting treatment of the goddess in the prologue is not an erratic phenomenon produced by his madness, for much earlier, in full control of his senses, he had insulted her in exactly the same way and in almost exactly the same words, as the messenger later tells us.[39] By his "dreadful words which should never have been spoken" Ajax provoked the anger of Athena, which she satisfies in the mockery of the opening scene.

But her attitude is not only consistent, it is also just. Ajax deserves punishment not only because of his slaughter of the cattle (the common property of the Achaean army) and the men in charge of them[40] (whom Ajax characteristically never even mentions), but also because the real objectives of his murderous onslaught were the sons of Atreus and Odysseus, the kings and commanders of the army. Athena in the prologue is a minister of justice. Her insistence, against the indignant and repeated protests of Odysseus, on exposing Ajax in his madness before his enemy is not merely vindictive: it is a necessary step in his condemnation. The proof of Ajax's deeper guilt, his intention to murder the kings, must come from his own mouth before a witness.[41] What Athena does is to prevent Ajax, by deluding his vision, from committing the great crime he had planned, and to reveal to Odysseus undeniable proof that the lesser crime he *has* committed would, but for her intervention, have been a slaughter of kings instead of animals. Surely this is the working of justice. The goddess thwarts and mocks her enemy, but it could also be said that she baffles and convicts a wrongdoer. The working of the fierce old code, in the action of the goddess, is the working of justice.

That she takes a merciless delight in his humiliation is, in terms of the accepted morality, natural and right; in theological terms it is at least logical. A strict conception of justice has no place for mercy, which might temper punishment and restrain exact retribution. That Athena, in addition to inflicting full punishment, also takes delight in the wrongdoer's fall is, for our modern Christian sensibility, hard to accept, and yet even the Christian consciousness, shot through as it is with the ideal of mercy, can on occasion feel something similar. In the *Divina Commedia*, Dante's savage mockery of the tortured Pope Nicholas is warmly approved by Virgil.[42] And the same *anima naturaliter Christiana* sharply reproves Dante's pity for the grotesquely mutilated prophets. This passage is an interesting parallel to the prologue of the *Ajax*. What excites Dante's pity is "our image so twisted," *la nostra imagine sì torta*—a feeling like Odysseus' sympathy for Ajax "yoked to cruel delusion." Virgil's reproof is harsh and bitter. "Are you still one of the fools, like the rest? Here pity is alive when it is truly dead": *Qui vive la pietà quand' è ben morta.*[43]

Athena's attitude is that of a merciless but just divinity who punishes the wrongdoer. At the same time it is the attitude of the victorious enemy who returns evil for evil and exults in the fall of his opponent. In this respect it is exactly that of Ajax, a point emphasized through the repetition of the same words and sentiments in the speeches of the goddess and the hero. "Is not laughter at one's enemies the kind that gives most pleasure?" Athena asks Odysseus, and Ajax describes an imaginary Odysseus awaiting torture inside the tent as "the prisoner who gives me most pleasure."[44] Athena ironically begs Ajax not to "humiliate" his prisoner, but this is exactly what she is doing to Ajax, as he realizes later: "the strong goddess, daughter of Zeus, humiliates me even to death."[45] In their uncritical adherence to the traditional code and their full exploitation of the harshness it enjoins, there is no difference between the goddess and the man.

But this does not constitute, as the modern reader instinctively feels it does (and as it would in Euripides),[46] a criticism of Athena. Rather, it is the measure of the heroic presumption of Ajax. He assumes the tone and attitude of a god. And in him this is no recent development. He has always felt and acted like this. When the messenger, later in the play, describes his insulting reply to Athena's encouragement before the battle, he defines the nature of Ajax's pride. Ajax was not "thinking like a man." And he also quotes the words of Calchas, which describe Ajax as one who, "born a man by nature, does not think as a man."[47] The tone of Ajax's speeches in the prologue is not the product of his delusion; it is the expression of his nature as it has always been.[48] And that tone is unmistakable. He talks and acts like a god; he assumes not merely equality with Athena, but superiority to her. Athena mockingly recognizes this conception of their relationship by her use of the word "ally" (σύμμαχος) to describe herself; the word in Athenian official parlance (it was the official designation of the subject cities and islands of the empire) suggests inferiority,[49] and it is clear that this is how Ajax regards her. He gives her orders, ἐφίεμαι (112), a strong word which he repeats a few lines later (116);[50] he roughly and insultingly refuses her request for mercy for Odysseus, and when she tells him to do whatever he sees fit, he condescendingly orders her to be just that kind of an ally to him always, that is, a subservient one.[51]

Ajax's assumption of godlike confidence is only an extreme expression of his fierce dedication to the traditional morality. In pursuing the heroic code to the bloodthirsty and megalomaniac extremes the prologue puts before us, he is acting not like a man but like a god. "May Zeus grant me," sang that bitter and vengeful poet Theognis, "to repay my friends who love me and my enemies who now triumph over me, and I would seem to be a god among men."[52] Ajax acts and thinks like a god among men. Like a god, he judges, condemns, and executes his enemies, with speed, certainty, and righteous wrath. The gods do indeed act like this, but they can do so because they have knowledge. "Learn," says Athena to Odysseus, "from one who knows."[53] But man is ignorant. "We know nothing clear," says Odysseus. "We are adrift." The same standard of conduct will not be valid for man in his ignorance and gods in their knowledge. What is wrong for one may be right for the other.

For the gods, in fact, the old rule to help friends and harm enemies is a proper rule. The proviso that Socrates adds to the rule in the *Republic*—"if our friends are good and our enemies bad"[54]—does hold true for the gods. Athena, in harming her enemy Ajax, is punishing a wrongdoer. And in her closing words she makes a claim to this general identification of friend with good and enemy with bad for the gods as a whole: "The gods love those who are self-controlled, and hate the bad."[55] But no man can make any such claim to distinguish certainly, as the gods can, between good and bad men. "We know nothing clear, we are adrift."

A man cannot know with certainty whether his friends are good or bad, and so with his enemies. But his ignorance is even more profound. He cannot even know for sure who his friends *are*, and by the same token, he cannot know who his enemies are either. Human relationships (and this is demonstrated by the action of the play) are so unstable, so shifting, that the distinction between friend and enemy does not remain constant. Human life is a flux in which everything is in process of unending change. "One day," says Athena, "brings to their setting and raises up again all human things."[56] The name of the flux in which all things human dissolve and reform is time, χρόνος. "All things long uncounted time brings forth from obscurity and buries once they have appeared. And nothing is beyond expectation." So Ajax tells us, in words which recall those of Athena.[57]

The statement is especially true of relations between man and man, friendship and enmity. In time, friends turn into enemies and enemies into friends. The *Ajax* itself is a bewildering panorama of such changed and changing relationships. Ajax came to Troy as the ally of the sons of Atreus, but he turned into their enemy and tried to murder them. "We expected," says Menelaus over Ajax's body, "that he would be an ally and friend of the Achaeans, but have found him ... a more bitter enemy than the Trojans."[58] Tecmessa, a Trojan, an enemy of the Greek invaders, saw her city destroyed by Ajax and became his prisoner and concubine. Yet she is the only one that truly loves him; the man that destroyed her city and enslaved her[59] is, she says, everything to her—mother, father, country, riches. Ajax and Hector were enemy champions and fought before the ranks of the assembled armies in single combat;[60] when the light failed and no decision had been reached, they exchanged gifts, in mutual respect, and parted friends. The sword which Ajax carries as he makes his great speech, on which he is in the end to kill himself, is the sword of Hector, his enemy-friend. Ajax and Odysseus, once comrades in arms and in the embassy to the tent of Achilles,[61] are now the bitterest of enemies. The most striking example of the mutability of human relationships offered by the play is one that Ajax will not live to see: Odysseus, his arch-enemy, feels pity for him and will fight for him against Agamemnon, to make possible the burial of his body. In human life, which is subject to time, nothing remains stable, least of all friendship and enmity. In such a world, "Help your friend and harm your enemy" is no use as a guide. How can a man help his friends and harm his enemies when they change places so fast?

Ajax comes at last to his moment of unclouded vision, in which he sees the world man lives in as it really is. He explores, for himself and for us, the nature of the ceaseless change which is the pattern of the universe. The famous speech in which he does so has caused a dispute among the critics which is still alive; there are two main schools of thought about it. One believes that the speech is a sincere recantation of stubbornness, a decision to submit to authority, human and divine, and so go on living. The other believes that the speech is a disguised and ambiguous reassertion of the hero's will for death, and though different critics of this majority school[62] differ in their estimates of how much of the speech is sincere and how much not, they are all united on the point that the speech is intended to deceive Tecmessa and the chorus.

The first of these two positions, most recently argued with his customary clarity and eloquence by C. M. Bowra, must face formidable objections. For one thing, it presents us with an Ajax who later, offstage and without preparation or explanation, changes his mind on the crucial issue of life or death, and Bowra can justify this only by assuming a fresh access of madness sent by Athena, for which of course there is no evidence in the Sophoclean text.[63] But, more important, this reading of the speech ignores completely the striking fact that the language of Ajax in these lines is that of a man obsessed by the thought of death; the words insistently and emphatically bring our minds back to the theme of death. He will "hide" his sword; time, as he has just told us in a phrase which refers to death, "hides all things once they have appeared," and later Tecmessa will find the sword of Hector "hidden" in his body.[64] "I shall go to bathe," πρός τε λουτρά. The word he uses is the regular word used to describe the washing of the corpse before burial and is so used at the end of the play when Teucer and the chorus prepare to bury Ajax.[65] "Let night and Hades keep it there below," he says of the sword, a phrase with ominous suggestions, for the word κάτω ("below") in Sophocles always refers, when it is used in this locative sense, to the dead, the underworld,[66] as it does in Ajax's last speech, where he announces that he will talk "to those below in the house of Hades," ἐν ῞Αιδου τοῖς κάτω (865).

These ominous phrases are typical of the speech as a whole;[67] everywhere in it the language hints, sometimes subtly, sometimes broadly, at death. If the speech is meant to convey a sincere decision to renounce suicide, reconcile himself with his enemies and the gods, and live, it uses strange terms—inept terms, in fact. Even in a lesser artist such an insensitive use of language would be remarkable. In Sophocles it is unthinkable.

Is the speech a *Trugrede*, then? Does Ajax intend to deceive his hearers, masking his unchanged purpose, death, with ambiguous words? There can be no doubt that he does deceive Tecmessa and his sailors; Tecmessa later complains bitterly that she was "cast out from his love and deceived."[68] But does Ajax consciously and deliberately deceive her and the chorus?[69] If so, we are faced with a problem as difficult as that raised by the other point of view—a serious inconsistency of character. The character of Ajax is Achillean; it may be all too easily tempted to extremes of violence, but not to deceit.

Many learned and subtle critics of the play have tried to skirt this difficulty, to present us with an Ajax who deliberately deceives and yet remains the simple direct outspoken hero of the tradition, but they are attempting the impossible. They succeed at best in finding a more complicated and euphemistic formula[70] for the fact that, according to this view, Ajax consciously and deliberately deceives his hearers. And that, as Bowra forcefully (and rightly) points out, is the last thing we can imagine Ajax doing.[71]

Not only does this intent to deceive strike us as uncharacteristic; it also seems insufficiently motivated. Why *should* he deceive his hearers? In the previous scene he made it perfectly clear that he intended to kill himself, announced his decision firmly, refused to argue the matter, and brutally silenced Tecmessa's attempt to dissuade him. Why should he conceal his intention now? The only plausible reason critics have been able to suggest is that he wishes to die alone in peace and must deceive Tecmessa and the chorus so that he will be allowed to go off alone, unmolested, with his sword. But this, especially when the scene is imagined theatrically, is not really adequate.[72] Would Tecmessa or the all too prudent sailors of the chorus dare oppose the will of this gigantic, imperious, raw-tempered, and raw-tongued man who has just come out carrying a naked sword? If he stalked off now announcing that he was going to find a lonely place to kill himself, can we really imagine the chorus and Tecmessa putting any effective resistance in his path? They appealed to him as strongly as they dared in the previous scene and were roundly told to mind their own business; one thing that emerges clearly from that scene is that Ajax of all men is master in his own house.[73] The idea that he would have to lie in order to escape from Tecmessa and his sailors is one that could never have occurred to Ajax. The intent to deceive is not only uncharacteristic of Ajax, it has no adequate motive in the dramatic circumstances.

All this merely replaces the dilemmas faced by previous critics with another dilemma, which appears to be equally insoluble. If Ajax is not trying to deceive Tecmessa and the chorus, masking an unbroken resolve for death with ambiguous phrases, and if he is not on the other hand trying to tell them, sincerely and without reservations, that he will make his peace with gods and men, and live, then what is he trying to tell them?

There is only one possible answer. He is not trying to tell them anything at all; he is talking to himself.[74] During the first part of his speech, he is oblivious of their presence,[75] totally self-absorbed in an attempt to understand not only the nature of the world which has brought him to this pass but also the new feelings which rise in him and prompt him to reconsider his decision for death.

This solution of the difficulty, that the first thirty-nine lines of Ajax's speech are soliloquy and therefore rule out the question of his intentions toward Tecmessa and the chorus, is suggested by an unusual feature of the speech, which has not been given the attention it deserves.[76] The speech comes directly after the closing lines of a choral stasimon and thus opens the scene. But contrary to usual practice, it plunges abruptly into the philosophical reflections on time, without any form of address to the chorus or Tecmessa. In the theater of Dionysus the vast size of the auditorium, the distance between even the closest spectators and the actors, and, above all, the masks excluded that play of facial expression which in the modern theater makes clear at once the direction of the actor's remarks; we can see and do not have to be told whom the actor is addressing. But the Athenian dramatist (and this was especially true of the opening moments of a new scene) felt obliged to establish firmly, clearly, and at once the relationship between the opening speaker and his dramatic audience. He put the opening speaker in some clear verbal rapport with the other person or persons on the stage or in the orchestra, by means of a choral introduction, a vocative formula, or a verb in the second person.[77] But in this speech there is nothing whatsoever to indicate whom Ajax is talking to, nothing until the fortieth line of the speech.

Such an opening speech is almost unparalleled in Sophoclean tragedy. In fact there is only one parallel. It is in this same play, the *Ajax*; it is the last speech Ajax makes. And here of course the absence of verbal rapport with the others is easy to understand; there *are* no others, not even the chorus. Ajax is alone on stage.

The opening lines of the great speech on time give the impression that Ajax is talking to himself, just as he does later when he *is* alone. And that impression is maintained. For thirty-nine lines there is no indication that he is talking to anyone else, no vocative formula, no verb in the second person. The only reference to anyone on stage, to Tecmessa, is a reference which makes it perfectly clear that at any rate he is not talking to *her*—"by this woman," he says, πρὸς τῆσδε τῆς γυναικός. "I pity her," he goes on, οἰκτίρω δέ νιν—as if she were not there at all. Finally he comes to the end of his reflections. His mind is made up. And now he turns to the others, and the words he uses sound like a formula of transition from private reflection to direct communication. Ἀλλ' ἀμφὶ μὲν τούτοισιν εὖ σχήσει: "Well, in these matters, it will turn out well." And then, σὺ δέ, "You"—at last he speaks to Tecmessa.

The speech is not a *Trugrede*, then; the first part of it is *selbstgespräch*, a soliloquy. Ajax is working out his own course of action with that same furious self-absorption we have already been shown in the previous scene, where he poured out his laments and curses unaffected by, hardly hearing, the questions and advice of the chorus.[78] Here, for the first thirty-nine lines of the speech, he is oblivious of the presence of anyone else; locked in the prison of his own passions, he fights his battle with the new feelings and the new vision of the world which have come to him since he made his decision to die. Only when at last he sees the nature of the world and his own best course of action does he recognize the presence of the others and give them their orders. In these final lines of his speech there is no ambiguity; his words are clearly a last will and testament, a handing over of responsibility. "Tell Teucer, if he comes, to take care of me, and of you. . . . " What else can this mean but "take care of my body and assume my responsibilities?"[79] Ajax never in his life asked anyone to take care of him; he was the one, as Teucer never tires of repeating later in the play, who rescued others. The harsh frankness of his closing lines surely rules out any possibility of intention to deceive in the earlier part of the speech; when he turns to Tecmessa and the chorus to give them their orders he speaks plainly enough. If they are deceived about his intentions because they misunderstood the course of the agonized self-communing through which he found his way to the decision, they have no one to blame but themselves. Though Tecmessa later complains with pardonable bitterness that she has been "deceived," the chorus blames not Ajax but itself. "I was completely deaf, ignorant, careless," ἐγὼ δ᾽ ὁ πάντα κωφός, ὁ πάντ᾽ ἄιδρις κατημέλησα (911–12).[80]

The great speech of Ajax, for most of its length, is not meant for anyone but himself; since he is a character in a play, that means that it is meant exclusively for us, the audience. He is not trying to deceive, but to understand, to understand the nature of the world which once seemed (and was) so simple, but in which he has now lost his way, to understand what his place is in this new-found, complicated world, and to decide on his next step. Ajax, we are told by the poet Pindar, who loved and admired his memory, was a man "with no gift of tongue, but stout of heart."[81] In this speech, the man whose hands had always spoken for him finds a tongue, and it is the tongue of a great poet. The lines in which he reassesses the world and time and his part in them are the first beam of light in the darkness of violence and failure which the play has so far imposed on us; in that light we can see in their true dimensions what has already passed and the greater things still to come.

The speech begins abruptly with a description of the action of time. "All things long uncounted time brings forth from obscurity and buries once they have appeared. And nothing is beyond expectation." This is a world in which anything can happen; in the course of time, things which appeared unconquerable find their master. "The dreadful oath and the heart hard as steel are overcome." These are not random examples. The oath Ajax swore, to be the loyal ally of the Atridae in their fight to recapture Helen, an oath mentioned later on by Teucer, has been broken by his attempt to kill them.[82] And his own heart, hard as steel, has been belatedly softened, in the interval since we last saw him announce that it was too late to educate him to new ways, by Tecmessa's appeals. "I pity her," he says, using the same words Odysseus used about him in the prologue. He feels this new compassion undermining his resolve to kill himself, and the discovery that he could be softened, deflected even for a moment from his chosen course by a woman's plea, leads him to understand the nature of the changing world, the uncertainty in which he lives. But the terms in which he expresses these new emotions betray the fact that they are rejected by his deepest instincts; the words which come to his lips to describe his new-found pity reveal that in the very attempt to formulate it, he has already left it behind. "I too, who was so dreadfully resolved just now, like iron in the dipping, I have had my edge softened by this woman here." His metaphor[83] is drawn from the sword he carries as he speaks, and the word he uses, ἐθηλύνθην (literally, "made effeminate"), is a word that Ajax can apply to himself only in contempt.[84] We can see, in the words he uses, the heart harden afresh, the sword regain its edge.

He cuts these disturbing reflections short with a decision to act. Ἀλλ' εἶμι—"I will go. . . . " He will go to the meadows by the shore, to bury in the ground the sword of Hector; let night and Hades keep it there below. The words he uses, as we have seen, are heavy with the sound of death; they stem from the deepest springs of his heroic nature. But the lines which follow show that, on the conscious level, he is still deliberating on his proper course. He gives his reason for wanting to bury the sword: "Since I received this sword from Hector, my bitterest enemy, I have got no good from the Argives." He looks back to the duel with Hector and sees the exchange of gifts as the turning point in his career, the beginning of his misfortunes. The sword of Hector, in the hands of Ajax, sought out and came near to killing the Atridae and Odysseus, Hector's enemies. Ajax now repudiates the gift of Hector: "The gifts of enemies are no gifts, and bring no good." His present troubles he now sees as caused by the sword, which, given to him by an enemy who turned into a friend, is a harsh reminder of the unpredictability of human relationships, a grim token of the inconstant shifting allegiances in which Ajax has lost his bearings. The possession of Hector's sword, the sword of the enemy commander and champion, had marked Ajax out as a man apart and alone among the Achaeans; it may have been the cause, he seems to feel, of the jealousy which lost him the arms of Achilles. To bury it might be seen as a gesture of his willingness to accept again the authority of the kings.

One thing is sure: the sword (and Hector's friendship) has brought him nothing but disaster. "Therefore" (τοιγὰρ), he goes on, "I shall in future know how to give in to the gods and show reverence for the sons of Atreus. They are the rulers, so one must give in to them. . . . " But once again he expresses his new feelings in words dictated not by the intelligence which has brought him to this conclusion but by the passion deep inside him which rejects it. "Give in to the gods and show reverence for the sons of Atreus." He should have said, as the scholiast points out,[85] "give in to the sons of Atreus and show reverence for the gods." The terms he uses are loaded with his passionate obstinacy; they make acceptance of authority appear harder than it really is, and this indicates his hardening resolve to refuse. "To show reverence for the sons of Atreus" is a hyperbolic phrase which presents submission in terms that Ajax of all men could never accept, and yet it also expresses a psychological truth. For Ajax, the mildest gesture of submission is as hard as abject surrender. And the phrase also indicates his instinctive realization of an objective truth. If he is to make his peace with the kings whom he tried to murder in their beds, he will have to renounce all pride, humble himself, and beg for mercy. These words express at once the nature of the action demanded by his new conciliatory mood and the psychological and objective impossibility of its fulfillment. The will to surrender is suppressed in the very moment and through the very process of its formulation. "Time," as Ajax told us, "brings things forth from obscurity and buries them once they have appeared."

The magnificent lines which follow, which state the argument for retreat, concession, and change, become, with this significant prologue, a description of the world in which Ajax, now that he has at last recognized its nature, cannot and will not live. "Things dreadful and most headstrong yield before prerogatives.... Winter which covers the paths with snow makes way for fruitful summer. The weary round of night stands aside for white-horsed day to set the light ablaze. The blast of dreadful winds puts to rest the moaning sea, and all-powerful sleep releases what he has bound, does not keep what he has taken forever." This is the world subject to time. The forces of nature, which govern the physical world, "things dreadful and most headstrong," observe discipline, withdraw, stand aside, to take their place in the pattern of recurring change, which is time. In such a world Ajax too, who is "dreadful and headstrong" like the forces of nature,[86] will have to bend and give way: ἡμεῖς δὲ πῶς οὐ γνωσόμεσθα σωφρονεῖν; "In such a world how shall I not be forced to learn discipline?"

Most translations and explanations of that line give us an Ajax who is reconciled (momentarily or ironically) to the necessity of surrender, but that is not what the words mean. The future of γιγνώσκω, wherever it occurs in Sophocles, has a special sense (dictated by the context)[87] of "learn against one's will, learn to one's cost," and so here: "How shall I not be forced to learn" or "learn to my sorrow," rather than Jebb's influential "Must we not learn discretion?" And σωφρονεῖν, to observe discipline, is in the context of this play a harsh word, which like γνωσόμεσθα marks one more stage in the hardening of Ajax's determination to repudiate not the sword of Hector but the world of time and change. It is used throughout the play to describe the attitude proper to a subordinate. Ajax himself uses it when he orders Tecmessa to leave him in peace: "Do not question or examine. It is good to observe discipline," σωφρονεῖν καλόν (586). It is the word which both the Atridae use to describe the attitude they think proper to inferiors. "Without fear," says Menelaus, "no army would be commanded in a disciplined fashion," σωφρόνως (1075). Agamemnon, telling Teucer that as a barbarian he has no right to speak, issues this word to recall him to a sense of his inferiority, οὐ σωφρονήσεις (1259). And it is the word Athena uses in her announcement that the gods love the "self-controlled," σώφρονας (132) and hate the bad; she is contrasting

Odysseus' acceptance of divine guidance with Ajax's rejection of it. These words, γνωσόμεσθα and σωφρονεῖν, like the use of the word σέβειν, reveal that Ajax's attempt to formulate the alternative to heroic suicide convinces him of its impossibility.

In the lines which follow, the description of what the pattern of eternal change means in the sphere of human relationships, Ajax's heart has hardened completely for death; the sarcastic contempt of these lines is unmistakable. "For I have recently come to understand that we must hate our enemy only to the extent permitted by the thought that we may one day love him, and I shall be disposed to serve and help a friend as one who will not remain my friend forever." His next words make it clear that this cynical prospect is for others, not for him. "For to the many, the harbor of friendship is untrustworthy." A world in which friends and enemies change places, and the old heroic code of "Harm your enemies, help your friends" is no sure guide, is no world for Ajax. He breaks off his absorbed reflection with a phrase that announces the end of his deliberation: "concerning these things, it will be well." He is satisfied and resolved on his course of action, and he now at last addresses Tecmessa and the chorus, for whom he has so far had no word. It is characteristic of him that when he does speak to them, it is to give them orders. They are clearly the orders of a man who is taking his leave and handing over his responsibilities: "Tell Teucer, if he comes, to take care of me...." He needs Teucer now to save his body from insult, but his reputation, his great name, he will save himself, by death. "You will soon hear that, unfortunate though I am now, I am saved." And he stalks off, carrying the sword of Hector.[88]

This great speech explores the dilemma posed by the changing nature of human relationships; the heroic code of friendship and enmity proves useless in a world where friends and enemies change places, a world in which nothing is permanent. Friendship and enmity, day and night, summer and winter, sleep and waking, one succeeds the other, and nothing remains forever, ὡς αἰὲν οὐ μενοῦντα. This word ἀεί, "always, forever," and its opposite οὔποτε, "never," are used, not only in Ajax's speech, but throughout the play, to point the contrast between time and eternity, between man's life and divine immortality.[89]

'Αεί, "always." It is the very first word of the play. "Always," says Athena, "I see you always hunting for some occasion against your enemies." It is true that this has always been typical of Odysseus, but on this occasion, when his enemy is offered up to him, mad and ruined, for his enjoyment, he suddenly and unexpectedly changes, and pities his enemy instead of mocking him. The word "always" is belied by the action of Odysseus. "Nothing is beyond expectation"; he defies expectation, ours and Athena's, deviates from what had seemed a permanent pattern. Ajax too belies the word. Tecmessa describes him weeping when he realizes that he has failed ignominiously in his attempt to kill his enemies. "Cries such as I never⁹⁰ heard from him before, ἃς οὔποτ' αὐτοῦ πρόσθεν εἰσήκουσ' ἐγώ (318) ... he used to explain that always laments like this were the mark of a cowardly and depressed spirit," κακοῦ τε καὶ βαρυψύχου γόους / τοιοῦσδ' ἀεί ποτ' ἀνδρὸς (319–20). "Kindness," says Tecmessa to an unrelenting Ajax, "always begets kindness," χάρις χάριν γάρ ἐστιν ἡ τίκτουσ' ἀεί (522)—she gets no kindness from him. On the lips of Ajax the word is of frequent occurrence; he is obsessed with the idea of permanence. "Here is my command to you," he says to Athena, "always to stand by me as an ally ... ," τοιάνδ' ἀεί μοι σύμμαχον παρεστάναι (117). Odysseus he sees as "the instrument of evil always," ἀεὶ κακῶν ὄργανον (379–80). He uses the word twice with hyperbolic exaggeration. "Will Teucer spend eternity on this raiding?" τὸν εἰσαεὶ ... χρόνον (342–43) he asks impatiently, and he commands that his son Eurysaces be taken home to his aged mother "to be her support in old age forever" (γηροβοσκὸς εἰσαεί, 570).⁹¹ In all these cases, the context casts an ironic light on the word; it is exposed as inappropriate by the reality. And in the great speech which shows us Ajax wrestling with the problem of man's life in time, he uses the word only with a negative: he speaks of the friend "who will not remain so forever" (αἰὲν οὐ μενοῦντα, 682), and of sleep, which "does not keep forever what he has taken" (οὐδ' ἀεὶ λαβὼν ἔχει, 676).

For human beings, subject to time, the word ἀεί, as Ajax realizes in his speech and as the play demonstrates in one passage after another, has no meaning. There is nothing in human life to which it can properly be applied, except to places—Salamis is "conspicuous to all men always," πᾶσιν περίφαντος αἰεί (599). But apart from the fixed unchanging landscape, a permanence to which Ajax turns in salutation in his farewell speech, "always" is the mode of existence not of man but of the gods, θεοὶ αἰὲν ἐόντες, and it is with them that the word is associated when it means what it says. Ajax's father told him, when he set out for Troy: "Wish to conquer, but to conquer always with the god's help," σὺν θεῷ δ' ἀεὶ κρατεῖν (765). Ajax rejected this advice with contempt and claimed that he would "snatch glory apart from them." But he has met defeat. And in his final speech he recognizes the connection between "always" and the gods; he calls on the Erinyes to avenge him, divinities who are "always virgin, always all-seeing," ἀεί τε παρθένους / ἀεί θ' ὁρώσας (835–36). And when later Teucer tries to explain the complicated process by which Hector and Ajax perished, each one through the other's gift, he says: "These things, and all things always, the gods contrive for men," Τὰ πάντ' ἀεὶ ... μηχανᾶν θεούς (1036–37).

Only for the gods do things "remain forever." "There is one race of men," says Pindar in a famous ode, "and one of gods. We breathe both from one mother. But there is a difference between us, in our power; the one is nothing, and for the other the brazen heaven, a sure foundation, remains forever," ἀσφαλὲς αἰὲν ἕδος μένει οὐρανός.[92] This phrase of Pindar's, ἀσφαλὲς αἰὲν ἕδος, is of course a reminiscence of a famous passage in the *Odyssey*, a description of Olympus, the home of the gods. Athena goes to Olympus, where, they say, is the sure foundation of the gods forever, ἕδος ἀσφαλὲς αἰεί (6.42). The next lines of the Homeric passage may well have been in Sophocles' mind when he wrote the lines in Ajax's speech which describe the alternations of the seasons. For on Olympus there are no seasons, no change. "It is not shaken by winds, or wet by rain, no snow falls on it, but cloudless air is spread there, a white radiance runs over it." There is no alternation of summer and winter, of night and day, no winds. When Ajax speaks of those conditions which on earth exemplify for man the imperative of change, he is emphasizing the difference between the human condition and the divine. The man who refuses to change, to conform to the pattern of alternation followed by the forces of nature more dreadful and headstrong than he is, is thinking not like a man, οὐ κατ' ἄνθρωπον φρονῶν, but like a god.

In the world of time and change, the world in which human beings act and suffer, nothing remains forever. Permanence, stability, single-mindedness—these are the conditions and qualities of gods, not of men. For man the word ἀεί is an illusion; man's condition is described by other words, words which define the fluctuating, unstable nature of human reality. The verb ἀλάσσειν, for example. The night brings a situation different from that of the day, ἐνήλλακται (208); "a god," says Menelaus, "has reversed the situation," ἐνήλλαξεν (1060), and the same speaker, gloating over the death of Ajax, which gives him his turn to use violence, sums it all up in a powerful phrase: "these things go by turn and turn about," ἕρπει παραλλὰξ ταῦτα (1087). The play is full of gnomic, antithetical lines which stress this theme incessantly: "everyone laughs and weeps, under the dispensation of the god"; "many are friends now and then bitter enemies." And Athena has stated it, in the prologue, as the gods see it: "one day brings to their setting and raises up again all human things."

In such a world, human attitudes do not remain fixed; they flow, like water. "The gratitude of one who has been loved flows away," Tecmessa says accusingly to Ajax, ἀπορρεῖ (523),[93] and Teucer similarly reproaches Agamemnon: "how swiftly among men the memory of gratitude felt to a fellow man flows away, and is proved traitor," διαρρεῖ (1267).[94] It is no accident that Ajax, in his last speech, dwells insistently on the fact that the sword on which he intends to throw himself is "set" and "fixed." "There it stands firm," ἕστηκεν (815), he says. "It is fixed in the enemy Trojan soil," πέπηγε (819). "I fixed it myself," ἔπηξα (821). The sword is still fixed in the earth, πηκτὸν (907) when Tecmessa finds him impaled on it. The repetition of this word (the natural opposite of ῥεῖν, to flow)[95] defines the context of Ajax's suicide. The steady immovable sword on which he kills himself is the one fixed point in a world of which change and movement are the only modes of existence.

The great speech of Ajax defines the world of time which is man's place and illustrates the impracticality of the traditional code. But it does something more. It discusses the plight of man, time's subject, not only in terms of his relation to gods and his private relation to other men, friends and enemies, but also in terms of his relation to the community. The dilemma of Ajax illuminates not only the metaphysical and moral aspects of man's life on earth, but also the political and social.[96]

Ajax is presented to us in this play as the last of the heroes. His death is the death of the old Homeric (and especially Achillean) individual ethos which had for centuries of aristocratic rule served as the dominant ideal of man's nobility and action, but which by the fifth century had been successfully challenged and largely superseded (in spite of its late and magnificent flowering in the poetry of Pindar) by an outlook more suitable to the conditions of the polis, an outlook which reached its most developed form in democratic Athens. Ajax is presented to us throughout in terms of this heroic morality; this is the function of the wealth of Homeric reminiscence which editors have noted in the language of the play. The words used by Ajax and about him recall the epic atmosphere of the heroic age, and since many of these words are spoken by his enemies, we are shown a full critique of the ideal, its greatness and also its limitations.

Ajax is μέγας, "big, great."[97] His whip in the first scene is big, and so are his words; his strength and courage are "the greatest," and for the sailors of the chorus he is one of the "great-souled" men on whose protection lesser men such as themselves depend.[98] But this word can be used by his enemies with a different emphasis; to them he is a "big body"—Agamemnon calls him a "big ox."[99] The great size of his physical frame and of his ambitions makes him a man apart, alone, μόνος. This is a word which is applied to him over and over again—in peace as well as war, he is a man alone.[100] He is a man of deeds, ἔργα,[101] not words, and when he does speak he speaks with an unassailable sense of his own superiority; his speech is κόμπος, the unabashed assertion of one's own worth.[102] His courage is described in words which recall the warriors of the *Iliad*: he is valorous, ἄλκιμος;

impetuous, θούριος; blazing, αἴθων; stout hearted, εὐκάρδιος; and terrible, δεινός.[103] His courage and audacity, τόλμη, θράσος, are exercised for a personal objective, fame, κλέος, εὔκλεια, and for the prize of supremacy in battle, ἀριστεία, of which he has been deprived by the award of Achilles' arms to Odysseus.[104] These are all qualities of a man who is self-sufficient; he has also the defects of these qualities. He has no sense of responsibility to anyone or anything except his own heroic conception of himself and the need to live up to the great reputation of his father before him. He is stubborn minded, στερεό-φρων, unthinking, ἀφρόνως, ἀφροντίστως, uncalculating, δυσλόγιστος, unadaptable, δυστράπελος, and, a word which is applied to him repeatedly, he is ὠμός, raw, wild, untamed—his nature is that of the wild animal, the figure in which he is seen in the hunting images of the prologue.[105]

Qualities and defects alike mark him as unfit for the type of ordered, cohesive society in which the individual's position is based on consent and cooperation. And this is brought home to us sharply by the presence of Odysseus, who is by nature most adapted to the conditions of life in the polis, the ordered society. All that we hear about Odysseus in the play comes from the lips of his enemies, so that the words which describe the man most adapted to society are all hostile estimates. But the words of Odysseus himself, and still more his actions, show us the other side of the coin. As in the case of Ajax and the heroic ideal, we are shown both the qualities and the defects of the Odyssean ideal.

Odysseus is willing to take direction from the goddess. "In all things," he says to her, "I am steered by your hand, as in the past so in the future."[106] There could be no clearer contrast with the unruliness of Ajax, as we see it in the prologue and hear of it later from the messenger. Ajax sums up this capacity of Odysseus to take direction in a contemptuous phrase: Odysseus, he says, is "the instrument of evil always." The chorus sees Odysseus as a man of words; "shaping whispered words, he persuades," and his lies are "persuasive."[107] Persuasion is of course the normal mode of operation for a man in an ordered and lawful society, and in the last scene of the play, where Odysseus persuades Agamemnon to allow burial for Ajax's body, we see this "persuasion" in a different and better light. To Ajax, Odysseus is a man who "would do anything,"[108] a man "who will put up with much," πολύτλας (a recurrent phrase used about Ajax by his friends is that he "would not have put up with...," οὐκ ἂν ἔτλη). But here again, in the last scene of the play we are shown another side of this tolerance; Odysseus will indeed "do anything"—he will go so far as to pity his enemy in distress and earn Agamemnon's contemptuous rebuke by fighting for that enemy's right to honorable burial. But it is only to be expected that Ajax should see all these qualities of Odysseus as defects, for he despises and rejects the conditions of human society in which they are the highest virtues.

Ajax, like Achilles before him,[109] is a law unto himself; his ideal is the Homeric one: "always to be best, and superior to the others." The virtues demanded of a man in a society of equals—tolerance, adaptability, persuasiveness—have no place in his make-up. In fact, the situation in which he finds himself at the beginning of the play is a result of his defiance of the community; he has reacted with violence against the decision of the judges who awarded the prize for bravery, the arms of Achilles, not to him but to his enemy Odysseus. Sophocles does not elaborate on the nature of the tribunal which made this award, but he describes it in terms which clearly associate it with the court of law as the fifth-century Athenian audience knew it: the words δικασταῖς (1136), ψηφίζειν (449), and κριταῖς (1243) do not occur in any other Sophoclean play, and they are all words which conjure up the atmosphere of the contemporary Athenian court.[110]

But Ajax recognizes no such communal authority. He sees things always in terms of individuals; for him the award of the arms of Achilles to Odysseus is the work of the Atridae, who "procured," ἔπραξαν (446) them for the man who "would do anything." If he had had his way, he says, they would never have lived to "vote such a judgment against any other man."[111] If Achilles had been alive to award the armor (again he sees it purely in terms of personalities), there would have been no question; "no one else would have seized, ἔμαρψεν (444) them but me"—the word betrays his natural violence and his utter incapacity to understand what the concept of communal decision means.

And yet, in this claim, he is surely right. Achilles *would* have recognized a kindred spirit. More, he would have recognized the truth that Ajax is the greatest of the Achaean warriors after him, a truth which Odysseus himself states at the end of the play, thereby admitting that the tribunal which awarded him the arms made the wrong decision.[112] It is no accident that Ajax, in the later fifth-century tradition, is the great prototype of the simple heroic man caught in the snares of the legal process; he appears in this context not only in Pindar,[113] but also in Plato's *Apology of Socrates*, where, together with Palamedes (another opponent of Odysseus), he is described as "one of the men of old who met his death through an unjust judgment."[114]

But the decision was to be expected. The appointment of a tribunal to award the armor of Achilles is a mythic event which marks the passing of the heroic age, the age which Achilles dominated while he lived, an age of fiercely independent, undisciplined, individual heroism. The rewards life has to offer will no longer be fought for and seized by the strongest, whose authority is his might, but will be assigned by the community. And once the decision is taken out of the hands of the individual and entrusted to a representative body, it is inevitable that the man most fitted to shine in courts and assemblies, to persuade, to yield at the right time, to control his feelings, to intrigue, to "do anything," will triumph over the man who lives by imposing his will on his fellow men and on circumstances by the sheer force of his heroic nature.

This political and social context of the dilemma of Ajax lies behind an important section of his great speech. His vision of the world as a pattern of change and concession, exemplified in the disciplined succession of the seasons, starts from and returns to the phenomenon of change in the relationship between man and man. And as is to be expected of an Attic dramatist writing in the fifth century B.C., this relationship is described in terms which recall Athenian democratic procedure. This part of Ajax's speech is full of words which for the audience were of contemporary significance. The Atridae, Ajax says (668ff.), are rulers, so one must give in to them: ἄρχοντές εἰσιν ὥσθ᾽ ὑπεικτέον. This use of the participle ἄρχοντες as a noun occurs only here in Sophocles and is of course the usual word for the Athenian magistrates.[115] The lines which follow, with their description of the orderly succession of the seasons, of night and day, reinforce the point, for the archons did not remain permanently in office but yielded annually to their successors. This implied comparison explains the appearance of the unexpected word τιμαῖς in vs. 670—a word which suggests the meanings "dignities, prerogatives, office."[116] Things dreadful and most headstrong yield to authority, to office. A few lines later "the weary circle of night *resigns* in favor of white-horsed day," for ἐξίσταται is a word frequently used of resignation, withdrawal, in a political context.[117]

Ajax's new vision of change in the natural world is expressed in terms that point to the operation of change and alternation in human society; these terms prepare our minds for what follows—his scathing rejection of the parallel phenomenon in human relations. "We must hate our enemy as one we will one day love, and I shall be disposed to serve and help a friend as one who will not remain so forever." It was notorious that in democratic states men changed sides (and with them friends and enemies) fast and lightly; later in the play Agamemnon describes this adaptability, shown by Odysseus, with the word ἔμπληκτος, "mobile, capricious"—the word Thucydides uses to characterize the swift shifting of allegiances in the bloody troubles at Corcyra.[118] The audience which heard Ajax speak these words had no doubt about his attitude to this mobility, for he was echoing a saying of

Bias of Priene, which they all knew: "Love as if you would one day hate. For most people are bad."[119] Ajax goes on to complete the quotation, and makes it clear that this cynical prospect is not for him. But Sophocles, by a seemingly insignificant change in the wording of the old saw, made it contemporary and pointed: "For, to the many, the harbor of friendship is untrustworthy." "To the many," τοῖς πολλοῖσι— this phrase is unexampled elsewhere in Sophocles—is a cliché of Athenian democratic language,[120] and it puts Ajax's contemptuous refusal to live as other men do in terms of the society of Sophocles' own time and place.

Ajax is indeed unfit for the new age, the political institutions which impose rotation and cession of power, which recognize and encourage change. "Unadaptable," δυστράπελος, the chorus calls him later in the play (914). It is a significant word (and occurs only here in the whole range of Greek tragedy), for it is the opposite of the word Pericles uses in the Thucydidean Funeral Speech to describe one of the key qualities of the Athenian democratic ideal—εὐτράπελος, "adaptable, versatile."[121]

Ajax belongs to a world which for Sophocles and his audience had passed away—an aristocratic, heroic, half-mythic world which had its limitations but also its greatness, a world in which father was like son and nothing ever changed, in which great friendships, and also great hatreds, endured forever.

But in the world as Ajax has at last come to see it, nothing remains forever, ὡς αἰὲν οὐ μενοῦντα. The man best equipped to live in that world is of course Odysseus. When Ajax makes his contemptuous formulation of the way the πολλοί must live, with a nicely calculated balance of love and hate, he is thinking above all of Odysseus. And the Odysseus of the play uses exactly the language which Ajax, with fierce sarcasm, rejects. "Many are friends now and then turn into bitter enemies,"[122] says Odysseus to Agamemnon. "I am ready," he says to Teucer, "to be just as much a friend now as I was an enemy then."[123] Agamemnon calls him "inconstant," ἔμπληκτοι (1358) and dismisses his attitude as selfish (1366). But in these circumstances, the attitude of Odysseus is noble. His change of sides, his renunciation of hatred for his dead enemy, is magnanimous and casts a fierce light on the triumphant hatred of the Atridae, who pursue the old morality to its logical and atrocious extreme—the exposure of the enemy's corpse. It is true that Odysseus explains his new attitude throughout in terms of self-interest. "I pity him ... considering my own case as much as his," he says to Athena. And to Agamemnon's indignant question, "You want me to allow him burial?" he answers, "Yes. For I too shall come to this." "Every man works for himself," says Agamemnon bitterly, and the answer of Odysseus is: "Who else should I work for?" Odysseus does not try, as the Atridae do, to dress his motives up as moral or political principle; he is thinking of himself, and he says so. But it is an enlightened self-interest. It stems from his vision and acceptance of the tragic situation of man, his imprisonment in time and circumstance. "We know nothing sure, we are adrift." "All of us that live are nothing but images, weightless shadows." These lines are the real basis of Odysseus' attitude. The ruin of an enemy, far from being an occasion for joy, is another human defeat, a portent of one's own inevitable fall. The recognition of time imposes a tolerance and restraint which is the mood of the new age and of Athenian democracy at its best. The individual can no longer blaze like Achilles, a star brighter than all the rest, but must take his place in a community, "observe degree, priority and place, office and custom in all line of order," adapt himself, learn discipline and persuasion, accept the yoke of time and change.

Menelaus and Agamemnon, like Ajax, hold fast to the old morality. They do what Athena does and what Odysseus will not do: they exult in Ajax's fall. They mock his corpse, are ready to trample on it, and intend to prevent its burial. They take full advantage of the circumstances which make them victorious over Ajax. "We couldn't rule him alive," says Menelaus shamelessly, "but we will dead." They accept the old morality, in their hour of triumph, for all it is worth. But their attitude does not stem from an obsession with permanence such as that which holds Ajax in its grip. They talk and act not in terms of heroic constancy, of "always," but in terms of Ajax's great speech of exploration and refusal; like Odysseus, they recognize and accept the world of time and change. But they are incapable of the tragic sense that world demands. Menelaus, like Odysseus, can see himself in his enemy's place. "If one of the gods had not extinguished his attempt on us, *we* would be lying there dead and disgraced," he says over Ajax's body. He understands even more. "These things go by alternation," he says.[124] "Before this *he* was the fiery pride and violence, and now *I* am the one with big thoughts." But from this vision of time's revenges he does not draw the Odyssean conclusion. "I forbid you to bury his body," he goes on.

And Agamemnon shows the same insensibility. "You rashly insult me, . . . " he says to Teucer, "in defense of a man who is dead, who is now a shadow."[125] That last word reminds us of Odysseus' description of all human beings—"images or weightless shadows." Agamemnon's words expose his failure to understand the attitude which acceptance of the world's change and flux demands.

The two kings bluntly and brutally enjoy their triumph in the name of the old morality. The ignobility of their attitude is emphasized by the tragic humility of Odysseus, who abandons the traditional code at the moment of victory and exultation, and even more by the stubborn defiance of Ajax, who reaffirms its validity in the moment of defeat.

Odysseus and the Atridae, with different reactions, recognize and accept the lot of man in time. Ajax recognizes it, in fact he is the one who defines it in his famous speech, but he will not accept it. He claims eternity, permanence, the absolute,[126] and if the world denies him what he asks, he will leave it. His son, after him, is to be like him: "Lift him up. He will not flinch at the sight of blood. . . . He must be broken like a colt to his father's raw ways, become like him in his nature. My son, be luckier than your father, but in everything else, like him." He is speaking in terms of ἀεί, "always." His son will carry on his personality. So will Teucer, who after Ajax's death is as intransigent and undaunted as his greater brother.

After the great speech of Ajax, the chorus impulsively concludes that he has come to terms with the world of change he describes so eloquently. They repeat his words.[127] "All things great time damps and fires.[128] I would say that nothing is impossible now that, beyond expectation, Ajax's mind has been changed." But we know that Ajax worked his way through to a knowledge of the world of time only to reject it. And we see him for the last time with the sword of his friend-enemy Hector, its hilt buried in the ground;[129] he makes his last speech not to men, but to eternal beings and things.

He calls on Zeus to bring Teucer to the defense of his body, on Hermes to put him to sleep easily, and on the Erinyes, ever-maiden, ever-seeing, for vengeance—vengeance on the sons of Atreus and on the whole Achaean army. As the confidence of Odysseus contracts, so that he cannot contemplate the suffering even of his worst enemy without pity, so the confidence of Ajax widens to include in his prayer for vengeance all those who, unlike him, accept the shabby world of time. He will be absolutely alone. His last words, the address to the sun and the farewell to the landscapes of home and of Troy, are the words of a man who is already beyond time. "I address you for the very last time and never afterwards again."[130] "Never" is as absolute a statement as "always": he used it boastfully to the goddess once,[131] but now it will not be contradicted by circumstances, belied by time. It lies in his power, and his alone, to make it true, and in a few moments, with a swift effortless leap,[132] he will do so. He has left men and time far behind; his final words are addressed to things eternal, unchanging, timeless. "Daylight, holy soil of my native Salamis, foundation of my father's hearth, famous Athens and its people, my kinsmen, streams and rivers of this place, and the plains of Troy, I address you all—farewell, you who have kept me alive. This is Ajax's last word to you. All else I have to say, I shall say to those below, in Hades." He is going, as he said himself, where he must go. "All-powerful sleep," he said in his great speech, "releases what he has enchained, does not keep forever what he has seized." But Hades does not release those he has taken; death holds them forever. In death Ajax enters the kingdom of "always." His tomb, as the chorus proclaims prophetically while the dispute about his burial is still going on, will be "remembered forever," ἀείμνηστος (1166).

The nature of man's life in time, its instability, is recognized by all three parties, Ajax, Odysseus, the Atridae. The only code of conduct proper to such a vision of the human condition is that of Odysseus, a tolerant and tragic humility. Ajax, who stubbornly maintains the old code and its claims for permanence, renounces life. But the Atridae, fully conscious of the instability of all things human, stick by the old code and blindly enjoy their moment of triumph. They condemn themselves out of their own mouths. Their calculating appeals to order, discipline, reasons of state, fail to mask the ignobility of their attitude, which is exposed by the tragic acceptance of Odysseus on the one hand and the tragic defiance of Ajax on the other.

Ajax's defiance of time and its imperative of change consists not in his suicide (which was in any case his only way of escape from ignominious death)[133] but in his final reassertion of hatred, his passionate vindication of the old heroic code. The problem which faces Ajax is not whether to live or to die, for die he must, but in what mood to die. He dies, as he had lived, hating his enemies. He does not know, and we are made to feel that he would not want to know, that his most hated enemy, Odysseus, will champion his cause against the Atridae. He would rather die than have to recognize Odysseus as a friend. He dies to perpetuate his hatred. His last fierce, vengeful, and beautiful speech is an attempt to arrest, for one man at least, the ebb and flow of relationship between man and man; he may be utterly alone, but he at least will hate his enemies forever.

His brother Teucer understands this. That is why he will not let Odysseus take part in the burial of Ajax. Ajax killed himself to defy a world in which he might one day have to help or feel gratitude to Odysseus. "I shrink from letting you put your hands on his body to help bury him. I am afraid it would offend the dead man."[134] Teucer is right, of course. Ajax hates Odysseus more than any other man. And these words of Teucer remind us, as they must have reminded and were doubtless meant to remind the Athenian audience, of Odysseus' own account, in Homer, of his meeting with the shade of Ajax in the lower world: "Only the shade of Ajax ... stood apart in anger.... 'Ajax,' I said, 'so you were not going to[135] forget your anger against me, even in death. ... Come here to me, my lord, hear what I have to say. Subdue your pride and noble spirit.' So I spoke to him. He made no answer, but strode off after the other shades to the dark house of the dead and gone." Οἴη ... νόσφιν ἀφειστήκει κεχολωμένη, alone, apart, in anger. This is the permanence Ajax has chosen. It is an eternity of hatred and loneliness, but it is the permanence he longed for—he will hate always, forgive never. His yearning for the absolute, the permanent, is fulfilled by his everlasting existence as a proud and silent hater of his enemy, alone, but free, free of the shifting pattern of constant change, free of time.

Notes

1. Σ on 1123.
2. F. Allègre, *Sophocle* (Lyon and Paris, 1905), p. 103: "méchante et cruelle ... partiale ... capricieuse enfin ... un fond de rancune qu'on ne pardonnerait pas à une mortelle." More recently John Moore, in the introduction to his excellent translation (*Sophocles II, The Complete Greek Tragedies* [Chicago, 1957]), describes the role of Athena as "perplexing, not to say fiendish" (p. 5).
3. The most extreme example of this attitude is to be found in Marshall MacGregor's *Leaves of Hellas* (London, 1926), pp. 83–109, "A Military Man."
4. Notable among recent discussions of the *Ajax* are: S. M. Adams, *Sophocles the Playwright* (Toronto, 1957), pp. 23–41; C. M. Bowra, *Sophoclean Tragedy* (Oxford, 1944), pp. 16–62; I. Errandonea, "Les Quatre Monologues de l'*Ajax* et leur Signification Dramatique," *Les Etudes Classiques*, 26, no. 1 (January 1958), pp. 21–40; J. C. Kamerbeek, *The Ajax of Sophocles* (Leyden, 1953); G. M. Kirkwood, *A Study of Sophoclean Drama* (Ithaca, N.Y., 1958), pp. 47–49, 101–10, 160–62; Richmond Lattimore, *The Poetry of Greek Tragedy* (Baltimore, 1958), pp. 62–80; F. J. H. Letters, *The Life and Work of Sophocles* (London and New York, 1953), pp. 123–46; Ivan M. Linforth, *Three Scenes in Sophocles' Ajax* (Berkeley and Los Angeles, 1954); C. H. Whitman, *Sophocles* (Cambridge, Mass., 1951), pp. 59–80 (cf. also index). See also (for bibliography as well as discussion) Albin Lesky, *Die Tragische Dichtung der Hellenen* (Göttingen, 1956), pp. 108–13.
5. H. D. F. Kitto, *Greek Tragedy: A Literary Study* (London, 1939).
6. Kitto, *Form and Meaning in Drama* (London, 1956), pp. 179–98.
7. Kitto, *Greek Tragedy*, p. 123; cf. also p. 122: "The end is rather the triumph of Odysseus than the rehabilitation of Ajax."
8. This point is emphasized by Teucer's διώκων κἀξιχνοσκοπούμενος (997), cf. ἰχνεύω πάλαι (20), κατ' ἴχνος ᾄσσω (32).
9. The words of lines 1319–24 define the tone for us: βοήν ... αἰσχίστους λόγους ... φλαῦρα ... ἔπη κακά ... αἰσχρά.
10. Apart from the *Ajax*, the only certain appearances of Olympian gods on stage in Sophocles (the deified Heracles of the *Philoctetes* belongs to a different category) occur in the *Scyrioi* and the *Ichneutae*, both of them satyr plays.
11. *Aj.* 683: ἄπιστός ... ἑταιρείας λιμήν. *O.C.* 611: βλαστάνει δ' ἀπιστία. *Aj.* 1359: ἦ κάρτα πολλοὶ νῦν φίλοι καὖθις πικροί. Cf. *O.C.* 614–15: ἐν ὑστέρῳ χρόνῳ τὰ τερπνὰ πικρὰ γίγνεται καὖθις φίλα.
12. In both X., *Mem.* 2.6.35 and Pl., *Men.* 71e, it is proposed as a definition of a man's *arete*, ἀνδρὸς ἀρετήν. In X., *Men.* 2.3.14 (and, for what it is worth, in Pl., *Clit.* 410a), it is attributed to Socrates himself. In X., *An.* 1.9.11, it is counted as a mark of the

greatness of the younger Cyrus that he followed this code. In the *Ch.* of Aeschylus (120–23), Electra asks the chorus whether a prayer for an avenger to kill in return is pious in the eyes of the gods (εὐσεβῆ θεῶν πάρα) and receives the indignant answer: "How could it fail to be? To repay one's enemy with evil!" (πῶς δ' οὔ, τὸν ἐχθρὸν ἀνταμείβεσθαι κακοῖς;). Cf. also Pl., *Cri.* 49b: ἀδικούμενον ἄρα ἀνταδικεῖν, ὡς οἱ πολλοὶ οἴονται, and Isocr. 1.26.

13. *LSJ*[9] 2.2 s.v.

14. Pl., *R.* 335e.

15. Archil. 65 (Bergk): ἓν δ' ἐπίσταμαι μέγα / τὸν κακῶς <με> δρῶντα δεινοῖς ἀνταμείβεσθαι κακοῖς.

16. Sol. 13.5ff. (Bergk): εἶναι δὲ γλυκὺν ὧδε φίλοις, ἐχθροῖσι δὲ πικρόν, / τοῖσι μὲν αἰδοῖον, τοῖσι δὲ δεινὸν ἰδεῖν.

17. 869–72: Ἕν μοι ἔπειτα πέσοι μέγας οὐρανὸς εὐρὺς ὕπερθεν ... εἰ μὴ ἐγὼ τοῖσιν μὲν ἐπαρκέσω οἵ με φιλοῦσιν / τοῖς δ' ἐχθροῖς ἀνίη καὶ μέγα πῆμ' ἔσομαι. Cf. also 337–39, quoted below, n. 52.

18. Pi., *P.* 2.83ff. (Bowra): φίλον εἴη φιλεῖν, ποτὶ δ' ἐχθρὸν ἅτ' ἐχθρὸς ἐὼν λύκοιο δίκην ὑποθεύσομαι. *I.* 4.52: χρὴ δὲ πᾶν ἔρδοντ' ἀμαυρῶσαι τὸν ἐχθρόν.

19. Apart from the passage referred to in Pl., *R.*, 331e (which seems to mean what Polemarchus says it does), Xenophon attributes the idea to Simonides in *Hier.* 6.12 and 2.2.

20. Matthew 5:43: Ἀγαπήσεις τὸν πλησίον σου καὶ μισήσεις τὸν ἐχθρόν σου.

21. Pl., *R.* I, 334c–35b.

22. cf. Ellendt-Genthe, *Lexicon Sophocleum* (Berlin, 1872), s.vv. ἐχθρός, δυσμενής, ἐνστάτης, πολέμιος, ἔχθρα, ἔχθω, ἐχθαίρω, ἐναντίος, φθόνος, and μισῶ (on which cf. Kirkwood, *Sophoclean Drama*, p. 231).

23. It still governs his mind in his search for a course of action; he rejects the idea of a glorious death attacking the Trojans because it would benefit his enemies, the Atridae (469: ἀλλ' ὧδέ γ' Ἀτρείδας ἂν εὐφράναιμί που).

24. 96: κόμπος πάρεστι ...

25. It is remarkable that Thucydides, in his description of the savage party strife on Corcyra, uses almost exactly the same phrase to describe recourse to violence (3.83.3): πρὸς τὰ ἔργα ἐχώρουν (contrasted to λόγοις in the preceding clause).

26. Sophocles makes this point with care. Athena describes her action in terms of Ajax's vision (cf. especially 51ff.: δυσφόρους ἐπ' ὄμμασι / γνώμας βαλοῦσα) and then reassures Odysseus by a promise of further action of the same kind (69–70: ὀμμάτων ἀποστρόφους / αὐγὰς ἀπείρξω σὴν πρόσοψιν εἰσιδεῖν. 85: ἐγὼ σκοτώσω βλέφαρα). Lattimore (*The Poetry of Greek Tragedy*, p. 67) speaks of her interference as "bewitchment, affecting not the heart and brain but the testimony of the senses."

27. cf. 51: ἀπείργω. 53: ἐκτρέπω. 60: ὤτρυνον, εἰσέβαλλον εἰς ἕρκη. 70: ἀπείρξω. See also 115: φείδου μηδὲν ὧνπερ ἐννοεῖς—the idea of whipping Odysseus is already in Ajax's mind. (Macbeth says to the vision of the dagger: "Thou marshall'st me the way that I was going.") When later Ajax lays the responsibility for his disgrace on Athena (401ff.), ἀλλά μ' ἁ Διὸς ἀλκίμα θεὸς ὀλέθριον αἰκίζει, he is blaming her not for his murderous attack, but for its failure, as is clear from his later statement (450ff.): ἡ Διὸς ... θεὰ / ἤδη μ' ἐπ' αὐτοῖς χεῖρ' ἐπευθύνοντ' ἐμὴν / ἔσφηλεν ἐμβαλοῦσα λυσσώδη νόσον. That is, the madness consisted of a failure of vision, a delusion, not the intent to murder. These passages make it clear that Athena's earlier statement, φοιτῶντ' ἄνδρα μανιάσιν νόσοις (59), is another reference to the distorted vision of the hero. Teucer (953–54) can use loose terms which suggest Athena's responsibility for the whole affair (τοιόνδε ... Πάλλας φυτεύει πῆμ' Ὀδυσσέως χάριν), but both Athena and Ajax know better.

28. 303: γέλων πολύν; cf. Kamerbeek, *The Ajax of Sophocles.*

29. This scene has an important dramatic function: how could the Achaeans learn that Ajax intended to kill kings, not cattle, without Ajax's self-exposure before Odysseus? Athena explains that Odysseus is to act as witness (67): ὡς πᾶσιν ᾿Αργείοισιν εἰσιδὼν θροῆς.

30. S. M. Adams sees a deeper meaning in the use of this word. "When she says she is Ajax's ally she is somehow speaking the literal truth" (p. 28). He states the "theme of the drama" as: "How Athena ensured that Ajax, though he had offended against her, should have honour after death" (p. 24).

31. cf. 38: φίλη δέσποινα, and 36–37.

32. 124: οὐδὲν τὸ τούτου μᾶλλον ἢ τοὐμὸν σκοπῶν.

33. 78: ἐχθρός . . . καὶ τανῦν ἔτι.

34. οἷον ἀφορῶν εἰς τὰ ἀνθρώπινα τὰ πάντων κοινά, says the scholiast on vs. 124.

35. 126: εἴδωλ᾿ ὅσοιπερ ζῶμεν καὶ κούφην σκιάν.

36. cf. Allègre, *Sophocle*, p. 104: "Sans le vouloir, Sophocle arrive au résultat qu'Euripide poursuivait de parti pris." Cf. also Bowra, *Sophoclean Tragedy*, p. 35.

37. cf. Σ on 79: σκληρὸν μὲν τὸ λέγειν ἐπεγγελᾶν τοῖς ἐχθροῖς ἀλλὰ θεός ἐστιν οὐκ εὐλαβουμένη τὸ νεμεσητόν. Lesky (*Die Tragische Dichtung*, p. 110) puts it well: "Die Sophrosyne ist bei Sophokles nicht Sache der Götter, die Menschen haben sie zu wahren. . . ."

38. Matthew 5:48.

39. Note ἄλλοισιν (774) and τἄλλα (112). In both cases he gives her permission to operate in spheres other than the one which directly concerns him.

40. 27: αὐτοῖς ποιμνίων ἐπιστάταις.

41. cf. n. 29.

42. *Inferno* 19.90ff.

43. *Inferno* 20.28.

44. 79: γέλως ἥδιστος. 105: ἥδιστος . . . δεσμώτης.

45. 111: αἰκίσῃ. 403: αἰκίζει.

46. The idea that gods should be better and wiser than men is a Euripidean commonplace. Cf., for example, E., *Hipp.* 120, *Ba.* 1348.

47. 777: οὐ κατ᾿ ἄνθρωπον φρονῶν. 760–61: ὅστις ἀνθρώπου φύσιν / βλαστὼν ἔπειτα μὴ κατ᾿ ἄνθρωπον φρονῇ.

48. Kirkwood (*Sophoclean Drama*, p. 102) claims that "the Ajax of the prologue is mad . . . in the rest of the play there is not the same blind passion." But in 387–91 Ajax wishes he could kill Odysseus, the Atridae, and finally himself, and in his last speech calls for vengeance on the whole Achaean army (843–44)—a vengeance far greater than the one he planned when mad.

49. cf. the common formula ᾿Αθηναῖοι καὶ οἱ σύμμαχοι, and especially Th. 5.47 (the text of the treaty between Athens and Argos): ἐπὶ ᾿Αθηναίους καὶ τοὺς ξυμμάχους ὧν ἄρχουσιν. . . . In Teucer's argument (1098), σύμμαχον clearly means "inferior, subordinate"; it is contrasted with αὐτοῦ κρατῶν (1099).

50. This is a word characteristic of Ajax; cf. also 991: ἐφίεθ᾿ ἀνὴρ κεῖνος.

51. 117: τοιάνδ᾿ ἀεί μοι σύμμαχον παρεστάναι.

52. 337–39: Ζεὺς μοι τῶν τε φίλων δοίη τίσιν οἵ με φιλοῦσιν / τῶν τ᾿ ἐχθρῶν μεῖζον, Κύρνε, δυνησόμενον / χοὔτως ἂν δοκέοιμι μετ᾿ ἀνθρώπων θεὸς εἶναι. . . .

53. 13: ὡς παρ᾿ εἰδυίας μάθῃς.

54. Pl., *R.* 335a: δίκαιον τὸν μὲν φίλον ἀγαθὸν ὄντα εὖ ποιεῖν, τὸν δ᾿ ἐχθρὸν κακὸν ὄντα βλάπτειν.

55. 132–33: τοὺς δὲ σώφρονας / θεοὶ φιλοῦσι καὶ στυγοῦσι τοὺς κακούς. These closing lines of the prologue, so emphatically placed and coming from so authoritative a source, cannot be ignored or passed over lightly. Whitman's subtle and eloquent attempt

(pp. 67–70) to limit and reduce their importance for the play is in the last analysis no more acceptable than Kamerbeek's cavalier dismissal (in *The Ajax of Sophocles*, p. 45): "These words are as devoid of import as the ferocious passage at the end of *Electra*."

56. 131: ἡμέρα κλίνει τε κἀνάγει πάλιν / ἅπαντα τἀνθρώπεια.

57. 647: φύει τ' ἄδηλα καὶ φανέντα κρύπτεται ...

58. 1052–54: ξύμμαχον τε καὶ φίλον ... ἐχθίω Φρυγῶν. Note ἐλπίσαντες 1052, and cf. 648: κοὐκ ἔστ' ἄελπτον οὐδέν....

59. 487: ἐλευθέρου ... πατρός. 489: νῦν δ' εἰμὶ δούλη.

60. This duel is mentioned by Teucer (1283ff.). Kitto (*Form and Meaning*, pp. 193ff.) attaches great importance to it; he sees Ajax's death on the sword of Hector and Hector's death dragged by the belt of Ajax as the completion of *Dike*: "They fought their duel; neither could prevail. Now each has killed the other; the interrupted pattern is complete."

61. In the *Iliad*, Ajax and Odysseus lead the embassy to Achilles (9), and later (11.484–86) Ajax covers the wounded Odysseus with his shield.

62. cf. Lesky (*Die Tragische Dichtung*, p. 112): "Der Gedanke wurde dann mehrfach variiert, aber im allgemeinen hat man daran festgehalten, dass es sich um eine richtige Trugrede handelt."

63. Bowra is of course conscious of this difficulty and states it frankly: "To our appalled surprise he has decided to kill himself" (*Sophoclean Tragedy*, p. 43); "Ajax's decision is intelligible only *on the supposition* that he is not master of himself but the victim of superior forces and powers. Naturally he does not understand this and cannot say anything about it. We *must base our conclusions* on the way in which he speaks and acts" (pp. 43–44); "We *may assume* that since Athene's anger is on him as it was when he was mad, it is again the cause of his fury" (p. 44). (Italics mine.)

64. 647: κρύπτεται. 658: κρύψω. 899: κρυφαίῳ.

65. 1404–5: τοὶ δ' ὑψίβατον / τρίποδ' ἀμφίπυρον λουτρῶν ὁσίων / θέσθ' ἐπίκαιρον. In Sophocles this word (with one exception, *Tr.* 634) refers either to libations for the dead (*El.* 84 and 434) or to the washing of the body (*Ant.* 1201, *El.* 445, 1139). In *O.C.* 1599, 1602, it refers to the preparations for death made by Oedipus. Cf. also E., *Ph.* 1667, *Hec.* 611, 780.

66. cf. Ellendt-Genthe, *Lexicon Sophocleum*, s.v.: "infra: item deorsum. Illud non dicitur nisi de inferis locis, mortuis, Dis"—a judgment borne out by his lists. In this passage he says of Ajax, "quasi inferis devoturus."

67. ἐκοίμισε (674) reappears in the final speech in a significant context (832): Ἑρμῆν χθόνιον εὖ με κοιμίσαι. Kitto (*Form and Meaning*, p. 190) points out that ἐκχωροῦσιν, ἐξίσταται (671, 672) are "ominous"; he translates them "make room" and "get out of the way."

68. 807–8: ἠπατημένη / καὶ τῆς παλαιᾶς χάριτος ἐκβεβλημένη.

69. This essential point is clarified by Kurt von Fritz, "Zur Interpretation des Aias," *Rheinisches Museum*, 83 (1934), 113–28.

70. The best known is Wolfgang Schadewaldt's description of the speech as a λόγος ἐσχηματισμένος in "Sophokles, Aias und Antigone," *Neu Wege zur Antike*, 8 (1929), 72–78: "Aias spricht eine figurierte Rede, einen λόγος ἐσχηματισμένος, wie die Rhetorik sagen würde ... So kommen wir zu dem Schluss: die Aiasrede ist ein λόγος ἐσχηματισμένος in dem der Dichter den Helden seinen Gesinnungswandel, mehr aus sich selbst als zu den anderen redend, darlegen und eben dadurch die Gefährten täuschen lässt." (In a note on p. 78, he puts it more simply: "'Täuschung' nicht 'Lüge' ist....."). The term is adopted from the late rhetorical treatise, περὶ ἐσχηματισμένων (*Dionysius of Halicarnassus*, ed. Usener, Radermacher [Leipzig, 1914], 3.295ff.), but Schadewaldt's importation of it into the argument simply substitutes a technical vocabulary for a moral one and solves nothing. The two examples of such λόγοι ἐσχηματισμένοι cited in support by Max

Pohlenz do not help either: "ein λόγος ἐσχηματισμένος, wie ihn bei Homer der als Bettler verkleidete Odysseus an seine Gattin richtet oder Agamemnon an das kampfesmüde Heer, wenn er es auf die Probe stellen will" (*Die Gr. Tragödie²* [Göttingen, 1954], p. 174; cf. also Erläuterungen, p. 74). The comparison of Ajax to Odysseus (and the Homeric Odysseus at that, whom Athena congratulates on his sharp practice, cunning, and tricks, 13.291–92) is not felicitous (cf. Kurt von Fritz [above, n. 69], p. 114), and the speech of Agamemnon in *Iliad* 2 is an attempt to gauge the temper of the army, a speech designed deliberately to produce a certain reaction against itself, a provocation, in fact. Even if Ajax's speech *is* meant to produce an effect on his hearers (but see below), the comparison of the two speeches does not seem as "lehrreich" as Pohlenz (Erläuterungen, p. 74) claims.

71. Bowra, *Sophoclean Tragedy*, p. 40.

72. cf. also D. W. Lucas, *The Greek Tragic Poets* (London, 1950), p. 122: "his possible fear that the Chorus might obstruct his suicide scarcely provides an adequate motive." Lattimore (cf. *The Poetry of Greek Tragedy*, pp. 69, 71, and 66, with notes) maintains that the chorus thinks Ajax mad throughout, and in order to get rid of them ("the shipmates of Ajax, who believe they are attending a madman, cannot plausibly let him go away unattended," p. 69), he must convince them he is sane. But at 481–82 they certainly do not talk as if they thought him mad, and in the ode which precedes his speech where they *do* talk in terms of madness, they are evidently prepared for his suicide, in fact vss. 635ff. sound almost like approval of the idea. (Cf. Σ on vs. 635) It is noticeable, too, that they put up no opposition to his going into his tent at 580ff., where he has made it clear that he is going to kill himself, and may very well do it inside the tent.

73. Impatient, harsh lines like 293, 342–43, 540, 543, and 586–95 have built up for us a picture of a man who is not likely to allow interference or even argument.

74. That this approach to the problem has not been explored may be due to the influence of Wolfgang Schadewaldt's authoritative *Monolog und Selbstgespräch* (Berlin, 1926), which rules out deliberative monologue for Sophocles ("die erhaltenen Stücke keine Erwägung in der Form der Selbstäusserung aufweisen," p. 91). Schadewaldt claims that *Selbstgespräch*, the earliest example of which is to be found in A. *Pr.* (88ff.; cf. Schadewaldt, *Monolog*, p. 51), was brought to its full development by Euripides (p. 93 and *passim*) but neglected by Sophocles: "Das Problem des inneren Zwiespaltes, solches die Vorbedingung für die erwägende Selbstäusserung ist, hat im Boden der sophokleischen Kunst nicht Wurzeln schlagen und sich zur Gestalt auswachsen können" (p. 91). But Schadewaldt's brilliant and sensitive monograph is not the last word. Many of his defining characteristics of *monolog* and *selbstgespräch* are highly subjective, and many of the general statements (like the one above on Sophocles) much too confident, given the nature of the evidence. And in the case of Ajax's speech, Schadewaldt neglects a formal characteristic (see below) which appears to me decisive. Interestingly enough, in his later "Sophokles, Aias und Antigone" he says of Ajax's speech, "mehr aus sich selbst als zu den anderen redend" (p. 78).

75. cf. Linforth, *Three Scenes*, p. 18: "All that Ajax has said so far [i.e., up to vs. 684] he has said in the hearing of his friends, but, whereas he spoke to them directly at the beginning, he has gradually drifted into the expression of his own inner reflections: he has been thinking aloud, mostly oblivious of his friends, heedless perhaps whether they hear and understand." The phrase "whereas he spoke to them directly at the beginning," for which (as we shall see) there is no evidence in the text, must be based on Linforth's idea that Ajax at the beginning of his speech is replying, as it were, to the final words of the choral ode: "The first words which Ajax speaks reveal that he has heard the closing strains of the choral song. Similarly, Oedipus' first words at his second entrance in *King Oedipus* (216) reveal that he has heard some of the prayers of the chorus in the preceding stasimon" (p. 11). But Oedipus begins by addressing the chorus (αἰτεῖς· ἃ δ' αἰτεῖς ...)

and continues to address the chorus in the second person throughout the speech (cf. 218, 223, 233, 252, 256, etc.). The comparison of these two speeches, in fact, makes clear the unique nature of Ajax's opening.

76. cf. Pohlenz, *Die Gr. Tragödie*², p. 176: "wenn dann zu der Täuschungsrede Aias mit Tekmessa aus dem Zelte tritt, zunächst jedoch nur in der dritten Person von ihr spricht, auch die Kameraden des Chores erst am Schluss anredet ... so ist das noch die archaische Technik, die uns bei Aischylos begegnete, die wir aber bei Sophokles später nie finden."

77. The Sophoclean scholia sometimes point out the dramatist's attention to this point; cf. Σ on *Aj.* 1, *El.* 1: πρὸς τίνα ὁ λόγος. . . .

78. cf. 372-76, 379-82, 387-91, 393-409, 412-27. He himself says (591), τοῖς ἀκούουσιν λέγε, and Menelaus says of him later (1069-70), οὐ γὰρ ἔσθ᾽ ὅπου / λόγων ἀκοῦσαι ζῶν ποτ᾽ ἠθέλησ᾽ ἐμῶν.

79. cf. Kamerbeek (*The Ajax of Sophocles*) on 688: "The instruction to Teucer falls outside the deceit." On 689: "This means of course that Teucer must see to Ajax's funeral and take over the care of his sailors." Kirkwood, p. 161: "At the end the meaning is so thinly veiled that except to Ajax's followers, who are ready to grasp at any straw, there can be no deception. When he bids his men to ask Teucer to 'take care of me and have good will toward you, for I am going whither I must,' he is scarcely practicing deception at all."

80. The difference between this statement of the chorus and Tecmessa's ἠπατημένη (807) is often overlooked. Errandonea, for example ("Les Quatre Monologues," p. 23), says: "De fait, tous deux, la femme et la choeur, en appelleront à la tromperie plus tard, devant le mort."

81. Pi., *N.* 8.24: ἄγλωσσον μέν, ἦτορ δ᾽ ἄλκιμον.

82. 649: χὠ δεινὸς ὅρκος. 1113: ἀλλ᾽ οὕνεχ᾽ ὅρκων οἶσιν ἦν ἐνώμοτος. This last passage must refer to the oath sworn to Tyndareus, the terms of which were (according to the scholium on this line): συναγωνίζεσθαι τῷ γαμοῦντι αὐτὴν καὶ συστρατεύειν εἴ τις ἁρπαγὴ γένοιτο περὶ τὴν Ἑλένην τῷ γήμαντι. For a different explanation of 649, cf. Linforth, *Three Scenes*, pp. 13-14.

83. For the suggestions of the word στόμα, cf. R. C. Jebb's note *ad loc.*

84. cf. E., *Fr.* 360 (*Erechtheus*) 28-29: τὰ μητέρων δὲ δάκρυ᾽ ὅταν πέμπῃ τέκνα/ πολλοὺς ἐθήλυν᾽ εἰς μάχην ὁρμωμένους. X., *Oec.* 4.2: σωμάτων ... θηλυνομένων as a result of καθῆσθαι καὶ σκιατραφεῖσθαι ... καὶ πρὸς πῦρ ἡμερεύειν.

85. Σ on v. 666: ἐπιφθόνως ἔφρασεν ἐν εἰρωνείᾳ ἀντιστρέψας τὴν τάξιν· ἔδει γὰρ εἰπεῖν θεοὺς μὲν σέβειν εἴκειν δὲ Ἀτρείδαις. For σέβειν in Sophocles, cf. Ellendt s.v. In the overwhelming majority of the cases where it is used, the word expresses religious awe for gods, temples, religious objects, and institutions. The only passages parallel to this use of σέβειν to express respect for *political* authority emphasize the violence of its use here. *Ant.* 166: τὰ Λαΐου σέβοντας ... θρόνων ... κράτη, a phrase of Creon's, whose fault is precisely that he demands "veneration" for the power of the state in preference to "veneration" for a corpse's right to burial; *Ant.* 744 (Creon again): τὰς ἐμὰς ἀρχὰς σέβων, a phrase which is rebuked by Haemon in the following line: οὐ γὰρ σέβεις, τιμάς γε τὰς θεῶν πατῶν; *Ant.* 730 (Creon again): τοὺς ἀκοσμοῦντας σέβειν, a hyperbolic, angry phrase—he is accusing his son of "veneration" for lawbreakers.

86. cf. Kamerbeek, *The Ajax of Sophocles*, on 669.

87. cf. S., *Ant.* 779, 998; *O.T.* 613; *O.C.* 852, 1197.

88. On the "theme of the sword," cf. Kirkwood, *Sophoclean Drama*, pp. 222-23.

89. ἀεί can of course mean, as Passow says, *jedesmalig* as well as *beständig*. But even such phrases as ὁ ἀεὶ βασιλεύων, ὁ ἀεὶ ἐπερχόμενος, express, as well as the impermanence of the individual concerned, the permanence or continuity of the office or action. The idea of continuity can also be limited, as in vs. 1031 of the *Ajax*: ἐκνάπτετ᾽ αἰὲν ἔστ᾽

ἀπέψυξεν βίον. But such phrases as θεοὶ αἰὲν ἐόντες show that the word can express also the idea of eternity, a permanent, infinite state.

90. For οὔποτε used confidently by Ajax about himself, cf. 98: ὥστ᾽ οὔποτ᾽ Αἴανθ᾽ οἶδ᾽ ἀτιμάσουσ᾽ ἔτι (a grimly ironical phrase, for the Atridae, who he thinks are dead, will in fact try to "dishonor" him in the future by refusing burial to his corpse). 775: καθ᾽ ἡμᾶς δ᾽ οὔποτ᾽ ἐκρήξει μάχη—a claim which is belied by the events of the *Iliad*, where Ajax too is driven back to the ships.

91. vs. 571: μέχρις οὗ (ἔστ᾽ ἂν Hermann, adopted by Pearson) μυχοὺς κίχωσι τοῦ κάτω θεοῦ is omitted by Jebb: "The verse is doubtless due to an interpolator who wished to limit εἰσαεί." This seems likely, for though ἀεί . . . ἔστε is common enough, εἰσαεί . . . ἔστε is not; in fact, I have not been able to find a parallel. The line does seem like what would be written in to soften the hyperbole, verging on oxymoron, of γηροβοσκὸς εἰσαεί used of an old woman. L. Radermacher, in *Sophokles, Aias* (Berlin, 1913), rejects it also.

92. Pi., *N.* 6.1–4.

93. Kirkwood (*Sophoclean Drama*, pp. 103–6) has some perceptive remarks on Tecmessa's speech.

94. It seems strange that Kamerbeek in his "Sophocle et Heraclite" (*Studia Volgraff* [Amsterdam, 1948], pp. 84–98), where he assembles the evidence for Heraclitean echoes and influence in Sophocles, omits these two emphatic occurrences of the Heraclitean key word.

95. Because of the sense "to freeze." Cf. A., *Pers.* 496–97: θεὸς . . . πήγνυσιν . . . πᾶν ῥέεθρον. So ποταμούς (Ar., *Ach.* 139); θάλασσα (Hdt. 4.28); πεπάγαισιν δ᾽ ὑδάτων ῥόαι (Al. 90 Diehl); ὕδωρ . . . πάγη (Anaximen., Diels, *Vorsokr.* A.7 19.5]); cf. Heraclit., Ibid., A.1 (55.26).

96. cf. Whitman's balanced discussion of the "peculiarly political mode of treatment" (*Sophocles*, pp. 64–66). The political tenor of the *Ajax* is discussed at greater length (and with less balance) by Norman O. Brown ("Pindar, Sophocles and the Thirty Years' Peace," *TAPA*, 82 [1951], 1–28), an article which, though severely censured by Victor Ehrenberg (*Sophocles and Pericles* [Oxford, 1954], pp. 178–82), has some valuable suggestions and formulations.

97. Lattimore (*The Poetry of Greek Tragedy*, p. 68) has a fine phrase for him: "gloomy giant."

98. cf. 205, 241, 386, 423, 502, 619, 154, 160, etc. At 169 the chorus calls him μέγαν αἰγυπιόν, possibly a reference to the other etymology of his name, for which cf. Pi., *I.* 6.49ff.

99. 1077: σῶμα . . . μέγα. 1253: μέγας . . . βοῦς.

100. For Ajax and μόνος, cf. 29, 47, 294, 467, 1276, 1283.

101. For Ajax and ἔργα, cf. 39, 439, 616, 116, 355; cf. also δρᾶν (120, 457, 468, 1280), χείρ (10, 40, 43, 50, 57, 97, 115, etc.).

102. cf. 96, 766, 770.

103. ἄλκιμος (1319), θούριος (1213), αἴθων (147, 222, 1088), εὐκάρδιος (364), δεινός (205, 312, 366, 650, 773).

104. τόλμη (46, 1004), θράσος (46, 364), κλέος (769), εὔκλεια (436, 465), ἀριστεῖα (464).

105. cf. 926, 766, 355, 40, 914. For ὠμός, cf. 205, 548, 885, 930.

106. 34–35: σῇ κυβερνῶμαι χερί.

107. 148–51: λόγους ψιθύρους πλάσσων . . . πείθει . . . εὔπειστα λέγει.

108. 445: παντουργῷ.

109. Achilles in *Iliad* 1 would have killed Agamemnon if Athena had not intervened; and she had to promise him a threefold recompense.

110. This atmosphere is maintained by other details through the play, e.g., ὀπτήρ, 29 (only here in S.; cf. Antiphon 5.27); τοὐπίτριπτον κίναδος, 103 (cf. And. 1.99); διωμόσω, 1233 (cf. Antiphon 5.12, Lys. 3.1, Pl., *Ap.* 27c, etc.); θόρυβος, 142 (cf. Kamerbeek, *The Ajax of Sophocles*, on 164). The "courtroom" atmosphere of the speeches of the second part of the play has often been remarked.

111. 448–49: δίκην ... ἐψήφισαν. The phrase shows that in Ajax's mind the Atridae voted, whereas we can see from what Menelaus says later that the kings were not part of the board of judges (1136: ἐν τοῖς δικασταῖς, κοὐκ ἐμοί, τόδ᾽ ἐσφάλη).

112. This is a much disputed point. Kirkwood (*Sophoclean Drama*, p. 72) is emphatic to the contrary: "For this assumption [that the award was an injustice to Ajax] there is absolutely no warrant in the play." He is right that vs. 1136 is no such warrant, but Odysseus' final admission, it seems to me, is. For whatever the nature of the board of judges, its criterion must have been *arete*.

113. Pi., *N.* 8.27.

114. Pl., *Ap.* 41b: διὰ κρίσιν ἄδικον....

115. In 1234, αὐτὸς ἄρχων ... ἔπλει, the participle is at least partly adjectival in function. The use of ἄρχων as a noun is more frequent in the other tragedians: A., *Th.* 674, *Pers.* 73; E., *H.F.* 38, *I.A.* 374, 375.

116. cf. Σ 669: τὸ δὲ τιμαῖς ὑπείκει ταῖς ἀλλήλων διανεμήσεσιν. Lattimore (*The Poetry of Greek Tragedy*, p. 70) translates: "give place in their succession." Cf. Schadewaldt, "Sophokles, Aias und Antigone," p. 73, n.4.

117. cf. Th. 4.28.3: καὶ ἐξίστατο τῆς ἐπὶ Πύλῳ ἀρχῆς (cf. ἐξανεχώρει in the same passage; in 2.63 it is used of abdicating from empire). Cf. also Pericles' phrase (2.61): ἐγὼ μὲν ὁ αὐτός εἰμι καὶ οὐκ ἐξίσταμαι.

118. Th. 3.82.4: τὸ δ᾽ ἐμπλήκτως ὀξὺ ἀνδρὸς μοίρᾳ προσετέθη.

119. D.L. 1.5.87: φιλεῖν ὡς μισήσοντας· τοὺς γὰρ πλείστους εἶναι κακούς.

120. The nearest parallel is also in the *Ajax* and also suggestive of the atmosphere of Athenian democracy (1243): εἴκειν ἃ τοῖς πολλοῖσιν ἤρεσκεν κριταῖς ... In Euripides the phrase is common; cf. *Or.* 772 (δεινὸν οἱ πολλοί), *An.* 336, *El.* 382, *Hec.* 257, etc. The political overtones of this speech are reinforced by the unique occurrence in Sophocles at vs. 683 of ἑταιρείας, which is the normal Athenian word for political faction or association (cf., e.g., Th. 3.82.5).

121. cf. Th. 2.41.1 ... τὸν αὐτὸν ἄνδρα παρ᾽ ἡμῶν ἐπὶ πλεῖστ᾽ ἂν εἴδη καὶ μετὰ χαρίτων μάλιστ᾽ ἂν εὐτραπέλως τὸ σῶμα ... παρέχεσθαι. Ael., *V.H.* 5.13: ἦσαν δὲ ἄρα Ἀθηναῖοι δεινῶς ἐς τὰς πολιτείας εὐτράπελοι καὶ ἐπιτήδειοι πρὸς τὰς μεταβολάς. ... If we read εὐτράπελον with M at Pi, *P.* 4.105 we have a significant context for the word; the heroic education will have none of it (cf. Pi., *P.* 1.92–93). For δυστράπελος, cf. Arist., *E.E.* 1234ᵃ5.

122. 1359: ἢ κάρτα πολλοὶ νῦν φίλοι καὖθις πικροί.

123. 1377: ὅσον τότ᾽ ἐχθρὸς ἦ, τοσόνδ᾽ εἶναι φίλος....

124. 1087: ἕρπει παραλλὰξ ταῦτα....

125. 1257: ἀλλ᾽ ἤδη σκιᾶς. The irony of this word in the play is complex; earlier Tecmessa spoke (unknowingly) of Athena as a "shadow" (σκιᾷ τινι, 301).

126. cf. G. Méautis, *Sophocle, Essai sur le Héros Tragique* (Paris, 1957), p. 40: "une âme éprise de l'absolu"; p. 46: "un pélerin de l'absolu."

127. cf. Σ on vs. 714: τὰ ὑπὸ τοῦ Αἴαντος διὰ πολλῶν εἰρημένα διὰ βραχέων διεξῆλθεν.

128. Kamerbeek, *The Ajax of Sophocles*, on 714, accepts τε καὶ φλέγει as "probably" belonging to the text, and explains the metaphor. Jebb is of course right when he says that the scholium on 714 does not "require" us to read τε καὶ φλέγει, but it certainly (as he

admits) encourages us to. Further, if we do, we have a double phrase which corresponds not only with φύει τ᾽ ἄδηλα καὶ φανέντα κρύπτεται but also with Athena's κλίνει τε κἀνάγει πάλιν (131).

129. On this scene, cf. the brilliant remarks of Lattimore, *The Poetry of Greek Tragedy*, pp. 75–77.

130. 858: κοὔποτ᾽ αὖθις ὕστερον.

131. 775: καθ᾽ ἡμᾶς οὔποτ᾽ ἐκρήξει μάχη.

132. 833: ξὺν ἀσφαδάστῳ καὶ ταχεῖ πηδήματι.

133. cf. 254: λιθόλευστον Ἄρη. 408–9: πᾶς δὲ στρατὸς δίπαλτος ἄν με χειρὶ φονεύοι.

134. 1394–95.

135. *Od*. 11.55: οὐκ ἄρ᾽ ἔμελλες ... This may be the model for *Aj*. 925. ἔμελλες, τάλας, ἔμελλες. ...

TWELVE

Review

SOPHOCLES' AJAX. Edited, with introduction, revised text, commentary, appendixes, and bibliography, by W. B. Stanford. Macmillan, 1963.

To his well-known and widely used editions of the *Odyssey* and the *Frogs* in the Macmillan series, Stanford now adds this edition of the *Ajax*. In its careful editing, its intelligently selective and often brilliant commentary, and its sensitivity to literary form and expression, it measures up to the high standard he has set for himself in his previous work.

A long introduction (fifty-five pages) deals thoroughly with the figure of Ajax in Homer and in the play, with the minor characters, and the structure; text history, meter, style, and date are dealt with fully in the appendixes, which also cover suicide in the ancient world, "anger and similar feelings" (a discussion of θυμός, etc.), and the crucial problem of the third monologue. Stanford weighs carefully the many views that have been put forward on this speech, especially the recent ones, and reasons his way to his own conclusion, which, with subtle differentiations, is the majority view: the speech *is* intended to deceive Tecmessa and the chorus. "Ajax now for the first and last time in his life stoops to deceit, out of pity.... If he had bluntly said, 'I am going away to kill myself...' what an agony of grief and frustrated affection he would have inflicted on his hearers" (pp. 286–87).

But even if we allow Stanford his point that "lies or deception intended either to help a φίλος or to harm an ἐχθρός were generally considered excusable and sometimes admirable" (though we might reply, "Yes, for Odysseus, but not for an Ajax or Achilles"), the trouble is that such a motivation has nothing noble about it; Ajax postpones the "agony of grief and frustrated affection" until such time as he will no longer be alive to face it in person. It is an evasion of the consequences of his decision, unworthy of the brutal but direct hero. And in any case such a "compassionate ambiguity" will in fact spare Tecmessa nothing; rather, it will in the end increase her suffering, when she realizes not only that Ajax is dead but that she has been (to use her

This chapter originally appeared in *Phoenix*, 18, no. 1 (1964). Reprinted by permission.

own words) "deceived and cast out from the love he once bore me long ago" (807–8).

The commentary is excellent throughout. Stanford has sown with the hand and not the whole sack: the "teachers and undergraduates" for whom the book was designed will be well served by this judiciously selective commentary, which deals frankly with difficulties, cites appositely the voluminous literature but avoids superfluous references and parallels, and shows the insight of a perceptive literary critic at every turn. Especially useful features are the careful treatment of the particles, the discussion of all the recent work on the play, and the imaginative suggestions on problems of staging.

The text is the first new text, strictly speaking, since Pearson's (1924, corrected 1928), for Kamerbeek's fine commentary (1953), though in effect it constitutes a text, does not print one. Since Stanford's edition will probably be the form in which English-speaking students will from now on make their first acquaintance with the *Ajax*, this text will be very influential and merits some discussion; we all know how hard it is to shake off the almost hypnotic authority of the text we studied in school, how easily even the most violent emendations assume in this way an air of solid, respectable tradition.

It is, fortunately, a conservative text, reflecting the prevailing tendency of modern scholarship. It differs from Pearson's text in some seventy-six places (omitting minutiae); a list of the differences, as in Kamerbeek's edition, would have been useful, for the series evidently does not allow the luxury of an *apparatus criticus*. In most of these places, Stanford rejects emendations and returns to the readings of the MSS. Six of Pearson's emendations fall by the wayside, as do four of Herrmann's, and the names of Elmsley, Thiersch, Reiske, Wakefield, Schaefer, Nauck, Dindorf, Schneidewin, Blaydes, and G. Wolff lose the honor they once had at the head of the entry in the apparatus. In almost all of these cases Stanford (anticipated in many of them by Kamerbeek) puts up a sound defense of the MSS reading and gives a satisfactory explanation. The most important are: 179 ἤ τιν', 208 ἀμερίας, 269 νοσοῦντες, 360 ποιμένων, 379 πάνθ' ὁρῶν, 387 προπάτωρ, 451 ἐπεντύνοντ', 571 μέχρις οὗ (but here it is better to delete the whole line, with Jebb), 624 ἔντροφος, 714 τε καὶ φλέγει is retained, rightly, 758 κἀνόνητα, 869 ἐπίσταται, 921 ἀκμαῖος, 966 ἤ, 1211 ἐννυχίου, 1268 ἐπὶ σμικρῶν λόγων, and 1357 νικᾷ.

A similar conservatism is displayed in Stanford's willingness to admit defeat where the MSS are badly corrupt. Unsatisfied (justifiably I think) by the various attempts to rewrite 600–604 (ἰδαία ... εὐνόμαι) and 1190 (ἀνὰ τὰν εὐρώδη Τροίαν), he encloses both passages in the "daggers of desperation." He marks 1416–17 with the same symbol, but his note suggests that they should rather be bracketed: "It seems to me, then, that Parker is right in rejecting both lines. . . . Presumably they are scribal annotations . . . which have displaced a single paroemiac (now lost). . . . "

Of particular interest are the passages where Stanford abandons both Pearson and Kamerbeek and returns to older editors or strikes out anew. Particularly important are the following: 98 οἶδ', which "adds a characteristic touch of confidence to Ajax's remark." 198 βακχαζόντων (the oldest tradition in the MSS according to Turyn). 330 φίλων γὰρ οἱ τοιοίδε νικῶνται φίλοι—"for it is by friends that such friends are overcome," though Stanford adds that perhaps Kamerbeek's νικῶνται, φίλοι is right. This is one case where faithfulness to the MSS seems to have been pushed too far. φίλοι is the *lectio difficilior* all right, but it seems too difficult; how many Greek scholars could make sense of φίλων γὰρ οἱ τοιοίδε νικῶνται φίλοι at first sight? The second φίλοι (which with Stanford's punctuation must refer to Ajax) makes a superfluous rhetorical point and in Kamerbeek's version, addressed to the chorus, it is weakly redundant, for Tecmessa has already addressed the chorus as ὦ φίλοι two lines previously.

Stobaeus' λόγοις is surely needed here; *ratio et res ipsa centum codicibus potiores.* 384 ἴδοιμί νιν νῦν certainly explains the omission of a long syllable, but it produces a peculiar word order. 427 πρόκειται is an improvement on πρόκειμαι. 450 ἀδάμαστος: Stanford makes a very good case for retaining the MSS reading. 496 ἤ (Bothe), rightly. 593 ξυνέρξεσθ'—"'be shut in together' ('you' being Tecmessa, the child and the attendants) makes good sense"; but surely Ajax is ordering the attendants to shut *him* in, repeating the impatient order he gave Tecmessa at 579 (πάκτου). 706 λῦσεν γὰρ (Turyn). 718 θυμῶν (Lloyd-Jones). 841–42: Stanford retains the MSS text entire.

His argument is not entirely convincing. The fact that "'this is a malediction, not a prediction' (Delcourt) so that the subsequent history of the Atridae is not necessarily relevant," is no argument for keeping the MSS text, for even with Pearson's τως ὀλοίατο, the wish of Ajax does not square with the known "facts" of Agamemnon's death. The choice is not between two references to the death of Agamemnon, one the canonical version and the other not, but between two references, both of which fail to coincide with the mythical facts. Since both versions are somewhat disturbing to the spectators (distracting attention at a moment of high dramatic tension), the choice must be for the shorter and less elaborate one, which also has the virtue of being clearly "wrong" and therefore clearly a wish and not a prophecy; the other looks as if it is going to be closer to the facts (as indeed it would be if only ἐκγόνων were for example ἐν γένει or some phrase which would include the idea "wife") and then starts off in a different direction. To have Ajax wish that the Atridae may die "by the hand of their nearest and dearest" and then go on to say "descendants," when the whole audience is confidently expecting a reference to Clytemnestra, would be singularly inept. In fact, the words Pearson excludes sound like a clumsy and unsuccessful attempt to make an original τως ὀλοίατο more congruent with the myth. 907 περιπετούς (Musgrave): Stanford's arguments are very persuasive here. 951 ἄγαν ὑπερβριθές ... ἄχθος: Stanford's suggestion of "a form ὑπερβάρητον" would have to be accounted for by assuming that ὑπερβριθές (a ἄπαξ λεγόμενον) was an intrusive gloss, which does not seem likely. 1022 ὠφελήσιμοι (*codd.*) is attractive, but the παῦρα, judging by normal usage elsewhere, would suggest "in few things" or "seldom" rather than "in short supply," as Stanford takes it. 1339 ἀντατιμάσαιμ' (Jebb, etc.) rightly, I think. Stanford is not entirely happy with it: "Ajax had not dishonoured Odysseus in any real sense." But the man who had seen Ajax in his mad fit and heard him boast that he intended to whip Odysseus to death could surely say, "I would not go so far in repaying insult for insult as to deny. . . . "

The very rare misprints (e.g., pp. lxii, lxiii) are lonely exceptions in this accurate printing of a complicated book; the only slips I noticed were the unattested form μειδᾶν (p. 188) and the reference to Beazley on p. 167, which should read: *The Development of Attic Black-figure*, 1951, plate 32.1.

THIRTEEN

Review

SOPHOKLES, ANTIGONE. Erl. u. mit einer Einl. versehen von Gerhard
Müller. Heidelberg, 1967.

This is certainly the fullest and most detailed commentary on the *Antigone*; its 287 large, closely packed pages of discussion (M. does not print
a text) invite comparison with Kaibel's famous edition of the *Electra*. A
foreword presents the main emphases of M.'s interpretation; an introduction discusses not only the main problems of the play but also the
myth and the date of production. The commentary itself is divided into
sections which correspond with the natural divisions of the play; each
section of Einzelerklärung is preceded by a more general discussion—
"Gedankengang und Funktion"—and, where relevant, a metrical analysis. This organization of the abundant material is admirable; it allows
separate and full discussion of those problems which transcend in
importance the sometimes minor details which give rise to them.

The first main objective of the commentary is stated as follows: "es
soll der so folgerichtig durchgeführte theologische Sinn der Tragödie
herausgearbeitet werden". M.'s point of departure is the work of
Bultmann and Reinhardt. Bultmann (in an essay now reprinted in Wege
der Forschung XCV) attributes Antigone's attitude to "the knowledge
that human existence and even the polis are limited by the otherworldly
[*jenseitige*] power of Hades"; Hades is defined as "the power from which
derives true justice and [here the English language fails me] durch die
alles menschlich-gesetzliche Recht relativiert wird." With this view, M.
combines the insight of Reinhardt that the tragic element in the play
springs from "the clash of fate-bound personalities who differ in essence
and represent different spheres, Creon the narrower, more limited,
Antigone the encompassing [*umgreifende*], which is related to the other
as the Conditioning to the Conditioned." M. finds support in both of
these scholars for his statement that "the two courts of appeal to which
Antigone resorts to ground her disobedience, Zeus and the unwritten
laws on the one hand, Hades and the rights of the underworld on the
other, are merely two sides of the same thing" (13).

This chapter originally appeared in *Gnomon*, 40 (1968).

The fundamental conception here is clearly Bultmann's. But his claim that Hades is the source of true justice stems from a translation of 451 which ignores the all-important definite article: ἡ ξύνοικος ... Δίκη is no warrant for his statement "und Dike gilt als die 'Genossin der Götter drunten'"—it means, as Jebb puts it, "the Justice which dwells with the gods below ... their personified right to claim from the living those religious observances which devote the dead to them." Hirzel's discussion (*Dike, Themis, und Verwandtes*, 138ff.), to which Bultmann refers, is so far from proving a fifth-century connection between the general idea of Dike and Hades that his only examples (apart from undatable Orphic hymns) consist of an Alexandrian dedication inscription and a personification of Isis as Dikaiosyne (149, n. 3). Bultmann himself admits that "es ist offenbar der dem Sophokles eigentümliche Gedanke, dass Dike, sonst die Tochter und Throngenossin des Zeus ... die ξύνοικος τῶν κάτω θεῶν ist" (23, n. 6). The truth is that Bultmann's presentation of Hades in the play, for all its eloquence and the incidental light it throws on certain passages, stems from a religious conception which has nothing to do with Sophocles; its Christian theological origin is more than once betrayed by phrases such as the characterization of Hades as "die das Leben beanspruchende und bestimmende Macht."

M. rightly contests the idea that Creon is the protagonist (with a reference to Diller's fundamental article in *Wiener Studien* [1956] 70ff.); he also states emphatically not only that Antigone is the hero of the play but also that she is absolutely right, in motive as in action, from beginning to end. A well-known American Sophoclean scholar once silenced a critic of Antigone's motives with the remark: "Sir, you are talking about the woman I love!" and M., though more serious, is of the same uncompromising school. "Über diesen Punkt darf nicht die leiseste Unklarheit bleiben ... Antigone hat ganz und gar recht, Kreon hat ganz und gar unrecht" (11). "Paien unt tort," the reader mutters to himself, "e chrestiens unt dreit," and turns to the commentary to find, as he expects, that 904–20 are athetized and 933–34 assigned to the chorus. With these unfortunate passages out of the way, M. can dismiss the followers of Hegel and Boeckh.

Hegel and Boeckh are not, however, the whole of the case M. is contesting. No one now denies that Creon was wrong to forbid Polynices' burial; by the end of the play, and even before, this is clear as day and it is equally clear that Antigone was right. But there are good grounds for thinking that the audience was allowed, if not encouraged, to think that Creon's position at the beginning of the play was not entirely wrong. Apart from the dramaturgical considerations (eloquently stated by Bowra, *Sophoclean Tragedy*, p. 67: "the audience must feel that the issue is difficult, that there is much to be said on both sides. ... Without this the play will fail in dramatic and human interest"), there is

the historical context of the work to be borne in mind. M. rightly rejects
H. J. Mette's suggestion (*Hermes* [1956], pp. 129–34) that Sophocles in
the *Antigone* is proclaiming a "new law" to replace the old—that those
guilty of ἱεροσυλία and προδοσία should not be buried in Attic
soil—but he does not pay sufficient attention to Mette's demonstration
that such a law existed. True, Creon exceeds the law by denying
Polynices' burial anywhere, but if the Athenians refused the body of
Themistocles burial in home soil because of suspected collaboration with
Pausanias, what would they have thought proper treatment for the body
of a man who led a foreign army in an assault on his own city?

The same indifference to historical background appears in M.'s
treatment of Creon's first speech; he has much to say of its ambiguities
but of the obvious, surface meaning only one thing: that Creon's
phrases "characterize him as verbose and tyrannical" (61). One could
not guess from M.'s discussion that 189–90 strongly resemble a famous
passage in Pericles' Funeral Speech or that almost exactly one hundred
years later Demosthenes had the clerk of the court read a large section
of it out loud to Aeschines and the Athenian jurors as an example of
the attitude proper for a loyal statesman. Clearly these lines (175–90) —
πεποιημέν' ἰαμβεῖα καλῶς καὶ συμφερόντως ὑμῖν, Demosthenes calls
them—were thought of as the epitome of democratic patriotism. The
story that Sophocles owed his election as *strategos* to the success of the
Antigone, whether true or not, makes little sense except in the light of
the lasting impression made by Creon's speech. M. consistently rejects
consideration of historical context in favor of the "zeitlos" (14); he
dismisses Ehrenberg's brilliant book in a rather contemptuous footnote
(14) and in another context (245) states his uncompromising principle:
"Grundsätzlich muss jedes zeitgeschichtliche Moment an Conception
und Durchführung der sophokleischen Tragödien geleugnet werden."
This seems an unlikely proposition for any fifth-century Athenian
writer, but especially so for one who was *Hellenotamias*, *strategos*,
probably *proboulos* in the critical situation that followed the Sicilian
disaster and, according to the ancient *Life*, ambassador.

As for Antigone, those who disagree with M. do so not on the
question of whether she was right or wrong but on the precise nature of
her motives and loyalties. Here of course M. makes it easy for himself
by cutting the Gordian knot at 904–20; only with this excision can he
maintain that, in contrast to Creon's speeches, "aus Antigones Worten
klingt keine Selbstzerstörung" (13) and justify his claim that Sophocles'
"gedankliche Konsequenz im Theologischen ist sehr gross und von
geradezu axiomatischer Strenge. . . . " (11).

The second and third of M.'s guiding principles are concerned with
"Doppelsinn." This means not merely the well-known Sophoclean irony
which, stemming from the contrast between the characters' ignorance

and the audience's knowledge of events to come, is as clear to the modern reader as to the ancient spectator, but also "ambiguity" in the sense it has assumed in the literary criticism of the English-speaking peoples since Empson defined its "Seven Types." This method of exploration in depth has undoubtedly added much to our understanding of poetry both modern and ancient, but it has often been pushed to and beyond the frontier of credibility. Of the first words of Genesis, St. Augustine remarks that Moses *sensit . . . in his verbis atque cogitavit, cum ea scriberet, quidquid hic veri potuimus invenire et quidquid nos non potuimus aut nondum potuimus et tamen in eis inveniri potest* (*Conf.* 12, 31). But there is room for doubt that God conferred the same gift of tolerant clairvoyance on mere mortal (not to mention pagan) poets; some of the products of the search for ambiguity would, one cannot help feeling, be greeted with quite unambiguous contempt by the poets on whom they are foisted. It is all too easy to discover ambiguities even in the simplest of texts. It is also just as easy to extract contradictory ambiguous senses as it is hard to establish an objective criterion for choosing between them. The resultant controversies often resemble Plato's malicious picture of the sophists improving on each others' fantastic distortions of Simonides' poem in the *Protagoras*.

M. (apparently without benefit of Empson and his school) manages to produce many subtle ambiguities, some of which will instruct and some appall, but he has found a solution for the problem which so puzzled Augustine, the difficulty of judging between the opposing interpretations which inevitably result once the plain sense of the text is transcended—*cum alius dixerit "hoc sensit quod ego" et alius "immo illud quod ego."* M. has encased the complicated play of ambiguity he uncovers in a cast-iron system which allows no disagreement about its ultimate meaning; "Doppelsinn" it may be, but not the kind that would allow a Hippias to say ἔστι μέντοι . . . καὶ ἐμοὶ λόγος περὶ αὐτοῦ εὖ ἔχων, for "in ihr fassen wir den theologischen Sinn des Stückes" (7).

The main source of Doppelsinn is of course the choral poetry of the play; the general, gnomic character of the language usually permits more than one particular application. M., however, takes as his basis Aristotle's statement (*Po.* 1456ᵃ) that the chorus should be "part of the whole and take a share in the action . . . as in Sophocles"; he insists that anything the chorus says or sings is in character and also strictly relevant to the action. But the chorus in this play is "der offizielle Vertreter der Bürgerschaft" and "in schlechthinniger Unterwerfung unter Kreons Willen" (16). Therefore, since Kreon "hat ganz und gar unrecht," the chorus is also wrong. "Nach dem Sinn des Dichters ist das konsequent durchgehaltene Verdammungsurteil [i.e., against Antigone] des Chors, das die ersten vier Stasima berherrscht, ein ungeheuerlicher Irrtum" (16). "Der Chor irrt, nicht gelegentlich und zufällig, sondern notwendig, weil aus einem falschen sittlichen Urteil" (16).[1] The chorus, then, insofar as it understands what it says, is wrong, and its opinion can be dismissed; any criticism it may make of Antigone is to be discounted as irrelevant for the interpretation of the play. Much of what the chorus says, however, can be easily understood as criticism (unconscious, of course) of Creon, and this, for M., is not only acceptable but is in fact the intention of the poet who "die sittlichen Vorwürfe des Chors gegen Antigone so zu formulieren weiss, dass ihre richtige Anwendung auf Kreon hindurchzuhören ist" (16).

It must be grudgingly admitted that this is methodologically a brilliant stroke; ambiguity is rigidly channelled along the lines of M.'s interpretation.[2] But there is more. The chorus not only, unbeknown to itself, condemns Creon, it also, in equally blissful ignorance, praises and mourns Antigone; all five stasima contain "ein weiterer Hintersinn, der den Ruhm von Antigones grosser Tat und Gesinnung zugleich mit der Klage über ihren Tod in sich birgt" (16).

A good example of how M. extracts from the text these three levels of meaning (one clear and false, the other two hidden but true) is his reading of the first stasimon. It is strictly relevant to the action; its point of departure is the report of the guard. The chorus attempts to explain the "sinful disobedience" of those who defied Creon's edict. Creon of course attributed it to bribery but the chorus explains the bold action "aus der unheimlichen Anstelligkeit der menschlichen Natur, aus ihrem raffinierten Geschick . . . " (83). It follows that the first three quarters of the stasimon cannot be, as most have thought, *in praise* of human ingenuity and achievement; on the contrary, "daring, world-mastery and effort to overcome all difficulties are presented in characteristic images in which the limits set by the gods to human endeavour are made clear. This and only this is the principle which governs the train of thought." There is, further, no trace of sophistic, of Protagorean, ideas. In fact (87), the thought of the stasimon springs from the tradition of ancient Greek poetry. "Die Gedanken dieses Stasimons . . . sind uralt" (88).

In support of this last startling statement, M. refers to Solon's "Musenelegie," to Alcman 1, Αἶσα [καὶ Πόρος] (cf. παντοπόρος. ἄπορος) and Simonides D 4.9, ἀμήχανος συμφορά. Even for those who may be inclined to welcome M.'s understanding of *Ant.* 332–64 as concerned more with limits than achievements, this is flimsy evidence, and M. feels the need to apologize: "Besässen wir von der Chorlyrik mehr als wenige Trümmer, so könnten wir gewiss die alkmanische Problematik [!] durch die Geschichte der Gattung hindurchverfolgen." (He seems to forget that we have a great deal of Pindar and Bacchylides.) But in fact M.'s interpretation of these Sophoclean lines is

achieved only by omission and special pleading. Of the first image, man
at sea, he has to admit (83): "Nicht unmittelbar ausgesprochen wird die
religiöse Scheu vor dem Element," and though he goes on to claim that
"mittelbar mag man sie aus der Ausmalung der Grenz-situation
herauslesen," few will be convinced; the lines clearly celebrate man's
courage and his triumph over the sea—of "Scheu vor dem Element"
there is not the slightest trace.

The second image, with its reference to the indestructible, inex-
haustible earth, gives M. a little more scope; man is up against the
Hesiodic Urmutter Ge. "Indem der Mensch tut, was er nach seiner
Natur und nach seiner Lage muss [but where is this to be found in the
text?] begegnet er doch einer Macht, die grösser und stärker ist als er,
und die seinem Streben eine Schranke setzt, die er niemals wird
überwinden können" (84). This seems to imply that man's purpose is to
wear out and destroy the earth (and so, presumably, starve to death).
But, as Sophocles presents it, the fact that the earth yields crops year
after year is due to human tools and skill (ἰλλομένων ἀρότρων ...
πολεύων).

The antistrophe of course gives M. no scope at all (this is admitted
in the skillful formula "in der ersten Gegenstrophe ist nicht mehr
ausdrücklich von Vordringen an Grenzen die Rede," which implies that
such a theme *has* been ausdrücklich in the strophe), but in the second
strophe, with the mention of Hades, M. has a last an undeniable
"Grenze" to offer. No one will quarrel with him, for it is here, almost
all critics agree, that the optimistic tone of the ode falters and begins to
change. But before he reaches that point, he manages to paraphrase the
magnificent confidence of παντοπόρος. ἄπορος ἐπ᾽ οὐδὲν ἔρχεται τὸ
μέλλον as follows: "gegenüber allem schlechthin das auf ihn zukommt
[τὸ μέλλον] bleibt seine unter der Not stehende Existenz zwangsläufig
durch die Fähigkeit bestimmt, Auswege zu finden." This smacks of
Heidegger's perverse (and almost unintelligible) version "überall hin-
ausfahrend unterwegs erfahrungslos ohne Ausweg kommt er zum
Nichts," and although syntactically speaking the words ἐπ᾽ οὐδὲν ... τὸ
μέλλον may be read ambiguously, in context they may not, for the
simple reason that unless they are read "im Sinne des auch zukünftig
unbegrenzten Fortschritts," the following μόνον (even if we allow M.
his μόνου) makes no conceivable kind of sense.

The second antistrophe is notoriously imprecise in reference; it has
been variously interpreted as critical of Antigone, of Creon, or of both.
For M. of course there is no problem. The chorus condemns Antigone
and is wrong. Since the poet's own meaning shines out "only *e
contrario*, in dialectical reversal" (85), the lines really condemn Creon.
But here, as all through the ode, there is still another meaning. "Soll

ich ihn Hintersinn oder Vordersinn nennen?" M. asks himself. This seems to herald something extraordinary, and indeed it does. The stasimon *does* after all turn out to be in praise of human greatness. "And this praise is deserved ... by Antigone." She faces the "Grenze," the danger of death, without flinching; from the "Grenze" of divine order she gives a higher norm to civic organization (and so is ὑψίπολις, and δεινή in the simple sense of "wonderful"); she is παντοπόρος, and ἄπορος—she finds a way to vindicate the eternal laws but cannot find a way to escape death; she can avoid incurable diseases (of the mind) ... and so on. M. does not find a way to have her sail the sea, plough the earth, catch birds and fish, tame the bull, and yoke the horse, not to mention teach herself speech, but the ingenuity of what he has managed to do is wonder enough: πολλὰ τὰ δεινά ...

Such a view of the meaning of this famous poem naturally rules out any possibility that Sophocles is using contemporary "Kulturgeschichte." M.'s main argument here seems to be that the typical historical sequence of the origins of human civilization is precisely what is avoided ("ist gerade vermieden" 83). Apart from the fact that there does not seem to be a "typical order" (comparison of the "Kulturgeschichten" in A., *Pr.*, E., *Supp.*, Pl., *Prt.* shows great variety, though it is true that navigation generally comes late rather than first), this is a lyric poem (a highly organized one, as M. expertly demonstrates in his metrical analysis), and the question of whether man invented agriculture before he built ships was not Sophocles' main concern.

It will not do either to dismiss Protagorean influence because Protagorean theory was optimistic whereas the Sophoclean ode finds in "the moral ambivalence of technical knowledge a source of tragic disaster" (89); this last statement is still true if the first three quarters of the ode seem to hold out an optimistic prospect, only to close in doubt and bewilderment—and that is infinitely more dramatic than the relentless sermon M. would have us read. In fact, what distinguishes this particular Kulturgeschichte from its fellows is precisely its secular tone: man "taught himself"—no Prometheus or Zeus was needed—and the list of what he taught himself does not include, as other accounts do, sacrifice and divination. Up to the mention of Hades 361, the lines present the proud and enlightened spirit of the sophist Erklärung at its best; the loss of confidence in the succeeding lines prepares us for the entirely different view of the human condition which will be forced on us by the events of the play.

The same methodical revelation and regimentation of Doppelsinn continues for the rest of the commentary, sometimes with results that verge on the grotesque, as for example in the explication of that recalcitrant poem, the fourth stasimon. The phrase used to describe

Danae's delicate condition (Ζηνὸς ταμιεύεσκε γονὰς, 949–50): "als Metapher aufgefasst, zu einer noch herrlicheren Auszeichnung Antigones wird" (214). For the benefit of those who have to rack their brains for the point of the comparison, M. explains later that "Zeus vertraute Antigone eine Aufgabe an...." The Lycurgus passage, though on the surface a comparison with Antigone as a sinner justly punished, is of course really a reference to Creon. Many would accept at least half of this statement, but M.'s proofs may cause them to waver. "Es ist nicht zu bezweifeln," he states confidently, "dass die Mänaden ... Antigone bedeuten" (17), and adds the rather pathetic detail that "den Musen tat Kreon weh mit seiner inhumanen Grobheit und Rohheit" (214).

In the third case, Cleopatra and the Phineidae, M. suggests a reason for the fact that more space is devoted to the misfortunes of her sons than to the imprisonment of Cleopatra (which is of course not mentioned at all and has to be assumed on the authority of Diodorus). It is that Cleopatra, like Antigone, brings about, through her imprisonment, sorrow for those nearest to her (217); the sons mourn the sorrowful sufferings of their mother—as Haemon does those of Antigone. What to most readers will seem far-fetched, indeed hard to understand, is so obvious to M. that he can comment: "sprechender kann die Hindeutung auf Haimon nicht sein."

M.'s highest flights of ingenuity occur in the attempt to demonstrate that even though Antigone is not on stage during the last part of the play, she is really foremost in Sophocles' mind and his presentation of the action. Since she is hardly mentioned (as M. frankly admits), this can only be achieved by a lavish helping of Doppelsinn. One example will suffice; *ex pede Herculem*. Eurydice (1282) is referred to as τοῦδε παμμήτωρ νεκροῦ and this, according to M., reminds us of Antigone— "Sie war in metaphorischem Sinne ganz Mutter des toten Polyneikes ..." (296). By the same reasoning, Creon's mourning over Eurydice, μᾶτερ ἀθλία (1300), also reminds us of Antigone. This is typical of the insights which embolden M. to claim that "was den zweiten Kommos angeht, so hätte, pragmatisch gesehen, die Leiche Antigones mit den beiden anderen vor Kreons Füssen niedergelegt werden können. Man kann nicht umhin, an den Schlussteil des Aias zu denken..." (20). This is taking the bull by the horns with a vengeance; unfortunately the bull refuses to move. We do indeed think of the closing scenes of the *Ajax*, but only to reflect that if Sophocles had wanted Antigone to dominate the final *commos* he would have had her body brought on stage with Haemon's rather than wait 2,500 years for someone to discover that τοῦδε παμμήτωρ νεκροῦ was meant to remind us of her and to realize that "die grosse Seele und ihr Geschick um so mächtiger gegenwärtig sind, je weniger an sie gedacht und von ihnen geredet wird" (20).

M.'s method as a whole reminds one irresistibly of Verrall's. But since, unlike Verrall's Euripides (who needed ambiguity to escape prosecution for impiety), M.'s Sophocles is on the side of the angels ("denn Sophokles ist als Dichter Theologe und macht theologische Aussagen," 11), the only reason one can think of for his insistence on disguising his meaning (M.'s explanation that it "hat ihren tiefliegenden Grund darin, dass der Gott, von dem Sophokles spricht, ein verborgener Gott ist" (18) leaves much to be desired) is Verrall's claim that the Athenians delighted in literature which was based on the principle "that the author ... must not be *plain* if he would, and would not if he might; that the simpler and clearer he seems, the closer you have to watch him, sure that at last his truest and gravest meaning will be found in a corner, or round a corner, so that (thank the gods!) it is worth a man's while to look for it" (*Euripides the Rationalist*, pp. 90–91).

97. Exit Antigone. An excellent suggestion; to M.'s reasons for it can be added the fact that only so can Antigone leave by the *parodos* without unduly delaying the entrance of the chorus. 99. M. takes φίλη as active, rightly. 114. M. uses Fraenkel's discussion of A., *A.* 358 to present a strong case for thinking στεγανός active in meaning here (against F.). 143. J. and E-G explain στυγεροῖν as "unglückliche." "Das kann das Wort nicht heissen," says M., rejecting J.'s parallel (*Ph.* 166) as corrupt. But cf., for example, *Tr.* 1017. 149. M. writes as if ἀντιχαρεῖσα were said by Creon instead of the chorus. 162. κοινῷ with πέμψας "absolut gebraucht" is not "witzlos"; it means "inclusive" — "a message sent to us all" (Campbell). 163–64. "Ton wahnhafter Zuversicht ... den die Laute σα–σει–σα–σα 163 und die fünf ω in 162–63 verschärfen." This description of the "klangliche Wirkungen" seems highly subjective. For example, 460–470 contain σοι–σα–σχε–σκα and *seven* ω, but the speaker is Antigone and though some might be tempted to hear a "Ton wahnhafter Zuversicht," M. would be the last to agree. 192. Excellent note on the construction κηρύξας ἔχω. 211ff. "Einer Erklärung, wie sie nicht unterwürfiger sein könnte" (61) is too strong; there is no opposition expressed, but J., Campbell, and Bruhn are right to recognize "secret misgiving," "barest acquiescence," etc. M.'s interpretation is dictated by the principle that "der Chor ... irrt konsequent." 311. Oversubtle interpretation of τὸ λοιπὸν ἁρπάζητε. This illogical use of τὸ λοιπόν is a Sophoclean cliche (cf. *O.T.* 1273, *Tr.* 911, and *Ant.* 717, which, however, M. eliminates by conjecture). 332. δεινά Like most commentators, M. sees a meaningful imitation of A., *Ch.* 585ff. But comparison with E., *Fr.* 1059, 1–4 suggests that it may be a variation of a well-known "priamel." 338–40. "Zehnfaches α, davon

dreimal im Anlaut, da, wo die Heiligkeit der Erde hervorgehoben wird."
The subjective nature of this type of interpretation of sound effect
(which is, incidentally, the fourth principal emphasis mentioned by M.
in his introduction) may be gauged by comparing Bruhn's equally
confident reaction to the same phenomenon: "Der Gleichklang malt das
rastlose Ringen des Menschen, die Erde zu seinem Besten zu bear-
beiten". 420. ἐν δ' ἐμεστώθη. M. is right (with J. against Bruhn) to take
this as *tmesis*, but his note goes on to class as *tmesis* or eliminate as
corrupt the other seven possible uses of ἐν adverbial in Sophocles. Since
it occurs in Homer, Herodotus, and Pindar, the attempt to abolish it in
Sophocles seems unnecessary. 522. M. rightly restricts the meaning of
συμφιλεῖν to the particular issue; Antigone's statement is not, as many
have implied, a rejection of hate, for she proudly states her hatred for
Creon, threatens Ismene with hatred, curses those who disturbed her
first burial of Polynices and prays for revenge on those who have
wronged her. 572. M. attributes to Antigone. He does not support his
assertion that τὸ σόν. 573. "Mag ... grundsätzlich verstehbar sein als
'die von der du sprichst'; *in concreto* ist es nicht so verstehbar." The
scholium explains it this way, and Bruhn's *Anhang* 80 gives sufficient
parallels. M.'s second reason that "this short spontaneous sentence
brings into the light more than a whole scene full of pathos the love
relationship which is of the greatest importance for the drama. ... If it
were less strong we would not understand Haimon's suicide" neglects
the fact that what is important for the action is Haemon's love for
Antigone; her attitude towards him is not relevant. The further
consideration that "'liebster Haimon' vor den Ohren seiner Verlobten
überhaupt nicht im Munde Ismenes möglich ist" can be dismissed in
view of the frequent occurrence of this form of φίλος as a common
salutation (Cadmus to Tiresias, E., *Ba.* 178, Chorus to Odysseus, *Cyc.*
767 etc.). M. adds one more argument, that "only if Antigone speaks
the line can Creon's answer 573 have a meaningful Sophoclean
Hintersinn"—Antigone and her betrothal will in fact bring Creon grief;
this is an argument which as M. says "für ebenso zwingend gelten muss
wie die genannten beiden." To the case against his attribution, one
might add that ἄγαν γε λυπεῖς is much more suitable if addressed to
Ismene, who has been speaking throughout (cf. *Aj.* 589, where the
identical phrase is used to silence Tecmessa at the end of an inter-
change). M. might have consulted with profit the excellent discussion of
the problem in Ivan M. Linforth's *Antigone and Creon* (Berkeley, 1961),
pp. 209–210. 806ff. (p. 183). Excellent discussion of Antigone's lamentation and the supposed contradiction with 463ff. 823ff. M. seems to imply
that Antigone's comparison of herself to Niobe had been suggested by
the chorus and was offensive to her. Niobe is "die grosse Frevlerin" (so

M., though there is of course no mention of this in the text) and "mit dieser Niobe in der Todesart und dessen argem Ruhm gleichgestellt zu werden, muss A. bitter empfinden." But there is no warrant for thinking that the chorus suggested Niobe or that A. rejects the comparison; on the contrary, A. makes the comparison herself and the chorus objects to it in the following lines. Electra too compares herself to Niobe (S., *El.* 149ff.), with no thought that she is a "grosse Frevlerin." On these two passages M. might have mentioned the interesting remarks of C. H. Whitman, *Sophocles* (Cambridge, Mass., 1951), pp. 93–94, 165. 891ff. A.'s last speech (what is left of it, that is, after M.'s surgery) is rightly characterized as a "quasi-monolog" (addressed to no one, though Creon is present) and compared to the first part of Ajax's speech (646–83). 1220–25. M. interprets correctly to mean that Haemon freed Antigone from the noose and laid her body on the ground. (Cf.. *O.T.* 1265ff.). The usual interpretation (e.g., J.'s "embracing her ... where she hangs lifeless") defies normal human instinct. 1258. διὰ χειρὸς ἔχων —"Kreon die Leiche seines Sohnes auf seinen Armen herbeiträgt." If so, he still has his fellow actor in his arms at 1297 ἔχω μὲν ἐν χείρεσσιν ἀρτίως τέκνον, and one wonders why Aeschines did not fall flat on stage in this role as he did in that of Oenomaus. "Natürlich handelt es sich um eine Puppe," says Bruhn, but one does not have to take these phrases literally (in spite of Σ 1279); cf. E., *Ba.* 969 (where the literal sense is Dionysos' dark meaning but to Pentheus ἐν χερσὶ μητρός must mean, as Dodds says, that "his mother will share his litter"), *Alc.* 19, 201; *Ion* 1440, 1443—"support, embrace"—so *Tro.* 377.

M. does not print a text; the commentary is followed by a list of 184 deviations from Pearson's. Of these, seventy-nine are M.'s own contribution (conjectures, adoptions of v. l., or, more rarely, return to the main manuscripts); the rest, with the exception of five proposals of Bruhn, were all available to (and most of them rejected by) Jebb.[3] In a short preface to the list (280–81), M. states his critical principle: "Ein Fortschritt in der Gestaltung des Sophoklestextes hängt vor allem an zwei Dingen, an einem verfeinerten Urteil bei der Auswahl der Varianten und an verständiger Konjekturalkritik." He pays little attention to the problem of the transmission, for he believes, with Pearson (preface VIII) "ἐκλεκτικοί, ut ita dicam, ... fieri debemus"; he treats all MS readings, variants, lemmata in the scholia, readings recorded or implied in their explanations, and citations in ancient authors on an equal basis—the truth may have been preserved in what the strict stemmatist would regard as very unlikely places. The pioneering work of Pasquali (whose results are confirmed by Dawes' brilliant book on the manuscripts of Aeschylus) makes this a more respectable point of view than our fathers would have thought it, but M.'s second critical principle will not be so widely welcomed. "Auch muss dem Vorurteil, eine Emendation sei erst dann voll gerechtfertigt, wenn der Weg von ihr zur Korruptel mit eindeutiger Notwendigkeit erhellt werden kann, immer wieder entgegengetreten werden" (34). His authority for this is Maas (*Textkritik* 1950[1], p. 11), but it seems unlikely that Maas could have intended his remarks to be taken as *carte blanche* for large-scale emendation free of paleographical scruples, especially in the hands of a critic who completely disregards Maas' cherished principle of *recensio*. What Pearson thought of this approach can be gathered from his comments (*CQ* 22 [1928], 182) on the type of conjecture M. so often adopts: "I cannot help thinking that the authors of such conjectures pay no regard to the improbability of their loss in the course of transmission." What M. has done, in fact, is to select the permissive element from the system of each of his two authorities and so write himself a charter for free-wheeling emendation the like of which has not been seen in the land since the spacious days of Blaydes.

But, though I doubt that many of M.'s proposals and revivals will find their way into the Sophocles texts of the next generation, his remarks deserve careful reading and consideration; he is a critic of great learning, of refined linguistic and stylistic sensibility, and he is also a forceful writer. Even if the solution he proposes does not often satisfy, he has a way of posing the problem in a challenging fashion; the reader will find himself forced to think again, and deeply, about many lines he has always taken for granted. M. might have quoted another passage of Maas' *Textkritik*; it is on p. 17 of the English edition and reads: "it is far more dangerous for a corruption to pass unnoticed than for a sound text to be unjustifiably attacked. For as every conjecture provokes refutation, this at all events advances our understanding of the passage. . . . "

4. ἀτημελές (M.) It seems doubtful that this could mean "Mangel an Pflege," even in the (unattested) passive sense; even if it could, such a meaning would be anticlimatic in an evocation of τῶν ἀπ' Οἰδίπου κακῶν. 24. Wunder's deletion (cf. Bruhn *ad loc.*) is dismissed on the grounds that "ἔκρυψε kann . . . ohne Zusatz nicht die Beerdigung ausdrücken." But cf. 285, *O.C.* 621. 57. ἐπαλλήλοιν (Hermann). Cf. Pearson *CQ* 22 (1928), 179. M.'s suggestion that the whole phrase refers also to the sisters—"so würden die Schwestern gemeinsam gleichsam von eigener Hand sterben, wenn Antigones Plan verwirklicht würde" (αὐτοκτονοῦντε) and that therefore the normal meaning of ἐπαλλήλοιν, "aufeinanderfolgend" is exact "auf die Schwestern angewendet, bei denen eine der anderen folgen würde" is based on nothing but fancy; the text contains not the slightest hint of any such suicide pact. 94. ἐχθρά . . . προσκείσῃ is admittedly unique usage, but L.

Dindorf's κάτω is no solution; the idea that Ismene will lie close to Polynices in the world below is not one that Antigone would be likely to entertain at this stage. 108. ὀξυτόρῳ, citing H. Lloyd-Jones *CQ* 1957, 12. 113. αἰετὸς ὡς γᾶν εἰς (M.) with ὑπεροπλίαις 130. It is true that ὡς should immediately follow the word it belongs to, but not so true that γᾶν εἰς "macht keine Schwierigkeit": M. cites *O.C.* 126 but cf. L. Campbell *ad loc.* In any case, two displacements are very awkward in so short a line. 138. ἄλλα μὲν ἄλλ' (Emperius) removes the need to understand (reluctantly, with J.) ἄλλα as "not as he had hoped" but produces four forms of ἄλλος in two short lines, which M. would have us understand as all referring forward (with no reference back to Capaneus) without "distributive Sinn." Perhaps Campbell's δεινὰ for ἄλλα in 138 (from V) deserves consideration. 140. δεξιόσειρος is indeed an uncomfortable bedfellow with ἐπενώμα and στυφελίζων but M.'s δεξιόχειρος (from Σ) in spite of the gloss περιδέξιος (cf. *Il.* Φ 163), can hardly have suggested the meaning "der gleichsam nur rechte Hände hat, dessen Linke also gleich viel leistet." A glance at the other δεξιο compounds will show the improbability. 150. χρὴ for ἐκ cures the hiatus (if indeed it needs curing), gives θέσθαι λησμοσύναν an object, and meets M.'s objection to the vulgate that the imperative infinitive is never used for "Selbstaufforderung." But no explanation of its loss can be imagined. M.'s second point would perhaps be answered by Blaydes' suggestion that ἐκ . . . θέσθαι λησμοσύναν is equivalent to ἐκλαθέσθαι with *tmesis.* 157. νεοχμοῖσι for νεαροῖσι (Nauck), solely on the grounds that "niemals scheint νεαρός in einem nicht positiven Sinne vorzukommen" and that consequently its presence here destroys the "tragisch ironischen Ausdruck der an unserer Stelle indiziert ist." By putting νεωστί into the lacuna 156 and reading with Schmid καινῷ for κοινῷ 162, M. manages to give us no less than four words for "new" in "einem nicht positiven Sinne" where the text had only one to start with. He might have remembered Corinna's advice to Pindar. 159. ἑλίσσων (Johnson) for ἐρέσσων. It is true that ἐρέσσω metaphorically expresses "das rhythmisch Lebhafte," but μῆτις can mean "plan" as well as "lautloses Überlegen" and "putting into motion what plan?" makes very good sense with the following words. 168. If κἀπεὶ introduces a third clause (so M. rightly with Bruhn against J.), then it is easy to understand e.g. τἀκείνου σέβοντας after 167 and unnecessary to suspect a lacuna after this line. M.'s statement that it is "erwünscht, dass jede der drei Regierungen in zwei Trimetern behandelt wird" adds nothing to his case. 172. παιθέντες (M.) He compares A., *Th.* 961, on which however see Groeneboom, who gives several examples of παίω and ἐπλήγην paired as here; note especially S., *El.* 1415 πέπληγμαι— παῖσον. 186. ἆσσον (Dobree). But for στείχουσαν ἀστοῖς cf. *O.C.* 1772 ἰόντα φόνον τοῖσιν ὁμαίμοις. J. gives an adequate explanation of Demosthenes' ὁμοῦ: ἀστοῖς would not have been clear in his context. 203. ἐκκεκηρῦχθαι λέγω (Nauck Carneadem secutus ap. D. L. 4.64). M. points out that Carneades' parody would hardly have been recognizable as such unless these two words were in the vulgate text of his time. It is difficult, too, to account for the unanimous ἐκκεκηρύχθαι of the codd. on any other basis. 241. M. puts a cogent case for τί φροιμιάζῃ; (Arist., *Rh.* 1415[b]21). His argument can be strengthened by the fact that the anonymous commentator on the *Rhetoric* (Rabe 234) also seems to have read these words and locates them more exactly in the Sophoclean context. The Aristotle passage continues with διὸ οἱ δοῦλοι οὐ τὰ ἐρωτώμενα λέγουσιν, ἀλλὰ τὰ κύκλῳ, καὶ προοιμιάζονται—the word κύκλῳ reinforces the reference to 241 of our play and the words οἱ δοῦλοι rule out the usual desperate referral of the passage (J., Cope, etc.) to E., *I.T.* 1162, since the person addressed there is Iphigenia. If, as J. thought, the Φύλαξ is a slave, the evidence that Aristotle read τί φροιμιάζῃ; here would seem overwhelming, but see the remarks of A. D. Fitton Brown on this point (*PCPhS* [1966], 19). 287. τιμὴν for καὶ γῆν M. But τιμὴν ἐκείνων i.e. θεῶν would mean not "die Ehre, die die heimatlichen Götter der Stadt und ihren Verteidigern ... erweisen ... " but "honors paid to the gods," as in 745. 343. A good defense of Nauck's ἀγρεῖ. 466. Against M.'s ἄλλως for ἄλγος see J. *ad loc.* on the characteristically Sophoclean sequence παρ' οὐδὲν ἄλγος ... κείνοις ἂν ἤλγουν. τοῖσδε δ' οὐκ ἀλγύνομαι. 467. ἄθαπτον [ὄντ'] ἠνεσχόμην with Blaydes (and, according to Campbell, Lushington). The form ἠνσχόμην is indeed without parallel, but on the attempts to emend it one is inclined to agree with J. that "the verses produced by these processes are wretched." M. takes the bull by the horns and claims· that θανόντ' ἄθαπτον ὄντ', far from being "wretched" is to be hailed as "hallender Hinweis auf Antigones schmerzhaftesten Zustand, der sie zu ihrer Tat trieb." One of his grounds for emending is that θανόντ' ... νέκυν is impossible; "ὁ κατθανὼν νέκυς ist homerische Formel, in der aber die Worte nebeneinanderstehen müssen." But on this basis, he should have emended θανόντα Πολυνείκους νέκυν 26 as well. 471. M. retains Blaydes τὸ γοῦν λῆμ', on which cf. Denniston *GP*[2], p. 459 ("not very attractive"). 506-7 deleted (Jacob) since they "stören den Gedankengang unerträglich." But they complete the thought of 504-5; ἔξεστιν corresponds to ἀνδάνειν and λέγειν θ' ἃ βούλεται to γλῶσσαν ἐγκλήοι Φόβος—the *tyrannos* can say and do what he pleases precisely because the people's mouths are closed by fear. The train of thought is continuous; τοῦτο 508 can refer back to τοῦτο 504 without "den Satz 506-7 zu überspringen." 536. ὁμορροθῶ (Nauck). "Die Wortbedeutung passt nicht zum blossen Ausdruck des Einverständnisses, aber sehr gut zu dem des Mittuns." But cf. E., *Or.* 530 and H. Lloyd-Jones' defense of ὁμορροθεῖ in *Gnomon*, 28 [1956], p. 109. 551. γελῶ γ' (Heath), rightly. 662ff. The case for Seidler's transposition will not generally be thought to be much advanced by the statement that "gerade diese Wiederholung (i.e. ἀνήρ 661 τοῦτον τὸν ἄνδρα 668) ist erwünscht; dieser Mensch, Antigone, erfüllt die sittliche Pflicht in der Familie...." J.'s careful paraphrase of the MS order and Fraenkel's objection (on A., *A.* 883) that Seidler's rearrangement destroys the reference in 672 to 669 both speak eloquently for the transmitted order. 674. τ' ἐν μάχῃ δορός is not "korrupt"; it is Pearson's conjecture. M. reads συμμάχους with Reiske; μάχῃ δορός is assailed as a "leere Dublette" but see Fraenkel on A., *A.* 439 for abundant examples of this phrase in tragedy. H. Lloyd-Jones (*Gnomon*, 28 [1956], p. 109) defends the MSS reading σὺν μάχῃ. 690. No lacuna. M. rightly rejects Pearson's suggestion that both speeches should be exactly the same length. 703. εὐκλείᾳ (Johnson), rightly. 717. τὸ πλοῖον (Hermann). στρέψας needs an object, says M, but ναῦν can easily be supplied from 715 (J. and cf. Σ). τὸ λοιπόν of something impossible is a regular Sophoclean irony cf. 31, *O.T.* 1273, *Aj.* 666. 718. εἶκε, θυμοῦ (M.) is an improvement on Dain's εἶκε, θυμῷ which left μετάστασιν without the necessary genitive (for which cf. E., *Andr.* 1003, *Hec.* 1266, *Fr.* 554). 749. M. follows Bruhn in adopting Enger's transposition—749. 757. 756. 755. For this, as for Bellermann's (Donner's)—754. 757. 756. 755—no paleographical explanation is offered. The object of Enger's transposition is to put 755 (which M. considers "der schärfste Angriff Haimon's") immediately before 758. One of the main reasons offered for this is that 756 is "eine viel zu zahme Reaktion" to 755. But J. has explained the force of the word—"cajole"; it refers to Haemon's εἰ μὴ πατὴρ ἦσθ'. Creon means: "do not pretend that you have any of the feelings with which a son ought to regard a father." As for Haemon's "schärfste Angriff," I should have thought it was 751 (which Creon takes as threat to his life). The transposition destroys the rhetorical contrast between νερτέρων and ζῶσαν, which seems to have little point if it comes after 757. 782. λήμασι (Dindorf). But what is wrong with κτήμασι in the sense "riches, possessions"? ἐμπίπτειν says M. "bedeutet: siegreich in ein Land einbrechen, über es herfallen". Precisely; from time immemorial victorious armies loot, plunder, "fall on possessions" (cf. E., *Hipp.* 538 Ἔρωτα ... πέρθοντα). The military metaphor (ἀνίκατε μάχαν, ἐννυχεύεις) is uninterrupted. There is no question (as in M.'s objection) of Eros attacking the rich rather than the poor. There is no need to press the metaphor—"Whose possessions?"—just as no one, mercifully, treats literally the metaphor of Eros the warrior standing night watch in the cheeks of a young girl. 797ff. M.'s ἀργὸς for πάρεδρος (παρεργος L^{ac}) is a courageous attempt; it improves the meter, and derives some paleographical support from Thgn. 584 (ἔργα codd. ἀεργά or ἀργά edd.). It is supposed to mean "dass die Macht des ἵμερος sich dispensiert von den θεσμά." But the two parallels cited for "sich dispensiert," A., *Th.* 411 αἰσχρῶν ἀργός and E., *I.A.* 1000 ἀργὸς τῶν οἴκοθεν, though they are often loosely translated "free from" etc., mean "not doing"; the genitive with this word always denotes activity of some kind (Pl. *Lg.* 806a ταλασίας, ib. 835d πόνων σφοδρῶν, Thgn. 1177 ἔργων). The Aeschylean phrase is the closest parallel, but even this depends on the possibility of ἐργάζεσθαι αἰσχρά. No analogous possibility exists for ἀργὸς θεσμῶν. 851–52. M. adapts Emperius' conjecture to produce (hesitantly for once): e.g., δύσταν' <οὔτε τούτοισιν ἔτ' οὔτε κείνοις>. This surely is a case for the obelus. 856. A defense of πολὺ προσέπαισας (pp. 190–91) remains impressive even if M.'s search for "den gewünschten ambivalenten Sinn" is discounted. 870. τάφων (Morstadt) for γάμων. "Denn was soll hier die argivische Hochzeit des Bruders...?" It is perfectly at home in a recital of the woes of the Labdacids which begins with the marriage of Oedipus and Jocasta, continues with the fact that Antigone will die unmarried, and ends with the marriage of Polynices which had such fatal consequences (δυσπότμων)—it brought the Argive army to Thebes.

904–920. *seclusi* (Lehrs). It is not likely that anyone will change his mind about this passage unless some new arguments are advanced or some new evidence offered, for acceptance or rejection depends on (and affects) not only the interpretation of the play as a whole but also the view to be taken of the history of the tragic texts in the fourth century. I cannot see that M. has anything new to offer, and we might well have been spared the familiar quotation from Goethe. M. does give an interesting summary and classification of the views of those who have defended the lines, (though he should have mentioned Bowra's eloquent explication in *Sophoclean Tragedy*, pp. 93–96). M.'s attack (apart from his total rejection of the lines on theological grounds) takes the form of pushing to its logical limits the awkwardness involved in adapting the arguments of the wife of Intaphrenes for the situation of Antigone. "Man muss weiterhin fragen, welcher Logik denn der Entschluss folgen würde, Polyneikes unbestattet liegen zu lassen im Hinblick auf einen noch zu erhoffenden Bruder?" (198) is a good example of the technique. But the speech is not logical; it is an almost hysterically hyperbolic expression of her love for the brother who in death, as in life, has every man's hand against him; the references to husband and child are not to be understood as a logical scheme of values but as an evocation of that life as wife and mother which she has sacrificed in order to bury her brother's body. It is true that the syntax of 905–912 is not as clear and full as it might be, but that does not make it unique in Sophoclean verse. And in any case it is not as bad as M. claims.

904. The position of εὖ (which must be taken with 'τίμησα) is not necessarily an "Unklarheit"; see Henri Weil, *Etudes sur l'antiquité grecque* (Paris, 1900), p. 248, "le vers récité comme il convient est très clair, et Sophocle écrivait pour le théâtre." 907. βίᾳ πολιτῶν expresses the only estimate of the situation A. can possibly make at this stage; the chorus has condemned her action and she has not heard Haemon's claim (693ff.) that the polis applauds her. The fact that Ismene used the same phrase (79) seems to me an argument for rather than against its appearance here. 908. νόμου ... πρὸς χάριν is rejected because the phrase "erfordert ... eine Person als Gegenüber ... ," but M.'s rule has to be supported by his elimination of πρὸς χάριν βορᾶς (30) and his dismissal of E., *Med.* 538 πρὸς ἰσχύος χάριν. He seems to have overlooked P., *O.* 8.8. On the line as a whole, M. quotes with approval J.'s remark: "a certain tone of clumsy triumph strongly suggestive of the interpolator who bespeaks attention for his coming point." It is rather a typical rhetorical question which does indeed bespeak attention for the coming point, but it is by no means unique in Sophoclean rhetorical style; is it so different from *O.C.* 1308? 909. The fact that the genitive of πόσις (which must be understood with κατθανόντος) does not occur, seems to be an argument (along the lines of *lectio difficilior*) against rather than for interpolation; an interpolator would have been more likely to write ἀνήρ or ἀνδρός. 912. M. objects that οὐκ ἔστ' ... ὅστις = keiner can only, in good style, be used in the sense: "es gibt keinen, von dem die und die Aussage gälte" (he compares 1156). But cf. E., *Med.* 1339. 913. ἐκπροτιμᾶν like so many other Sophoclean verbs compounded with two prepositions, is a ἅπαξ λεγόμενον (cf. 218, 1202, *Aj.* 736, 922, *Tr.* 759, *Ph.* 668, 991, *O.C.* 1025, 1648). It does not suggest the hand of the interpolator.

929–30. αὐταὶ ψυχῆς omitted (Dindorf). With M.'s attribution of 933–34 to the chorus, this omission gives a neat metrical "Responsion" to the whole passage. But the words must stand. "Die metaphorischen ἀνέμων ῥιπαί können nicht ohne Schaden für den Stil im gleichen Satz erläutert werden" says M.: on the contrary, the phrase needs explanation, for the metaphorical use of ῥιπαί is paralleled (as far as I know) only by 137, where it is explained by ἐχθίσταις and ἐμπνέων. The attribution of 933–34 to the chorus is of course dictated by M.'s view of Antigone: "Im Munde Antigones wäre der Ausruf ... unwürdig. ... " But ταύτῃ 936 does not have to be referred to Antigone; M. dismisses J.'s "on this wise" but *Ph.* 1448 and *O.C.* 1300 speak eloquently for it. 966. πάρα (M.), which is supposed to stand for πάρεισιν. The construction is compared to the well-known type ἀκτή τις ἔστ' Εὐβοιὶς ἔνθ' ... But such formulas do not use πάρεστι, and the τις is regularly added; furthermore the subject is always singular, but here there are two subjects, one of them plural. 980. ἔχοντος (M.) for ἔχοντες. This is supposed to agree with ματρός. M. cites six tragic passages where a masculine participial form is used for feminine. But even if, after reading Barrett's critical review of these cases (on E., *Hipp.* 1102ff.) the reader still accepts E., *Hel.* 1630 (on which however see now A. M. Dale's edition) and A., *A.* 560 as genuine and not accounted for by construction κατὰ σύνεσιν there is still no instance anywhere near as violent as the agreement (and juxtaposition) of a masculine participle with that eminently feminine word ματρός. 1029. νουθετοῦντι (Wecklein), on the grounds that "τῷ θανόντι ist unerträglich neben artikellosem ὀλωλύτα." But νουθετοῦντι without an article is no better and in any case the text makes good sense; "surrender to the dead man" and "do not stab a corpse" are rhetorical variations of the same idea. 1080–1083. Omitted (Wunder) as "funktionslos in der Rede und im Stück" (M. rejects J.'s interpretation of τῶν ἐχθρῶν κακά 10). But J. gives a cogent defense of the relevance of these lines; cf. especially "the prophet ... having foretold a dramatic sorrow for the father ... now foreshadows a public danger for the king." Creon is to be a failure not only as a father but also as a statesman.

The length of this review is a tribute wrung from an unfavorable witness to the power of the attack which M. has launched against the accepted text and most of the current interpretations of the *Antigone*. Even those who reject his methods will still have to consult his commentary; there is hardly a passage in the play which from now on can be properly discussed without at least a reference to this immensely learned, brilliant, and infuriating book.

Notes

1. M. implies ("er irrt ... konsequent und das ist für den sophokleischen Chor überhaupt charakteristisch", 16) that this is a general principle of Sophoclean dramaturgy. Like the old view that the chorus always expressed the opinion of the poet, this is too rigid a rule to be true.

2. Only rarely does a possible Doppelsinn escape the imperatives of M.'s system; in such a case the possibility of ambiguity has to be denied. At 44, for example, ἀπόρρητον πόλει can perfectly well, grammatically speaking, mean "forbidden by the city" as well as "to" or "for." Here M. gives a ruling *ex cathedra*: the dative cannot be a dative of agent for "der Urheber ist zunächst und noch 47 Kreon."

3. "Dieser Kommentar ist entstanden aus dem Bemühen, alles, was man in den letzten Jahrzehnten über Sophokles' tragische Kunst hinzugelernt hat, in eine Überprüfung sämtlicher Diagnosen zum Text hineinzunehmen, die der Kommentar von Richard Jebb vor fast 80 Jahren gegeben hat" (7).

FOURTEEN

Review

*SOPHOCLE, POETE TRAGIQUE. By Gilberte Ronnet. Paris, Editions E.
de Boccard, 1969.*

From the general renewal of interest in Sophoclean tragedy which
followed the First World War and which shows no signs of losing its
momentum, France, as the author remarks in her preface, has remained
somewhat apart; the reappraisal of the Sophoclean tragic view has been
carried on mainly in German, English, and Italian. Ronnet's book "has
no other purpose than to acquaint French-speaking students with this
fermentation of ideas expressed in foreign languages" (p. ix)—an
overmodest assessment, for her running dialogue with Adams, Bowra,
Kirkwood, Kitto, and Maddalena (to name only the most frequently
cited critics) is a byproduct of her own original discussion of the nature
of Sophoclean tragedy.

The most striking feature of her presentation is the division of the
seven plays into two groups. The first (*Tr.*, *Ajax*, *Ant.*, *O.T.*) is the
product of Sophocles' maturity; it consists of plays that are structurally
similar and present a fully tragic vision of the world. These plays are
studied together from different viewpoints in separate chapters "Dramatic Structure," "Characters," "Chorus," "Destiny and the Gods."
The other three plays, the work of Sophocles' old age, depart from the
formula of the first group ("the partly voluntary annihilation of a
superior being before the eyes of an uncomprehending crowd," p. 314)
to present an action no longer subordinate to the will of the hero, who
now does not have to make the tragic choice between death and
dishonor but on the contrary finds, in the denouement, satisfaction (p.
315). The differences between the two groups of plays are so great that
we are led "to consider two different Sophocles, one after the other" (p.
333).

Such a view of Sophoclean *évolution* owes something to Whitman
and the development of Whitman's ideas by Torrance in his brilliant
article in *HSCP*, LXIX (1965). But Ronnet's presentation of "deux

This chapter originally appeared in the *American Journal of Philology*, 92, no. 4 (1971).
© 1971 by The Johns Hopkins Press. Reprinted by permission of the *Journal*.

Sophocles" is elaborated in full detail and with logical consistency. The first Sophocles (age thirty to sixty) is the incarnation of the Periclean spirit; he is a democrat, hostile to Sparta, a lover of liberty, but also, like Pericles, an "aristocrat" in the moral sense of the word. His heroes are "l'homme supérieur" who exists in a "univers moral hiérarchisé" which corresponds to the spirit of Periclean democracy—"une hiérarchie des honneurs et des pouvoirs fondée sur le mérite" (p. 335). This Sophocles shares with Pericles his "foi en l'homme"; the greatness of man, however, consists, for Sophocles, not in his martial prowess or his capacity for technical progress but in his free decision, in the face of suffering and death, to remain faithful to his ideal, be it honor, love, or truth. The gods, who face the hero with this choice, are either indifferent or hostile; Sophocles, by his humanism, turns against the religious thought of the preceding generation, as we see it in Aeschylus.

Sophocles II is a very old man who has "survived his century." He is still a democrat in the depths of his heart, but Periclean democracy has vanished forever, and the Theseus of the *Oedipus at Colonus* is a mere nostalgic image of a glorious past. In the Athens of the last years of the war, Sophocles began to represent men "as they are": the adversaries of the hero are now disloyal, with a taste for lies, whereas before they had been brutal, but frank; the heroes themselves are "violent, vindictive, pitiless"—"beings not devoid of nobility, but embittered, full of hate, stained with cruelty" (p. 338). "It seems as if the poet has lost his confidence in what the Pericles of Thucydides calls the 'nobility of soul' [τὸ εὔψυχον, II, 39, 1] of the Athenians and, consequently, his faith in human nature." In compensation he takes a more confident view of life, writing not tragedies but plays which, with their "happy end [sic]," are a lesson of hope; the mood is one of measured optimism founded on the feeling that undeserved suffering cannot last forever. The gods are no longer cruel or indifferent; one can even speak of a certain benevolence on their part.

There is obviously some truth in this view (which I have tried to summarize without distortion); everyone feels that there is a difference between, for example, the *Ajax* and the *Philoctetes*. And Ronnet has pointed out an interesting structural difference between the two groups: in the later plays "l'action n'est plus subordonnée à la volonté du héros." The active character in *Electra* is Orestes, in *Philoctetes*, Neoptolemus; in the *Oedipus at Colonus* all the characters are in action around the unmoving old man who waits for the fulfillment of the oracles and contributes to it only by his very immobility (p. 314). This is a valuable observation and its further extension—that in the early plays the tragic situation destroys a past which was happy or at least tolerable, whereas in the late plays the heroes are marked by a long past of undeserved suffering—is slightly less valuable only because Deianira (in spite of Ronnet's "entourée d'estime au milieu de ses enfants," p. 317) could on this score be classed with the later rather than the earlier plays.

But the sharp and systematic differentiation between the four "tragedies" and the later plays, one which Ronnet extracts from a detailed consideration of all their aspects, depends on interpretations which are in many cases controversial. The *Electra*, for example, can be assigned to the second group under the rubric "happy end" only by claiming firmly that its theme is not the punishment of Agamemnon's murderers but the "liberation" of Electra. Ronnet quotes Waldock approvingly: "not only are the Erinyes not lurking; they are not on the visible horizon." But they do not need to be. In any Athenian dramatization of the Orestes story, their intervention was so taken for granted by the audience that it had to be explicitly denied if it was not to be assumed; the reason for this is not the authority of the *Oresteia* (still less the "recent revival" of it which so many critics, with no evidence whatsoever, accept as proved) but the fact that Orestes' flight to Athens was firmly based in local Athenian cult. Every member of the audience took part once a year in the festival of the Choes (a month or so before the Dionysia) and knew that the official explanation of its ritual was the presence in Athens long ago of Orestes, a polluted murderer, seeking judgment and absolution. For Sophocles' audience, a hint of the consequences of his action was enough and Sophocles had given hints aplenty. Ronnet (following Bowra) refuses to admit that Aegisthus' double-edged remark (1498) can refer to anything besides Aegisthus' own impending death (but then what is the point of Orestes' γοῦν in his reply?); she dismisses (with Maddalena) the ambiguity of the repeated καλά in 1425 (in spite of the fact that it is a striking echo of the sinister word-play on καλῶς in 790–93); and she sees no significance in the correspondence between Clytemnestra's prayer for the death of her enemy (637) and Electra's prayer to the same god for the same blessing (on which see C. P. Segal, "The *Electra* of Sophocles," *TAPA*, XCVII, [1966] 525).

But if the *Electra* is made too cheerful ("le 'message' de Sophocle ... est essentiellement pratique: quelles que soient les circonstances, il ne faut jamais désespérer," p. 236), the *Trachiniae* (as a play by Sophocles I) is made unnecessarily grim. Ronnet denies that there is any hint in the text of Heracles' imminent deification on Mount Oeta. It is of course true that Heracles in the play has no foreknowledge of this development (as is clear from νέρθεν, 1202), but Bowra has pointed out that his elaborate directions for the building of the pyre (1159 ff.) must have reminded the audience of that final scene of the Heracles saga, so familiar from the vase paintings of the sixth century on.

There is another feature of the dialogue between Hyllus and Heracles which points even more firmly in the same direction.[1] Heracles, after extracting an oath of obedience from a reluctant Hyllus, orders him to build the pyre, place his father's body on it, and then fire it. When Hyllus refuses to carry out the culminating action, Heracles merely reassures himself that Hyllus will at least build the pyre and declares himself content with that (ἀρκέσει καὶ ταῦτα, 1216). And not a word more is said about who will set it alight. Here the familiar doctrine, so often invoked in Sophoclean criticism, that everything we need to know is contained in the text of the play, breaks down in spectacular fashion. If the audience is not supposed to know already who *did* put the torch to the pyre, Sophocles is at best an incompetent bungler, for he has raised the question in most emphatic terms. But of course he is not, and of course the audience knew that Philoctetes did it, receiving the bow and arrows as his reward—and this is all part of the story of Heracles' ascent to Olympus.

In the treatment of the characters, Ronnet makes a clear distinction between early and late. The heroes of phase 2 are distinguished by their "dureté égoiste" from those of phase 1 with their "généreuse abnégation" (p. 318). Oedipus at Colonus is a "vieillard aigri et haineux" (p. 306); Philoctetes is the victim of "une obstination aveugle, fondée à la fois sur un faux orgueil et sur la peur" (p. 258); Electra is "obsédée par la haine" (p. 223). But Ajax, Antigone, Deianira, and Oedipus Tyrannus "incarnent . . . ce qu'on pourrait appeler l'homme idéal, en tout cas, un type d'homme supérieur qui suscite l'admiration" (p. 314). Needless to say, this thesis is maintained in its entirety only by Procrustean operations; one example will suffice. "Jamais," says Ronnet, speaking of Oedipus' curse on Polynices, "Sophocle n'avait décrit un tel paroxysme de haine et de cruauté" (p. 301). She seems to have forgotten Ajax, who in his last speech calls on the Erinyes not only to destroy the Atridae but also (in a phrase which foreshadows Oedipus' prophecy that his corpse will drink Theban blood) to "feed on (γεύεσθε) the whole army, all its people." Ronnet, in her summary of this scene (pp. 33–34), omits this ferocious curse, but Jebb, comparing the two passages (*Ajax*, p. xxxix), finds Oedipus' imprecations "appalling" but Ajax' "vindictiveness . . . monstrous." Whatever attitude one takes towards these examples of heroic rage, it seems idle to deny that they come from the same mold.

Ronnet's handling of Heracles shows signs of a similar distortion which derives, partly at any rate, from the imperatives of her thesis. According to this, the hero in early Sophocles is posed (except in the case of the *Oedipus Tyrannus*) against his enemies, the cause of his misfortune—the Atridae, Creon, Heracles. "Placing Heracles on the same plane as the Atridae and Creon," Ronnet admits frankly, "logically leads us into the camp of those who see the basis of his character as a monstrous selfishness" (p. 94). It does indeed. Heracles "n'est qu'une brute," "inhumain," "monstrueux," a "grossier personnage": his fall is due to "l'*hubris* de toute une existence livrée aux débordements de la violence et de l'instinct." But if Heracles is no more than this, the play presents us with an implausible situation; how could Deianira love such a man so passionately—"the best of all men" she calls him—that she would have recourse, in spite of misgivings, to a love philter to win him back? Ronnet's presentation gives no impression of the powerful effect of the last scene of the play. The actions of Heracles which have led to the catastrophe certainly deserve her harsh comments, but the last moments of Heracles on stage show us the superhuman strength of will, the irresistible energy that had enabled the hero to perform his famous labors. "Il ne fait que subir, . . . " says Ronnet; but in fact, once he has recognized the fulfillment of the prophecy, he turns from lamentations and thoughts of vengeance to imperious action, as he forces on a reluctant Hyllus not only the building of his funeral pyre but also the marriage with Iole and then gives his marching orders to the funeral procession which is to place his still living body, racked with pain, on the pyre. Ronnet makes an excellent case for claiming that Deianira is the "hero" of the play, but there is no need to deny Heracles heroic stature—he is obviously cut from the same cloth as Ajax and old Oedipus.

It will perhaps be obvious by this point that Ronnet is prone to psychological analysis of a type which has in recent years been viewed with increasing skepticism. She is inclined to create out of bare dramatic hints fully developed personalities with psychological histories and this sometimes, especially in the case of minor characters, gets out of hand. Haemon, for example, in the *Antigone*, is found to be:

> not just the lover who refuses to survive his love; he is also, perhaps above all, the son who discovers the unworthiness of his father and for whom the whole moral universe in which he had lived up to now collapses suddenly—filial piety, justice, piety towards the gods, all the values which formed a harmonious whole in which his love was framed are now torn apart by Creon's action. Haemon staggers under the shock of his discovery; the condemnation of Antigone is more than a wound for the lover, it is the symbol of this shattered world which opens up before him and which he instinctively refuses ... when he breaks with his father, shouting to him—ambiguous phrase—that he will never see his face again, Haemon says "No" to what his life used to be but also to Life [mais aussi à la Vie, 84].

This seems clearly out of proportion to Haemon's one scene in which most of what he says to his father is general rather than personal; I have cited it (well, most of it) because it is used later to buttress a suggested explanation of a familiar enigma of the *Antigone*—what on earth went on in that tomb? "Le récit du messager n'est pas clair." How did Haemon get in there? "Ne pourrait-on comprendre qu'Hémon, comme Aïda dans l'opéra de Verdi, s'est introduit secrètement dans le tombeau, avant qu'on y amène Antigone, pour y mourir avec elle?" (p. 85). The dazzled reader naturally begins to imagine them singing "O terra addio, addio valle di pianti, ... " but Ronnet's next sentence shows that the suggestion is serious. "Une telle décision serait l'aboutissement logique de l'état d'âme que nous venons d'analyser."[2]

A similar emphasis on psychology also pervades the treatment of the chorus. It is not the "porte-parole du poète" but "must be studied as a collective personality, its character analyzed and its place in the architecture of the play determined." Such a study is "en grande partie psychologique" (p. 134). The difficulties that arise from such an approach become clear at once, as the author proceeds to discuss the chorus of the *Trachiniae*. It is composed of young girls, sympathetic to Deianira, able to comfort her but too young and inexperienced to advise her. But by the second stasimon the chorus has already stepped out of character. "Par une inadvertance du poète, le choeur, un court instant, perd sa personnalité." But this is not the only "inadvertance du poète" in his presumed use of the chorus as a "personnage collectif"; another has to be pointed out in the note on page 135. And in the last stasimon of the play, the chorus "does not reveal its feelings," the ode "is of an extreme banality and is merely a transition which allows us to await the arrival of Heracles" (p. 140). Things are no better in the *Antigone*: its stasima "risquent à chaque instant d'apparaître comme de simples intermèdes entre deux épisodes," the last one, in particular, with its "vide absolu de pensée et de sentiment" is an "entr'acte en musique." It begins to look as if the principle that the chorus in Sophocles "est toujours un personnage, plus ou moins lié au héros, plus ou moins intéressé à l'action, mais réagissant en fonction de son caractère et de sa situation" (p. 167) is, like so many generalizations about the Sophoclean chorus, another of those literary canons which critics persist in extracting from their author's text and proclaiming to the world, only to have to admit, more in sorrow than in anger (and usually, unlike Ronnet, in a footnote) that the benighted author, on more than one occasion, failed miserably to live up to his own standards.

When the chorus does not seem to be reacting "en fonction de son caractère," Ronnet has unkind words for its efforts (*banalité, médiocrité de pensée*, etc.); but where (according to her) it *does*, we are presented with some novel psychological insights. That same chorus of Trachiniae, for example, comes in for some harsh criticism. Their reaction to the true story of Iole's arrival (the second stasimon) "has no word of pity for the betrayed wife or blame for the unfaithful husband." This can be explained only by their "youth and naïveté." They sing about the struggle between Heracles and Achelous for the hand of the young Deianira; it is "the terrified meditation of young girls discovering to what excesses men are led by sensuality." This is buttressed by the speculation that "perhaps in their heart of hearts they are more sensitive to the misfortune of Iole, who was, like them, a young girl, than to that of the rejected wife." Later on, after Hyllus' tirade against his mother, they keep silence; and yet, according to Ronnet, this would have been the moment to inform the young man of his mother's innocent intentions. "So the chorus abandons Deianira to her death, at the moment when it could have saved her." But how could it have saved her? And for what? We realize later that she was lucky not to fall into Heracles' hands alive. This is a nonexistent issue if ever there was one, but Ronnet feels called upon to explain their omission. It is due "not to lack of sympathy, but because the chorus is disoriented by the swiftness of events and their failure to understand the heroine's thoughts. Psychologically this passivity is not implausible—they are young girls" (p. 138). Later, they fail to understand Deianira's motive for suicide "which they condemn by calling it hubris"; but surely Jebb is right to point out that this means merely "violent deed." Later still, "as if they felt resentment towards the dead woman, they refrain from defending her memory; it is at the very moment when Heracles hurls the fiercest threats at his wife that they begin to lament the fate of 'this hero.'" They are "unfaithful friends," who "at the testing time reveal their mediocrity" (p. 140). Needless to say, their final remarks about Zeus do not have to be taken seriously. "Nothing, as we have seen, gives the chorus the authority necessary to express a philosophy. Composed of inexperienced girls, its reactions are limited by the bounds of its intelligence and sensitivity...."

These are typical results of Ronnet's insistence that the chorus always reacts in function of its character (except where the poet obviously let the side down). But why this passion for uniformity? It seems much more sensible to suppose that Sophocles was as flexible in his use of the chorus as he was in his subtle handling of meter, that he used whatever means or mode was appropriate to the dramatic situation. He could indeed create a choral character that was consistent in its every utterance, lyric or iambic—he did so in *Philoctetes*; but in other plays, and especially in *Trachiniae* and *Antigone*, he used the chorus sometimes in this way and sometimes with little regard for its "character" (or none at all), to illuminate the action by suggesting new perspectives or recalling mythical background, to prepare the audience for a change of emphasis or direction, to lull it into a false sense of security before the catastrophe. Certainly he tried to "characterize" his chorus, but it was always (unlike the Erinyes or Hiketides of Aeschylus) a minor character and one he was prepared to sacrifice for an important effect. When, to take one of Ronnet's problems, the chorus of young girls who have so far been sympathetic to Deianira, weep for Heracles as if they had never known his wife, they do so because Sophocles wants the audience to think now not of Deianira's innocence but of the greatness of the dying hero and, quite clearly, he was not at all worried that the audience would concern itself with what had happened to the "character" of the chorus.

"Destiny and the Gods" is the fourth of the rubrics under which the plays are considered, and here, as in the matter of structure and character, Ronnet finds a difference between the mature Sophocles and the old man who wrote the last plays. The gods of the early plays are no comforting pantheon. Zeus in the *Trachiniae* shows an "injuste indifférence"—"in this drama in which everyone speaks of his power, he seems as passive and remote as the gods of Epicurus will be in their *intermundia*" (p. 177). Athena in the *Ajax* is vindictive and cruel; she detests in Ajax the man who invited her to take her encouragement elsewhere ("C'est la réaction d'une coquette, blessée de voir ses avances repoussées"). She has "an incredible contempt for men"; in fact, Ronnet compares her to the Zeus of the *Prometheus Bound*. In the *Antigone* the gods are like Zeus in the *Trachiniae*—remote and indifferent, without pity for human suffering. Apollo in the *Oedipus Tyrannus* is like Athena in the *Ajax*, only worse: "a divinity who plays a game with a good man, has him unconsciously commit a crime and then amuses himself by having him discover it...." Small wonder that the discussion of the role of the divine in this play ends with the words: "le pessimisme est maintenant total" (p. 198). "Faut-il alors voir dans ces quatre tragédies une sorte de procès des dieux?" Ronnet asks, but finds that to seek to justify or condemn "the gods" is not the right way to formulate the problem, for the gods "are forces which are at play in the course of events ... their cruelty, their injustice signify that life can be cruel and unjust" (p. 204).

In the last three plays, things are slightly less desperate, but this seems to have little to do with the gods. In the *Electra* "the gods are as far-off as in the *Trachiniae*" but "life is not as cruel as it appeared in the preceding plays." In the *Philoctetes*, Heracles brings about a happy conclusion, but he does not act in the name of the gods (who remain "remote and indifferent"); he is moved by friendship alone (p. 274). The *Oedipus at Colonus* gives Ronnet some awkward moments, but the gods are finally cut down to size, though it has to be admitted that in the matter of the heroization of Oedipus "Sophocle fait appel aux croyances les plus antiques ... aux formes les plus primitives de la religion." But this, it appears, is not to be taken at face value: "n'y a-t-il pas un sens caché?" Of course there is. "Si, pour la première fois dans son théâtre, le poète déchaîne sur la scène les prestiges du surnaturel, le foudre de Zeus et le tonnerre de Hadès, ce n'est pas pour saluer l'élévation d'un homme au ciel, mais pour célébrer l'élection divine d'Athènes" (p. 312). The difference between early and late presentation of the gods is after all negligible. "If in the later plays the gods appear more benevolent" they are still "little more than the symbols of everything in the world that is independent of the human will, the order (or disorder?) of things. ... The punishment of the guilty no longer involves the ruin of the innocent ... the poet deliberately chooses subjects in which the course of events stops at a fortunate moment" (p. 341).

Even those who feel, with Ronnet, that "on a peine à imaginer qu'un Sophocle ait partagé avec les plus humbles de ses contemporains ces antiques croyances" will view with dismay the arguments which are used to make the case for this secular Sophocles and his metaphorical gods. Quite apart from the sleight of hand which tries to reduce to purely human terms the intervention of Heracles in the *Philoctetes* and the diversion of the religious element in the *Oedipus at Colonus* to the political sphere, Ronnet's treatment neglects the importance of those divine oracles which, in play after play, frame the action and are always fulfilled. In the case of the *Oedipus Tyrannus*, where they cannot be neglected, she takes the bull by the horns and speculates that the play may express the irritation of the Athenians with the Delphic oracle because of its support of Sparta in 432; "in a deliberately ambiguous manner, Sophocles would in this case be taking a stand against belief in oracles and against the institution which seemed likely to injure Athens in the great adventure in which it was about to engage" (p. 330).

The final chapter ("Conclusions") has been cited often in the course of this review for general statements summarizing the argument; it also contains an attempt to establish the dates of the four plays for which there is no external evidence. The method proposed is based on the discovery of contemporary references in the text. Ronnet points out such references in the dated plays: Creon in the *Oedipus at Colonus* and Odysseus in the *Philoctetes* ("if one admits that he is the son of Sisyphus, therefore a Corinthian") both typify cities the Athenians had reason to hate at the time of production, and the *Antigone* seems to her to echo the arguments of the political struggle between Pericles and Thucydides, son of Melesias. Two "methods" are therefore available for tackling the undated plays. Either one can try to locate, by reference to foreign policy, the moment at which Athens found itself on bad terms with the people represented by the unpleasant character of the play, or one can utilize what we know of the political and intellectual battles in Athens to see what confrontations the play can bear witness to (p. 323).

This is a bad start, but the end is worse. The "personnage antipathique" of the *Trachiniae* is of course Heracles. He is a Theban hero, but since Thebes was always hostile to Athens the "method" offers no precise information. However there was another place for which Heracles was a protecting deity—Thasos; he had a temple there and was figured on its coins. Thasos revolted from the Athenian alliance in 465 and was finally reduced to subjection in 463 by Cimon. The *Trachiniae* "composed about 464–2 is near in date to Sophocles' first production *Triptolemos* (468).... That celebration of the civilizing Athenian hero is balanced by the presentation of the 'prétendu héros dorien ... comme un homme égoiste et bestial.' " The *Trachiniae* is a "sort of cultural manifesto, the work of a poet still young, who expresses the thought of the new generation and takes issue with the Dorian ideal of the archaic age" (p. 224).

The other dates suggested are based on similar fantasies. *Ajax* is connected with the suicide of Themistocles (the date of that event of course is not known, but Ronnet puts it in 456). "Le pièce n'a-t-elle pas l'air d'une demande de réhabilitation de Thémistocle?" Well ... no. If one could ask a typical group of fifth-century Athenians what mythical type they associated with Themistocles, I suspect that his enemies would plump for Thersites or Sisyphus and his friends would claim Odysseus, but surely no one in this world or the next could think of Themistocles, son of Neocles, as Ajax, son of Telamon. *Electra* (following a suggestion of L. A. Post) is assigned to 411 or 410; it celebrates the "liberation" of Electra from her oppressors and so refers to the overthrow of the 400. Orestes is presumably Theramenes and Aegisthus Antiphon or Phrynichus. Surprisingly enough, the one contemporary reference in Sophoclean tragedy which can be taken seriously, even by those who do not accept it (the plague in the *Oedipus Tyrannus*), is rejected by Ronnet in favor of the fact that the hero's enemy in the play is Apollo and so the play is dated to a time when Athens felt angry at Delphi, that is to say 431. It so happens that this is one of the few years in which it can be said with confidence that the *Oedipus Tyrannus* was *not* produced, for we know that in that year Sophocles came second in the competition after Euphorion and we also know that when he produced the *Oedipus* he was beaten by Philocles.

Like many French books, this one has no index, but an analytical table of contents is of some help for reference. Misprints are few, but the reader may be confused by "d'Ulysse" (p. 39), which should read "d'Ajax," and "Crotoniates" for "Coloniates" (p. 291). On page 13, something seems to have gone wrong with the syntax of the third sentence—perhaps the printer omitted a line—and the quotation from Sainte-Beuve on page 7 should, I suspect, read "Je sais" rather than "Je suis." There are also one or two slips on the part of the author that should be corrected. It is not true that (p. 157) nowhere in the *Oedipus Tyrannus* are we told that the chorus consists of old men; they are addressed as *presbeis* by Oedipus in v. 1111. It is not true that Creon makes two appearances in the play (p. 76); he makes three entrances—Ronnet overlooks the prologue.

This review has concentrated on the main argument in an attempt to expose its weak points; it is only fair to conclude by saying that Ronnet's book is fresh, stimulating, and provocative throughout, and that its lively prose and logical presentation make it a pleasure to read.

Notes

1. For this argument I am indebted to a lecture given by Prof. Hugh Lloyd-Jones; it can now be consulted in his book, *The Justice of Zeus* (Berkeley and Los Angeles, 1971), p. 127.

2. Haemon's presence in the tomb before Antigone gets there leads to the gruesome suggestion that "Hémon aurait alors aidé Antigone à se pendre...." How *do* you help your love to hang herself?

FIFTEEN

Review

SOPHOCLES: A READING. By G. H. Gellie. Melbourne University Press, 1972.

Gellie writes for "scholars, undergraduates and senior school-children as well as the people who are interested in the active theatre" but addresses himself "most of the time" to "the growing group of undergraduates who know no Greek but want to read Greek plays" (p. vii). This group is admirably served—Gellie writes with clarity and wit—but scholars too will find much to reckon with in this incisive survey of the Sophoclean tragedies. The first half of the book examines "the way in which each speech, scene or ode ... makes its contribution to the play as a whole," taking plays in chronological order of production (*Trachiniae* between *Antigone* and *O.T.*). The second half contains chapters on plot, character, chorus, gods, and poetry; it "takes soundings from all the plays on a range of topics" and tries "to plot the directions in which a dramatist has moved over the course of his writing career." Nineteen pages of notes deal with controversial points and the views of other scholars; a full bibliography (eight pages) lists books and articles referred to in the text and notes.

The standpoint from which Gellie analyzes the plays is almost exclusively that of dramatic effect; he tries always to imagine himself in the place of the working dramatist, with problems of theatrical economy paramount in his mind. He is clearly much influenced by H. D. F. Kitto (a debt he acknowledges freely) and of course by the pioneering study of Tycho von Wilamowitz. His preoccupation with dramaturgical imperatives is clear from the frequency of such phrases as "the needs of the play," "the way the plays must work," "at this point the play badly needs an injection of new material," and (an almost metaphysical concept) "Jocasta is being used by the play."

For his purpose, a reading of the plays for a modern audience unschooled in the Greek language and unacquainted with the religious and social background of the plays, this is of course the right (and probably the only) way to begin. But though Gellie pays little attention

This chapter originally appeared in *Antichthon*, 7 (1973). Reprinted by permission.

to the historical circumstances (the references to contemporary politics in his discussion of *Philoctetes* stand out as a rare exception), his analysis of the dramaturgical problems leads in every case to an intelligent and suggestive discussion of the moral and religious issues posed by the plays. Nor are these two separate spheres; the shape of the play is seen as an essential element of the statement the play is making or the question it poses. The result is a reading of the plays which is sensitive, often enlightening, always interesting, but which is also at times limited by the basic criterion with which Gellie is working. It is with these limitations that this review is concerned.

It is to be expected that criticism which emphasizes theatrical imperatives will regard with suspicion elaborate analysis of character, especially if it seeks overall psychological consistency. In this Gellie is of course in very good company, and such a reaction was desirable, even necessary, against the nineteenth-century predilection for carefully constructed life histories, in Shakespeare as in Greek drama. The reaction went too far (Zürcher, for example, claimed that "for Sophocles the conception of a genuine 'character' is from the point of view of intellectual history [*aus geistesgeschichtlichen Gründen*] quite impossible"), and the concern of most critics now working in this area is to find formulas which will fit the undeniable fact that Sophoclean drama is based on impressive individual personalities into the context of the rudimentary psychology of the fifth century, the operation of divinity in human life, and the strangeness of the dramatic structures in which those personalities are displayed in action. Gellie makes a notable contribution to this discussion. He distinguishes between the earlier and the later Sophoclean plays; in *O.C.*, *Philoctetes*, and *Electra*, "character is now being used for cause and justification," whereas in *Ajax*, *O.T.*, *Trachiniae*, and *Antigone* the characters are "different because their stories are different . . . the differences between them lie not so much in personality differences as in the different things they do . . . " (p. 209). Gellie illustrates this point with a fascinating comparison—the reclining "Dionysus" figure on the Parthenon pediment. Why is he reclining? "A number of reasons can be supplied . . . people recline when they are tired, when they have fallen over. . . . But if we fasten on any one of these reasons and say that Dionysus' tiredness is important for our interpretation of the pediment, that interpretation may be a strange one. We know perfectly well that the real reason for his reclining is the fact that he is in a corner of a pediment" (p. 212). This is a brilliant analogy, and Gellie's development of it should be read in his own words; it is too long to quote here. (The fact that he uses it specifically to explain a "problem" in Sophocles' presentation of Antigone which does not seem to me to be a problem at all does not detract from the value of his insight.) And yet, cogent as it is, it needs qualification.

The story (and this is the pediment—Eteocles in the *Seven* "is killed by the shape of his myth," p. 206) is never as rigidly demanding as the architectural form. Antigone did not have to die (she survived in Euripides' version) and Jocasta did not have to hang herself (she is still alive in Euripides' *Phoenissae*). If the dramatist is indeed working in a pediment frame, he does not have to put his figure in the corner but may move him to the center, where there is more freedom of movement.

The point Gellie is making (the subordination of character to *praxis*—to use John Jones's terms) is buttressed by a reference—to Aeschylus, who does not blunt his point by building up the personality of Orestes. Such a development might have tempted us to wonder whether Orestes was killing his mother because he had been an unhappy child, because he idolized his father, or because he was ambitious to rule in Argos. But leave him without a definite character and there can be only one reason for the killing of his mother: the "senseless shape of things" (p. 208). This is oversimplification, however; Aeschylus has Orestes tell us why he kills his mother—not the "senseless shape of things" but (*Cho.* 300–301) "the god's commands, the great sorrow for my father and the pressure of lack of money" (i.e., "his ambition to rule in Argos").

For a student who reads the plays in translation the main difficulty, as Gellie is aware, is the chorus. His chapter on the subject will be very helpful to his readers; his analysis of the many different uses to which Sophocles puts this relentlessly undramatic feature of the tragic festival is full of perceptive remarks. He is (quite rightly) averse to seeing in the choral odes the "judicial voice of the poet" (p. 225) and though he points out that in *Ajax*, *Antigone*, and *O.T.* the "public dimension" of the chorus enables it "to take on an identity", even a "character" (p. 241), he warns against overestimating their contribution to the play. "Their gnomic utterance is an expression of time-honoured truth, the best thinking yet achieved before an Antigone or an Oedipus has carried forward the moral boundary" (p. 242). This is an admirable statement, but in practice Gellie is much harsher in his judgment of choral poetry than this balanced phrase would suggest. The last stasimon of *O.T.*, for example, is not the final word about the meaning of Oedipus' fall (as the last scene shows), but it cannot be dismissed with phrases like "the cliches of Greek pessimism ... the best aid to digestion" (p. 99). And the great second stasimon of the *Antigone* (which Gellie rightly recognizes as an "Ode to Man which opens on a note of guarded admiration," p. 36) cannot be justly characterized as "a piece of conventional good sense" (p. 243).

Gellie is conscious that in the body of the book he has had to write as if the plays (to quote Lattimore) "were written in plain prose." In a final chapter, he gives us a careful analysis of his own literal translation of one iambic and one choral passage, which are first-class demonstrations of what can be achieved by close *explication de texte* in this unlikely medium. But he lays too much stress on the simplicity of Sophocles' language in the dialogue passages. He begins by quoting Earp, "who found only one simile and seventeen metaphors in the 1,530 lines of *Oedipus the King.*" But Earp's figures refer only to dialogue, not the whole play, and in any case he is a short-sighted guide in this territory—he does not see anything metaphorical in lines 4, 24, 45, 67, 73, 109, 111, 121, or 138 (to take only the prologue).

SIXTEEN

Review

SOPHOCLES, WOMEN OF TRACHIS. Translated by C. K. Williams and
Gregory W. Dickerson. Oxford University Press, 1978.

SOPHOCLES, OEDIPUS THE KING. Translated by Steven Berg and
Diskin Clay. Oxford University Press, 1978.

With the publication of these two volumes, the Oxford series *Greek
Tragedy in New Translation* is roughly one-third of the way along its
course: eleven down, twenty-one to go. It is a distinguished enterprise;
on the whole, the translators have amply satisfied the demand of the
general editor, William Arrowsmith, for "language, rich and vivid as
poetry," which "is equally effective as dialogue actors can speak,
naturally and with dignity." The project has even higher ambitions: "Its
aim is to re-create the entire extant corpus of Greek tragedy as though
it had been originally written by ancient masters at home in the English
language of our time." This is a job for poets, and though there are a
surprising number of Greek scholars who are also published poets (six
of the eleven translations have only one name on the title page) the
work often has to be done, as in the case of the two Sophoclean
tragedies under review, by a poet in collaboration with a scholar.

Such collaboration is not necessarily a matter of sweetness and
light. That there were impediments to the marriage of true minds in the
Williams-Dickerson team is admitted by Mr. Arrowsmith in his foreword, which explores in eloquent terms the problems presented by such
an operation—"like marriage, tandem translation is a tricky, even risky
business"—and it is an open secret that the honeymoon in the Berg-
Clay ménage was short. The poet, intent on creating dramatic poetry in
his own idiom, will tend to follow his muse where she leads; the
scholar, anxious trustee of the ancient legacy and apprehensive of the
judgment of his colleagues, will try to restrain the poet's more erratic
flights. From this tension (present also but perhaps less violent in the
mind of the scholar-poet) Mr. Arrowsmith hopes to see emerge what he
claims to have found in the Williams-Dickerson *Women of Trachis*:
"hard-won unity, as real as it is precarious, in which it is possible to feel

both the turbulence of the original and the poet's final successful effort to bring that turbulence under firm artistic control." For these two translations, Mr. Arrowsmith's claim is only partly justified. Though both are phrased in vivid and forceful English and run trippingly upon the tongue (in the actors' dialogue, at any rate; the choral odes are another matter), they have their failures too, and some of them stem from what looks remarkably like a lack of firm control.

It must be conceded that the problems facing a translator of Greek tragedy are numerous and formidable, especially formidable when the poet is Sophocles. His dramatic style, pitched midway between the opulence of Aeschylean imagery and the comparative sobriety of Euripidean rhetoric, can conjure out of highly formal language the illusion of passionate, unpremeditated speech; it can also invest a simple statement with reverberating ironies as well as a characteristic grave music. In addition, the tragic genre itself presents sobering challenges. The spoken sections of the play are encased in lines which are metrically as inexorably regular as the Alexandrines of Racine (by comparison, Shakespeare is a maverick), and extended passages of dramatic dialogue consist of line-for-line exchanges. The sections which were sung (some of them, the choral odes, were also danced) are framed in rhythmic structures of an intricate exactness which is completely alien to the genius of English verse.

C. K. Williams's attack on the first of these problems, the style of Sophoclean dialogue, is to sacrifice everything else for speed and directness; his speakers are no-nonsense characters whose language rarely rises above the level of the prosaic and the colloquial. As a result he is at his best in the speeches of the interfering messenger, the lying herald, and above all the brutal dying Heracles, whose paroxysms of rage and agony, modulating to a tone of otherworldly authority when he finally accepts his destiny, are successfully brought over into English. But Mr. Williams's Deianira lacks the radiance Sophocles has given to so many of her lines. "I'm afraid / " she says, "to say how much I miss him / until I'm sure it's the same there." This is an honest translation, but no one could guess from it what exquisite cadences haunt the three lines of Greek it represents and how subtly the Greek words suggest passion and reticence combined.

Steven Berg is more ambitious; his dialogue, though still direct and forceful, is pitched in a higher poetic key. And there are passages where he succeeds brilliantly. In the counterspeeches of Oedipus and Tiresias, for example, he manages to transpose into speakable and memorable English both the fierce eloquence of Oedipus' accusation and the demonic authority of the blind prophet's reply. But Mr. Berg has the defects of his qualities. Even in this scene there are a few self-indulgent touches: a superfluous image at the end of Tiresias' speech ("an ember of pain. Ashes"), a three-line expansion of the hint of desolation conveyed to the Greek audience by the one word *Kithairon* (some explanation was justified, but not three lines). Elsewhere and often, Mr. Berg allows himself much more license: "I am afraid, afraid / Apollo's prediction will come true, all of it, / as God's sunlight grows brighter on a man's face at dawn / when he's in bed, still sleeping / and reaches into his eyes and wakes him." The Sophoclean original runs: "Yes, afraid that Apollo will turn out to be correct." This interpolation is all the more distressing because it interrupts a swift sequence of dramatic revelations which in the original is couched in the cut and thrust of single-line dialogue.

In their approach to this problem, the strict regularity of the iambic speeches, Mr. Berg and Mr. Williams both renounce any attempt to reproduce the form of the original; they use an elastic line. Mr. Berg's, in fact, runs the gamut from one syllable to twenty. This freedom of maneuver removes the temptation to pad out the line, a temptation to which earlier translators often succumbed in their efforts to reproduce, line for line, those series of rapid question and answer which sometimes strike the modern ear as faintly comic. (Housman's brilliant parody of the results was enough to put an end to the practice: "*Alcmaeon*: A shepherd's questioned mouth informed me that— / *Chorus*: What? For I know not yet what you will say. / *Alcmaeon*: Nor will you ever if you interrupt.") Both our translators sacrifice formal balance for dramatic economy and cut to the bone where they think they see fat. In the *Women of Trachis*, for example, Heracles asks his son Hyllos if he knows the daughter of Eurytus, and Hyllos answers: "You mean Iole, if I am not mistaken." Mr. Williams translates: "Iole." In *Oedipus the King*, Kreon leads up to his defense against Oedipus' charges with a series of rhetorical questions to which the answer, as both men know, is "Yes." "Are you married to my sister?" asks Kreon, and Oedipus answers with a line which would not be unfairly represented by: "A negative answer to your inquiry is out of the question." Mr. Berg translates: "I married Jocasta." If these exchanges had been written by Euripides it is likely that there would have been cause for surgery, but Sophocles is a subtle operator and should be approached with caution. In the first case, the hesitation and apparent obtuseness of Hyllos is fully dramatic; he has promised his father a favor, but now, with the mention of the girl who has, in all innocence, destroyed his parents, he half foresees the outrageous demand which is to follow. And the periphrases of Oedipus' reply reflect a sarcastic impatience with Kreon's pettifogging courtroom techniques.

It is, however, in the translation of the allusive, lyrical odes that the poets come into their kingdom; here the more literal the rendering the less effective it is likely to be. Paradoxically enough, Mr. Berg, who is so generous with his own contributions in the dialogue, here shows restraint; except for some overemphases and undue expansions in the climactic ode which comes after the revelation scene, he has written moving poetry which re-creates much of the power and beauty of the original. Occasionally, in fact, it comes close to perfection, as in the lines on the plague: "and lives one after another split the air / birds taking off / wingrush hungrier than fire / souls leaping away they fly / to the shore / of the cold god of evening / west." The principles which underlie these lyric translations are explained in the preliminary notes, which contain a valuable discussion of the nature of Greek choral poetry and the aim of the translators: "to reproduce in English, which has no tradition for this kind of song, the essential gaps and ambiguities of Greek choral song by a kind of Broken Poetry."

Mr. Williams, too, explains his method; it is perhaps significant that the "we" of the Berg-Clay discussion is replaced by the first person singular. Sounding the familiar note that we have lost the music and the dance which made these choral poems so powerful a medium for the ancient dramatist and citing the notorious difficulty of producing effective unison delivery from a speaking chorus, he attempts to "make at least a facsimile of the basic musical experience of the chorus ... by using many repetitions, generally of single words, but, occasionally, of phrases and whole line units." He also breaks the choral utterance down into extremely short lines, each of which "represents an *individual* voice, coming from a spatially distinct point on the stage." For this particular idea, he gives credit to an exercise developed by Peter Brook: the words of a Shakespearean line are distributed among a group of actors, one word each, and they "attempt to reproduce the line as it would be spoken by an individual."

What the effect of the resulting compositions would be on stage I have no idea, but in cold print they do not inspire enthusiasm. The repetitions are exhausting. "O let him / let him get / here. Here! Let / the oars not / stop, never / stop, not / until / he gets / here, not./ Let him leave / that island, island— / fires, / leave the / sacrifice he's / doing / and get here, get / here, get here, / here." Space forbids reproduction of the typography; some idea of the look of the page can be obtained by imagining the mouse's tale in *Alice* extended over several pages (though without the steady reduction in type size). Occasionally, as in the rendering of the great opening chorus on the mutability of all human fortune, there are lines which can stir emotion, but there are many more which inspire only dismay. "Now watch / this! Watch / this have me! / I'm letting it / have me! / It has / me. Look! / Soaring! ME!/ Can't think! / JOY! ME!" It is true that the original here is not

Sophocles at his greatest, but it deserves a better version than something that sounds like a series of captions for Jules Feiffer's spindly danseuse in one of her self-admiring ecstasies.

These two translators are the most daring and experimental the series has so far presented. It is the fate of such innovators to rise high above the norm when successful and fall just as far below it when they fail. Messrs. Berg and Williams are no exception. Like the little girl of the nursery rhyme, when they are good, they are very, very good . . .

It would be unfair to conclude without mention of the scholars. Gregory W. Dickerson and Diskin Clay have added valuable notes on the plays, many of which will command the attention of their professional colleagues, and they have written perceptive and innovative introductions. These lucid but profound explorations of the Sophoclean tragic vision are the distillation of their long study of the text, and they are authoritative critical statements: Mr. Dickerson's a revealing vindication of a play which has been strangely neglected, Mr. Clay's an arresting reassessment of an acclaimed masterpiece.

Part IV: Euripides

SEVENTEEN

The Hippolytus *of Euripides*

The usual critical treatment of the *Hippolytus* of Euripides is an analysis in terms of character, an analysis which, whatever its particular emphasis, is based on the Aristotelian conception of tragic character and the relation between character and reversal of fortune. In the case of the *Hippolytus*, this analysis, far from arriving at a generally accepted line of interpretation, has produced nothing but disagreement. Is Hippolytus the tragic hero,[1] destroyed by an excess of chastity, a fanatical devotion to the goddess Artemis? Or is Phaedra the tragic heroine,[2] and the conflict in her soul the tragic conflict of the play? The claims of Theseus should not be neglected; his part is as long as Phaedra's, and the Aristotelian word *hamartia* is used to describe his conduct by the goddess Artemis.[3]

Such divergence of views is natural in a play which develops so many characters so fully; though literary statistics are distasteful, the size of the parts in this play (an important statistic for the actors, at any rate) shows how difficult the problem of emphasis is. Hippolytus speaks 271 lines,[4] Phaedra and Theseus 187 apiece, and, surprisingly enough, the Nurse has more lines than either Phaedra or Theseus: 216.[5] The attempt to make Phaedra the central figure of the play seems perverse — why not the Nurse? She too has her conduct described as *hamartia*[6] — and even Hippolytus is not a central figure on the scale of Medea, who speaks 562 lines in a play of similar length, or Oedipus, who has 698 in the *Oedipus Tyrannus*, a play which is a little longer. The search for a central tragic figure in this play is a blind alley. When the action is so equally divided among four characters, the unity of the work cannot depend on any one, but must lie in the nature of the relationship of all four. In the *Hippolytus*, the significant relationship between the characters is the situation in which they are placed. It is exactly the same situation for each of them, one which imposes a choice between the same alternatives — silence and speech.

And we are shown that their choice is not free. Aristotle's comments on the tragic character assume, to some extent, that the

This chapter originally appeared in *Yale Classical Studies*, 13 (1952). © 1952 by The Yale University Press. Reprinted by permission.

human will is free to choose. But the freedom of the human will and the importance of the human choice are both, in the prologue of the *Hippolytus*, expressly denied. In no other Greek tragedy is the predetermination of human action by an external power made so emphatically clear. In the *Oresteia*, where each word and action is the fulfillment of the will of Zeus, the relation between human action and divine will is presented always in mysterious terms; the will of Zeus is an inscrutable factor in the background which is clearly revealed only at the close of the trilogy. And while Clytemnestra is on stage in the *Agamemnon*, we are not distracted by any feeling that her purpose as a human being is not decisive; in fact, it is the most important thing in the play. Sophocles' Oedipus has fulfilled and is still fulfilling the oracles of Apollo, but it is Oedipus, a human being making human decisions, who commands our undivided attention. And significantly, the prophecy of Apollo is presented as exactly that, a prophecy and not a determining factor; Apollo predicts, but does no more—it is Oedipus who acts.

Both the *Oedipus* and the *Agamemnon* may be ultimately, in logical (though not necessarily religious) terms, determinist, but dramatically they emphasize the freedom of the human will. But the *Hippolytus* begins with a powerful presentation of an external force which not only predicts but also determines; Aphrodite tells us not only what will happen but announces her responsibility and explains her motives. It is a complete explanation and one which (even if it were not confirmed in every particular by another goddess at the end of the play) we are bound to accept. Aphrodite is one of the powers which rule the universe; and though what she says may shock us, we must accept it as true.

The play, from this point on, should be simple, the unrolling of an inevitable pattern. But Euripides has a surprise in store. As we watch the human beings of the drama, unconscious of the goddess's purpose, work out her will, we are struck by their apparent freedom. In no other Greek tragedy do so many people change their minds about so many important matters. Here again Euripides is departing sharply from the procedure of his fellow dramatists. Clytemnestra's purpose in the *Agamemnon*, concealed from the chorus and her victim by the resolution of that male-thinking brain, dangerously close to the ironic surface of her speech of welcome, triumphantly achieved when she stands over Agamemnon's body—this inflexible purpose is the straight line along which the whole play moves. Oedipus' determination to know the truth, carried relentlessly to the brink of the abyss and beyond, is the line of development of the greatest plot in western tragedy. But in the *Hippolytus* the line of development of the characters' purposes is a zigzag. Phaedra resolves to die without revealing her love, and then makes a long speech about it to the chorus. The Nurse urges her to reveal it, regrets her action when she hears her mistress speak, and then returns to urge Phaedra on to further lengths of speech. And Hippolytus, when he learns of Phaedra's passion, first announces his intention to tell Theseus the truth and then changes his mind and keeps silent.

"In this world, second thoughts are best," says the Nurse.[7] Three of the principal characters have second thoughts (the Nurse, in fact, has not only second but third and fourth thoughts); the play makes an ironic juxtaposition of the maximum dramatic complication of individual choice with a predetermined and announced result. The choice of one alternative then the other, the human mind wavering between moral decisions, accepting and rejecting in a complicated pattern which emphasizes the apparent freedom and unpredictability of the human will—all this is the fulfillment of Aphrodite's purpose.

The choice between speech and silence is the situation which places the four principal characters in significant relationship and makes an artistic unity of the play. But it does much more. The poet has made the alternations and combinations of choice complicated. Phaedra chooses first silence then speech; the Nurse speech then silence, then speech, then silence; Hippolytus speech then silence; the chorus silence; and Theseus speech. The resultant pattern seems to represent the exhaustion of the possibilities of the human will. The choice between silence and speech is more than a unifying factor in the play; it is a situation with universal implications, a metaphor for the operation of human free will in all its complicated aspects. And the context in which it is set demonstrates the nonexistence of the human free will, the futility of the moral choice.

The goddess Aphrodite presents the issue and announces the outcome. Her preliminary work is done ($\pi\acute{\alpha}\lambda\alpha\iota$ $\pi\rho\text{οκ}\acute{ο}\psi\alpha\sigma$', 23); the moment has arrived for the consummation of her design, the punishment of Hippolytus ($\tau\iota\mu\omega\rho\acute{\eta}\sigma\text{ομαι}$, 21). But there is still one recalcitrant detail, Phaedra's determination to remain silent. "She, poor woman, is dying in silence. No one in the house shares the secret of her disease":

$\dot{\eta}$ $\tau\acute{\alpha}\lambda\alpha\iota\nu$' $\dot{\alpha}\pi\acute{ο}\lambda\lambda\upsilon\tau\alpha\iota$
$\sigma\iota\gamma\hat{\eta}$· $\xi\acute{\upsilon}\nu\text{οιδε}$ δ' $\text{ο}\ddot{\upsilon}\tau\iota\varsigma$ $\text{οἰκετ}\hat{\omega}\nu$ $\nu\acute{ο}\sigma\text{ον}$ (39–40).

But this last obstacle will be removed; things will not fall out this way, $\dot{\alpha}\lambda\lambda$' $\text{ο}\ddot{\upsilon}\tau\iota$ $\tau\alpha\acute{\upsilon}\tau\eta$ $\tau\acute{ο}\nu\delta$' $\ddot{ε}\rho\omega\tau\alpha$ $\chi\rho\dot{\eta}$ $\pi\text{εσε}\hat{\iota}\nu$ (41). The truth will come out, $\kappa\dot{\alpha}\kappa\phi\alpha\nu\acute{\eta}\sigma\text{εται}$ (42). And Theseus will kill his son.

In the scene between Phaedra and the Nurse, we are shown the first stage of the accomplishment of Aphrodite's purpose—Phaedra's change from silence to speech. Her words are the involuntary speech of delirium, the breakout of her suppressed subconscious desires. But this delirium is also the working of the external force, Aphrodite, who predicted this development and now brings it about before our eyes. Phaedra's wild fantasies make no sense to the Nurse and the chorus, but their meaning is clear to the audience. Her yearning for the poplar and the grassy meadow, for the chase and the taming of colts on the sand, is a hysterical expression of her desire for Hippolytus.[8]

The Nurse calls her outburst madness (μανία, 214), that is, meaningless speech, and Phaedra, when she comes to her senses, calls it madness too (ἐμάνην, 241), but in a different sense, passion. She has revealed nothing, but she has for the first time put her desire into words, and broken her long silence. Her passion (ἐμάνην) has overcome her judgment (γνώμη, 240); in her case the choice between silence and speech is also a choice between judgment and passion. In the next few lines she defines her dilemma, poses the alternatives, and sees a third course open to her:

> τὸ γὰρ ὀρθοῦσθαι γνώμαν ὀδυνᾷ.
> τὸ δὲ μαινόμενον κακόν· ἀλλὰ κρατεῖ
> μὴ γιγνώσκοντ' ἀπολέσθαι (247–49).

To be right in judgment (ὀρθοῦσθαι γνώμαν), that is, in her case, to remain silent, is agony (ὀδυνᾷ); passion (τὸ μαινόμενον), in her case, speech, is evil (κακόν). Better (ἀλλὰ κρατεῖ) to make no choice and perish (μὴ γιγνώσκοντ' ἀπολέσθαι) —to perish unconscious of the alternatives, to abandon judgment and choice, to surrender free will.[9] This is what she comes to in the end, but she has not yet reached such desperate straits. She is still in the no man's land between the alternatives of speech and silence, for her delirious outburst has not revealed her secret to the Nurse. But it has brought her a momentary relief and thus weakened her determination. She is now less able to withstand the final assault on her silence which the Nurse, at the request of the chorus, proceeds to make.

The Nurse has little hope of success; she has tried before and failed—πάντα γὰρ σιγᾷ τάδε (273), "Phaedra keeps silent about it all," she tells the chorus. But she makes a last attempt. The essence of her practical viewpoint can be seen in her reproach to Phaedra when she gets no answer; for her there is no problem which cannot be resolved by speech. "Well, why are you silent? You should not be silent, child. Either you should refute me, if I say something wrong, or, if I say what is right, you should agree with my words":

> εἶεν· τί σιγᾷς; οὐχ ἐχρῆν σιγᾶν, τέκνον,
> ἀλλ' ἤ μ' ἐλέγχειν, εἴ τι μὴ καλῶς λέγω,
> ἢ τοῖσιν εὖ λεχθεῖσι συγχωρεῖν λόγοις (297–99).

She gets no answer still, and in an angry reminder to Phaedra that she is ruining her children's future, she mentions, without realizing its significance, the name Hippolytus. This fortuitous thrust provokes a cry of agony and a plea for silence. "I beseech you, in future, be silent about this man," τοῦδ' ἀνδρὸς αὖθις λίσσομαι σιγᾶν πέρι (312).

The Nurse does not realize the reason for Phaedra's agitation, but she senses the moment of weakness and presses her advantage. She now makes a frontal attack on Phaedra's silence; throwing herself at her mistress' feet, she seizes her hand and knees. It is the position of the suppliant, the extreme expression of emotional and physical pressure combined, and it is enough to break Phaedra's weakened resolution. "I will grant your request," δώσω (335). "My part is silence now," replies the Nurse, "and yours is speech," σιγῷμ' ἂν ἤδη· σὸς γὰρ οὐντεῦθεν λόγος (336).

Phaedra finds speech difficult. She invokes the names of her mother and sister, examples of unhappy love, and associates herself with them. But she finds it hard to speak plainly. "If only you could say to me what I must say myself," πῶς ἂν σύ μοι λέξειας ἁμὲ χρὴ λέγειν (345). This is her wish, to break silence and yet not speak, and she actually manages to make it come true. In a dialectic maneuver worthy of Socrates himself, she assumes the role of questioner and makes the Nurse supply the answers and repeat the name Hippolytus, this time in a context which leaves no doubt about its significance. "You have said it," she says to the Nurse, "you did not hear it from me," σοῦ τάδ' οὐκ ἐμοῦ κλύεις (352).

This revelation is more than the Nurse had bargained for. She who saw only two attitudes toward speech for Phaedra—rebuttal or agreement—can adopt neither herself; she has no advice to give, no solution to propose. She is reduced to despair and silence; she who reproached Phaedra for wishing to die now resolves on death herself. "I shall find release from life in death. Farewell. I am no longer living":

ἀπαλλαχθήσομαι
βίου θανοῦσα. χαίρετ'· οὐκέτ' εἴμ' ἐγώ (356–57).

The full meaning of her words to Phaedra is now clear to us and to her. "My part is silence now," σιγῷμ' ἂν ἤδη. "Speech from this point on is yours," σὸς γὰρ οὐντεῦθεν λόγος.

Speech is Phaedra's part now, and she pours out her heart to the chorus. The relief of speech, which first forced itself on her in a delirious outburst, is now the product of conscious choice. She tells the chorus the path her judgment followed, τῆς ἐμῆς γνώμης ὁδόν (391): first of all, to hide her sickness in silence, σιγᾶν τήνδε καὶ κρύπτειν νόσον (394). But this proved insufficient; more was needed, to subdue her passion by self-control, τὴν ἄνοιαν εὖ φέρειν / τῷ σωφρονεῖν νικῶσα (398–99). And when this failed, she resolved on a third course, to die. She is still resolved to die; her change from silence to speech has made no difference to the situation, for she can depend on the silence of the chorus and the Nurse. But she has had the comfort of speech, told her love and despair to a sympathetic audience, and what is more, an admiring one. "Honour? Who hath it? He that died o' Wednesday," says Falstaff, and this is the essence of Phaedra's dilemma too. She has resolved to die in silence to save her honor, to be εὐκλεής. But this very silence means that she cannot enjoy her honor while living, and it will not even be appreciated after her death. No one will ever know the force she overcame and the heroic nature of her decision. Death in silence involved an isolation hard for any human being to bear, and she makes it clear that her desire to be appreciated was one of the forces driving her to speech. "May it be my lot," she says, "not to pass unnoticed when I act nobly, and not to have many witnesses when my acts are disgraceful":

ἐμοὶ γὰρ εἴη μήτε λανθάνειν καλὰ
μήτ' αἰσχρὰ δρώσῃ μάρτυρας πολλοὺς ἔχειν (403–4).

Now she can act nobly, die rather than yield to passion, and yet not pass unnoticed. The chorus, the representatives of the women of Troezen,[10] recognize and praise her nobility (431–32). Phaedra can have her cake and eat it too. But it is not destined to end this way, ἀλλ' οὔτι ταύτῃ τόνδ' ἔρωτα χρὴ πεσεῖν, said Aphrodite in the prologue.

For the Nurse now intervenes again. Her passion and despair silenced her and drove her from the scene when she realized the nature of Phaedra's sickness. But she has changed her mind. She has now rejected silence, which abandoned Phaedra to her death, and chosen speech, which is designed to save her life. "In human life," she says, "second thoughts are somehow best":

κἀν βροτοῖς
αἱ δεύτεραί πως φροντίδες σοφώτεραι (435–36).

Phaedra's silence was γνώμη, judgment; her speech was at first μανία, passion. But in the Nurse's case these relationships are reversed. Her passion, despair, drove her to silence, and her speech now is the product of γνώμη, judgment. It is speech (λόγος) in both senses of the Greek word, speech and reason; the nurse here represents the application of human reason to a human problem.

The "reason" behind the Nurse's lines is one stripped bare of any restraint of morality or religion, though it uses the terms of both. The speech is a masterpiece of sophistic rhetoric, in which each argument points toward the physical consummation of Phaedra's love. But this is a conclusion which the nurse is clever enough not to put into words. She leaves the implied conclusion to work on Phaedra's weakened resolution and contents herself, to conclude her speech, with specific advice in which every phrase is an ambiguity: τόλμα δ' ἐρῶσα (476), "bear your love (as you have so far)" or "dare to love"; τὴν νόσον καταστρέφου (477), "subdue your love (as you have so far)" or "make it subject to you, turn it to your own good"; ἐπῳδαὶ καὶ λόγοι θελκτήριοι (478), "incantations and charmed words," to cure her of her passion[11] or to make Hippolytus love her. The Nurse is probing to see what effect her speech will have on Phaedra; she does not dare commit herself fully yet.

She gets a violent reaction. These are οἱ καλοὶ λίαν λόγοι (487), too fair-seeming words; Phaedra asks for advice that will save her honor, not please her ears. But she has made an important admission; the Nurse's words did please her ears: τὰ τοῖσιν ὠσὶ τερπνά (488). The Nurse sees the weakness in Phaedra's defense and pushes hard. She speaks bluntly and clearly now. "You need not graceful words [so much for honor] but the man":

οὐ λόγων εὐσχημόνων
δεῖ σ' ἀλλὰ τἀνδρός (490–91).

This is plain speaking, and Phaedra replies with an angry and agonized plea for silence, οὐχὶ συγκλῄσεις στόμα (498). But the Nurse presses her advantage and pushes the verbalization of Phaedra's suppressed wishes to a further stage; she has already mentioned "the man," τἀνδρός, and now she invokes "the deed," τοὔργον (501)—the act of adultery itself.[12] This word brings out into the open the consummation which Phaedra rejected with such horror in her speech to the chorus (413–18), but now it is attractive as well as repulsive—like love itself, ἥδιστον ... ταὐτὸν ἀλγεινόν θ' ἅμα (348)—and Phaedra now reveals that if the Nurse continues to put evil in a fair light, τᾳσχρὰ δ' ἢν λέγῃς καλῶς (505), she will come to it and be consumed in what she now flees from, εἰς τοῦθ' ὃ φεύγω νῦν ἀναλωθήσομαι (506).

The Nurse is clever enough to return to ambiguities, the love charms, φίλτρα ... θελκτήρια (509), which will relieve her sickness without disgrace or damage to the mind. The Nurse thus returns to her original proposal; this is the same circular movement of her earlier interview with Phaedra, in which the name "Hippolytus" was the point of departure and return. And here, as there, the closing of the circle with the repetition makes clear the meaning of the words. Phaedra must know now, after all that has been said, what the Nurse means by "love charms." But the ambiguous phrasing is a triumph of psychology on the Nurse's part. She remembers how Phaedra tried to evade responsibility by a verbal fiction before—"If only you could say to me what I must say myself" and "You have said it. You did not hear it from me"—and she gives her mistress the same opportunity again. And Phaedra takes it. Her question is not "What will be the effect of this love charm?" but "Is it an ointment or something to drink?" πότερα δὲ χριστὸν ἢ ποτὸν τὸ φάρμακον; (516). She has abandoned her critical intelligence, γιγνώ-σκειν, γνώμη, and surrendered control over her own choice; she is now following the third and most desperate of the three courses she saw before her. "To be right in judgment is agony, passion is evil, best of all is to perish without judgment or choice," μὴ γιγνώσκοντ' ἀπολέσθαι.

That she surrenders control of her actions here is made clear and also plausible by the relationship between Phaedra and the Nurse which the words and tone of the next few lines suggest. She is now a child again, and the Nurse does for the grown woman what she had always done for the child—evades her questions, makes light of her fears, relieves her of responsibility, and decides for her. "I don't know," she says, in answer to Phaedra's question about the nature of the love charms. "Don't ask questions, child. Just let it do you good," οὐκ οἶδ'· ὀνάσθαι μὴ μαθεῖν βούλου, τέκνον (517). To Phaedra's expression of fear that her secret will be revealed to Hippolytus, the nurse replies, "Leave that to me, daughter," ἔασον ὦ παῖ. "I'll take care of that," ταῦτ' ἐγὼ θήσω καλῶς (521). With a prayer to Aphrodite, συνεργὸς εἴης (523), "cooperate with me," and a statement that she will tell her thoughts to "friends within the house," the Nurse goes into the palace. And Phaedra lets her go. She has gone through the cycle of conscious choice, first silence, then speech, and come at last to abandon choice all together and entrust her destiny to another. And the result will be, as she said herself, destruction, μὴ γιγνώσκοντ' ἀπολέσθαι.

For that result she does not have long to wait. "Silence," Σιγήσατ' ὦ γυναῖκες (565), is the word with which she follows the closing line of the choral stasimon to open the next scene. She is listening to what is happening inside the house, where Hippolytus is shouting at the Nurse. What Phaedra both feared and longed for has come true; Hippolytus knows of her love.

The opening lines of the ensuing dialogue show Hippolytus in his turn confronted with the same choice, between silence and speech. He must choose between telling Theseus what he has heard, and remaining silent, as he has sworn to do. His first reaction is a passionate announcement that he will speak, an appeal to earth and sun to witness what he has just heard:

ὦ γαῖα μᾶτερ ἡλίου τ' ἀναπτυχαί
οἵων λόγων ἄρρητον εἰσήκουσ' ὄπα (601–2).

To the Nurse's plea for silence, σίγησον ὦ παῖ (603), he replies, "Impossible. What I have heard is dreadful. I cannot keep silence," οὐκ ἔστ' ἀκούσας δείν' ὅπως σιγήσομαι (504). This impulse to speak is, as in Phaedra's case, passion overriding judgment, but the passion which inspires him is not the same. Behind Phaedra's delirious words and subsequent conscious surrender to the Nurse's questioning, we can see the power of Aphrodite working in her. But Hippolytus' outburst is the shocked and incredulous reaction of the virgin mind, the working of Artemis in him. And in his case, as in Phaedra's, the passionate impulse endangers the chief objective of the conscious mind; Phaedra's speech endangers her honor, that εὔκλεια which is her life's aim,[13] and Hippolytus' speech endangers his highest ambition, reverence, εὐσέβεια,[14] for it involves breaking the oath he swore to the Nurse. Though they make their choices in different order (Phaedra choosing first silence, then speech; Hippolytus first speech, then silence), the parallel is striking. And the agent who brings about the change of mind is in each case the same, the Nurse.

The connection between the two situations is emphasized not only verbally and thematically but also visually. For the Nurse now throws herself at the feet of Hippolytus, as she did at Phaedra's, and clasps his hand and knees, as she did hers. The supreme gesture of supplication is repeated, to meet with the same initial resistance and final compliance. But this time she begs not for speech but for silence.

Hippolytus rejects her request with the same argument she herself had used against Phaedra's silence. "If the matter is good," he says, "it will be better still when published," τά τοι κάλ' ἐν πολλοῖσι καλλίον λέγειν (610)—a line which recalls what the Nurse had said to Phaedra, "Then you will be even more honored if you tell," οὔκουν λέγουσα τιμωτέρα φάνῃ (332). Hippolytus launches on his passionate denunciation of women. The violence of his speech relieves the passion which made him ignore his oath, and he ends his speech with a promise to keep silence, σῖγα δ' ἕξομεν στόμα (660). He will respect the oath. "Don't forget this, woman," he says to the Nurse, "it is my reverence which saves you," εὖ δ' ἴσθι τοὐμὸν σ' εὐσεβὲς σῴζει, γύναι (666). Hippolytus too changes his mind: "in this world second thoughts are somehow wiser."

But Phaedra's situation is desperate. She does not believe that the disgust and hatred revealed in Hippolytus' speech will remain under control—"He will speak against us to his father," she says, ἐρεῖ καθ' ἡμῶν πατρί (690)—and even if she could be certain of Hippolytus' silence, she is not the woman to face Theseus with dissimulation. She wondered, in her long speech to the chorus, how the adulteress could look her husband in the face (415–16), and even if she had the necessary

hardness, the situation would be made difficult, to say the least, by
Hippolytus' announced intention to watch her at it (661–62). Now she
must die, as she intended from the first, but she can no longer die in
silence. That would no longer be death with honor—τοιγὰρ οὐκέτ᾽ εὐ-
κλεεῖς / θανούμεθ᾽ (687–88). Speech has brought her to this pass, and in
order to die and protect her reputation she now needs more speech.
"Now I need new words," she says, ἀλλὰ δεῖ με δὴ καινῶν λόγων (688).

"May I not pass unnoticed when I act nobly," she said in the
beginning, "nor have many witnesses when I act disgracefully" (403–4).
She got the first half of her wish—the chorus was witness to her noble
resolution to die in silence—but the second half was not granted.
Hippolytus is a witness to her weakness, and he must be silenced. To
this motive for action against him is added the hatred of the rejected
woman who has heard every word of his ugly speech.[15] The "new
words" which she finds, the letter to Theseus accusing Hippolytus of an
attempt on her virtue, will save her reputation and satisfy her hatred.
They will guarantee the ineffectiveness of Hippolytus' speech, if speak
he does, and they will also destroy him.

But there are other witnesses to be silenced too, the chorus. She
asks them to hide in silence what they have heard, σιγῇ καλύπτειν
ἀνθάδ᾽ εἰσηκούσατε (712), and they agree. They bind themselves to
silence by an oath. Thus the chorus, like the three principal characters
so far seen, chooses between the same two alternatives, and seals its
choice, silence, with speech of the most powerful and binding kind, an
oath. The chorus will not change its mind.

The preliminaries are now over, and the stage is set for Hippolytus'
destruction. Phaedra commits suicide, and Theseus finds her letter.
What happens now, whether Aphrodite's purpose will be fulfilled or fail,
whether Hippolytus will live or die, depends on whether Theseus
chooses silence or speech. He does not keep us waiting long. "I cannot
hold it inside the gates of my mouth," he says, τόδε μὲν οὐκέτι
στόματος ἐν πύλαις / καθέξω (882–83). But it is not ordinary speech. By
the gift conferred on him by his father, Poseidon, he can speak, in
certain circumstances, with a power that is reserved for gods alone—his
wish, expressed in speech, becomes fact. In his mouth, at this moment,
speech has the power of life and death. And he uses it to kill his son.
"Father Poseidon, you gave me once three curses. With one of these,
wipe out my son":

ἀλλ᾽ ὦ πάτερ Πόσειδον, ἅς ἐμοί ποτε
ἀρὰς ὑπέσχου τρεῖς, μιᾷ κατέργασαι
τούτων ἐμὸν παῖδ᾽ . . . (887–89).

Here the last piece of the jigsaw puzzle of free will is fitted into place to complete the picture of Aphrodite's purpose fulfilled. And Theseus' curse is at the same time a demonstration of the futility of the alternative which the second thoughts of Phaedra, Hippolytus, and the Nurse have suggested. "Second thoughts are somehow wiser"—they were not for these three. Perhaps first thoughts are best: μὴ γιγνώ-σκοντ', as Phaedra said. But Theseus is the one person in the play for whom second thoughts would have been wiser, and he gives himself no time to have them. He acts immediately, without stopping to examine the case or consider alternatives: μὴ γιγνώσκοντ' ἀπολέσθαι, to abandon judgment and perish—Phaedra's last desperate course—is Theseus' first impulsive action.

The alternatives before these human beings—first and second thoughts, passion and judgment, silence and speech[16]—are chosen and rejected in a complicated pattern which shows the independent operation of five separate human wills producing a result desired by none of them, the consummation of Aphrodite's purpose. The fact that the moral alternatives are represented by silence and speech is not merely a brilliant device which connects and contrasts the situations of the different characters; it is also an emphatic statement of the universality of the action. It makes the play an ironical comment on a fundamental idea, the idea that man's power of speech, which distinguishes him from the other animals, is the faculty which gives him the conception and power of moral choice in the first place.

This Greek commonplace is most clearly set forth in a famous passage of Aristotle's *Politics* (1.1.10). "Man alone of the animals possesses speech [λόγον]. Mere voice [φωνή] can, it is true, indicate pain and pleasure, and therefore it is possessed by the other animals as well ... but speech [λόγος] is designed to indicate the advantageous and the harmful [τὸ συμφέρον καὶ τὸ βλαβερόν] and therefore also the right and the wrong [τὸ δίκαιον καὶ τὸ ἄδικον]: for it is the special property of man, in distinction from the other animals, that he alone has perception of good and bad [ἀγαθοῦ καὶ κακοῦ] and right and wrong [δικαίου καὶ ἀδίκου] and other moral qualities [καὶ τῶν ἄλλων]."[17]

It is clear that Euripides was familiar with the idea, for he makes at least one ironical reference to the contrast between man, who has speech, and the animals, which do not. Hippolytus, in his furious invective, wishes that women could be provided with dumb animals instead of servants like the Nurse. "Animals with bite instead of voice should be housed with them, so that women could neither speak to anyone nor get speech back in return":

ἄφθογγα δ' αὐταῖς συγκατοικίζειν δάκη
θηρῶν, ἵν' εἶχον μήτε προσφωνεῖν τινα
μήτ' ἐξ ἐκείνων φθέγμα δέξασθαι πάλιν (646–48).

Here he wishes that speaking beings could be made dumb, but in his own moment of trial and agony before Theseus he reverses his wish, and begs an inanimate object, the house, to speak in his defense. "House, if only you could somehow send forth a voice and bear witness . . .":

ὦ δώματ' εἴθε φθέγμα γηρύσαισθέ μοι
καὶ μαρτυρήσαιτ' . . . (1074–75).

Speech is what distinguishes man from the other animals. But in the *Hippolytus* its role is not simply to point out the distinction between right and wrong. It is presented not as the instrument which makes possible the conception of moral choice and expresses moral alternatives, but as an explosive force which, once released, cannot be restrained and creates universal destruction. Ποῖ προβήσεται λόγος; (342): "To what length will speech go?" asks the Nurse, when she has finally succeeded in opening Phaedra's lips. It goes far enough to ruin all of them. It assumes many forms: Phaedra's delirium, the Nurse's cynical argument, Hippolytus' invective, Phaedra's letter, Theseus' curse—and in all these forms it is the instrument of Aphrodite's will.

The *Hippolytus* is a terrible demonstration of the meaninglessness of the moral choice and its medium, speech. But it is not a mechanical demonstration; the unifying and meaningful situation is the key to the play, but that does not mean that character is unimportant. The demonstration is in fact powerful precisely because the choices and alternations of choice made by the human beings are in each case the natural expression of the individual character. As has often been remarked, if the prologue were removed, the action would still be plausible. The external directing force works not against but through the characteristic thoughts and impulses of the characters involved. But the brilliant delineation of character in the *Hippolytus* does more than motivate the action plausibly. The characters, like the situation, have a larger dimension of meaning than the purely dramatic; they are individual examples which illustrate the fundamental proposition implied in the situation—the futility of human choice and action.

The four characters involved are very different: different in purpose, action, and suffering. But they all go through the same process. Action in each case, far from fulfilling conscious purpose, brings about the opposite of that purpose. The individual purpose is the expression of a view of human life and a way of living it; in each case this view is exposed, by the individual disaster, as inadequate. And the view of human life implies, in turn, an attitude toward the gods; these attitudes are in each case proved unsound. The human beings of the world of the *Hippolytus* live out their lives in the darkness of total ignorance of the nature of the universe and of the powers which govern it.

Phaedra's purpose and way of life can be summed up in one word, the word which is so often on her lips: εὐκλεής, "honorable."[18] She has a code of honor proper for a princess, an aristocratic and unintellectual ideal. From first to last this is Phaedra's dominant motive, except for the fatal moment when she surrenders her initiative to the Nurse. It is to preserve this honor that she takes her original decision to die in silence; to enjoy appreciation of her honor she indulges in the luxury of speech to the chorus; and to rescue her honorable reputation from the consequences she ruins Hippolytus and brings guilt and sorrow on Theseus. But it is all to no purpose. In the end her conspiracy of silence is a failure and her honor lost. Hippolytus and the chorus keep the oaths that they have sworn and remain silent; the house cannot speak; but the goddess Artemis coldly reveals the truth to Theseus, who learns not only that his wife had a guilty passion for Hippolytus but also that she has tricked him into killing his innocent son. Phaedra's attempt to save her honor has proved an expensive failure.

Not only is her purpose baffled and her code of conduct shown to be inadequate; her concern for her honor is dismissed by the gods as irrelevant. Both Aphrodite and Artemis treat Phaedra's honor with complete indifference. "She is honorable—but still, she dies," ἡ δ᾽ εὐκλεὴς μέν, ἀλλ᾽ ὅμως ἀπόλλυται (47), says Aphrodite, and when Artemis reveals the truth to Theseus she makes it clear that she is concerned with the reputation not of Phaedra, but of Hippolytus. "I have come," she says to Theseus, "to show that his mind was just, so that he may die in honor" ὡς ὑπ᾽ εὐκλείας θάνῃ (1299)—to save his reputation. Phaedra's passion, far from being buried in silence so that she can be honored after death, will be the subject of song in the ritual cult of Hippolytus. "It shall not fall nameless and be silenced, Phaedra's passion for you":

κοὐκ ἀνώνυμος πεσών
ἔρως ὁ Φαίδρας ἐς σὲ σιγηθήσεται (1429–30).

Phaedra's purpose, to save her honor, is one consistent with her ideal of conduct and her life as she has lived it so far. It is characteristic of the Nurse that her purpose has nothing to do with ideals; it is specific and practical—she wishes to save not Phaedra's honor but her life, and to that end she will use any means which promise success. Her love for

Phaedra is the motive for her actions from first to last. But in the end she succeeds only in destroying Phaedra's honor and her life as well; she hears herself rejected utterly and cursed by the person to whom she has devoted her entire life and whose well-being is her only objective.

The Nurse has no aristocratic code of conduct. Her word is not honorable, εὐκλεής, but λόγος,[19] speech, reason, argument. She believes in, and tries to effect, the settlement of human problems by human reason, λόγος, expressed in speech, λόγος, which influences others as argument, λόγος. This is in fact not an aristocratic attitude but a democratic one, and the Nurse has another quality characteristic of Athenian democracy, flexibility.[20] She can adapt herself quickly to new situations, seize a new ground of argument—a capacity illustrated by the fact that she shifts her ground in the play not once, like Phaedra and Hippolytus, but three times. She is in fact so flexible that her attitude is not a consistent moral code at all, but merely a series of practical approaches to different problems. It is natural therefore that the Nurse should be made to speak in terms that clearly associate her with the contemporary sophists, who, like her, had a secular and confident approach to human problems, the rhetorical skill to present their solution convincingly, and a relativism which, expressed as the doctrine of expediency, enabled them to shift their ground, as the Nurse does, from one position to another.

For the Nurse, when she first talks to Phaedra, the choice between speech and silence is meaningless. She believes only in the choice between speech and speech. "You should not be silent, child. But either refute me if I speak badly, or agree if I speak well" (297–99). This implies her basic confidence that no problem is beyond the power of human reason, but when she hears the first hints of what is wrong with Phaedra (337–42), her confidence begins to falter. Ποῖ προβήσεται λόγος; "to what lengths will speech go?" she asks. And when she understands the truth, she tries to stop Phaedra's speech, οἴμοι τί λέξεις; (353). "Oh. What will you say?" She abandons hope of saving Phaedra's life, and consequently has no further use for her own. She goes off to die.

She comes back with her confidence renewed. She is now ashamed of her emotional reaction, her inadequacy, νῦν δ' ἐννοοῦμαι φαῦλος οὖσα (435). Second thoughts are best. What has happened to Phaedra is not ἔξω λόγου (437), not something beyond the powers of reason and speech.

The powerful speech into which she now launches is easily recognizable as contemporary sophistic rhetoric at its cleverest and worst; it is a fine example of "making the worse appear the better cause." It is the devil quoting scripture; she cynically accuses Phaedra of ὕβρις (474), insolence and pride toward the gods. She uses the stock sophistic argument to justify immoral conduct, the misdemeanors of the gods in the myths. And she reveals, in her description of the way of the world—the husbands who conceal their wives' infidelities, the fathers who connive at their sons' adulteries—a cynicism which is the well-known result of sophistic teaching, the cynicism of a Cleon, a Thrasymachus. Only a hardened cynic, in fact, could fancy that Hippolytus could be corrupted. And the Nurse's argument takes this for granted. Speech is all that is needed, λόγοι θελκτήριοι, winning words and in a double sense—the love charms and also her pleading the cause of love which will charm Hippolytus into compliance.

When we next see her, she is begging for silence. Ποῖ προβήσεται λόγος; was a prophetic question. Speech has unloosed forces beyond her control—ἔξω λόγου, and she now persuades Hippolytus to remain silent. But Phaedra has overheard their interview and now resumes control of the situation. She pours out on the Nurse all the fury and hatred which Hippolytus' terrible denunciation has roused in her. She uses the verbal loophole the Nurse so cleverly left her; "Did I not tell you to be silent?" οὐκ εἶπον ... σιγᾶν; (685–86) and curses her terribly, calling on Zeus to blast her with fire and destroy her root and branch:

$$\text{Ζεύς σε γεννήτωρ ἐμὸς}$$
$$\text{πρόρριζον ἐκτρίψειεν οὐτάσας πυρί (683–84).}$$

But the nurse is still not silenced. "I can make a reply to this, if you will listen," ἔχω δὲ κἀγὼ πρός τάδ', εἰ δέξῃ, λέγειν (697), she says, and she maintains her practical, unprincipled viewpoint—"If I had succeeded, I would be one of the clever ones," εἰ δ' εὖ γ' ἔπραξα κάρτ' ἂν ἐν σοφοῖσιν ἦ (700). And desperate though the situation is, she still has a way out. "There is a way to save you, even from this situation, my child," ἀλλ' ἔστι κἀκ τῶνδ' ὥστε σωθῆναι, τέκνον (705). But the Nurse, her way out, and the whole concept of λόγος, reason and speech, for which she stands, are rejected by Phaedra in one biting phrase—παῦσαι λέγουσα, "Stop talking" (706). And we hear no more of the Nurse.

The worldly, practical approach to the problem has proved no more successful than Phaedra's simple code of honor. The Nurse's one purpose, to save Phaedra's life, has, when translated into action, ensured her death. And the Nurse's outlook implies a view of the gods, a skeptical view, which is ironically developed in a play which has begun with the appearance of the goddess Aphrodite in person. The Nurse reveals her basic skepticism in her opening speech (176–97), in which she dismisses speculation about future life as unprofitable. Life as we know it is painful, she says (189–90), but as for some other thing, dearer than life, darkness enfolds it and hides it in clouds (192–93). There is no revelation of what lies beneath the earth, κοὐκ ἀπόδειξιν τῶν ὑπὸ γαίας (196). Later, when she recognizes the power of Aphrodite, she still expresses her belief in "scientific" agnostic terms. "Cypris was no god, then, but something greater, whatever it may be, than a god":

> Κύπρις οὐκ ἄρ' ἦν θεός
> ἀλλ' εἴ τι μεῖζον ἄλλο γίγνεται θεοῦ (359–60).

This rationalism of hers is the most unsound of all the views of the order of the universe expressed or implied by human beings in the play, and by a supreme irony this representative of skeptical thought is chosen to be the most important link in the chain of events which Aphrodite has forged. The Nurse's "reason" is the driving force in the process which brings Phaedra and Hippolytus to their deaths.

Hippolytus' purpose and his ideal is put before us early in the play; it is to live a life of piety and devotion to the virgin goddess Artemis. "I am in your company, and exchange speech with you," he says to the statue of Artemis. "I hear your voice though I may not see your face. May I round the final mark of the course of my life even as I have begun":

> σοὶ καὶ ξύνειμι καὶ λόγοις ἀμείβομαι,
> κλύων μὲν αὐδήν, ὄμμα δ' οὐχ ὁρῶν τὸ σόν·
> τέλος δὲ κάμψαιμ' ὥσπερ ἠρξάμην βίου (85–87).

He hopes to round the final mark, to run the full course of a life of reverence and piety, but his prayer is to be ironically fulfilled this very day. At the end of the play, he hears Artemis' voice though he cannot see her face, and exchanges speech with her as he lies dying, but he has been cut off in full career, his chariot wrecked. And before that he will have suffered the spiritual agony of seeing his father condemn and curse him as a hypocritical adulterer, a man whom it would be a mockery to associate with Artemis.

Like Phaedra, he is an aristocratic figure; in fact, most of the commonplaces of the aristocratic attitude are put into his mouth in the course of the play.[21] But he is also an intellectual and a religious mystic.[22] His principles, unlike Phaedra's, are clearly and consistently formulated; for him the most important thing in life is εὐσέβεια, reverence toward the gods.[23] "I know first of all how to treat the gods with reverence," ἐπίσταμαι γὰρ πρῶτα μὲν θεοὺς σέβειν (996), he says when defending himself against his father's attack. Except for the moment of passion when he threatens to break his oath and speak, he is guided in every thought and action by his εὐσέβεια. And when he finally decides for silence and his oath, he emphasizes this motive: "Know this, woman, it is my reverence which saves you," εὖ δ' ἴσθι τοὐμὸν σ' εὐσεβὲς σῴζει, γύναι (656), he says to the Nurse. He might have said, "It is my reverence which destroys me," for all through his father's bitter onslaught he stands by his principles, respects his oath, and keeps silent about Phaedra's part in the affair. As was the case with Phaedra and the Nurse, it is the central concept of his whole life and character which destroys him.

And, like them, he represents an attitude toward the gods. It is a religious position which is intellectual as well as mystic. His reverence for the gods manifests itself mainly in the worship of one goddess, Artemis; he completely rejects another, Aphrodite. The position is logical; on the intellectual plane, the worship of Artemis is clearly incompatible with the worship of Aphrodite, and acceptance of the one does constitute rejection of the other. The mass of humanity can ignore the contradiction, as the old servant does in the opening scene and just as most Christians manage to serve Mammon as well as God. But for the man who has dedicated his life to God, or to a goddess, there can be no compromise. Hippolytus must choose one or the other, "Man must choose among the gods as the gods choose among men," ἄλλοισιν ἄλλος θεῶν τε κἀνθρώπων μέλει (104), he says to the servant.[24] And Hippolytus has chosen Artemis. It does not save him. He dies in agony in the prime of youth, and before he dies he has to go through the mental agony of hearing himself, the virgin soul, πάρθενον ψυχὴν ἔχων (1006), treated by his father as a lustful hypocrite. And he sees himself in the end as a man who has spent his life in vain, ἄλλως: "In vain have I toiled at labors of reverence before mankind," μόχθους δ' ἄλλως / τῆς εὐσεβίας εἰς ἀνθρώπους ἐπόνησα (1367–69). He even goes so far as to wish that human beings could curse the gods, and though he is reproached by Artemis for this sentiment, he shows his disillusion in his farewell to her. "This great companionship of ours, you find it easy to leave," μακρὰν δὲ λείπεις ῥᾳδίως ὁμιλίαν (1441).[25] His reverence is inadequate, not merely as a way of life but also as a religious belief; it cannot stand unmoved in the face of reality—the knowledge that his privileged association with Artemis made him not a man to be envied but a pitiful victim, and that all the goddess can do for him is promise to kill another human being to avenge him.

Theseus is an early Attic king, but with the customary anachronism of Athenian tragedy, he is presented as a fifth-century statesman. His characteristic expression of thought and feeling is that of the man in the public eye, the man who is always conscious of his audience. When he states the charge against his son and invokes Poseidon's curse, he calls on the city to hear, ἰὼ πόλις (884), making it an official act. Even in his mourning for Phaedra he is conscious of his public stature, ἔπαθον ὦ πόλις (817), and in his tirade against Hippolytus he speaks to the audience as often as he does to his son, σκέψασθ' ἐς τόνδε (943), προφωνῶ πᾶσι (956). And he supports his action by an appeal to his reputation; if he is worsted by Hippolytus, the monsters he conquered in his heroic youth will no longer serve as proof that he is harsh to evildoers (976–80). His life is devoted to the maintenance of a reputation; even in his private sorrow he never forgets that the eyes of Athens are upon him.

He is a statesman, but not, like his son, an intellectual. He is the man of action; this point is emphasized by his impulsive act, his appeal to his heroic past, and his contempt for speech (λόγος). This appears clearly in his attack on his son; he describes Hippolytus as one who pursues evil with "pious words," σεμνοῖς λόγοισιν (957). "What words," he says, "can argue more effectively than this woman's corpse?" κρείσσονες τίνες λόγοι τῆσδ' ἂν γένοιντ' ἄν; (960–61) "Why do I try to compete with you in words on this matter?" τί ταῦτα σοῖς ἁμιλλῶμαι λόγοις; (971). He follows this last remark with action, the proclamation of banishment; he is a man not of words but of deeds. When he called Poseidon's curse on his son he did not wait, as Artemis reminds him later, for proof or prophecy or cross-examination, but followed his impulse. He is like another Athenian statesman, Themistocles, who, says Thucydides, was best at intuitive action in an emergency, κράτιστος ... αὐτοσχεδιάζειν τὰ δέοντα, and the best man to decide immediate issues with the least deliberation, τῶν ... παραχρῆμα δι' ἐλαχίστης βουλῆς κράτιστος γνώμων (1.138); Theseus acts with the swift decision of a Themistocles, an Oedipus. But he is wrong. And his mistake destroys the thing to which he has devoted his life. It is a mistake he can never live down, his public reputation is gone, as Artemis coldly tells him: "Hide yourself in shame below the depths of the earth, or take wing into the sky ... among good men there is now no portion you can call your own" (1290–95).

Theseus, too, has a distinct religious attitude. His is the religion of the politician, vocal, formal, and skin-deep, verbal acceptance but limited belief. He first appears on stage wearing the wreath of the θεωρός, the state visitor to an oracle, and he can roundly recite the names of the gods in public proclamation or prayer—"Hippolytus ... has dishonored the awful eye of Zeus," τὸ σεμνὸν Ζηνὸς ὄμμ' ἀτιμάσας (886), but he only half believes in all this. He prays to Poseidon to kill his son, and before the day is out, but when the chorus begs him to recall his prayer he replies: "No. And in addition, I shall exile him from this land," καὶ πρός γ' ἐξελῶ σφε τῆσδε γῆς (893). That revealing phrase "in addition" is expanded in the succeeding lines. "Of these two destinies he will be struck by one or the other," δυοῖν δὲ μοίραιν θατέρᾳ πεπλήξεται (894). Either Poseidon will strike him down or he will live out a miserable life in exile. The hint of skepticism is broadened when the messenger arrives to announce the disaster. He claims that his news is of serious import (μερίμνης ἄξιον, [1157]) to Theseus and all the citizens of Athens, but Theseus' first thought is of political news: "Has some disaster overtaken the neighboring cities?" (1160–61). Informed that Hippolytus is near death he asks, "Who did it? Did he get into trouble with someone else whose wife he raped, as he did his father's?" (1164–65). And only when the messenger reminds him of his curse does he realize the truth. "O gods, Poseidon, then you really were my father, you listened to my curses" (1169–70). It is a revelation which proves the unsoundness of his skepticism, and he accepts it with joy. But he will live to regret it and wish his prayer unspoken. "Would that it had never come into my mouth," ὡς μήποτ' ἐλθεῖν ὤφελ' ἐς τοὐμὸν στόμα (1412).

Theseus has gone through the same cycle as the other characters of the play. All four of the characters live, and two of them die, in a world in which purpose frustrates itself, choice is meaningless, moral codes and political attitudes ineffective, and human conceptions of the nature of the gods erroneous. But two of them learn, at the end of the play, the truth which we have known from the beginning, the nature of the world in which they live. They learn it from the lips of Artemis, as we have already heard it from the lips of Aphrodite. Artemis comes, like Aphrodite, to reveal (ἐκδεῖξαι [1298], δείξω [9]); she confirms, expands, and explains the process of divine government, of which the prologue was our first glimpse.

These two goddesses are powers locked in an eternal war, a war in which the human tragedy we have just witnessed is merely one engagement. In this particular operation, Aphrodite was the active agent and Artemis the passive; Artemis now informs us that these roles will be reversed—there will be a return made for this in which Artemis will assume the active role and Aphrodite the passive. The terms in which she explains her passivity in this case to Theseus make clear that this is permanent war, an eternal struggle in which the only losses are human lives.

"This is law and custom for the gods," she says, θεοῖσι δ' ὧδ' ἔχει νόμος (1328). "No one wishes to stand hostile against the energy of a god who has a desire—we stand aside always":

οὐδεὶς ἀπαντᾶν βούλεται προθυμίᾳ
τῇ τοῦ θέλοντος ἀλλ' ἀφιστάμεσθ' ἀεί (1329–30).

The authority for this law and custom, as Artemis makes clear, is Zeus himself; but for her fear of Zeus, she says, she would not have allowed Hippolytus to die. What has happened, then, is no anomaly, but the working of the system of divine government of the universe, an eternal pattern of alternate aggression and retreat. And we can see from what Artemis says that when she has the active instead of the passive role, she will be as ruthless as Aphrodite was in this case.

The words which describe Aphrodite's direction of human affairs are thus equally applicable to Artemis; they constitute a description of the function of divine government as a whole. And there are two words, repeated throughout the play at crucial moments and in significant contexts, which characterize the nature of the government of the universe. One of these words, σφάλλειν, describes the action characteristic of the gods, and the other, ἄλλως, describes the human condition which results from that action.

Σφάλλειν, to trip, throw, cast down. It is Aphrodite's own word for her action in the play. "I throw down those who despise me," σφάλλω δ' ὅσοι φρονοῦσιν εἰς ἡμᾶς μέγα (6). The literal accomplishment of this metaphorical threat comes when the bull from the sea "throws" the horses of Hippolytus' chariot, ἔσφηλε κἀνεχαίτισεν (1232). But this action is not confined to Hippolytus. The word recurs in connection with all the principal characters of the play. "You are quickly thrown," ταχὺ γὰρ σφάλλῃ (183), says the Nurse to Phaedra in her opening speech. She is referring to Phaedra's sudden changes of mind, the capriciousness of the sick woman who vacillates between staying indoors or out, but the words have a terrible significance in the light of what happens later when Phaedra changes her mind about something more important. Speaking of her own love for Phaedra and wishing, for her own peace of mind, that she did not love her so much, the Nurse laments the fact that "consistent conduct in life," βιότου δ' ἀτρεκεῖς ἐπιτηδεύσεις (261), "brings, so they say, not pleasure but overthrow," φασὶ σφάλλειν πλέον ἢ τέρπειν (262). It is true enough; the one consistent attitude in her, her love for Phaedra, brings her to ruin, and the words describe more exactly still the attitude and practice of Hippolytus, who is as consistent as the Nurse is flexible, as single-minded as the Nurse is versatile.

Phaedra, after she has heard Hippolytus denounce her and all her sex, sees herself as "thrown," σφαλεῖσαι (671). As Theseus reads the fatal letter, the chorus prays to an unnamed god, ὦ δαῖμον, not to throw the house, μὴ σφήλῃς δόμους (871). And when Theseus explains to Hippolytus how he could curse and condemn him, he uses the same word; "I was tripped and thrown in my opinion by the gods," δόξης γὰρ ἦμεν πρὸς θεῶν ἐσφαλμένοι (1414). It is this remark of his which provokes Hippolytus' wish that the human race could curse the gods.

The goddess trips, throws, leads astray, frustrates—all these are meanings of σφάλλειν, and the word which describes the operation of the human will in these circumstances is ἄλλως—otherwise, differently, wrongly, in vain. This adverb is used to describe the operation of human will throughout the tragedy; the character's actions produce results opposite to their purpose, things turn out "otherwise." "Our labor is all in vain," ἄλλως τούσδε μοχθοῦμεν πόνους (301), says the Nurse of her efforts to make Phaedra speak; the word has a double sense here, for the Nurse succeeds in her final attempt, but the results are not what she intended. "Vainly," says Phaedra to the chorus, "have I pondered in the long watches of the night, seeking to understand how human life is ruined":

ἤδη ποτ' ἄλλως νυκτὸς ἐν μακρῷ χρόνῳ
θνητῶν ἐφρόντισ' ᾗ διέφθαρται βίος (375–76).

This understanding she never attains, but it is given in all its fullness to Theseus and Hippolytus at the end of the play. "In vain, in vain,"[26] chants the chorus, "does the land of Greece increase sacrifice of oxen to Zeus and Apollo. . . . ":

ἄλλως ἄλλως παρὰ τ' Ἀλφεῷ
Φοίβου τ' ἐπὶ Πυθίοις τεράμνοις
βούταν φόνον Ἑλλάς <αἶ'> ἀέξει (535–37).

"In vain," says Hippolytus in his agony, "have I performed labors of reverence before mankind":

μόχθους δ' ἄλλως
τῆς εὐσεβίας
εἰς ἀνθρώπους ἐπόνησα (1367–69).[27]

And the Nurse, speaking specifically of humanity's ignorance of anything beyond this life, characterizes the whole human situation with the same word. μύθοις δ' ἄλλως φερόμεσθα (197), "We are carried off our course, led astray, supported vainly, by myths." In the context, it is of course a rationalist criticism of popular beliefs, but the verbal pattern of the whole poem invests it with a deeper meaning. We are borne astray, carried to a destination we did not intend, by myths, myths in which the Nurse does not believe, but which the appearance and actions of the two goddesses in the play prove to be not myths in the Nurse's sense, but the stuff of reality. The underlying meaning of the Nurse's words is brought out by the emphatic manner in which both goddesses are made to emphasize their connection with myth; myth, μῦθος, is the word they use of their own speech. "I will quickly reveal the truth of these words [myths]," δείξω δὲ μύθων τῶνδ' ἀλήθειαν τάχα (9), says

Aphrodite; Artemis, after telling Theseus the truth, asks him cruelly, "Does my word [story, myth] pain you?" δάκνει σε Θησεῦ μῦθος; (1313). Human beings are indeed borne astray by myths, the goddesses who trip their heels and thwart their purpose. Humanity is merely the "baser nature" which "comes between the pass and fell-incensed points of mighty opposites."

Of the nature and meaning of Aphrodite and Artemis in this play much has been written, and there is little to add. They have many aspects; they are anthropomorphic goddesses, myths, dramatic personalities with motives and hostile purposes and they are also impersonal, incompatible forces of nature. They are indeed "mighty opposites," and that opposition may be expressed in many terms—positive and negative, giving and denying, increase and decrease, indulgence and abstinence—but what Euripides has been at some pains to emphasize is not their opposition, but their likeness. The play is full of emphatic suggestions that there is a close correspondence between them.

When Hippolytus describes the meadow sacred to Artemis from which he has made the wreath he offers to her statue, he mentions the bee, μέλισσα (77), which goes through the uncut grass in spring. It is an appropriate detail, for the name μέλισσα, bee, was given to priestesses of Artemis,[28] and the bee is in many contexts associated with virginity.[29] But some five hundred lines later the chorus compares Aphrodite to a bee, "She hovers like a bee," μέλισσα δ' οἷα τις πεπόταται (562–63). This transference of symbol from the appropriate goddess to the inappropriate one is strange, and it is reinforced by another striking correspondence. The chorus, early in the play, describes Artemis, under one of her many titles, Dictynna. "She ranges through the marsh waters, over the land and over the sea, in the eddies of the salt water":

> φοιτᾷ γὰρ καὶ διὰ λίμνας
> χέρσον θ' ὑπὲρ πελάγους
> δίναις ἐν νοτίαις ἅλμας (148–50).

And later, the Nurse, describing the power of Aphrodite to Phaedra, uses similar language; "She ranges through the air, and she is in the wave of the sea":

> φοιτᾷ δ' ἀν' αἰθέρ', ἔστι δ' ἐν θαλασσίῳ
> κλύδωνι (447–48).

The function of these surprising echoes[30] is to prepare us for an extraordinary feature of Artemis' concluding speeches: she repeats word after word and phrase after phrase of Aphrodite's prologue. These two polar opposites express themselves in the same terms. "I gained a start on the road long ago," πάλαι προκόψασ᾽ (23), says Aphrodite, and Artemis uses the same unusual metaphor—"And yet I shall gain nothing, and only give you pain," καίτοι προκόψω γ᾽ οὐδέν, ἀλγυνῶ δέ σε (1297), she says to Theseus. "I shall reveal," δείξω (6), says Aphrodite; and Artemis says that she comes "to reveal," ἐκδεῖξαι (1298). "I am not unnamed," κοὐκ ἀνώνυμος (1), says Aphrodite, and Artemis takes up the phrase; "not unnamed (κοὐκ ἀνώνυμος) shall Phaedra's love for you fall and be silenced." Both of them claim, in similar words and with opposite meanings, that they reward the reverent and punish the wrongdoer (5–6 and 1339–41), and each of them, with the same characteristic word, τιμωρήσομαι (21 and 1422), announces her decision to kill the other's human protégé.[31]

They are opposites, but considered as divinities directing human affairs, they are exactly alike. The repetitions emphasize the fact that the activity of Aphrodite and the passivity of Artemis are roles which will be easily reversed. And the mechanical repetition of Aphrodite's phrases by Artemis depersonalizes both of them; we become aware of them as impersonal forces which act in a repetitive pattern, an eternal ordered dance of action and reaction, equal and opposite. From the law which governs their advance and retreat there can be no deviation; Artemis cannot break the pattern of movement to save Hippolytus, nor can she forgive Aphrodite. Forgiveness is in fact unthinkable in such a context; it is possible only for human beings. These gods are, in both the literal and metaphorical senses of the word, inhuman.

Artemis does indeed tell Hippolytus not to hate his father, πατέρα μὴ στυγεῖν (1435). But this merely emphasizes the gulf between god and man. She does not, on her plane, forgive Aphrodite; rather, she announces a repetition of the terrible events we have just witnessed: a new human victim is to die to pay for the loss of her favorite. "The anger of Cypris shall not swoop down on your body unavenged. For I shall punish another man, with my own hand, whoever chances to be most loved by her of mortals, with these inescapable arrows":

ἐγὼ γὰρ αὐτῆς ἄλλον ἐξ ἐμῆς χερὸς
ὃς ἂν μάλιστα φίλτατος κυρῇ βροτῶν
τόξοις ἀφύκτοις τοῖσδε τιμωρήσομαι (1420–22).

This, together with the promise that his memory will be the myth of a virgin cult, is the consolation she offers Hippolytus for the fact that she stood aside and allowed him to be destroyed. She cannot weep for him—that is the law which governs the nature of gods (κατ᾽ ὄσσων δ᾽ οὐ θέμις βαλεῖν δάκρυ [1396])—nor can she stay by him as he dies. "It is not lawful for me to see the dead and defile my eye with their dying breath":

ἐμοὶ γὰρ οὐ θέμις φθιτοὺς ὁρᾶν
οὐδ' ὄμμα χραίνειν θανασίμοισιν ἐκπνοαῖς (1437–38).

And she withdraws, leaving father and son alone.

It has often been remarked that this disturbing play ends on a note of serenity. Méridier's comment is typical: "le dénouement s'achève, grâce à la présence d'Artémis, dans un rayonnement de transfiguration. Et cette scène finale, où la tristesse déchirante s'épure peu à peu et s'apaise dans une sérénité céleste. . . . "[32] The ending is serene, but the serenity has nothing to do with Artemis, who throughout her scene with Hippolytus coldly and insistently disassociates herself from him,[33] so that he bids her farewell with a reproach. The serenity comes not from the goddess but from the two broken men who are left on stage after she withdraws.

Hippolytus forgives his father. To err is human, as Artemis says to Theseus:

ἀνθρώποισι δὲ
θεῶν διδόντων εἰκὸς ἐξαμαρτάνειν (1434);

but to forgive is not divine. It is an action possible only for man, an act by which man can distinguish himself from and rise above the inexorable laws of the universe in which he is placed. And though Hippolytus recognizes that he is following Artemis' advice,[34] he shows too that he is fully conscious of the fact that in forgiving he is doing what she cannot do. As he forgives his father, he calls to witness his sincerity "Artemis of the conquering arrow," τὴν τόξοδαμνον Ἄρτεμιν μαρτύρομαι (1451). The epithet is not ornamental; it recalls vividly Artemis' announcement of her intention to repay, twenty-five lines before—"with these inescapable arrows [τόξοις ἀφύκτοις] I shall punish another." Hippolytus calls to witness his act of forgiveness the goddess who cannot herself forgive.

It is significant that Artemis leaves the stage before the end of the play; her exit closes the circle which began with Aphrodite's entrance. Within its circumference, the human beings of the play fulfilled through all the multiple complications of choice an external purpose of which they were ignorant. But Aphrodite's purpose is now fulfilled; she has no further use for these creatures, and Artemis has gone. The play ends with a human act which is at last a free and meaningful choice, a choice made for the first time in full knowledge of the nature of human life and divine government, an act which does not frustrate its purpose. It is an act of forgiveness, something possible only for human beings, not for gods but for their tragic victims. It is man's noblest declaration of independence, and it is made possible by man's tragic position in the world. Hippolytus' forgiveness of his father is an affirmation of purely human values in an inhuman universe.

Notes

1. "The chief character is Hippolytus, and it is around him that the drama is built." G. M. A. Grube, *The Drama of Euripides* (New York, 1941), p. 177. See also L. Méridier, *Euripide* (Paris, 1927), Tome 2.19.

2. See David Grene, "The Interpretation of the *Hippolytus* of Euripides," *CP* 34 (1939), 45–58.

3. vs. 1334.

4. This and the following figures are based on Murray's Oxford text.

5. This figure does not include vss. 780–81 and 786–87, which Murray, with several manuscripts and the support of the scholia, assigns to the Nurse. It is dramatically more effective that the Nurse should disappear from the play after Phaedra's dismissal—ἀλλ' ἐκποδὼν ἄπελθε καὶ σαυτῆς πέρι φρόντιζ' (708–9). In any case, the phrasing of the verses which Murray assigns to the Nurse indicates a speaker who did not know that Phaedra was going to commit suicide; the Nurse knew this only too well (cf. 686–87).

6. By Phaedra in vs. 690.

7. vs. 436: αἱ δεύτεραί πως φροντίδες σοφώτεραι.

8. ὑπό τ' αἰγείροις ἔν τε κομήτῃ
λειμῶνι κλιθεῖσ' ἀναπαυσαίμαν; (210–11).

Both λειμών and κομήτης have sexual associations; see E. *Cyc.* 171 for λειμών and Ar. *Lys.* 827 for κομήτης. The taming of πῶλοι (231) is a common sexual metaphor (cf. Anacreon 75).

9. For a different interpretation of the force of ἐμάνην, μανία, and τὸ μαινόμενον, see E. R. Dodds, "The ΑΙΔΩΣ of Phaedra and the Meaning of the *Hippolytus*," *CR* 39 (1925), 102–10.

10. This is emphasized by the formal opening of Phaedra's address to them (373–74):

Τροζήνιαι γυναῖκες, αἳ τόδ' ἔσχατον
οἰκεῖτε χώρας Πελοπίας προνώπιον.

Cf. also παῖδες εὐγενεῖς Τροζήνιαι (710), when she makes her final request to them for silence.

11. For φίλτρα with deterrent effect, see, for example, Tibullus 1.2.59–69; Nemes., *Buc.* 4.62ff.

12. For this sense of ἔργον, see *LSJ sub verbo* 1.3.c.

13. See below, n. 18.

14. See below, n. 22.

15. See Méridier's excellent comments in *Euripide*, p. 19.

16. Though the choice between silence and speech has no further significance for the action—which has been determined beyond recall by Theseus' curse—it still recurs as a reminiscent theme in the second half of the play. Thus, Hippolytus urges his silent father to speak, σιγᾷς· σιωπῆς δ' οὐδὲν ἔργον ἐν κακοῖς (911), in words clearly designed to recall the Nurse's plea to Phaedra, εἶεν· τί σιγᾷς; οὐκ ἐχρῆν σιγᾶν, τέκνον (297). And the bull which comes from the sea to fulfill Theseus' curse announces its appearance with φθόγγος (1205) and φθέγμα (1215) but does its deadly work in silence, σιγῇ πελάζων (1231).

17. cf. Isoc., *De Antidosi* 253–57, *Nicocles* 5–9; X., *Mem.* 1.4.12.

18. cf. 423, 489, 688, 717; also 405 (δυσκλεᾶ). In 47 Phaedra is called εὐκλεής by Aphrodite.

19. cf. 288 to 514 *passim*.

20. cf. Th. 2.41, τὸν αὐτὸν ἄνδρα παρ' ἡμῶν ἐπὶ πλεῖστ' ἂν εἴδη καὶ μετὰ χαρίτων μάλιστ' ἂν εὐτραπέλως τὸ σῶμα αὐταρκὲς παρέχεσθαι.

21. For example, 79–81, 986–89, 1016–18.

22. But not an "Orphic"; that ghost is laid by D. W. Lucas in *CQ*, 40 (1946), 65–69.

23. cf. 84, 656, 996, 1309, 1339, 1368, 1419, 1454.

24. This is one, at least, of the meanings of this compressed statement.

25. The words recall Aphrodite's comment on the relationship between them: μείζω βροτείας προσπεσὼν ὁμιλίας (19).

26. ἄλλως ἄλλως corresponding to Ἔρως Ἔρως in the strophe.

27. The verbal context of this last appearance of ἄλλως is almost identical with that of its first, the ἄλλως τούσδε μοχθοῦμεν πόνους of the Nurse (301).

28. cf. scholia ad Pi., *P.* 4.106; Ar., *Ra.* 1274 (= A., *Fr.* 87).

29. cf. Verg., *G.* 4.197ff.: "quod neque concubitu indulgent nec corpora segnes in Venerem solvunt."

30. They are pointed out by Grube, *The Drama of Euripides*. He remarks on the "ominous similarity" of 148 and 448 and the "interesting echo" (μέλισσα).

31. cf. also μῦθος (9 and 1313) and βουλεύμασι (28 and 1406).

32. Méridier, *Euripide*, p. 24. For a similar view, more fully and more soberly developed, see S. M. Adams, "Two Plays of Euripides," *CR* 49 (1935), 118-19.

33. cf. 1396, 1404 (where ξυνάορον dispels the ambiguity of Hippolytus' τρεῖς ὄντας ἡμᾶς [1403]), 1436, 1437–39.

34. cf. 1442–43.

EIGHTEEN

Second Thoughts
in Greek Tragedy

"In human life," says the Nurse in Euripides' *Hippolytus* (435–36), "second thoughts are somehow wiser." Like many another character in Euripidean tragedy, she has just changed her mind, and, in true Euripidean style, she justifies her action with a generalization. It is not a generalization which would have recommended itself to Aeschylus and Sophocles; before Euripides, change of mind is a rare phenomenon on the tragic stage.[1]

Aeschylus, as Bruno Snell has demonstrated, broke new ground in Greek poetry with his explicit presentation of a conscious human choice between alternatives, a free human decision which commits its taker to a tragic course.[2] The responsibility the hero thus assumes, and the complex relation of his choice to the will of the gods and his own heredity, allow little scope for a change of mind. Aeschylean drama is linear; its principal figures, their decision once made, pursue their chosen course to the bitter end.[3]

In *The Persians*, which is the tragedy of a whole people rather than an individual, and which furthermore works through retrospect and prophecy rather than through present action, a change of mind is excluded by the nature of the dramatic organization. In the *Seven against Thebes*, Eteocles, at the end of a slow, almost static, preparation, makes his swift decision to fight against his brother; it is a decision, but not a change of mind—he had already decided to fight in person at one of the gates (282), and the gate where Polynices awaits him is the last remaining assignment. Once he has announced his passionate and fatal decision, the chorus tries to persuade him to change his mind, but without success. He sticks to his resolve, which is also the working of his father's curse. In *The Suppliants* there are no changes of mind. The chorus, in its unshakeable determination to prevent a marriage with the sons of Aegyptus, is one of the most demonically inflexible characters in Aeschylean tragedy. The king of Argos makes his hard decision, but

This chapter originally appeared in *Greek, Roman and Byzantine Studies*, 7, no. 3 (1966). Reprinted by permission.

once it is made he does not waver; he defies the herald of Aegyptus, and, as we know from other accounts, stakes his life on the issue and loses it.

In the *Agamemnon*, Clytemnestra's concealed purpose is the line along which the action inexorably moves: there will be no wavering in the heart of the woman who plans like a man. Agamemnon, however, after announcing emphatically that he will not walk on the tapestries spread before him (921ff.) yields to her persuasion and changes his mind. In the *Choephoroe*, Orestes hesitates when his mother bares her breast before his avenging sword—"Pylades, what shall I do?" τί δράσω;—but Pylades' three lines extinguish any hope that he will spare her. The *Eumenides*, however, ends with a dramatic change of mind; the Erinyes, persuaded by Athena, exchange their baleful threats against the Athenian land and people for hymns of blessing. The Erinyes, of course, are not human beings; neither is the hero of *Prometheus Bound*. He is one of the most inflexible figures in all Greek tragedy, but, although he will not change his mind, the action of the play consists of a series of attempts to make him do so, by persuasion, guile (the Oceanus scene), and force. The play, in fact, presents a Sophoclean hero in a Sophoclean situation, a hero whose greatness lies in his steadfastness and who is subjected, unsuccessfully, to tremendous pressure to make him change his mind.[4]

The mainspring of Sophoclean tragedy is the hero's stubborn refusal to change, no matter what force, persuasion, or deceit is used against him.[5] Ajax does not change his mind, though Tecmessa and the chorus think for a short while that he has. In the famous speech which has caused so much controversy, he contemplates the possibility, but in terms so negative that there is never for a moment any room for doubt that he rejects it.[6] Electra and Oedipus, in the two plays named after him, resist all attempts to make them change their minds on important issues (though Oedipus, unlike Electra, makes minor concessions).[7] Antigone resists even greater pressure without flinching, but her antagonist Creon, whose speeches are as full of heroically inflexible formulas as hers, finally cracks, surrenders, and changes.[8] In the *Philoctetes* (a very late play, 409) the hero is so stubborn that it takes a god come down from heaven to make him change his mind, though in the same play young Neoptolemus does completely reverse himself and Odysseus is so flexible that he seems to be infinitely changeable.

In Aeschylus and Sophocles, then, a change of mind is a rare phenomenon; when it does occur, it is either attributed to a secondary character or affects a secondary issue. The two older poets apparently found a change of mind either difficult to manage or downright undesirable on their tragic stage: it did not fit the tragic situations which they created and explored. The idea has to be expressed, of course, especially by Sophocles, in whose heroic plays the attempt to change the hero's mind is the mainspring of the action, but it is remarkable that the ordinary prose words for changing one's mind (μεταγιγνώσκω, μεταβάλλομαι, μεταβουλεύω etc.)⁹ hardly ever appear. Instead, the idea is expressed by phrases which present a change of mind not as a personal decision but as something imposed from outside or else in pejorative metaphors which suggest that it is a thing to be avoided, above all by heroes.¹⁰

The harshest of those expressions which suggest that a change of mind is imposed, not spontaneous, are drawn from the vocabulary of war. The change may be designated as conquest or domination. When Clytemnestra urges Agamemnon to walk on the tapestries she has spread for him, she tells him, "For those who are wealthy and powerful it is a fitting thing to be conquered," τοῖς δ' ὀλβίοις γε καὶ τὸ νικᾶσθαι πρέπει (941). And when the king gives way to her imperious will, he echoes her metaphor: "Since I have been subdued to obey you in this matter . . . ," ἐπεὶ δ' ἀκούειν σου κατέστραμμαι τάδε . . . (956).¹¹ When the chorus urges Ajax to reconsider his decision for suicide, they say: "Grant to your friends victory over your mind," δὸς ἀνδράσιν φίλοις γνώμης κρατῆσαι (483–84). "Such men as this," says Tecmessa in an appeal to the chorus, "are conquered by the words of friends," φίλων γὰρ οἱ τοιοίδε νικῶνται λόγοις (330).¹² Odysseus, in the same play, says to Agamemnon: "You are victorious, if you are conquered by your friends," κρατεῖς τοι τῶν φίλων νικώμενος (1353). And old Oedipus at Colonus, prevailed on by his daughters to see his son Polynices, says to them: "You conquer me by your speech," νικᾶτέ με λέγοντες (1204–5).

Similar to this military metaphor is the Sophoclean formula which is the keynote of all six of the heroic plays—the summons to the hero to yield, to surrender, εἴκειν, ὑπείκειν, etc.¹³ The demand is made to Ajax, Antigone, Philoctetes, Electra, and Oedipus, and in each case it is answered with defiance. But there is one character in Sophocles who does surrender to the pressure of circumstance, Creon, in the *Antigone*. He is urged to surrender by his son Haemon, to be like the tree that yields to the river in flood, ὑπείκει (713), unlike the sailor who does not yield to the wind, ὑπείκει μηδέν (716), and Tiresias bids him "surrender to the dead man," εἶκε τῷ θανόντι (1029). He refuses with heroic firmness, but in the end he does yield, and when he does, it is a swift and sudden collapse. "To yield is a dreadful thing," τὸ δ' εἰκαθεῖν γὰρ δεινόν (1096), he says, but yield he must. "I shall obey," πείσομαι (1099). But this word really means "I shall be persuaded," and it is indistinguishable in Greek from the future tense of the verb πάσχω—"I shall suffer, something will be done to me." He finds it hard to surrender, μόλις μέν, but he will "resign his heart's wish," καρδίας δ᾽ ἐξίσταμαι (1105), a word found in prose with connotations such as "resign from office," "give place to others," and even "degenerate."[14] "My thought," says Creon finally, "has been turned [ἐπεστράφη] in this direction." The passive nature of these formulas for change of mind recalls the only use in early Sophoclean drama of a form of the normal prose word μεταγιγνώσκω. The chorus of the *Ajax*, in ignorant jubilation, declares that Ajax "has been converted from his anger," μετανεγνώσθη (717); the complex compound μεταναγιγνώσκω occurs only here in extant Greek, and the passive of μεταγιγνώσκω does not seem to occur at all. In both cases, Creon and Ajax, the simple ways of expressing the concept of change of mind which lay ready to hand in everyday language seem to be deliberately avoided; the expressions used convey by their awkward distortion of plain speech the strain which a change of mind imposes on the tragic character.

There are other words which present change of mind as something imposed in even more violent metaphors. "Love," sings the chorus of the *Antigone*, "you wrench aside the minds of the just to injustice," δικαίων ἀδίκους φρένας παρασπᾷς (791–92). And Oedipus at Colonus is reassured by Antigone that Polynices will not "violently wrench him aside from his purpose," οὐ ... σε ... πρὸς βίαν παρασπάσει γνώμης (1185–86). In a similar phrase, Creon in the *Antigone* speaks of money which "warps honest minds to set themselves to shameful actions," παραλλάσσει φρένας (288).

A more gentle form of pressure to produce change (apart from the neutral and frequent πείθω, "to persuade") is the metaphor of "enchantment, bewitchment." This is how the Erinyes announce their change of mind towards Athens. After the repeated persuasive speeches of Athena, they explore her offer and then move towards acceptance. "I think you will charm me, and I turn from anger," θέλξειν μ᾽ ἔοικας καὶ μεθίσταμαι κότου (900). Here a normal prosaic word (μεθίσταμαι) appears (the only time it does appear in this sense in Aeschylus),[15] but it is introduced by the metaphor of enchantment. Antigone at Colonus urges Oedipus to listen to his son: "When men are given advice, their nature is enchanted by the incantations of those they love," νουθετούμενοι φίλων ἐπῳδαῖς ἐξεπᾴδονται φύσιν (1193–94).[16] Prometheus protests that Zeus will not "enchant" him "with the honey-tongued incantations of persuasion," μ᾽ οὔτι μελιγλώσσοις πειθοῦς ἐπαοιδαῖσιν θέλξει (172–73), and Athena, in her litany of persuasive appeals to the Erinyes, speaks of the "honied enchantments" of her tongue, γλώσσης ἐμῆς μείλιγμα καὶ θελκτήριον (886).

A second class of expressions presents a change of mind in pejorative metaphors. Eteocles rejects the chorus's appeal to avoid the fight with his brother as "blunting" the keen edge of purpose. "I am a sharp edge, you will not blunt it with words," τεθηγμένον τοί μ' οὐκ ἀπαμβλυνεῖς λόγοις (716). When Prometheus prophesies the murder of their husbands by the Danaids, he speaks of one who will change her mind: "One of the daughters love will charm not to kill her bedmate, the edge of her purpose will be blunted," μίαν δὲ παίδων ἵμερος θέλξει τὸ μὴ κτεῖναι ξύνευνον ἀλλ' ἀπαμβλυνθήσεται γνώμην (865–67). And Oedipus at Thebes reproaches the chorus for urging him to spare Creon's life: "You blunt the edge of my heart," τοὐμὸν ... καταμβλύνων κέαρ (688). "To bend" is another such metaphor. "Zeus," says the chorus of the *Prometheus Bound*, "has set his mind unbending," θέμενος ἄγναμπτον νόον (163), but he is no more unbending than his great adversary: "None of this will bend me," γνάμψει γὰρ οὐδέν τῶνδέ μ' (995), Prometheus replies to Hermes. He will not be "moistened" either, τέγγῃ γὰρ οὐδέν (1008), says Hermes to Prometheus. The metaphor suggests softening by moisture as well as tears. "Nor are you softened by prayers," οὐδὲ μαλθάσσῃ λιταῖς, he continues, using a metaphor drawn from softness of touch (of fabrics, flowers, etc.), and this metaphor (formations of μαλθακός, μαλακός) is very frequent. "Zeus will be soft-hearted some day," μαλακογνώμων (188), says Prometheus, predicting his adversary's defeat. "Zeus is not softened by such words," οὐχὶ μαλθακίζεται (952), says Hermes, and Kratos accuses Hephaestus, when he feels pity for Prometheus, with the words: "You grow soft," σὺ μαλθακίζου (79).[17] "In the gods' name, soften," πρὸς θεῶν μαλάσσου, says Tecmessa to Ajax (594), but a fragment of a lost Sophoclean play gives the proper heroic answer: "The heart of noble men does not grow soft," ἀνδρῶν γὰρ ἐσθλῶν στέρνον οὐ μαλάσσεται.[18]

The words μαλακός, μαλθακός, and their derivatives often suggest effeminacy in fifth-century usage,[19] and sometimes this suggestion that a change of mind is unmanly is made more explicit. "I shall not become woman-minded," θηλύνους γενήσομαι, says Prometheus (1003), and Ajax in his monologue despises himself for the momentary weakness stirred in him by Tecmessa's appeal: "My mouth was made effeminate by this woman here," ἐθηλύνθην στόμα πρὸς τῆσδε τῆς γυναικός (651–52). Similar to these expressions is the conception of a change of mind as "corruption" or "destruction": "Know this," says Agamemnon, as Clytemnestra bids him walk on the tapestries, "that I shall not corrupt my purpose," γνώμην μὲν ἴσθι μὴ διαφθεροῦντ' ἐμέ (932).[20]

This list is not complete (and I have reserved for later discussion some expressions which need special treatment), but it is representative, and the general picture is clear. A change of mind appears in Aeschylean and Sophoclean drama as something imposed and hence a sign of weakness, or it is expressed in pejorative metaphors—in any case, it is rarely presented on stage.[21]

One material reason for this feature of early tragedy may well have been the actor's mask. With the face of the tragic character fixed in one mold which announces his station and essential characteristic, without the play of facial expression which we take for granted on the stage, rapid emotional change and swift shift of purpose must have been difficult to present clearly in the vast theater of Dionysus. This, however, was only an inhibiting, not a prohibiting, factor, for Euripides overcame the difficulty, but it may help partially to explain the relative inflexibility of resolve and consistency of purpose in pre-Euripidean tragedy. But there are deeper causes. They lie in the poets' conception of human nature and heroic action and the place of these things in the cosmic framework.

In Aeschylus there are many interweaving strands in the fabric of human action. Eteocles' decision to fight his brother at the seventh gate is his own personal choice; we can see its motive in the bitter hatred he reveals in his great speech. It is also the product of chance—for he might have chosen to fight at any one of the gates, and chance, in Aeschylus, is the working of the will of Zeus. It is also the action of the curse his father pronounced on both his sons. In such a complex pattern of individual will, divine dispensation and hereditary curse, there is little room for change of mind. And indeed, the only significant change of mind in Aeschylean drama is that of the Erinyes who, though also subject to the mysterious processes of the will of Zeus, are not human at all.[22]

The inflexible resolution of the Sophoclean hero stems from a different conception, the aristocratic idea of a man's φύσις, his "nature." "*Physis*," says Albin Lesky, "is a man's permanent possession, his inalienable and unchanging inheritance . . . what man inherited through his descent determined his essence once and for all."[23] In the *Philoctetes* (409 B.C.), Sophocles gives us, in the person of a secondary character, Neoptolemus, son of Achilles, a picture of a man who betrays his φύσις, though he returns to it before the play is over. In this play, and in connection with this character, some of the phrases used to express the phenomenon of change of mind, though they are still not the neutral, prosaic formulas Euripides had been using for many years, are yet devoid of the pejorative connotations usual elsewhere in Sophoclean drama. "Curse you," says Philoctetes to the young man. "No, not yet, not until I learn if you will transfer your purpose back again," εἰ καὶ πάλιν γνώμην μετοίσεις (961–62). "Is it not possible," says Neoptolemus to Philoctetes, "to change one's mind back again?" μεταγνῶναι πάλιν; (1270). The reason for these neutral formulas is clear: Neoptolemus' change of mind is desirable. It is a change of mind *back* (πάλιν) to a position he should never have deserted, his reintegration in the heroic mold of his father Achilles. "Everything is difficult," he says earlier, "when one leaves behind his own φύσις and does what is not appropriate to it" (902–3).²⁴ He returns to it and is welcomed by Philoctetes as his father's son. "You have shown the φύσις from which you sprang" (1310–11). This return to heroic standards is in startling contrast to the attitude of the third principal figure in the play, Odysseus, who has no φύσις at all. "Where such men are needed, such a man am I," οὐ γὰρ τοιούτων δεῖ, τοιοῦτός εἰμ' ἐγώ (1049); he is whatever the changing circumstances demand. He can be anything because he is nothing, and he disappears ignominiously from the play, running away from the arrows of Philoctetes (1305–7).²⁵ He is not mentioned in the final speech of Heracles, who reserves his blessing for the young man who has recovered his heroic constancy and the sick hero who changed his mind only at the last moment at the express command of a god.²⁶

When the *Philoctetes* was first produced, Euripides had been Sophocles' competitor at the annual tragic festival for more than forty years.²⁷ There is no historical gap between them; in fact the younger poet was the first to die and Sophocles wore dark clothes at the *proagon* in 406 to mourn his rival's death. But in the earliest Euripidean play we have, the *Alcestis* (438), we can sense a complete change of atmosphere.

Admetus, the Thessalian king, the generous host *par excellence*, changes his mind in spectacular fashion, and it is emphasized for us by emphatic verbal repetitions. To mark his mourning for the wife who dies in his place, he promises her never to marry again, to put an end to revels, παύσω δὲ κώμους (343), to gatherings of friends drinking together, συμποτῶν θ' ὁμιλίας (343), to wearing of garlands and to music which has filled his house, στεφάνους τε μοῦσαν θ' ἣ κατεῖχ' ἐμοὺς δόμους (344). His wife consoles him. "Time" she says, "will soften you," χρόνος μαλάξει σ' (381). And it does. In the very next scene he welcomes into his house a friend, Heracles, who proceeds to revel, κώμου (804), drink, πίνει (757), wear a garland, στέφει δὲ κρᾶτα (759), and make music—drunken music, for he "howls out of tune," ἄμουσ' ὑλακτῶν (760). And before the play is over, Admetus accepts from Heracles an unidentified veiled young woman in a scene that suggests a marriage ceremonial. "Time will soften you," χρόνος μαλάξει (1085), says Heracles, as Alcestis had said before him. But of course the veiled woman is Alcestis back from the dead, so the play has a happy ending.

The formula for change of mind, μαλάσσω, is the familiar pejorative metaphor of the heroic tradition, but here it has a new content. Far from describing an attack on an iron determination, it expresses a new reality. The underlying assumption is that Admetus not only can change his mind but probably will. And he does. We are in a different dramatic world, no longer a heroic one.

The *Alcestis* is a substitute for a satyr play, but with the *Medea* (431) we are in an unmistakably tragic atmosphere; the central figure is built along Sophoclean lines, a dominating forceful personality whose purpose, once fixed, nothing can move, not the appeals of the chorus nor the screams of her children. Nothing can move her, but her resolution can be shaken, not by any external agency or circumstance but by the conflicting passions in her soul. The play from the very beginning emphasizes the instability of human decisions. The Nurse, for instance, regales us with some sociological reflections about changing one's mind—it is hard for the upper classes. "The spirit of royal persons is a strange and terrible thing: they have no discipline and much power, and they find it hard to change their tempers":

δεινὰ τυράννων λήματα καί πως
ὀλίγ᾽ ἀρχόμενοι πολλὰ κρατοῦντες
χαλεπῶς ὀργὰς μεταβάλλουσιν (119–21).

This is the first appearance of this word μεταβάλλω in this sense in extant Greek tragedy.[28] It is one of the most frequent prose words for "change," especially change of mind, and, as we shall see, it is one of Euripides' favorite words, together with its abstract noun μεταβολή. Unlike the metaphorical words generally used in such a context by Aeschylus and Sophocles, μεταβάλλω has no connotation of softening, weakening, yielding, or the like: it is a neutral word which accepts the phenomenon it describes as natural and normal.[29]

Creon announces Medea's sentence of immediate exile in uncompromising terms, ruling out any possibility of reprieve. "It is better to earn your hatred now than to be softened and later lament loudly," κρεῖσσον δέ μοι νῦν πρός σ᾽ ἀπεχθέσθαι ... ἢ μαλθακισθένθ᾽ ὕστερον μέγα στένειν (290–91). But "softened" he is. "My spirit is not at all that of a king," ἥκιστα τοὐμὸν λῆμ᾽ ἔφυ τυραννικόν (348), he says, unconsciously echoing the Nurse's reflections on royal tempers.

Creon changes his mind (and to his cost), but Medea resists Jason's appeals to self-interest and good sense. When she wishes for love rather than wealth (598–99), he suggests a different formula, introducing it with the words "Why don't you change your wish?" οἶσθ᾽ ὡς μετεύξαι; (600). This verbal compound may very well be a Euripidean invention; at any rate, it does not appear elsewhere in the whole of Greek literature as we have it.[30] In the next scene, Medea appears to change her mind: it is part of her plan to lure Jason into the trap. She confesses with apparent humility that she was wrong and has now come to better thoughts, φαμεν κακῶς φρονεῖν τότ᾽ ἀλλ᾽ ἄμεινον νῦν βεβούλευμαι τάδε (892-93). "My anger," she says, "has changed," μεθέστηκεν χόλος (898). Jason takes up her word. "Your heart," he says, "has changed for the better," ἐς τὸ λῷον σὸν μεθέστηκεν κέαρ (911). This word μεθίστημι is another of the normal prose words used for change;[31] it occurs rarely in this sense in Aeschylus and Sophocles[32] and first appears fully at home in the verse of Euripides.[33]

This whole scene, with Medea's feigned change of mind brilliantly acted out to deceive Jason, her maneuver to assure herself of Jason's love for the children (she calls them out of the house to embrace him [895] and then hears him speak with pride and love of the great future he will ensure for them [914ff.]), and her unfeigned sorrow when this reaction on his part finally seals their death warrant (922ff.)—this complex fabric of lies and truth (the lies believed, the truth unrecognized) shows an extraordinary dramatic ingenuity. It is the first time in our extant plays that a feigned change of mind is used to impose on another character, and it shows not only brilliant technique but also a new view of human nature. It has no precedent (unless with some critics we take Ajax's great speech as a deliberate attempt to deceive Tecmessa and the chorus);[34] but it had imitators. Surely Sophocles, in the scenes where Neoptolemus feigns initial reluctance to take Philoctetes aboard ship before consenting (519-25) and repeats the deception when Philoctetes urges immediate departure (635-45), had learned from this scene of the *Medea*.

Medea has pretended to change her mind, but when the moment comes to crown the deaths of Creon and his daughter with the murder of the children, she hesitates, and this is no pretense. The pressure on her to change her mind is not from without but from within; the form is soliloquy, not dialogue.[35] Like Orestes faced with his mother, she wavers, but, unlike him, needs no Pylades to bring her back to her purpose. In this famous speech, Euripides is breaking new dramatic ground; he shows us a heroic soul at cross-purposes with itself. She uses Orestes' words: "What shall I do?" τί δράσω; (1042). And her courage fails. "Farewell, my former plans," χαιρέτω βουλεύματα τὰ πρόσθεν (1044-45). And once again, "Farewell, my plans," χαιρέτω βουλεύματα (1048). What restores her resolution is not the voice of a god or his human spokesman, but the thought that she will be a laughingstock to her enemies if her plans for revenge fail. She exclaims at her own cowardice in admitting "soft words," μαλθακοὺς λόγους (1052), to her heart. She will not "weaken, corrupt," διαφθερῶ (1055) her hand.

But once again the sight of the children is too much for her feelings, and she falters a second time. This time, however, she recognizes the struggle in her own soul, for it is to her θυμός, her passion, that she appeals for the children's lives. "No, my passionate heart, do not do this," ... μὴ δῆτα θυμέ ... (1056). The appeal is refused, her θυμός takes full control, and now she swears by the avengers below in Hades that the children will die. And with no further hesitation she bids them a poignant farewell; the next time she sees them it will be with sword in hand (1278).

This speech was undoubtedly a new experience for the Athenian audience. The dramatic wavering back and forth between alternatives—four complete changes of purpose in less than twenty lines—marks the beginning of an entirely new style of dramatic presentation. Even six years later, in *The Acharnians*, Aristophanes is still regaling the audience with parodies of this speech. Dicaeopolis nerves himself for his ordeal with an address to his θυμός: "Forward now, my passionate soul, πρόβαινε νῦν ὦ θυμέ. Here's the starting line. You hesitate, do you? Drink your dose of Euripides down and take off! Good, that's right. And now, O suffering heart, be off in the same direction ... " (483–86).

It is excellent fooling, but shows clearly that the scene in the *Medea* has made an indelible and disturbing impression. It has on modern critics too. Bergk[36] (and Wecklein was inclined to approve)[37] wanted to cut out the second half of the speech and leave only two changes of mind instead of four.

Medea pretends to change her mind and then, at the critical moment, falters in her purpose, but she overcomes her doubts and sweeps on to her revenge. But in the *Hippolytus*, produced three years later (428), the classical ideal of heroic φύσις is completely dissolved. The characters of this play change their minds in a bewildering crisscross pattern which works out to their destruction and the fulfillment of Aphrodite's revenge.[38] Phaedra has made a heroic resolve—to die rather than reveal her love for Hippolytus. The Nurse, even before she begins what is to be a successful attempt to break that resolve, gives us the first explicit formulation of the new Euripidean view of human nature and conduct, the unheroic creed. "That one's behavior in life should be rigid (strict, exact) brings, they say, disaster rather than joy," βιότου δ' ἀτρεκεῖς ἐπιτηδεύσεις φασὶ σφάλλειν πλέον ἢ τέρπειν (261–62). "The Nurse," says Barrett, rightly, "produces this maxim simply apropos the present question of sticking to one's friends through thick and thin. But Euripides (not the Nurse) has another application in mind: Phaedra's present trouble is the result of sticking to her principles, of her refusing to give way to her love.... " The Nurse's attack begins. Phaedra is to "loosen the path of her thoughts," λύσασα ... γνώμης ὁδόν (290), and the Nurse, abandoning the incorrect path along which she followed

Phaedra before, will turn to another, better word, ἐπ' ἄλλον εἶμι βελτίω λόγον (292). A chance mention of the name Hippolytus breaks Phaedra's silence, and soon the truth is out. The Nurse, who was so sure that λόγος ("speech, reason") would solve the problem (297–99), now abandons herself to despair and wishes for death (353–57). But Phaedra, still resolved to die, now has the comfort of speech and pours out her story to the sympathetic ear of the chorus. She is still resolved; she states her principles in full confidence that she will never betray them. "Since this is how I think, there is no charm [φαρμάκῳ] that could make me desert them [διαφθερεῖν] so as to think the opposite," ὥστε τοὔμπαλιν πεσεῖν φρενῶν (388–90). She is wrong, and with magnificent poetic economy Euripides has contrived that what she rejected in the old metaphor "to change her mind through a charm," φαρμάκῳ διαφθερεῖν, comes about in fact: it is the Nurse's promise of a love charm which engineers her weak consent to her own betrayal (516).

The Nurse recovers from her dejection; she changes her mind and presents us with a more explicit version of her previous generalization. "In mortal life second thoughts are somehow wiser," κἀν βροτοῖς αἱ δεύτεραί πως φροντίδες σοφώτεραι (435–36). It does not look as if they are. Phaedra's second thoughts, and the Nurse's, lead straight to disaster. Hippolytus, in a famous line, threatens to break his oath of silence but then changes his mind; his second thoughts seal his death warrant, for when Phaedra dies by the rope and accuses him in a letter to Theseus (third thoughts! καινῶν λόγων, 688), he has no means of defense. Theseus has his second thoughts much too late: he calls down Poseidon's fatal curse on his son before he even questions him. "Take that prayer back," ἀπεύχου . . . πάλιν (981), cries the chorus, but he will not, and Aphrodite's purpose is fulfilled.

The chorus, lamenting the fate of Hippolytus, who remained true to the oath he had sworn, comes to the same conclusion as the Nurse and echoes the key word of her speech: "May my thoughts be neither rigid [ἀτρεκής] nor false. May I change my ways easily [ῥᾴδια δ' ἤθεα . . . μεταβαλλομένα] to fit the next day's span . . . " (1115–16).

This is an astonishing statement to come from the mouth of a tragic chorus. A choral ode is not of course to be lightly taken as the meaning of the play; it is a part of the total dramatic structure. But this stasimon is especially emphatic. It is the last one in the play; it is apparently sung by two choruses, one of men and one of women,[39] in responsion, and its moving, eloquent phrases bear directly on a central theme of the play which has been repeatedly introduced by the actors. Though it does not proclaim the time-serving creed of the Odysseus of the *Philoctetes*—"May my thoughts be neither rigid *nor false*"—it certainly abandons heroic consistency and the aristocratic ideal of human φύσις.

Like many another stasimon in Greek tragedy, it questions the dispositions of the gods and emphasizes that the life of man is nothing but change; what is new is the doctrine that human nature too is and must be nothing but change, in constant adaptation to circumstances.

In all of the plays which follow the *Hippolytus*, the instability of the world is paralleled by the instability of the human beings who live in it. The words for change of mind, those new prosaic words which Euripides introduced into tragic diction, occur from play to play. Change is the mode of operation of the universe, of chance, τύχη, of the gods; μεταβολή—a word which occurs with increasing frequency in Thucydides' account of the war as it pursues its course—is the key word of later Euripidean tragedy. "O Chance," says Ion when he discovers the strange story of his life, "you who have through change brought it about that tens of thousands of mortals suffer misfortune and then again fare prosperously . . . ":

> ὦ μεταβαλοῦσα μυρίους ἤδη βροτῶν
> καὶ δυστυχῆσαι καὖθις αὖ πρᾶξαι καλῶς
> τύχη (1512–14).

Change is painful, αἱ μεταβολαὶ λυπηρόν (*HF* 1292); it is also sweet, μεταβολὴ πάντων γλυκύ (*Orestes* 234). A whole range of words new in the mouths of tragic actors and chorus is employed to express the shifting, various nature of the world we live in: μεταπίπτω, μετατίθημι, etc.[40] One of them, περιπετής, appears for the first time in tragedy in the sense of "turning round, reversing" in *Andromache* 982, περιπετεῖς τύχας, a forerunner of Aristotle's celebrated formula περιπέτεια.

The gods, like the universe they direct, are changeable too. Poseidon accuses Athena in the *Troades* prologue: "Why do you leap so now to one temper, now to another?" τί δ' ὧδε πηδᾷς ἄλλοτ' εἰς ἄλλους τρόπους; (67). Later in the play, Hecuba, without benefit of this conversation, correctly guesses the nature of the universe: "Chance events, like a man who quickly changes his mind,[41] leap now here, now there," τοῖς τρόποις γὰρ αἱ τύχαι, ἔμπληκτος ὡς ἄνθρωπος, ἄλλοτ' ἄλλοσε πηδῶσιν (1204–6). And the chorus of the *Helen* sings of the dilemma faced by the thinker who tries to determine the nature of the gods, when "he sees the various dispensations of heaven leaping first here and then there and back again with contrary and unlooked-for results":

> . . . τὰ θεῶν ἐσορᾷ
> δεῦρο καὶ αὖθις ἐκεῖσε
>   καὶ πάλιν ἀντιλόγοις
> πηδῶντ' ἀνελπίστοις τύχαις . . . (1140–43).

The action of men in such a world is described in similar terms. The neutral, factual words for changing one's mind, μεθιστάναι, μετατίθεσθαι, μεταβάλλεσθαι, occur frequently. In *The Suppliants* 1083 we are given another version of the Nurse's δεύτεραι φροντίδες: "by later counsel we are set right," γνώμαισιν ὑστέραισιν ἐξορθούμεθα. The *Andromache* (1003–4) gives us the nearest Greek equivalent of our phrase "change of mind," μετάστασις γνώμης, and in the *Orestes* even the word μεταβουλεύομαι[42] is fitted, not, it is true, into iambic trimeters, but into trochaic tetrameter. Orestes, playing his contemptible game of cat and mouse with the Phrygian slave, spares his life, but then pretends to change his mind, ἀλλὰ μεταβεβουλευσόμεσθα (1526). In the *Bacchae* these same formulas for change of mind are used with a new and terrible content; under Dionysiac possession and in their recovery from it, the characters "change their mind" in more than one sense of the phrase. "I approve of your change of mind," αἰνῶ δ' ὅτι μεθέστηκας φρενῶν (944), says Dionysus to Pentheus;[43] more is involved than a normal change of mind, for Pentheus' next words are, "Couldn't I carry on my shoulders the valleys of Cithaeron, Bacchants and all?" And so in the reverse process, when Agave recovers from her Bacchic frenzy to realize that the lion's head she carries is the head of her son, "I have become somehow sane," γίγνομαι δέ πως ἔννους, she says, "changed from my former mind," μετασταθεῖσα τῶν πάρος φρενῶν (1269–70).

The *Bacchae* was one of the final group of plays Euripides wrote just before his death in Macedonia; the other one which has survived is the *Iphigenia at Aulis*. And in this play Euripides fills his stage with human beings who react to changing circumstance with swift and frequent changes of mind which are presented not as deviations from a heroic standard but as normal human behavior.

The one thing everybody knows about this play is that Aristotle disapproved of it. "In connection with characters, there are four things that should be aimed at, . . . " he says in the *Poetics* (1454ᵃ26). "The fourth is consistency [τὸ ὁμαλόν]. For even if the person being imitated is of an inconsistent sort and that kind of character has been posited,[44] still he should be consistently inconsistent [ὁμαλῶς ἀνώμαλον]. An example . . . of inconsistency is the *Iphigenia at Aulis*, for the girl who makes the speech of supplication bears no resemblance to the later one."

This comment of Aristotle's is not surprising, for in his discussion of tragedy one of the things he does not seem to make allowance for is that heroes or heroines might change their minds.[45] But one cannot help feeling that he might have picked a better example, for Iphigenia's change of mind has been well prepared for in Euripides' play—it comes as the climax of a series of swift and sudden changes of decision which is unparalleled in ancient drama.[46]

Agamemnon, at night in the camp at Aulis, has been writing a letter. The old man who speaks to him in the prologue describes his actions. "You are writing a letter, this one you hold in your hand now. You erase over and again the same written words, you seal it and open it again, and throw the tablet to the ground . . . " (35–39). Agamemnon explains to his servant the whole story—the demand for Iphigenia's sacrifice, the plot to entice her to Aulis with a false story of marriage to Achilles, and the letter he himself wrote to Clytemnestra with instructions to send her daughter to the camp. But he has changed his mind. "What I wrote then was wrong. I have rewritten it well, to the opposite effect," αὖθις μεταγράφω καλῶς πάλιν (108).[47] And he sends the old man off to Argos with the counterorder—to keep Iphigenia at home.

The word μεταγράφω occurs only here in tragedy, and this has been seized on as one more proof of fourth-century interpolation or revision for the fourth-century stage.[48] It proves nothing at all. This word μεταγράφω is the normal fifth-century word for "to correct a draft, to rewrite," and if it does not occur elsewhere, that is most likely because no one before Euripides wanted to have one of his principal characters write two or more versions of an important letter.

Menelaus intercepts the new letter and faces his brother with what he regards as evidence of treachery. In the excited, brilliantly written trochaic dialogue which follows, the attack on and defense of Agamemnon's change of mind shows, through the naturalness of the language and the ease of the swift transitions, that in this last play Euripides handles with faultless ease the problem of presenting on the tragic stage human beings who twist and turn, leap from one position to another— men "not as they should be, but as they are."

Menelaus' furious assault paints Agamemnon as a vacillating trickster. "Your thoughts are crooked, one thing now, another then, yet another soon," πλάγια γὰρ φρονεῖς, τὰ μὲν νῦν, τὰ δὲ πάλαι, τὰ δ' αὐτίκα (332). "Your mind is not stable," νοῦς δέ γ' οὐ βέβαιος (334). He reproaches his brother for the change that high office has produced in him. When he campaigned for the command of the Achaean host, he was humble and approachable—"but then, when you got the command, you changed to different ways," μεταβαλὼν ἄλλους τρόπους (343). The good man, says Menelaus, should not, when in high office, "change his ways," τοὺς τρόπους μεθιστάναι (346), but should be "reliable," βέβαιον (347). The indictment proceeds. When the fleet was held up at Aulis, Agamemnon was in despair and confusion, but when Calchas prophesied that the sacrifice of Iphigenia would speed the fleet to Troy, he was joyful and sent a letter summoning his daughter. "And now I have caught you turning back," ὑποστρέψας λέλησαι, "changing what you wrote to something else," μεταβαλὼν ἄλλας γραφάς (363).

It is a powerful speech, and, apart from personal attacks on Menelaus (which Agamemnon does not omit), there is only one real answer: that the change of mind was justified. And Agamemnon finally says so: "If I made a bad decision then and later changed to good counsel, am I therefore mad?" εἰ δ' ἐγὼ γνοὺς πρόσθεν οὐκ εὖ μετετέθην εὐβουλίαν, μαίνομαι; (388–89).

The quarrel is interrupted by the arrival of a messenger; Iphigenia, Orestes, and Clytemnestra have arrived at Aulis. The first letter has done its work, and Agamemnon has no way out now—he is under "the yoke of necessity," ἀνάγκης ζεύγματ' (443). But his laments are interrupted by Menelaus. The man who so bitterly attacked Agamemnon's instability of purpose, who praised the "reliable" mind, has suddenly changed his attitude. "I stand apart from what I said before," τῶν παλαιῶν ἐξαφίσταμαι λόγων (479). Disperse the fleet, he says, let it sail home from Aulis (495): "Have I changed from my fierce words?" ἀλλ' ἐς μεταβολὰς ἦλθον ἀπὸ δεινῶν λόγων; "What has happened to me is natural," εἰκὸς πέπονθα. "I have changed over to feel love for my brother," τὸν ὁμόθεν πεφυκότα στέργων μετέποσον. And then, in a generalization which justifies his conduct: "Such changes are not the mark of the evil man," ἀνδρὸς οὐ κακοῦ τροπαὶ τοιαίδε (500–4).

But nothing can save Iphigenia now; the army insists on her sacrifice, as Agamemnon well knows. Clytemnestra makes one last attempt to save her by enlisting the aid of Achilles, the prototype of heroic φύσις. He promises to defend her, to defy the army. But in this play even the greatest hero of them all is a different man. After promises, made in high, astounding terms, he advises Clytemnestra to make one last attempt to persuade Agamemnon to change his mind. "What prudent advice!" she says to him, ὡς σῶφρον' εἶπας (1024). Nobody ever had occasion to speak like that to Achilles before.

When, later, he comes in pursued by his own troops, there is clearly no way out. And Iphigenia, who earlier in the play made her marvelous speech of supplication to Agamemnon begging for her life—"Had I the speech of Orpheus, father," εἰ μὲν τὸν Ὀρφέως εἶχον ὦ πάτερ λόγον (1211ff.)—now changes her mind and resolves to die willingly, κατθανεῖν δέ μοι δέδοκται (1375). Inconsistent? It is one more change of mind, no more violent than those we have seen earlier in the play. And if Aristotle means that it is unmotivated (and his statement has been so interpreted), he has overlooked something. Right from the beginning of the play, through the speeches of the actors and the lyrics of the chorus, Euripides has emphasized the Panhellenic nature of the expedition, presenting it as a holy war of all Greece united against the barbarians. This is the content of Iphigenia's speech (1378–1400). In 406 B.C., it was a theme heard in many quarters in a Greece ravaged by internecine war,[49] and when Iphigenia states it so simply and nobly, there can have been few in the audience who did not feel its power.

Achilles, overcome with admiration at Iphigenia's courage, offers to protect her if she should change her mind again, ἴσως γὰρ κἂν μεταγνοίης τάδε (1424). He seems to expect that she will, but she does not and goes off to what she fully expects will be her death.

It is typical of the paradoxical nature of Euripidean drama that the poet who in his plays destroyed the old ideal of heroic φύσις, the god-given, unchangeable nature of a great individual, and filled his stage with irresolute, changeable human beings in whom we can more easily recognize ourselves, should in this last play have presented us with a truly heroic action which springs not from stubborn resolution but from a change of mind.

Notes

1. This essay is concerned not with fundamental change of character nor with regret for past action (μετάγνοια, μεταμέλεια), but solely with "change of mind," understood as the dramatic presentation and formulation of a new decision or attitude which supplants and reverses a previously determined course of action.

2. cf. Bruno Snell, *Aischylos und das Handeln im Drama* (*Philol.* Supplement b.20, Heft 1) (Leipzig, 1928); *The Discovery of the Mind*, trans. T. G. Rosenmeyer (Cambridge, Mass., 1953), pp. 101–8; *Scenes from Greek Drama* (Berkeley and Los Angeles, 1964), pp. 1–22.

3. cf. Snell, *Discovery*, p. 107: "Pelasgus, Achilles, Eteocles, Orestes, all the Aeschylean heroes cannot be made to swerve from their course of action, however powerful the motives operating against it may be."

4. cf. B. M. W. Knox, *The Heroic Temper: Studies in Sophoclean Tragedy* (Berkeley and Los Angeles, 1964), pp. 45–50.

5. Ibid., pp. 8–44.

6. T. B. L. Webster, *An Introduction to Sophocles* (Oxford, 1936), pp. 96–97, and C. M. Bowra, *Sophoclean Tragedy* (Oxford, 1944), pp. 39–43, seem to be alone in their conviction that Ajax seriously renounces his intention to kill himself.

7. *O.T.* 669; *O.C.* 1204–5.

8. cf. Knox, *The Heroic Temper*, pp. 67–75; Hans Diller, "Über das Selbstbewusstsein der sophokleischen Personen," *Wiener Studien*, 69 (1956), 82–83.

9. μεταγιγνώσκω Hdt. 1.40, 86, 7.15; Th. 1.44, 3.58 and μεταβάλλομαι Hdt. 5.75; Th. 1.71, 8.73, 90. μεταβουλεύομαι Hdt. 1.156, 7.12, 8.57; μετανοέω does not occur in extant tragedy (though Heimsoeth tried to introduce it at E., *I.A.* 1207).

10. I omit consideration of words which mean "cease from," etc. (λήγω, παύομαι, μεθίημι); they imply a change of mind but do not explicitly present the substitution of a new course of action.

11. cf. Eduard Fraenkel, *Aeschylus, Agamemnon* (Oxford, 1950), *ad loc.*

12. The last word of the line is φίλοι in all the mss; Bodleian c89 records a variant λόγοις, which is found also in Stobaeus. W. B. Stanford, *Sophocles' Ajax* (London, 1963), *ad loc.* argues for φίλοι, but cf. chapter 12 of this book.

13. cf. Knox, *The Heroic Temper*, pp. 15–17; Diller, "Über das Selbst.," 75ff.

14. cf. e.g., Th. 2.63, 4.28; S., *Ph.* 1053, *Aj.* 672; Pl., *R.* 380d.

15. It does not occur in Sophocles in this sense.

16. cf. F. Ellendt-Genthe, *Lexicon Sophocleum* (Berlin, 1872), s.v. ἐξεπάδω: "Accusat. additur quod *mutatio animi* facta significatur, velut sagae et praestigiatores ipsam rerum naturam convertere credebantur."

17. cf. also A., *P.V.* 379, ἐάν τις ἐν καιρῷ γε μαλθάσσῃ κέαρ.

18. Pearson *Fr.* 195 ('Επίγονοι).

19. For a discussion of the meaning of the words in an earlier period, cf. Max Treu, *Von Homer zur Lyrik* (Munich, 1955), pp. 183–88.

20. Although Fraenkel is undoubtedly right in his interpretation of παρὰ γνώμην in 931, there does not seem to be any reason (except Fraenkel's admiration for the "*gentilezza* of the utterances of the king and queen") why 932 should not mean "I will not change my mind." In fact, the only parallels, E., *Med.* 1055 χεῖρα δ' οὐ διαφθερῶ and *Hipp.* 389 διαφθερεῖν (on which cf. W. S. Barrett, *Euripides Hippolytos* [Oxford, 1964], ad loc.) clearly refer to a change of mind.

21. There are some phrases which do not fit either of these categories but yet betray by the very complication of their expression the difficulty posed for the poet by the content. For example, S., *Ph.* 1191–92, τί ῥέξοντες ἀλλοκότῳ γνώμᾳ τῶν πάρος ὧν προφαίνεις; which really means "To do what? Have you changed your mind?" and *Aj.* 736, νέας βουλὰς νέοισιν ἐγκαταζεύξας τρόποις (ἐγκαταζεύγνυμι seems to occur only here.).

22. At A., *A.* 218ff. the chorus describes Agamemnon's dilemma and decision at Aulis; the phrase φρονεῖν μετέγνω employs a normal prosaic word meaning "change one's mind." But the context makes it quite clear that this is not a change of mind from one decision to another, but from indecision to decision. "(He) decided instead to entertain thoughts of the utmost audacity . . . " is the paraphrase suggested by J. D. Denniston and D. L. Page, *Aeschylus Agamemnon* (Oxford, 1957), on 221. Fraenkel's translation—"he reversed his mind"—implies that he had previously decided *not* to sacrifice Iphigenia, and of this decision there is no trace in the text. In fact, Agamemnon states this alternative in terms which make it clear that he rejects it—"the possibility is dismissed as unpractical" as Page puts it (p. xxvi). Fraenkel formulates the meaning of μετέγνω more precisely in his note on 221; in his explanation of A., *Supp.* 110 (2.219 n.1) he says: "to pass from a normal state of mind into a condition in which he is ready to commit a crime, a man must have undergone a μεταγνῶναι . . . " The only other occurrence of this word in Aeschylus (μεταγνούς *Supp.* 110) is also puzzling. In the context, ἄταν δ' ἀπάτᾳ μεταγνούς cannot mean "he has changed his mind to his own infatuation and destruction . . . " (Fraenkel on *A.* 221) but must mean simply "resolving on infatuation etc." This is in fact how it is taken by the authorities Fraenkel cites: N. Wecklein, *Aischylos, Die Schutzflehenden* (Leipzig, 1902), ad loc., "er hat sich . . . statt zum Heilsamen zu seinem Verderben entschlossen"; Wilamowitz-Moellendorff, *Aischylos Interpretationen* (Berlin, 1914) p. 31, n.3, "entscheidet sich das falsche urteil der menschen für ἄτη." Buecheler's interpretation (*RhM* 41 [1886], 8), in which according to Fraenkel "the passage is rightly explained," suffers from his insistence that ἄτη means loss of a lawsuit (as opposed to νίκη); he renders "damnum tulisse ita eos poenitet non ut peccare caveant sed ut porro nitantur ad fraudem."

The context in both passages seems to suggest that for Aeschylus μεταγιγνώσκω does not mean "to change one's mind" but something like "to decide one way instead of the other."

23. Albin Lesky, *Die Griechische Tragödie*[2] (Stuttgart, 1958), p. 163.

24. For a comic version of the same thought cf. Ar., *V.* 1457, τὸ γὰρ ἀποστῆναι χαλεπὸν φύσεος ἦν ἔχοι τις ἀεί.

25. As he had previously retreated before the prospect of combat with Neoptolemus (1257).

26. Philoctetes' change of mind is expressed in the old formula, "I shall not disobey your words," οὐκ ἀπιθήσω (1447).

27. He first competed in the Dionysia in 455 (with the *Peliades*) and was awarded third prize. cf. the "Life," L. Méridier, *Euripide* I⁴ (Paris, 1956), 2.

28. Not in Aeschylus, once in Sophocles (*El.* 1262), but in the sense of "exchange."

29. It is common in Aristophanes: μεταβάλλεσθαι τοὺς τρόπους *V.* 1461, *Ra.* 734, 1451, *Pl.* 36.

30. Similar in meaning is the phrase ἀπεύχου ... πάλιν *Hipp.* 891.

31. e.g., Hdt. 1.65, 118; Th. 4.76, 6.89, 8.48; and cf. Ar., *Eq.* 397, *V.* 748, 1451, *Pl.* 365, 994.

32. A., *Eu.* 900, *Pers.* 158; S., *Fr.* 646.6. In *Ant.* 718 μετάστασιν δίδου—introduced by εἶκε (cf. Jebb *ad loc.*)

33. e.g., *Alc.* 174, *Heracl.* 487, 796, 935, *Ion* 1506, *Ba.* 296 etc.

34. cf. chapter 11 of this book. Stanford sums up recent discussion in *Sophocles' Ajax*, app. D, pp. 280–88. Cf. also chapter 12 of this book.

35. The classic discussion of this monologue is Wolfgang Schadewaldt, *Monolog und Selbstgespräch* (Berlin, 1926), pp. 193ff. For some salutary corrections to the *geistes-geschichtliche* inferences often drawn from this speech, see Eilhard Schlesinger, "Zu Euripides' Medea," *Hermes*, 94 (1966), 28ff.

36. Theodor Bergk, *Griechische Literaturgeschichte* III (Berlin, 1884), p. 512, n. 140, "der Schluss der Monologes der Medea (1056–80) nur die Gedanken wiederholt welche schon vorher ausgesprochen waren; dies ist weit mehr geeignet den Eindruck abzu-schwächen als zu steigern."

37. cf. Wecklein, *Euripides, Medea*³ (Leipzig, 1891), pp. 26–30 (two versions of the *Medea*) and p. 150 on vss. 1056–80.

38. cf. chapter 17 of this book.

39. See Barrett's full discussion *ad loc.*

40. μεταπίπτω, E., *Alc.* 913, *Ion* 412, *I.A.* 502 (not in Aeschylus or Sophocles but cf. Ar., *V.* 1454, *Av.* 627). μετατίθημι *Or.* 254, *I.A.* 388, *Rh.* 131 (not in Aeschylus, once in S., *Ph.* 515 but in an unusual sense, cf. Jebb *ad loc.*).

41. For this meaning of ἔμπληκτος (which the context demands) see LSJ s.v. 2 and cf. esp. S., *Aj.* 1358. The modern editors and translators are almost unanimous in their interpretation of the word as "crazed, mad," e.g., Barnes (1788) "*veluti furens homo,*" Paley (1892) "crazy," Tyrrell (1921) "like an idiot," Lattimore (1959) "a madman." L. Parmentier and H. Grégiore, *Euripide IV* (Paris 1959), have the correct translation, "un homme fantasque," which is the ancient explanation too, cf. Σ *ad loc.* (Schwartz II, p. 374).

42. Not in Aeschylus or Sophocles but already in *Od.* 5.286 μετεβούλευσαν θεοὶ ἄλλως; cf. Hdt. 1.156, Ar., *Ach.* 632.

43. cf. E. R. Dodds, *Euripides Bacchae*² (Oxford, 1960), *ad loc.*

44. ὑποτεθῇ with R. Kassel, *Aristotelis De Arte Poetica Liber* (Oxford, 1965).

45. Horace makes explicit the underlying assumption of the Aristotelian passage: "sibi convenientia finge ... servetur ad imum qualis ab incepto processerit et sibi constet" (*A.P.* 119, 126–27).

46. cf. Markland's brilliant note on E., *I.A.* 1375.

47. Reading, with John Jackson, *Marginalia Scaenica* (Oxford, 1955), p. 209, Μενέλεως <ἐγώ> θ'. ἃ δ' οὐ / καλῶς τότ', αὖθις μεταγράφω καλῶς πάλιν—a correction of Vitelli, incorrectly reported by Murray (who seems to have reproduced the mistake of E. B. England).

48. D. L. Page, *Actors' Interpolations in Greek Tragedy* (Oxford, 1934), p. 138.

49. cf. e.g., Ar., *Lys.* 1133–34, ἐχθρῶν παρόντων βαρβάρων στρατεύματι / Ἕλληνας ἄνδρας καὶ πόλεις ἀπόλλυτε; X., *H.G.* 1.6 (Callicratidas in the Aegean, 407 B.C.); and see R. Goossens, *Euripide et Athènes* (Brussels, 1962), pp. 683ff.

NINETEEN

Euripidean Comedy

"The most tragic of the poets," Aristotle called him (whatever he may have meant by it),[1] and succeeding ages have agreed; the great Euripidean tragedies, *Hippolytus*, *Medea*, *Bacchae*, *Trojan Women*, show us a world torn asunder by blind, disruptive forces, which affords no consolation, no compensation for suffering, no way to face it except resigned endurance, a world which reduces man from the status of hero to that of victim. But Euripides had another side to his genius: he introduced to the theater of Dionysus new forms of drama, the *Iphigenia in Tauris*, the *Helen*, the *Ion*, plays which critics and scholars have labored in vain to define. They are clearly a radical departure from Euripidean tragedy (from any of our notions of tragedy, for that matter), but the search for a term which adequately describes them has resulted only in a confusing assortment of vague categories: they have been called romantic tragedy, romantic melodrama, tragicomedy, romances, romantic comedy, *drames romanesques*, *Intrigenstücke*, to list only the most influential attempts at nomenclature. One cannot help suspecting that what everyone would really like to call these plays (at least the *Ion*) is comedy (though no one, to my knowledge, has taken the plunge).[2] There are, of course, good reasons for such hesitation. But I should like to suggest that they are not good enough, that provided the word "comedy" is understood in modern, not ancient terms, Euripides, in these plays but especially in their culmination, the *Ion*, is the inventor, for the stage, of what we know as comedy.

One reason for stopping short of this word is of course the certainty that Euripides himself would have repudiated it with some indignation. "Comedy," he would have said, "is an entirely different kettle of fish: it is what my friend Aristophanes writes." In fifth-century Athens the two genres were rigidly separate, and comedy—a high-spirited combination of unbridled personal lampoon, literary burlesque, indecent buffoonery, brilliant wit, and lyric poetry of the highest order—had its own recognizable conventions of plot, language, dance, and meter, which were quite distinct from those of tragedy. When at the end of a long

This chapter originally appeared in *The Rarer Action: Essays in Honor of Francis Fergusson*, ed. Alan Cheuse and Richard Koffler (New Brunswick, N.J., 1970). © 1970 by Rutgers, The State University of New Jersey. Reprinted by permission of Rutgers University Press.

night of revelry, drinking, and conversation, Socrates in Plato's *Symposium* proposed and defended the thesis that the same man could be capable of composing both tragedy and comedy, we are left in no doubt that his hearers, a comic and a tragic poet, are reluctant to accept this surprising idea. "They were being forced [ἀναγκαζομένους] to this conclusion," says Plato, "but they could not follow his argument too well, for they kept drowsing off—Aristophanes went right off to sleep first, and Agathon went the same way just as dawn was breaking."[3] Only Socrates could have proposed such a paradox; for the fifth-century Athenian, tragedy was tragedy and comedy comedy, and never the twain should meet.

But Aristophanic comedy has had no descendants, and comedy for us is something different. It comes to us from the Greeks all right, but not from Old Comedy; it descends through Plautus and Terence to the Renaissance dramatists from Menander, the Athenian comic poet of the fourth century, and his plays in turn derive from those plays of Euripides in which the prototype of modern comedy is to be found. In this, as in so many ways, Euripides is prophetic, the poet of the future; what he invents is the prevailing drama of the next century, the domestic comedy of manners and situation, of family misunderstandings (between father and son, husband and wife) of mistaken identity and recognition, of lost children reclaimed and angry fathers reconciled to spurned suitors finally revealed as long-lost sons of wealthy friends—the comedy of misapprehension, recognition, and restoration, of Menander and Philemon, which is also the main tradition of modern European comedy from Shakespeare to Oscar Wilde.

Of course, the mere fact that these Euripidean plays have a happy ending is not enough to justify the term "comedy." Aristotle preferred tragedies which end in misfortune, but his statement clearly implies that some sort of happy ending was far from rare and did not disqualify a play as tragedy. And this would have been clear even without Aristotle, for the *Oresteia* of Aeschylus and the *Philoctetes* of Sophocles, to take only two examples, do not end in misfortune, and yet no one has ever thought of them as comedies. Such a term for these Euripidean plays could be justified only by the appearance in them of a treatment of situation and character differing sharply from the tragic norm. And Euripides does indeed in these plays (and, for that matter, in others) introduce to the tragic stage an entirely new attitude to human nature and action. It has been called "realistic," but it is not hard to show that the term is inadequate. To avoid begging the question, it is perhaps better to demonstrate the nature of Euripides' untragic tone, not from one of the plays in question, but by reference to the opening scenes of a play which, taken as a whole, clearly belongs to the tragic canon, the savage *Electra*. It is a shocking play. What in Aeschylus was the just punishment of a father's assassins by a god-driven son and in Sophocles the crowning achievement of a heroic daughter's lonely endurance becomes in Euripides a pair of sordid murders: Aegisthus ignominiously butchered by the guest he had invited to the sacrificial feast, Clytemnestra lured to her death through her solicitude for her daughter's feigned pregnancy. These actions are of course the climax of the play and are written in Euripides' grimmest mood. But the opening scenes are a surprising contrast.

The prologue speech is delivered by an unnamed character, a small farmer, who gives us the astonishing news that he is Electra's husband. Not that he has presumed to exercise his marital rights, he goes on: he has too much respect for Agamemnon's line (lines 43ff.). The situation is piquant, to say the least, but we have no hint yet of a real departure from the heroic mode which has always been appropriate for this particular story—except one. Aegisthus, the farmer tells us, forbade Electra's marriage to a noble suitor, for fear of a son who would avenge Agamemnon (22ff.). But then he decided to kill her anyway because of a fear "that she would bear children to one of them secretly" (26).[4] This slight hint of scandalous possibilities is all we are given to prepare us for the shock provided by Electra's entrance. She comes on stage as no tragic heroine we know of ever did before—balancing a jug on her head in the immemorial fashion of Greek village women on their way to the spring. "O dark night," she sings, "keeper of the golden stars, in which carrying this jug balanced on my head, I go to fetch water from the river" (54ff.). Perhaps, we think, we are meant to be moved to pity at the depths of poverty to which this princess has been reduced: this is one more pathetic prop—like the rags of Telephus, Oeneus, Phoenix, and many another Euripidean hero.[5] But Electra goes on: "Not that I have reached any such degree of poverty—it is so that I may show the gods the savagery of Aegisthus" (57–58). Just in case we don't get the point, her husband asks her why she goes to all this trouble, "even though I tell you not to" (66). She replies that she wishes to repay his kindness by helping him, by sharing his labors. "You have work enough in the fields. It is *my* duty to prepare everything inside the house. When the workman comes home, it is pleasant for him to find everything shipshape inside." "Well," says her husband, "go ahead, if you insist. The spring is not far from the house in any case" (71ff.). And in any case, Electra has a servant with her.[6] "Take this jar off my head and put it down," she commands later (140), as she sings her solo aria recounting the sorrows of her life. Quite apart from the extraordinary visual detail of the water jug, the tone of this scene is unmistakable. It is *domestic*: we are being invited not to identify ourselves with the passions and destinies of heroic souls but to detach ourselves and observe the actions and reactions of ordinary human beings in a social situation with norms and customs we are only too well acquainted with. And this domestic realism, which might have served simply to deepen the pathos of the heroine's situation, is made, by ironic comment and juxtaposition, to expose not merely the sordid details of Electra's misery, but also her pretenses and affectations.

This scene is only the beginning; there is much more to come. To the chorus which invites her to accompany them to the great festival of Hera, Electra replies not only with a recital of her wrongs and a repetition of her determination to mourn Agamemnon's death forever, but also with a more mundane excuse. "Look at my hair; it's dirty. Look at these rags of clothes. Are they fit for Agamemnon's royal daughter?" (184ff.). These sentiments are couched in faultless glyconics but they still mean nothing more than "I haven't a thing to wear," and in case we had any doubt the chorus offers to lend her something. "Borrow from me fine-woven dresses to wear and these golden ornaments to go with them—do please accept" (191–93).

Fewer than two hundred lines later, Electra is standing at the door of the house talking to Orestes and Pylades (she does not yet know who they are) when her husband comes back from his work (for his lunch presumably). He is certainly a patient husband, but even he is upset. "It's disgraceful—a wife standing around with men." "Dearest," replies Electra, "don't get suspicious of me." The strangers are emissaries of Orestes come to see the sorrows of her life. "Well," says her husband, "some of them they can see, and I'm sure you are telling them the rest";[7] he is, of course, quite right. He invites the strangers into his house. Orestes, in a long speech, admires his nobility, but Electra takes a different view. When husband and wife are alone together, she proceeds as follows: "You rash fool, you *know* how poor your house is; why did you invite in these strangers who are of a higher station than you?" "Why not?" says the farmer reasonably. "If they are as noble as they seem, they will be as content in humble circumstances as in high." "Humble's the word," says Electra.[8] "You made a mistake. Now go off and find the old man who used to look after my father ... tell him to bring some food for my guests." "All right," says her long-suffering husband, "I'll go. Now *you* go inside, and fix things up. You know very well that a woman, if she wants to, can always find something extra to piece out," προσφορήματα, a word which occurs nowhere else in Greek literature. And in the next scene the old man, complaining about his bent back and wobbly knee, comes in loaded with food and drink (487ff.). "Here, daughter, I've brought you a newborn lamb from my flocks, and garlands for the guests, and cheeses I took out of the buckets and this wine—vintage stock of Dionysus—such a bouquet—not much of it, but sweet stuff—just pour a cup of this into some weaker brew ... "

The comic effect of much of this is unmistakable;[9] but the play of course does not continue long in this vein. True, there is still the burlesque of Aeschylus' recognition scene to come,[10] with the old man pleading for one after the other of the three traditional recognition tokens, only to have them all contemptuously dismissed by Electra as foolishness. But Orestes finally *is* recognized by a scar on his forehead, and after that, brother and sister plan and carry out the two treacherous, brutal murders. The effect of the domestic atmosphere of the first half of the play is to strip every last shred of heroic stature from Electra and Orestes, so that we see their subsequent actions not as heroic fulfillment of a god's command, but rather as crimes committed by "men as they are," to use Sophocles' description of Euripides' characters, by people like ourselves. After we have seen a shrewish and snobbish Electra scold her husband for not knowing his place in society, we are not likely to see her murder of her mother as anything else than what it is, an unnecessary act of paranoiac jealous hatred.

The comic tone is used here for a purpose which has nothing to do with comedy. But as social comedy the opening scenes of the play are brilliant,[11] and since they are the first extant appearance of such scenes on the tragic stage, they invite careful examination. The most novel and incongruous element in them is the repeated emphasis on the everyday details of domestic life, on meals and their preparation, the need to carry water and bring food, not to mention wine. This is a new note. In Greek tragedy before this (what we have of it), references to food and drink are scarce, short, incidental, and frequently negative;[12] certainly no tragic heroines before Electra balance water pitchers on their heads, quarrel with their husbands about whether there is enough food for the guests, and send them off to procure cheese, lamb, and wine. All this smacks of comedy, where people eat and drink with gusto, prepare enormous meals and drink gigantic quantities of wine, where menial tasks (from pouring gravy on a pancake to feeding a giant dung beetle) are the order of the day. But such matters also bulk large in satyr plays,[13] and, although Euripides did not write comedies in the ancient sense of the word, he did, like Aeschylus and Sophocles, write satyr plays. In the only specimen of this extraordinary genre which has survived complete, the *Cyclops* of Euripides, food, drink, and domestic chores are very much to the fore. "Here I am at my work," says the prologue speaker, Silenus, "filling sheep troughs and sweeping floors. I wait on that godless Cyclops at his unholy meals. And now I must follow orders, and scrape out the cave with this iron rake." Odysseus arrives; thinking he is in book 9 of the *Odyssey*, he begins in heroic style, but breaks off at the sight of the satyr chorus. Soon he is exchanging his wine for the Cyclops' food—meat, cheese, and milk. And so it goes on, including, before the climax (the blinding of Polyphemus), a drunken symposium, with Silenus stealing the drunken Cyclops' wine, which ends as Polyphemus, announcing that Silenus is his Ganymede, carries him off protesting into the cave.

We have, of course, one other Euripidean play which, if not strictly satyric, was at any rate performed fourth after three tragedies, the *Alcestis*. It has no chorus of satyrs, and, though it has a contrived happy ending it is a poignant and bitter play. In fact, the only thing which reminds us that this is a substitute for Silenus and the "foreheads villainous low" of the satyr chorus is the scene in which, after the servant describes the difficulty of waiting on Heracles at table (he is an importunate guest who, not content with what is offered, demands more, and a hard-drinking guest as well), the hero himself emerges to berate the servant for his gloomy looks and expound his philosophy of eat, drink, and be merry in almost the same terms Cyclops uses to Odysseus.[14] Here we are for a moment back in the world of food and drink and domestic detail, but it is only a moment, and we cannot help wondering what the Athenian audience thought of this Euripidean experiment, the first of many. What he has done in *Alcestis* is to present a satyr play completely transformed by the introduction of tragic situation, character, chorus, and style. And if he could do that, why could he not do the opposite? In the *Electra*, I suggest, he has completely transformed the first half of the tragedy by the introduction of situation, character, and style proper to a satyric play.

This transformation of the tragic atmosphere by the introduction of domestic detail did not, of course, escape the keen eye of Euripides' constant critic. Aristophanes, in the *Frogs*, puts into his mouth the boast that he had improved tragedy by "bringing in household matters, things we use and live with," οἰκεῖα πράγματ᾽ εἰσάγων, οἷς χρώμεθ᾽ οἷς συνέσμεν (959–60), and taught the Athenians to "run their houses better than before." Dionysus' reply to this claim dots the i's and crosses the t's:

So now the Athenian hears a pome
of yours and watch him come stomping home
to yell at his servants every one
"Where oh where are my pitchers gone?
Where is the maid who has betrayed
my heads of fish to the garbage trade?
Where are the pots of yesteryear?

> Where is the garlic of yesterday?
> Who hath ravished my oil away?"[15]

In the opening scenes of the *Electra*, the domestic, light tone prevails, but they are an introduction to the grim horrors of the denouement. It is in such plays as *Iphigenia in Tauris* and *Helen*, which present not tragic catastrophe but hairsbreadth escape from it, that the new spirit achieves its full expression and dominates the whole play. These two plays are generally admitted to be a new departure. They are the ancestors of a whole genre of western melodrama in which captured white adventurers avoid a gruesome death by playing on the ignorance and superstition of the savages. They have a neat formula: part one, the recognition; part two, the escape by trickery (in both plays the woman provides the brainwork).[16] But the only thing that puts these plays in the tragic category is the fact that they were entries in the tragic competition at the festival of Dionysus.

What Euripides has done in them is to eliminate from tragedy what previously had been its essence: τὸ ἀνήκεστον—"the incurable" (it is Aristotle's word, and Nietzsche's).[17] He has suppressed the action which cannot be recalled, which allows no escape from the consequences—the meeting of the hero and the absolute situation and his decisive act which changes, "incurably," his world. If Iphigenia had actually sacrificed Orestes, that would have been incurable and could have been tragic. If all three of the protagonists had been recaptured and killed, that would have been incurable and possibly tragic. But Athena intervenes, they all get away, and furthermore the chorus of captured Greek girls get to go home, too.

The essence of this new dramatic form is that the characters are set to walk on the thin ice which separates them from the dark tragic waters; though they may crack the surface, they never quite break through. The genre is a virtuoso exercise in the creation of suspense, which ends with a happy escape from the incurable tragic act and suffering. But this new dramatic purpose is still expressed in and to some extent hampered by tragic form. There is still a chorus, for example (which has to be rescued *en masse* in *Iphigenia in Tauris*). But if the main purpose of the dramatist is to generate excitement from the danger and eventual escape of the protagonists, how can the chorus do what it has always done?[18] How can it illuminate the deeper meaning of the action, trace its roots in the mythic past, explore its wider significance as a paradigm of man's condition, his relationship to his city and his gods? What has it to sing about? Nothing. And that is what it does sing about, very beautifully, with late-Euripidean lyric elegance, but it is still singing about nothing at all.[19] "Why should I dance the

choral song?" the chorus of *Oedipus the King* asks. That question raises
the main issue of the play and is answered in unmistakable terms by the
outcome of the action. But this is a question which the choruses of the
Iphigenia in Tauris and *Helen* had better not ask; it would only remind
us that their choral songs are on the way to becoming mere musical
interludes, the ἐμβόλιμα of Agathon, which could be put anywhere in
the play or, for that matter, in any play.

The chorus is not the only awkward impediment to Euripides' new
dramatic design; there is also the myth. The end of the road on which
he has taken the first step, suppressing the dignity and terror of the
tragic action, is the abandonment of myth altogether. This was of course
the achievement of his younger contemporary, Agathon, who produced
the first tragedy based on invented characters. But Euripides puts his
new wine in the old bottles, and though he chooses his myths carefully
for their outlandishness (among Taurians, Egyptians, and, in the
Andromeda, Ethiopians) and for their unfamiliarity to the audience
(both Iphigenia and Helen have to explain their situation at length and
with precision), the mythical figures and their associations keep suggesting that there are greater dimensions to the action—a suggestion
which true tragedy can exploit, on which, in fact, it relies, but which
now saddles Euripides with an incongruous element, a hint of serious-
ness clashing with the bright swiftness of his plot and the wit that
distances us from his characters. In the *Helen* the heroic aspects of the
Trojan myth are played down as much as possible except where they are
used to pose a comic contrast; Menelaus, ordered off by an old
gatekeeper woman who talks to him as if he were a beggar, recalls with
regret his "famous armies," only to be told: "you may have been an
important figure *there*, but you're not *here*" (453–54). And in the
Iphigenia, Euripides allows the myth to add a sort of false profundity to
the action, false because unrelated: the themes of Greek versus
barbarian ideas of morality, of human sacrifice and divinity and so on,
like the antiquarian disquisitions on the Athenian Choës or the Artemis
cult at Brauron, are grace notes, not a tragic bass.

Though these two plays brilliantly exploit the new tone and
techniques, their exotic setting works against too heavy an emphasis on
the domestic detail, the everyday round. But this is well to the fore in
the *Ion*, a play which, in a sense still to be defined, is full-fledged
comedy—a work of genius in which the theater of Menander, almost a
hundred years in the future, stands before us in firm outline.

Like the *Iphigenia* and the *Helen*, its plot depends on ignorance of
identity, *agnoia*, and recognition, *anagnorisis*. A man comes from
ignorance to knowledge, solves the mystery of his birth, and knows for
the first time who he is. That is the plot of the *Ion* and also of

Sophocles' *Oedipus the King*. The resemblances between these two plays are, in fact, remarkable.[20] Both turn on oracles of Apollo, both contain a mother who exposed the child which she has now every reason to think is dead (but is alive); in both the hero fears that his unknown mother may turn out to be a slave (but in fact she is a queen); Oedipus killed his father and Ion threatens to kill his (supposed) father Xuthus. But between the two plays there is all the difference in the world. For the recognition, which is the catastrophe of the one, is in the other the happy solution of the potentially tragic deadlock. *Oedipus the King* presents the tragic spectacle of man's recognition of his real status, not god but man, not ruler but ruled, blind, not all-seeing. But the *Ion* presents a similar situation in fundamentally different terms: the recognition, the hero's realization of his identity, is not a tragic climax but a happy ending—what made Oedipus the King an outcast makes Ion the slave a king.

The play begins with a prologue spoken by a god, Hermes. But this is not the dread Hermes, conductor of the dead, invoked by Orestes in the *Choëphoroe*: he introduces himself as "manservant of the gods," δαιμόνων λάτριν (4), as he recounts the background events in which he played a part—the part of "manservant" to his elder brother Apollo. He carried off the child of Apollo and Creusa (whom the mother had abandoned) and "doing my brother a favor," as he puts it, left the child on the steps of the temple at Delphi, where he was rescued by the priestess and brought up as a temple servant. Creusa (who returned to find the child missing) was later married to a foreign prince, Xuthus. But the marriage is childless, and they are on their way to Delphi to consult Apollo, Xuthus hoping for a son of his own to be born to Creusa, while she hopes that in some miraculous fashion Apollo will restore to her the vanished child. And that, Hermes tells us, is just what Apollo plans to do; he will give Ion to Xuthus as his own son (Hermes does not tell us how this delicate operation will be performed—Euripides holds that in reserve), Creusa will be told the truth when she gets home to Athens, Creusa's (and Apollo's) indiscretion will remain concealed from the world (and especially from Xuthus), and everything will be for the best. But here comes the boy himself, Hermes tells us: "I'll step aside into the laurel grove here, to find out what happens to him." And as he does, as Ion, a temple slave equipped with a broom made of laurel branches (103), some kind of water container (105–6), and a bow and arrows (108), comes out of the temple.

This is a very unusual beginning. Gods as prologue speakers are no strangers to the Euripidean stage, but this Hermes is a world away from the menacing Aphrodite of the *Hippolytus*, the vengeful Dionysus of the *Bacchae*, the august figures of Poseidon and Athena, who in the *Trojan Women* prologue plan the destruction of the Greek fleet. For one thing, unlike all these deities, who have urgent personal motives for appearing, Hermes has no business here at all. "I have come [ἥκω] to Delphi," he says, echoing similar formulas used by Poseidon and Dionysus, but unlike them, he does not tell us why; the only reason suggested (faintly) is curiosity about the outcome, "to learn what happens to the boy" (77) — an interesting statement in view of the fact that Apollo has planned everything down to the last detail. But even this suggestion is a mere dramatic pretext, for like his successors in New Comedy (Pan in the *Dyscolus*, for example, and Tyche in the *Aspis*) Hermes has no part in the action and promptly vanishes from the play. His sole function is to explain the situation, and for that purpose, since the situation involves rape (11), concealment (14), and deceit (71), no better spokesman could be imagined than the "manservant of the gods" — λάτριν, a word which Aeschylus' Prometheus (966) used to insult him, but which this Hermes complacently applies to himself.[21]

Ion's monody opens with a brilliant evocation of sunrise at Delphi which is justly famous, but as it proceeds we learn that his duties, which he is performing, are to sweep the approach to the temple, water down the dust, and keep the birds away from the statues. He even sings a lyrical address to his broom (112ff.), in which phrases like "O fresh-blooming instrument of service made of beautiful laurel . . . with which I sweep the floor of Phoebus all day long" remind us irresistibly of Aristophanes' merciless parody of Euripidean monody (*Frogs*, 1331ff.), the point of which is precisely the ludicrous effect produced by the combination of high-flying lyric form and earth-bound content. The resemblance of all this to Electra and her water jug and still more to Silenus and his rake is only too clear, and the dithyrambic grace of Ion's warnings to the various birds he threatens with his arrows does not disguise the obvious fact that if he fails to keep them away from the statues he will soon be cleaning up bird droppings just as surely as Silenus is raking out sheep dung.

It might be expected that the entry of the chorus would at last strike the solemn note appropriate to tragedy, but this chorus, maid-servants of Creusa, reinforces the holiday mood which has so far prevailed. Delphi was a tourist center in the ancient world as it is in the modern, and the girls are sightseers,[22] excitedly calling each other's attention to the pedimental sculptures, identifying the figures for all the world as if one of them had a *Guide Bleu* in hand. Finally in an inspired bit of by-play, they ask the museum attendant, Ion, if they can go inside, and like so many of their modern counterparts, get a short negative answer.[23]

Creusa and Ion feel an immediate sympathy; he admires her nobility of appearance and she his courteous manner. She tells him, in answer to his questions, the story of her marriage to Xuthus, a foreigner (he expresses polite surprise, 293), and of their childlessness; Ion, questioned in turn, confesses that he has no name, no known parents, and is a temple slave—his mother must have abandoned him. This reminds Creusa of a friend of hers, who abandoned her child; he would now have been about the same age as Ion, and his father—well, his father was Apollo. Suddenly the real purpose of her presence here is revealed: while Xuthus is off making preliminary inquiries at the oracle of Trophonius, she has come to make a secret inquiry about the child—her friend's child—and asks Ion to take the matter up with the Pythia. He points out that such a request would put Apollo in an awkward position, and no servant of the god will run the risk of doing that. As Xuthus comes on stage, Creusa hurriedly begs Ion not to say a word about the matter; Xuthus might not approve, and the thing might get out of hand. She is afraid that "the story might develop along lines other than those we have pursued" (396–97)—an admirably diplomatic formula.

Xuthus goes in to consult the oracle and comes out wild with excitement to meet Ion, whom he rushes forward to embrace, for, as we learn later, he has been told by Apollo that the first man he meets will be his own true son. The ensuing dialogue, in racing tetrameters, here for the first time employed in tragedy for undeniably comic effect, is one of Euripides' most brilliant scenes. One feature of it which has not been sufficiently emphasized (in fact it has often been suppressed) is the ambiguity of the word Xuthus uses to address Ion in the opening lines, τέκνον. It can mean "son" but it can also mean simply "child" or "boy."[24] Since in the dramatic circumstances it cannot possibly occur to Ion that it means "son," the only explanation of Xuthus' conduct likely to recommend itself to him is that this middle-aged man is making vigorous sexual advances to him. This too is the only valid explanation of the violence of Ion's reaction (524). If an older man rushes toward you asking to kiss your hand and embrace you, you might well think him crazy and push him away if he also addresses you as "my son," but it is only if he calls you "boy" that you will threaten him with a weapon. The ambiguity is essential to an understanding of the opening lines, and yet it is ignored in most commentaries[25] and suppressed by translators, who consistently have Xuthus hail Ion as his son in the opening line. There is no excuse for this; it was clearly explained by Wilamowitz long ago,[26] and he is certainly right; no one conversant with fifth-century Athenian ways can doubt it, and the art of the period is rich in apposite illustrations, from the red-figure vases on which bearded men court boys with gifts of tame birds and unmistakable gestures, to the self-satisfied smile on the face of the terra-cotta Zeus at Olympia as he carries Ganymede off in his arms.

But let the scene speak for itself. The rough translation which follows, far from exaggerating the comic element, falls far short of it for want of a modern English tragic style to accentuate the contrast between form and content:

Xuthus.   Boy, be happy. That's the only
    formula that fits the case.
Ion (retreating).   I'm quite happy. You be quiet
    and we'll both be better off.
X. Let me kiss your hand, enfold you
  in my arms in fond embrace.
I. Are you in your right mind, stranger?
  Has the god deranged your wits?
X. Right mind? I've just found my dearest.
  Why not rush into his arms?
I. (still retreating).   Stop it! Don't you paw me. You'll
    destroy Apollo's laurel wreaths.
X. I *will* touch you. I'm not stealing;
  you're my dearest, found at last.
I. (picks up bow and arrow).
  Get your hands off me or you'll get
  arrows in those lungs of yours!
X. Why do you repel me? Don't you
  recognize your dearest love?
I. One thing I *don't* love is putting
  crazy foreigners in their place.
X. Kill me, burn me, then, your father,
  that's who you'll be murdering.
I. You my father? How can that be?
  You my father? What a laugh![27]
X. Wait. If you'll just listen to me
  I'll explain my point of view.
I. What have you to say?
       X.   Your father—
I'm your father, you're my son.
I. Who says so?
      X.   The god Apollo
brought you up, but you're my son.
I. Don't you need another witness?
X. Just Apollo's oracle.
I. You misunderstood some riddle.
X. Not if I can trust my ears.
I. Exactly what *did* Phoebus tell you?

X.   That the first man I should meet—

I.   Where and when?

                    X.   Coming from the temple,
from the oracle of the god—

I.   Well, and what's supposed to happen?

X.   —that man is my own true son.

I.   Yours by birth or a gift in some way?

X.   A gift, and yet my very own.

I.   And I'm the first one you ran into?
No one else?   X.   Just you, my child.

I.   That's a curious combination.

X.   Yes. I'm overwhelmed myself.

I.   Yes, but, in that case, who's my mother?

X.   There you have me, I don't know.

I.   Phoebus didn't tell you?   X.   I was
so delighted I didn't ask.

I.   Earth must be my mother.   X.   Hm.
The earth does not bear children, though.

I.   How *can* I be yours?   X.   I don't know.
I refer it to the god.

I.   Well, let's try investigation.

X.   Anything you say, my son.

I.   Did you have an affair with someone?

X.   Yes, when I was young and wild.

I.   Before you married Erechtheus' daughter?

X.   Naturally. I've since reformed.

I.   That was when you got me, was it?

X.   Yes ... the times *do* coincide.

I.   In that case how did I get to Delphi?

X.   I don't have the slightest clue.

I.   It's a long way from Achaea.

X.   Yes, that's what is puzzling *me*.

I.   Did you ever come here to Delphi?

X.   Yes, for Bacchus' festival.

I.   And you stayed with one of the locals?

X.   Yes. There were some Delphian girls ...

I.   He introduced you to their circle?

X.   Yes, and to their Bacchic rites.

I.   And you, how were you, drunk or sober?

X.   Well, I wasn't feeling pain.

I.   That's *it*—the hour of my conception!

X.   Fate has found you out, my son.

Ion rather reluctantly accepts his new father, but when told he is to come to Athens, he speculates gloomily on his status there as an outsider, the base-born son of a foreigner, and on the fact that his situation vis-à-vis Creusa will be, to put it mildly, delicate. But Xuthus has it all figured out (like Apollo). He will take Ion along with him "as a sightseer," θεατὴν (656), and then, on some propitious occasion, he'll tell Creusa the truth. He's sure he can bring her around. He orders the chorus, on pain of death, to keep Creusa in the dark and rushes off to prepare a huge feast. But the chorus does tell Creusa, and there is nothing comic about the tormented aria in which she blurts out the whole story of her lost child and reproaches Apollo for his heartlessness. The chorus and the old man she has brought with her—the tutor of Erechtheus, a fierce guardian of the blood purity of the royal line—are appalled. But the old man, though he had trouble climbing the steep approach to the temple, is not slow to urge action ("I may be slow in the foot," he says, "but I'm quick in the head," 742), and he proposes revenge on the god who has acted unjustly. "I am a mere mortal," Creusa replies. "How shall I prevail against higher powers?" The old man's answer suggests that we are not to take all this too seriously. "Burn down the holy oracle of Apollo!" "I am afraid," she says. "I've got trouble enough already," καὶ νῦν πημάτων ἅδην ἔχω (975). She rejects the suggestion that she kill Xuthus, for he was good to her once, but she accepts with alacrity the idea of killing the boy; Ion, the bastard son of a foreign interloper, shall never reign in Athens. The old man is sent off to poison Ion's wine at the feast Xuthus has prepared.

The attempt fails, the old man confesses, and Ion leads the hue and cry after Creusa, who takes refuge at the altar. The deadlock is resolved by the priestess who once found the child on the temple steps; hearing that Ion is leaving for Athens, she comes to bring him the cradle in which he was left—it may help him some day to find his mother. Creusa recognizes it and by describing its contents convinces Ion that he is her child. But it is not so easy to convince him that Apollo is his father; he knows that Apollo told Xuthus a different story. He goes toward the temple to resolve his doubts "whether the god is a true prophet or a false" (1537). But this potentially embarrassing interview never takes place; Athena appears, to speak for Apollo, since, she says, the god himself thought it better not to face them, "lest blame for things past should come into the open." But all will be well. Ion will go to Athens, succeed to the throne, and become the ancestor of all the Ionians. Xuthus will never know the truth about Ion, but Creusa will bear him sons, Dorus and Achaeus, who will be the ancestors of the rest of the Hellenic nation.

This play is clearly a step beyond the plays of recognition in far-off lands and escape from the barbarians. The scene is Delphi, the background Athens and Athenian patriotic myth; the familiarity of the surroundings is emphasized by insistence on domestic detail. And the pattern of recognition followed by deceit has been transformed: here the recognition is delayed until near the end of the play,[28] while deceit, used not by Greeks against barbarians, but by husband against wife, wife against husband, son against father, mother against son, and Apollo against them all, winds its complex threads throughout the entire play. There is only one reminiscence of the old pattern; in the end one character remains deceived—Xuthus, and he is, if not a barbarian, at least a foreigner.

It is time to document the claim that this extraordinary play is the prototype of comedy in the modern sense of the word. Definitions of comedy are notoriously inadequate, and I do not propose to attempt a new one; I shall be content if I can demonstrate that the *Ion* is the first drama we know of which contains in combination those elements which characterize the standard comic form as we see it in Menander, Plautus, Shakespeare, Molière, and all the way to Oscar Wilde.

First and foremost is the undeniably comic element of scenes which provoke laughter. No matter how ambitious or intellectual comedy may aim to be, it cannot dispense with this element; even *The Tempest* has its drunken butler and mooncalf, *Dom Juan* its Sganarelle, *Tartuffe* its Orgon. The *Ion* has not only its broadly comic Xuthus-Ion scene but a score of light touches here and there which must have caused, if not outright laughter, at least a smile. This laugh, even the smile, is something tragedy at its most intense dare not risk. There is no humor in *Oedipus the King*; one smile would have dissipated the almost unbearable tension on which Sophocles relies to sustain belief in the hopelessly improbable situation, and one good laugh would have shattered the illusion once and for all.

Second, the action is set in a context which emphasizes domestic realities—food and drink, clothing and shelter, cooking and cleaning, the normal human round. Ion's humble duties are emphasized not merely in the opening scene but throughout: the chorus identifies him for Creusa as "that young man who was sweeping the temple" (794–95), and the play contains a long description of a feast (Ion's birthday party) at which the wine flows freely. This emphasis is constant in comedy: Caliban has to "scrape trenchering" and "wash dish," and his reply to Prospero's threats is "I must eat my dinner"; Falstaff's tavern bill shows "one half-penny-worth of bread to this intolerable deal of sack," and in *The Merry Wives* he is hidden in a laundry basket and covered with foul linen; Dom Juan is eating (and Sganarelle is trying to) when the statue knocks on the door, and no one is likely to forget the cucumber sandwiches of *The Importance of Being Earnest*.

These two elements of comedy, broad humor and the emphasis on mundane detail, are Euripides' most striking innovations, and their source is not in doubt; they are both regular ingredients of the satyr play. The next feature of this prototype of comedy, the hair's-breadth escape from catastrophe, appears also in the plays of recognition and escape, the *Iphigenia in Tauris* and the *Helen*. This close brush with the incurable tragic act—Ion and Creusa narrowly avoid the fates of Orestes and Medea—becomes a standard feature of comedy, which generates the excitement of tragic potentiality but spares us the pity and fear caused by its fulfillment. Hegio in Plautus' *Captives* is on the point of killing his son Tyndareus but relents and sends him off to the quarries to be recognized and welcomed later. Antonio and Sebastian are about to kill Alonso—"then let us both be sudden"—when Ariel intervenes. Tartuffe's triumph is complete, but the police official, to his surprise (and ours) arrests *him* instead of Orgon. Macheath is led off to be hanged, but the Player objects—"Why then, friend, this is a downright deep tragedy. The catastrophe is manifestly wrong"—and Macheath is spared. Tom Jones tumbles into bed with one Mrs. Waters and it turns out that she is probably his mother and Tom a sort of Gloucestershire Oedipus, but it's all right—she's not. Comedy skirts the edge of the tragic frontier but retreats just in time.

The next significant feature of the *Ion*, the presentation of the recognition not as catastrophe (*Oedipus the King*), nor as the prelude to the tragic action (the three Electra plays), or escape (*Iphigenia in Tauris* and *Helen*), but as the happy ending, seems to have no precedent in drama but becomes, from this point on, through Menander, Plautus, Terence, *Twelfth Night*, *Cymbeline*, *L'Avare*, and *The Importance of Being Earnest*, the stock comic solution, "la fin d'une vraie et pure comédie," as Mascarille introduces the double recognition which ends Molière's *L'Étourdi*. The delayed prologue of Menander's *Perikeiromene* is delivered by a goddess who had neither temple nor priest—Agnoia, mistaken identity; she mercifully explains the extremely complicated situation for which she is responsible. In Greek society, exposure of unwanted children and enslavement by war or piracy gave a certain plausibility to the recognition of a slave girl as an heiress or a temple slave as a prince; in modern comedy the effect is usually obtained by disguise, as with Viola and Sebastian in *Twelfth Night* (they almost kill each other in a duel), or by robbing the cradle (as in *Cymbeline*). It takes an Oscar Wilde to have his hero left by the charwoman in a bag at the Victoria Station cloakroom. Of course, to bring about the recognition there must be some stage property left with the baby to be brought out at the critical moment, like the cradle and the snake bracelet in the *Ion*, or, as in *Cymbeline*, "a most curious mantle, wrought by the hand of his queen mother, which, for more probation, I can with ease produce" (act V, scene 5).

In the *Ion*, ignorance of identity is dramatically exploited in virtuoso fashion. The unknown identity is that of Ion—only Apollo and Hermes know it. Before the play is over, we have seen a false as well as a true recognition; Ion has been taken for the son of three different mothers and two fathers. The happy solution has an ironic twist: both Xuthus and Creusa accept Ion as their son, each one thinking (correctly, in Creusa's case) that the other is deceived. This ending is like that of *Tom Jones*. Is Tom a bastard or a true man? He ends up a squire, but he is still a bastard. Only, like Ion, he happens to be the bastard son of the right person.[29]

The happy ending of comedy is, as in the *Ion*, a restoration of normalcy, an "integration of society," as Northrop Frye puts it, "which usually takes the form of incorporating a central character into it."[30] Ion is restored to his proper station, in his family (son returns to mother) and his city (from slavery to freedom, indeed to royalty). This characteristic of comedy was long ago remarked by Euanthius ("illic prima turbulenta, tranquilla ultima"),[31] and the restoration may take many forms: of individual to proper status, of balance between the sexes (*The Taming of the Shrew*), of order in the state (the return of the Duke in *Measure for Measure*), or a deeper spiritual restoration, as in the finale of *The Tempest*:

> In one voyage
> did Claribel her husband find in Tunis
> and Ferdinand her brother found a wife
> where he himself was lost; Prospero his dukedom
> in a poor isle, and all of us ourselves
> where no man was his own.

Further, this restoration of normalcy reaffirms, as in the *Ion*, the traditional values of society. Tragedy presents the hero overthrown, though he is magnificent in defeat; a world collapses in and with him, never to be restored. It is the rejection of all normal standards of success, of all comforting moralities, the naked exposure of the fault in things, a view of the abyss. But comedy leaves us with a sense that the standards of this world, though not perfect, are sound: there is no flaw in the universe, only misunderstandings, maladjustments; once restoration is achieved, all is peaceful, *tranquilla ultima*, and everyone gets his just deserts. "Voilà par sa mort un chacun satisfait," says Sganarelle as

Dom Juan goes down in flames. "Ciel offensé, lois violées, filles séduites, familles déshonorées ... maris poussés à bout—tout le monde est content." The chorus closes the *Ion* with a similar assurance that justice governs the universe:

> In the end the good and noble all enjoy their just reward,
> but the low and evil natures never prosper in this world.

This uninspired jingle (translation for once offers no insoluble problem) is a far cry from the lines that end the *Bacchae*:

> Many are the shapes of divine dispensation
> many the unexpected decisions of the gods.
> What we expected is not fulfilled
> for what we never thought of the god found a way.

Furthermore, in comedy as in the *Ion*, the traditional values which are reaffirmed are those of an exclusive group—social, racial, or national. Comedy depends on a feeling (shared by the audience) of cohesion and exclusiveness, of a common identity which resents and repels outsiders; part of the pattern of restoration, in fact, is the expulsion of the intruder, balancing the readmission of the lost or disguised group member. This intruder is of course the most comic figure in the cast, the pretender, the *alazon*, and at the end of the play he is restored to his proper (lower) station—like Parolles, the "gallant militarist," who is exposed as a "past-saving slave"; Malvolio, who, believing that greatness is thrust upon him, is "most notoriously abused"; and Falstaff, who cried, "The laws of England are at my commandment!" but was greeted by his "sweet boy," now king, with the words, "fool and jester." In the *Ion* this figure is, of course, Xuthus, the only character who is presented in broadly comic vein; he is a foreigner in an Athenian society which jealously guarded the privileges of hereditary citizenship (therein lies the relevance of Ion's long speech about the trials that await him in Athens), and Xuthus' final deception is accepted as just return for his presumption—his plan to put what he thinks is his illegitimate son on the throne of Athens. Xuthus' foreignness is emphasized by Creusa, the old man, Ion, and by Xuthus himself, who quickly dismisses Ion's suggestion that the earth may have been his mother, though Athenian tradition (recited not once but almost *ad nauseam* in the play) claimed just such a birth for Erichthonius, Creusa's grandfather.

Xuthus, the intruder, the comic butt, has one more characteristic which is to become a standard ingredient of the comic recipe—his wife is the mother of someone else's child. The real father is a god, and of course many tragic husbands found themselves in the same position—

Amphitryon, for example, in the *Heracles*. But Amphitryon knew that he was "the bed-fellow of Zeus" and was proud of it. Xuthus is ignorant of Ion's true paternity, and, what is more, he is tricked by the real father, who has an oracle at his disposal, into believing (though everyone else in the play finally knows the truth) that Ion is his own flesh and blood. Such a situation of blissful ignorance is a constant fear of the comedy father, in Athens as elsewhere. "We none of us know whose son we are," runs a fragment from Menander's *Carthaginian*; "we just suspect or believe."[32] And a fragment attributed to both Euripides and Menander runs: "The mother loves her child more than the father; she knows it's hers and he just thinks it's his."[33] The Athenian marriage formula ran, "for the begetting of legitimate children"[34]—a formula which Molière could not have known but which sounds very like Mascarille's prayer before his marriage: "que les Cieux prospères / nous donnent des enfants dont nous sommes les pères." Around the head of Xuthus, the deceived but happy husband, floats a prophetic aura of things to come; he is the prototype of the farcical St. Joseph of the medieval mystery plays and of Machiavelli's Messer Nicia.

All this, taken together, seems to justify the claim that in the *Ion*, Euripides invented what was to become the master pattern of western comedy. The ingredients of the comic mixture come from different sources: from tragedy, from satyr play, from his own invention. The real originality lies in their combination, and the success of that combination can be judged from the fact that down through the centuries comic dramatists have returned to the formula time and again.

And yet Euripides did have a model, a predecessor, though he was not a dramatist. As in almost every field of Greek poetry, the great original is Homer. The *Iliad* is the model for tragedy (especially for Sophocles), and the *Odyssey* contains almost all of the elements Euripides combined to create dramatic comedy. The emphasis on domestic routine and food is remarkable throughout; Eumaeus tends swine, Eurycleia washes the beggar's feet, while Odysseus himself announces frequently that man's hungry belly is what drives him on,[35] and as for the meals, Fielding called the *Odyssey*, not without justice, the "eatingest epic." The hair's-breadth escapes are many and various, though the crucial one stems from Odysseus' decision not to go straight to the palace; he goes disguised as a beggar and mistaken identity is followed by recognition, which is the happy ending—the slaughter of the suitors and Odysseus' restoration as husband and king. The suitors are upstart intruders, usurping the place of a hero of the Trojan War, and they are very definitely put in their places, though they are not treated comically. But there is an occasional touch of broad humor, the most remarkable being the song of Demodocus about Ares and Aphrodite trapped in the golden web, and this even presents us with a deceived husband. Finally, the normal, popular standards of justice are reaffirmed; everyone gets his just deserts. And on this point Aristotle remarked: "The poem has a double plot and also an opposite catastrophe for the good and the bad ... the pleasure, however, derived from this is not that of tragedy. It is proper rather to comedy."[36]

There is, of course, one aspect of the *Ion* which I have neglected entirely, an important one—for some critics, in fact, it is the most important one of all. I mean the religious problem posed by the play: what are we to make of Apollo? The play begins with a description of a god's intention and plan, a clear, logical design. So does the *Hippolytus*. But in that play the plan works inexorably through to its hideous end. In the *Ion* it comes completely unstuck: everything goes wrong. Mother and son come within an ace of killing each other, and though this unforeseen calamity is avoided, the whole story of Creusa and Apollo is published to the world, whereas its continued suppression, Hermes told us, was one of Apollo's principal objectives—γάμοι τε Λοξίου κρυπτοὶ γένωνται (72–73). And in the end, when Ion goes to the temple to demand the truth from Apollo, Athena prevents the confrontation: Apollo, for fear of "blame for the past," does not appear.

Explanations of this treatment, unique in tragedy, of a major Olympian figure[37] fall into three main groups. Verrall and many who follow his lead but avoid his excesses see Euripides the rationalist at his most trenchant, exposing the absurdity not only of the myth but also of the Olympian religion. Wilamowitz and many after him see political factors involved; Apollo had predicted a Spartan victory in the war and was a safe target. A modern school of interpreters, stressing the emphasis on religious and mythical motifs in the play, tries to reclaim it as religious in feeling; Apollo's divine benevolence is almost foiled by human ignorance and folly.[38]

These explanations remain unconvincing: each is a partial solution which only throws more emphasis on those aspects of the play it fails to explain. But once we regard the play as an entirely new medium, a tragedy written in the comic mode, the whole problem disappears. For in comedy the gods are neither attacked nor defended; they take their place with human beings in a world where nothing too much is expected except that things shall turn out right in the end—*tranquilla ultima*. Aristophanes can present Dionysus in his own theater as a coward and buffoon (a blasphemous buffoon at that)[39] or Zeus overthrown by a couple of Athenian tax dodgers in *The Birds*, without anyone's believing that he is trying to undermine religion. On the contrary, Aristophanes is always given full marks, not always deserved, for religious and political conservatism. Here again, Euripides seems to have taken a hint from the comic poets. Ironic, but also sympathetic, his new vision embraces gods as well as men: the acceptance of limitations, weakness, passions, and mistakes extends even to Olympus. To err may be human, but in the *Ion* it is also divine.

In a papyrus fragment, discovered early in this century, of a life of Euripides by Satyrus, the following headless sentence occurs: "towards wife, and father towards son, and servant towards master and also the whole business of vicissitudes, raping of young women, substitutions of children, recognitions by means of rings and necklaces. For these are of course the main elements of the New Comedy, and Euripides brought them to perfection." D. L. Page, with that confidence we cannot help but admire, once proposed a correction—"Menander" for "Euripides"[40]— but no one seems to have followed his lead. And Philemon, who in the fourth century put into the mouth of one of his characters the lines,

> If I were sure of life beyond the grave
> I'd hang myself—to meet Euripides,[41]

was not a tragic, but a comic, poet.

Notes

1. In the context, it would seem to refer to the prevalence of unhappy endings in his plays: αἱ πολλαὶ αὐτοῦ εἰς δυστυχίαν τελευτῶσιν (1453ᵃ25). But as D. W. Lucas (Aristotle, *Poetics* [Oxford, 1968]) points out (p. 147): "it is not clear that Euripides was addicted specially to the unhappy ending." (He quotes Gudemann's computation: "unhappy Soph. 43, Eur. 46; happy Soph. 16, Eur. 24.") Lucas himself thinks that "taken in its context this famous aphorism must mean that Euripides excels in arousing pity and fear" and interprets: "most tragic in the sense that he is the most heart-rending of the poets." He rejects R. C. Jebb's "most sensational" (*Attic Orators*, I, ci) on the grounds that this meaning of τραγικώτατος is "unexampled at this date." But Jebb cites Hyperides 3, col. 37, τραγῳδίας (which J. O. Burtt in the Loeb edition renders as "theatrical complaints"), and he might have added the similar [τραγ]ω(ι)δίας γράψαι in 2, col. 10, as well as D. 18.13, ἐτραγῴδει; 19.189, τραγῳδεῖ.

2. Some critics have come close to the edge. L. Parmentier, *Euripide IV* (Paris, 1925), p. 186 (preface to the *Electra*): "Euripide ... a écrit pour ses contemporains les plus épris de la nouveauté, et, pressentant la sorte de théâtre que réclamerait bientôt son peuple, il a introduit dans certains de ses drames le genre d'intérêt et le ton qui devaient aboutir bientôt à la comédie moyenne et à la comédie nouvelle." W. H. Friedrich, *Euripides und Diphilos* (Munich, 1953), Zetemata V, p. 10: "Keine der erhaltenen attischen Tragödien ist geeigneter als diese [i.e., the *Ion*] den Übergang zur Komödie, insbesondere zu Menander, zu bilden."

3. cf. J. P. Mahaffy, *A History of Classical Literature* (London, 1891), I, part II, 5: "Plato hazards as a mere drunken fantasy what Shakespeare has realized for us—the compatibility of tragic and comic genius in the same poet."

4. The new *Aspis* of Menander gives us a comic parallel for this phrase: the cook lists among the kinds of domestic events which cancel feasts and deprive him of a job, ἢ

τέτοκε τῶν ἔνδον κυοῦσά τις λάθρᾳ (*Menandri Aspis et Samia I*, ed. C. Austin [Berlin, 1969], p. 12, l. 218).

5. Ar., *Ach.* 418ff.

6. Even if the other imperatives are thought of as addressed by Electra to herself, θές with ἐμῆς in l. 140 must be addressed to someone else. J. D. Denniston in *Euripides, Electra* (Oxford, 1939), pp. 64–65, presents the opposing views on this point and comes (reluctantly) to the conclusion that Electra does have an attendant. "Certainly, an attendant is somewhat superfluous in this scene, and the presence of one impairs the emotional force of Electra's outburst. But these considerations cannot outweigh the linguistic intractability of ἐμῆς. Θές, then, must be addressed to the attendant."

7. 355, οὐκοῦν τὰ μὲν λεύσσουσι, τὰ δὲ σύ που λέγεις.

8. The translation attempts to reproduce the effect of ἔν τε μικροῖς (407) ἐν σμικροῖσιν (408).

9. It has, however, been variously appraised. Denniston, *Euripides, Electra*, p. xxxi, finds the scene in which Electra scolds her husband "charmingly done" and the farmer's comment at 77–78 a "delightful touch," but Keene's commentary, *The Electra of Euripides* (London, 1893), is unrelievedly serious throughout, as is that of G. Schiassi, *Euripide, Elettra* (Bologna, 1955). H. D. F. Kitto, *Greek Tragedy* (3d. ed., London, 1961), p. 333, n. 1, refers under the heading "Realism" to "the invitation to the festival (167ff.), Electra's nagging of her husband (404ff.), and the general atmosphere of domesticity." Parmentier, *Euripide IV*, p. 179, speaks of "un ton de parodie ... nous avons la fille acariâtre qui se trouve si malheureuse d'être mal mariée, mal vêtue, mal parée et mal coiffée ... nous avons la martyre avouant qu'elle va sans nécessité puiser elle-même l'eau à la rivière." Schlegel, of course, thought the *Electra* the "allerschlechteste" Euripidean tragedy precisely because of the untragic treatment of the situation: "Durch seine Absichten ist es wenigstens keine Tragödie geworden, er hat es vielmehr auf alle Weise zum Familien-gemälde, in der heutigen Bedeutung des Wortes, heruntergearbeitet" (*Vorlesungen über dramatische Kunst and Literatur*, Erster Teil [Stuttgart, 1966], p. 120).

10. This scene has always been a stumbling block for admirers of Euripidean tragedy, and in many an embarrassed defense of it we can almost read between the lines Goethe's fervent wish for *Antigone*, 904ff.: "I would give a good deal if some qualified philologist could prove to us that it is an interpolation." A learned and powerful attempt to do so was made by Eduard Fraenkel in an appendix to his edition of *Aeschylus, Agamemnon* (Oxford, 1950), 3.815–26; he revives and reinforces a suggestion by A. Mau as a necessary corollary of his own condemnation of the corresponding portion of the recognition scene in the *Choëphoroe*. His arguments are respectfully but efficiently countered by H. Lloyd-Jones in *CQ*, n.s. XI (1961), 171–81. F. Solmsen, in a careful and enlightening analysis, "Electra and Orestes: Three Recognitions in Greek Tragedy," *Mededelingen der Koninkluke nederlandse Akademie van Wetenschappen, A. Lett. Nieuwe Reeks, Deel 30, no. 2* (Amsterdam, 1967), demonstrates the dramatic appropriateness of the three tokens of recognition in each of the two scenes.

11. I have mentioned only the high points, but of course there is much more: the farmer's down-to-earth reflections on the uses of wealth, 426ff., for example; Electra's fierce rejection of the idea that Orestes would come back in disguise for fear of Aegisthus (524ff.); Orestes' inquiry about the old man (553–54) which runs (the translation is Denniston's): "To which of your friends, Electra, does this ancient relic of humanity belong?"

12. A., *Pers.* 490 (the Persians short of food on the retreat), *A.* 331 (the Greeks breakfast in Troy), 1597 (the banquet of Thyestes), 1621–22 (Aegisthus threatens the chorus with starvation); S., *Ant.* 775 (the food to be left in Antigone's prison-tomb); E., *Hipp.* 112 (H. will eat before feeding the horses), 275 (Phaedra will not eat; cf. *Med.* 24), *Supp.* 864–66 (Capaneus a moderate eater).

13. cf. V. Steffen, *Satyrographorum Graecorum Fragmenta* (Posen, 1952): Aristias, *Frs.* 3, 4; A., *Frs.* 39, 46, 47, 75–76; S., *Frs.* 8, 40, 42, 47, 89, 123, 130, 131, 147, 158; E., *Frs.* 12, 31, 39, 43; Ion, *Frs.* 10, 11, 18; Achae., *Frs.* 1, 5, 7, 12, 14, 21, 31.

14. E., *Alc.* 780ff., *Cyc.* 336ff.

15. Ar., *Ra.* 980ff., tr. Richmond Lattimore.

16. See the fundamental article of Solmsen, "Zur Gestaltung des Intrigenmotivs in den Tragödien des Sophokles und Euripides," *Philologus*, LXXXVII (1932), 1–17, reprinted in *Euripides*, ed. Ernst-Richard Schwinge, Wege der Forschung LXXXIX (Darmstadt, 1968).

17. Aris., *Po.* 1453^{a}35, Nietzsche, *Menschliches Allzumenschliches*, 2.23, "unheilbar."

18. cf. Kitto, *Greek Tragedy*, 3d. ed., pp. 339ff.: "The Chorus in New Tragedy."

19. In *Helen* the first regular stasimon is not sung until 1107. Its last stanza (1151ff.) speaks of the folly of the war at Troy, but the connection of this sentiment with the events witnessed on stage is artificial, to say the least. The next stasimon (1301ff.), which describes the sorrows of Demeter (Cybele), makes some kind of connection between this theme and Helen's situation, but the text is corrupt and obscure, and we do not know and cannot guess what it was. Much has been made of this vexed passage but the most recent comment on it, by A. M. Dale, *Euripides. Helen* (Oxford, 1967), p. 147, seems the soundest: "There is no room for more than a hint, and indeed more would only have emphasized the complete irrelevance of this motif to all the rest of the play.... The ode is in fact introduced for its own sake." The third and last stasimon is elegant embroidery. In the *Iphigenia in Tauris* the first two stasima express in varied ways the nostalgia of the chorus; the third and last tells how Apollo slew the dragon Python and took over the oracle at Delphi. The relevance of this is far to seek; arguments that begin like Seidler's (summarized by Paley) "as the plot of the play turns on Apollo's oracle being proved right ... " only serve to point up the contrast between this play and the *Oedipus the King*, where the truth of Apolline prophecy really is an issue and is so treated.

20. cf. D. J. Conacher, "Some Profane Variations on a Tragic Theme," *Phoenix*, 23.1 (1969), 26–33.

21. The same word is twice applied to Hermes in Sophocles' *Inachus*, where he helps Zeus in his love affair with Io. Cf. D. L. Page, *Greek Literary Papyri* (Cambridge, Mass., and London, 1941), p. 24, Διὸς ... λάτρις, and Steffen, *S. Gr. Fr.*, p. 170, Ζηνὸς ... λάτριν. Whether the *Inachus* was a tragedy or a satyr play is still a question; cf. W. M. Calder III, "The Dramaturgy of Sophocles' *Inachos*," *Greek and Byzantine Studies*, 1.2 (1958), 137ff., and R. Pfeiffer, "Ein neues Inachos-Fragment des Sophokles," *Bayerische Akademie der Wissenschaften Philosophisch-Historische Klasse* (Sitzungsberichte-Jahrgang, 1958) heft 6, who thinks that the new fragment reinforces his earlier opinion (*Bay. Ak.* etc., II [1938], 26–62) that it was a satyr play. Pfeiffer's view is reinforced (by reference to vase paintings) by C. Pavese, "L'Inaco di Sofocle," *Quaderni Urbinati di Cultura Classica*, III (1967), 31–50.

22. Euripides repeats this device in *I.A.*: the chorus consists of wives (176) from Chalcis (168) who have come over to see the Greek fleet in which their husbands will go to Troy. They give an exhaustive account (some critics have thought it exhausting—and interpolated) of their sightseeing.

23. 221, οὐ θέμις, ὦ ξέναι.

24. For τέκνον used as a simple form of address by an older man to a younger, cf. S., *Ph.* 130 (Odysseus to Neoptolemus); 141 (chorus to Neoptolemus), 300 (Philoctetes to Neoptolemus); and E., *El.* 605 (old man to Orestes).

25. An exception is G. M. Grube, *The Drama of Euripides* (New York, 1941), p. 266.

26. Wilamowitz, *Euripides. Ion* (Berlin, 1926), p. 111.

27. 528, ταῦτ' οὖν οὐ γέλως κλύειν ἐμοί;

28. See Solmsen, "Euripides' *Ion* im Vergleich mit anderen Tragödien," *Hermes*, LXIX (1934), 390ff. (also reprinted in *Euripides*, ed. Schwinge, Wege der Forschung LXXXIX).

29. cf. Friedrich, *Euripides und Diphilos*, Zetemata V, p. 10: "Die Handlung ... endet schliesslich in Eironeia—in Vorsicht, Verschwiegenheit und sanftem Betrug." He compares the ending of *Hecyra*.

30. Northrop Frye, *Anatomy of Criticism* (Princeton, 1957; Atheneum ed., 1965), p. 43.

31. Euanthius, *Excerpta de Comoedia*, pp. 13–31 of Donatus, *Commentum Terenti*, ed. P. Wessner (Leipzig, 1902), vol. 1. The citation is on p. 21 and is worth quoting in full. "Inter tragoediam autem et comoediam cum multa tum imprimis hoc distat quod in comoedia mediocres fortunae hominum, parvi impetus periculorum laetique sunt exitus actionum, at in tragoedia omnia contra, ingentes personae, magni timores, exitus funesti habentur; et illic prima turbulenta tranquilla ultima, in tragoedia contrario ordine res aguntur; tum quod in tragoedia fugienda vita in comoedia capessenda exprimitur."

32. Ed. Koerte-Thierfelder, *Menander, Reliquiae*, 2, fr. 227,

αὐτὸν γὰρ οὐθεὶς οἶδε τοῦ ποτ᾽ ἐγένετο
ἀλλ᾽ ὑπονοοῦμεν πάντες ἢ πιστεύομεν.

33. August Nauck, *Tragicorum graecorum fragmenta*, 2d. ed., fr. 1015,

αἰεὶ δὲ μήτηρ φιλότεκνος μᾶλλον πατρός·
ἡ μὲν γὰρ αὑτῆς οἶδεν ὄνθ᾽, ὁ δ᾽ οἴεται.

34. Koerte-Thierfelder, *Menander*, 2, fr. 682, παίδων ἐπ᾽ ἀρότῳ γνησίων, and elsewhere. (It now turns up again in the new papyrus of the *Samia*—727 in Austin's edition.)

35. *Od.* 15.344; 18.53–54; 17.286. This last example,

γαστέρα δ᾽ οὔ πως ἔστιν ἀποκρύψαι μεμαυῖαν
οὐλομένην, ἡ πολλὰ κακ᾽ ἀνθρώποισι δίδωσι,

was closely imitated by Euripides in an unknown play (Nauck, *Fragmenta*, 2d. ed., fr. 915):

νικᾷ δὲ χρεία μ᾽ ἡ κακῶς τ᾽ ὀλουμένη
γαστὴρ ἀφ᾽ ἧς δὴ πάντα γίγνεται κακά.

This passage in turn was quoted with approval:

εὖ γ᾽ ὁ κατάχρυσος εἶπε πολλ᾽ Εὐριπίδης
νικᾷ κτλ,

by the comic poet Diphilus (ed. Theodor Kock, *Comicorum Atticorum Fragmenta*, fr. 60).

36. Arist., *Po.* 1453ᵃ30ff.

37. Apollo's oracle is condemned by the Dioscuri in *El.* 1245ff., but the tone and the occasion are serious. In the *Eumenides* he is outmaneuvered in the trial scene by the Furies (640ff.), but there is no loss of dignity comparable to that presented by the finale of the *Ion*. There Apollo is challenged in his own house of prophecy by his own dedicated servant but fails to appear. Instead, Athena comes "at a run" (1556) to speak for him: Apollo "did not think it right [the word could also mean "did not deign" or simply "refused"] to come before your sight, lest blame for things past should come into the open" [or "come between you and him"—less likely]. Athena's statement that Apollo "has done all things well" (1595) is followed by a justification which cannot gloss over the fact that the prophetic god *par excellence* failed to foresee the reactions of the human beings concerned to his plan for their welfare.

38. F. M. Wassermann, "Divine Violence and Providence in Euripides' *Ion*," *Transactions and Proceedings of the American Philological Association*, LXXI (1940), pp. 587–604; Anne Pippin Burnett, "Human Resistance and Divine Persuasion in Euripides' *Ion*," *CP* LVII (1962), 89–103. Burnett's article, though it speaks of "man-made tragedy ... transformed into providential comedy" (p. 101) takes the role of Apollo very seriously; he is "the one god who could embody the idea of mercy" and who "is chosen to represent the divinity which can restore life where death is threatened, and change guilt to blessedness" (p. 101). Even for those who cannot accept this conclusion, the article is valuable for its perceptive discussion of individual passages, its subtle analysis of the dramatic structure, and also for the magisterial way in which it finally disposes of those Victorian moralistic attitudes towards Apollo's way of a god with a maid, which still, after all these years, confuse the issue.

39. Ar., *Ra.* 479, is the most obvious example.

40. D. L. Page, *Actors' Interpolations in Greek Tragedy* (Oxford, 1934), p. 220: "Εὐριπίδης appears to be an error for Μένανδρος."

41. Kock, *Comicorum atticorum fragmenta*, 2, fr. 130.

TWENTY

Euripides' Iphigenia in Aulide 1–163 (in that order)

When Murray,[1] following England's example,[2] printed the iambic trimeters before the anapaests in what was to become the standard text, and so presented generations of students with two incomplete prologues (imposing on the nonconformist much page turning and mental gymnastics), he was simply reflecting the almost unanimous consensus of European scholarship. Ever since Musgrave in 1762 expressed doubts about the anapaests[3] and suggested that two and a half lines cited by Aelian (*N.A.* 7.39) from Euripides' *Iphigenia* came from a genuine, lost prologue, the great figures of European scholarship had wrestled with the problem in languages ancient and modern. Musgrave's championship of the Aelian fragment as part of a lost prologue was soon (for obvious reasons)[4] abandoned,[5] but his attack on the form of the traditional opening was pressed home by other scholars with new and sharper weapons. Explanations varied (two editions,[6] two separate plays,[7] a manuscript left unfinished by Euripides and completed by his son[8]), as did tastes (some saw Euripides' hand in the trimeters and some in the anapaests), but agreement was almost universal[9] that the prologue in its traditional form could not be Euripidean, that the same man could not have written both anapaests and iambics to run in their present sequence.

Since Murray's text was published, this point of view has been reaffirmed (with some new arguments and a judicious pruning of the old) by two acute and learned critics, D. L. Page[10] and Eduard Fraenkel.[11] Their two independent discussions—Fraenkel (1956) does not mention Page (1934)—present what may be regarded as the definitive indictment of the prologue; it seems unlikely that even the most careful scrutiny will discover fresh grounds for condemnation.[12] The prosecution may well rest content with its case; what follows is a plea for the defense which, in the course of a critical examination of the arguments against authenticity, draws attention to some significant structural features which seem to have been overlooked.[13]

This chapter originally appeared in *Yale Classical Studies*, 22 (1972). © 1972 by the Cambridge University Press. Reprinted by permission.

The counts against the manuscript prologue, old and new, great and small, may be conveniently summarized and listed as follows:

(1)   There is no parallel in fifth-century tragedy for a prologue which opens with anapaestic dialogue.

(2)   There is, *a fortiori*, no parallel for a prologue consisting of anapaestic dialogue with an expository iambic speech inserted in it.

(3)   The transition from anapaests to iambics (48–49) is extremely clumsy.

(4)   The text contains major corruptions which come close to producing unintelligibility (especially 107).

(5)   The anapaests and iambics are incoherent (107 and 124 are especially irreconcilable).

(6)   Anapaests and iambics repeat the same material (see 35–48 and 107–14).

(7)   Crude imitation of other Euripidean passages betrays the interpolator's hand in the iambics (73ff., 112ff.).

(8)   The opening lines of the iambics are clearly intended as the opening lines of the play.

(9)   Agamemnon's decision to read the letter to the old man is unmotivated (contrast *I.T.* 760ff.).

(10)   The text of letters in tragedy should be given in iambics, not, as in 115–16 and 118–23, in anapaests.

(11)   Unusual vocabulary is used (see especially μεταγράφω 108).

This is an impressive bill of attainder, but it is not as damning as it at first appears, for Fraenkel and Page, though they have added new items to the list, have seriously weakened, if not destroyed, the cogency of some of the old arguments.

The Unparalleled Anapaestic Dialogue of the Opening Lines

This is what originally aroused Musgrave's suspicions.[14] He rejected the obvious answer (that *Rhesus* has such a prologue)[15] with a reference to the hypothesis of that play, which speaks of not one, but two, iambic prologues, now lost.[16] There is in any case some ground for thinking that the *Rhesus* we possess may not be the play Euripides wrote;[17] to rely on this parallel would clearly be a desperate resort. But there *is* a firm parallel for a Euripidean anapaestic prologue in dialogue form: the *Andromeda*, produced in 412. The Ravenna scholiast to Aristophanes' *Thesmophoriazusae* informs us that the anapaestic lines, ὦ νὺξ ἱερά κτλ.,[18] were the beginning of the prologue, τοῦ προλόγου 'Ανδρομέδας εἰσβολή.[19] G. Dindorf first cited this passage in connection with the *I.A.* prologue,[20] and Welcker accepted it, but, as Fraenkel points out, the great authority of Wilamowitz (who to the end of his life defended his friend Carl Robert's support of Hartung's idea that *Andromeda* must have begun with an iambic prologue spoken by Echo)[21] had such overriding influence that "for many representatives of modern research," the fact revealed by the Aristophanic scholium "ceased to exist."

Fraenkel has rightly reasserted its validity and he justly remarks, on the idea that Echo could speak the prologue, that "a Greek knew Echo all too well to imagine that one whose nature is such that she is incapable of saying anything except to answer could once for a change speak first."[22] He emphasizes the vital point that Andromeda's opening anapaests were not a "monody" (as they are sometimes described)[23] but part of "an anapaestic duet"; the fact that Echo's part in the exchange was limited to repetition does not alter the fact that the play began with anapaestic dialogue and so gives us a precedent for the anapaestic dialogue of *I.A.* It is, as a matter of fact, a much bolder experiment than the dialogue between Agamemnon and the old man; the Andromeda-Echo dialogue must have walked along the bare edge of the ridiculous, and Aristophanes did not have to push it very hard to produce the hilarious parody scene in the *Thesmophoriazusae.*

The Lack of Parallel for a Prologue Consisting of Anapaestic Dialogue Interrupted by an Iambic Speech

It cannot be denied that there is no parallel at all for an anapaestic dialogue interrupted by an iambic speech and then resumed, all this in the prologue. Hermann referred to the delayed expository prologues in Plautus[24] (*Cistellaria, Miles*), and of course the same thing occurs in Aristophanes (*Equites, Vespae,* etc.) and Menander (*Perikeiromene*). The parallels from Aristophanes may be discarded at once, for they involve a characteristically Aristophanic rupture of the dramatic illusion, a specific reference or appeal to the audience, unthinkable in tragedy. The Menandrian and Plautine instances are not contemporary, nor are they cogent parallels;[25] they present a prologue speech delivered in a separate scene by a new speaker, whereas the Euripidean opening involves not only a movement from dramatic exchange to expository narrative and back again in one short scene but also a corresponding alternation of meters. It should be frankly admitted that there is nothing in the extant remains of fifth-century tragedy which will make it easier for us to accept the uncompromising novelty of this experiment. If it is genuine Euripides, it is a bold departure from "the form of opening he consistently employed, whose stereotyped use is attested by the ancient witnesses."[26]

However, it is a departure for which, in this particular case, compelling motives can be adduced. If Euripides planned to begin the play with an anapaestic dialogue designed to reveal the torment in Agamemnon's soul by dramatic rather than expository technique, he was faced with the problem that this play, above all others, needed a full expository speech as well.[27] Not only was it based on a myth known to the audience in many different versions, it also presented a fast-moving, complicated plot which was kept in motion by a succession of sudden changes of mind in the principal characters[28] and depended for its effect, in some of the most exciting scenes, on the participants' knowledge or ignorance of the real situation in which they were acting. Euripides had to make sure that the audience was given, right at the start, a complete and precise understanding of the initial situation; an expository speech of some length was indispensable. If the experimental anapaestic dialogue of the *Andromeda* was to be repeated, this time to reveal the dilemma of Agamemnon, only Agamemnon could deliver the expository speech. To put it first would destroy the dramatic and poetic power of the anapaests;[29] to put it after them was clearly impossible, since the scene must end with Agamemnon's new instructions to the old man and the old man's exit with the letter. There was only one place to put the expository speech—where it is.

There are some significant structural features of the prologue (discussed below) which suggest strongly that the present arrangement is the work not of a clumsy interpolator but of a conscious artist who took great pains to reinforce and normalize the unprecedented form which he invented to answer his dramatic needs. And after all, we cannot be sure that it *was* unprecedented; we have only a remnant of fifth-century tragedy. "For one who works in a ruin," says Groeneboom, discussing a similar problem, "it is extremely dangerous to 'correct' the scant remains of the building."[30] The objection has been made that Euripides, though an innovator in many ways, was a conservative in dramatic form, at least in the larger forms;[31] but this observation stands contradicted by many features of the late plays. If the *Orestes* had not survived intact, who would have dared surmise that one of the most stereotyped, routinely regular of Euripidean dramatic forms—a messenger speech—was in this case couched in astrophic lyric meter and dithyrambic language and put in the mouth of a Phrygian slave?

The Awkwardness of the Transition from Anapaests to Iambics (48–49)

This was singled out for criticism as early as Bremi and Welcker and has been a favorite target ever since; the objection finds its most pungent formulation in Fraenkel (p. 298). "When the king is asked (43ff.) 'What is troubling you? What new turn in your affairs? Come, share the story with me ... ,' he cannot possibly (unless of course he exists in a world not of thinking and feeling human beings but of marionettes) reply with the words (49): 'Leda daughter of Thestios had three girls ... ' "

This criticism, however, ignores the fact that there are many occasions in Greek (and especially in Euripidean) tragedy when the characters seem to modern readers to be speaking more like marionettes than living, feeling human beings. Later in this same play, Clytemnestra anxiously demands from Agamemnon detailed information about the pedigree of her prospective son-in-law. "I know the name of the boy to whom you have given your consent," she says, "but I would like to know who his father is and where he comes from" (695–96). The answer she gets is: "Aegina was born daughter to her father Asopus"—an answer beginning *ab ovo* in the same fashion as Agamemnon's answer to the old man. But such stichomythic catechisms[32] are not the only type of what appears to us stilted formalism; there is also the beginning of the messenger speech. In the *Orestes*, for example, Electra, informed by the messenger that she and Orestes have been condemned to death, begs him to tell her how they are to die. By stoning? Or will she be allowed to commit suicide? This rather urgent question receives an answer which begins: "I happened to be just inside the gates on my way in from the countryside ... " (866); Electra finally learns that she has narrowly escaped death by stoning some eighty lines later (946). This is, of course, routine technique in Euripidean messenger speeches; no matter how anxious and pressing the inquiry, the messenger begins at the beginning with a narrative sentence that makes it clear he has plenty of time and intends to use it.[33] The regularity of this phenomenon shows that this was a dramatic convention, perfectly familiar to Euripidean audiences, for dealing with a situation in which a direct question required a long narrative answer. But that is precisely the situation created by the insertion of a narrative prologue-type speech in a dialogue. When Euripides decided to open his play with a dramatic dialogue which included an expository narrative, a familiar, well-understood convention lay ready to hand.

In any case, the transition is not quite as abrupt as Fraenkel suggests. For the old man continues speaking after asking his question and mentions (46) the name of Tyndareus, which affords a natural transition to Agamemnon's "Leda" (49).

Major Corruptions Producing Unintelligibility

The biggest problem is vss. 106–7: "We alone among the Achaeans know how this matter stands, Calchas, Odysseus, and Menelaus." As Jackson remarks, "Since not even the shyest of men can omit himself when tabulating the subjects of a plural verb in the first person, it is necessary to introduce ἐγώ."³⁴ That is not difficult and the remedy is paleographically acceptable; it was done by Vitelli, but Murray (following England) reported the emendation incorrectly and Jackson revived the original version:

Κάλχας 'Οδυσσεὺς Μενέλεως <ἐγώ> θ'· ἃ δ' οὐ
καλῶς τότ', αὖθις μεταγράφω καλῶς πάλιν.³⁵

Besides this corrupt passage in the iambics, there are two in the anapaests. In vss. 149–51 sense is restored by the corrections of Bothe and Blomfield-Wecklein. At 115ff. it seems clear that Reiske's transposition must be adopted; the old man's λέγε καὶ σήμαιν' must follow immediately the end of Agamemnon's iambic speech.

This gives us three passages in 163 lines where the text has to be restored or rearranged. But in a play which depends solely on LP (or rather, as Zuntz has shown, on L alone in an intermediate stage of Triclinian recension),³⁶ this is not a figure which should raise doubts about authenticity. The first eighty-one lines of the *Ion*, for example, have an omitted pronoun (81, cf. *I.A.* 106) and two lines (1 and 3) which set textual problems not yet solved—Murray marks both passages with the obelus. The first 177 lines of *I.T.* (which contain anapaests and iambics in roughly the same proportion as the *I.A.* prologue) make sense and meter in Murray's text only with the aid of two excisions (142, 146); two insertions (150, 154); conjectures (omitting obvious and minor corrections) by Badham (3), Scaliger (58, 118), Canter (62), Markland (125), Heath (172), Sallier (98), Murray (156–57), and Porson (176); and the bracketing of 38–39 and 59–60. As if that were not enough, Murray labels 134–35 *vix sani*. Compared with these two typical examples from "alphabetic" plays, the text of the *I.A.* prologue seems remarkably healthy; as an argument against authenticity, textual corruption is clearly irrelevant.

The Incoherence of 107ff. in the Iambics
with 124ff. in the Anapests

In 87ff. Agamemnon describes the causes of the agony of indecision which the old man has asked him to explain. Calchas demanded the sacrifice of Iphigenia to Artemis as the price for favorable winds. Agamemnon at first refused and was ready to disband the army, but Menelaus persuaded him to obey. Agamemnon sent a letter to Clytemnestra summoning Iphigenia to Aulis on the pretext that she was to marry Achilles. "Alone among the Achaeans," he says, "Calchas, Odysseus, Menelaus, and I know how this matter stands," ὡς ἔχει τάδε

(106). And now Agamemnon has changed his mind again, and intends to send the old man off with a second letter, countermanding the first.

What exactly is meant by ὡς ἔχει τάδε? The four conspirators share a secret of which the rest of the army, and in particular Achilles, are ignorant. Clearly the most important thing that has to be kept secret is that the proposed marriage is merely a pretext, ψευδῆ ... γάμον (105). But what about the rest of the story? At this point, it is not clear from what Agamemnon says whether Achilles and the army think that Iphigenia is coming to Aulis but do not know that the marriage is a mere pretext or whether Achilles and the army do not know anything at all—that they are not even aware Iphigenia has been sent for. Of course, it later becomes clear that the second alternative is the correct one, but at this point, for the audience, Agamemnon's words are utterly ambiguous.

And yet one critic after another has assumed the words are clear as day and mean the second and only the second alternative, that Achilles and the army were completely in the dark. Consequently, when the old man, informed of the contents of the new letter, bursts out that Achilles will rise up in anger against Agamemnon because of the loss of his bride, these same critics find an intolerable incoherence, a fresh proof of clumsy patchwork—or else try to defend the passage on the grounds that Agamemnon says 106–7 as an aside (Hermann)[37] or that the old man "manque un peu d'attention ou d'intelligence" (Weil). But there is no ground for such an assumption.[38] At vs. 106, some members of the audience may well have thought that Achilles knew of the proposed marriage, others that he did not, while still others may have realized that Agamemnon had not committed himself on the point; most of them, in all probability, did not give the matter a moment's thought.[39] But the old man's question directs the audience's full attention to this matter; all of them—those who share the old man's misunderstanding, those who did not but perhaps now wonder if they were wrong, those who realized that the question had been left in the air, and those who had not thought about it at all—wait impatiently to hear Agamemnon's answer. It is unequivocal this time, clear as crystal: "Achilles contributes not his action, just his name; he knows nothing of the marriage, nothing of what we are doing."

This is a fact of the utmost importance for Euripides' play and had to be impressed on the audience by the most striking means available. The ground had to be laid for the brilliant scene which was to come later—the meeting of Clytemnestra and Achilles, a scene of Menandrian comedy based on *agnoia* which would have missed its mark, in fact been unintelligible, if the audience had not been made fully aware that Achilles had never heard of the marriage project. Of course, Euripides could have made Agamemnon say explicitly at 106ff. that Achilles knew nothing. But what he has done is to make the point by dramatic exchange rather than expository explanation and so drive it home more effectively.[40]

The temporary ambiguity is not by any means alien to the spirit of Euripidean dramaturgy, for in the prologue scenes of *Hippolytus* and *Ion*, Euripides "is not straightforward" but "is concerned ... to mislead and mystify without outright misstatement," as Barrett puts it.[41] And the particular technique of this passage, the creation of ambiguity, even possible misapprehension, to produce, by correction, full clarity on a major issue is to be found also in the intellectual dramas of Plato. "The dramatic misapprehension by the interlocutor is one of Plato's methods for enforcing his meaning," says Paul Shorey, "the dramatic misunderstanding forestalls a possible misunderstanding by the reader."[42]

In any case, it speaks volumes for the dramatic viability of the traditional text in this passage that even so severe a critic as Page finds no difficulty in the coexistence of 98ff. and 124ff.—though he does not admire the technique and dismisses 105ff. as an interpolation on other grounds.[43]

Anapaests and Iambics Repeat the Same Material (Especially 35–48 and 107–14)

The end of Agamemnon's iambic speech (107–14) repeats much of the material and some of the words of the concluding lines of the old man (35–48) which bring the first anapaestic system to a close. Fraenkel, who thinks that Euripides wrote a complete anapaestic prologue (stage 1), that someone else later wrote a complete, but dull, iambic prologue to replace it (stage 2) and that a third person cut and combined the two to produce what we have now, sees in these resemblances a proof that the writer of the iambic prologue (stage 2) simply transposed, as it were, the brilliant anapaests into the wooden iambics. It is instructive to compare Page's analysis. He too posits three authors for the prologue: Euripides, X, and Y. Euripides wrote a complete iambic prologue (of which we have only part—and 106–14 is not by Euripides), X (a good poet of the fourth century—"one thinks of the romantic atmosphere of Chaeremon") wrote an alternative complete anapaestic prologue (of which we have only part) and Y ("an excellent editor, no doubt, but a bad poet and a worse dramatist") combined them in the form preserved in LP, removing some superfluous anapaests (e.g., 110 deliberately copied from the sense of 38, and 114 from 45).

There are obviously subjective judgments at work here, but both critics agree that the verbal resemblances are suspicious. But it does not seem to have been noticed that the repetitions can be fully justified; they perform a necessary function. The repetition, at the end of an expository narrative digression, of the subject matter and very often the actual words with which the digression began—ring composition—is a well-known feature of archaic style which has been fully explored in Homer, Herodotus, and Aeschylus in a series of publications by W. A. A. van Otterlo.[44] His examples from tragedy, however, all consist of single speeches in which the closing repetition and the initial statement, which is repeated, are both pronounced by the same speaker. This is of course not the case in the passage which concerns us here. But a type of ring composition in which the closing words of the digression echo the words and matter of the immediately preceding speech which gave rise to it is also to be found in tragedy. In the prologue of Sophocles' *Electra*, Orestes ends his long discussion of his mission and his plans for its fulfillment with the words καιρὸς γὰρ ὅσπερ ἀνδράσιν / μέγιστος ἔργου παντός ἐστ' ἐπιστάτης (75–76), which echo the closing lines of the preceding speech of the *paidagogos*: ὡς ἐνταῦθ' ἐμὲν / ἵν' οὐκέτ' ὀκνεῖν καιρός, ἀλλ' ἔργων ἀκμή (21–22).[45] Similarly, in Euripides' *Orestes*, the speech of Apollo which, interrupting action at a point of high excitement, announces the fate and future of the participants, ends, ὅς νιν φονεῦσαι μητέρ' ἐξηνάγκασα (1665) with an echo of the last line of Menelaus' preceding speech, αἷμα μητρὸς μυσαρὸν ἐξειρ- γασμένος (1624).

There are many more such passages,[46] but these two will suffice to make the point. In both of them the repetition restores dramatic continuity, returning the action to the point at which it was abandoned for exposition. So the last words of Agamemnon's speech, recalling the closing words of the old man, mark the end of the static exposition, the resumption of dramatic action. Once again Euripides solved the technical problem raised by his insertion of an expository speech in a dramatic dialogue by adapting a familiar convention, this one as old as Homer.

Repetitions and Imitations Which Betray the Hand of the Interpolator

Fraenkel cites in particular two passages in the iambics: 71ff. and 112ff. The first, a description of Paris, ἀνθηρὸς μὲν εἱμάτων στολῇ / χρυσῷ τε λαμπρὸς βαρβάρῳ χλιδήματι, has often been compared with the description of the same person which appears in *Troades* 991ff. (βαρβάροις ἐσθήμασι / χρυσῷ τε λαμπρόν), but for Fraenkel the relationship between them is dependence, not resemblance. The descrip- tion of Paris and of the excitement his appearance aroused in Helen is, as Fraenkel says, fully appropriate in Hecuba's speech, "but," he goes on, "when the prologue-speaker in *I.A.*, in his summary of the preceding events, descends to such details as these ... the broad depiction of things that are utterly inessential here is completely at odds with Euripidean narrative prologue style."

It could be argued that since the play's dilemma will finally be solved by Iphigenia's decision to die willingly and so unite the pan-Hellenic fleet in its determination to sail against the barbarians, this detail is not inessential at all, but rather the first statement of a theme, the contrast between Greek and barbarian, which is given repeated and increasing emphasis throughout the play[47] to prepare our minds for Iphigenia's *coup de théâtre*. But Fraenkel's real objection is that the *I.A.* passage is a mere imitation of the lines in *Troades*: "For the man who wrote εἱμάτων στολῇ etc. ... the attractiveness of βαρβάροις ἐσθήμασι etc. ... was irresistible, and that man was certainly not Euripides." To which the simple answer is that combinations of these words χρυσο-, στολή, λαμπρός, and χλιδή in various forms constitute a regular Euripidean cliché—they turn up together again and again (*Bacch.* 154, Τμώλου χρυσορόου χλιδᾷ; *Andr.* 2, σὺν πολυχρύσῳ χλιδῇ, 147, κόσμον μὲν ἀμφὶ κρατὶ χρυσέας χλιδῆς, στολμόν τε; *Elec.* 966, στολῇ λαμπρύνεται; *Helen* 423–24, λαμπρά τ᾽ ἀμφιβλήματα χλιδάς τε; *Fr.* 688, στολὴν ἰδόντι λαμπρός).[48]

The second passage, 112–13,

ἃ δὲ κέκευθε δέλτος ἐν πτυχαῖς
λόγῳ φράσω σοι πάντα τἀγγεγραμμένα,

is almost identical with *I.T.* 760–61,

τἀνόντα κἀγγεγραμμέν᾽ ἐν δέλτου πτυχαῖς
λόγῳ φράσω σοι πάντ᾽,

and for Fraenkel the explanation is simple: the lines in *I.A.* were "skrupellos geplündert." But this judgment overlooks the fact that the language of Attic tragedy from Aeschylus to Euripides uses these same words whenever writing is mentioned: δέλτος, πτυχαί, ἐγγράφω etc. are words which can hardly be avoided, as the following passages make clear: Aesch., *Supp.* 946 πίνακιν ... ἐγγεγραμμένα, 947 ἐν πτυχαῖς βίβλων; *Eumen.* 275 δελτογράφῳ ... φρενί, *Prom.* 789 ἐγγράφου ... δέλτοις; Soph., *Trach.* 157 δέλτον ἐγγεγραμμένην, 683, ἐκ δέλτου γραφήν, *Fr.* 144 γραμμάτων πτυχάς; Eur., *I.T.* 727 δέλτου διαπτυχαί, 763, τἀγγεγραμμένα, 787 τὰν δέλτοισιν ἐγγεγραμμένα, 793 γραμμάτων διαπτυχάς, *I.A.* 324 τἀγγεγραμμένα, *Fr.* 506.2–3 ἐν Διὸς δέλτου πτυχαῖς γράφειν. And even λόγῳ φράσω seems to be common Euripidean formula, as appears from *Fr.* 621 φράσαι λόγῳ and *Fr.* 1083.10, λόγῳ φράσαι.

The Opening Lines of the Iambics Suggest
That This Is the Beginning of a Play

This argument, often advanced and often rejected, is forcibly restated by Page (p. 139): "the detail of 49–51 implies that nothing had gone before, e.g. the self-announcement involved in ἐμὴ ξυνάορος is wholly superfluous, especially after τῇ σῇ τ᾽ ἀλόχῳ 46." But in fact nothing in the way of necessary information *has* gone before; all we know at vs. 48 is that Agamemnon is at Aulis, that it is almost dawn, and that he has been writing and rewriting a letter in great distress. The opening anapaests have done their job brilliantly—they have created a mood; the speech which now begins will give us the information we need. In any case, the "self-announcement" involved in the phrase ἐμὴ ξυνάορος, if it is to be the first hint we are given of Agamemnon's identity, is not in line with normal Euripidean practice. In his prologues, the opening speakers are identified by this inferential method only when like Medea's nurse, δέσποιν᾽ ἐμὴ Μήδεια (6–7) or the farmer in the *Electra*, ἡμῖν δὲ δὴ δίδωσιν Ἠλέκτραν ἔχειν / δάμαρτα (34–35), they have no name of their own.[49] The phrase is not a "self-announcement" but (with the following line) the first identification of the imposing and important lady who is to bulk so large in the action of the play.

Page's further objections, that in the iambic speech Agamemnon is not addressing the old man and in any case tells him nothing he does not know, apply too rigid a standard of stage realism. Deianira's long prologue speech in *Trachiniae* shows just as little consciousness of the presence of her nurse, who has however listened to it, as her first lines show; Iolaos in the *Heraclidae* tells his children (whom he finally addresses at vs. 48) a great many things they must know already, and Amphitryon's account of the woes of Heracles' family in the *Heracles* prologue can scarcely have been news to Megara.

Agamemnon's Decision to Read the Letter
to the Old Man Is Unmotivated

This objection is as old as Dindorf but is most forcibly stated by Fraenkel. In the corresponding passage in *I.T.*, he points out, there is an excellent motive for Iphigenia's reading of her letter: Pylades must know the contents in case the letter is lost with the ship at sea—if that were to happen he could keep his solemn oath to deliver the letter only if he knew what it said. "Here the motivation is fully established," says Fraenkel, "but of such a meaningful motivation there is in the corresponding passage of the trimeter prologue not the slightest trace" (p. 301).[50]

No motive is stated, but one leaps to mind. The old man is ordered to deliver to Clytemnestra a letter which will surprise and shock her; her questions will be many, sharp, and urgent, for the letter gives no reason for Agamemnon's change of plan. If the old man does not know the contents of the letter, he may be driven to indiscretions; Agamemnon does not want him to reveal that the marriage of Iphigenia was a fraud, still less that she was to be sacrificed. The mission is a delicate one; the old man, when questioned, must say just what is in the letter, no more, no less—consequently, he must know what it says.

There is a passage in Xenophon's *Cyropaedia* which provides a parallel situation and even some verbal parallels. It was cited by Markland long ago, and England saw its significance, but it is worth quoting again since another relevant passage, further on in Xenophon's text, was overlooked. After a victory of Cyrus over the enemy, won while his commander, King Cyaxares, is feasting, the king sends a messenger to Cyrus rebuking him for his independent action and ordering the recall of his troops. Cyrus detains the messenger and sends a trusted man of his own back with the answer; since he intends to continue independent action, the letter calls for diplomatic skill—it has to be conciliatory in tone and firm in purpose. The messenger will have a difficult embassy; the king is angry and he is in any case ὠμὸς ... καὶ ἀγνώμων (4.5.9). Cyrus reads his letter to the messenger (*Cyr.* 4.5.26): ἀναγνῶναι δέ σοι καὶ τὰ ἐπιτελλόμενα, ἔφη, βούλομαι, ἵν᾽ εἰδὼς αὐτὰ ὁμολογῇς ἄν τί σε πρὸς ταῦτα ἐρωτᾷ. And then after reading the letter, he says: ταύτην αὐτῷ ἀπόδος, καὶ ὅ τι ἄν σε τούτων ἐρωτᾷ, ᾗ γέγραπται σύμφαθι (ibid., 34). The messenger of Cyrus had a delicate and dangerous mission; it was vital that when questioned he should take the same line as the letter he carried. This is exactly the case of the old man, and the words he uses, ἵνα καὶ γλώσσῃ / σύντονα τοῖς σοῖς γράμμασιν αὐδῶ—correspond to Xenophon's ἵν᾽ εἰδὼς αὐτὰ ὁμολογῇς and still more to ᾗ γέγραπται σύμφαθι.

Letters in Tragedy Are Generally Phrased in Iambic Trimeter

This is a new argument, developed by Fraenkel in support of his contention that there was once a complete iambic prologue in existence.

> The composer of the trimeters cannot possibly have intended to have the reading aloud of the letter in anapaests. If there is any form of communication in drama for which according to Greek and for that matter Roman feeling for style the character of plain everyday speech must be preserved and for which accordingly that meter is preferable which, as Aristotle says, partakes most of the nature of τὸ λεκτικόν—it is the letter form (p. 300).[51]

It follows, he goes on, that the writer of the iambics must have written a complete prologue, containing the reading aloud of Agamemnon's letter in iambic trimeter.

This argument seems to turn in its user's hand, for of course the anapaests, which Fraenkel attributes to Euripides, do contain the text of the letter and Fraenkel, in his reconstruction of the lost anapaestic prologue, retains these lines. It seems to follow that Euripides was perfectly willing to have a letter read aloud in anapaests, but the writer of the trimeters was not. Unfortunately the reason given for his reluctance is so general that it would surely have restrained Euripides as well.

But in any case, how many letters are read aloud in extant Greek drama? There seem to be only two certain examples: the anapaestic letter in *I.A.* and the iambic letter in *I.T.*[52] Possibly (though it does not seem to have been suggested) Theseus at *Hipp.* 855–56 is quoting Phaedra's letter; if so we have another iambic letter (two lines long). But the more one considers these two lines, the more they look like what Barrett and other editors assume them to be—the words of Theseus. Clearly the evidence for Fraenkel's generalization, as far as Greek tragedy goes, is slim.

μεταγράφω *(108) Occurs Here Only in Poetry*

This is one of Page's arguments for rejecting 106–14, but it is not cogent. If the occurrence of a word which is found elsewhere only in prose is to be reckoned as a count against authenticity, one trembles to think of the fate of, e.g., Sophocles, *Trachiniae* 873–91. It contains three words which occur elsewhere only in prose (and late prose) if at all; καινοποιηθέν 873 does not reappear until Polybius; διηΐστωσε 881 is found nowhere except as a conjecture of Grenfell and Hunt at Pindar, *Paeans* 6.96 (rejected by Bowra and not recorded by Snell) and χειροποιεῖται 891 does not seem to turn up again until it is used by Epiphanius,[53] Bishop of Constantia in Cyprus, who died in 403 A.D. Agamemnon's μεταγράφω is much easier to defend. It is a good fifth-century word (Thucydides uses it of the same circumstances and in the same sense—a change in the text of a letter),[54] and it is used by Xenophon of changing the text of treaties and by Demosthenes of changing the text of judicial verdicts.[55] If Euripides wanted his Agamemnon to speak of revising the text of a letter, what other word was there to use?

To sum up: the case for the defense states that the objections to vocabulary (11), style (7), and meter (10) are invalid, the appeal to textual corruption (4) irrelevant, the allegations of incoherence (5) and lack of motivation (9) short-sighted, the claims that the opening anapaests cannot (1) and that the opening iambics must (8) constitute the beginning of a play unfounded, and the complaints about awkward transition (3) and repetition (6) a failure to recognize the dramatist's adaptation of existing tragic conventions for a prologue which, it has to be admitted, has no formal parallel (1).

The case for the defense, then, requires further only that the reader entertain the possibility that Euripides, for understandable dramatic reasons, experimented with a new form of prologue: an anapaestic dialogue enclosing an iambic expository speech. If this seems a large demand, it should be remembered (though it seems to be generally forgotten) that the prosecution's demands on the reader's imagination are incomparably greater. They ask us to believe that Euripides wrote a complete anapaestic (or iambic) prologue, that someone else later wrote a complete alternative iambic (or anapaestic) prologue, and that still a third person cut pieces off both prologues and fitted the bits together to form what we have now (perhaps writing some dull verses himself to bridge the gaps he had created). There is no doubt which of these two explanations would have appealed to William of Occam. But the three-hand theory, apart from its assumption of pluralities, creates some problems its champions do not attempt to answer.[56] Why did the third man, faced with two perfectly good prologues, mutilate and combine them to create something which both Page and Fraenkel regard as a sorry product? What on earth was his motive? And secondly, if someone so perverse and stupid really existed, why is it that his version of the prologue and his alone has survived?[57]

But there is a much graver objection to the theory of triple authorship. Leaving the question of his purpose aside, it does not seem beyond the bounds of possibility (though Friedrich finds it so)[58] that the third man could have carved and glued the two prologues so skillfully that the resulting amalgam would contain all the information necessary for the audience's understanding of the subsequent action. What does seem incredible is that he should have done so and at the same time created the remarkable formal symmetry which distinguishes the prologue in its present form. It does not seem to have been noticed, but it is a fact, that the anapaestic systems on either side of the iambic speech are of exactly the same metrical length.[59] Further (and this seems to have been overlooked, too), Agamemnon's speeches in the first half of the second anapaestic system, and there only, are melic anapaests; this medium for expressing heightened emotion, especially sorrow, is used for his reading of the letter (115–16), his assurance that Achilles is ignorant of the proposed marriage (128–32), his desperate regrets (137–38), and his urgent command to the old man not to delay *en route*

(141–42). This change of meter, coming immediately after the iambic speech in which Agamemnon confides in the old man the full desperation of his situation, is in exactly the right place.

It does not seem likely that such formal symmetry and such precise metrical organization can have resulted from the activities either of Fraenkel's "Bearbeiter" who "pasted up [zusammengeklittert] the product that has been preserved for us," for he was a fast and careless worker ["er hat hastig gearbeitet"], or of Page's editor, who was "a bad poet and a worse dramatist." It seems much more likely that the two anapaestic systems were written to stand exactly where they are, fore and aft of the iambics, and if so there seems no good reason to doubt that the poet who arranged the three elements of the prologue so artfully also wrote them or that the poet in question was Euripides.[60]

Notes

1. Murray, *Euripidis Fabulae* III (Oxford, 1909).

2. E. B. England, *The "Iphigenia at Aulis" of Euripides* (London, 1891), p. xxv. "I have in the arrangement of the text endeavoured to restore the 'erratic block' to its original position though I cannot hope to remove all traces of its long sojourn on foreign soil, nor to efface the scars which its intrusion has left in its unnatural position. That is, I have printed the iambics first and left a lacuna in the middle of the anapaests." Hartung (*Euripidis Iphigenia in Aulide*, [Erlangen, 1837]) had previously rearranged the text of the prologue, but in a more eccentric manner: 49–109, 1–48, 110–14, 115–63, with minor transpositions and lacunae.

3. S. Musgrave, *Exercitationum in Euripidem Libri Duo* (Leyden, 1762), pp. 25ff.

4. Musgrave himself realized that such a speech made by Artemis to Agamemnon in the prologue would make nonsense of the subsequent action; he offered the rather feeble suggestion that "fieri . . . potest ut quae citavit Aelianus ad Agamemnonem vel absentem vel non audientem dicta sint" (26).

5. It is difficult to see how it could have formed part of an epilogue either, unless the whole of the final messenger speech in our text is a later addition. However, Page's brilliant discussion (*Actor's Interpolations in Greek Tragedy* [Oxford, 1934], pp. 196–99) shows that even the last part of the speech (1578ff.), which is usually dismissed as Byzantine forgery, contains enough good whole lines and left-hand line beginnings to suggest that it is rather a Byzantine attempt to restore a faded and damaged page of an ancient codex (though Page thinks the original was fourth century or later, not Euripidean). He dismisses the lines quoted by Aelian as non-Euripidean; his main reasons are that "φίλαις is the adjective of a much inferior poet" and that "there are only two parallels to σήν prospective at the end of an iambic in E., *Alc.* 658, *Supp.* 1010 . . . in each of these two the sequent noun follows immediately at the beginning of the next verse" (p. 200). It must be conceded that φίλαις is weak and tasteless, but the second argument will not hold water. W. Morel in *Ph. W.* (1935), 401ff. produced a parallel to the Aelian passage with ἐμήν, but closer parallels lie ready to hand. *Hec.* 405 and *I.A.* 1202 both end with prospective σόν not followed immediately by its noun and *Alc.* 1072 ends with a σήν which looks forward to its noun (γυναῖκα) at the beginning not of the next trimeter but the one after that.

6. A. Boeckh, *Graecae Tragoediae Principum etc.* (Heidelberg, 1808), pp. 214ff.

7. One by Euripides and one by Euripides junior (H. Zirndorfer, *De Euripidis Iphigenia Aulidensi*, [Marburg, 1838]).

8. A. Matthiae, *Euripidis Tragoediae et Fragmenta* (Leipzig, 1823), VII, p. 326. "Hanc fabulam quae non vivo Euripide sed post eius mortem demum acta sit, ab auctore imperfectam et inchoatam relictam esse, ita ut nonnulla quidem cum cura elaborata essent, alia vero secundis curis relicta, nonnulla etiam fortasse bis diverso modo scripta, quae deinde auctor retractans ea eligeret quae maxime probaret; quae reperiri poterant, ea deinde ab Euripide minore ita coagmentata esse ut iusta fabula agi posset."

9. Two outstanding exceptions to the general trend were Henri Weil, *Sept Tragédies d'Euripide* (Paris, 1879), and C. G. Firnhaber, *Euripides Iphigenia in Aulis* (Leipzig, 1841). Weil's defense of the prologue (309ff.) is rather dogmatic and he falls back on an inane explanation of the contradiction he thought inherent in 105ff. and 124–25 (on which see below). Firnhaber (xxiv ff.) gives an excellent summary of the argument up to his time. More recently the prologue has been defended by W. H. Friedrich, "Zur Aulischen Iphigenie," *Hermes* 70 (1935), 86ff.

10. *Actors' Interpolations* (Oxford, 1934), pp. 138–40.

11. "Ein Motiv aus Euripides in einer Szene der Neuen Komödie," *Studi in Onore di Ugo Enrico Paoli* (Florence, 1956), pp. 293–304.

12. H.-M. Schreiber, *Iphigenies Opfertod* (dissertation, Frankfort on the Main, 1963), discusses the prologue at some length and rejects it in its present form but, apart from polemic against Friedrich and Page, does not add anything to the argument. M. Imhof, *Bemerkungen zu den Prologen der sophokleischen und euripideischen Tragödien* (Winterthur, 1957), rejects the iambic passage as post-Euripidean because it does not measure up to the artistic standards he discovers in his valuable analysis of the Euripidean prologues. "Es fehlt ihr die lebendige rhythmisch gegliederte, in Wellen an die Gegenwart heranführende Gedankenbewegung. Das ist ein rein erzählende, sachlich vorbereitende, exponierende Prologrede, schon stärker aus der Illusion herausfallend als bei Euripides" (104). But this criticism has point only if the iambic passage is treated as a separate unit (in which case it also has to be considered incomplete); as a narrative speech inserted into "einer dialogisch-anapästischen Szene von stark stimmungshaftem Charakter" (105), it cannot and should not be judged by criteria appropriate for complete iambic prologues.

13. The argument on both sides is limited to internal evidence; early citations are rare. The anapaests were known to Chrysippus and Machon. Murray's apparatus cites Arist., *Rh.* 3.11 for vs. 80 in the trimeters, but Fraenkel (p. 302, n. 3) reminds us that τοὐντεῦθεν οὖν in that passage was introduced by Victorius from the Euripides line; the rest, as Fraenkel judiciously remarks, "may, with slight lapse of memory, refer to *I.A.* 80, but certainly does not have to."

14. Musgrave, *Exercitationum*, p. 26, "Accedit etiam quod systema Anapaesticum nusquam alibi ab Euripide in initio Tragoediae positum sit."

15. Similar, but not, as W. Ritchie (*The Authenticity of the Rhesus of Euripides* [Cambridge, 1964], p. 102f.) points out, comparable.

16. The hypothesis attributed to Aristophanes of Byzantium, however, clearly refers to the text we have: ὁ χορὸς συνέστηκεν ἐκ φυλάκων Τρωικῶν, οἳ καὶ προλογίζουσι.

17. Ritchie's careful and instructive examination of the whole problem leads him to the conclusion that the play we have is indeed the *Rhesus* of Euripides and that it was written very early in his career, in fact before the *Alcestis* (438). His analysis of style and vocabulary demonstrates that many of the objections along these lines were ill-informed or purely subjective; the demonstration still retains much validity after the searching criticism of this part of the book by E. Fraenkel in *Gnomon* 37 (1965), 228ff. His book has put the question of authenticity on a sounder, more objective basis, but it has not settled it. Even if it had, the *Rhesus* would not be a relevant parallel for the *I.A.* prologue, for even Ritchie believes that it started with a trimeter prologue, now lost.

18. They appear to be "melic" anapaests (for which see the excellent description in A. M. Dale, *The Lyric Metres of Greek Drama*[2] [Cambridge, 1968], pp. 50ff.).

19. Fraenkel (p. 304) rightly rejects suggestions that εἰσβολή may not mean "the opening line" and refers to A., *Fr.* 143 N.[2] Further confirmation of his point is to be found in the Venetus scholia to Ar., *Ra.* 1 (p. 274, ln. 27 Dübner): εὐθὺς ἐν τῇ εἰσβολῇ διαβάλλει τούς τε κωμῳδοὺς κτλ. and 1219 Σθενεβοίας δὲ ἡ ἀρχή. διαβάλλει δὲ τὴν ὁμοειδίαν τῶν εἰσβολῶν τῶν δραμάτων.

20. According to Firnhaber (xxvi) it was E. Müller (1838), but Fraenkel points out that the third volume of the Dindorf edition of Euripides (in which the parallel is cited) has a preface dated 1837.

21. For references to Welcker, Hartung, Robert, and Wilamowitz, see Fraenkel's notes 3 to 6 on p. 303.

22. "L'idée est plaisante," says Weil (p. 309, n. 2) of Hartung's proposal.

23. e.g., England (p. xxii) "This passage is a monody." The incredible proof he gives is that Mnesilochus in the Aristophanic parody says ὦ 'γάθ' ἔασόν με μονῳδῆσαι to Euripides.

24. *Euripidis Iphigenia in Aulide* (Leipzig, 1831), p. x, "Neque ea res sine exemplo videtur fuisse quum etiam in Plauti fabulis, quae ad mediae sunt comoediae similitudinem factae, quaedam prologum non habeant in ipso initio."

25. For a discussion and defense of the use of parallels from comedy, see Friedrich, "Zur Aulischen Iphigenie," *Hermes* 70 (1935), pp. 92–93 and M. Andrewes, "Euripides and Menander," *CQ* 18 (1924), 8–9.

26. W. Nestle, *Die Struktur des Eingangs in der Attischen Tragödie* (Stuttgart, 1930), p. 133. He is discussing the *Andromeda* prologue, which he does not believe can have begun with anapaests. (He does not attempt to discuss the opening of *I.A.* "weil die sich auf die Form ihres Eingangs beziehenden Fragen nur in Zusammenhang mit den übrigen Schwierigkeiten des Stücks erörtert werden können" [p. v].)

27. For an eloquent presentation of this point, see Friedrich, pp. 87–88.

28. cf. B. Snell, *Aischylos und das Handeln im Drama*, *Philol.* Supplement 20, 1 (Leipzig, 1928), pp. 148ff.; A. Lesky, *Die Griechische Tragödie*[2] (Stuttgart, 1958), p. 246; chapter 18 of this book.

29. Max Pohlenz, *Die Gri. Tragödie*[2] (Göttingen, 1954), II, p. 183: "Diesem [i.e., the anapaestic dialogue] noch eine Prologrede nach dem üblichen Schema vorauszuschicken war dann kaum möglich. Hätte Agamemnon selbst zuerst in ruhig-sachlichem Tone zum Publikum gesprochen, musste die folgende Schilderung seine Seeleszustandes ihre ganze Wirkung verlieren."

30. P. Groeneboom, *Aischylos' "Perser"* (Göttingen, 1960), part 2, p. 30. He is discussing O. Müller's widely followed transposition of 93–101 to a position after 102–13. "Es mag auf den ersten Blick verlockender erscheinen die Mesodos nicht nach zwei, sondern—in der Form einer Epode—nach drei Strophenpaaren folgen zu lassen, weil drei Strophenpaare in der älteren Dichtung des Aischylos oft ein Ganzes bilden; entscheidend ist dieses der äusseren Form des Liedes entnommene Argument jedoch bei dem spärlichen Vorrat an Vergleichsmaterial nicht: für den, der in einer Ruine arbeitet, ist es äusserst gefährlich die geringen Reste des Gebäudes zu 'korrigieren.'"

31. Imhof (above, n. 12), p. 106: "Auch die Iphigenie in ihrer dramatischen Beweglichkeit und Lebendigkeit zeigt den neuen Geist, den neuen letzten Stil. Aber in den grossen Formen ist dieser gerade nicht neuernd, sondern archaisierend."

32. A more extended (and by modern standards of realism even more absurd) example is A., *Supp.* 290ff., where the chorus, challenged to prove its claim of Argive descent, asks the king a series of leading questions to which he supplies unnecessarily full answers; he finally volunteers information without being asked (311) before he himself turns questioner.

33. cf., e.g., *Ba.* 1041–43, *El.* 772–74, *Andr.* 1083–86, *Hipp.* 1171–73. This abrupt opening which, with no concern for dramatic illusion, ignores the interlocutor's question and insists on telling the story from the very beginning is strictly Euripidean technique. In Sophocles in every case where a long narrative answers a question, there is a preliminary passage (sometimes only one line) which provides a transition from dialogue to narrative. The most striking example is *O.T.* 1237 (the chorus' question is answered at once, out of time sequence) but cf. also *Aj.* 284, 748, *El.* 680, *Ant.* 1192ff., *Tr.* 749, 899, *O.C.* 1586.

34. John Jackson, *Marginalia Scaenica* (Oxford, 1955), p. 209.

35. "Neither the enjambement nor αὖθις πάλιν nor the quasi-zeugma (ἅ δ᾿ οὐ καλῶς τότ᾿—sc. ἔγραψα—αὖθις μεταγράφω) needs any vindication," ibid.

36. G. Zuntz, *An Inquiry into the Transmission of the Plays of Euripides* (Cambridge, 1965).

37. *Euripidis Iphigenia in Aulide*, p. xii: "Agamemno . . . ea quae arcana sunt aversus ab sene et submissiore voce ut ille non audiat putandus est dicere."

38. W. Friedrich (see n. 9) defends the present form of the prologue but admits "Inkonsequenzen"—in particular the clash between 106–7 and 124ff. However, he explains this as a result of the fact that Euripides wavers throughout the play between two different versions of the saga. Here the old man's question "hängt . . . in der Luft" (p. 79) because "der Dichter hat ihn unwillkürlich mehr wissen lassen als er wissen kann. Der Alter fragt aus einer un- oder voreuripideischen Situation heraus, jedenfalls, um ganz vorsichtig zu reden, aus einer Situation, die dem Dichter so nahe lag, dass er sich ihrer offenbar mit Selbstverständlichkeit bediente wenn er sie brauchte." But this theory of a different "Sagenversion die ab und zu in das Drama hineinspukt" (p. 80) merely explains one inconsistency (for so Friedrich thinks it) by pointing to others and claiming that the poet is inconsistent throughout; a reference to Wilamowitz's book on Sophocles inevitably follows (p. 81). M. Pohlenz, in his second edition of *Die Gr. Tragödie*, came round to the opinion that both anapaests and iambics were written by Euripides, but finding these two passages "sachlich unvereinbar," fell back on the theory that Euripides composed an anapaestic prologue, then realized that a more complete exposition was needed and composed the iambics: "doch ist er nicht mehr dazu gekommen, diese organisch mit dem ersten Entwurf zu verbinden und innerlich auszugleichen."

39. Weil's full comment is revealing. "En disant, au vers 106 sq., que Calchas, Ulysse et Ménélas étaient seuls dans le secret, Agamemnon entendait que tout le reste de l'armée ignorait non seulement que le projet de mariage fût un vain prétexte, mais encore qu'il fût question d'un tel projet et que le roi eût mandé sa fille. Ceci est évident pour quiconque lit la narration d'Agamemnon avec une attention réfléchie." Apart from the fact that even a reading "avec une attention réfléchie" does not settle the question at all, the phrase shows that Weil was thinking of the scholar in his study, not of the audience at the Dionysia.

40. C. Headlam, *Euripides, Iphigenia in Aulis*[4] (Cambridge, 1922) speaks of "an artistic device for restating a fact on which he wishes to lay special stress."

41. W. S. Barrett, *Euripides Hippolytos* (Oxford, 1964) on vs. 42. (The *Bacchae* prologue also "misleads," cf. vss. 50ff.)

42. P. Shorey, *The Republic of Plato* (Loeb Classical Library, Cambridge, Mass.), vol. II (1935) on 523b and 529a. (He compares also *Lg.* 792b–c.)

43. His reasons for this are given on p. 138. They are: "(1) impossible omission of ἐγώ from 106–7; only violent emendation can restore it. (2) μεταγράφω; word here only in poetry. (3) Indicative εἰσεῖδον very rare in Euripides (v. England). (4) 112–13 owe much to *I.T.* 760–61. (5) Weak redundancy of ἅ δὲ κέκευθε δέλτος with τἀγγεγραμμέν᾿. (6) General lameness of the verses." On (1) see above, on (2) below. As for (3) England was dead wrong, as a glance at the Allen and Italie *Concordance* will show. On (4) see below. The redundancy condemned in (5) is no weaker than that presented by τἀνόντα κἀγγεγραμμέν᾿ in the *I.T.* passage.

44. (1) *Beschouwingen over het archaïsche element in den stijl van Aeschylus* (Utrecht, 1937) gives examples from Sophocles and Euripides on pp. 23–26 and discusses the technique in Aeschylus on pp. 76–105. (2) *Untersuchungen über Begriff, Anwendung und Entstehung der griechischen Ringcomposition* (Amsterdam, 1944) is concerned mainly with Herodotus and Homer. (3) *De Ringkompositie als Opbouwprincipe in de Epische Gedichten van Homerus* (Amsterdam, 1948) (with French résumé, pp. 87–92).

45. This repetition seems to have escaped the notice of commentators (even of Kaibel); the only remark on it I have found is G. Schiassi, *Sophoclis Electra* (Florence, 1961): "La chiusa del discorso di Oreste fa eco a quella del discorso del pedagogo; ritorna il motivo del 'momento buono' che è quello dell'azione."

46. e.g., E., *I.T.* 258~59~337–39, *Ph.* 1087~1196, *Tr.* 633~681, 352~405, *H.F.* 1254~1310, *Supp.* 406~425; S., *O.T.* 582~615, *Ant.* 1032~1047, 1063~1090; A., *Pers.* 352~431, *Ag.* 280~316, 550~581.

47. cf. 52, 65, 71, 74, 77, 80, 92, 190ff., 272, 295ff., 308, 324, 350, 370, 410, etc.

48. *Fr.* 7 (N.²) κρεῖσσον δὲ πλούτου καὶ βαθυσπόρου χθονός (from Orion) turns up in Stobaeus with the ending πολυχρύσου χλιδῆς. Cf. also E., *Rh.* 305–6 πέλτη ... χρυσοκολλήτοις τύποις ἔλαμπε.

49. Apollo in *Alcestis* and Silenus in *Cyclops* are identified by inferred self-announcement, but in both cases their identity was clear from their costume.

50. Fraenkel's objection unfortunately applies also to the hypothetical complete anapaestic prologue he tries to reconstruct. "Der Dichter der Anapäste lässt ... den alten Mann sagen: 'lass mich den Inhalt des Briefs erfahren, damit ich ihn genau wie du ihn geschrieben hast wiedergeben kann (falls der Brief verloren geht).'" But why on earth should the old man be afraid of losing the letter? Unlike Pylades, he is not going by sea; he is supposed to intercept Clytemnestra's chariot (149ff.).

51. Fraenkel refers to his *Iktus und Akzent im lateinischen Sprechvers* (Berlin, 1928), p. 93. The examples given there are of course all from Roman comedy.

52. G. Monaco, in an interesting article on the use of letters in ancient drama ("L'epistola nel teatro antico," *Dioniso* 39 [1965], 334–51), points out that the letter in *I.T.* is not read aloud by Iphigenia (she couldn't write as is clear from 584ff., so presumably she couldn't read either) and that in fact part of what we hear is her memory of what she dictated to the prisoner who once wrote it for her and part paraphrase adapted to the dialogue with Pylades. "Il messaggio ... è esposto in forma diretta (cioè com'è stato dettato al volenteroso prigionero poi ucciso) ma inframezzata da qualche riferimento che non sembra testuale (come τοῖς ἐκεῖ del v. 771 ...) ... Dopo la parte in forma diretta, che occupa i vv. 770 sg., 774–776, 778 sg., il resto è parafrasato" (p. 347).

53. And even there only in the active voice: *Haer.* II. lxiv 31. 32 (p. 633 of Dindorf II).

54. 1.132.5 παρασημηνάμενος σφραγῖδα ἵνα, ἣν ψευσθῇ τῆς δόξης ἢ καὶ ἐκεῖνός τι μεταγράψαι αἰτήσῃ, μὴ ἐπιγνῶ, λύει τὰς ἐπιστολάς. Cf. *I.A.* 37ff. γράμματα ... σφραγίζεις λύεις τ' ὀπίσω.

55. Cf. LSJ *ad verb.* But the entry cites the *I.A.* passage under the meaning "copy, transcribe." It should come below under "rewrite, alter or correct what one has written." (The new supplement does not note this error.)

56. The three-hand theory also presents us with the *disiecta membra* of two once-complete prologues. Fraenkel offers us the hacked remnants of a splendid Euripidean prologue in anapaests, Page the truncated corpse of a (possibly) Euripidean prologue in trimeters embedded in two pieces of a fine fourth-century anapaestic prologue. Both, when they have separated the wheat from the chaff, are forced to appeal to presumably lost lines for completeness. Our present prologue is at least complete; if it could take voice it might say to us, adapting the words of a recent American President "I'm the only prologue you've got."

57. The play was famous in the fourth century and often produced. The Alexandrians knew that there were in existence three different prologues to *Rhesus*; it seems strange that if there were three versions of the prologue of *I.A.* no Alexandrian comment on the fact survives.

58. Friedrich, p. 91, n. 2, "Man bedenke, mit welcher Häufung von Zufällen man rechnen müsste: Zufällig enthalten die Trimeter, wie zugegeben wird, gerade das, was den Anapästen fehlt. Zufällig fangen die Trimeter genau an dem Punkte an, wo die Mitteilungen erwartet werden, die Agamemnon in seiner Rede macht usw."

59. This is obscured by Murray's colometry (which departs from that of Barnes but retains his numbering). But the important point is that counting paroemiacs (more frequent in the second system because of Agamemnon's melic anapaests) as dimeters, there are exactly eighty-eight anapaestic dimeters on each side of the trimeters.

60. This article had already been in the editor's hands for some time before the appearance of Gudrun Mellert-Hoffmann's *Untersuchungen zur "Iphigenie in Aulis" des Euripides* (Heidelberg, 1969). The second part of this work, pp. 91–155, contains a vindication of the *I.A.* prologue in its present form with a careful consideration of all the objections which have been advanced against it and an especially valuable examination of the attacks on its language and style. Naturally enough, some of the material of the present article is there anticipated, but it also presents new arguments which, if generally accepted, will serve to reinforce Mellert-Hoffmann's impressive demonstration.

TWENTY-ONE

The Medea *of Euripides*

In 431 B.C. Euripides competed against Sophocles and Euphorion with three tragedies, *Medea*, *Philoctetes*, and *Dictys*, followed by a satyr play, *Theristae*; he was awarded the third prize.[1]

But his *Medea* left a deep and lasting impression in the minds of his Athenian audience; comic parodies,[2] literary imitations,[3] and representations in the visual arts[4] reflect its immediate impact and show that the play lost none of its power to fascinate and repel as the centuries went by. It struck the age as new, but like all innovative masterpieces, it had its deep roots in tradition; it looks back to the past while it gropes for the future. In it we can see what Euripides took over from his predecessors and contemporaries, how he transformed what he learned from them, and what he invented and was to refine and develop as his own unique tragic vision in the last twenty years of his long dramatic career.

He had been fascinated by this story from the very beginning. His first offering in the Dionysiac contest (in 455 B.C., only three years after the staging of Aeschylus' *Oresteia*) included the *Peliades*, the story of Medea at Iolcos, her deceitful promise to rejuvenate old Pelias, its king, and the king's death at her hands. Some time later (we do not know the date—it may have been before the *Medea* or after it),[5] Euripides produced the *Aegeus*, the story of Medea at Athens, married to old Aegeus, its king, and her unsuccessful attempt to engineer the death of his son Theseus. In 431 B.C., twenty-four years after his first production, he staged the play we have, the story of Medea and Jason at Corinth.

We know that the version of the myth which he used in this play was not imposed on him. The many variants of the legend which can still be found in ancient mythographers and commentators as well as in the fragments of lost epics show that he had a wide freedom of choice.[6] One account had Medea kill her children unintentionally (she was trying to make them immortal and something went wrong with the formula); in another the children were killed by the Corinthians in a revolt against Medea, whom they had appointed queen of Corinth; in yet another

This chapter originally appeared in *Yale Classical Studies*, 25 (1977). © 1977 by the Cambridge University Press. Reprinted by permission.

Medea killed Creon, left her children in the temple of Hera, and fled to Athens—whereupon Creon's kinsmen killed the children and spread the rumor that Medea had done it. At least two of these versions (and probably more besides) were available to Euripides, but he made his own by combination, addition, selection. In it, Medea, far from being queen of Corinth, is a refugee there. Deserted by her husband, Jason, she is to be deported, but she kills Jason's bride, the bride's father (Creon, king of Corinth), and her own children, whose bodies she leaves in the temple of Hera Akraia before she departs for Athens. And it seems to be suggested by the evidence that the murder of the children by Medea herself is Euripidean invention.[7]

Out of the old stories available to him, Euripides created a new one—a version more shocking, more physically and psychologically violent than anything he found in the tradition. What is even more remarkable is the way he handles it. How was he to present such a shocking series of actions to an Athenian audience in the theater of Dionysus?

There were several possibilities open to him. He might have made Medea a Clytemnestra figure—a magnificent criminal whose violence represents the primitive past of the race, posed against the civilized, rational values of male democracy, represented in this case by Jason. He might have created a version of the story in which Medea was punished for her crimes and so have shown the working of the justice of the polis,[8] represented by Creon, or of Zeus, announced by a god from the machine—Hera, perhaps, would have been appropriate, or that old standby, Apollo. He might have presented us with a Medea who murdered her children while insane, like Ino (who is actually referred to in the play), or one who murdered in cold blood but was then consumed by everlasting remorse, like Procne. But he did none of these things: what he did was, like the endings of so many of his plays, unexpected.

The prologue introduces the situation swiftly—a wife abandoned with her children for a royal bride in a foreign city. Medea will take no food, listen to no comfort, no advice: she will only weep and rage. But it soon becomes clear that she is no passive sufferer. "I am afraid," says the Nurse; "she is planning something dreadful." As the action develops, we begin to feel the brooding menace of the unseen figure behind the stage door; she is planning suicide or revenge and the Nurse fears for the children's lives. Soon we hear Medea's desperate cries from inside the stage door, her curses, her wishes for death and general destruction.

This is no ordinary woman wronged: in fact, the stage situation may have reminded the audience of a play they had (probably) seen some years before[9]—the *Ajax* of Sophocles. There too we hear the hero's desperate and terrifying cries from inside the stage building,[10] where, like Medea, he lies, refusing food;[11] there too a woman fears for the protagonist's child (and has had it taken away to safety).[12] And there are many other resemblances. Both Ajax and Medea fear more than anything else in this world the mockery of their enemies;[13] for both of them a time limit of one day is set;[14] both in a set speech explore the possible courses of action open to them and, rejecting alternatives, decide—the one for suicide, the other for revenge.[15] And these similarities are enforced by some striking verbal parallels between the two plays.[16]

These resemblances are not coincidence. Medea, in fact, is presented to us, from the start, in heroic terms. Her language and action, as well as the familiar frame in which they operate, mark her as a heroic character,[17] one of those great individuals whose intractable firmness of purpose, whose defiance of threats and advice, whose refusal to betray their ideal vision of their own nature, were the central preoccupation of Sophoclean tragedy. The structure and language of the *Medea* is that of the Sophoclean heroic play. This is the only extant Euripidean tragedy constructed according to the model which Sophocles was to perfect in the *Oedipus Tyrannos* and which, through the influence of that supreme dramatic achievement and its exploitation by Aristotle as a paradigm, became the model for Renaissance and modern classical tragedy: the play dominated by a central figure who holds the stage throughout, who initiates and completes—against obstacles, advice and threats—the action, whether it be discovery or revenge.[18] Other Euripidean tragedies are different. *Hippolytus* is a drama with four principal characters.[19] Hecuba, who is on stage throughout *The Trojan Women*, is no dominating figure but a passive victim, as she is also in the play named after her, until she turns into a revengeful Medea figure at the end. Pentheus, Heracles, and Andromache are victims rather than actors. Electra in her own play comes nearest to Medea in stage importance, but she cannot act without Orestes, and in the *Orestes* he shares the stage with her. *Phoenissae* has no central character at all and the *Ion, Iphigenia in Tauris,* and *Helen* are plays of a different type, in which the "incurable" tragic act is avoided.[20] The *Medea* is the only Euripidean tragedy (in the modern sense of that word) which is tightly constructed around a "hero": a central figure whose inflexible purpose, once formed, nothing can shake—a purpose which is the mainspring of the action.

Medea is presented to the audience in the unmistakable style and language of the Sophoclean hero.[21] These have been isolated and discussed elsewhere;[22] all that is necessary here is to demonstrate their presence and function in the *Medea*. She has the main characteristic of the hero, the determined resolve, expressed in uncompromising terms: the verbal adjectives *ergasteon* (791), "the deed must be done," and *tolmeteon* (1051) "I must dare"; the decisive futures—especially *kteno*, "I shall kill"—this word again and again. The firmness of her resolve is phrased in the customary Sophoclean terms *dedoktai* (1236), *dedogmenon* (822)—"my mind is made up." She is deaf to persuasion; she will not hear, *akouei* (29). She is moved by the typical heroic passions, anger, *orge* (176 etc.), wrath, *cholos* (94 etc.). She exhibits the characteristic heroic temper daring, *tolma* (394 etc.), and rashness, *thrasos* (856 etc.). She is fearful, terrible, *deine* (44 etc.) and wild, like a beast, *agrios* (193 etc.). She is much concerned, like the heroes, for her glory, εὐκλεέστατος βίος (810); she will not put up with injustice, οὐδ' ἀνέξεται (38), and with what she regards as intolerable, οὐ . . . τλητόν (797). Above all, she is full of passionate intensity, that *thumos* which in her case is so marked a feature of her make-up that in her famous monologue she argues with it, pleads with it for mercy, as if it were something outside herself. Like the heroes, she feels that she has been treated with disrespect, *etimasmene* (20), *atimasas* (1354 etc.); wronged, *edikemene* (26 etc.); and insulted, *hubriz'* (603 etc.). Her greatest torment is the thought that her enemies will laugh at her, *gelos* (383 etc.). Like the Sophoclean heroes, she curses her enemies (607 etc.) while she plans her revenge. She is alone, *mone* (513) and abandoned, *eremos* (255 etc.), and in her isolation and despair she wishes for death.

Like the Sophoclean tragic hero, she resists alike appeals for moderation and harsh summonses to reason. She is admonished, *nouthetoumene* (29) by her friends but pays no more attention than a rock or the sea waves. She is begged to "consider," *skepsai* (851), but to no avail: she cannot be persuaded, *peithesthai* (184) or ruled, *archesthai* (120). The chorus beg her as suppliants, *hiketeuomen* (854) to change her mind, but to no effect. To others her resolution seems to be stupidity, folly, *moria* (457 etc.), and self-willed stubbornness, *authadia* (621);[23] she is like a wild animal, a bull (92 etc.), a lioness (187 etc.).

As in Sophoclean heroic tragedy, there is also a secondary figure whose pliability under pressure throws the hero's unbending will into high relief. It is not, in this play, a weak sister, like Ismene or Chrysothemis, but a man, like Creon in the *Antigone*; in fact, he has the same name, Creon; he is king of Corinth. He comes on stage, his mind made up: he has proclaimed sentence of immediate exile for Medea. She must leave at once: he is afraid of her. Her eloquent appeal falls on deaf ears: his resolve, he says, is fixed, *arare* (322). She will never persuade him, οὐ γὰρ ἂν πείσαις ποτέ (325). But she does. He yields, though he knows that he is making a mistake, and gives her one more day.

However, the structure of the *Medea* does differ from that of the Sophoclean hero play in one important respect: the hero (like Clytemnestra in the *Agamemnon*) must conceal her purpose from everyone else in the play, except, of course, the chorus, whom (unlike Clytemnestra) she must win over to her side. Consequently, a characteristically Sophoclean scene is missing: the two-actor dialogue in which the heroic resolve is assailed by persuasion, threat, or both—Ismene to Antigone, Creon to Antigone, Chrysothemis to Electra, Tecmessa to Ajax. But there *is* a speech in the *Medea* which rolls out all the clichés of the appeal to reason, the summons to surrender which, in Sophocles, all the heroes have to face. It is typical of Euripides' originality, of the way he makes things new, that this speech is delivered by Medea herself.

It is her false declaration of submission to Jason, her fulsome confession that she was only a foolish emotional woman, the speech that lures him to his doom. "I talked things over with myself," she tells him, "and reproached myself bitterly." As she reports her self-rebuke, she pulls out all the stops of the Sophoclean summons to reason. "Why do I act like a mad woman [*mainomai* 873] and show hostility to good advice [τοῖσι βουλεύουσιν εὖ 874]? Shall I not rid myself of passion [*thumou* 879]? I realize that my judgment was bad [*aboulian* 882]. . . . I raged in pointless anger [μάτην θυμουμένη 883] . . . I was mindless [*aphron* 885]. . . . I confess I was full of bad thoughts then . . . but have come to better counsel now [κακῶς φρονεῖν τότ' . . . ἄμεινον . . . βεβούλευμαι 892–93]. My anger has subsided [μεθέστηκεν χόλος 898]." And later, when Jason accepts her apologies, she says, "I shall not disobey you [*apisteso* 927]. What you did was best for me [*lōista* 935]."[24]

Jason is understanding and sympathetic. "I congratulate you on your present frame of mind—and I don't blame you for things past. Anger is something you have to expect from a woman. . . . But your mind has changed for the better [ἐς τὸ λῷον 911]." As he turns from Medea to his sons, Euripides puts in his mouth a subtle variation on a Sophoclean theme: the threat to the hero that he or she will realize the need for surrender in time, γνῶναι . . . χρόνῳ.[25] "You have realized what the best decision is," he says to her, "though it took time [ἔγνως . . . τῷ χρόνῳ 912]." He has swallowed the bait—hook, line, and sinker: the way is now prepared for the murders that will wreck his life.[26]

This speech is part of Medea's grand design; these formulas of dissuasion masquerading as terms of submission are the instruments of her revenge. As if this were not a sufficiently daring adaptation of the patterns of the heroic play, Euripides presents us with another. There *is* one person who can and does pose a real obstacle to Medea's plans, who can effectively confront her with argument—Medea herself.[27] In the monologue she delivers after she hears that her fatal gifts have been delivered into the princess's hands by her children, she pleads with herself, changes her mind, and changes again and then again to return finally and firmly to her intention to kill them. When the children look at her and smile, she loses her courage. "Farewell, my plans!" (1048). But then she recovers. "Shall I earn the world's laughter by leaving my enemies unpunished? No, I must dare to do this!" (1049–51). Then a sudden surge of love and pity overcomes her again and she addresses herself to her own *thumos*, her passionate heroic anger, as if it were something outside herself. "Do not do it. Let them go, hard-hearted— spare the children!" (1056–57). But her *thumos* will not relent: the children must die. In this great scene the grim heroic resolve[28] triumphs not over an outside adversary or adviser but over the deepest maternal feelings of the hero herself.

This presentation in heroic terms of a rejected foreign wife, who was to kill her husband's new wife, the bride's father, and finally her own children, must have made the audience which saw it for the first time in 431 B.C. a trifle uneasy. Heroes, it was well known, were violent beings and since they lived and died by the simple code "help your friends and hurt your enemies" it was only to be expected that their revenges, when they felt themselves unjustly treated, dishonored, scorned, would be huge and deadly. The epic poems do not really question Achilles' right to bring destruction on the Greek army to avenge Agamemnon's insults, nor Odysseus' slaughter of the entire younger generation of the Ithacan aristocracy. Sophocles' Ajax sees nothing wrong in his attempt to kill the commanders of the army for denying him the armor of Achilles; his shame springs simply from his failure to achieve his bloody objective. But Medea is a woman, a wife and mother, and also a foreigner. Yet she acts as if she were a combination of the naked violence of Achilles and the cold craft of Odysseus, and, what is more, it is in these terms that the words of Euripides' play present her. "Let no one," she says, "think me contemptible and weak, nor inactive either, but quite the opposite— dangerous to my enemies, helpful to my friends. Such are the qualities that bring a life glory" (807ff.). It is the creed by which Homeric and Sophoclean heroes live—and die.[29]

She is a hero, then, but since she is also a woman, she cannot prevail by brute strength; she must use deceit.[30] She is, as she admits herself, a "clever woman," *sophe*, and this cleverness she uses to deceive everyone in the play, bending them to her frightful purpose. Creon is tricked into giving her one day's grace; she knows that his initial bluster hides a soft heart[31] and fawns on him (her own term, *thopeusai* 368) to gain time. Aegeus is tricked into promising her asylum in Athens: tricked is the word, for if he had realized that she intended to destroy the royal house of Corinth and her own children, he would never have promised her protection. She knows this, and that is why she binds him by a solemn oath. And Jason she takes in completely by her assumption of the role of repentant wife: she showers him with such abject self-abasement, such fawning reiteration of all the male Greek clichés about women (she even says: "A woman is female—it's her nature to weep," 289),[32] that one wonders how Jason can believe it. But she knows her man. "That's the way a sensible woman *should* act," he says, γυναικὸς ἔργα ταῦτα σώφρονος (913).

And so the poisoned gifts are taken to the new bride; Medea, when she hears that they have been delivered and accepted, successfully resists the temptation to spare the children, and then, after savoring at length[33] the messenger's frightful description of the poison's effects, she kills her sons. Her revenge is complete when Jason comes to save them; she holds their bodies in the chariot sent by her grandfather Helios, and, safe from Jason, taunts him with the wreck of all his hopes, his childlessness. The end of the play sees her leave to deposit the children's bodies in Hera's temple and then go off to Athens.

She triumphs.[34] She will always suffer from the memory of what she did to the children, as she grudgingly admits to Jason (1361–62),[35] but she has her full and exquisite revenge. "These children are dead," she says to him, "that is what will torment you" (1370). And she escapes the consequences of her action, goes safely to Athens.

This is very unlike what happens to most Sophoclean heroes. Ajax triumphs in a way, but he is dead; Oedipus wins a kind of victory, but he is blind; Antigone's victory comes after she has hanged herself. This complete success of Medea is connected with another feature of the way she is presented which is also in sharp contrast with the Sophoclean hero. She is quite sure, from start to finish, that the gods are on her side.

All the Sophoclean heroes feel themselves, sooner or later, abandoned by gods as well as men: their loneliness is absolute, they can appeal only to the silent presence of mountains, sea, and air.[36] But Medea from her first appearance has no doubts that the gods support her cause. She appeals to Themis (ancestral law) and Artemis (woman's help in childbirth!) to witness Jason's unjust action (160); she calls on Zeus, who, she says, knows who is responsible for her sorrows (332), swears to avenge herself in the name of Hecate,[37] "the mistress I revere above all others, my chosen helpmate" (395ff.). She asks Jason if he thinks the same gods by whom he swore fidelity no longer reign in power (493), appeals again to Zeus (516), and calls exultantly on "Zeus, the justice of Zeus and the light of the Sun" (764), as she sees her plans for revenge ensured by Aegeus' promise of shelter in Athens. After the murder of the children she is still confident, in her

confrontation scene with Jason, that Zeus is on her side (1352), and she
makes plans to deposit the bodies of her sons in the temple of Hera
Akraia (1379). When Jason appeals to the avenging Erinyes and blood
retribution (*Erinys . . . Dike* 1389f.), she dismisses his claim to divine
protection with scorn: "What god or spirit listens to *your* prayers?"
(1391). She never wavers from her faith that what she does has divine
approval.[38] She can even say, to the messenger who brings the news
from the palace which seals the fate of the children: "These things the
gods and I, with my evil thoughts, have contrived [ταῦτα γὰρ
θεοὶ / κἀγὼ κακῶς φρονοῦσ' ἐμηχανησάμην 1013–14]."

"The gods and I"—she sees herself as their instrument and
associate.[39] And the play gives us no reason to think that she is wrong.
On the contrary, it confirms her claim in spectacular fashion. All
through the play, appeals are made to two divine beings, Earth and Sun.
It is by these divinities that Aegeus is made to swear the oath that he
will protect Medea from her enemies once she reaches Athens; it is to
Earth and Sun that the chorus appeals at the last moment, begging
them to prevent the murder of the children, and Jason, in the last
scene, asks Medea how, with her children's blood on her hands, she
can look at Earth and Sun. "What Earth will do we shall not be told,"[40]
but Helios, the Sun, is clearly on Medea's side. Not only are the
poisoned gifts sent to the princess an inheritance from Helios (and the
poison acts like a concentration of the sun's fire), but, more important,
it is Helios who sends Medea the chariot on which she escapes to
Athens. "In the gods' name," says Jason, "let me touch the soft skin of
my sons" (1402–3). But *his* appeal to the gods has no effect; "Your
words are wasted" (1404), Medea tells him, and draws away in her
chariot as Jason appeals again to Zeus. The chorus ends the play with
lines which appear in our manuscripts at the end of several other
Euripidean plays; some critics have thought them inappropriate here,[41]
but they are obviously and squarely in their right place:

> Zeus on Olympus has many things in his store-room:
> the gods bring to pass many surprising things.
> What was expected is not fulfilled.
> For the unexpected the gods find a way.
> So this story turned out.

Medea's appearance as a heroic figure, as the murderer of her
children who escapes the consequences of her actions, apparently with
the blessing of the gods, must have seemed to the audience surprising
beyond description. Euripides himself, like the gods, has many things in
his store room; he has defied expectation and found a way for the
unimagined.

II

But he has another surprising thing in his store room: Medea's final appearance. She has been on stage since near the beginning of the play; she leaves only toward the end, when she goes through the palace door to murder her sons. When she enters again, to face Jason, she is on the chariot sent by Helios, her grandfather, high up in the air. This last detail is not clearly stated in the text, but no other stage arrangement would explain why Jason cannot reach her and must beg her to let him touch the bodies of his sons. She must be either on the roof of the stage building (but that would present mechanical difficulties) or in the *mechane*—her chariot swung out over the stage area on a crane.[42] In either case, she is high up and out of reach. But this is the place reserved in Attic tragedy for gods; this is not, as the chorus of the *Electra* says, the pathway of mortals, οὐ γὰρ θνητῶν γ' ἥδε κέλευθος (1235–36). And as the scene progresses, this hint that she has become something more than mortal is confirmed. Her situation, action, and language are precisely those of the divine beings who in so many Euripidean plays appear at the end in power[43] to wind up the action, give judgment, prophesy the future, and announce the foundation of a religious ritual.[44]

From her unapproachable position on high, she interrupts and puts a stop to the violent action of the human beings on the lower level (Jason is trying to break down the palace door). In this she is like Apollo in the *Orestes*, Athena in the *Ion* and *Iphigenia in Tauris*, the Dioscuri in *Helen*, and Hermes in the *Antiope*.[45] She justifies her savage revenge on the grounds that she has been treated with disrespect and mockery (1354–55), like Dionysus in the *Bacchae*; in this she is like Aphrodite in the *Hippolytus* prologue, Athena in the prologue to the *Troades*. She takes measures and gives orders for the burial of the dead (her own sons 1378ff. and the princess 1394)[46] like Thetis in the *Andromache*, Athena in *The Suppliants* and *Erechtheus*, Hermes in the *Antiope*, and the Dioscuri in the *Electra*. She prophesies the future (the ignominious death of Jason) like Thetis in the *Andromache*, Athena in *The Suppliants* and *Ion*, the Dioscuri in *Electra* and *Helen*, Apollo in *Orestes*, and Dionysus in the *Bacchae*.[47] She announces the foundation of a cult (for her own children in Corinth 1382ff.) like Artemis in the *Hippolytus* and Athena in the *Iphigenia in Tauris* and *Erechtheus*.[48] She announces her departure and destination (1384ff.) like the Dioscuri in *Electra* and Apollo in *Orestes*.[49]

And Medea speaks in phrases which recur in the pronouncements of the gods from the machine. "Why are you trying to break down the doors with crowbars?" she asks Jason. "Stop!" *pausai* (1319). "Why are you directing a pursuit?" Athena asks Thoas at the end of the *Iphigenia in Tauris*. "Stop!" *pausai* (1437). So Apollo speaks to Menelaus in the *Orestes*: *pausai* (1625). This is not the only command Medea issues from the *mechane*: like the gods she is prone to imperatives. She dismisses Jason. "Go!" she says to him, "and bury your wife," *steiche* (1394). So Athena in the *Ion* dismisses Ion and Creusa: "Go!" *steicheth'* (1616), and the Dioscuri in *Electra* send Orestes on his way to Athens with the same word: "Go!" *steich'* (1343).[50]

Medea shows the same merciless, even vindictive, attitude toward Jason that characterizes the Euripidean gods. "The children are dead. This is what will give you pain," she says to him, using the same word, *dēxetai* (1370), that Artemis uses in the *Hippolytus* when she rebukes Theseus: "Do my words pain you?" *daknei* (1313). Like Artemis, she holds out the prospect of more suffering to come. "Listen to what comes next—you will cry out in even greater agony," says Artemis (1314), and Medea tells Jason: "You are not sorrowing yet. Wait until you are old" (1396).[51] A statement of Artemis about the ways of gods with men sums up what Medea might have claimed: "Those who are evil we destroy, children and home and all" (1340–41)—except that Medea's more exquisite revenge is to leave Jason alive and alone amid the ruin of his hopes for his sons and his marriage.

Medea is presented to us not only as a hero, but also, at the end of the play, by her language, action, and situation, as a *theos* or at least something more than human. She does not start that way, but that is how she ends. Ends, that is to say, in *this* play:[52] she is going to Athens, as she tells us, and what form she will assume there we are not told. It is not likely that Euripides' audience was worried about that point: they must have been sufficiently taken aback by the appearance of Medea, the murderer of her sons, in the "habiliments of the goddess," assuming the attitude and using the language of the stage *theos*.

It is very hard to imagine what it meant to them (and what it should mean to us), for there is no parallel to it in Attic drama. Peleus in the *Andromache* is told that he will become a *theos* (1256) and is given a rendezvous for his apotheosis (1265ff.), but it does not take place on stage. Helen, at the end of the play which bears her name (1667), is given a similar assurance (not fulfilled on stage) and in the *Orestes* she actually appears on the right hand of Apollo, on her way to rejoin Castor and Polydeuces in the heavens (1631ff.), but she does not say anything. There *are* two cases in which a human being at the end of the play performs one of the functions of the *deus ex machina*. In the *Heraclidae*, Eurystheus, on the point of death, gives instructions for his burial (1036) and reveals a Delphic oracle which gives his buried corpse protective powers for Athens in future wars (1032ff.). (However, he expressly forbids a cult of his grave 1040–41.) In the *Hecuba*, the blinded Polymestor prophesies the transformation of Hecuba and the deaths of Agamemnon and Cassandra (1259ff.). These are faint and partial approximations, but there is nothing remotely comparable to Medea's full exercise of all the functions of the *theos* and her triumphant godlike departure through the air.

The effect of this investment of Medea with all the properties and functions of stage divinity must have been to bring home to the audience the conviction that Medea is not merely an individual woman wronged and revengeful; she is, at the end, a figure which personifies something permanent and powerful in the human situation, as Aphrodite clearly does, and Dionysus also. These two were Olympian deities, worshiped in state cult and portrayed in temple sculpture, but the Greek imagination created many other *theoi*, was apt, in fact, to see a *theos* in every corner. "All things are full of gods," said Thales, and from Hesiod on through the fifth and fourth centuries, Greek literature presents us with *theoi* who represent almost every phase of human activity and circumstance—poverty, plague, reputation, force, helplessness, ambition, time, and sorrow, to name just a few. A sentence of Menander gives a clue to what lies behind this proliferating theogony: adding a new *theos* to the unofficial pantheon—shamelessness (*Anaideia*)—he says: "Whatever has power is now worshipped as a god."[53]

Medea, in her last appearance, certainly has power but it is not easy to define exactly what she represents. There is a *theos* in Aeschylus which bears some resemblance to her: the house-destroying *theos* of the *Seven against Thebes*, τὰν ὠλεσίοικον θεὸν οὐ θεοῖς ὁμοίαν (720–21). But this *theos* is almost immediately (723) identified as an *Erinys*, and that will not do for Medea; in fact, as a spiller of kindred blood, she should be their allotted victim, as Jason vainly hopes she will be (1389).[54] Revenge—*dike* in the simplest sense—certainly has something to do with it, but she is more than Lesky's "Dämon der Rache";[55] there would have been no need to give her the style and appurtenances of a *theos* for that—as seems clear from the figure of Hecuba in the last scenes of the play which bears her name. Perhaps the appearance of this ferocious incarnation of vengeance in the place of an Olympian god is meant to reinforce in the audience's mind that disconcerting sense of the disintegration of all normal values which the play as a whole produces, to emphasize visually that moral chaos which the chorus sang of earlier:

The spell cast by sworn oaths has faded; respect for others no longer remains anywhere in Greece, it has taken wing up to the sky. (439ff.)

But Medea as *theos* must also represent some kind of irresistible power, something deeply rooted in the human situation, as dangerous as it is universal. It has something to do with revenge for betrayal, but its peculiar ferocity must stem from the fact that before she was a hero and through her action became a (stage) *theos*, she was a woman.

It is clear from Medea's very first speech that this strange drama, which uses Sophoclean heroic formulas to produce a most un-Sophoclean result, is grounded in the social reality and problems of its own time. There can be no doubt, to anyone who reads it without prejudice, that the *Medea* is very much concerned with the problem of woman's place in human society. I do not of course mean to revive the idea, fashionable in the early years of this century, that Euripides is a feminist.[56] Even though tradition has it that speeches from the *Medea* (in the translation of Gilbert Murray) were read aloud at suffragette meetings (a careful selection, no doubt), it is not likely that Sylvia Pankhurst would have admitted Medea to membership in her league. Euripides is concerned in this play not with progress or reform[57] but (just as in the *Hippolytus* and the *Bacchae*) with the eruption in tragic violence of forces in human nature which have been repressed and scorned, which in their long-delayed breakout exact a monstrous revenge. The *Medea* is not about woman's rights; it is about woman's wrongs, those done to her and by her.

III

This aspect of the play is usually ignored or dismissed—on the grounds that Medea is atypical: she cannot be considered a figure relevant to the problems of Athenian society because she is an oriental barbarian and also a witch.[58] "Because she was a foreigner," says Page, "she could kill her children: because she was a witch she could escape in a magic chariot."[59] The second half of this magisterial pronouncement kills two birds with one stone; in addition to denying the play any relevance to Athenian society, it also disposes of the awkward questions raised by Medea's appearance as the *theos* on the machine—she is just a witch on a glorified Hellenic broomstick. Since Page gives no other evidence that Medea is a witch, what he seems to mean is rather: "since she can escape in a magic chariot, Medea is a witch." But supernatural winged chariots are hardly an identifying mark of witches: they are properties, in Greek mythology, of gods, of Apollo, of the Attic divinity Triptolemos, above all of Helios, the sun (who is, of course, Medea's grandfather). And yet Medea as a witch or sorceress appears as a regular feature of most discussions of the play.[60] There are of course passages in ancient literature which present us with lurid pictures of Medea as a figure resembling our conception of a witch. In the following lines, for example, she addresses her prayer to Hecate:

> For thee, my hair flowing free as is the custom of my race, I have paced the sacred groves barefoot. I have called down rain from dry clouds, driven the waves to the sea-bottom ... changed the order of the seasons ... brought wheat to harvest in the winter time.

Another poet gives us a detailed description of the witches' brew she cooks for old Aeson:

> And all the while the brew in the bronze cauldron boiled and frothed white: in it were herb-roots gathered from Thessaly's lonely vales ... and hoar-frost taken at the full of the moon, a hoot-owl's wings and flesh, a werewolf's entrails also, and the fillet of fenny snake, the liver of the stag.

The first of these passages is from the *Medea* of the Roman dramatist Seneca[61] and the second from the *Metamorphoses* of Ovid.[62] It is, in fact, in the Roman poets of the first centuries B.C. and A.D. (Horace, Virgil, and Lucan) that something resembling our conception of a witch first appears, to give literary shape to the medieval witch of Christian times who serves the devil instead of Hecate but claims the same powers to raise the dead, curse, blight, transform, and prophesy. From the contents of Ovid's cauldron to that of Shakespeare,

> Finger of birth-strangled babe
> ditch-delivered by a drab
> make the gruel thick and slab,[63]

there runs an unbroken line. But it does not go back as far as the fifth century B.C. The term "witch," with its medieval overtones of black magic, ugliness, and malevolence, has no place in a description of Euripides' Medea.

There is, however, one incident in Medea's career, well-known to the fifth-century audience, which, though it does not justify the anachronistic use of the term "witchcraft," does associate her with the use of magic—her deliberately unsuccessful attempt to rejuvenate old Pelias by cutting him into pieces and boiling him in a pot. Interestingly enough, this is not magical practice, but a deliberate murder which uses other people's belief in magic to mask its real nature. Still, it is at any rate a magical context for Medea and it was a popular story; Sophocles dramatized it in his *Rhizotomoi*,[64] and it was the subject of the *Peliades* at the very beginning of Euripides' career as a dramatist. It would therefore have been very easy for him to emphasize this aspect of Medea's action: the material was familiar, needing only an emphasis on the dramatist's part to bring it to the surface of the audience's memory and cast a baleful spotlight on Medea the sorceress. But he hardly mentions it, and when he does, it is in the blandest of terms. It is described simply as a murder—"I killed Pelias, the most painful way to die, at the hands of his own daughters" (486ff.)—without any of the sensational details. In fact, when one thinks how naturally a scathing reference to this episode would have fitted into Jason's desperate invective at the end of the play,[65] it seems as if Euripides was doing his best to avoid the subject altogether.

And in any case, in the play Euripides wrote, Medea has no magical powers at all. Until she is rescued by the god Helios, and is herself transformed into some kind of superhuman being, she is merely a helpless betrayed wife and mother with no protection of any kind. She has only two resources, cunning and poison.

Perhaps it is the use of poison which has led so many critics to use the word "witch." For the only fifth-century Greek word for witch that the dictionaries can suggest is *pharmakis*, which means of course a woman who deals with love charms, drugs, and poisons. This certainly applies to Euripides' Medea,[66] but it has nothing to do with witchcraft. Love charms, drugs, and poisons are the age-old last recourse of the unloved or vengeful wife in fifth-century Athens, modern Egypt, nineteenth-century India, or for that matter Victorian England[67]—everywhere in fact before the scientific detection of poisons made these things too dangerous (for the poisoner) to use. And Medea is not the only *pharmakis* in Athenian literature. Deianira in Sophocles' *Trachiniae* tries to win back her husband's love with a love charm which, like Medea's gift to the princess, is a poisoned robe (and has the same effect on its victim).[68] The stepmother, in Antiphon's speech, gives her husband a love charm (drinkable this time) which kills him; the prosecution claims that was exactly what she intended.[69] The Athenian princess Creusa (no barbarian witch this one) uses in Euripides' *Ion* a poison just as magical as Medea's[70] to try to kill the boy she thinks is her husband's bastard son. All three of these ladies use poison, intentionally or not, to redress the balance of their unequal struggle with their husbands, but no one dreams of calling them witches.

Of course, Greek men did not approve of such feminine initiatives, but they did not invest them with the supernatural and diabolical associations of the modern word "witch." In any case, the particular function of the medieval witch—cursing, producing barrenness in women, a murrain on the cattle, disease and death for whole families—was in the ancient world not the province of specialists but the normal recourse of ordinary individuals. This is all too clear to anyone who studies the hate-filled inscriptions known as *defixiones*, which show, from the fifth century on, ordinary persons, in Greece and elsewhere, solemnly recording on tablets of lead or pieces of broken pottery their spells for the painful destruction of their neighbors and business rivals. "I call down on Androtion a fever to recur every fourth day until he dies," runs one of the milder specimens—scratched on a fifth-century Athenian potsherd.[71]

Medea then, in the body of the play, has no supernatural powers or equipment. All she has is a very powerful poison, but this merely puts her in the same class as Deianira and Creusa. These are of course not the parallels cited by the proponents of Medea the witch. They cite Circe and Hecate. But Hecate is a great goddess and of course Circe is a goddess too, as Homer plainly tells us.[72] The Medea of the body of the play is not comparable in any way with these powerful figures.

But if to call Medea a witch falsifies the situation, she is also, according to many modern critics, a barbarian, an Oriental, and therefore equally irrelevant to the problems of Greek society. This case is most eloquently argued by Page.

> She is just such a woman as his audience would expect a foreign princess to be. She has nearly all the features of the type—unrestrained excess in lamentation, a readiness to fawn on authority, the powers of magic, childlike surprise at falsehoods and broken promises. . . . It was natural then that Medea should be unrestrained in the expression of her sorrow, like a Phrygian or a Mysian . . . she was like a wild beast in her grief and anger. And then in a moment she changes her mood and cringes before the King . . . a second time . . . before Aegeus, a third time before Jason. Respect for authority was the primary cause. The Oriental was accustomed to despots whose word was law. . . . Broken promises Medea finds it . . . difficult to forgive. . . . The contrast of truthful barbarian and lying Greek had long been a commonplace.[73]

The case could not be more eloquently stated, but it is flawed. Medea is indeed unrestrained in the expression of sorrow, but the comparison should be "like Ajax, Odysseus, Achilles, Heracles."[74] She is compared to a wild beast, but so, sooner or later, are all the Sophoclean heroes.[75] The way she fawns on Creon, Aegeus, and Jason has nothing at all to do with respect for authority; she is deceiving them all, and two of them she is luring to their ruin.[76] As for her "childish surprise at falsehoods and broken promises," this is a trait she shares (apart from the prejudicial adjective) with Creusa, Philoctetes, and of course the Greek chorus of the *Medea*.

Page finds that "above all the inhuman quality of the child-murderess was a typically foreign quality. The chorus could think of only one other example in the legends of Greece—Ino" (though, as he points out in a note, "they might have added at least Agave and Procne"). But Page does not produce any eastern stories which will serve as cogent parallels. In fact, as an example of the "appalling cruelty" of "foreign countries," he cites Astyages, who "set a Thyestean feast before Harpagos." But the adjective "Thyestean" gives the game away—that's a *Greek* story!—and the list of Persian atrocities which follows contains nothing which cannot be paralleled, or for that matter bettered, from Greek myth and history.[77]

"No *Greek* woman would have had the heart to do what she has done"; Page quotes Jason to sum up his case. But dramatic characters do not necessarily speak for their creator. And this speech is neatly cancelled out by one of Thoas', the barbarian king in the same dramatist's *Iphigenia in Tauris*. Informed that the captured Orestes has murdered his mother, he exclaims (using exactly the same verb as Jason, *etlē*) "Apollo! Not even among the barbarians would anyone have the heart to do what he has done" (1174).

In any case, there is no suggestion in the play that anyone regards Medea as a barbarian, except of course, in the end, Jason. The chorus of Corinthian women fully approve of her first announcement that she plans revenge on her husband (267–68). When she makes clear that this means death not only for Jason but also for the king of Corinth and his daughter, they raise no objections. In fact, in the choral ode which follows they sing exultantly of honor coming for the female sex. When she tells them that her plans have changed—she will now kill the princess, "whoever touches her," and also Jason's sons—they cry out in protest. But it is only the murder of the children which appalls them. Their protest brushed aside, they say only that she will be the unhappiest among women. Where they could have intervened decisively—the scene in which Medea entraps Jason by feigned humility—they remain silent. Finally, after listening to the messenger's ghastly account of the deaths of the king and his daughter, their only comment is: "It seems as if heaven today were bringing much evil on Jason—as he deserves!" (1231–32).

The chorus obviously feel that Medea's situation might well be their own: as far as they are concerned, she speaks like and for them, and when after the offstage murder of the children they sing their antistrophe, far from suggesting that she is a witch and oriental barbarian (and surely this was the place to make Page's point), they find a parallel in their own Greek tradition. "Only one woman, only one, have I heard of who in time past raised her hand against her children. It was Ino, driven mad by the gods" (1282ff.). The foreignness of Medea was fixed in the legend and it suited Euripides' purpose, since it made possible the liquid fire and the chariot of the sun, but Euripides' Medea, in her thought, speech, and action is as Greek as Jason, or rather, as Ajax and Achilles.

IV

But she is a woman and her first speech, that of a woman speaking to women, exploits and appeals to their feelings of sympathy. It is of course one of the most famous speeches in Greek tragedy. No more howls of despair, or threats of suicide—she comes out of the house to win the support of the chorus for her still nebulous plan for revenge. She is apologetic, conciliatory, a foreigner who must carefully observe the proprieties. But her life, she says, has been destroyed; her husband, who was everything to her, has turned out to be the vilest of men.

"Of all the creatures that have breath and intelligence, we women are the most afflicted." We buy our husbands with our dowry—her argument proceeds—not knowing if they will be good or bad, go into a new home unprepared for the new life. If we work hard and make a success of it, we're lucky; if not, death would be better. The man, when he tires of our company, can go out for distraction; we are forced to keep our eyes steadily on one single human being. They say we live at home in safety, while *they* fight the wars—what fools! I'd rather stand in the battle line three times than go through child-bearing once.

It is magnificent rhetoric, and it wins their heart. But it is not, as has so often been claimed, *just* rhetoric. It has its vital function in the construction of the drama, but it must also reflect some contemporary reality, for dramatists, especially the greatest dramatists, are not philosophers, not original thinkers; they reflect and use, dramatize and intensify, the thought and feeling of their time. And in fact there are many signs that in the intellectual ferment of late fifth-century Athens, the problem of women's role in society and the family was, like everything else, a subject for discussion and reappraisal. In Euripides' *Melanippe Desmotis*, for example, someone (presumably the heroine) makes a long polemical speech demonstrating woman's moral and religious superiority to man (Page, *GLP* 112). The *Lysistrata* of Aristophanes is of course a hilarious comedy, but it has a deeply serious undercurrent of feeling, and the heroine of the play, the woman who organizes her sex on both sides to stop the war, is wholly sympathetic—it is quite clear that her creator admired her. J. H. Finley long ago drew attention to the resemblances (some of them verbal) between Medea's speech and the arguments against marriage set forth (from the man's point of view) by Antiphon the sophist.[78] And one cannot help suspecting that much later, Plato, when he says in the *Republic* that to divide mankind into male and female for the purposes of public life or education or anything, except the begetting and bearing of children, is just as absurd as to divide it into the long-haired and the bald,[79] may well be adapting to his own purpose, as he so often does, ideas that were first put into circulation by the sophistic radicals of the fifth century.

Even if it is conceded that the role of women in family and society was a problem under discussion in fifth-century Athens, it may be objected that it was a theme a tragic poet might well avoid, and that even if he did choose to handle it, he would never take as his protagonist a woman who butchered her own sons. Yet this same strange combination of infanticide and programmatic speech about the lot of women appears in another tragedy produced before 414 (how many years before, we do not know).[80] Its author is none other than Sophocles. His *Tereus* told the story of the Athenian princess Procne, married to Tereus, king of Thrace. She persuaded him to bring her sister Philomela from Athens to join her. Tereus, on the way home, raped Philomela, and then cut out her tongue so that she could not denounce him. But Philomela wove the story of the outrage on a piece of embroidery and so Procne learned the truth. She killed her son by Tereus (his name was Itys), cut up the flesh, cooked it, and served it up to Tereus who ate it. The gods, in pity and disgust, changed all three of them into birds: Tereus to a hoopoe, Philomela to a swallow, and Procne into a nightingale, whose song is a perpetual mourning for Itys.

This metamorphosis almost certainly did not take place on stage (though Tereus in *The Birds* of Aristophanes complains that Sophocles gave him a beak), and in fact we have very little idea of how Sophocles treated this horrendous tale. But among the few fragments that survive there is one speech of Procne, the wronged wife, which runs as follows:[81]

> Now, separated (from my family), I am nothing. Many a time I have observed that in this case our sex, the female sex, is nothing. When we are children, in our father's home, our life is the most pleasant in the world; young girls grow up in thoughtless delight. But when we reach maturity and intelligence, we are expelled, bought and sold, far away from the gods of our fathers and from our parents, some to barbarians, some to houses where everything is alien, others to houses where they meet with hostility. But all this, when one night has joined us to our husband, we must acquiesce in, and pretend that all is well.

We do not know the context of this speech but its content is astonishingly close to Medea's opening address to the chorus, and it is made by a woman who, like Medea—but in even more gruesome circumstances—kills her child to punish her husband. The attribution of such sentiments to two such similar characters by two different playwrights suggests that the lot of women was, in late fifth-century Athens, very much a question of the day, and also a subject that fascinated the tragic poets.

Even those who recognize that Medea's speech is not merely the rhetoric of an oriental witch but a reflection of Athenian social conditions, usually tamp down its explosive potential by explaining that since women in fifth-century Athens (unlike women today) were confined to the home, children, and servants, excluded from active social, economic, and political life, some such protest was only natural in the work of an intellectual dramatist. Though this view of woman's lowly position in fifth-century Athens has been doubted by influential scholars in recent years,[82] it seems to me, on the whole, to be fairly close to the truth. But what is no longer true is the implied comparison which makes our own society look extremely advanced in this matter and permits smug and carefully qualified understanding of Medea's protest as a historical curiosity. For our own complacency about the freedom of women in modern industrial democracy has been exploded by the literature of the militant women's movement of the last decade. In fact, almost everything the play says about women's position in society is still relevant (except perhaps for the dowry, but that is still an important matter in France, Italy, and, above all, in Greece), and the startling universality of Euripides' play is clear from the fact that it says some things that do not seem to have occurred to anyone again[83] until Simone de Beauvoir wrote *Le Deuxième Sexe.*

Medea's speech wins over the chorus, but now she has to deal with Creon and his sentence of immediate expulsion. He is afraid of her, and one thing which contributes to his fear is the fact that, as he says himself, she is a clever woman, σοφὴ πέφυκας (285).[84] "Clever" is not an adequate translation of *sophe*—but then, there isn't one. It is a word used in the fifth century to describe not only the skill of the artisan and the poet, not only the wisdom won by experience and reflection, but also the new intellectual, enlightened outlook of the great sophistic teachers and the generation they had taught. This is why Creon fears her; it is on this point that she must reassure him, and she does. She admits that she is *sophe*—an intellectual, a person of great capacity—but points out that it has not done her any good. She speaks in generalities, but it is clear enough what she is talking about. Men distrust superior intelligence in general, but they really fear and hate it in a woman. *Sophos*, a clever man, is bad enough, but *sophe*—a clever woman!

This is not the first time, Creon—it's one of many—that my reputation thwarts and harms me. No one who has his wits about him should have his children taught to be unusually clever (*sophous*). They will be called lazy, indolent, and, worse than that, they'll win the jealous hatred of their fellow-citizens. If you offer new and clever ideas to fools, they'll think you good for nothing, not clever. And then again, if the city at large ranks you above the recognized intellectuals, *they*'ll be your bitter enemies. This is what has happened to me, exactly this. I am clever; some hate and envy me; others find me withdrawn, others just the opposite, and still others offensive. I am not so clever.

These lines have sometimes been seen as Euripides' bitter reflections on his own isolation as an advanced and intellectual poet. There is much truth in this view, but the lines are also Medea's, the complaint of a woman of great intellectual capacity who finds herself excluded from the spheres of power and action.

She wins her one day's delay from Creon and tells the chorus her plans; so far, they do not include the murder of the children. The chorus evidently approve, for they plunge straight into the great ode which celebrates the new day coming for the female sex.

> The waters of the sacred rivers run upstream;
> the right order of all things is reversed.
> Now it is *men* who deal in treachery:
> now covenants sealed in heaven's name are worthless.

So much for Jason's betrayal. But they go on.

> Legends now shall change direction,
> Woman's life have glory.
> Honor comes to the female sex.
> Woman shall be a theme for slanderous tales no more.
>
> The songs of poets from bygone times shall cease
> to harp on our faithlessness.
> It was not to our minds that Phoebus, lord of melody,
> granted the power to draw heavenly song from the lyre:
> for if so, we would have chanted
> our own hymns of praise
> to answer the race of man.
>
> Time in its long passage has much to tell
> of our destiny as of theirs.

This is an extraordinary passage. All the songs, the stories, the whole literary and artistic tradition of Greece, which had created the lurid figures of the great sinners, Clytemnestra, Helen, and also the desirable figures (from the male point of view) of faithful Penelope and Andromache—all of it, Hesiod's catalogues of scandalous women, Semonides' rogues' gallery of women compared to animals, is dismissed; it was all written by men. The chorus has suddenly realized the truth contained in the Aesopian story of the man and the lion who argued about which species was superior.[85] Shown as proof of man's dominance a gravestone on which was carved a picture of a man downing a lion, the lion replied: "If lions could carve sculptures, you would see the lion downing the man."

Xenophanes had remarked that if cows, horses, and lions had hands and could paint pictures and carve statues, they would have made gods looking like themselves. It took Euripides to apply the revolutionary implications of that statement to the relation between men and women. "Legends now shall change direction; woman's life have glory," sings the chorus, but the future tense is unnecessary. Euripides' play itself is the change of direction.[86]

For though he has spared us no detail of the hideous revenge Medea exacts from her enemies, he has presented that revenge in heroic terms, as if she were not a woman but an Achilles or Ajax. She has no doubts about the rightness of her course—her one moment of hesitation she dismisses as cowardice. Like Achilles in his rage against Hector, she surpasses the bounds of normal human conduct: Achilles wishes that his spirit (*thumos*) would drive him to strip Hector's flesh from his body and eat it raw, and he does treat his enemy's body shamefully. Medea kills her sons to make Jason a lonely, childless man. The one is as heroic, and tragic, as the other.

But Achilles relents. Medea does not. Her final words to Jason are full of contempt, hatred, and vindictive triumph: her rage is fiercer than the rage of Achilles, even of Ajax: it has in the end made her something more, and less, than human, something inhuman, a *theos*.

But this was only to be expected. For Ajax and Achilles have run their full course as men in the world of men, earned their share of glory, used to the full the power and skill that was theirs, before their time came to die. But Medea is a woman: no matter how great her gifts, her destiny is to marry, bear and raise children, go where her husband goes, subordinate her life to his. Husband, children, this is all she has; and when Jason betrays her, the full force of that intellect and energy, which has nowhere else to go, is turned against him.

One passage in their last confrontation is revealing. "Did you really think it right to kill them," he asks her, "just because of what goes on in bed?" (*lechous*, 1367).[87] And she answers: "Do you think that is a small suffering for a woman?" It is a great suffering—for she has nothing else. It was to this marriage that she devoted all the courage, skill, and intellect she possessed—to save Jason in Colchis, to murder Pelias, for his sake, in Iolcos; to this marriage she has devoted all her energy, all her power. She could have been a queen, and who knows what besides, in her own country; she gave it up for her marriage. And when that was taken away from her, the energy she had wasted on Jason was tempered to a deadly instrument to destroy him. It became a *theos*, relentless, merciless force, the unspeakable violence of the oppressed and betrayed, which, because it has been so long pent up, carries everything before it to destruction, even if it destroys also what it loves most.

Notes

1. cf. the *hypothesis* attributed to Aristophanes of Byzantium. Sophocles came in second.

2. cf. Ar. *Th.* 1130, *Ran.* 1382; Eupolis, *Demoi* K90; Strattis, *Medea* K33–35 (apparently a full-length travesty); Plato K30; Eubulus K26; Alexis K176; Philemon K79. Cantharus K, 1, p. 764 *Medea.*

3. W. H. Friedrich's "Medeas Rache," in *Vorbild und Neugestaltung, Sechs Kapitel zur Geschichte der Tragödie* (Göttingen, 1967), pp. 7–56, now reprinted in Wege der Forschung LXXXIX, *Euripides*, ed. E.-R. Schwinge (Darmstadt, 1968) pp. 177–237, is a brilliant comparative study of later versions of the *Medea* which works backwards ("Von Grillparzer zu Euripides") to an illuminating discussion of all features of the Euripidean original.

4. L. Séchan, *Etudes sur la tragédie grecque dans ses rapports avec la céramique* (Paris, 1925, repr. 1967), pp. 396–422; D. L. Page, *Euripides, Medea* (Oxford, 1938), pp. lvii–lxviii; A. D. Trendall and T. B. L. Webster, *Illustrations of Greek Drama* (London, 1971), pp. 96–97.

5. There seems to be a consensus that the *Aegeus* was produced before the *Medea*: see, for references, A. Lesky, *Die Tragische Dichtung der Hellenen* (Göttingen, 1972), p. 305, n. 27. There is, however, no external evidence for the date except vase paintings (on which see T. B. L. Webster, *The Tragedies of Euripides* (London, 1967), pp. 79–80, 297–98). But the argument from vase paintings assumes too much; how do we know that the representations, frequent after 430, of Medea at Athens were not inspired by the *Aegeus* of Sophocles? Or of some other dramatist? Or by no dramatist at all? The fragments themselves are insignificant, and dates based on metrical statistics are in this case quite worthless.

6. See the discussion in Page, *Euripides, Medea*, pp. xxi ff.

7. I am convinced by Page's demonstration (pp. xxx ff.) that Neophron's *Medea* is later than that of Euripides. (For a survey of the controversy see Lesky, *Tragische Dichtung*³, p. 301; Lesky agrees with Page.) K. v. Fritz, *Antike und moderne Tragödie* (Berlin, 1962), p. 386 (reprint of an article published in 1959), believes that Neophron's careful motivation of Aegeus' appearance was known to Euripides but deliberately avoided by him ("mit einer gewissen absichtlichen eigenwilligen Nichtachtung") for a purpose. This argument is developed by H. Rohdich, *Die Euripideische Tragödie* (Heidelberg, 1968), pp. 51ff. Euripides' Medea does not even offer to interpret the oracle Aegeus has received from Delphi; Neophron's Aegeus says he has come to Corinth expressly to ask her to do so. Euripides' purpose in abandoning the plausible motivation for Aegeus' entrance provided by his predecessor was, according to Rohdich, "to protect his Medea from the

suspicion that her *sophia* was something extraordinary and superhuman.... His Medea remains completely in the realm of the human" (p. 52). But this seems to load the Euripidean passage with more weight than it can bear. It needs no superhuman wisdom to interpret the oracle give to Aegeus; everyone in the audience would have understood at once the patently sexual purport of it. And there was sufficient reason why Medea should *not* interpret the oracle. The birth of Athens' patron hero Theseus was to follow from Pittheus' misinterpretation of it (Plutarch, *Theseus* 3); if Medea explains to Aegeus that he is not to have sexual intercourse before returning to Athens, he will never get to Troezen and Aethra. (One wonders, in fact, what Neophron did about this.) According to E. Schlesinger, "Zu Euripides' Medea," *Hermes* 94 (1966), 47, Euripides wants the audience to think that Aegeus did not go on to Troezen but returned at once to Athens (to be on hand for Medea's arrival). "Euripides gibt ja deutlich zu verstehen, dass er mit einer anderen Sagenform arbeitet." It is true that Euripides presents us with an Aegeus already married, that Medea promises to cure his sterility by *pharmaka*, and that the chorus's farewell to Aegeus can be interpreted (though it need not be) as a hint that he will go directly to Athens. But the exploits of the young Theseus on his way from his home in Troezen to Athens were so central to Athenian patriotic saga, so familiar to the audience (cf. Bacchylides, Dithyramb 18; Euripides, *Hippolytus* 976ff. for example) that it is hard to imagine Euripides "working with a different version of the saga" which had Theseus born elsewhere than Troezen.

8. In the *Medea* of Carcinus there seems to have been a trial: Medea used the argument κατὰ τὸ εἰκός (Arist., *Rh.* 1400^{b}9).

9. On the date of the *Ajax* see now Lesky, *Tragische Dichtung*[3], p. 180, n. 2.

10. S., *Aj.* 333, 339, 342–43.

11. E., *Med.* 24 κεῖται δ᾽ ἄσιτος; S., *Aj.* 323 κείμενος, 324 ἄσιτος.

12. S., *Aj.* 531, 533, 535.

13. E., *Med.* 383, 404, 797, 1049, 1355, 1362; S., *Aj.* 367, 382, 454, 961, 969, etc. The four resemblances between the two plays discussed above are noted by A. Maddalena, "La *Medea* di Euripide," *RFIC* (1963), 137–38.

14. E., *Med.* 355 ἐφ᾽ ἡμέραν μίαν; S., *Aj.* 756 τήνδ᾽ ἔθ᾽ ἡμέραν μόνην.

15. E., *Med.* 364–409; S., *Aj.* 430–80.

16. E., *Med.* 974 ὧν ἐρᾷ τυχεῖν (vengeance): S., *Aj.* 685 τοὐμὸν ὧν ἐρᾷ κέαρ, 967 ὧν γὰρ ἠράσθη τυχεῖν (suicide). E., *Med.* 93 ὥς τι δρασείουσαν: S., *Aj.* 585 δρασείοις, 326 ὥς τι δρασείων κακόν. (This is a rare verb: in S. only here and *Ph.* 128; in E. only here and *Ph.* 1208; not in Aeschylus; in paratragic passages Ar., *Pax* 62, *V.* 168.) Compare also E., *Med.* 47–48 and S., *Aj.* 552ff. (children unconscious of the sorrows of their elders), E., *Med.* 173ff., and S., *Aj.* 344ff. (the chorus feels that the protagonist's passion will be calmed by their presence).

17. Maddalena, "La *Medea*," pp. 133–34, draws attention to Medea's concern for τιμή. "Disonorata: ἀτιμάζω o ἀτιμάω è la parola greca che indica l'offesa all'onore: è la parola usata da Omero nell'*Iliade* a dire l'offesa recata all'onore di Achille: è la parola usata da Sofocle nell'*Aiace* a dire l'offesa patita da Aiace. È anche la parola usata da Euripide nella *Medea*. Diversi e simili sono l'Achille omerico, l'Aiace sofocleo e la Medea di Euripide: diversi nei fatti ma simili nell'animo."

18. W. Steidle, *Studien zum antiken Drama* (Munich, 1968), p. 152, n. 1: "rechnet man die Chorverse ab, so umfassen ihre [d.h. Medeas] Äusserungen mehr als ein Drittel des Stücks, was ihre ungewöhnliche beherrschende Rolle hinlänglich deutlich macht." V. di Benedetto, *Euripide, Teatro e Società* (Torino, 1971), p. 31: "La *Medea* ... è dominata dal principio alla fine, in una misura che non trova riscontro in nessuna delle tragedie euripidee a noi pervenute, dalla personalità della protagonista."

19. cf. chapter 17 of this book.

20. cf. chapter 19 of this book.

21. In 431 B.C., of course, the only Sophoclean hero plays we can be certain Euripides knew are the *Ajax* and *Antigone*. The characteristic mood, language, and situation of this type of drama were however, already present in the Aeschylean *Prometheus Bound* and in any case stem from Homer's *Iliad*. (Cf. B. M. W. Knox, *The Heroic Temper* (Berkeley and Los Angeles, 1964), pp. 45–52.) The case for Sophoclean influence on the *Medea* is strengthened by the fact that no other extant Euripidean play deploys the full armory of Sophoclean heroic situation and formula.

22. Knox, *Heroic Temper*, pp. 10–44.

23. On this word cf. Friedrich, *Vorbild und Neugestaltung*, pp. 51–52 (Wege der Forschung LXXXIX, *Euripides*, pp. 233–34).

24. Rohdich, *Euripideische Tragödie*, p. 59, n. 78, draws attention to almost all the words cited above and characterizes Medea's speech as one "die den Nützlichkeitsaspekt der intellektuell fundierten σωφροσύνη auch terminologisch gänzlich übernommen hat." His Jason represents "die vom Intellekt kontrollierte, auf den Nutzen gerichtete σωφροσύνη" — the fifth-century sophistic claim to intellectual mastery of the world ("in ihm steht die sophistische Idee intellektuell geführter Weltbewältigung auf der tragischen Bühne," p. 58) which is to be revealed as a mere illusion by Medea's action ("ist der Triumph des Untragischen nur verblendender Schein," p. 59).

Rohdich's theory of Euripidean tragedy is an attractive one, brilliantly presented: but in this case the fact that the "terminology" of *Nützlichkeit* is employed also against Prometheus and the Sophoclean heroes suggests that it has older sources than the fully developed sophistic claims of the late fifth century.

25. Knox, *Heroic Temper*, pp. 25–26.

26. On Jason's "Blindheit" with regard to Medea see von Fritz, *Tragödie*, pp. 349ff.

27. cf. D. J. Conacher, *Euripidean Drama* (Toronto, 1967), p. 195: "Medea herself is really the only one capable of resisting Medea."

28. cf. Schlesinger, "Euripides' Medea," p. 30, on the conflict in Medea's monologue as:

> der Widerstand des Glücksstrebens des gewöhnlichen Menschen in ihr gegen das Los das ihr zugefallen ist, Taten von übermenschlichem Ausmasse zu vollbringen, heroische Taten im griechischen Sinn des Wortes. Im Grunde wird hier in der Sprache der zweiten Hälfte des 5. Jhs. nichts anderes gesagt als das, was im Monolog Hektors in X und in Achilleus' grosser Rede in I ausgesprochen ist.

29. cf. Lesky, *Tragische Dichtung*³, p. 306, "einen Satz alter Adelsmoral"; Schlesinger, "Euripides' Medea," p. 53, "Das ist die gewöhnliche Sprache der Heroen. Ihr θυμός verlangt nach κλέος, nach dem εὐκλεέστατος βίος, und dies ist nach griechischem Empfinden eine durchaus edele Haltung."

30. cf. von Fritz' brilliant analysis (*Tragödie*, pp. 361ff.) of lines 407–9. Women are not capable of ἐσθλά — "die grossen, die herrlichen Taten, die Heldentaten, die von jedermann bewundert werden" — their position in life makes that impossible. But they understand κακά — "die krumme Wege." Jason, by breaking his oath, has descended to such means, and by them he will be defeated. But Medea speaks also of her τόλμα and εὐψυχία:

> Auch darin enthüllt sich also eine Umkehrung der traditionellen Wertungen und Begriffe. So wie hinter den ἐσθλά, die Iason vollbracht zu haben scheint, sein κακία zum Vorschein kommt, so verbirgt sich hinter den κακά, die Medea vollbracht hat und noch vollbringen will, ihre τόλμα, ihre εὐψυχία, in gewisser Weise ihre πίστις, alles Dinge, die eigentlich zu den ἐσθλά gehören, die in der Tradition als dem männlichen Geschlecht vorbehalten gelten.

31. cf. von Fritz, *Tragödie*, pp. 395ff. (with a defense of the last two lines of Creon's speech, athetized by some critics).

32. γυνὴ δὲ θῆλυ. "The neuter θῆλυ is contemptuous here" (Page, *Euripides, Medea*). Cf. S., *Tr.* 1062 γυνὴ δέ, θῆλυς οὖσα κοὐκ ἀνδρὸς φύσιν.

33. 1133–34 ἀλλὰ μὴ σπέρχου, φίλος, / λέξον δέ.

34. cf. W. Steidle, *Studien*, pp. 166–67; H. Diller, *Entretiens sur l'antiquité classique* VI (Geneva, 1960), p. 32.

35. cf. Steidle, *Studien*, p. 167, n. 90: "Wie wenig die moralische Seite des Muttermords eine Rolle spielt, zeigt der geringe Raum, der ihr gewidmet ist."

36. Knox, *Heroic Temper*, pp. 33–34.

37. This invocation of Hecate is often cited as part of the evidence that Medea is presented throughout as a sorceress, a witch. Cf. Page on line 364; on line 367 he cites *Ion* 650 (which must be a misprint for 1050), but that passage is an invocation of Kore in her aspect of *Einodia*, not Hecate, and asks her aid for Creusa's plan to poison Ion. (For "witchcraft" and poison, see below, section III). But there was an aspect of Hecate which had nothing to do with sorcery or poison but rather with the home and woman's functions in it. An effigy of Hecate stood in front of every house door (A., *Fr.* 742 Mette, Ar., *V.* 804, *Ra.* 366), women asked Hecate's advice as they left the house (Ar., *Lys.* 64), and played games with their daughters in her honor (*ibid.* 700—"hausliche Kult der Hekate" says Wilamowitz *ad loc.*); women called on her in childbirth (A., *Supp.* 676ff. Ἄρτεμιν δ' Ἑκάταν γυναικῶν λέχος ἐφορεύειν). Hecate is obviously an ambiguous figure, and Medea's devotion to her cannot be interpreted as an attitude typical of a sorceress unless reinforced by the context (which it is not).

38. cf. also 22, 169, 209, 1372.

39. It is typical of Jason's blind misunderstanding of his situation (and Medea's) that he can call her, in the teeth of the evidence, ἐχθίστη γύναι / θεοῖς (1323–24).

40. H. D. F. Kitto, *Greek Tragedy* (3d. ed., London, 1961), p. 199.

41. "Here they seem a little inapposite," Page, *Euripides, Medea*; "Die Schlussverse des Chores . . . haben hier bestimmt nichts zu suchen," Lesky, *Tragische Dichtung*[3], p. 309.

42. cf. Page, *Euripides, Medea*, at 1414; Séchan, *Etudes*, p. 416, n. 7; Steidle, *Studien*, p. 166.

43. cf. M. P. Cunningham, "Medea ΑΠΟ ΜΗΧΑΝΗΣ," *CP* 49 (1954), 152: "Medea appears aloft in the place and after the manner of a *theos*. She appears as a *theos* appears; she acts as a *theos* acts and she says the sort of thing a *theos* says."

44. The argument which follows in the text assumes that the appearance of a *theos* on the *mechane* was a spectacle familiar to the audience of 431 B.C., though it is of course true that all the extant examples of this phenomenon are dated (some certainly, the others probably) later than the *Medea*. (The first version of the *Hippolytus*, however, probably had a *deus ex machina*—cf. Webster, *Tragedies of Euripides*, pp. 65, 70—and may have preceded the *Medea*.) It seems unlikely, in view of the exact correspondence of all the features of Medea's final appearance with the functions of the *deus* in the later plays, that this can have been the first use of this device. The *mechane* itself was used in the Aeschylean *Psychostasia* and possibly in his *Carians or Europa* (cf. T. B. L. Webster, *Greek Theatre Production* [London, 1956], p. 12), and the appearance of a god at the end of the play to bring a conclusion occurs in the Aeschylean *Prometheus Bound* and (probably) in the lost *Danaides*.

45. cf. D. L. Page, *Greek Literary Papyri* (Cambridge, Mass., and London, 1941), p. 68. One may compare also the end of the *Erechtheus* of Euripides (C. Austin, *Nova Fragmenta Euripidea* [Berlin, 1968], p. 36), where Athena intervenes to prevent Poseidon from destroying Athens by earthquake.

46. 1394 θάπτ' ἄλοχον. This is, in its context, a savage, exultant rejoinder to Jason's reproaches, but it is also a regular feature and formula of the address of the *theos*. Cf. E.,

Andr. 1239–40 γόνον / θάψον; E., *Erechtheus* (Austin fr. 65, vs. 67) θάψον νιν; E., *Antiop.* (Page, *Greek Literary Papyri*, p. 68), ὅταν δὲ θάπτῃς ἄλοχον; E., *El.* 1278–80 μητέρα ... Μενέλαος ... Ἑλένη τε θάψει; E., *I.T.* 1465 οὗ καὶ τεθάψῃ κατθανοῦσα.

47. An unidentified divine figure seems to have prophesied at the end of the *Phaethon*; cf. J. Diggle, *Euripides' Phaethon* (Cambridge, 1970), pp. 44ff., 53.

48. According to a papyrus *hypothesis* of *Rhadamanthys* (Austin, *Nova Fragmenta Euripidea*, p. 92, no. 14), Artemis, ἐπιφανεῖσα, orders the foundation of cult (τιμάς) for the Dioscuri.

49. cf. also E., *Ion* 1616 ἕψομαι δ' ἐγώ (Athena); E., *I.T.* 1488 συμπορεύσομαι δ' ἐγώ (Athena); E., *Hel.* 1665 πέμψομεν (the Dioscuri).

50. cf. also E., *Ion* 1572 χώρει, Κρέουσα; E., *El.* 1289 χώρει; E., *I.T.* 1448 χώρει; E., *Or.* 1678 χωρεῖτε; E., *Antiop.* (Page, *GLP*, p. 68, v. 81) χωρεῖτε; E., *Andr.* 1263 ἀλλ' ἕρπε; E., *Hel.* 1663 πλεῖ.

51. Compare Medea's "Too late!" νῦν σφε προσαυδᾷς, νῦν ἀσπάζῃ, τότ' ἀπωσά-μενος (1401–2) with Dionysus' ὄψ' ἐμάθεθ' ἡμᾶς, ὅτε δὲ χρῆν, οὐκ ᾔδετε (E., *Ba.* 1345).

52. cf. Cunningham, "Medea," p. 159: "Although this final appearance of Medea involves an illusion that she is a *theos*, we are also reminded that it is not a true apotheosis.... She is going off to Athens to live with Aegeus there."

53. A. Koerte, *Menandri quae supersunt. II* (Leipzig, 1959), fr. 223 τὸ κρατοῦν γὰρ νῦν νομίζεται θεός.

54. ἀλλά σ' Ἐρινὺς ὀλέσειε τέκνων. It is true that the chorus, at the height of its frenzied appeal to Helios to prevent the murder of the children, uses language which is generally thought to describe Medea as an Erinys: ἀλλά νιν ... κάτειργε κατάπαυσον, ἔξελ' οἴκων τάλαιναν φονίαν τ' Ἐρινύν (1258ff.). The words ἔξελ' οἴκων, however, seem rather inapposite if the object is Medea herself, and would make more sense as a wish to clear the house of the spirit of vengeance. So the scholiast understood it: αὐτὴν φησι τὴν δαίμονα, οὐ τὴν Μήδειαν. ὑπείληπται γὰρ τῶν τοιούτων κακῶν αἰτία εἶναι ἡ Ἐρινύς. Cf. A., *A.* 1571f.

55. Lesky, *Tragisch Dichtung³*, p. 309.

56. L. Bloch, "Alkestisstudien," *Neue Jahrbücher*, band 7 (1901), p. 30: "In seinem Herzen, stand er auf der Seite des damals gerade in mächtiger Bewegung aufwärtsstre-benden Geschlechtes." Bloch refers with approval to Ivo Bruns' "feine und richtige Beobachtung" (in *Frauenemancipation in Athen* (Kiel, 1900), p. 9) "dass Euripides die an Zahl noch geringe fortschrittliche Partei der athenischen Frauen in den Chorliedern der 'Medeia' zu Worte kommen lässt."

57. cf. K. J. Reckford, "Medea's First Exit," *TAPA* 99 (1968), 239: "This is not to say that Euripides is acting as the women's champion ... or writing social criticism or pleading for some reform."

58. W. Schmid, *Geschichte der griechischen Literatur*, band III (Munich, 1940; repr. 1961), p. 360: "den lässt der Dichter noch wissen, dass sie als Barbarin eine Tat verüben konnte, der eine Griechin nicht fähig gewesen wäre und dass die Täterin eine Zauberin ist, d.h. er stellt sie ausserhalb des Kreises normaler griechischer Weiblichkeit."

59. In view of the total disagreement with Page's overall conception of the *Medea* expressed in this article, it seems only fair to acknowledge at this point my deep indebtedness to his masterly commentary on the text.

60. This is especially true of critics writing in English and French. See, for example, G. M. A. Grube, *The Drama of Euripides* (New York, 1941; repr. 1961), pp. 152–54; A. Elliot, *Euripides' Medea* (Oxford, 1969), on lines 395, 1317; D. W. Lucas, *The Greek Tragic Poets²* (London, 1959), p. 199: "a genuine witch"; Conacher, *Euripidean Drama*, pp. 188–89; Cunningham, "Medea," p. 153; Reckford, "Medea's First Exit," pp. 333, 374; L. Méridier, *Euripide*, t. I (Paris 1926; repr. 1965), p. 119: "une magicienne redoutable" etc.

The evidence is surveyed in C. Headlam's edition of the play (ΕΥΡΙΠΙΔΟΥ ΜΗΔΕΙΑ [Cambridge, 1904]) as an appendix, "Medea as a sorceress" (pp. 105–7). Headlam's conclusion is that "Euripides . . . in his play wisely keeps this occult power somewhat in the background and it greatly conduces to the dramatic effect that his heroine impresses us as a woman, not as a witch."

In recent German (and more rarely Italian) literature, the normal, human aspects of Euripides' Medea have been emphasized (see Rohdich, *Euripideische Tragödie*, pp. 44–46, for citations and discussion). Rohdich himself speaks of "das Bemühen des Dichters seine Medea der ihr vom Mythos her anhaftenden Monstrosität zu entkleiden und als normale Frau für den Zuschauer verbindlich zu machen" (p. 41). Thi goes too far in the opposite direction; Medea is not a "normale Frau" but an extraordinary one, as her presentation in heroic terms makes clear.

61. lines 752ff. (excerpted).

62. 7.262ff. Translated by Rolfe Humphries, *Ovid's Metamorphoses* (Bloomington, Ind., 1957).

63. *Macbeth* 4.i.30ff.

64. The three surviving fragments (A. C. Pearson, *The Fragments of Sophocles* [Cambridge, 1917], pp. 534–36) contain in their 14 lines more of the atmosphere of sorcery than can be found in the 1,420 lines of Euripides' play.

65. Jason mentions her betrayal of her father and murder of her brother (1332–34) but then proceeds directly to the murder of his own sons.

66. cf. Rohdich, *Euripideische Tragödie*, p. 48: "Auch hier zeigt sich Euripides bemüht . . . die das Normale übersteigenden Fähigkeiten Medeas auf die Kenntnis der φάρμακα zu beschränken."

67. cf. Friedrich (*Vorbild und Neugestaltung*, p. 37, Wege der Forschung LXXXIX, *Euripides*, p. 216): "Denn die 'Weisheit' mit der sie ihre Widersacher zugrunde richtet, ist nicht göttlicher als die der Locusta, der Brinvillière und der Giftmischerinnen unserer Tage, die mit Pflanzenschutzmitteln und Pralinen arbeiten."

68. The messenger speeches describing the effects of the poison in both plays have often been compared: see, e.g., Page, *Euripides, Medea*, p. xxvi, n. 4.

69. Antiphon, 1.14ff.

70. E., *Ion* 1003ff.

71. M. P. Nilsson, *Geschichte der griechischen Religion*[3], vol. I (Munich, 1967), p. 801 (with illustration). Theocritus' jilted girl Simaetha (Idyll 2) is a literary example of such private initiative. She is not a "witch"; she is (to quote Gow's characterization) "poor . . . perhaps an orphan, presumably bourgeoise; she is not a ἑταίρα (41). Her position appears to be that of several young women in the New Comedy" (A. S. F. Gow, *Theocritus* [Cambridge, 1965], vol. II, p. 33). For an act of sorcery performed by a whole community, see the inscription from Cyrene (R. Meiggs and D. Lewis, *A Selection of Greek Historical Inscriptions* [Oxford, 1969], 5ff.): κηρίνος πλάσσαντες κολοσὸς κατέκαιον ἐπαρεώμενοι πάντες συνενθόντες καὶ ἄνδρες καὶ γυναῖκες καὶ παῖδες καὶ παιδίσκαι. τὸμ μὴ ἐμμένοντα τούτοις τοῖς ὁρκίοις ἀλλὰ παρβεῶντα καταλείβεσθαί νιν καὶ καταρρὲν ὥσπερ τὸς κολοσός. A. D. Nock (quoted by Meiggs and Lewis, *Greek Historical Inscriptions*) says of this extraordinary procedure that the community "reinforces the magical potency of the curse with a magical act, identical with the practice of what we regard as anti-social black magic." (The inscription is dated to the fourth century B.C. but the ceremony described may be as old as the seventh century.)

72. *Od.* 10.136, 220, 297, etc.

73. Page, *Euripides, Medea*, p. xix; cf. Méridier, *Euripide*, p. 118: "Il ne faut pas oublier d'ailleurs que Médée n'est pas grecque mais une Barbare. . . . De la Barbare elle a la ruse et la puissance de dissimulation; l'élan sauvage de sa passion, la cruauté raffinée de

ses plans, l'énergie farouche dont elle en poursuit l'exécution, s'expliquent par son origine."

74. V. di Benedetto (*Euripide*, p. 33) takes issue with Page on this point: "almeno per questo rispetto il personaggio di Medea non è meno 'greco' di Alcesti e Fedra."

75. cf. Knox, *Heroic Temper*, pp. 42–43.

76. cf. di Benedetto, *Euripide*, pp. 37–38, on Medea's "freddo calcolo e ragionata astuzia."

77. There is a passage in the *Andromache* which charges the barbarian races with incest (father and daughter, mother and son, brother and sister) as well as murder of kin: but the speaker is Hermione who, with her father Menelaus, kidnaps Andromache's child, forces her to leave sanctuary by threatening to kill it, breaks the promise made to spare its life, and would have murdered mother and child if not prevented.

78. J. H. Finley, *HSCP* 50 (1939), 65ff. = *Three Essays on Thucydides* (Cambridge, Mass., 1967), pp. 92–94. Cf. also Reckford, "Medea's First Exit," pp. 336ff.

79. Pl., *R.* 5.454c–e.

80. The date of production of Aristophanes' *Birds* (414) is the *terminus ante quem*. T. B. L. Webster, *An Introduction to Sophocles*[2] (London, 1969), p. 4, dates it before 431 on "external evidence" which (pp. 176–77) turns out to be its resemblance in theme and (reconstructed) "diptych form" to the *Trachiniae*, which he also dates before 431. W. Buchwald, *Studien zur Chronologie der attischen Tragödie* (Königsberg, 1939), pp. 35ff., also puts it before *Medea*: it was the model for Medea's murder of her sons. Others, basing their proposals on "contemporary allusions," have dated it nearer to 414. There is no certainty, or even probability, here: "Keine der angeführten Datierungen kann Sicherheit beanspruchen" (Lesky, *Tragische Dichtung*[3], p. 262).

81. Pearson, *Fragments of Sophocles*, p. 583. I follow Jebb's interpretation of the difficult opening lines.

82. A. W. Gomme, "The Position of Women in Athens," *CR* 20 (1925), 1–25 (reprinted in *Essays in Greek History and Literature* [Oxford, 1937]); H. D. F. Kitto, *The Greeks*[2] (Harmondsworth, 1957), pp. 219–36.

83. With the startling exception of Geoffrey Chaucer; cf. n. 85.

84. σοφὴ πέφυκας καὶ κακῶν πολλῶν ἴδρις. This phrase is taken by many proponents of Medea the witch as evidence for their case. But, though "wise woman" meant "witch" in seventeenth-century English, the Greek word *sophe* has no such connotation. The *sophia* Creon fears is the craft that rescued Jason from his pursuers at Colchis and brought death to Pelias: these are *kaka* in the sense defined by von Fritz (cf. n. 30). Medea of course deliberately misunderstands his drift, but the charge she is evading is not "witchcraft." And her argument, after all, is soundly based. Her *sophia* has brought her to her present state, a woman abandoned in a hostile country.

85. Hausrath Hunger 264: cf. Babrius 194 (Crusius) and Chaucer, *Wife of Bath's Prologue* 692ff.

> Who peyntede the lioun, tel me who?
> By god, if wommen hadde written stories
> As clerkes han withinne hire oratories
> They wolde han written of men more wikkidnesse
> Than all the mark of Adam may redresse.

86. cf. I. Caimo, *Dioniso* 6 (1937–38), 4: "in realtà l'inno che celebra la donna e suona per contro l'ignominia all'uomo è già qui nel suo nucleo primordiale."

87. cf. Rohdich, *Euripideische Tragödie*, pp. 59ff.: "Die Antithese: λέχος und Affekt."

TWENTY-TWO

Review

EURIPIDEAN DRAMA: MYTH, THEME, AND STRUCTURE. By D. J. Conacher. University of Toronto Press, 1967.

D. J. Conacher's stimulating and thoughtful study deals with the whole body of extant Euripidean drama (except for *Rhesus*, on which, not completely convinced by Ritchie's book, Conacher suspends judgment). It is an attempt "to relate the varied and often novel structures and techniques of Euripidean drama to the varied and often novel themes which the dramatist has chosen to expound" (vi). In an introductory chapter which compares Euripides' approach to tragedy with that of Aeschylus and Sophocles, Conacher defines six different types of Euripidean drama (14–15), and it is under these headings that he groups and discusses the plays in the rest of the book. These divisions are: first, "those plays which may properly be called 'mythological'" (*Hippolytus* and *Bacchae*), to which is added the "near-mythical" *Heracles*; secondly, political and social tragedies (*The Suppliants, Heraclidae*); third, tragedies of "war and its aftermath" (*Troades, Hecuba, Andromache*); fourth, "realistic tragedy" (*Medea, Electra, Orestes*); fifth, "romantic tragedy" (*Ion, Helen, I.T.*); and sixth and last, "satyric and prosatyric" (*Cyclops, Alcestis*). Two plays (*Phoenissae* and *I.A.*) which, "while they lack the credibility and thematic concentration of tragedy nevertheless contain certain paratragic effects and are quite different in substance and tone from romantic tragedy" are discussed under the somewhat prejudicial rubric *tragédie manquée* (227–64).

Conacher is aware that, "among plays which operate on the same general level of reality," these distinctions are not always crystal clear; "the groupings ... are intended as a critical convenience rather than as rigid and mutually exclusive categories" (15). On the other hand he can claim, with some justification, that "distinctions between plays clearly opposed in mythical approach (the *Hippolytus* and the *Helen* for example) or in the kind of reality they treat (the *Bacchae* and the *Troades* for example) are readily recognizable."

This chapter originally appeared in the *University of Toronto Quarterly*, July 1968. Reprinted by permission of the University of Toronto Press.

Some kind of division into groups is of course forced on any open-minded reader of the whole of Euripides. Perhaps it is due merely to the caprice of ancient selection and the hazards of medieval transmission which gave us so many more of his plays, but whatever the reason, no one can fail to recognize the extreme diversity of method, structure, and approach exhibited in the surviving plays of Euripides, as compared with the seven Sophoclean plays. Even in the case of Sophocles we have come to realize that we should not assess the unity and cohesion of the *Trachiniae* by standards derived from the *Oedipus Tyrannus*; the need for critical flexibility is even clearer when we consider the obvious differences in tone as well as structure between, say, the *Medea* and the *Helen*. Conacher approaches each play as an individual problem and investigates in each case the relation between theme and structure; his arrangement is not based on any theory of the development of Euripides' thought or method ("these divisions do not correspond very precisely to any historical grouping of the poet's plays") but results from the detailed and often subtle discussion of the structural and thematic complexities of each individual work.

In his exploration, Conacher has deserved well of the general reader and the scholar alike; his discussion is clear, well informed (a valuable feature of the book is his wide-ranging review of modern Euripidean criticism), and often original. Though the reader may sometimes look in vain for an exact definition of the theme which is supposed to explain the structure (as, for example, in the chapter on *The Suppliants*), or may find the proposed theme rather vague (as, for example, in the case of the *Andromache*) or unsatisfactory (the theme of the *Orestes* seems to be "revelation of the essential Orestes"), he will often reach the end of Conacher's chapters with new insight into a play (the theme of *charis* in the *Heraclidae*) or a fresh appreciation of its complexities (the *Phoenissae* for example), and always with great respect for Conacher's selective intelligence and good judgment (the chapter on the *Medea* is especially satisfying). Conacher does his duty as a critic to both author and reader: he sends the one back to the other with a head full of questions, new perspectives, and fresh lines of inquiry.

Conacher's handling of myth will raise the most questions in his reader's mind. He does not define the term, and the meaning he attaches to it (a rather idiosyncratic one) emerges gradually. Only *Hippolytus* and *Bacchae* are "mythological" (though the *Heracles* is "near-mythical"); this obviously calls for a narrower definition of myth than the accepted one, for all the tragedies are based on myth. The appearance of gods on stage is not the criterion, for *Troades*, with its prologue spoken by two gods, turns up among the tragedies of "war and its aftermath," and the *Ion* (which, like the *Hippolytus* has one god in the prologue and another in the epilogue) is discussed under "romantic tragedy." In what sense are the *Troades* and *Ion* not mythological? The answer to this question seems to be implied in Conacher's discussion (13) of Euripides' "varied approaches to myth," in which he detects a major dualism. "On the one hand Euripides devoted a certain measure of his dramatic energy to the ridicule of, and satire on, literal belief in the traditional gods of myth" (which is sometimes incidental, as in *Helen* or *I.T.*, sometimes "bound up with the whole play," as in *Ion*). "On the other hand in a few plays (such as the *Hippolytus* and *Bacchae*) Euripides takes myth seriously and uses anthropomorphic gods to symbolize certain real forces. . . . In between these two extremes there are certain plays (such as the *Heracles* and the *Troades*) which are undeniably tragic in their effect and yet which *do* involve a negative or sceptical attitude to the gods of mythology" though "in such plays . . . the mythical element is not, in itself, of any real significance in the tragic action." From all this it appears that what Conacher means by myth is the existence and efficacy of the Olympian gods—what Heracles (1346) calls "horrid tales made up by poets." Euripides' attitude toward these tales is not just skeptical, it is satiric; his literal portrayal of the Olympians "must be taken as an attempt to impugn, by a sort of *reductio ad absurdum*, the old anthropomorphism (which was by no means dead) and all its implications" (29). It is a scornful repudiation (46) of mythological nonsense (81). "Euripides devoted a considerable portion of his energies as a dramatist to showing that Greek myth, literally understood, presented a conception of the gods which was unworthy of belief by a civilized people" (83). Conacher is thoroughly consistent on this point; even the mythological plays (in which the gods are used "to symbolize certain real forces") can still satirize the literal existence of those gods. Aphrodite in the *Hippolytus* is intentionally overdrawn and unconvincing (16)—the prologue is an example of "the simple trick of ruining an idea by overstatement—in this case of casting doubt on the less credible features of myth by an exaggerated emphasis upon them" (28).

Conacher has two main grounds for this view of Euripides' attitude toward the gods he so frequently brings on stage. The first is that the Euripidean gods, conceived on the Homeric model (28) and indeed as an exaggeration of the Homeric (50), are an apparent regression from the presentation of the divine in Aeschylus and Sophocles, "coming at the end of a tradition which had sought to save the mythological gods from such attacks as Xenophanes had made on them" (29). Such a literal and primitive view of the gods is inconceivable on the part of a fifth-century intellectual (50) and would have been disturbing to an Athenian audience. (This at any rate seems to be the meaning of

Conacher's remark [28]: "If we observe the contrast between ... this bludgeoning of the audience with the crudest form of divine motivation ... and ... the approaches of Aeschylus and Sophocles, surely we must see the effect which this neo-Homeric primitivism would have had on a fifth-century audience.") The second basis is that time and time again in the plays, human beings express ideas about the gods which transcend such crude notions and demand a higher moral standard for gods than for men (the servant in *Hippolytus*, Cadmus in the *Bacchae*, etc.); the views expressed in these passages "all contradict the mythical situation on which their plays are based but are nevertheless endorsed by the final effect which these plays have on us"; therefore "it seems reasonable to conclude that they are the poet's own" (52).

If this conclusion is correct, Conacher's thesis is proved up to the hilt, for these passages do more than simply demand higher standards of divine governance than the plays present. They implicitly (and in one case, the *Heracles*, explicitly) deny the truth of the whole mythological framework and the very existence of the Olympian gods as they were visualized and worshiped in fifth-century Athens. The idea of course is not new (Conacher is clearly much influenced by Norwood and—though he repudiates his wilder flights—Verrall), but the presentation of it here is well thought out, restrained, and remarkably consistent, for Euripides' attitude toward the gods, in Conacher's view, is the same in the romantic and political as in the mythological tragedies—the only change from one type of play to another is in tone. (However, he does make an exception for the *Bacchae*, in which "Euripides is prepared to forego that rationalistic iconoclasm which he uses with such telling effect on various tales of the Olympian gods.") From start to finish, Euripides was "attempting to show citizens bred in the traditional views ... that such conceptions of the gods *should* offend them" (51).

Conacher's argument on this fundamental question, though lucidly expressed, has had to be put together from scattered passages; I sincerely hope I have summarized it fairly before raising what seem to me two insuperable objections to it. The first is a feature of many Euripidean plays which is not accounted for by his explanation and which is mythological *par excellence*. Conacher refers to it (apparently without sensing any contradiction) on page 304: "it was a favourite device of the dramatist's to provide explanations, some of which were original, of perplexing cults and cult objects." Such etiologies are in fact very frequent; they are usually announced by a goddess, and they occur at the end of plays belonging not only to mythological tragedies (*Hippolytus*), but also to realistic (*Medea*), romantic (*I.T.*), and even political plays (the patriotic legend of the tomb of Eurystheus in *Heraclidae* and now, in the new Paris papyrus of the *Erechtheus*, the foundation of the cult of the Hyakinthides by Athena). By these injunctions to found religious rites or in other cases (as, for example, *Ion*) by divine prophecies embodying Athenian patriotic traditions, Euripides often linked the action of the play to cults in which many of his audience had taken part and national traditions which they all accepted. These etiologies are inseparable from the old anthropomorphism which, according to Conacher, Euripides was attempting to impugn. But there can surely be no question of an attempt to ridicule or satirize contemporary religious cult, still less patriotic traditions; Athens was engaged, during the period which saw the production of nearly all these plays, in a war which put her very existence in danger, and the tragic festival itself was not only a religious ceremony but also a competition for the applause and favorable judgment of the audience. Nor can this Euripidean device be explained away as empty formality or mere conformity to tradition. On the contrary, it is, in the extant remains of Greek tragedy, peculiar to Euripides and may very well have been his own invention.

But the basic flaw in Conacher's view of what Euripides meant by his insistence on the stage presence of the Olympian gods becomes clear only when we see the plays not as written texts but as theatrical performances. Conacher appeals to the "final effect which these plays have on us." This is of course a highly subjective criterion, but there is one undeniable effect which he neglects: the visible, audible, living presence on stage of those gods the dramatist is supposed to be arguing out of existence. Heracles may comfort himself by claiming that the strife between Zeus and Hera which has brought him to disaster is merely part of "the horrid tales made up by poets," but we have seen and heard Lyssa and Iris, experienced fully the shock of their sudden appearance, and sensed in the rhythm of Lyssa's racing trochaics the pulse of the madness which before our eyes descends into the house to fasten on its innocent victim. If Euripides had wanted us to share Heracles' belief that such things are impossible, why did he bring them on stage with such dramatic power? Heracles can talk like this because he has not seen and heard Lyssa and Iris, but we have. And since everything that appears on stage is equally real, the final effect in this case is that Heracles is, quite simply, wrong. So are the characters in the other plays who assume that gods are better than men. The divine framework in which a typical Euripidean tragedy is enclosed does indeed contradict the beliefs and aspirations of the human beings who are its victims, but its reality cannot be denied; it is the power structure of a harsh world which men may believe or wish better than it is, but only until (like Hippolytus, Cadmus, and many another) they are confronted with the truth. This is indeed a retrogression (real, not apparent) from the presentation of the divine in Aeschylus and Sophocles: men have changed beyond all recognition, but the gods remain Homeric. But we are not entitled to assume that such an attitude is "inconceivable on the part of a fifth-century intellectual." By his juxtaposition of cruel gods and men who assume or demand a just and ordered universe, Euripides is only producing by dramatic means the same shattering effect Thucydides creates by taking us without a break from the Periclean funeral speech straight into the description of the horrors of the plague. There is a tragic gulf between man's ideals and the brute fact of his powerlessness in the face of merciless, irrational forces. If Euripidean tragedy is a repudiation, it is not so much of mythological nonsense as of human illusions.

This is, of course, a controversial matter on which no two critics see quite eye to eye, and the disagreement expressed above does not affect the real merits of Conacher's book. He has undertaken to present a consistent and balanced picture of Euripides' work as a whole (how much easier it is to deal with only one side of it!), and he has handled his complicated subject skillfully and fairly, sometimes with original insight, always with good sense. The book has an excellent bibliography, and would have been improved by an index. It also contains three valuable appendices which discuss critical and semantic problems in *Hippolytus* and *Bacchae*.

TWENTY-THREE

Review

CATASTROPHE SURVIVED: EURIPIDES' PLAYS OF MIXED REVER-SAL. By Anne Pippin Burnett. Clarendon Press and Oxford University Press, 1971.

This book has been awaited with impatience by all those who have read with profit and pleasure (though not necessarily with complete agreement) the author's articles on Euripides in the pages of *Classical Philology*.[1] Their great expectations will not be disappointed. This is at once the most stimulating and the most important book on Euripides that has appeared in many years. It tackles the central problem posed by Euripidean drama (concentrating on the most problematical of the plays) and applies a method of analysis which, though it is not entirely original,[2] produces in Burnett's subtle, learned, and rigorous exploitation of its possibilities what is in effect a new set of criteria for the evaluation not only of Euripides but of Attic tragedy as a whole. This is not to say (as will become clear later) that these criteria are always and equally valid, or that they are in every case correctly applied, but there is no doubt that Burnett has opened up a rich new vein in what had seemed to be a largely worked-out claim.

The central problem posed by Euripidean drama lies of course in what we have come to call "tone" — "the attitude of a work as revealed in the matter rather than stated," to quote a convenient capsule definition.[3] Inseparable from this is the problem of the author's intention, which some modern critics have declared impenetrable and in any case irrelevant, but which can hardly be avoided in the case of state-financed competitive performances aimed at a mass audience. In the case of drama which works, as Plato put it, "through imitation" rather than through "the narration of the poet himself,"[4] the problems of tone and intention are especially difficult; in Euripides they appear, to judge from the critical literature, to be close to insoluble. Readers may often disagree about the attitude of the poet to his creatures and their actions in Aeschylus and Sophocles, but "disagreement" is far too mild a word

This chapter originally appeared in *Classical Philology*, 66, no. 4 (1972). © 1972 by The University of Chicago. Reprinted by permission.

for the polar contraries of reaction produced by such plays as the *Heracles* or the *Ion*. A cursory glance at a collection of critical essays such as that of J. R. Wilson on the *Alcestis*[5] is, to use Kitto's phrase, to "contemplate Chaos."[6] Even in the pitifully small number of plays by the two older dramatists which have survived the centuries, we can discern patterns of action, thought, and feeling which help us find our bearings in the interpretation of any single play. The Euripidean corpus, however, though we have almost three plays for each one by the other poets, gives us no such help; we are adrift, without map or compass. It seems impossible to establish agreement on the fundamental question: what effect did Euripides intend to produce on the Athenian audience for which these plays were designed? In the absence of such agreement, the field is wide open for every man to make his own Euripides—the rationalist, the irrationalist, the political dramatist, the philosopher, the feminist, the radical, the reactionary, or the mere bungler.

This disarray of modern critical opinion is partly due to the literary sophistication and artistic self-consciousness which distinguish Euripides' work. Aristophanes mocked his reliance on books for his plots, and Euripides was not above giving his actors lines which criticized the technique of his fellow dramatists or even made subdued fun of the tragic conventions in which they themselves performed. The irony of situation which Sophocles exploits with such demonic expertise, playing on the audience's knowledge of the outcome to invest his character's ignorant pronouncements with tragic significance, becomes in Euripides an irony of form, which poses the all-too-human motives and actions of the characters against the audience's expectation of the required heroic tone and counts on their familiarity with the conventional tragic plots and roles to ensure appreciation of his deformations, ranging from subtle to outrageous, of the norms.

This familiarity with the conventions and "inner fictional imperatives" of the old stories recast as tragic plots is the base line of Burnett's attack on the problem. Tragedy had been a regular feature of the Athenian year since before the beginning of the fifth century. The audience was attuned to themes and variations; they were "veterans," as Aristophanes called them in *The Frogs*.[7] "The tragic plots were few, even the fictions were few, and the poet, choosing among them, knew that each would evoke once more a unanimous trained emotion and a wealth of predictable association" (p. 16). Though Burnett realizes the difficulty of isolating these "norms of tragic action" (which are "of course never to be found in a pure form"), she deduces "from surviving tragedy the general outline of six favorite hypothetical plots." These are three representatives of "negative overturn"—actions of punishment (of the principal), vengeance (exacted by the principal), and willing sacrifice (of the principal)—and three of "positive overturn"—plots of suppliants raised, of rescue, and of return. The expectations aroused by each of these plots are built on by Euripides as he combines two or more of them in each of the seven plays that Burnett, after her introductory chapter, proceeds to discuss: the *Alcestis, Iphigenia in Tauris, Helen, Ion, Andromache, Heracles,* and *Orestes.*

She establishes and isolates the basic components of each play and then uses them as a control to assess the "distorted and aberrant stage forms" which Euripides has created; she analyzes with insight, wit, and precision the kaleidoscopic changes of tone which are the results of their juxtaposition and interweaving. Though her method has its failures as well as its successes, and though there are many details in her interpretation at which one reader or another may balk, these chapters open up new perspectives in Euripidean criticism and exploit in masterly fashion an aspect of his dramaturgy which has been widely ignored, or at best dimly seen, but must now take its place in the forefront of the critic's preoccupations.

Her analysis of the *Iphigenia in Tauris* as a rescue play (with no fewer than ten examples of the rescue of human beings[8]), containing in its center a negative (interrupted) action, "technically one of vengeance," throws a revealing light on the dramatic rhythms of the play (as, for example, in her discussion of the two messenger speeches, pp. 61–62) and also on many details of action, motivation, and exposition which have seemed to many critics jarring or irrelevant but are here elegantly fitted into their exact position in the complex structure. Her summary of that structure deserves citation as a typical example of her keen insight and her gift for spare but eloquent formulation. The play "tells a story of two fraternal pairs, one divine and one mortal, a group of four who have so assorted themselves that the brother god Apollo is the patron of the mortal brother Orestes, while his sister Artemis stands in the same relation to the mortal sister Iphigenia. The final achievement of the play is double, as each brother rescues his sister in a mirroring pair of actions that are simultaneous and interdependent" (p. 48). The *Helen* she sees as a "suppliant-rescue play"; the Theonoe episode constitutes an intrusive "tragedy of idealism and self-sacrifice" which is "miraculously interrupted"—a reading of this strange scene which makes better dramatic sense than previous attempts to deal with it. The *Helen* is a drama in which everyone recognizes an artistic self-consciousness at work (or rather play), and Burnett's approach is fully vindicated by the frequent passages in which the actors seem to criticize their own roles or lines (e.g., 1056). Euripides here rings the changes on the dramatic stereotypes in virtuoso fashion almost to the point of parody, and Burnett's loving and witty analysis of his deformation of the familiar is a sure guide through this hall of distorting mirrors. The *Ion* is "a mixture of return, rescue and vengeance ... but the vengeance plot is one in which the catastrophe is interrupted.... The interruption of the vengeance plot and the fulfillment of the other two depend ultimately upon recognition and the play is so organized that when the heroine of the vengeance piece shall recognize the hero of the return, the rescue will come about and the plots will melt together" (p. 101). Burnett's deft handling of these interlocking complications brings to a high polish many obscure facets of this jewel of Euripidean dramaturgy. The *Andromache* "begins with a suppliant tragedy played by a helpless heroine ... and is followed at once by a rescue piece" which is "broken in on by a third drama, a tragedy of divine punishment" (p. 131). In this chapter, Burnett develops a useful concept, "the peculiarly Euripidean practice" of role changing, the creation "of a kind of repertory situation in which a character may, while keeping the same stage name, appear now in one and now in another of the conventional parts during the course of the play" (Hermione, for example, is first a tormentor of the helpless heroine and then the helpless heroine herself). This chapter also contains, in Burnett's discussion of the "thumbnail rescue-piece" (the Orestes-Hermione scene, a notorious stumbling block for the critics), one of the best examples in the book of the way she uses the dramatic norms to put a disconcerting scene in perspective and so make it dramatically intelligible. Her analysis of the *Heracles*, where she finds three combined plots—suppliant drama, divine punishment, and rescue piece—instead of the usual two "halves" of the play (which critics have deplored, tried to link thematically and symbolically, or hailed with enthusiasm as a deliberate "formal rift"), is by far the most satisfying presentation I have seen of the mechanism of this extraordinary tragedy. In the *Orestes* (to which she devotes two chapters) she deals convincingly with "Euripides' most difficult play," sorting out its varied and transformed components into a suppliant action, a rescue, and a mixed rescue and vengeance action, "every one of which fails" (p. 184).

No one will read these chapters without occasional or even frequent disagreement, but no one can fail to learn from them, to acquire a fresh and sharpened sense of the mechanics of Euripidean drama and of the way the plays *work*. Indeed, it is no small tribute to the efficacy of Burnett's method that in the adverse criticism of the following paragraphs some of the objections urged against her interpretation rest on details the critic would never have seen if he had not learned from her what to look for.

She sometimes seems to misread the results of her own method, and sometimes, too, the basic plot pattern she uses as a control rests on too flimsy a basis. Both failings (and also a success) are visible in her treatment of what is admittedly the most baffling play of the lot, the *Alcestis*. It is a combination of "a tragedy of willing sacrifice" with a "rescue piece." The ideal form of the sacrifice tragedy is described for us on pages 22–25: "The action in a sacrifice play is . . . openly identified with the concerned will of a god. . . . Its causal beginning lies normally in an express divine command." It

> describes the death of an appropriate victim, a perfect individual. . . . There is no question of *hamartia* because this act of divine destruction . . . has . . . a positive, ritual purpose; it alleviates some evil abroad in the world. . . . There is always a dissuader, for otherwise the decision of the principal cannot be depicted in action, but, if this character is seriously debased his true function is undermined, since there is no special glory in resisting the temptations of the craven.

Burnett applies these canons of the sacrifice plot to the situation and speeches of Alcestis and Admetus. She demonstrates, in a serried series of comparisons between Alcestis on the one hand and Macaria, Antigone, Polyxena, Iphigenia, Menoeceus, and Praxithea[9] on the other, that Alcestis is "given a strong outward conformity to that of her prototype," and that Alcestis' "sacrifice tragedy is apparently in perfect ethical agreement with other plays of the type." This is a valid and important demonstration; Burnett shows irrefutably the irrelevance of the complaints so many modern critics have made about the coldness and self-centeredness of Alcestis[10]—the realistic rehearsal of alternatives and the calculation of what her sacrifice will accomplish are both proved to be normal constituents of the principal's main speech in this type of play.

Admetus, however, is "the dissuader . . . whose character cannot be seriously debased," and, as before, Burnett tries to establish her claim by appeals to parallels. This time they are not so cogent:

> He takes the part of an Iolaus or a Hecuba or a Clytemnestra and is the one who tries to keep the sacrifice from taking place. . . . Like Iolaus he cannot quarrel with a god's command, but, like Hecuba and Clytemnestra, he bewails his own fate since he must lose a loved one, complaining that he is destroyed and begging the victim not to abandon him. . . . Like Polyxena's mother, he would cling to the sacrifice and die with her and he must be told by others that this cannot be. . . . Like Iolaus he hails the virtues of this female savior and promises to honor her . . . like him he is reluctant later to admit to an outsider that a victim has been sacrificed. [p. 27]

But the lines of Admetus (420–21) which are cited to buttress the statement that "he cannot quarrel with a god's command" do not mean or imply anything of the kind. The chorus tells him that everybody has to die and he replies, "I know." And the "reluctance to admit that a victim has been sacrificed" is in the case of Iolaus (*Heracl.* 634) a matter of no consequence, a mere dramaturgical dismissal of the previous scene, whereas in the case of Admetus it is a major structural element, a deception of Heracles which makes possible the happy ending (and at the time earns him a harsh reproof from the chorus). But much more disturbing than these details is the inadequacy of the parallel as a whole. For Admetus is not and cannot be the "dissuader"; he has accepted the sacrifice long ago and it cannot now be reversed. In addition, he differs from the dissuaders cited to explain his case in the crucial fact that unlike them he is the beneficiary of the sacrifice: it is his own life which that sacrifice saves. At one point, speaking of the *Helen*, Burnett announces that Euripides expects of the audience "an almost Japanese finesse," but to think that they would not sense the jarring incongruity of Admetus' appeals to his wife not to die calls for an audience of almost Bradfordian[11] stolidity. In fact, the resemblances (such as they are) between Admetus' speeches and those of Hecuba, Iolaus, and Clytemnestra seem to me to emphasize the incongruities; the audience's recognition of the convention to which Euripides is appealing could only have heightened their appreciation of the hideously false position in which the dramatist saw fit to place his hero. Burnett lays much stress on the fact that Alcestis gives her life not so much for Admetus as for the *oikos*, the continuity of the family, the inheritance of her children, and the argument has great force. But it is still humanly and dramatically true that the one person who cannot possibly beg Alcestis not to abandon him and beg to be buried with her is her husband Admetus. And there is one fairly regular element of the dissuader's role in the sacrifice play (not mentioned by Burnett) which is missing from the speeches of Admetus. Of the three examples cited of the "one who tries to keep the sacrifice from taking place" (Iolaus, Hecuba, Clytemnestra), two (*Heracl.* 451ff., *Hec.* 385ff.) offer their own lives in place of that of the sacrificial victim. It is easy to see why even Euripides did not put *that* offer in the mouth of Admetus;[12] it would have pushed the formal irony too far, to make the scene skirt the borderline of parody.

There is, however, one character in the play who calls a spade a spade: Pheres, the father of Admetus. In the sordid exchange of insults between father and son, Euripides throws on the husband's acceptance of his wife's sacrifice the spotlight of ordinary unheroic humanity's feelings about the individual's right to life. "I brought you into the world," says Pheres. "Do I have to die for you as well? ... Lucky or unlucky, your life is your own.... Don't die instead of me, I won't die instead of you." These are home truths indeed and it is hard to see why, if Euripides wanted the audience to see Admetus as the Iolaus or Hecuba of this play, he could have allowed himself to include so devastating a scene.

Burnett's ingenious explanation of the presence of Pheres in the play invokes the audience's understanding of the form of the second component of the *Alcestis*, the "rescue piece." This type of play "presupposes a victim immobilized and in danger from a threatening creature; ... after a prologue of lament, the normal stage action begins with the arrival (properly accidental) of the hero.... Since the true *agon*, the struggle with the monster, must occur offstage ... it may be replaced in the staged action with a second encounter between the champion and someone who does not wish to release the victim even when the danger is past. The proper ending of the play is some form of translation ... often associated with marriage" (p. 30). Much of this seems both well grounded and also germane to a discussion of the *Alcestis*. The Thanatos of the prologue is a "threatening creature" all right; the *agon* takes place offstage, and the ending of the play is certainly a "translation ... associated with marriage." But where is the "second encounter between the champion and someone more ordinary who does not wish to release the victim even when the danger is past"? According to Burnett, this scene "has not been left out but has been played by proxies in a substitute scene of conflict." It is the quarrel between Pheres and Admetus.

It seems unlikely that even Japanese finesse would have enabled the audience to deal with this set of Chinese boxes: Admetus and Pheres are "proxies" for Heracles and some hypothetical character in a scene which is a "substitute" for a "second encounter" which itself "replaces" the *agon* between Heracles and Thanatos. If Euripides really wanted the audience to feel that the Admetus-Pheres scene was meant to "replace, in the emotional economy" of the action, "the struggle with the monster," he could surely have found some means less riddling than this; the appeal to scene typology breaks down here.

The breakdown is revealed as even more serious when the evidence for the typology, especially that of the "second encounter" (which is vital for Burnett's thesis), is subjected to close scrutiny. In her outline of the normal sacrifice plot, Burnett had evidence to spare, but the "second encounter" of the rescue plot turns out to have a name but no local habitation. "Enough survives of the Euripidean *Andromeda* to allow certain general assumptions and to encourage a reconstruction of the satyr-play *Hesione* whose preparations are shown on the Pronomos vase ... in addition we can recognize the rescue action in its masculine form in the *Philoctetes* and the satyr *Cyclops* and can use it perhaps as a hypothesis for the *Prometheus Luomenos*" (p. 30). These are, alas, slim pickings. Exhibit A, the satyr-play *Hesione* ("the parallel with the *Hesione* is the closest," p. 31), which is to be reconstituted on analogy with general assumptions allowed by the remnants of the Euripidean *Andromeda*, is already a desperate expedient even before one remembers that we have no evidence for the existence of such a play (except of course for a fourth-century comedy of that title by Alexis). The Pronomos vase does not name the play or the heroine, still less give even the faintest idea of the plot.[13] Even if we accept the archaeologists' stab in the dark that the play is about Hesione, Burnett's statement that, after being rescued by Heracles, Hesione "then had to be wrested from her ungrateful family" (so providing a substitute *agon* scene for the hypothetical play), assumes a version of the story found only in late and notoriously unreliable mythographers;[14] in Homer the reward refused to Heracles was not the hand of Laomedon's daughter but his horses. This substitute *agon* is in fact not fully substantiated anywhere in our texts. There seems to be some evidence for such a scene in the fragments of the *Andromeda*, but the reconstruction of lost Euripidean plays is a hazardous business, as Burnett herself demonstrated so incisively in her review of T. B. L. Webster's *Tragedies of Euripides* in *CP*, LXIII (1968), 310ff.). The *Philoctetes* is not mentioned again; the lost *Prometheus Luomenos* gives us a Prometheus "rescued from the eagle by a champion, who still had to deal with Zeus." (But for the last seven words there is no evidence at all—perhaps it was Prometheus who had to deal with Zeus.) In the *Cyclops*, "since the monster may appear on stage ... there is no need for a second scene of resistance to the rescue action" (p. 31). The hypothetical second *agon* has for its base only a few uninformative fragments of the *Andromeda*; something much more solid is required if the searing realism of the Pheres scene is to be effectively discounted.

The book has been discussed so far as if its only concern were an understanding of the dramatic conventions in which Euripides worked. But there is much more to it than this; it offers also a theory of fundamental intention, a Euripidean theology, or rather, a theodicy. "Each play shows human exertion to be blind and ineffective at best, sordid sometimes, and occasionally contemptible and cruel. And each play meanwhile depicts a divine pity and purpose that can, when it is ready, turn disaster into bliss" (p. 14). There is not too much to quarrel with in the first of these two sentences (though they hardly cover the cases of Alcestis and Theonoe), but the second is another matter.

Burnett fully justifies her statement for the *Alcestis* and *Helen*, and the brilliance of her analysis of the *Orestes* comes close to persuading even this skeptical reviewer that the "finale is meant as a fully functioning part of the drama and must be taken seriously" (p. 212). In the chapter on the *Iphigenia in Tauris*, her explanation of the aborted escape—"Euripides has indulged in this play in an almost Pelagian celebration of the virtue and wit of man, but he has found, in the gigantic wave, a remedy for his near-heresy" (p. 68)—will appeal more to readers steeled in the school of old Aquinas than to the laity, but she does succeed in demonstrating the pervasive importance of Apollo in the play with a cogency that will cause those who have ignored or belittled it (this reviewer included) to reconsider the question. The apologia for Apollo in the *Ion*, however, leaves much to be desired. She makes a strong case for Apollo's guiding providential hand at work throughout (the dove, for example, is "the agent of Apollo,"[15] p. 118), but she has to admit that "the plot does seem, by its very structure, to question his absolute foresight and control." Her attempt to palliate this awkward aspect of Euripides' presentation of the god of prophecy *par excellence*—"he can foresee the massive shapes that loom in the future" (the coming history of the Aegean)[16] but not "mortal actions"—is self-defeating. An Apollo who "does not know the strength of passion in the human heart" and so produces obstructions to his plan which "he has in a sense created but seems not to have foreknown" cannot be the god whom Greeks and barbarians made long journeys to consult about the future results of their "mortal actions," and who foresaw that Oedipus would be born, survive exposure, kill his father, and marry his mother. The *Andromache* is also a difficult play to reconcile with Burnett's formula: the murder of Neoptolemus has to be justified by reasoning which will leave many readers unsatisfied. True enough, Neoptolemus is a *theomachos*, like Pentheus (p. 152); he once demanded satisfaction from Apollo for his father's death. But he has "changed his mind" (*Andr.* 1003), and when he goes to Delphi in the play it is to offer an apology for this fault. His assassination in the god's temple with the god's encouragement is, as Burnett says, "a cruelly ugly thing," but she justifies it by claiming that "even in his attempted conciliation he re-enacts his first ineradicable crime." The explanation of this enigmatic statement is that "his very prowess serves to remind us of the Neoptolemus who outraged Priam and Astyanax" (matters on which Euripides is silent)[17] and that his prowess "once again involves him in acts of desecration." These, it appears, are "actually 'sacking' Apollo's shrine (note *katharpasas* 1121–22, cf. 1095), seizing arms that had been dedicated to the god and using them in a battle with Apollo's priests. He sweeps the sacred objects from the altar and takes his stand upon it and ... fills the peaceful shrine with a rowdy ill-omened din (1144–45)." Since Neoptolemus is under attack by an armed lynch mob encouraged by the god in his "peaceful shrine," one can hardly call all this a "new crime"; Burnett would have done better to rest her case on the ineradicable nature of the first one.

The play which above all others challenges Burnett's assumption of a "divine pity and purpose that can, when it is ready, turn disaster into bliss" is of course the *Heracles*; here she has taken on a task worthy of the hero himself. I do not think she has succeeded; it is here that her arguments are at their most subtle and least convincing. There are two main problems: the deaths of Megara and the children (among the most ghastly in Greek tragedy) and the suffering of Heracles, who, seized by god-sent madness, slaughters his wife and sons. Both of these fates must, to sustain Burnett's thesis, be shown as in some way deserved. She does not tackle the problem of the hideous deaths of the children (and in any case they are not characterized and their fate is a pendant to those of Megara and Heracles), but she has harsh words for their mother and only slightly less harsh words for Amphityron. Their fault is that they "easily agree to leave their sanctuary" (p. 159). They refuse the "essential suppliant choice—to die, if die one must, as a consecrated being and as a sure agent of destruction for the enemy." They "willingly divest themselves of all their supernatural force and choose to die as ordinary secular victims" (p. 161).

The responsibility for this choice is Megara's; she persuades Amphityron to yield. "She is wanting in the primary quality of the suppliant, awareness of the divine." She is "a materialist" (p. 162); "her doctrine of Necessity and her conversion of Amphityron are reminiscent of Jocasta's temptation of Oedipus in the *Tyrannus*" (p. 166). Burnett does not actually say in so many words that the deaths of Megara and her children are their punishment for these "offences," but this is clearly implied in her statement that Heracles punishes the offenses of his family against the gods (p. 171) and in her interpretation of the messenger's account of the slaughter inside the house. "The poet has unobtrusively insisted that this fate was not only necessary to heaven but truly chosen by those who have suffered it." That insistence has never been more unobtrusive appears from her explanation. "He has imaged Heracles like an Erinys with a torch (928)" (there is no mention of the Erinys in the text and the torch is a normal instrument of the sacrifice) "and has made him call up the very *Keres* that Megara has chosen for her sons (870, cf. 481)" (but Megara did nothing of the sort—she claimed that *Tyche* assigned the *Keres* instead of the portions their father had intended for them); "he has also shown the principals of the first action now vainly hiding at an altar (974, 984)" (but both passages refer to the children, who are hardly the "principals") "or vainly supplicating the mortal champion they had preferred to Zeus Soter (986ff.)" (one of the children again, who had no voice in the decision). It is clear that here Burnett is building with straws, and one indication of the dilemma to which her argument has brought her is her elevation of the barely sketched figure of Megara (whose "doctrine of Necessity" is a bundle of tired clichés) to the status of Sophocles' Jocasta, who is not only an unforgettable dramatic creation but also the spokesman for a "doctrine" of *Tyche* which for the first time in our literature envisages a meaningless, accidental universe.

A similar exaggeration is to be seen in the claim that the suppliants' fault is to leave sanctuary prematurely. For these suppliants are in the most desperate case in all Greek tragedy. They are without food, water, or clean clothes; they sleep on the bare ground (*H.F.* 52). Their one hope of rescue has gone, not to some place from which it might be hoped that he will return, but to Hades. They are not, as Andromache was, merely threatened with death by fire; the orders are given on stage and no one doubts that the tyrant Lycus will see them carried out. And they have the children with them. (Andromache defied Hermione's threat to burn her alive, but her child—so she thought—was safe.) In these extreme circumstances, Megara's wish to die with dignity and less painfully seems understandable. Even though it does display a certain lack of faith in divine providence, this does not seem an adequate justification for the horror which ensues. One does not of course expect the justice of a Greek god to be tempered with mercy; one should in fact expect it to be harsh, especially where the god's prerogatives are threatened or his *timê* denied.[18] But so extreme a disproportion between offense and punishment suggests that Euripides was not thinking in such terms here—a suggestion supported by the fact that, as we learn clearly from the divine creatures who later walk the stage, the deaths of Megara and the children are merely incidental, part of the attack on Heracles. One cannot help suspecting that these suppliants have offended not so much against the gods as against Burnett's Rules of the Drama, and this suspicion is confirmed by a phrase of the author herself: "their movements are in glaring violation of the rules of the suppliant plot" (p. 160).

But the main problem is what happens to Heracles. What has he done to deserve, in any dispensation that can be thought of in terms of justice (there is no question of turning "disaster into bliss" in *this* play),[19] the madness that impels him to slaughter his wife and children? The first count against him in Burnett's explanation is the killing of Lycus, a "crime against the suppliant plot" (p. 177) which "ends in the villain's defeat but not as a rule in his death" (p. 165). Burnett admits, however, that this action "was, in a primitive sense, just" and proceeds to explain that "he then made a parody of that deed, with all its violence and unreason highly exaggerated, in the 'Mycenean' killing of

Eurystheus and his sons," but this "is at best only a symbolic crime and is plainly the effect not the cause of the heavenly intervention." The real reason is the wrath (*cholos*) of Hera, announced (and shared) by Iris. This wrath, according to Burnett, has nothing to do with Hera's jealousy as a deceived wife (Heracles specifically claims [1309–10] that it has, but Burnett is not impressed, since he utters these words at "his most faithless point of despair"); it is "the magnificent almost personified wrath that sometimes comes upon a Homeric hero from outside." The wrath is in fact theological in origin: "Hera's general intention is to defend the grandeur of the gods by defeating an attempt at grandeur on the part of man (841–42) ... such a punishment presumes a Heracles whose constant good fortune and freedom from stain constituted a kind of conspiracy against Olympus." The nature and purpose of this conspiracy are left to the reader's imagination; perhaps they can be deduced from a later passage: "His deeds, his aspect and his singular good fortune constitute a threat in themselves, for if they are thought to be attributes of his mortal part, he will inspire, as Megara's example shows, a Pelagian worship of man and spread the godless doctrine of Necessity" (p. 179).

This is subtle doctrine, but the text of the play offers little support for it. If these were Hera's reasons for destroying Heracles, why did she try to kill him in the cradle, before he attained such threatening stature (1266ff.)? His "singular good fortune" consisted of a series of dangerous labors that even Iris calls "bitter" (*pikrous*, 826), and we have it from no less an authority than Lyssa that one reason she is reluctant to carry out Hera's orders is that Heracles, in the course of his labors, "single-handed restored the worship of the gods which had been overthrown by impious men" (852–53)—a strange activity for a Pelagian hero. It may be true that the word *cholos* "has nothing of sexual vindictiveness in it" (though it is used six times by and about Medea) and that Heracles' reference to Hera's jealousy comes from the depths of despair, but these are not reasons to dismiss so lightly, in favor of fine-spun metaphysics, a motive stated in the play with such dramatic and rhetorical force. "Let the glorious wife of Zeus stamp her foot in the dance ... for she has accomplished her purpose, brought down the foremost man of Greece in ruin. Who would pray to such a goddess? Jealous of Zeus, for his union with a mortal woman, she has destroyed the benefactor of Greece, though he gave her no cause" (1303ff.). I do not know any fully satisfactory way of reconciling these sentiments with the famous passage which follows much later, in which Heracles repudiates tales of adultery and violence among the gods as the lies of the poets, and it is one of the merits of Burnett's chapter that she tries to do so. But her explanation as a whole demands a resolute determination to see unmerited evil as incomprehensible good, an attitude which is to be seen at its most tragic and religious in Claudel, at its most comic and secular in Doctor Pangloss,[20] but nowhere, so far as I can see, in any writer who used the Greek language before the triumph of Christianity.

It is in the nature of the critic's function that he should attack weak points as well as celebrate strengths; it is also inevitable that the attack should occupy a disproportionate amount of his space, for it demands detailed discussion and the citation of chapter and verse. It will perhaps redress the unavoidable imbalance of this review to end by saying that Burnett's book will delight the discerning reader by the wit and concision of its prose and command his unremitting concentration by the logic of its argument and the learning with which it is supported. For any serious student of Euripides, the book's originality and real achievements make it, quite simply, indispensable.

Notes

1. *CP*, LV (1960), on the *Helen*; LVII (1962), on the *Ion*; LX (1965), on the *Alcestis*; LXV (1970), on the *Bacchae*. The first three are among the plays discussed in the book under review, but the reader need not fear duplication of already published material; they are here treated from a different point of view, fully integrated in the structure of the book, and made to yield fresh insights.

2. Burnett acknowledges indebtedness to Lattimore and Friedrich (p. viii).

3. J. T. Shipley, ed., *A Dictionary of World Literature* (New York, 1943).

4. *R.* 394c.

5. J. R. Wilson, ed., *Twentieth-Century Interpretations of Euripides' Alcestis* (Englewood Cliffs, N.J., 1968).

6. H. D. F. Kitto, *Poiesis* (Berkeley and Los Angeles, 1966), p. 1.

7. *Ra.* 1113.

8. One of these, the rescue of Thoas "from his barbarity," might be quietly dispensed with.

9. This particular comparison is a little disturbing, since Praxithea is sacrificing not herself but her daughter.

10. For example, C. F. Beye, who speaks of the "lifeless and selfish grounds upon which Alcestis has chosen to die" (*GRBS*, II [1959], 124).

11. In the early decades of this century, the city of Bradford in Yorkshire was known to the actors of itinerant companies—because of the imperturbability of its audiences—as "the comedian's grave."

12. He does, of course, wish that he had the tongue and song of Orpheus, to charm the powers below, but this would still preserve his own life—and in any case, wishes are not horses.

13. All the Pronomos vase tells us is that the play represented (if indeed one particular play *is* represented—the experts disagree) had a chorus of satyrs and two actors, one clearly identified as Heracles, the other an unnamed king (?) whose mask has an oriental tiara. It shows also a woman (not, therefore, an actor) holding a similar oriental mask. In the center are two figures, one identified as Dionysus, the other presumed (because she appears on the other side of the vase) to be Ariadne; most interpreters

consider that these figures have nothing to do with the "play." The king (?) is generally taken to be Laomedon, the woman Hesione (though Bieber, for example, following Bulle, thinks she is Paidia holding the mask of Hesione). Buschor thinks that though the chorus represents a satyr play, the actor figures stand for "tragedy" (not a particular tragedy but "the higher spheres of drama"); Arias-Shefton, accepting this view, concluded that the "complete dramatic tetralogy is present"! The *Hesione* is clearly no firm foundation on which to build.

14. The main source is Hyginus, on whose reliability as a basis for reconstructing lost plays Rose justly remarks: "vix ulla est earum fabularum quin aliqua saltem ex parte a tragoedia quam aut nunc habemus aut qualis fuerit ex fragmentis dispicere possumus, discrepet" (H. J. Rose, *Hygini Fabulae*[3] [Leyden, 1967], p. x).

15. Her account of this episode is, however, a little fuzzy. This "redeeming bird" is recognized as the god's contrivance to save Ion's life—its "death purchases a new life for him." But his life was saved not by the dove but by the ill-omened word which prompted him to pour the poisoned wine on the ground (or by the piety which inspired that action). The dove's function is to reveal the murder plot.

16. Which is, however, prophesied by Athena.

17. The murder of Astyanax is mentioned by Andromache (vss. 9–10), but she does not attribute it to Neoptolemus. If Euripides had wanted his audience to think of Neoptolemus as the killer of the boy, he would have mentioned it in Hermione's tirade against the *amathia* of Andromache. It would have been even more rhetorically effective than what she does say: "You sleep with and bear sons to the son of the man who killed your husband" (170ff.).

18. See now the wide-ranging and masterly discussion of this problem by H. Lloyd-Jones, *The Justice of Zeus* (Berkeley and Los Angeles, 1971).

19. Burnett tries to introduce some bliss by claiming that once the play is over "then the spectator begins to recall once more all that he knows about Heracles' life on Olympus"; she illustrates by quoting some lines of Hesiod which mention among other blissful details that Hera now loves Heracles and honors him far above all the rest. (Bentley, one cannot help remembering, changed the last words of *Paradise Lost* from "their solitarie way" to "with Heavenly Comfort cheered.") She has to admit, however, that the play itself hardly encourages the audience to put on rose-tinted spectacles as the chorus marches off; to counter what she truly calls "the desolate effect of the final exit of the principal," she can marshal only "muffled hints" (some of them effectively muffled to the point of inaudibility).

20. I am not dragging Doctor Pangloss in by his coattails; Voltaire is invoked by Burnett herself in her discussion of the view that the play is "the poet's open satire on the gods": "it is surely a mistake in method to attribute this Lisbon earthquake style of thinking to a poet who has never for a moment shown that he found the existence of evil on earth incompatible with the idea of the existence of a god in heaven" (p. 176, n. 24). She is right to dismiss the idea that the play is a satire or a rationalist tract, but the question at issue is not the *existence* of gods but the nature of their dealings with humanity—specifically, the reasons for Hera's ferocious intervention.

TWENTY-FOUR

Review

EURIPIDES: IPHIGENEIA AT AULIS. Translated by W. S. Merwin and George E. Dimock, Jr. Oxford University Press, 1978.

IPHIGENIA. A film directed by Michael Cacoyannis, 1977.

In the early spring of 406 B.C., as the three Athenian poets selected to compete in the dramatic festival announced the subjects of their plays and presented their actors and choruses to the public at a preliminary ceremony known as the Proagon, the news reached Athens that Euripides had died in Macedonia, far to the north. As a tribute to his fellow tragedian, who had been his younger rival for nearly half a century, Sophocles, who was not to outlast the year himself, appeared dressed in black and brought his actors and chorus on without the customary festive garlands on their heads. Euripides, according to a later tradition, had been killed by a pack of hunting dogs.

Scholars are justifiably wary of the sensational stories of the death of poets current in antiquity (Sophocles for example is presented in one account as a victim of his own punctuation—he lost his breath reading aloud a long passage from *Antigone*), but anyone who has ever been chased on a Greek hillside by shepherd dogs will not dismiss the story out of hand. It has, in any case, a symbolic rightness: Euripides had for close to fifty years played the part of Athens' bad conscience, perplexing, shocking, and depressing his contemporaries. "He was a harsh man," writes Seferis, "and his friends were few. / The time came, and the dogs tore him to pieces."

But the news of his death (whatever the manner of it may have been) was not the last Athens was to hear of him. He left behind him three new plays, which were produced in Athens by his son, Euripides the Younger. One of them has not survived; another, the *Bacchae*, is universally recognized as a masterpiece; the third, *Iphigenia at Aulis*, has met with a mixed reception.

It is an exploration in depth and at considerable length of the situation recalled by the old men of the chorus in the opening stasimon of Aeschylus' *Agamemnon*: the Greek fleet, poised for the invasion of

This chapter originally appeared in the *New York Review of Books*, February 9, 1978.

Troy but held fast at Aulis by adverse weather; the dilemma of Agamemnon—to sacrifice his daughter and thus release the ships or to disband the army. The king faces an agonizing decision—"Pain both ways and what is worse? Desert the fleets, fail the alliance?"—but when he makes up his mind, his mood hardens: "once he turned he stopped at nothing, seized with the frenzy."[1]

Euripides' Agamemnon, however, is made of softer stuff: the play is full of indecision, its psychological plot line is, in fact, a series of sudden changes of mind. Before the play's opening, Agamemnon has already sent for his daughter Iphigenia, with the false promise (kept secret from the prospective bridegroom) that she is to marry Achilles. In a brilliantly poetic prologue, a night scene in the windless calm at Aulis, he changes his mind abruptly and sends a trusted servant with a letter to his wife, instructing her to keep the girl in Argos. The letter is intercepted by Menelaus; a furious quarrel between the brothers is interrupted by news of Iphigenia's arrival at the camp. She is accompanied, to Agamemnon's dismay, by her mother Clytemnestra. The king's despairing reaction to this news stirs Menelaus to pity and a change of heart: he withdraws his opposition and urges Agamemnon to disband the army and save his child.

But Agamemnon fears it is now too late. Even if the brothers kill the priest, Calchas, who made the prophecy about the wind, Odysseus is also privy to the secret and might disclose it. The truth will come out, and the army will demand the sacrifice; if opposed, it may well kill both kings and sack Argos too. When Iphigenia and her father meet, her innocent, loving questions are answered with grimly ambiguous phrases; the husband's attempt to send his wife home fails miserably—Clytemnestra insists she will preside at the wedding and questions Agamemnon about Achilles, her future son-in-law.

In the next scene, unexpectedly, she meets Achilles as he storms into the royal enclosure to demand action; his troops are on the verge of mutiny. Her coy references to his coming marriage to her daughter are met with a blank incomprehension which turns to alarm as he misinterprets her attempt to take his hand; just as they realize that they have both been deceived, Agamemnon's old servant enters to tell them how and why. Achilles makes a gallant offer to protect Iphigenia by force of arms but urges a last appeal to Agamemnon by mother and daughter. Euripides was a master of dramatic rhetoric; Clytemnestra's speech, a magnificent tirade which combines appeals to justice and self-interest with menacing reproaches, is followed by Iphigenia's heart-breaking plea for her life: "If I had the tongue of Orpheus, Father ... " But Agamemnon repeats his argument that the army will have its way by force and adds a patriotic note: "Greece must be free / if you and I can make her so."

Achilles is now the only hope, but he comes on stage pursued by his own mutinous troops. He is ready to fight, one man against an army, and tells Clytemnestra to hold her daughter close, but Iphigenia refuses his help. Since she must die, she will die nobly, for Greece: the destruction of Troy will be her monument, her wedding. She goes off alone to the altar and a messenger comes to tell Clytemnestra that at the last moment, as the sacrificer's knife struck, the girl vanished and a deer lay bleeding on the altar in its death throes; the goddess Artemis, who had demanded the sacrifice, has spared the human victim. (It is not mentioned here, but in an earlier Euripidean play Iphigenia was transported to the land of the Taurians, in what is now the U.S.S.R., to preside over human sacrifices offered to Artemis by the local barbarians.)

Iphigenia at Aulis is remarkable not only for its variety of incident and its series of harshly dramatic—some critics have said melodramatic—confrontations but also for its presentation—unprecedented in extant tragedy—of sudden changes of mind and the atmosphere of social comedy which envelops the meeting of Clytemnestra and Achilles: in these and other ways it foreshadows the New Comedy of the next century. It is clearly the mature conception of a great dramatist: it has even some claim to be considered, like the *Bacchae*, a masterpiece. But if so, it is, at least in its present shape, a flawed masterpiece.

Its present shape is that preserved by two fourteenth-century Byzantine manuscripts which are our only authority for nine of Euripides' surviving plays. All nine of these texts have been damaged to some extent by textual corruption and interpolation, but the *Iphigenia at Aulis* is a major casualty. The last part of the messenger speech which concludes the play contains lines that betray total ignorance of the elementary rules of ancient Greek versification; there is at least one passage where two versions of the same short speech suggest that we are dealing with an uncorrected draft; there are structural anomalies in the brilliant prologue; a rather monotonous "catalogue of ships" in the first stasimon has often been dismissed by editors as the work of a later interpolator. In addition, there are places throughout the play where "the line thickens," where illogical transitions, clumsy phrasing, and inept or unusual stage action make us doubt that the sure-footed poet of the *Bacchae* is here in full control of the material.

We may have a text Euripides left unfinished at his death (some have even tried to pinpoint the line, like the famous bar in *Turandot*, where the master breathed his last). The play may have been put together from first drafts and completed by his son; worse still, we may be reading lines, even whole scenes, which were fabricated by later, fourth-century, actor-producers; quite certainly the conclusion of this play, whether it was from Euripides' pen or not, was so badly damaged in the long handwritten transmission that some Byzantine scholar tried his clumsy hand at filling the gaps. The play has long been an irresistible challenge to the textual critic; one of the greatest classical scholars now living, Sir Denys Page, gave the world the first glimpse of his immense learning, critical acumen, and brilliant prose style in a book called *Actors' Interpolations in Greek Tragedy*, of which the subtitle runs: *Studied with special reference to Euripides' Iphigenia at Aulis.*[2]

In the manuscripts the prologue, for example, consists of an initial dramatic exchange (in anapaestic rhythm) between Agamemnon and his old servant, an expository iambic speech by Agamemnon, and a concluding dramatic exchange in anapaests which sends the old man on his way with the letter to Clytemnestra. The standard modern text of Euripides, Murray's Oxford edition, prints anapaests and iambics as two different prologues, both incomplete; this represents the editor's belief that two poets were at work here, their efforts perhaps combined by a third. But a translator who wants the play to be read and performed cannot afford such scholarly purity; he is likely to view more favorably than textual critics do the idea, once proposed by the present reviewer, that if the prologue could find a voice it would say (with acknowledgments to Lyndon Baines Johnson): "I'm the only prologue you've got."[3]

W. S. Merwin and George E. Dimock have given us the prologue as it stands in the manuscripts and have followed a similarly conservative policy consistently throughout; this translation presents, in so far as modern scholarship can reconstruct it, the full text as it left the hands of the Alexandrian scholars of the third century B.C. Merwin is an old hand at poetic translation and his version performs in exemplary fashion the difficult task which William Arrowsmith, the general editor of the series, defined for his poets: to produce "dramatic poetry ... realizing itself in words and actions that are both speakable and playable."

The translator of Euripides does not have to wrestle with the involved imagery and "high astounding terms" of Aeschylean diction, or renounce in desperation any attempt to reproduce the undefinable poetic radiance given off by almost every Sophoclean line, but he has his difficulties none the less. Euripides developed a conversational style for his characters which was closer to normal speech than anything previously heard on the Attic stage, a style perfectly suited to the unheroic figures and situations of his drama. Yet, though the style sometimes verges on the prosaic, the diction is still artificial; the plain surface is cleverly contrived, as Aristotle pointed out. "The best concealment of art," he says, "is to compose by selecting words from everyday speech, as Euripides does." The danger facing the translator as he tries to produce in English, as Euripides did in Greek, "language" (to quote the general editor again) "that actors could speak, naturally and with dignity," is that he will lapse into dullness or vulgarity. Merwin triumphantly avoids both extremes and presents a version which is remarkably faithful to the original and is also, in its short but subtly varied lines, as elegant in meter as it is forceful and flowing in style.

The translators' decision to stay with the text holds good even for the final messenger speech, the last half of which is a mosaic of late antique and Byzantine iambics, overlaid with modern corrections. This was too much for their predecessor in the University of Chicago series, Charles Walker,[4] who cut his translation short at the point where Iphigenia goes off to be sacrificed and printed a version of the rest in an appendix. Dimock, the scholar of the Oxford Press team, justifies acceptance of the present end of the play by referring to Page's demonstration that the Byzantine scribes were copying and supplementing a damaged and partly illegible last page (though Dimock claims more than Page did when he says that "even where our copies have not preserved the exact words Euripides wrote or would have written, they have faithfully kept his conception").

In any case, the decision to cut or retain this ending usually depends more on overall interpretation than scholarly evidence. Walker, citing the "practice of most modern translators (Schiller among them)," omitted the happy ending because "the whole force of the play collapses if the heroine is hastily called up to heaven at the last minute." Dimock's important and challenging introduction to the new translation argues that Euripides did indeed end his play with the rescue of Iphigenia but that "the 'happy' ending is undercut in typically Euripidean fashion." Clytemnestra's doubts about the truth of the messenger's report — "how can I know / that this is not all a lie, made up / to silence my bitter grieving?" — reinforce earlier hints in the play that "the old tales are not true". In any case, "Artemis' alleged rescue of Iphigenia" is not "a sign of moral approval on the playwright's part ... the information is presented in a way and in a context which only deepen the negative implications of the sacrifice, indicting gods as well as men for the insanity of aggressive war."

For Dimock (as for many others), the play is above all an indictment of wars of aggression. There is much to be said for this view. When Euripides left for Macedon in 408, Athens had been at war for over twenty years. After fighting Sparta to a stalemate peace in the first ten years of the war, the Athenians had lost their fleet and the pick of their fighting men in a megalomaniac attack on Syracuse in far-off Sicily and since then had carried on a desperate struggle on the Aegean against Spartan fleets subsidized by Persian gold. In 406, when Euripides died, Athens was still fighting; he had seen the democratic assembly, buoyed by temporary success, refuse one opportunity after another to make peace on realistic terms. The Athenian situation of the last years of the war is reflected in the play, not only in the sarcastic portrayal of the Mycenaean king Agamemnon as a candidate for election to the generalship—"touching hands / keeping open house to the whole citizenry"—but also in the brooding menace of the war-hungry masses Agamemnon does not dare to disobey—"in an army of tens of thousands," Euripides had written in an earlier play, "the mob is uncontrollable, the indiscipline of sailors fiercer than fire."[5]

The war against Troy is presented all through the first part of the play in the blackest of terms, as a war fought to recapture a worthless woman, to satisfy the ambition of a time-serving monarch and the greed of a piratical host. Even its champion, Agamemnon, explaining to his daughter that she must die to make it possible, can do no better than to say: "Being Greeks / we must not be subject to Barbarians / we must not let them carry off our wives." It is all the more astonishing, then, that Iphigenia ends by launching into a full-scale patriotic justification of the war to explain her proud acceptance of death. This was a problem notorious enough in antiquity for Aristotle to cite it as a classic illustration: "an example . . . of inconsistency, the *Iphigenia at Aulis*. For the girl who pleads with her father for her life bears no resemblance to the later Iphigenia." Aristotle was not the last to find the transition from heartbreaking supplication to patriotic, not to say jingoistic, acceptance of self-sacrifice psychologically unacceptable.

Aristotle, who was the tutor of Alexander, the future conqueror of Persia, probably found nothing objectionable in the patriotic antibarbarian terms of Iphigenia's speech and was castigating only the sudden switch from one position to another. But most modern critics have found the speech intolerable in its own right, and Dimock is no exception. Iphigenia is the victim of an illusion—"she has been brought up under the heroic code"—and goes to her death as the willing sacrifice for a cause which the whole of the play indicts as a monstrous fraud. In fact, the play's "caricature of pro-Hellenic anti-barbarian chauvinism" shows that it is, among other things, a response to the proposal of the sophist Gorgias, made in a famous speech at Olympia, that the Greeks cease fighting each other and unite to fight the barbarian Persians. "The remedy," says Dimock, "must have seemed to Euripides worse than the disease."

This is an interesting idea, but a good case can be made for exactly the opposite point of view—that Iphigenia's speech is a reinforcing echo of Gorgias' appeal. The loss of Athens' fleet in Sicily in 413 gave Sparta its first chance to challenge Athens at sea, as it had to do if it was to win the war. But Spartan naval power was financed by the Persians, whose fee was the return to Persian rule of the Greek cities along the Asia Minor littoral. Since then, the war had depended entirely on Persian subsidies, offered mostly to Sparta, though on one occasion Athens too had hoped to be the beneficiary. Both sides were in effect dancing to the Persian tune.

Gorgias' voice was not the only one raised against this ignominious situation. In 407, the Spartan admiral Callicratidas, shabbily treated by the Persian satrap he had asked for funds, complained that the Greeks were in miserable condition, fawning on barbarians for money, and said that if he got home alive (he didn't) he would do all that he could to reconcile Athenians and Spartans. And in Aristophanes' *Lysistrata*, the heroine's great harangue to the Spartan and Athenian commissioners contains the reproach that they fight and destroy each other "with the barbarians, your enemies, armed and looking on." Evidently this idea of union against Persia as a way to achieve peace among Greeks was in the air, and Euripides, far from thinking it worse than the disease, may have seen it as the lesser evil. For it is very doubtful that the Greeks, reconciled on such terms, would have had the energy or the resources to mount an effective offensive against Persia; it was only with Persian backing that they could fight each other.

Dimock's thoughtful analysis goes farther, however, than the contemporary political situation; he finds in Euripides' treatment of the theme implications of profound ethical and philosophical significance. "Euripides identifies the essential cause of aggressive war as *philotimia*, the urge to be thought superior." This is indeed, as he points out, a key word in the Greek text and a basic ancient (and for that matter modern) Greek imperative; it is the essence of the heroic code, a fundamental assumption of heroic myth. "*Philotimia* and belief in destiny are related. Both are rooted in acceptance of the truth of the Greek myths. . . . By questioning the myths our play potentially destroys the basis both for *philotimia* and for belief in destiny."

In a penetrating analysis of the working of heroic ambition in all of the characters and its disastrous effects in action, Dimock suggests that "the play offers an escape from the clutches of *philotimia* and fate." The myths may not be true, but even if they are, the fact that human feelings can occasionally and temporarily prevail, as they do in Agamemnon and Menelaus, encourages us "to resist the supremacy of *philo-*

timia," just as their casting doubts on the "efficacy of prophecy" encourages resistance to "the idea of mythological necessity." The play demands that we ask questions: Who knows whether Iphigenia's death would make the wind blow? What would have happened if the two kings had tried to silence Calchas and Odysseus, or thrown themselves on the mercy of the army, or fled to Mycenae? And there are more questions besides, all of them in plangent discord with the overt themes of the myth.

This view of the play's effect on the audience is very far from the Aristotelian formula; in fact it is reminiscent of the theory and practice of the author of *Uber eine nichtaristotelische Dramatik*:

> *The spectator of the dramatic theater says*: "Yes, that's what I have often felt myself—I'm like that—That's only natural—That's how it will always be—The suffering of this man moves me deeply, because there is no way out for him."

> *The spectator of the epic theater says:* "I never thought of that— That's not how one should act—That is extremely surprising, almost unbelievable—That ought to stop—The suffering of this man moves me deeply because there could after all be a way out for him."[6]

As Dimock sees our play, the Athenians, like Brecht's audience for epic theater, were supposed to learn something—to "refuse to play the game of heroic superiority" and, in more limited terms, to see that nothing could be worse than to continue their now hopeless war. Dimock even feels that in the end "the Athenians did give evidence that they had understood what Euripides was saying." When the surrender came in 404, one of the conditions was the destruction of the walls which connected Athens with the sea; it was done "to the music of flute girls and with rejoicing"—by the Athenians *en masse*, as Dimock evidently reads the passage in Xenophon which describes the event. But what Xenophon says is this: "Lysander sailed into the Piraeus, and the exiles returned and began to demolish the walls to the music of flute girls and with enthusiasm, believing that day was the beginning of freedom for Greece." "Freedom for Greece" was the banner under which Sparta had fought the twenty-seven-year war, and the run of the sentence suggests strongly that the only Athenian members of the happy wrecking crews were the pro-Spartan exiles.

In any case, the questioning, probing reaction to drama which Dimock prescribes for the audience of this play is possible, as Brecht never tires of repeating, only if the spectator remains detached, emotionally uninvolved with the characters, if "instead of empathy *Verfremdung* [alienation] is introduced."[7] But *Iphigenia at Aulis* is a play that takes the spectator by the throat from the very beginning and forces him to identify not only with the wronged mother and the threatened girl but even, in his turn, with the cowardly royal father. This is demonstrated, with terrifying intensity, in Michael Cacoyannis' powerful film *Iphigenia.*

This is not, of course, his first film version of a Greek tragedy. His most recent effort along this line, *The Trojan Women,* was a rather wooden affair; a series of academic performances by American and English actresses on their best classical behavior—only Irene Papas as Helen succeeded in giving life to Edith Hamilton's bland translation. This was a disappointment after the same director's much earlier *Electra* (based on Euripides' play, Papas in the title role): a film remarkable for its skillful use of the Greek landscape, its imaginative handling of the chorus, its evocation of the unchanging realities of life in a Greek village, and, above all, its faithful re-creation against this rich background of Euripides' tormented and murderous heroine. The sound track of *Electra* was Greek, and so is that of *Iphigenia*; perhaps it was the English dialogue of *Trojan Women* which inhibited the director; however that may be, he has now recaptured the passion and vitality of the earlier film. The giant Antaeus was a wrestler who had a fresh access of energy every time he touched the earth; perhaps Cacoyannis has drawn strength from his return to Greek actors and the Greek language—which is, even after 2,500 years, still recognizably the language of Euripides.

He works with a succinct modern Greek version of Euripides' play; the speeches are reduced but the essentials are all there. The great scenes lose none of their power and those between father and daughter produce that almost unbearable pathos which explains Aristotle's statement that Euripides, in spite of his faults, is the most tragic of the poets. I heard the same judgment, expressed in different terms, from the Washington cinema owner who organized the premiere of the film at the Kennedy Center prior to its exclusive run at one of his theaters: "It's a four-handkerchief movie." It certainly sends audiences out red-eyed, and much of the credit for this is due to the cast, especially to the frail beauty of the young Tatiana Papamoskou and the magnificent acting of Irene Papas, whose Clytemnestra starts as a proud and loving mother and ends as a desperate, bereaved, menacing presence. Her drawn face looking back at Aulis as the warships sail for Troy is the last frame of the film.

The film's pictorial richness (it looks as if it has indeed been shot at Aulis, the mountains of Euboea in full view across the straits) is enhanced by color; this is brilliantly used, even when, in the outdoor sequences, the fierce Greek sun seems at times to leach the colors of the film as it does those of the air, exposing a landscape of rock and stunted shrub which glares, almost colorless, in the heat. To his credit, Cacoyannis has not allowed the availability of color to tempt him with visions of reconstructed Mycenaean palaces; when the action is not outdoors or in Agamemnon's hut, an adroit use of carefully angled shots of real Greek ruins suggests the palace at Argos (one of these buildings has Roman-style arches but only archeologists will be offended).

Euripides' play, of course, has no scenes set in Argos, but it is the privilege and the duty of the camera to extend the dramatic frontier out beyond the three walls of the modern and the one wall of the ancient stage, and Cacoyannis presents us with a great deal of action which the original audience did not see. In fact, the first half hour of the film consists, except for a few tiny fragments, of material which does not correspond to anything in the Euripidean text.

In the opening section, Cacoyannis tries to do two things: to give visual and dramatic shape to what in Euripides is an unseen but deadly menace—the army—and to explain why Agamemnon was faced with the oracular command to kill his daughter in the first place. Cacoyannis' army is a magnificent bunch of bearded cutthroats whose mutinous impatience grows visibly as the windless heat blazes on and the rations run low. A near riot over the bad food drives Agamemnon to desperate measures; he leads his mounted archers to a pastoral sanctuary where priests tend their sheep and orders his men to kill the livestock. Unfortunately, they go too far and kill a deer which is sacred to the goddess Artemis. The high priest Calchas confines his reaction for the moment to baleful looks, but soon, at night, he brings the oracle to Agamemnon in his tent. The goddess will send the winds if he will sacrifice his daughter, and meanwhile the army, ignorant of the real nature of the sacrifice demanded, waits impatiently for Agamemnon to act.

This section of the film is full of action; in fact there is so much horseback work in it that at times one seems to be present at the creation of a new genre—the souvlaki Western. But it is sad to note that when Cacoyannis leaves Euripides behind and takes off on his own, he sometimes teeters on the verge of the ridiculous. The priests, for example, are barefoot, clothed in skin-tight long cotton robes and have their heads shaved; all they need to be contemporary is a saffron robe, a begging bowl, and a mantra or two. The army has in its ranks a large number of experts on the bongo drums, who rattle away on them as the sun sinks and Agamemnon in his tent cries: "Those infernal drums!" If he had not been speaking Greek, one would have expected him to continue: "the natives are restless tonight, Carruthers."

These are minor matters; more important is the purpose behind this lengthy and emphatic presentation of the reasons for Agamemnon's dilemma. Euripides devotes four iambic lines to them and even at that does not offer an explanation. The lines merely state that Calchas told Agamemnon the price he would have to pay for Troy: his daughter. It is as if Euripides were saying: "There is no need to explain it. This is the way of the world; if you are a man in the seats of power, sooner or later you will face a choice just like this one." But Cacoyannis bears down heavily on the point and leaves the spectator with the feeling that there is more here than meets the eye. Calchas is presented not as the impartial spokesman of a goddess but as a man deeply insulted and fiercely angry. The goddess was evidently not responsible for the doldrums in the first place; yet now she speaks as if she controlled the winds. There are unanswered questions here, disturbing hints of what looks like wavering direction. But all this is left behind as a firm hand takes over. Agamemnon comes out of the tent and calls the old man; Euripides' play has begun.

At the end of the film it appears that the suspicions aroused by Cacoyannis' prologue were justified. The army, now informed of the terms of the oracle by Odysseus, has insisted on its fulfillment. As they wait for Iphigenia, who has claimed the glory of self-sacrifice, there is a conspiratorial exchange between Odysseus and Calchas: "The wind is rising; we had better hurry." And indeed it is. Before Iphigenia is actually seized by the Hare Krishna priests, it is blowing with gale force and Agamemnon dashes up the steps to the high altar to save his daughter. He is, of course, too late.

What is all this about? The oracle, it now seems, had nothing to do with the goddess; it was invented by Calchas. Why? To revenge the insult to *him*, to satisfy his *philotimia* (a priestly trait of character referred to by Menelaus, as Dimock points out). But what about Odysseus? Why does he go along with the scheme? Speculation along these lines is useless. The real question is: why does Cacoyannis give the story a final twist of his own invention, to make Iphigenia the victim not of a harsh destiny but of a peevish act of retaliation? Only one answer suggests itself: to underline even more heavily the irony of Iphigenia's acceptance of self-sacrifice. She was even more deluded than we thought. It was not even for a predatory army launched on an aggressive war that she died; she died to settle a personal score.

This part of the film, like the long beginning, is all Cacoyannis; it is his interpretation of the play and some may admire it. But even those who do not should be thankful to him for his faithful and visually overwhelming presentation of the play Euripides wrote. It is hard to see how it could be better done.

It is done so well, in fact, that it provides a unique opportunity to test Aristotle's famous verdict on the inconsistency of Iphigenia's character. Quite apart from any ironic reflection on the war which may or may not be intended, can we believe that Iphigenia, after her impassioned plea for life, would then decide to accept her death in the triumphantly patriotic terms she uses in the play? Accept her death she must, and one can imagine many ways she could find to reconcile herself to it, but would she say: "I will be the one / to protect our women in the future / if the barbarians dare to come near"? The film here is faithful to the text, the dramatic tension has been expertly built toward this point, and the actors and supporting cast are all that could be desired, but I, for one, could not believe she would speak like that. I can think of many reasons, some better than others, why Euripides, at the time, might have put these words in her mouth, but I have to agree, reluctantly (as so often), with spoil-sport Aristotle: this sounds like a different girl. It is another flaw in the masterpiece—as if there were not enough already.

But this extraordinary play remains, like Euripides, intensely tragic in spite of its faults. It deserves a place in the modern repertoire, and Dimock and Merwin have now provided an English version which will be welcomed by readers and actors alike. And Cacoyannis' film, for all its aberrations, recreates for the modern audience that irresistible, unbearable assault on the emotions that was Euripides' special skill and that made him, in his own time, a poet greatly loved but also feared.

Notes

1. Robert Fagles, trans., *The Oresteia* (New York, 1975), pp. 99–100.
2. Oxford, 1934.
3. cf. chapter 20 of this book.
4. Walker, like his friend Edmund Wilson (see *NYR*, March 3, 1977, pp. 13–14), had studied Greek as an undergraduate; he had also produced and directed plays in the thirties.
5. *Hec.*, 606ff.
6. Bertolt Brecht, *Werkausgabe* (Frankfort on the Main, 1967), vol. 15, p. 265.
7. Ibid., p. 301.

Part V: Coda

TWENTY-FIVE

The Tempest *and the Ancient Comic Tradition*

In *The Tempest* Shakespeare abandons the three familiar *milieux* in which most of his plays are set (classical antiquity, medieval England, and Renaissance Europe)[1] for a nameless island remote even from that Tunis which is itself, according to Antonio, "ten leagues beyond man's life." This island is not only uncharted, it is one on which anything can happen; "All torment, trouble, wonder, and amazement / Inhabits heere." The poet places his characters in a world which seems to be purely of his own creating; it seems in this respect significant that, in spite of prodigies of *Quellenforschung*, no satisfactory source of *The Tempest* has yet been identified.

In the so-called "romances" of Shakespeare's last period there is an accelerated flight from probability; it is a movement beyond the "probable impossibility" to the complete impossibility. In *The Tempest* the laws which govern objects existing in space and time as we know them are imperiously suspended. Until the solemn moment when Prospero abjures his rough magic, the action develops in a world which defies nature: "These are not naturall evens, they strengthen / From strange, to stranger." One wonders how Prospero can keep his promise to the bewildered Alonso "I'le resolve you / (Which to you shall seeme probable) of every / These happend accidents."

A recent production by the Yale Dramatic Association presented *The Tempest* as "science-fiction"; the shipwreck scene took place in a space ship, and the action which takes place away from Prospero's cell was seen on a gigantic television screen, tuned in by a Prospero, who sat before a control board which buzzed and flashed green light. The point was well-taken: Shakespeare has in fact done what the modern science-fictioneers do—substituted for the normal laws of the operation of matter a new set of laws invented for the occasion.

Such a substitution creates great possibilities for what Aristotle called "spectacle," and if the Yale Dramatic Association developed

This chapter originally appeared in W. Wimsatt, *English Stage Comedy* (New York, Columbia University Press, 1955). Reprinted by permission.

those possibilities somewhat exuberantly along modern lines they at least did no worse than Dryden and Davenant in 1667, whose stage direction for Act I, scene I, reads, in part: "This Tempest ... has many dreadful / Objects in it, as several / Spirits in horrid shapes flying down among the / Sailers, then rising and crossing in the Air. / And when the / Ship is sinking, the whole / House is darken'd, and a shower of / Fire falls upon 'em."

But novel and fantastic effects (and in this play it is clear that Shakespeare was interested in producing them) have their dangerous side; they may, by trading too much on it, destroy that willing suspension of disbelief on which every dramatic performance depends. The audience may come to feel, with Gonzalo, "Whether this be / Or be not, / I'le not sweare." The dramatist, by asking too much, may lose everything. Such a defiance of the normal laws of cause and effect in the operations of nature is especially dangerous in comedy, for comedy's appeal, no matter how contrived the plot may be, is to the audience's sense of solid values in a real world, to a critical faculty which can recognize the inappropriate. Tragedy, which questions normal human assumptions, may introduce the super- and the hypernatural more safely than comedy, which depends on the solidity of those assumptions for a response. A comic poet who sets his characters in action not in the world as we know it, but in one which defies our expectation, must compensate for the strangeness of the events by making the essences and relationships of the characters immediately and strikingly familiar. To put it another way, the fantasy and originality of the setting must be balanced and disciplined by a rigid adherence to tradition in character and plot.

This, I suggest, is a valid formula for *The Tempest*. It has certainly the most extraordinary and fantastic setting, for the sorcery of Prospero is a stranger thing than the familiar English fairy magic of *The Midsummer Night's Dream*. But in other ways it is the most rigidly traditional of all Shakespeare's comedies—with one exception. The exception is *The Comedy of Errors*, which is, however, apprentice work, a typical Renaissance *remaniement* of a Plautine original. *The Tempest* is as original as *The Comedy of Errors* is imitative, and yet they are the beginning and end of the same road. For the traditional foundation on which *The Tempest*'s cloud-capped towers are raised is the ancient comedy of Plautus, Terence, and (though the name would not have meant much to Shakespeare) Menander.

Like all proper foundations, this one is not conspicuous. But there are odd corners where its outline is visible in the superstructure. This, for example:

Prospero (to Ariel):   She did confine thee
By helpe of her more potent Ministers,
And in her most unmittigable rage,
Into a cloven Pyne, within which rift,
Imprison'd, thou didst painefully remaine
A dozen yeeres: within which space she di'd,
And left thee there: where thou didst vent thy groanes
As fast as Mill-wheeles strike.

The groans of a disobedient spirit imprisoned in a cloven pine by a "blew ey'd hag" come "as fast as Mill-wheeles strike": the simile illustrates the unfamiliar by appeal to an aspect of ordinary experience. Yet not, presumably, Ariel's ordinary experience: there are no mills in the strange economy of Prospero's island. The simile illustrates by an appeal from one world to another, with an anachronism that is the reverse of those Homeric similes which compare conditions of the heroic age to those of the poet's own time. (Homer compares the voice of Achilles to a trumpet, an instrument which the embattled heroes of his poem never mention or use, almost certainly because it had not yet been invented.) The mill wheels of Shakespeare's simile come not from his own world but from the world of Plautine comedy, where with monotonous frequency the rebellious slave is threatened or actually punished with an assignment to the brutal labor of the mill. And in this fantastic context, where Ariel ("my slave, as thou reportst thyselfe") is reminded of his punishment for former disobedience and threatened with even worse punishment for present disobedience, the simile gives a touch of familiarity and proportion to the outlandish details of Ariel's nature and status.

Here the classical precedent is for a moment distinctly visible, but in general it does its work the more efficiently because it is not obtrusive. Below the strange and brilliant surface composed of medieval magic and Renaissance travel tales, the initial situation, the nature and relationships of most of the characters, the development of the action and its final solution are all conjugations of the basic paradigms of classical comedy.

One of the most influential of these paradigms relates to the existence in ancient society of a dividing line stricter and more difficult to cross than any social barrier has been since: the distinction between slave and free. The free man could not imagine a misfortune worse than slavery, nor the slave a greater blessing than freedom. Slave and free were not so much separate classes as separate worlds: Aristotle could go so far as to claim that they were separate natures. This division was the most important sociological datum of ancient society, affecting men's attitude toward each other with a power almost as great as that of natural differences of sex or color. Among other things it provided a fixed contrast of condition and standards on which comedy could be based.

Ancient tragedy at the height of its development ignores the division and deals only with free men; Attic tragedy did not deal with slaves until Euripides introduced them, and this innovation was one of the main grounds for the conservative attack on him. The place for slaves was comedy, which, says Aristotle, "is an imitation of characters of a lower type," and the lowest type imaginable was the slave. Comic slaves could be beaten, could curse, lie, cheat, be drunken, lecherous, and cowardly to the limit of the free audience's capacity for laughter without offending its sense of propriety and human dignity. Such an exhibition might in fact be considered to have a moral effect; in Plutarch's *Life of Lycurgus* (ch. 28) we are told that at Sparta the ephors introduced into the military dining halls Helots who had been deliberately inebriated as a spectacle to teach the young what drunkenness was like. They also made the Helots learn songs and dances that were, to quote Plutarch again, "ignoble and ridiculous."

This was of course, not a real dramatic performance (though there is evidence of some kind of comic performance at Sparta from quite early times); at Athens the picture is clearer. It is perhaps only a coincidence that the chorus of satyrs in the only two surviving specimens of the humorous satyr play are, in the plot of the plays, temporarily enslaved, but it is evident that typical Athenian Old Comedy depended heavily on the laughter to be extracted from the low proclivities and activities of slaves. Aristophanes is not typical, but he indicates what is typical in a famous passage of self-congratulation which sets forth his claim to have ennobled comedy. Among other things he claims to have "liberated the slaves, whom the poets always brought on stage howling, all for the sake of the same old joke, so that a fellow-slave could make fun of their stripes, and ask them, 'What happened to your hide, poor devils? Were your sides assaulted by a whiplash army that cut down the trees on your back?'" Aristophanes did not, of course, dispense entirely with servile humor; rather, he seems to have adapted it to subtler purposes by introducing witty contrasts between slave and free. In *The Knights*, for instance, he brings on stage all the prominent Athenian politicians of the day as slaves in the house of a bad-tempered old man called Demos: in this comedy Demosthenes, Nicias, and Cleon fight, cheat, drink, spy, play the coward, curse, bawl, lie, and rant as valiantly as any slave ever born. Here the humorous aspects of servile behavior are used to make a satiric point, that the free men behave like slaves. *The Frogs* makes the opposite point by ringing the changes on the contrast between the master Dionysus and his slave Xanthias, who repeatedly exchange identities—with the surprising result that the slave emerges as his master's superior in wit, courage, and incidentally, literary taste, for Xanthias cannot abide Euripides.

In the comedy of the fourth century the magnificent fantasy and political wit of Aristophanes are sadly lacking, but the theme of contrast between slave and free remains. In the domestic comedy of Menander and his contemporaries (the models of the Roman comic poets) the theme crystallizes into a variety of stock patterns, which have exerted enormous influence on comedy ever since.

In this comedy, the master design is always more or less the same. A domestic problem involving the free members of the household (usually, in Menander, a marriage or a seduction—sometimes both) is eventually solved through complicated intrigues which involve the slave members of the household. The comedy proceeds on two social levels which interpenetrate, often on two plot levels as well, which also interpenetrate. The slave characters (and a host of technically free but hardly distinguishable lower-class types such as parasites, butlers, cooks, and pimps) have their own problems (the attainment of freedom, a free meal or a free drink), the solution of which is artfully made to depend on the solution of the problem of the free characters. A typical paradigm is the plot in which a clever slave, by intelligent initiative and intrigue (often directed against his less intelligent fellow slaves) solves his master's problem (which may range from finding a wife to marrying off a child) and, as a reward for his services, gains his private objective, his liberty.

This is a slave who has the intelligence of, and eventually attains the status of, a free man, but there is another type of slave who is a convenient vehicle for the traditional servile humor. This one provides the sullen bad temper, the cursing, the drunkenness, the indecency, thievishness, and cowardice which are the traditional characteristics of the comic slave. He may have the same ambition as his cleverer fellow, but not the same capacity; he forms grand designs, but through stupidity (often through the direct intervention of the clever slave) he fails miserably and is humiliated and punished with blows or a stint at the mill.

While the slaves, in aspiration and action, trespass on the confines of the free world, the freeborn may find themselves—as foundlings, kidnapped children, or prisoners of war—temporary denizens of the slave world; their identification and restoration to freedom (and usually marriage) is the play's denouement and usually coincides with, and balances, the liberation of the clever slave or the restoration of the stupid slave to his proper station, or both. Together with these contrasts of condition, there are deeper contrasts of nature: free men can think and act like slaves and slaves can rise superior in intelligence or emotion to their masters. One of the most searching and profound of Roman comedies is Lessing's favorite, *The Captives* of Plautus, in which master and slave, both enslaved as prisoners of war, exchange identities so that the master (as the slave) can be released to take the ransom demand home, while the slave remains in slavery (as the master), risking and, as it turns out, suffering terrible punishment when the truth is discovered. The nobility displayed by the slave is, characteristically enough, justified at the end of the play by the discovery that he was really born free, and his liberation is balanced by the punishment of the slave who originally kidnapped and sold him into slavery. In this and in practically all Roman comedy, the finale is a restoration of the characters to their proper status; in the typical pattern, the restoration of one of the two young lovers to freedom makes possible their marriage, and the stern father releases the clever and independent slave who has been instrumental in bringing about the happy conclusion.

When the dramatists of the Renaissance began to imitate the Roman comedies, slavery was a thing of the past in Europe (though not a few Elizabethan worthies made their fortunes by introducing it into the West Indies), but the ancient comic design was easily adapted to the conditions of a society which, like that of Elizabethan England, was based, however insecurely, on hierarchical social categories. Shakespearean comedy abounds in brilliant adaptations of the basic formula: the cruel reduction to his proper station suffered by Malvolio, who had "greatnesse thrust" upon him; the exposure of Parolles "the gallant militarist" as a "past-saving slave"; above all the magnificent interpenetration of the two worlds of court and tavern in *Henry IV*. Falstaff acts the role of the king in the Boar's Head, runs his sword through Hotspur's corpse at Shrewsbury, and sets out for London crying, "The Lawes of England are at my commandment"—only to be brusquely restored to his proper station as a "Foole and Jester." Prince Hal, like some foundling (as his father suggests), begins as "sworn brother to a leash of Drawers," sounding "the very base-string of humility," but in the end restores himself to his proper station, "to mock the expectation of the world."

But in *The Tempest*, a Utopia which Shakespeare invented for himself (as Gonzalo invents his in the play), there is no need to translate the classic form: it can be used literally. Prospero is master (and incidentally an irritable old man with a marriageable daughter), and Ariel and Caliban are slaves. Prospero as sorcerer has the power to enslave and release the free men too; this contrast is relevant for all the characters of the play—one of its main components is what Brower has called "the slavery-freedom continuity." "The 'slaves' and 'servants' of the play," he points out, "suffer various kinds of imprisonment, from Ariel in his 'cloven pine' to Ferdinand's mild confinement, and before the end of Act IV everyone except Prospero and Miranda has been imprisoned in one way or another. During the course of Act V all the prisoners except Ferdinand (who has already been released) are set free."[2]

After the long expository scene between Prospero and Miranda (itself a typical Plautine delayed prologue), we are presented with an interview between master and intelligent slave:

All haile, great Master, grave Sir, haile: I come
To answer Thy best pleasure; be't to fly,
To swim, to dive into the fire: to ride
On the curld clowds: to thy strong bidding, taske
Ariel, and all his Qualitie.

This is servile enough, and comparable to many a hyperbolic declaration of availability made by Roman comic slaves; its comic tone is pointed up by the fact that the moment Ariel is asked to make good some of these fine promises, he rebels. "Is there more toyle?" he asks:

Since thou dost give me pains,
Let me remember thee what thou hast promis'd
Which is not yet perform'd me.
Prospero: How now? moodie?
What is't thou canst demand?
Ariel: My Libertie.

Some critics have been disturbed at the vehemence of Prospero's reaction, and it is true that phrases such as "Thou liest, malignant Thing"—"my slave, as thou reportst they selfe"—and "Dull thing, I say so" sound more suited for Caliban than delicate Ariel. Yet it is not really surprising that Prospero should display what Wilson calls "ebullitions of imperious harshness" toward a slave who, after such an enthusiastic declaration of willingness to serve his master, balks at the first mention of "more worke."

Prospero does more than chide; he threatens punishment. Sycorax punished Ariel with confinement in a cloven pine—"it was a torment / To lay upon the damn'd"—but Prospero threatens to go one step farther: "I will rend an Oake / And peg—thee in his knotty entrailes." Ariel begs for pardon and promises to be "correspondent to command." He is rewarded with a fresh promise of freedom—"after two daies / I will discharge thee"—and sent about his master's business with renewed imperiousness:

>   goe take this shape
> And hither come in 't: goe: hence
> With diligence.

"*Exit*," reads the stage direction.

From this point on Ariel is correspondent to command, and his first service is to bring Ferdinand into the presence of Miranda. It is the traditional role of the intelligent slave to further his master's marriage projects, and Ariel fully regains Prospero's favor and gets a renewed promise of the traditional reward. "Delicate Ariel, / Ile set thee free for this." In fact, Ariel gains a remission of part of his stated time: "Ile free thee / Within two dayes for this."

Throughout the rest of the play Ariel acts as Prospero's eyes and ears, but, as befits the clever slave, with a certain initiative too. He rescues Alonso and Gonzalo from the conspirators, and his words suggest that, though he has a general commission to protect Gonzalo at any rate, the methods have been left to him. "Prospero my Lord, shall know what I have done." His mischievous action against Caliban and the two Neapolitans is apparently his own idea, for Prospero later asks him where they are, and Ariel gives a full report of the chase he has led them. Yet the comic aspects of the relationship between master and slave are not neglected in the swift action of the play's central section. Ariel, ordered to produce spirits for the masque, replies:

> Before you can say come, and goe,
> And breathe twice: and cry so, so:
> Each one tripping on his Toe,
> Will be here with mop, and mowe.

This sounds remarkably like the half-ironical servile exaggeration of the Plautine slave promising miracles of speed. Charmides orders his slave to go from Athens to Piraeus—*I, i, ambula, actutum redi*, "Go on, go on, start walking, come back right away"—and gets the answer, *Illic sum atque hic sum*, "I'm there and back again." And that same Ariel who asks, "Doe you love me Master? no?" at the end of the jingle quoted above, can also admit that he fears his master's temper:

> Prospero: Spirit: We must prepare to meet with Caliban.
> Ariel: I my Commander, when I presented *Ceres*
> I thought to have told thee of it, but I fear'd
> Least I might anger thee.

The comic aspects of Ariel's slavery are balanced by those of Prospero's mastery. This is not the only reference to Prospero's short temper. "Why speakes my father so ungently?"—"he's compos'd of harshnesse" — "your fathers in some passion" — "never till this day / Saw I him touch'd with anger, so distemper'd." These observations only confirm the impression made by Prospero's outbursts of fury against his slaves. There is more than a touch in him of the Plautine old man, the irascible *senex* (*severus*, *difficilis*, *iratus*, *saevus*, as Donatus describes him),[3] who may in the end turn out to have a heart of gold but who for the first four acts has only a noticeably short temper and a rough tongue.

This anger of Prospero's is of course much more than a reminiscence of the irascibility of the stock comic figure: he is a man who has been grievously wronged and who now, with his enemies at his mercy, intends to revenge himself. That this has been his intention is made perfectly clear in the speech in which that intention is forever renounced:

> Thogh with their high wrongs I am strook to th' quick
> Yet, with my nobler reason, gainst my furie
> Doe I take part: the rarer Action is
> In vertue, then in vengeance.

And this renunciation takes place when the slave rises superior to his master, setting an example of noble compassion:

> Ariel: ... your charm so strongly works 'em
> That if you now beheld them, your affections
> Would become tender.
> Prospero: Dost thou thinke so, Spirit?
> Ariel: Mine would, Sir, were I humane.
> Prospero: And mine shall.

This is a magnificently imaginative version of the scenes in which the comedy slave surpasses the master in qualities which are traditionally those of the free man: in intelligence, courage, self-sacrifice. Here the nonhuman slave surpasses his human master in humanity.

As the play draws to a close, the recognition of Ariel's services and the renewed promises of liberation increase in frequency to become an obsessive burden:

> thou
> Shalt have the ayre at freedome: for a little
> Follow, and doe me service.
> quickly Spirit,
> Thou shalt ere long be free.
> I shall misse
> Thee, but yet thou shalt have freedome.
> Bravely (my diligence) thou shalt be free.

"The reluctance of the sylph to be under the command even of Prospero," says Coleridge, "is kept up through the whole play, and in the exercise of his admirable judgement Shakespeare has availed himself of it, in order to give Ariel an interest in the event, looking forward to that moment when he was to gain his last and only reward—simple and eternal liberty." He might have added that what Shakespeare "has availed himself of" is a dramatic design as old as European comedy.

Ariel, the slave whose nature is free, is balanced by Ferdinand the free man and prince, who is enslaved. Accused as "spy" and "traitor," he is subdued by Prospero's magic. But there is nothing magical about the entertainment he is promised:

> Ile manacle thy necke and feet together:
> Sea water shalt thou drinke: thy food shall be
> The fresh-brooke Mussels, wither'd roots, and huskes
> Wherein the Acorne cradled. Follow.

This is a Shakespearean version of the chains-and-prison diet with which the ancient comic slave is so often threatened, and of which he so often complains. And Ferdinand's next appearance shows him performing servile tasks:

> I must remove
> Some thousands of these Logs, and pile them up,
> Upon a sore injunction.

The work he is doing is in fact Caliban's work (*"Enter Caliban with a burthen of wood"* is the stage direction for the preceding scene), and Ferdinand himself describes it as "wodden slaverie." But whereas Caliban has just declared his independence and Ariel longs to be free, Ferdinand the free man is for the moment content to be a slave:

> all corners else o' th' Earth
> Let liberty make use of: space enough
> Have I in such a prison.

The service which he so willingly accepts is of course not that of his master, but that of his mistress:

> The verie instant that I saw you, did
> My heart flie to your service, there resides
> To make me slave to it, and for your sake
> Am I this patient Logge-man.

And the multiple wit of these variations on the theme is dazzlingly displayed when he and Miranda plight their troth:

Miranda: to be your fellow
You may denie me, but Ile be your servant
Whether you will or no.
Ferdinand: My Mistris (deerest)
And I thus humble ever.
Miranda: My husband then?
Ferdinand: I, with a heart as willing
As bondage ere of freedome: heere's my hand.

He accepts marriage (that is, bondage) with a heart "as willing as bondage ere of freedome" (as willingly as Ariel, for example, would accept his liberty), but this acceptance, overheard by Prospero, is the signal for his release from the "wodden slaverie" in which he is now bound.

Ferdinand, as we have seen, is contrasted to Ariel, but Ariel's real opposite is Caliban, "my slave, who never / Yeelds us kinde answere." Caliban's employment is menial: while Ariel treads "the Ooze of the salt deepe," Caliban "do's make our fire / Fetch in our wood, and serves in Offices / That profit us." It is remarkable that, on an island where spirits can be made to produce banquets and perform masks, Prospero should need the services of Caliban to "fetch in firing ... scrape trenchering" and "wash dish," but so it is. "We cannot misse him."

Caliban, besides being a "Tortoys," "Hag-seed," "delicate Monster," "Moone-calfe" "debosh'd Fish," and "borne Devill," is also a slave—a poisonous, lying, and abhorred slave, to quote Prospero. His first speech (offstage)—"There's wood enough within"—and the on-stage curses which follow it are enough to suggest a familiar frame of reference for the first appearance of this outlandish figure: he is the surly, cursing slave of the old tradition.

Caliban's curses are highly original in expression—"language as hobgoblin as his person," says Dryden justly. Shakespeare has created a special vocabulary of invective appropriate to the savage apprehension of nature, but the expressions have the same dramatic characteristics as their venerable ancestors. The cursing seems to be a thing in and for itself—it violates plausibility, for one thing. Why should Prospero put up with it and counter it with threats of punishment that sound curiously like it? And Caliban is made to refer to another aspect of this improbability: "his Spirits heare me / And yet I needes must curse." He "needes must curse" because his cursing is vital to the comic essence of his nature; the scene in which he exchanges curses for Prospero's threats of punishment is a traditional feature of the comedy of master and slave.

Caliban is a sullen slave (a Sceparnio), a cursing slave (a Toxilus), and also a lecherous one. The only touch of low sexual humor in *The Tempest* is Caliban's unrepentant laughter when reminded of his attempt on Miranda's virtue. But that one laugh is enough to remind us that he has an ancestry reaching back through scurrilous Plautine slaves and Aristophanic comic actors wearing a leather *phallos* to the ithyphallic satyrs of the Greek vase paintings.

Caliban's meeting with Trinculo and Stephano is a servile parallel and parody of Miranda's meeting with Ferdinand; both mistress and slave are overcome with wonder at the vision of their counterparts in Neapolitan society. Miranda's worshiping remark "I might call him / A thing divine" is echoed in Caliban's "that's a brave God, and beares Celestiall liquor"; Ferdinand's "My Language? Heavens" finds a base echo in Stephano's "where the divell should he learne our language?" Stephano and Trinculo—"two *Neapolitanes* scap'd"—are to Ferdinand as Caliban is to Miranda: creatures of a lower order. And Stephano the "drunken butler" is a familiar figure; the slave in charge of his master's wine who drinks most of it himself is a standard character of the old comedy. In one of the better-known Plautine plays, the *Miles Gloriosus*, there is a scene with not one but two drunken butlers, one dead drunk on his back inside the house, the other drunk on his feet outside.

But the drunkenness of Stephano is surpassed by that of Caliban. His extravagant admiration of Stephano, as Trinculo perceives, is more than savage simplicity: "The poore Monster's in drinke." In his drunken fit he thinks of the primary objective of all slaves, his freedom. Unlike Ariel, he cannot hope to win it by delicate service; he can gain his freedom only by working against his master or by running away from him. He deserts Prospero, "the Tyrant that I serve," for Stephano, and the service of this new master turns out to be perfect freedom, which he proceeds to celebrate in song and dance: "Freedome, high-day, high-day, freedome." It is the traditional servile drunken exhibition and it is grotesquely funny, but it is only the other side of the coin which shows us Ariel, moody, demanding his liberty. Ariel and Caliban are as opposite as earth and air, but they are both enslaved, and in this they are alike. One suspects that Caliban speaks something close to the truth when he tells Stephano that Prospero's power depends on one thing only, his "Bookes":

> without them
> Hee's but a Sot, as I am; nor hath not
> One Spirit to command: they all do hate him
> As rootedly as I.

"They say there's but five upon this Isle," says Trinculo. "We are three of them, if th' other two be brain'd like us, the State totters." Of the three of them, the one with the most brains is Caliban. With servile flattery and cunning, he supplants Trinculo in Stephano's graces, securing a series of reprimands and eventually a beating for his fellow slave:

> Beate him enough: after a little time
> Ile beate him too.

He is now Stephano's "lieutenant," but he knows what must be done to guarantee his new-found dignity: he must encompass Prospero's death. And so the "foule Conspiracy" is formed. The slaves indulge their exaggerated fantasies of freedom and sovereignty: "Monster, I will kill this man: his daughter and I will be King and Queene, save our Graces: and *Trinculo* and Thy selfe shall be Vice-royes." It is a servile parody of the more serious conspiracy of the free men, Antonio and Sebastian.

The drunken butler dreams of a kingdom; he is not the first. It is instructive to compare his plans with those of Gripus, the Plautine slave who has fished a treasure out of the sea and intends to hang on to it:

> When I'm once free, I'll equip myself with property, an estate, a house. I'll go into trade with great ships; I'll be considered a King among Kings. . . . I'll build a great city, and call it Gripus, after myself, a monument to my fame and doings. And in it I'll set up a great Kingdom . . . And yet, King though I am, I must make my breakfast on sour wine and salt, no relish for my bread.

This comic incongruity between the present and the imagined future, between station and ambition, is carried to hilarious lengths in the climactic appearance of Caliban and his associates. They "do smell all horse-pisse," but Stephano's royal dignity is undisturbed. "Wit shall not goe unrewarded while I am King of this Country," he says, and Trinculo hails him in the titles of the old ballad, "O King *Stephano*, O Peere: O worthy *Stephano*." Standing at the entrance to Prospero's cell, King Stephano talks like a tragic hero: "I do begin to have bloody thoughts." And Caliban's urgent warnings are rejected in royal style: "Monster, lay to your fingers . . . or Ile turne you out of my Kingdome."

A few seconds later Stephano's kingdom melts into thin air. And on his last appearance he and Trinculo are ordered off with Caliban to perform menial tasks; no distinction is made between them:

> Goe Sirha, to my Cell,
> Take with you your Companions: as you looke
> To have my pardon, trim it handsomely.

The stupid slaves, their wild ambitions foiled and their presumption suitably punished, are restored to their proper place and function.

Prospero has already been recognized as "sometime *Millaine*" and restored to *his* proper station—"thy dukedom I resigne." The marriage of Ferdinand and Miranda is arranged; all that remains is to free the clever slave—"to the elements Be free, and fare thou well." Then the play, except for a version of the conventional Plautine request for applause, is over, the traditional paradigm complete. Gonzalo is given the speech in which the loose ends are tied together and the pattern of restoration spelled out:

> In one voyage
> Did *Claribell* her husband finde at *Tunis*,
> And *Ferdinand* her brother, found a wife,
> Where he himselfe was lost: *Prospero* his Dukedome
> In a poore Isle:

So far we are still within the recognizable limits of the ancient plan, but Gonzalo's closing words (though they continue the metaphor of liberation) can serve to remind us that this plan is only the bare outline of a poetic structure which in feeling and imagination as far surpasses Plautine comedy as "great'st do's least":

> —*Prospero* his Dukedome
> In a poore Isle: and all of us, our selves,
> When no man was his owne.

Notes

1. cf. Gilbert Highet, *The Classical Tradition* (Oxford, 1949), p. 194.
2. R. A. Brower, *The Fields of Light* (Oxford, 1951), p. 110.
3. cf. George F. Duckworth, *The Nature of Roman Comedy* (Princeton, 1952), p. 242, n. 14.

INDEX

Library of Congress Cataloging in Publication Data

Knox, Bernard MacGregor Walker.
  Word and action.

  Includes index.
  1. Greek drama (Tragedy)—History and criticism—Collected works. I.
Title
PA3133.K6   882′.01′09   79-11277
ISBN 0-8018-2198-3